Revolutionary Constitutions

Revolutionary Constitutions

Charismatic Leadership and the Rule of Law

BRUCE ACKERMAN

The Belknap Press of Harvard University Press
CAMBRIDGE, MASSACHUSETTS
LONDON, ENGLAND · 2019

Design by Dean Bornstein

Library of Congress Cataloging-in-Publication Data

Names: Ackerman, Bruce A., author.
Title: Revolutionary constitutions : charismatic leadership and the rule of law / Bruce
    Ackerman.
Description: Cambridge, Massachusetts : The Belknap Press of Harvard University
    Press, 2019. | Includes bibliographical references and index.
Identifiers: LCCN 2018048881 | ISBN 9780674970687 (hardcover : alk. paper)
Subjects: LCSH: Populism. | Personality and politics. | Constitutional law. | Constitutions. |
    Revolutions. | Charisma (Personality trait)—Political aspects. | Political leadership.
Classification:
LC record available at https://lccn.loc.gov/2018048881

For Susan, with love

Contents

Introduction: Pathways / 1

Part One: Constitutional Revolutions

1   Constitutionalizing Revolution? / 27

2   Movement-Party Constitutionalism: India / 54

3   Struggling for Supremacy: South Africa / 77

4   From the French Resistance to the Fourth Republic / 116

5   Constitutional Revolution in Italy / 131

6   A Progress Report? / 157

Part Two: Elaborations

7   De Gaulle's Republic: The Outsider Returns / 169

8   Reconstructing the Fifth Republic / 199

9   Solidarity's Triumph in Poland / 227

10 Solidarity's Collapse: The Perils of Presidentialism / 255

11 The Race against Time: Burma and Israel / 282

12 Constitutionalizing Charisma in Iran / 324

13 American Exceptionalism? / 361

Notes / 405

Acknowledgments / 443

Index / 447

Revolutionary Constitutions

Pathways

Law legitimates power. Constitutionalism is part of this larger dynamic—and it has played an increasingly dominant role over the past century. Its world-wide rise has profoundly reshaped modern notions of authority.

But how?

Lots of historical studies provide insights into the rise of constitutionalism in one or another polity or region. Yet it has been tough to organize the be-wildering complexity of global experience into a compelling comparative framework. We can make life easy for ourselves by supposing that constitu-tionalism is a one-size-fits-all ideal that animates a common project throughout the world. But this seems unlikely to be true (to put it mildly).

Once we recognize the reality of deep differences across the globe, a large problem emerges: How do we distinguish the accidental from the truly fundamental?

Max Weber asked himself a similar question when confronting an earlier political universe. He too rejected the idea that political power appealed to a single, legitimating logic—famously distinguishing between the very different appeals of tradition, charisma, and bureaucratic rationality. This trichotomy remains relevant, but it fails to recognize the distinctive attractions of constitutionalism.

I aim to fill this gap. This is the first in a series of volumes that will explore three different pathways through which constitutions have won legitimacy over the past century. Each pathway generates a distinctive ideal type—with its own set of attractions and problems.

I will not pass philosophical judgment on the ultimate merits of one or another ideal type.[1] I want to understand the different historical and cultural dynamics that have transformed each of them into powerful engines of le-gitimation over the course of the twentieth century.

A deeper understanding of the past is especially important at this moment. With constitutional crises erupting throughout the world, it is tempting to believe that all of them are symptoms of the same disease—so-called populism—and can be cured in similar ways.

This is a mistake. Countries that have traveled down the three different paths to constitutionalism confront very different crises. While I will be considering a variety of reform measures, what is needed more urgently is a diagnosis of the different predicaments confronting countries traveling each path—so that citizens and political leaders might gain a deeper sense of the challenges they confront in sustaining their distinctive traditions into the twenty-first century.

My three ideal types will also enable a more discriminating form of transnational learning. If, as I suggest, the leading countries of Europe emerge from different constitutional pathways, these differences should be treated with respect if the European Union is to sustain itself as a vital force in the coming generation. I will also try to persuade you that my three ideal types deliver powerful insights into the dilemmas confronting leading nations in Africa, Asia, the Middle East, and South America. These types enable comparative insights into common dilemmas that would otherwise escape the attention of national politicians transfixed by the seemingly unique features of their domestic crises.

To emphasize this point, I will be concluding this book with a discussion of the United States. Rather than celebrating my own country as exceptional, I will be asking this question: How do the patterns of constitutional development in the rest of the world enlighten modern American experience?

My project is ambitious. But it should not be confused with more ambitious ones. For starters, I want to distinguish my inquiry from a larger effort to clarify the ideal of the rule of law. Constitutionalism, as I understand it, involves the imposition of significant legal constraints on top decision-makers. But the broader "rule of law" ideal deals primarily with the techniques by which top decision-makers try to control everybody else.

Many autocratic regimes have found the rule of law an extremely useful device in governing their societies. Under this setup, the autocrats assert their arbitrary right to establish the rules, but require the bureaucracy and the judiciary to implement their commands in a consistent and principled fashion.

So understood, the rule of law is a fundamental legitimating principle in its own right—providing legal equality for all, regardless of social position. If the autocratic regime fulfills its promise, it may well persuade its inhabitants of the legitimacy of the system. Evenhanded administration also has great instrumental value—facilitating the effort by top decision-makers to realize their values and programs in an efficient fashion.

It was this promise of legitimacy and efficiency that inspired the great Enlightenment monarchs of eighteenth-century Europe; and it has been pursued ever since by many autocracies throughout the world, with mixed results. But for now, it is enough to emphasize that even an enlightened autocracy remains an autocracy—not a constitutional state.

By the same token, it's quite possible for constitutional regimes to fall dramatically short of rule-of-law principles. The United States, for example, tolerates a lot of legal arbitrariness from juries and low-level bureaucrats. Nevertheless, elites at the top of the executive, judicial, legislative, and military hierarchies confront fundamental constraints on their freedom of action. Using my ideal types, I hope to clarify why this is so—and why very different legitimating logics prevail in different systems.

At the same time, I will not try to provide a complete causal account of the conditions under which political regimes sustain themselves over time. Even a constitutional government that generates broad belief in its legitimacy may be crushed by military defeat or economic depression or some other catastrophe. The reverse may also be true: virtually everybody may believe that the Constitution is a sham and yet continue to support the system as long as it delivers prosperity and national security.

Nevertheless, the presence or absence of a widespread belief in constitutional legitimacy can play an important—sometimes, all-important—role in shaping political and social life. So the different dynamics that can generate such commitments are worthy of sustained study.

Three Ideal Types

Let's begin with a sketch of the three paths. In the first scenario, a revolutionary movement makes a sustained effort to mobilize the masses against the existing regime. In most cases, this leads to bloody repression and the reinforcement of the status quo. But I will focus here on success stories—ones in which revolutionary outsiders have managed to oust establishment insiders from political authority in places like India, South Africa, France, Italy, Poland, Israel, and Iran.

Despite their obvious differences, the constitutions of all these nations are rooted in a common experience. In each, revolutionary insurgents manage to sustain a struggle against the old order for years or decades before finally gaining political ascendancy.

We will call this Time One—its more particular definition will serve as a recurring concern in our case studies. But for now, only one point needs emphasizing. During their respective Time One, insurgents do not merely rely on brute force in their battle against the status quo. They also denounce the existing regime as *illegitimate,* and call upon their fellow citizens to join in resisting the existing order. Indeed, these revolutionary declarations of principle play a central role in sustaining the movement, especially during periods of adversity. During dark moments, activists face the prospect of detention or death at the hands of the old regime. Nevertheless, they refuse to give up their struggle with a government they consider deeply illegitimate—and it is only natural for them to tell the world why they are right to think so.

These revolutionary pronunciamentos set the stage for the construction of the new regime at Time Two. The Founding is typically a time of high-energy politics, in which leaders and followers are bound together by long years of common sacrifice. Now that the insurgent movement has gained power, a distinctive option emerges: it may translate its high-energy politics into a constitution that seeks to prevent a relapse into the abuses of the past and commits the republic to the new principles proclaimed during the long hard struggle of Time One. To invoke a much-abused Weberian term—which I will define more precisely later—call this the *constitutionalization of revolutionary charisma.*

This is an option, not an imperative. We will be considering cases in which the ascendant movement fails to take advantage of its Time Two opportunity. But I have said enough to contrast this revolutionary scenario with two very different pathways that have also generated successful constitutional constructions over the course of the twentieth century.

In my second ideal type, the political order is built by pragmatic insiders, not revolutionary outsiders. When confronting popular movements for fundamental change, the insider establishment responds with strategic concessions that split the outsiders into moderate and radical camps. Insiders then invite moderate outsiders to desert their radical brethren and join the political establishment in governing the country. This co-optation strategy culminates in landmark reform legislation that allows the "sensible" outsiders to join the establishment—and thereby reinvigorates the establishment's claims to legitimate authority.

Great Britain provides a paradigmatic example. During the Napoleonic Wars, its governing elite repudiated revolution as a model for legitimate transformation. But over the next generation, the establishment refused to support hard-liners, like the Duke of Wellington, who were determined to suppress all efforts at fundamental change. Instead, "moderate" insiders reached out to "sensible" outsiders to support the Reform Act of 1832. This set the stage for further acts of strategic co-optation at later moments of popular confrontation. During the twentieth century, perhaps the most salient example was the Parliament Act of 1911, which legitimated the politics of redistribution characteristic of the modern welfare state.

Such landmarks represent fundamental elements of the British constitution, but they lack ringing statements of principle like those found, say, in South Africa's revolutionary Bill of Rights. Nor were they adopted in the name of a mobilized movement that committed the People to a "new beginning" in its political life. They emerged instead as strategic concessions adopted through the pragmatic adaptation of preexisting lawmaking institutions to accommodate the demands of "sensible" outsiders-turned-insiders.[2]

These great reform statutes seem so different from revolutionary constitutions that scholars often deny that the British have a constitution at all. This claim might make sense if constitutionalism designated a one-size-fits-all ideal type. But this is precisely what I deny. Countries traveling down the establishment track do indeed place great value on achievements like the Parliament Act. As later generations are socialized into the governing elite, they are trained to use these *precedents of responsible government* in dealing with the populist challenges of their own time.

Britain's example of pragmatic adaptation has influenced many parts of the Commonwealth—most notably Australia, Canada, and New Zealand, which share a distrust for ringing revolutionary principles, and emphasize the importance of prudent adaptation. Other forms of establishment-constitutionalism have emerged in Scandinavia, Latin America, and Asia. We will be studying their distinctive variations on common themes in the next volume. But this second ideal type will also provide a reference point in the present study—since revolutionary movements will often confront efforts to co-opt them into established regimes, and their responses can profoundly shape their success in constitutionalizing their charisma when they finally succeed in gaining control over the commanding heights.

Revolutionary Outsiders versus Responsible Insiders: the first two ideal types emerge out of high-pitched struggles, but generate different outcomes. Under the insider scenario, the political establishment makes strategic concessions that undermine outsider momentum; under the outsider scenario, the establishment is overwhelmed by a revolutionary constitutional order.

But regime change sometimes occurs without the pressure of a massive popular uprising, and this requires the addition of a third ideal type. Let's call it *elite construction*.

Under this scenario, the old system of government begins to unravel, but the general population stays relatively passive on the sidelines. The emerging power vacuum is occupied by previously excluded political and social elites, who serve as a principal force in the creation of a new constitutional order.

Sometimes the new constitution allows the old elites to retain a significant share of power; sometimes it doesn't. But whatever the particularities, the key point is that the new regime is an elite construction, not a revolutionary creation.

Elite constructions are also distinguishable from insider constitutions. Under the insider scenario, the political establishment remains in control of the situation, making strategic concessions that take the wind out of the sails of the insurgent movement. In the third model, the existing regime is experiencing such a severe crisis that political insiders can hope to retain a share of power only by making an elaborate compact with outside elites.

This insider-outsider compact generates a constitution that looks very different from the jumble of reform statutes that serve as precedents of responsible government in the establishment model. It is instead an elaborate document in which both sides define, and commit themselves to, the new rules of the game.

In developing these texts, elite protagonists may borrow heavily from provisions originating elsewhere—often from constitutions that have previously emerged from the revolutionary pathway. For example, their constitutions will typically claim to speak in the name of the People. Despite such rhetorical assertions, the rising elites have not, in fact, been propelled into existence by a mass movement of citizen-activists who have struggled in the People's name.

Spain provides a revealing example. Franco's death propelled the Falangist regime into a succession crisis. Haunted by memories of the Spanish Civil War, moderates led by King Juan Carlos preempted another revolutionary upheaval by reaching an accommodation with Franco's bitterest enemies. Resisting hard-line pressures, the young king appointed Adolfo Suárez prime minister, who reached out to bitter opponents—most notably Santiago Carrillo, leader of the illegal Communist Party. With the support of the army chief of staff and the leader of the Spanish Church, Suárez prevailed upon the Falangist legislature to pass a Law for Political Reform, setting the stage for free elections that included the Communists. When the electorate gave left and right extremists low levels of support, elite moderates were in a position to elaborate a democratic constitution, which was overwhelmingly approved by the voters at a referendum.

These votes were important, but they should not be confused with the kind of mass mobilization that serves as the primary engine of revolutionary constitutionalism. It was instead the king's decisive action in 1981—thwarting a military coup against the elected government—that consolidated the elite Constitution into a crucial legitimating element of the emerging system.[3]

The Spanish case has served as a central reference point for scholarly discussion of the great democratic wave that reached its climax with the fall of the Soviet Union after 1989. But these recent events should not overshadow an earlier turning point at which elitist dynamics played a key role. Most notably, the postwar constitutions of Germany and Japan were constructed by elites at a time when the masses were overwhelmed by the devastation of defeat. But in contrast to Spain, the German and Japanese elites were under the humiliating supervision of foreign occupiers. Despite this fact, these constitutional constructions have proved remarkably robust for more than two generations.

Nevertheless, they display legitimation problems that are closer to the Spanish case and very different from constitutions emerging from the first two pathways. Our next task is to diagnose these differences.

Different Types, Different Problems

Constitutionalizing Charisma

The great problem looming down the pathway of revolutionary constitutionalism is the specter of totalitarian dictatorship. Lenin and Mao—no less than Nehru, Mandela, De Gasperi, de Gaulle, Wałesa, Ben-Gurion and Khomeini—gained power after revolutionary challenges to the ancien regime. Yet the constitutions generated by the Communist Party served as mere propaganda devices for Stalinist and Maoist terror, and failed to impose significant constraints on the subsequent authoritarianisms of Nikita Khrushchev or Xi Jinping.

For a very long time, these Communist shams were viewed as the almost inevitable consequences of "real" revolutions. But this is a Cold War distortion—as I aim to show in the case studies that follow. At present, I will defer comparisons between constitutional and totalitarian revolutions, and focus on the way in which constitutional revolutions face a characteristic set of legitimation problems that are very different from those confronting countries traveling down establishmentarian and elitist pathways.

These problems arise from the distinctive dynamics involved in the constitutionalization of charisma—a notion I will be invoking to suggest an analogy with a similar, but different, process that Weber famously portrayed in describing the *bureaucratization* of charisma over time. I will be emphasizing two fundamental aspects of this dynamic: one, political; the other, legal.

My political analysis emphasizes the way in which the revolutionary legitimacy of the founding generation fades over time. During Time One, the very act of joining the revolutionary party was dangerous—risking violent repression from the old regime. The experience of common sacrifice establishes a charismatic bond between revolutionary leaders and their followers that legitimates their new constitutions at Time Two. This bond between high-energy movement and legalistic text is important, but it only serves as the initial stage of a longer-term process. So long as the revolutionary generation lives, the vivid memories of their struggle against the old regime are a key resource through which the revolutionary government legitimates its use of power; the proud pronouncements in the constitutional text play only a secondary role.

But as the founding generation dies off, the revolutionary regime confronts a *legitimacy vacuum* at Time Three. On the one hand, the rising generation has a very different understanding of the role of the political parties that spearheaded the earlier revolution. During the days of insurgency, the simple decision to join the movement was dangerous, carrying the risk of arrest or jail or worse. But now the former revolutionary party serves as a pathway to power. This means that it will attract countless opportunists who care little about the old ideals—although there will be other, more idealistic types who will seek to reinvigorate them. Nevertheless, second-generation idealists can't claim the charismatic authority earned by their predecessors. After all, the first generation didn't just talk revolution; they risked a lot to make it happen. But the idealists of the rising generation are all too aware that they are building on the founding legacy.

An analogous process is also occurring among millions of ordinary people who lived through the revolution. While they pay minimal attention to current politics in the distant capital, for them the revolution remains a vital reality during Time Two, with parents regaling their children with (often-embroidered) accounts of their own small sacrifices on behalf of the insurgency during its times of trial. But these vivid accounts begin to fade as the old-timers die and leave their children with half-forgotten memories.

In short: at both elite and mass levels, political authority moves toward *the normalization of revolutionary politics.*

The opposite is true among the lawyers and other professionals who are charged with interpreting the enduring meaning of the constitution. Lawyers earn their pay by persuading powerful officials to vindicate their clients' interests. This means that during Time One, most professionals were deeply enmeshed in mastering the dominant legalisms of the old regime. Once this regime has been repudiated at Time Two, these old-timers will have problematic claims to authority as they adapt their legal arguments to take account of the new revolutionary legal order.

There will be exceptions. Some radical lawyers will have supported the movement during Time One, and may win great prominence in the constitutional drafting process at Time Two. But even after their revolutionary text is proclaimed in the name of the People, there will be lots of work to do before the profession as a whole can fully assimilate the revolution's constitutional principles into its repertoire of legal argument. By definition, the radical principles announced at the Founding disrupt many older legal notions—and it takes a great deal of time for lawyers and judges to reorient their older notions to build new doctrinal solutions to a host of practical problems. During the early decades, this will lead to a good deal of caution in dealing with potential confrontations with the charismatic governmental leaders in charge of the political branches—who will predictably accuse the judiciary of playing politics if it tries to use its old-style legalisms to veto key initiatives advanced by the movement party in power. Rather than risk institutional humiliation, courts will typically develop their early constitutional doctrines in less provocative settings—building up an increasingly elaborate body of authoritative opinions that will serve as the basis for greater professional self-confidence as the years go by. While Time Two jurists are exquisitely aware of the fragility of their efforts to come to terms with the revolutionary constitution, lawyers and judges at Time Three use these early judgments with growing self-confidence as authoritative precedents in their efforts to resolve hot-button disputes between rival politicians.

This means that Time Three will be marked by a series of succession crises—in which an increasingly confident judiciary will confront an increasingly normalized political class in an intensive struggle to occupy the legitimacy vacuum left by the preceding generation. On the one hand, the politicians will continue to assert that the old political parties still are the principal carriers of the revolutionary spirit; on the other, the legal professionals will insist that their constitutional doctrines are more deeply rooted in the Founding than anything the second-generation politicians have to offer.

These struggles for authority take different forms in different places, but in many cases the judiciary successfully manages to get the political branches grudgingly to recognize the judges' claims to ultimate constitutional authority. This breakthrough at Time Three, however, remains vulnerable for quite some time—and its ultimate fate depends on the success of legal professionals in consolidating the high court's assertions of supremacy over the next few decades during Time Four.

We will be exploring crucial variations on these themes in the chapters that follow. But one point will suffice for now: The four-stage process raises legitimation problems that are categorically different from those arising in polities traveling down the two other constitutional pathways.

Disestablishment

Consider the insider paradigm of responsible government. These regimes dismiss the very idea that a mass movement led by outside agitators can legitimately speak for the People. Serious government cannot be based on such populist claptrap. It is grounded instead in the capacity of seasoned elites to convince "sensible" outsiders to abandon rabble-rousing extremists and join the old establishment in pragmatically adapting the system to meet the changing "needs of the times."

Within this framework, there is no room for judges to invalidate legislation by claiming that it violates fundamental principles established "by the People" at the Founding—for the simple reason that no such revolutionary transformations are recognized as legitimate. Instead, talk of popular sovereignty is dismissed as a legal fiction concealing the crucial role of statesmanlike elites in the democratic process. On this understanding, voters confront competing Election Manifestos, prepared by leaders of rival political parties, describing their action plans if they gain the support of the voters at the next election. When their party does indeed triumph on election day, its leaders have *earned* the democratic right to enact its manifesto into law. Once the new prime minister gains the support of parliament, she has every right to insist on the enactment of her party's initiatives even if they repudiate significant legislation passed by earlier parliaments. It is utterly undemocratic for courts to strike down these new statutes as inconsistent with inherited "constitutional norms" based on older legislation.

It follows that claims to judicial supremacy have no proper role within this second ideal type. Nevertheless, the paradigm does provide a space for the judiciary to play an important, if secondary, function within the evolving system. After all, judges are very much part of the governing establishment. By temperament and training, they have a comparative advantage in reflecting upon the meaning of the great constitutional settlements of the past, and they are frequently called upon to apply their understandings of these precedents in the resolution of concrete cases. As a consequence, their judicial opinions can alert the political leadership to the presence of fundamental legal issues that they might otherwise ignore as they deal with current concrete problems.

Nevertheless, and in contrast to the revolutionary model, there is a definite limit to the court's authority. Judges may be allowed to insist that the sitting parliament take a hard look at fundamental legal questions raised by its statutory innovations. But if the prime minister gains parliamentary support a second time around, the courts should call a halt to their resistance. While judges may play a constructive role by returning a problematic statute for reconsideration, they must recognize parliament's democratic authority to demand that the courts faithfully implement the new legislation the second time around. While one round of back-and-forth may play a useful role, a second round would amount to outright defiance of the mandate that the party has won in the last election.

This "soft form" of judicial review is categorically distinct from the "hard form" affirmed by courts during Times Three and Four in the political life of revolutionary regimes. In countries traveling down this pathway, the death of the Founding generation opens a legitimacy vacuum which courts have successfully filled by asserting that they serve as *superior* defenders of the legacy left by the revolutionary constitution—and that the more opportunistic political leaders of the new generation should indeed defer to the judiciary's professional efforts to safeguard core principles motivating the earlier struggle for liberation.

The distinction between "hard" and "soft" judicial review has become increasingly important during the postwar era, in which both national and international charters of human rights have gained increasing political salience. This has provided an opening for judges in Great Britain, the Commonwealth, and other establishmentarian jurisdictions to engage in different forms of "soft" review requiring democratically elected governments to reconsider proposed legislation which threaten to undermine the emerging consensus on fundamental human rights. Nevertheless, this soft form of judicial review is categorically different from the claims to judicial supremacy that are common in other systems. It serves to complement, not challenge, the basic premises of establishmentarianism—so long as the courts make it clear that they will defer to parliamentary sovereignty in the end.[4]

In contrast, the rise of popular referenda does raise a fundamental challenge to establishmentarianism—and one that has no counterpart within revolutionary regimes. Because type-one constitutions are grounded in narratives based on earlier acts of collective sacrifice against illegitimate governments, their drafters will not raise principled objections to the use of referenda at later points in constitutional development. When properly structured, they can serve as a focus for revitalized grassroots movements to express the will of "We the People" on future occasions when elected politicians assault foundational understandings. The only question within the revolutionary paradigm is prudential: Is it possible to design the referendum process so that it can be triggered by broadly based movements, but not by special interests?

The referendum represents a far deeper threat to the establishment tradition. Rather than allowing the time-tested parliamentary leadership the chance to hammer out sensible solutions to pressing problems, referenda open the way for demagogic appeals to ordinary citizens who lack the time and knowledge required for such fateful choices.

For present purposes, the recent British vote endorsing exit from the European Union suggests the depth of the legitimation crisis that referenda can generate. For starters, the Westminster government's decision to call a referendum in 2016 owes absolutely nothing to the revolutionary spirit that leads popular movements to entrench referenda in their type-one constitutions. To the contrary, the British decision was the product of short-term decisions by no-nonsense politicians who chose to use the referendum device without regard to its long-term constitutional implications.

The roots of the tragicomedy of 2016 go back to the early 1970s, when Prime Ministers Edward Heath and Harold Wilson convinced the British to join Europe in the first place. Up to this point, the Westminster establishment had looked with disdain on the Continental tendency to call national referenda when the going got tough. As a consequence, when Prime Minister Heath triumphantly brought home an agreement with Brussels to join the Common Market, he did not seriously consider offering it up for approval at a special referendum. Instead, he followed the tradition of the Great Reform Acts and presented the basic terms of his bargain with Brussels to Parliament for its approval—only to encounter fierce opposition in the House of Commons.

While most of the Nos came from the Labour Party, a few Conservative nationalists also defied their own party's prime minister and joined the opposition. Nevertheless, Heath pushed his initiative through Parliament by razor-thin margins. On January 1, 1973, Great Britain entered Europe in a fashion that vindicated the Westminster tradition of responsible government.

The tradition began to unravel, however, when Heath called a snap election in early 1974, expecting that his dramatic European achievement would be rewarded by a ringing endorsement at the polls. This didn't happen. Harold Wilson instead promised the voters that he would get a better deal from Brussels if they put him in power. When his Labour Party emerged from the election with the most seats, Wilson became prime minister; but he confronted a special problem: though he had come out on top, his party had fallen thirty-three seats short of the 334 members of Parliament (MPs) required for a clear majority in the Commons. Given his shaky control over Parliament, he was then obliged to rely on Conservative votes to gain majority support for the new EU deal that he managed to negotiate in Brussels. Yet this appeal to Tory MPs alienated many of his Labour MPs, threatening his government with imminent collapse.

This prospect led Wilson to call a referendum on his New Deal with Brussels. Under this scenario, he could stave off a no-confidence vote long enough to ask voters to give their support to his European initiative; if he succeeded, he could then reassert his authority over his fragile parliamentary coalition on the ground that they should respect the "judgment of the People," and move on to other issues on which they were united.

Wilson's end-run around Parliament succeeded. His New Deal for Europe gained 2-to-1 support from the voters, allowing him to stagger on as prime minister for a while.[5] In turning to the referendum, however, Wilson paid absolutely no heed to the dangers it posed to fundamental principles of Westminster democracy. It was only his short-term problem of coalition management that led him to break with the Westminster tradition exemplified by the Great Reform Bill of 1832 and the Parliament Act of 1911. Indeed, his statute calling for a referendum formally designated it as merely advisory. This stat-utory caveat, however, only demonstrated Wilson's characteristically British contempt for abstract constitutional principles. He did not take seriously the possibility that if his opponents won the referendum, they might insist that Parliament was *obligated* to heed the "judgment of the People."

Moreover, the 2-to-1 Yes vote seemed to redeem Wilson's disdain for coun-terfactuals. Perhaps it would turn out that his one-off use of the referendum had managed to resolve the European question once and for all. For all any-body could tell at the time, Wilson's maneuver revealed the establishment's remarkable capacity to "muddle through" constitutional crises with great suc-cess, precisely by refusing to indulge the French habit of fierce debate over abstract constitutional principles.

It didn't turn out that way. The Brexit referendum is forcing Britain to con-front the legitimation crisis that Wilson managed to evade in 1975. Forty years later, David Cameron found himself in precisely the same position as Wilson. He was a pro-European prime minister at the head of a party with a powerful anti-European faction—whose opposition to the European Union was making it increasingly difficult for him to govern effectively at Westmin-ster. Like Wilson, he tried to obtain a better bargain from Brussels that would satisfy his opponents' increasingly vociferous complaints. But when his critics refused to be pacified, he desperately clung to power by invoking Wilson's precedent and calling a referendum in the hope of leading a multiparty pro-European coalition to victory. Like his predecessor, he did not seriously con-sider the deeper constitutional implications of a No vote.

In this respect at least, Cameron's establishmentarian tendencies were even more pronounced than Wilson's. The Conservative leader came from a wealthy family. Young David was educated at Oxford, where his outstanding perfor-mance allowed him easy entry into the higher reaches of the Conservative Party, culminating in his election as its leader. This paradigmatic member of the British establishment was unprepared to take seriously the notion that dissident Conservatives and outraged UK Independence Party members (UKIPers) might succeed in their rabble-rousing efforts to exploit mass prej-udices for a No vote against the prime minister's sensible effort to renegotiate Britain's deal with Brussels.

Like Wilson, Cameron was careful to specify, in the special statute calling for a referendum, that its results were strictly advisory. But once the polls closed, the victorious "populists" insisted that their 52–48 victory represented an authoritative decision by the British People that Westminster could not legitimately ignore. They also took the strongest possible view of the meaning of the popular verdict—insisting on a "hard" Brexit in which Britain would break all ties with the European Union.

Constitutional chaos ensued as Cameron resigned in disgrace, opening up a space for one of his leading opponents to take his place. But then something quite revealing happened. After some frantic maneuvering, the Conservatives turned away from the leading Brexiteers, who had stabbed Cameron in the back, and embraced yet another member of the governing establishment. The new prime minister, Theresa May, had loyally served Cameron as home secretary, and had loyally supported his pro-European position during the referendum campaign. But as she positioned herself for the top job, she suddenly switched sides, and now endorsed the "hard" Brexit demanded by the populists. Her dramatic turnaround set the stage for yet another time-honored effort at establishmentarian co-optation. By turning to her as prime minister, the establishment gave due recognition to the populist impulse— just as it had at crucial turning points beginning with the Reform Act of 1832. But it nevertheless hoped to sustain its grip on authority by presenting a paradigmatic member of the establishment as a humble servant of the People's will.

Once installed as prime minister, the establishment's new leader refused to allow her parliamentary critics to block the quick implementation of the 52–48 vote. She insisted instead that she could simply tell Queen Elizabeth to exercise her Royal Prerogative to inform the European Union that Britain was leaving, without any need for legislative approval at Westminster.

May's effort to short-circuit Parliament harkened back to a pre-democratic era when kings had real power, but over the centuries the Royal Prerogative had become merely symbolic, with the queen deferring to the prime minister as the authoritative spokesperson for the Commons. By ignoring the grounds for this modern convention, May was proposing to use the Royal Prerogative—of all things—as a battering ram to vindicate popular sovereignty over the deeply entrenched principle of parliamentary sovereignty.

In characteristically British fashion, May was entirely uninterested in confronting the constitutional paradoxes that she was provoking. So far as she was concerned, the prerogative had appeal simply as a solution to a very practical problem: given the strong pro-European sentiment of many MPs, it wasn't clear that she could win majority support for Brexit in the Commons, and the Royal Prerogative would permit her to avoid a humiliating defeat that might lead to her downfall.

Yet the self-aggrandizing character of her proposal generated loud protests elsewhere—leading to an equally remarkable effort to use the courts to stop her royalist/populist initiative dead in its tracks. This appeal was itself deeply problematic—at no time in recent history had the judges claimed the authority to serve as the final arbiters of the meaning of the British constitution. Nevertheless, within six months of the June referendum, the Supreme Court made precisely this claim, invalidating Ms. May's proposed use of the prerogative as an unconstitutional assault on the principle of parliamentary sovereignty.

The scene was set for a mind-blowing confrontation: The Court rising to the defense of Parliament while the queen asserted the supremacy of popular sovereignty—with the prime minister cheering her on.[6] How to resolve this struggle over the fundamental principles of the British constitution?

It was handled in characteristically British fashion: by muddling through under establishment leadership. Rather than escalating the crisis further by denouncing the Court's decision as illegitimate, May returned to Westminster without further comment on constitutional first principles and managed to push her Brexit bill through Parliament. Nevertheless, despite her critics' failure to block the enactment of a strong bill, their vocal opposition put her on notice that she could not count on Parliament to ratify the exit agreement she hoped to negotiate with Brussels.

This led her, paradoxically, to take a step that further exacerbated Britain's constitutional predicament. She called a "snap" parliamentary election in June 2017, appealing to the voters to ratify their Brexit decision by enhancing her Conservative majority.

May had every reason to expect success. Both pollsters and pundits were united in predicting a landslide victory over her fragmented and demoralized opposition. Yet they were wrong once again. Instead of giving the prime minister their overwhelming support, the voters returned a "hung parliament"—in which the demoralized Conservatives lost their majority—and May could no longer hope to cobble together a coalition in Commons that would approve the sweeping legislation required for her decisive break with the Continent.

It is anybody's guess what this will mean for Britain's future relationship to the European Union. But for present purposes, I am more interested in emphasizing how this latest turn of the wheel deepens Britain's constitutional confusion. To put the issue in bold relief, begin with a counterfactual: Suppose the snap election had indeed generated a Conservative landslide. Under this scenario, the new Parliament would have endorsed May's position that it had an obligation to heed the 2016 referendum and rubber-stamp the sweeping legislation required for a "hard" Brexit. This would have created a decisive precedent for the future—establishing that Westminster had a constitutional responsibility to follow through on the judgment of the People expressed at referenda.

The "hung parliament" will instead force an agonizing reappraisal. It will require the general public and the political classes to ask a very different question: Which has priority in determining Britain's constitutional future—the 2016 vote in the referendum or the 2017 vote for Parliament?

Even more importantly: How will this question be resolved—through another snap election to Parliament or another referendum or some combination of both?

The British may well rise to the occasion and respond in relatively decisive fashion. Under these optimistic scenarios, we will see either the revitalization of the country's long-standing tradition of parliamentary government or the construction of a twenty-first-century version of popular sovereignty—or some hybrid containing both elements. Whatever the details, Britain would emerge with a constitutional paradigm that has broad credibility among the general public and governing elite.

There is also a darker scenario looming on the horizon. In this alternative future, Britain's political establishment fails to muddle its way through to a sensible resolution of the Brexit problem. Instead, the competition between rival parties only generates a pattern of "hung parliaments" and indecisive referenda that lead to escalating confusion—further exacerbated by agonized Supreme Court pronouncements along the way. Over the coming decade, the very notion that British government can rely on a relatively coherent constitutional legacy will seem increasingly problematic—leading to deep confusion among political elites and broad-ranging alienation by the general public.[7]

In raising this prospect, my aim isn't to predict the future, but to invite you to consider a fundamental issue. After all, the establishmentarian version of Westminster democracy has been one of the greatest success stories of the past two centuries. Yet the Brexit episode teaches that great historical success may not suffice to propel a legitimation paradigm forward into the future. Sometimes muddling through may suffice if a nation is lucky; but there are occasions when political leaders must look beyond short-term self-interest to sustain the legitimacy of their larger governing framework. *Constitutional statesmanship can play a key role in sustaining political legitimacy, and its failure may undermine the most entrenched paradigms.*

Authenticity

With this in mind, let's turn to our final ideal type. Elite constructions lack the legitimation resources available to constitutions generated by the two preceding paradigms. On the one hand, the drafters can't claim that they represent revolutionary movements that have carried on a sustained struggle for the principles enshrined in their new system of higher law; on the other hand, they don't represent an established political elite that has successfully guided the nation for generations. How, then, is the elitist constitution to generate support for its legitimacy among the general population?

With difficulty.

Let's call it the authenticity problem, and we see it on display in Spain today. Despite its relatively good performance over the past generation, the Constitution crafted in Madrid in the 1970s has met with broad resistance in the Basque country for decades. It has more recently provoked an even more acute crisis in Catalonia—with a revolutionary movement party for Catalan independence insisting that the Spanish Constitution is a top-down assertion of power that does not represent the authentic will of the Catalan nation.

I will defer a sustained analysis of the Spanish case to the next volume. For present purposes, it serves as a contemporary example of authenticity problems confronting many other countries. The issue arises most acutely when, in contrast to Spain, the new Constitution is the product of military defeat and foreign occupation. In this scenario, domestic elites hammer out the terms of their "new beginning" under the direct supervision of their military conquerors. In such cases, why should these elite constructions continue to win the support of the general public once the military occupation comes to an end and the Constitution must sustain itself on its own, despite its stigmatizing association with humiliating defeat?

Sometimes this question has no answer. Consider the constitutional collapses that recently occurred in Iraq and Afghanistan once these regimes were obliged to fend for themselves after America withdrew most of its military forces.

Sometimes the question arises after a long period of quiescence. Consider today's Japan, where the Abe government is challenging the Peace Article of the Constitution imposed by General MacArthur. If Abe succeeds, this may well be the opening gun in his larger campaign for a sweeping repudiation of the MacArthur Constitution as an inauthentic expression of Japanese values.[8]

But in some cases this question is buried so deeply in political consciousness that it fails to provoke collective anxiety. This is precisely the situation in Germany today. How has the country avoided a serious confrontation with the fact that its Basic Law of 1949 was created under military conditions that severely compromised its claims to authenticity?

To be sure, Allied occupation of Germany wasn't quite as omnipresent as it was in Japan. But it was still overwhelming. At the end of the war, the Four Powers each controlled a separate part of Germany—and none were willing to allow their residents to craft their own form of government. While the Soviets went their own way, the three Western allies met in London to establish the conditions under which West Germans would be allowed to proceed. The London Protocol, as it was called, was addressed to the leaders of the newly created governments in the American, British, and French zones. They were told to send representatives to a Parliamentary Council, which would submit the Constitution for approval at a referendum. By insisting on a popular vote, the Allies aimed to safeguard the new Constitution against later charges of inauthenticity.

Nevertheless, the Parliamentary Council rejected this demand. Although its leaders owed their positions of political prominence to the Allies, they refused to call a referendum, and emphasized that they did not believe that their charter deserved the status of a Constitution. This is why they called it a "Basic Law" instead, and asserted in its Final Article that a truly authentic Constitution could only be achieved when East Germans could free themselves from Soviet control and join the Westerners at a new constituent assembly speaking for the entire German Nation.[9]

When faced with this remarkable act of defiance, the Allies found it prudent to back down. Nevertheless, they were right in believing that this exacerbated their authenticity problem. A leading scholar, Donald Kommers, reports, "Opinion polls showed that . . . a majority of the respondents were not even aware of the Parliamentary Council's existence. In May of 1949, a survey found that two-thirds of them were not sure what the Basic Law was." He rightly concludes that in losing the chance to approve the Basic Law, "West

German voters were depriv[ed] of the knowledge they might have gained . . . had a popular campaign for ratification taken place."[10]

Within this context, the Basic Law's most famous constitutional innovation takes on a paradoxical appearance. In ringing provisions, its "eternity clauses" declare that human dignity, democracy, and the rule of law serve as bedrock principles of the new republic, and can *never* be undermined by later amendments. But what does it mean for an emphatically provisional "Basic Law" to insist that human dignity is an eternal value of the Republic? Or that democracy is eternal, when Germans were not allowed to vote on the Basic Law itself?

The authenticity problem arose again in 1989. With East German street demonstrators challenging Communist rule by proclaiming "We are the People," the vice president of the West German Constitutional Court, Ernst Gottfried Mahrenholz, insisted that the Final Article of the Basic Law required Chancellor Helmut Kohl to convene a Constituent Assembly of the *entire* German people to hammer out a true Constitution.[11] While Mahrenholz presented the case most persuasively, many others made similar demands.

Helmut Kohl was not among them. The last thing he wanted was a lot of East German Communists and West German leftists entering a Constituent Assembly to challenge the legitimacy of his government. He refused to heed the Final Article, and engineered reunification through one of the most curious international agreements in legal history. The standard treaty is negotiated by sovereign states to regulate future relationships with one another. But the so-called "Reunification Treaty" extinguished the existence of the DDR at the very moment it signed the agreement. I know of no other "treaty" that has operated as a suicide pact.[12]

Yet a quarter century later, Germany has managed to forget the fact that, in both 1949 and 1989, its political elite refused to place the Constitution before the voters for their considered judgment.

How to account for this act of collective amnesia?

During the 1950s and 1960s, it was the Economic Miracle, not the Basic Law, that played the central role in legitimating the rise of the Federal Republic from the ashes of the Nazi catastrophe. If there was a single preeminent symbol of the New Germany during this period, it was the deutsche mark, not the "eternity clauses." It was only during later decades that the German Constitutional Court successfully transformed the Basic Law into a central element of German political identity—so much so that the replacement of the deutsche mark by the euro in the 1990s could occur without the national trauma that would have accompanied a similar displacement in the 1960s.

But once again, the Court's role in Germany was very different from the roles played by judiciaries emerging out of the previous two scenarios. It did not root the Basic Law in the revolutionary achievements of the constitutional past—since there weren't any. Nor did it engage in a collaborative enterprise with the established political branches, as the judiciary did in Great Britain and the Commonwealth. Its path to success was exceedingly complex, and I will try to do it justice in the next book.[13] In this Introduction, it's more important to consider how the elitist origins of German constitutionalism fit into my trinitarian analysis of the distinctive predicament confronting the European Union's quest for legitimacy.

The EU Crisis: A Cultural Diagnosis

There is an ongoing disagreement over the nature of the European Union. Some believe it is broadly comparable with other great federations—most notably the United States. Others view it as unique.

My argument leads me into the uniqueness camp. The leading nations of Europe come to the Union along different paths: the Constitutions of Germany and Spain are elite constructions; France and Italy and Poland have moved down the revolutionary path; Great Britain emerges from the establishmentarian tradition.

Little wonder these countries have trouble finding a common pathway to a more perfect union. For the French and Italians, it is perfectly acceptable for a popular movement to launch a transnational movement for a more United Europe—and if this movement gains traction, it can prepare the way for a Constituent Assembly that could legitimately present a new federal Constitution for ratification by the People of Europe at referenda.

Germans, however, see EU-wide referenda as vehicles that would permit demagogic populists to repudiate fundamental human rights in the name of the People. Given this clear and present danger, it is wiser to rely on constitutional courts to serve as the final arbiters in conflicts between the European Union and its member states.

Britain will go down a third pathway if it reconsiders Brexit and reenters the Union. Instead of looking to the courts, or to referenda, to resolve fundamental issues of principle, it would encourage political leaders on the Continent to muddle their way through to no-nonsense solutions.

In contrast, the United States does not display a similar split when it comes to the fundamental question of legitimacy. From the Founding onward, the revolutionary paradigm has remained central to the American experience—with mobilized political movements repeatedly transforming fundamental principles during Reconstruction, the New Deal, and the Civil Rights Revolution.[14]

This revolutionary tradition hardly immunizes the United States from the crises of the twenty-first century—endless war, escalating economic inequality, intensifying cultural division, looming ecological catastrophe. But a common paradigm organizes the collective American effort to confront these problems. We repeatedly see popular movements of the Right and Left appealing to their fellow citizens to repudiate the "Washington establishment" from power and generate deep and broad support for a decisive break with the corrupt past. The great question is which movement party will succeed in mobilizing the People in the manner of George Washington, Abraham Lincoln, Franklin Roosevelt, or Martin Luther King Jr.

Today's Americans, like those of earlier centuries, currently confront the challenges posed by the charismatic movement politics of revolutionary reform—and the final chapter of this book will explore how this paradigm gives a distinctive shape to the profound predicaments the country confronts in the age of Trump.

But for now, the key point to emphasize is that the crisis of the European Union has a very different shape. Because its member states emerge from different legitimation-paradigms, they don't even agree on the appropriate path to take in resolving the crises that threaten to rip the Union apart—with Germany, France / Italy / Poland, and Great Britain predisposed to respond very differently to common problems.

These deep conflicts might have been ameliorated if recent European history had taken a different turn. A decade ago, the member states of the European Union met at the Brussels Convention to launch an appeal to the Peoples of Europe to ratify a Constitutional Treaty. If this campaign had succeeded, Europe would have been in a much better position to deal with the escalating crises threatening the Union's future.

This point is ignored by scholars who emphasize that, after the voters in France and the Netherlands rejected the proposed treaty, political elites met in Lisbon and hammered out a new agreement that contained many of the same terms and that currently provides the basic framework for the Union. But the Lisbon agreement and later accords were elite constructions that tried to avoid self-conscious consideration of their merits by ordinary citizens. This decade of evasion is allowing rising protest movements to portray the European Union as an alien force dominated by harsh technocrats, with EU politicians serving as pseudo-democratic ornaments.

Is there a way out of this impasse?

I do not know. My aim is diagnosis, not cure. There is some consolation, however, in reflecting on a basic limitation of my analysis. As Weber emphasized, no real-world polity perfectly expresses any ideal type. One type may predominate—in the case of the European Union, that type is elite constitutionalism—but particular historical experiences may well generate counterthemes from competing paradigms. Rather than yearning for the purity of a single ideal type, the path of statesmanship may well involve the creative synthesis of cross-cultural themes with broad resonance throughout the Union.

We will be in a better position to explore this possibility at the end of the second book, once we have worked our way through case studies exploring the constitutional dynamics that have propelled different member-states in such different directions.

Only one thing should be clear: it is better to be self-conscious about the European Union's trilemma than to pretend it doesn't exist.

❀ PART ONE

Constitutional Revolutions

CHAPTER 1

Constitutionalizing Revolution?

Classical Greek thought is thoroughly unsympathetic to the notion of sudden political change. For Plato and Aristotle, a dramatic breach with the past placed the polity on the threshold of catastrophic decline.

The Semitic religions reversed the relationship between past and future. For Moses, Jesus, and Mohammed, the idol-worshipping past was the problem, not the solution. The challenge was to repudiate its temptations and transform secular authority so that it respected the Word of God. The revolutionary present, marking the revelation of the divine will on Earth, represented a triumphant "new beginning," not a catastrophic moment of political disorder.

A successful break with the political past would not suffice to ensure salvation. Final redemption could come only by transcending the temporal world entirely—and gaining one's rightful place in the eternal order. But so long as humanity remained trapped within its mortal coil, the challenge for secular government was to break with the pagan past, embrace the divine truth marked out by the holy scriptures and prevent future relapses into the bad old days.

The European Enlightenment launched an assault on the Semitic religions by regrounding political authority on the will of the People, not the will of God. But Enlightenment revolutionaries did not go further to reject the Jewish / Christian / Muslim understanding of the relationship between past, present, and future. From 1776 onward, they refused to succumb to neoclassical fears of sudden political change. They insisted that it was right and proper for the People to rise up against the injustices of the ancien regime, and create a revolutionary "new beginning" that would break with the past and set a brave new course for the future.[1]

This secular relegitimation of a revolutionary "new beginning" has had a massive impact over the past 250 years—generating a complex pattern of achievement and catastrophe throughout the world.[2] My central aim is to identify and analyze these legitimation patterns.

I will be dividing modern revolutions into two broad types. In the *totalizing variant,* the mobilized movement of the People aims for a root-and-branch reconstruction of all aspects of social and political life. This aspiration legitimates the worst pathologies of the twentieth century. If the aim is to build an Enlightenment Paradise on Earth, it must be led by a revolutionary Party dedicated single-mindedly to this awe-inspiring task—relentlessly crushing reactionary dissent and purging Party members who deviate from the sacred mission. The Party-state may also promulgate a constitution expressing its guiding ideals, but it does not allow "bourgeois legalism" to block ongoing efforts by the revolutionary vanguard to redeem the judgment of History.

We see this logic at work in the Reign of Terror during the French Revolution. But it reaches its peak with Stalin and Mao—who claimed "scientific" Marxism as a warrant for the death and degradation of tens of millions in the Party's struggle to ensure the triumph of the Working Class.

Once the Communists legitimated the totalizing reconstruction of society, the same logic was appropriated by its most determined opponents. Most obviously, Adolf Hitler repudiated the Marxists' universalistic appeals to the workers of the world, but shared their belief that Party dictatorship was the only serious way to establish Heaven on Earth.

I invoke these notorious examples to emphasize the contrast with the second kind of revolution whose dynamics we shall be analyzing in the chapters which follow.

Revolution on a Human Scale

Revolutions on a human scale are very ambitious affairs—indeed, they are the most ambitious collective enterprises that human beings can ever realistically execute. But they do not attempt a total makeover of society. They focus on *particular sphere(s) of social or political life,* and mobilize activists to repudiate currently dominant beliefs and practices within *the target of revolutionary concern* while leaving intact prevailing mores in other spheres.

The revolution succeeds when it *fundamentally* reorganizes dominant beliefs and practices in a *relatively* short period of time. Over the longer run, radical reorganization in the target domain(s) may lead to significant transformations in other spheres—but this is not inevitable. To the contrary, these relatively intact spheres of social life may remain robust for a very long time to come. In contrast to the totalizers, no revolution-on-a-human-scale marks the End of History.

This is why a constitution is so important. Once revolutionaries gain power, it makes sense to hammer out the particular commitments that inspired their movement to make such sacrifices to destroy the old regime during Time One. The constitutional text commits the new regime to a series of *revolutionary reforms,* not a totalizing transformation, of the old order.

To put the point more affirmatively, the constituent assembly will serve as a central forum for a broader debate that tries, first, *to target* the spheres of political and social life where deep-cutting reform is most imperative, and, second, *to specify* the particular constitutional commitments necessary to achieve the requisite revolutionary reforms.

There are no easy answers. Some revolutionaries will aim for bigger changes; some will focus on narrower targets. The crucial question is whether the different elements of the leadership can hammer out terms that can gain the broad support of the grassroots movement. If the revolutionary coalition succeeds, Time Two culminates in a Constitution broadly recognized as the work of We the People; if not, the regime must legitimate itself at later moments without the resources provided by this early success.

I have packed a lot into the last five paragraphs. Let's go over the same ground more carefully.[3]

"Political" Revolutions

Modern political and social life organizes itself into relatively autonomous spheres. At any given time and place, the principles and practices prevailing in particular spheres differ dramatically—the way you are expected to behave within the family differs radically from the norms prevailing at work or school or church or the sports field. "Normal" people are constantly making the requisite shifts as they move from one sphere to another in daily life. While negotiating the imperative demands of their "life world," they may sometimes take a look at a newspaper or internet site to keep up with political battles going on in the distant capitol. Most of the time they are content to remain on the sidelines while engaged in the more pressing demands of everyday life. Nevertheless, they may well be open to the appeals of movement-activists who aim to recruit them to their ongoing effort to overcome the resistance of these remote power centers and respond affirmatively to their demands for a revolution on a human scale.

Consider the women's movement and its challenge to deeply rooted forms of male domination in different spheres of economic life. If women had contented themselves with micro-changes in their ordinary lives, the current generation would have witnessed only gradual shifts in a vaguely egalitarian direction. Instead we see something more much ambitious. Throughout the world, women are building sociopolitical movements that self-consciously insist on fundamental reforms in the institutionalized expectations prevailing in sphere after sphere. It takes real courage for activists to join these campaigns—since the men in charge often respond by punishing them for their disruptive challenges to the status quo. Yet the activists persist, linking their demands at home, at work, and other crucial spheres to a larger vision of a more just society. This multi-sphere mobilization has had very different consequences in different parts of the world—in some places, generating a fierce backlash; in others, a revolution on a human scale.

Yet, even where it has been most successful, the women's movement has by no means demanded a total revolution against all forms of economic and social oppression, nor has it even insisted on a fundamental transformation of the political system. This might indeed be necessary in traditionalist monarchies like Saudi Arabia. But in many other places, the movement's success in mounting the necessary constitutional and legislative changes may serve to confirm the legitimacy of the transformed political order—by demonstrating its responsiveness to fundamental changes in social attitudes and practices.

This book deals, then, with a special case—in which the transformative target is the political regime itself. In focusing on the state, revolutionaries on a human scale in India, South Africa, and elsewhere will often find themselves struggling against totalizing competitors, who denounce them as "mere" reformers who lack the courage of their convictions. But despite these predictable attacks, the revolutionary regime-transformations achieved by the Indian and South African Congress Parties were not acts of cowardly betrayal of the Leninist / Maoist ideal. To the contrary, they proceeded from the recognition that only gods can successfully revolutionize everything at once, and that mere mortals will achieve greater progress by focusing their energies upon constitutional transformations that enable the new regime to target those deeply entrenched injustices whose reform is most urgently required at their particular moment in history.

Now that we have located revolutionary constitutionalism as a species of a familiar genus, it will pay to elaborate its distinctive features.[4]

Self-Consciousness

A movement can't be revolutionary without presenting itself as the bearer of great and exigent principles that require a break with the current regime. Not only must movement leaders advance a public critique which indicts the existing regime as illegitimate. The critique must gain the self-conscious endorsement of grassroots activists, who deploy it in their ongoing campaigns to generate broad public support. Of course, different protagonists will differ in their attention to movement principles—with many spending much more of their time on the urgent business of defending the insurgency against the old regime's effort to destroy it. Nevertheless, even the most hard-nosed militants need to believe that their sacrifices are worth it—otherwise, they would give up the struggle. It is precisely the aim of the movement's self-conscious critique to reassure them on this crucial matter.

The "self-consciousness" requirement may be fulfilled by many different ideologies, so long as they remain on a human scale. An appeal to national liberation may serve as a key element, as in India or Poland, but a revolution may also appeal to imperial grandeur, as in Gaullist France. It may be social democratic, as in most of our cases; or it may be neoliberal, as in Poland. It may issue a sweeping condemnation of deeply entrenched practices of social domination, as in India and South Africa, or it may turn a blind eye to the country's past history of racial injustice, as in Poland; it may combine liberal and egalitarian themes in a host of variations, or it may repudiate Western ideals of secularism in a collective effort to build a constitution worthy of an Islamic Republic, as in Iran.

For now, it is more important to contrast the revolutionary mode of self-presentation with another familiar ideal type: the *evolutionist* who denies that she is doing anything novel and describes herself as proposing a few pragmatic alterations in the status quo. Sometimes this modest form of self-presentation may well yield big results in the real world—indeed, we shall be surveying a number of such "success stories" in the next volume, where I will investigate establishmentarian (Type Two) and elitist (Type Three) pathways to constitutional government. But the fact that these pathways are sometimes successful doesn't imply that revolutionaries are bound to fail in constructing constitutional governments—as our case studies show, this simply isn't true.

Movement Parties

Most revolutionary movements fail. For starters, it's never enough for the masses "spontaneously" to heed the call for change by flooding into the streets for a day or a week of demonstrations. Each of our success stories involves years of dedicated organizational activity. This is the common feature connecting the movements led by the Congress Parties of India and South Africa, those led by the French and Italian Resistance against the Nazis and Fascists during the Second World War, the Solidarity movement's struggle against Polish Communism, and the joint effort by secular and religious movements to overthrow the Shah. During their sustained period of rebellion (Time One), movement activists not only risk death or imprisonment by engaging in a host of brave acts of opposition. They build movement-party organizations that link grassroots activists to revolutionary leaders emerging on the regional and national levels. These institutional connections generate a collective sense of joint engagement in a collective project to win control of the state in the name of the People. If this weren't so, how else to explain the willingness of activists—on both grassroots and leadership levels—to endanger their lives for the common good?

Dilemmas of Revolutionary Transition

So far as the old regime is concerned, all this revolutionary agitation is the work of demagogues who have exploited the discontent of the ignorant masses—and the existing government will predictably try to crush the movement in the name of law and order.

But sometimes the ancien regime will have little choice but to retreat before the rising movement party. The British had been so weakened by their "victory" in World War II that they could no longer maintain their authority over India. Similarly, the defeat of the Nazis opened the way for the Resistance movement parties to fill the vacuum left by the fall of Vichy France and Fascist Italy; the sudden collapse of the Shah's regime created a similar legitimacy vacuum in Iran.

In other cases, the established regime engages in a continuing struggle with the insurgents—before it is ultimately defeated by its revolutionary antagonists. The dynamics of takeover look very different in Mandela's South Africa, de Gaulle's France, and Wałesa's Poland. Yet once again, common themes emerge that elude the totalitarian vision. On the Leninist-Maoist view, "real" revolutionaries fight the existing regime to the bitter end. Once they have destroyed the opposition on the battlefield, there are only two ways to deal with defeated antagonists—kill them or send them to "reeducation camps" until they emerge as brainwashed supporters of the new regime. My alternative model emphasizes less coercive possibilities—most notably, the path to a negotiated transition—that generate very different legitimation issues.

Consider *the problem of democratic reorganization*. During Time One, the old regime has done its best to drive the revolutionaries underground in its effort to reestablish its authority. As a consequence, the insurgents' sense of a larger unity is sustained by the personal charisma of a few distant leaders—typically in prison or exile—whose great sacrifices express the imperative need to continue the revolutionary struggle in the name of the People.

As the old regime reluctantly recognizes that it must negotiate with its antagonists, and revolutionary leaders go to the bargaining table, the organization of a new round of elections will loom large on the agenda. The rising leadership needs electoral victories to establish that it does indeed have a popular mandate to transform the status quo in fundamental ways.

Yet the shattered revolutionary organization is poorly prepared for an exercise in democratic politics. If top leaders hope to win the elections, they must build a nationwide network that can nominate a credible set of candidates and get their grassroots supporters to the polls on election day—and they must succeed in a matter of months, not years.

Failure comes at a heavy price. On the one hand, the fractured organization may generate a host of revolutionary parties that challenge the top leadership's authority to speak for the People. The escalating struggle might make it impossible for the competing factions to hammer out a constitution that expresses the principles motivating the great sacrifices of Time One. Even worse, the revolution might be hijacked by better-organized opponents who are hostile to the entire effort to break with the past.

De Gaulle, Mandela, and Wałesa struggled with this predicament in different ways. The key point to emphasize is that their legitimation problem is categorically different from the "negotiated solutions" emerging from polities traveling down other pathways to constitutionalism. In countries where the masses remain passive on the sidelines—as in post-Franco Spain or postwar Germany and Japan—elites could construct their new constitutions without worrying whether their deal would be disrupted by revolutionary mobilization. Even though they had many other problems, they could safely assume that they were the dominant operational actors.

Revolutionary leaders face a different reality. When they confront the old regime at the bargaining table, it won't be enough to strike a transitional deal that they consider satisfactory. They will be exquisitely aware that, beyond the bargaining table, there are rival revolutionaries who may condemn them for consenting to a "corrupt bargain" with their bitter antagonists. If this charge of betrayal resonates among grassroots activists, it will make it much harder for the movement party to emerge with a landslide victory in the transitional elections that loom ahead. One of the rewards of comparative analysis will be a glimpse into the paradoxes generated by very different efforts to solve such *dilemmas of revolutionary transition.*

Fundamentality

Once outsiders finally manage to gain power at Time Two, how big a change must they enact in the Constitution before the new regime can count as "revolutionary"?

Since revolutions on a human scale don't aim for a totalizing break with the past, the new Constitution may well incorporate older constitutional understandings and governmental practices. But these traditional elements operate in ways that would have previously seemed deeply problematic or utterly scandalous.

I will call this *unconventional adaptation:* older traditions continue to operate, but only in ways that recognize the legitimacy of the revolutionary effort to mark a "new beginning" in political time. Each of our case studies will reveal variations on this unconventional theme. They will also raise a larger issue: Does the emerging ensemble of old and new constitutional elements represent a *sufficiently fundamental* break with the past to count as truly "revolutionary"?

Given the human scale of the enterprise, there can be no hope for a hard-and-fast answer. Even at the moment of its initial adoption, "radicals" will be denouncing the new Constitution as a "betrayal" of the movement's grander ambitions, whereas "conservative" revolutionaries will predictably dissent from one or more of its efforts to transform the foundations of political and social life.

There is no point in taking sides in these inevitable debates. In a revolution on a human scale, the "fundamentality" of the transformation is essentially contestable. So long as revolutionaries of all stripes are dominating the process of constitutional redefinition, and bitter-end defenders of the old regime have been pushed to the sidelines, the key question is whether the newly ascendant revolutionaries can hammer out a constitution that is plausibly related to the vision of the public good that animated their long struggle in the wilderness.

This point is sufficient for my purposes. I do not aim to pass moral judgment on particular revolutionary regimes. My goal is to understand the legitimating dynamics through which one or another Constitution gains its central claim to authority in organizing the new regime—both for the newly ascendant governing elites and for the millions of followers who supported the collective effort to revolutionize the system.[5]

Two Forms of "Charisma"

"Charisma" will be playing a central role in my analysis, so it won't hurt to take a preliminary stab at clarifying this notoriously slippery notion.

I will be distinguishing two forms. Call the first *organizational charisma:* activists at the grassroots level come to identify deeply with their movement party's struggle for political ascendancy. They do not view organizations like Solidarity in Poland, India's Congress Party, or South Africa's ANC as special interest groups engaged in arcane maneuvers in distant halls of power. They view them as the organizational means through which their own grassroots struggles can transform the state into an engine for legitimate social change. Over time, local activists engage in an ongoing effort to persuade their friends and neighbors to join their movement-party organization, and to make small and large sacrifices for the public good (as the ongoing movement-party dialogue defines and redefines it over time).

Leadership charisma is a distinct phenomenon. It should not be confused with the Madison Avenue charisma displayed by glamorous movie stars and such. Many revolutionary leaders—Nehru and Mandela and De Gasperi, for example—were utterly lacking in glitzy glamor. They owed their symbolic centrality to the story that movement activists tell themselves about the origins and objectives of their revolutionary struggle. Others—like de Gaulle or Wałesa or Khomeini—generated special forms of political electricity, but so did potential rivals.

The thing that set all of them apart was that they found themselves at the right place at the right time in the revolutionary struggle—and their decisive acts of sacrifice served as paradigmatic examples for the broader struggle for a "new beginning" in the political life of the nation. To put the point in non-charismatic terms: Symbolic leaders owe their centrality to the role they play in the *revolutionary narrative* that ordinary people tell themselves about the meaning of their larger collective struggle for political redefinition.

The relationship between organizational and leadership charisma is complex. Sometimes symbolic leaders will do everything possible to enhance the charismatic appeal of their movement parties; sometimes they will do the opposite and destroy their movement organizations to build up their own cults of personality. But at all times, the relationship between the leadership and grassroots organizations will play an important role in the dynamics through which charisma is or is not constitutionalized at Time Two.

The Revolutionary Challenge to Standard Approaches

My inquiry is similar to, but different from, the conventional way lawyers ordinarily think about constitutional change. The reigning professional paradigm is provided by legal positivism. This school of thought has developed lots of competing variants, but all insist that law is analytically distinct from other sources of normative commitment.

Given this premise, positivists try to provide a "rule of recognition" that enables citizens to understand what "the law" requires of them. This master rule enables everybody, regardless of their particular moral convictions, to recognize what they must do in order to qualify as law-abiding citizens of their particular state. Of course, the laws may turn out to be so unjust that residents may refuse to obey them. But the positivist insists that even when citizens engage in acts of civil disobedience, they can still distinguish between the requirements of the "law" and the demands of "personal morality"—if only to declare that personal morality requires them to disobey the law.

My view is positivistic in one key respect. I will be analyzing revolutionary developments even if they launch the People in the "wrong" direction—as defined by my own moral ideals. I will be bracketing my own philosophical commitments to make a different point. Regardless of whether they are "right" or "wrong," revolutionary movement parties confront *the same* series of legitimation problems in constitutionalizing their charisma over time.

I part company with the positivist when it comes to defining the nature of constitutional revolution. This is because we are asking different questions. The positivist doesn't ask how a regime legitimates itself. He simply wants to identify the fundamental rules by which a particular regime distinguishes law from non-law. If, for example, the state is suddenly dominated by lawmakers who transform basic principles in a big way, the positivist doesn't count this change as "revolutionary" if it is enacted in conformity with the preexisting Constitution. It's only when these foundational rules are broken that the positivist recognizes that something "revolutionary" is going on.

Here is where we part company. The positivist definition is both over- and under-inclusive for my purposes. It is too broad because a decisive break with the established "rule of recognition" may be achieved down all three pathways. Suppose, for example, that the new constitutional order is an elite construction that has been imposed in violation of the old rule of recognition. This is enough to make it revolutionary for the positivist, but it fails my test because the new regime is not the product of a mobilized movement that has self-consciously repudiated the old regime to demand a "new beginning" in the name of the People.

Positivism is also under-inclusive. Some insurgent movements at Time One manage to constitutionalize their revolutions at Time Two *without* breaking any of the old regime's rules for formal amendment. This happened in South Africa, for example. Nevertheless, the formal legality of Mandela's rise to the presidency was not the reason millions of ANC activists hailed it as legitimate—nor was it the reason many defenders of apartheid recognized it as worthy of respect. Although a revolutionary regime's legalistic link to the past may play a secondary role in gaining constitutional legitimacy, the relationship between its experiences at Time One and Time Two is far more important. As we shall see, success in constitutionalizing charisma at Time Two will set up a distinctive set of legitimation problems at later stages of development—especially when the founding generation begins to die off (Time Three) and its successors seek to carry on the principles of the revolution canonized by the Constitution (Time Four).

Rethinking Comparative Law?

My four-stage dynamic also challenges a second reigning paradigm. For a very long time, comparatists have begun their labors by dividing the legal universe into two distinct spheres—the common-law culture of the English-speaking world and the civil-law culture on the Continent.

This familiar approach doesn't get to the heart of the matter. The constitutions of India and South Africa emerge from the common law; those of France, Italy and Poland, from the civil law. These different legal traditions did shape each revolutionary regime's distinctive responses to the challenges of constitutionalizing charisma. Yet they played secondary roles. The fate of the regime crucially depended on the modes of constitutional politics through which movement parties and political institutions confronted the four-stage dynamic propelling the legitimation process forward. The distinctive contributions of common-law and civil-law traditions can be assessed only within this larger framework.

This leads me to a related critique. Traditional approaches adopt a court-centered approach. This focus then makes it seem sensible to deploy the common-law / civil-law split as the baseline for comparison—because it helps account for big differences that undoubtedly do exist in Anglo-American and Continental styles of judicial review.

In contrast, I begin with the problem of legitimating the regime as a whole—including all key institutions in the rising revolutionary regime. My challenge is to explore the dynamic process through which courts might—or might not—play an increasingly legitimate role in the evolving system over time.

More broadly still, I will show that regimes traveling down the pathways described by the establishmentarian and elitist pathways (Types Two and Three) confront legitimation challenges that are very different from those encountered along the revolutionary track—and that judges play different roles in meeting these challenges. In contrast, much recent work obscures these differences, and treats constitutional courts as if they were engaged in a worldwide conversation about the meaning of "free speech" or "human dignity." This is a mistake.

A "Third Wave"?

Comparative constitutionalism is a booming academic business nowadays.[6] Since I am hardly the first to propose a new way forward, it will help to note some salient ways in which my approach differs from those of my fellow trailblazers.

Recent work in law and political science has focused on more elitist pathways. Current scholarship has been profoundly shaped by Samuel Huntington's *Third Wave,* published in 1991. As the Berlin Wall was falling, Huntington linked the astonishing events in the Communist world to then-recent democratic transitions in Latin America and Southern Europe. He believed they amounted to a "third wave" of constitutionalism, which differed from its predecessors precisely in its reliance on elite bargaining to smooth the way to a successful democratic transition. Huntington's views were reinforced by the pathbreaking comparative studies of Juan Linz and Alfred Stepan, who also emphasized the central role of "pacted transitions" in recent moves to liberal democracy.[7]

This book emphasizes different constitutional experiences. Revolutionaries in postwar India or France managed to hammer out constitutions without serious bargaining with representatives of the old regime. When revolutionaries do negotiate with the old regime, as in South Africa or Poland, the bargaining process is profoundly shaped by the high-energy politics in the larger society.

To explore these complexities further, consider the influential work of Tom Ginsburg and his associates. They have dominated the scholarly agenda over the past decade by marrying "Third Wave-ism" with "rational actor" models of political behavior. Their studies focus on the moment when the old regime begins to bargain with constitutional reformers on a peaceful transition to democracy. As the two sides start wheeling and dealing, they will find that they share a common interest. As they look ahead to a new era of free elections, rival politicians can't be sure how they will fare at the ballot box. Given the uncertainties of transition, both sides run a serious risk that they will lose key elections, and find themselves at the mercy of the majority.

To reduce the risk of worst-case outcomes, both sides may find it advantageous to limit the power of the elected majority to do grievous damage to their fundamental interests—and empower an independent constitutional tribunal to enforce these constitutional limitations against the electoral winners in the democratic sweepstakes. Ginsburg called this the "insurance rationale" for constitutional restrictions on majority rule by an independent judiciary.[8]

Ginsburg's analysis is insightful, but it doesn't do justice to the dilemmas of revolutionary transitions. As our case studies will show, leaders like Mandela or Wałesa can't allow rivals to denounce them for negotiating with widely despised representatives of the existing order—and this profoundly reshapes the character of their confrontations with the old regime at the bargaining table in ways that the conventional wisdom can't explain.

Professor Ginsburg has also taken the lead in a second interdisciplinary venture, which seeks to harness the computer revolution to comparative constitutional analysis. He has led an effort to construct an elaborate database, containing all the constitutions created worldwide over the past two centuries.[9] To permit computer manipulation, the constitutions are treated in a severely reductionist fashion. Each text is cut up into bits and pieces—so that similar clauses in different constitutions can be identified across time and culture. Similarly, the only larger themes considered are those reducible to formalistic terms: Was the constitution parliamentary or presidential? Was it approved in a referendum? And so forth.

Computer runs on these bits and pieces can bring to light interesting patterns of evolution over time. But they cannot substitute for holistic approaches that focus on efforts by engaged participants to legitimate their authority in particular cultures and historical contexts. As they hammer out their founding drafts, culturally rooted protagonists do not look upon bits and pieces of text as ends in themselves—but as elements in their larger effort to gain broad recognition of their constitutional authority.

Yet the computer-driven analyst is encouraged to ignore precisely this dimension of the legitimation process—because it cannot be expressed quantitatively. Instead, Ginsburg's methods predispose him to theories of constitutional change that trivialize the role of revolutionary self-sacrifice and collective agency.[10]

Constituent Power?

This reductionist approach is also characteristic of contemporary efforts by leading political theorists to justify systems of checks and balances. Most notably, Jan Elster rejects the very idea of collective agency that is central to the revolutionary project—once again adopting a rational-actor account.

In his view, constitutional designers confront a problem similar to the classical dilemma faced by Ulysses as he considers steps to preempt the Sirens' effort to lure his ship into disaster. To deflect this threat, Ulysses orders his seamen to put wax into their ears so that they will not hear the Sirens' song.

Elster advises constitution makers to take similar precautions. They should design the modern ship of state recognizing that citizens may succumb to moments of passion in the future—and create a system of fundamental rights, and institutional checks, that will permit the government to stay more or less on course until the wave of emotion subsides.[11]

But in the revolutionary scenario we will be exploring, the constitution emerges from a period of passionate insurgency against the old regime. The movement leadership enters the constituent assembly with pride in the great sacrifices their followers have made for the common good; they do not view passionate commitment with fear and trembling; they insist that it is their high obligation to constitutionalize the principles motivating their past liberation struggle in the name of the People.

To put it mildly, this is not the mind-set captured by Elster's invocation of Ulysses and the Sirens. Nevertheless, the revolutionary pathway has in fact generated constitutional arrangements that have imposed powerful constraints on would-be autocrats. The challenge is to understand how and why this has happened repeatedly over the course of the twentieth century.

❀ ❀

If, however, we move back a generation or three, we do indeed confront major thinkers whose writings remain of enduring importance. One of Hannah Arendt's great contributions to political thought was to present a vibrant defense of revolutions on a human scale. I follow her in refusing to allow the catastrophes that followed upon the totalizing visions of a Lenin or a Hitler to lead us to reject the very ideal of revolutionary constitutionalism. Like her, I insist that citizens can achieve a precious sense of collective agency as long as they limit their transformative ambitions.

But I disagree with the way Arendt defines these limits. She insists that would-be revolutionaries should resist the temptation to place the problem of social and economic justice at the center of their program. Rather than emphasizing "social questions," as she calls them, they should concentrate on building new political institutions that will provide a space for ongoing citizenship engagement. In her view, it was precisely the American revolutionaries' exclusive concern with the construction of political institutions that accounted for their great success in founding their new Republic. In contrast, their fellow revolutionaries in France lost their Republic when they allowed themselves to be diverted by demands for social and economic equality—these larger aspirations destroyed their common sense of citizenship, and split them into a host of contending factions.[12]

Arendt, however, does not move beyond the late eighteenth century to test her thesis against the experience of more recent revolutions on a human scale. This is precisely my project here—and it establishes that Arendt's fear of the "social question" cannot do justice to the facts. The struggles of India's Congress Party and of South Africa's ANC against social and economic injustice were central to their ultimate success in legitimating their new Constitutions in the name of the People. After the Second World War, the constitutional "new beginnings" achieved in France and Italy were legitimated by Resistance movements in which Social Democrats and Communists played central roles.

With the exception of South Africa, these counterexamples were available to Arendt. But writing during the Cold War struggle against Communism, she failed to appreciate the constitutional achievements of social democracy. Instead, she treated the eighteenth-century revolution in America as if it were the great exception to the totalitarian revolutions of modernity. But once we look at the twentieth century as a whole, it is clear that the "social question" has propelled constitutionalism forward on many occasions.

My analysis of these constitutional revolutions also requires me to confront the claims of a very different theorist: Carl Schmitt. Like him, I emphasize the distinctive charismatic bonds linking a revolutionary movement to its leadership. For Schmitt, however, the very idea of "constitutionalizing charisma" is an oxymoron, concealing a dichotomous choice—*either* the governing elites sacrifice their authentic link to the People by following the constitutional "rule of law" *or* they cede power to a Supreme Leader who can inspire his People to commit themselves to totalizing self-transformation. So far as Schmitt is concerned, it is the masses shouting "Heil Hitler" that are the only true foundation of a revolutionary regime. But once again, the examples of a Nehru or Mandela serve to refute this either / or approach.[13]

The tragic temptations of hero worship have sometimes shattered the constitutional foundations of revolutionary regimes. But this is not inevitable. Schmitt, like Arendt (but for very different reasons), is simply wrong on the facts. Time and again, we will see movement leaders, in collaboration with grassroots activists, channel their high-energy politics into constitutions that *credibly* serve, both to elites and ordinary citizens, as an enduring legacy of their great acts of collective sacrifice.

For all my differences with Arendt and Schmitt, we start from the same place—the significance of revolutionary politics in coming to terms with modernity. In contrast, a third great political thinker, Joseph Schumpeter, wanted to banish the very idea of a revolution on a human scale from serious scholarly conversation. On his view, only disaster awaits nations that rely on the People to authorize a new beginning in their political life. Because voters are basically "unintelligent and irresponsible," taking their judgments seriously "may prove fatal." The only sound form of government is based on the disciplined judgments of well-trained elites. Regular elections may sometimes sweep entrenched politicians from power, and disrupt existing corrupt arrangements. But while random shocks may clear the deck, the system's operation won't be improved if victors take popular sovereignty seriously. Instead of pandering to the ignorant prejudices of the masses, they should rely on the creative energies of free-market entrepreneurs and civil society innovators to propel their nations forward.[14]

Over the past generation, neo-Schumpeterianism has enjoyed a great intellectual renaissance, with social scientists elaborating mathematical models that treat voters as spectacularly uninformed consumers in a political "marketplace" dominated by elite actors offering competing "brands" designed to further their narrow self-interest.[15] This interdisciplinary effort has greatly reinforced similar tendencies in comparative constitutional law—where, as we have seen, breakthrough scholarship is dominated by big-data analyses testing a range of hypotheses based on narrow self-interest.

I aim to show, however, that revolutionary constitutionalism has been a dynamic force in the twentieth century and remains a powerful present-day reality. To confront this fact, we must turn from economics to sociology for interdisciplinary insight. Over the past generation, the study of social movements has gained a central place in the discipline—which has already led to a promising series of boundary-crossing conversations with legal scholars.[16] I very much hope that this book will encourage a more intensive collaboration in the future.

The Case Studies: An Overview

I have thus far contented myself with an abstract sketch of the four-phase dynamic of revolutionary constitutionalism—proceeding from mobilized insurgency (Time One) through constitutional founding (Time Two) through succession crisis (Time Three) through consolidation (Time Four). But it is time to get more specific.

Part 1 of this book fills in this abstract account with case studies from four countries on three continents, making my case in pairwise fashion. It starts off with a comparison between revolutionary "new beginnings" in India (Chapter 2) and South Africa (Chapter 3); and then moves to consider the efforts by the Resistance movements in France (Chapter 4) and Italy (Chapter 5) to vindicate their struggles for national liberation in postwar constitutions. Despite the enormous differences in social and economic conditions, and political and legal cultures, all four countries represent variations on the four-stage dynamics exhibited by revolutions on a human scale.

India is the largest constitutional democracy in the world. It displays plenty of imperfections, but so do lots of other countries. Yet nobody can deny that its Constitution of 1950 continues to provide core legitimating structures for its democratic government in the twenty-first century.

This simple point poses a big problem for conventional wisdom. For starters, India lacks what the standard literature endlessly calls the "preconditions for democracy." Its overwhelming poverty, illiteracy, and caste system seem to condemn the country to an authoritarian system where elections are regularly rigged and courts fail to constrain the power of entrenched political elites.

Prospects look even grimmer once India's ethnic and linguistic diversity is taken into account. In Europe, such diversity is typically treated as a major factor undermining the movement toward a stronger European Union. Yet it has not defeated the operation of a powerful central government on a subcontinent containing twice the Union's population.

No need to exaggerate. New Delhi has engaged in long military struggles against rebellious minorities. The real-world operation of its constitutional system is deficient in fundamental respects. But this is also true in the United States, Europe, and Latin America. The question is not whether India, or any other polity, perfectly fulfills its ideals. The real-world issue is: How has India's constitutional order sustained its broad-based legitimacy under such uncongenial circumstances?

The puzzle can be solved only if we take seriously both the Congress Party's revolutionary role in mobilizing a vast popular movement in support of national independence, and its success in constitutionalizing its high-energy politics during the Nehru era. These achievements laid the foundation for a remarkably creative resolution of a succession crisis after Nehru's death, enabling the emergence of the Indian Supreme Court as the ultimate defender of the nation's revolutionary constitutional legacy.

India's four-stage process played itself out over a century—stretching from Mahatma Gandhi's transformation of Congress into a well-organized movement in the early twentieth century through the constitutional consolidations of the early twenty-first century—and it has not yet come to an end. To the contrary, it provides essential background for an assessment of the current effort by Prime Minister Narendra Modi, and his Hindu Nationalist movement, to revolutionize the Supreme Court's entrenched understandings of the nation's founding principles.

India's century-long history not only frames its current constitutional predicament. It also serves as a benchmark for analyzing other countries that have experienced more recent revolutions—and so have not fully confronted succession crises or later efforts at consolidation. South Africa provides a case in point. Its Constitution only dates to 1996, and the country remains in the grip of an escalating struggle by political rivals seeking to fill the "legitimacy gap" left behind by Nelson Mandela. It is too soon to say whether the rising generation will meet the challenges of statesmanship required to sustain the constitutional order.

Nevertheless, a systematic comparison with Indian developments at Times One, Two, and Three will generate a host of insights. Like its Indian counterpart, the African National Congress gained power only after decades of mobilization and struggle against the established regime. There are also many parallels in the ways Mandela / ANC and Nehru / IC transformed their revolutionary charisma into constitutional authority in their ascent to power.

There are differences as well. The ANC's military arm, the Spear of the Nation, played a critical role in the ANC's victory, since only a sustained guerilla war against the apartheid regime forced it to accept the need for negotiations. The IC's revolutionary campaign for independence was far less violent—in part because Britain's response was less repressive. Even though the Raj repeatedly imprisoned Gandhi and Nehru and countless followers for their acts of civil disobedience, the Congress Party could propel its movement forward without engaging in the guerilla warfare endorsed by the ANC. Moreover, Congress gained power after the Second World War without the elaborate negotiations required in South Africa, since it did not confront anything resembling the entrenched opposition of the apartheid regime. Instead, the government of Clement Attlee decided that Britain had been so weakened by the Second World War that it could no longer maintain its Indian empire, and that the IC was the only well-organized movement party that could plausibly avoid total chaos.

Both India's "declining empire scenario" and South Africa's "revolutionary-bargaining scenario" will reemerge in later cases—so this initial pairwise comparison will serve to develop questions for further elaboration in Part 2 of the book.

The same is true of the succession crises the regimes have encountered after Nehru and Mandela left the political stage—creating "legitimacy vacuums" that rival politicians have sought to fill with their own claims to leadership. Different rivals have different kinds of qualifications—some have a family connection to Nehru / Mandela; others have honed superbureaucratic skills during the previous period of IC / ANC government; others have gained charismatic authority from their grassroots activities. It makes a big difference which type wins in the ensuing struggle—and how the losers handle their defeats. But it also matters how the constitutional courts respond to the opportunities and dangers offered up by the escalating competition among the political elite.

While Indian constitutionalism managed to survive its succession crisis of the 1970s, South Africa's struggle is only now reaching its climax. As always, I do not suggest that my comparisons with India permit confident predictions about the fate of the constitutional legacy left behind by Mandela and his revolutionary generation. But I hope that the systematic comparisons with India provide insights that would be missed by standard analyses that focus more narrowly on South African developments.

The South Africa / India discussion sets the stage for the second pairwise comparison in Part 1: the constitution-building efforts in France and Italy after the Second World War. Once again, we see insurgent movements leading their Peoples to a "new beginning"—this time, in their struggles to repudiate the authoritarian regimes of Marshal Petain and Benito Mussolini. But in contrast to the ANC / IC, no single movement party played a dominant role in mobilizing wartime opposition to the two pro-Nazi governments. Instead, the Resistance in both countries emerged from three distinct political parties—Communist, Socialist, and Christian Democratic—with competing ideologies, leaderships, and organizations. Once the Allies decisively defeated Germany in 1945, the three parties of the Resistance confronted an obvious question: Would they continue to collaborate long enough to hammer out a constitutional framework that would define the "new beginning" for which their activists in the underground had sacrificed so much? Or would they immediately begin to compete with one another and lose the chance to organize their followers into a broad-based popular campaign for a Resistance Constitution that crystallized the principles of their common struggle?

Call this the *coordination problem*—and it would not be easy to solve. In both cases, the three-party coalition rose to the challenge—first working out an agreement on a common constitutional text and then gaining majority support at popular referendums marked by extraordinary levels of popular participation and political self-consciousness.

Nevertheless, there was a big difference. In France, but not in Italy, the civilian leaders of the Resistance were challenged by a military commander, Charles de Gaulle, who claimed superior authority to speak for the People. In this respect France resembles South Africa more than Italy: Nelson Mandela also confronted formidable challenges in gaining the support of the powerful military force, the Spear of the Nation, which played a central role in the insurgency. Nevertheless, he finally managed to gain the Spear's assent for his constitutional initiatives.

This didn't happen in France. The General emerged as the leading opponent of the proposed Constitution that the three-party civilian coalition offered up to the People at a national referendum. On de Gaulle's view, the Communist/Socialist/Christian Democratic draft that gained the consent of the Constituent Assembly had not gone far enough in revising the parliamentary system of the Third Republic. He called upon the People to repudiate the coalition's initiative at the polls, thereby opening up the path for popular endorsement of his own proposal for a more sweeping constitutional revolution. He insisted that only a very different, "semi-presidential" framework, granting broad powers to the chief of state, could enable France to thrive in the postwar world. Needless to say, the General believed that his wartime role made him the obvious person to serve as the nation's first president.

After a fierce political struggle, the parties of the Resistance gained the upper hand at the polls. Nevertheless, the General refused to recognize the legitimacy of the Fourth Republic, and organized a Gaullist movement party to overwhelm the civilian parties at the initial elections organized under their Constitution. But when his new party ran out of steam in the early 1950s, the General seemed doomed to political irrelevance. He retreated to his country estate at Colombey-les-Deux-Églises and remained aloof from the party competition he despised—until the entire regime confronted a grave crisis that finally led him to end his self-imposed political exile, and return to power as the Hero of the Resistance.

As a consequence, the French and Italian stories diverge at a critical juncture. In Italy, we will be observing variations on the multistage dynamic that played itself out in India and South Africa—with the Italian constitutional court emerging from a succession crisis to gain broad political recognition as a privileged legal guardian of the nation's revolutionary principles.

Matters took a different turn in France. The country's devastating defeat at Dien Bien Phu in 1954 was followed up by a series of humiliating military setbacks in North Africa. Increasingly, the army high command began to blame its civilian masters for their failure to give full support to their mission—and when the government did not satisfy their demands, they finally organized a serious attempt to seize power in Paris. In a desperate effort to deflect a military coup, the leaders of the Fourth Republic turned to de Gaulle, who saw this as his last chance to redeem the vision of strong presidential government that the voters had previously rejected a decade before.

Acting with blinding speed, the General assumed power in late 1958 and gained a sweeping victory for his revolutionary Constitution at a popular referendum the following year—following up this victory with his election as the first president of the Fifth Republic.

Part 2 begins by analyzing de Gaulle's belated triumph. I will be inviting you to reflect on some striking parallels to our previous cases—in particular, events in India that ultimately enabled its Supreme Court to establish itself as key defender of its revolutionary Constitution of 1950. If I succeed in persuading you that the Gaullist Republic confronted similar legitimation crises at critical turning points, this will reinforce my basic thesis. After all, France and India are vastly different from one another—culturally, economically, socially. Even if we limit ourselves to political and legal factors, striking differences remain. The Indian system is parliamentary; the French, presidential. Indian courts operate on common-law premises; the French judiciary operates as a paradigmatic civil-law system. Yet the four-stage revolutionary dynamic still provides organizing insights that cut across these classical lines of comparison.

I make out my case in two chapters. Chapter 7 is devoted to de Gaulle's efforts to constitutionalize his presidentialist Republic during his time in power; Chapter 8 considers his successors' ongoing struggle to deal with the legacy he left behind. Their relative success in sustaining the legitimacy of the Fifth Republic has had a worldwide impact—more than thirty-five countries have adopted the Gaullist model of "semi-presidentialism" over the past sixty years.

When viewed from afar, the new French model promised to avoid the dangers of more familiar alternatives. On the one hand, European parliamentary systems have frequently experienced great instability—with multiparty cabinets repeatedly losing the support of key members of their governing coalitions. By comparison, a French-style presidency promises greater stability over the middle run. On the other hand, American-style presidential systems notoriously have led to paralysis if the presidency and legislature are controlled by antagonistic political parties. In contrast, the French model promised a new way out of these logjams—most notably, by authorizing the president to threaten the early dissolution of Parliament unless its leaders adopt a more collaborative approach. Stability + collaboration = who could ask for anything more?

My case study of Poland (Chapters 9 and 10) serves as a call for reappraisal. Solidarity was one of the largest revolutionary movements of modern times—with millions of activists engaging in a decade of struggle before forcing the

Communists to retreat in 1989. Reflecting the broad appeal of the French model, Solidarity's national leadership adopted a semi-presidential system in negotiating their peaceful transition to power in 1989.

With disastrous results. They didn't recognize the danger at the time, but their "semi-presidential" design created a structure that encouraged the revolutionary leadership to split into rival factions—tempting both Lech Wałesa and his longtime associate, Tadeusz Mazowiecki, to compete for the presidency. When Wałesa emerged victorious, he claimed that the voters had given him a special mandate to govern in their name—only to find that Solidarity's parliamentary leadership rejected his privileged claim to speak for the People. The ongoing competition between president and parliament made it impossible for the two sides to work out a new Constitution to bring before the Polish people.

Even worse, the bitter factional conflict generated widespread alienation among the general public. After all, Wałesa, Mazowiecki, and other leaders had helped inspire millions of ordinary Poles to join Solidarity's struggle against Communism, sometimes at great personal sacrifice, during the 1980s. Yet the struggle between president and parliament made it appear that these very same leaders had forgotten the reason they organized Solidarity in the first place. By 1995 the voters were thoroughly disgusted and swept the old revolutionaries from power—replacing them with politicians who had visibly collaborated with the old Communist regime. Yet at least these "reformed Communists" promised to end the backbiting and to provide sober and stable government. Once in power, the post-Solidarity leadership took the opportunity finally to advance a new Constitution for Poland—which was narrowly approved in a referendum characterized by widespread apathy and voter abstention. Semi-presidentialism, in short, played a central, if under-acknowledged, role in Solidarity's failure to constitutionalize its charisma.

Suppose you are convinced. Even so, this only raises a larger question. To put the point in ideal-typical terms: Even if Poland's Constitution of 1997 is best viewed as an elite construction of Type Three, rather than a revolutionary constitution of Type One, is this shift in pathways really that important?

We will consider this question in dealing with the last two decades of Polish constitutional politics (Chapter 10), but it also looms large in our next pair of case studies. For all sorts of reasons, comparatists aren't in the habit of comparing constitutional developments in Iran and Israel. Yet both of those governments were born in revolutions—with the Shia in Iran and the Zionists

in Palestine struggling to establish a "new beginning" in their nation's political identity. The two revolutionary polities begin to diverge at Time Two,
but in a counterintuitive way.

The Israeli Declaration of Independence publicly committed the provisional Zionist government to the rapid promulgation of a constitution—yet
David Ben-Gurion repudiated this promise once he emerged victorious at the
polls and his movement party, Mapai, became the decisive actor in Israel's constituent assembly. Instead, he convinced the Knesset to defer constitutionalization to the indefinite future. As we shall see in Chapter 11, the construction
of a serious system of checks and balances was not taken up in earnest until
a generation later, at Time Three, when the country confronted its own
version of a succession crisis.

In contrast, as we shall see in Chapter 12, Ayatollah Khomeini took a very
different course. His revolutionary opposition to the Shah had forced him into
exile for thirteen years—so that he was still living in Paris when the Shah's
authority was visibly disintegrating. As he prepared for his triumphant return,
Khomeini turned to a trusted associate, Hassan Habibi, to prepare a draft constitution to present to the nation upon his arrival in the homeland. This
"Paris draft" advanced the key claim that revolutionary Iran should transform
itself into an Islamic *Republic*—committed both to Islamic values and to republican self-government. Upon his arrival in Iran, the Ayatollah gave high
priority to realizing this constitutional vision. His provisional government
quickly called for elections to a constituent assembly, known as the Council
of Constitutional Experts, and a revised version of the "Paris draft" was advanced as the basis for popular debate in the run-up to this election. This was
the first time Iranians would elect representatives since the fall of the Shah,
and the Council's sole mission was to frame the constitutional meaning of
the high-energy politics that was propelling the revolution forward. Once it
convened, the Council spent three months debating the provisional draft,
leading to its fundamental revision. The Council then put its final proposal
before the voters, who approved it in a landslide in December 1979—only ten
months after the Ayatollah had returned to his homeland.

We come, then, to our first paradox: in Israel it was liberal Social Democrats like David Ben-Gurion who passed up on the opportunity to constitutionalize his movement's revolutionary charisma; while it was the Supreme
Religious Leader of the Iranian People who followed the likes of Mandela and
de Gaulle and took advantage of the founding moment to establish the Islamic
Republic's constitution on the basis of popular sovereignty.

This first paradox leads to another. As I have suggested, the adoption of semi-presidentialism in Poland was a root cause of Solidarity's failure to mobilize broad popular consent for a revolutionary constitution at Time Two. Yet the adoption of French-style semi-presidentialism accounts for Iran's remarkable success in sustaining a constitutional system of checks and balances over the long term.

The original draft of Iran's Constitution was not only written in Paris; it was largely the handiwork of Hassan Habibi, who had received his doctorate in law and sociology from the Sorbonne. It was only natural that Habibi would turn to the form of government he knew best—the French Fifth Republic—as a source of inspiration. His draft drew heavily—in both language and structure—from the Gaullist original. Over the course of debates in 1979, the Council of Constitutional Experts revised Habibi's draft to emphasize the Islamic character of Iran's "new beginning"—most notably, by incorporating the position of Supreme Leader into the Gaullist framework. But it did not attempt a thoroughgoing revision of the substantive and structural provisions that Habibi had borrowed from the Fifth Republic. As a consequence, a popularly elected president, along with other French-inspired institutions, retained a prominent place in the Iranian constitutional order.

The French-style presidency would play a decisive role over the longer run. When the Ayatollah died in 1989, his passage from the scene generated a characteristic succession crisis. As in the cases of Nehru and Mandela, De Gasperi and de Gaulle, there was nobody in the Iranian revolutionary elite who could remotely match the personal charisma of the departed Khomeini. What is more, Ali Khamenei, his successor as Supreme Leader, was deliberately chosen despite his lack of high religious credentials. The selection of a second-rate cleric opened the way for popularly elected French-style presidents to claim mandates from the voters to pursue policies opposed by the not-so-Supreme Leader. As election followed election, the balance of authority between Leader and President has shifted back and forth—depending on the character of particular presidential mandates and Khamenei's skill in manipulating the formidable levers of institutional power that are available to him. Nevertheless, Iran currently stands as a paradigmatic Islamic *Republic*—with the Supreme Leader's claim to represent the Will of God in an ongoing contest with the President's claim to represent the Will of the People. It is a big mistake to confuse this system of checks-and-balances with the authoritarian regimes that prevail in Saudi Arabia and elsewhere in the Mideast.

It turns out, then, that the negative Polish experience with the French model cannot be generalized into a hard-and-fast rule. Sometimes semi-presidentialism undermines revolutionary constitutionalism; sometimes it promotes it. But we must await the full development of our Polish and Iranian case studies before we can engage in a disciplined analysis of the factors that play a positive or negative role in the overall process of legitimation.

Up to this point in the argument, I have been looking backward to some of the greatest constitutional revolutions of the twentieth century. My aim is to invite you to join in the effort to construct a framework that will permit new insights into their distinctive character. If my Four Time model proves to be revealing, however, it should also provide a better grasp of the fundamental problems confronting twenty-first century exercises in revolutionary constitutionalism.

Chapter 11 explores this possibility by considering the ongoing predicament confronting Aung San Suu Kyi in Burma. Beginning in 1989 she spent most of her time in prison or under house arrest after the military brutally suppressed a popular insurgency supporting her call for a "new beginning." But a resurgent revolutionary movement forced the military to retreat and grant her a central position in the current government. Yet her effective authority is deeply constrained by the Constitution that the generals imposed on the nation in 2010. As a consequence, she confronted some fundamental questions as she assumed power: Should she mobilize her movement behind a demand for a new constituent assembly that could sweep away these limitations—but at the risk that the military might respond with another brutal round of repression? Or should she defer the effort to constitutionalize her movement's charisma, and engage in an elitist bargain with the generals that might smooth the path to a negotiated transition to democracy?

There is no easy answer to such questions—it required Aung San Suu Kyi to weigh the risks of military repression against the benefits of calling upon her movement to repudiate the general's Constitution of 2010 and undertake a revolutionary "new beginning" in the country's constitutional identity. Nevertheless, our twentieth-century case studies clarify the stakes involved, and suggest how Suu Kyi's choice of an elitist path set the stage for the tragic expulsion of hundreds of thousands of Rohingya refugees from the country.

I turn finally to my own homeland, the United States, and consider how this book's investigations into the "new beginnings" attempted in Africa, Asia, and Europe enlighten an understanding of the country's constitutional crisis in the age of Trump. Is there anything really distinctive about the great turning points in American constitutional development? Or are they best understood as variations on themes played out in other parts of the world during the twentieth century?

In other words: Is America really exceptional?

I invite my readers to ask themselves this question as they move onward to consider the concrete case studies. I'll sketch out my own answers in Chapter 13.

CHAPTER 2

Movement-Party Constitutionalism: India

There are three bastions of democratic constitutionalism in Asia: India, Japan, and Australia / New Zealand. Each system is anchored in many decades of successful practice, and large consequences would follow if these countries fail to reinvigorate their twentieth-century legacies. Such setbacks would not only cast a shadow on more recent constitution-building efforts in the region. Major failures will have world historical significance, given Asia's rise to world power in the twenty-first century.

Asia, like Europe, is a place of many paradigms. India's constitution is revolutionary; Japan's is an elite construction. Australia and New Zealand have adapted establishmentarian traditions inherited from Westminster. It would be a mistake to launch our investigation with loose talk about "Asian constitutionalism." The subject is best approached by considering each major regime as an exemplar of its respective ideal type.

Given my concern with revolutionary constitutionalism, I will focus here on India and defer other Asian regimes to later volumes. India's experience provides a particularly useful starting point, since it permits a multigenerational perspective on the four-stage dynamic characteristic of this ideal type. We begin at Time One, with Gandhi and Nehru transforming the Congress Party (known simply as Congress) into a mass movement during the first half of the twentieth century—and then turn to the Time Two effort to constitutionalize Congress's revolutionary politics at the Founding, and then move to the bitter succession crises of Time Three and finally to the Supreme Court's effort at Time Four to establish itself as the leading defender of the constitutional principles left behind by the revolutionary Constitution established by the Founders.

This century-long history will serve as a reference point throughout this book, but it will be particularly useful in our second case study: South Africa. There are some striking similarities between the African National Congress and its Indian counterpart. Yet the two national liberation movements take different shapes during their periods of insurgency—partly because of the very different ways in which the British and Afrikaner regimes confronted emerging revolutionary threats.

Speaking broadly, governments respond to insurgencies by mixing two strategies: coercion and cooptation. But the mixes can be very different. The British frequently used force in India, but they also tried to tame Congress by offering it a secondary role in imperial government. Gandhi initially resisted these offers, but Congress under Nehru accepted the British invitation and vigorously participated in elections for consultative assemblies set up by the Raj. This not only required Congress to engage in the hard political work involved in organizing a movement party. The party's victories at the polls allowed its leaders to use the colonial assemblies as platforms for legitimating their claims to speak for the People.

South Africa's apartheid regime was much more brutal. It launched an intensive military effort to crush the ANC. This made it impossible for the insurgents to establish a well-organized movement party of the Indian type. Instead, Afrikaner suppression split the ANC's leadership in two. Nelson Mandela and his fellow revolutionaries were thrown into captivity on Robben Island, while Oliver Tambo pieced together an ANC-in-exile out of very disparate movements. At the same time, ANC sympathizers at home were driven underground, and lacked the capacity to coordinate their local efforts with fellow activists in other cities and regions.

Along with its continuing campaign of suppression, South Africa's governing National Party did make intermittent efforts at cooptation. But its heavy reliance on brute force undermined the trust necessary for the ANC to take these gestures seriously. Instead, the regime's systematic violence provoked the ANC to sponsor a formidable guerilla army, the Spear of the Nation—which the ANC's civilian leadership had difficulty controlling.

These different patterns of movement development in India and South Africa made a big difference at Time Two—when the two revolutionary movements hammered out constitutions in the name of the People. Nelson Mandela confronted problems in gaining the backing of his fragmented supporters on a scale that Nehru and his allies did not encounter. Mandela's response to this "coordination problem" will set the stage for an analysis of analogous problems raised by similar splits in later case studies.

The Indian case provides a second orienting perspective. South Africa's experiment in constitutional democracy has now lasted a quarter century.

While all presidents of the revolutionary Republic played significant roles in the liberation struggle, none possessed Mandela's charismatic centrality. His departure from office has led to a series of succession crises as leading contenders competed for ascendancy.

This was also true in India—which experienced a particularly explosive crisis. While South Africa's transition to Time Three remains in doubt, India's much longer history permits us to see how it managed to resolve its dilemma in a way that enabled the Supreme Court, and other independent institutions, to establish themselves as the preeminent defenders of the nation's revolutionary legacy.

But enough of coming attractions.

Time One: The Transformation of Congress

When Congress was founded, it had neither revolutionary ambitions nor mass appeal. It was the creation of Anglophile Indian elites in the late nineteenth century—who were inspired by the ideas of John Stuart Mill and other liberals to join the British in governing the subcontinent. The elites entering the imperial civil service and colonial assemblies in response to Westminster's invitation confronted a formidable obstacle: the subcontinent's extraordinary linguistic, religious, political, and social diversity seemed to doom such a grand project. To bridge the enormous gaps that separated particular communities, elites could settle for nothing less than a fundamental reappraisal of their relationship to traditional society. While their families had previously played a leading role within the dominant cultures of their region, they would have to prepare themselves to engage in the great project of constructing an Enlightened India that embraced the entire subcontinent.[1] The Congress Party served as a primary vehicle for coordinating these Westernizers' efforts to participate in the government of the empire.

Once Gandhi returned home in 1915, he increasingly challenged this elitist evolutionary vision. He called on Congress to repudiate the British legacy of top-down government and engage in a bottom-up mobilization for the construction of an independent India based on the rich diversity of village and regional life.[2]

Gandhi's rise to the presidency of the Congress Party in 1921 signaled a victory over the old guard, but it did not secure the decisive triumph of his vision. To the contrary, younger leaders like Nehru and other democratic socialists saw Gandhi as an impractical romantic. On their view, his idealization of village life concealed the pervasive ignorance, inequalities, and religious hatreds that were everyday realities of lived experience.

Their solution: maintain the earlier Congress's emphasis on gaining control of state institutions, but this time for revolutionary purposes. It was not enough to collaborate with the British, or even break free of the empire and declare independence. The challenge was to build a strong social democratic state that could take the lead in transforming entrenched patterns of caste and class that generated mass oppression.[3]

Given their profound disagreement, the conflict between Gandhians and Nehruvians might have split Congress into rival organizations championing competing visions. But this didn't happen. Gandhi's campaigns of civil disobedience served the short-term purposes of both decentralizers and centralizers—disrupting British claims to authority in ways that mobilized increasing mass support for fundamental change.

The British also helped keep Congress together. The Raj responded to mass demonstrations with violence and detentions—emphasizing the need for both wings to join forces in a common struggle for independence. But repression was not so pervasive as to destroy Congress's reality as a social presence. Gandhi, Nehru, and many others went to jail repeatedly, but they regularly returned to lead further rounds of protest, catalyzing countless bottom-up demonstrations at the local level.

Although the movement maintained its momentum, the British failed to offer the Congress Party a serious role in imperial government. During the first third of the century, only a tiny minority of natives—amounting to 3 percent of the population—were allowed to choose representatives in the consultative assemblies the British had constructed to help govern the subcontinent. Even this small group could only choose a minority of delegates—the majority were appointed by the Raj, without any pretense of popular participation.[4] This made it easy for Gandhi to persuade Congress to denounce the imperial elections as shams and organize boycotts at the polls to protest their fraudulent character.

But the conflicting visions advanced by Gandhi and Nehru were put to the test with the passage of the Government of India Act of 1935. The new initiative expanded the suffrage to 29 percent of the population and opened up all seats in the provincial assemblies to popular vote.[5] If Congress fielded its own candidates, it could use the assemblies as platforms to broaden its mass appeal.

As early as 1929, the 62-year-old Gandhi had handed on the presidency of Congress to the 40-year-old Nehru; but in 1934 Gandhi resigned from

Congress entirely, divorcing himself from the next generation's effort to gain democratic control of the commanding heights.[6] This marked a critical moment at which Congress self-consciously turned itself from a *protest movement* into a *movement party* aiming to win control of the state. This transformation provoked a massive increase in popular engagement. As Congress fielded candidates for the new assemblies, membership in the party skyrocketed from 500,000 in 1935 to 4.5 million in 1938. When the votes were counted, the movement party dominated eight of eleven provincial assemblies, and gained control of half the seats opened for popular election in the central legislative assembly in New Delhi.[7]

Despite Gandhi's opposition to centralized bureaucratic government, he had prepared the ground for this success. During his time of leadership, he had developed elaborate consultative networks that linked Congress's national leadership to provincial and local organizations.[8] He also remained a charismatic figure long after his formal resignation from the party's presidency—playing a central role in massive "Quit India" demonstrations during the Second World War.[9]

Nevertheless, Congress's sweeping electoral victories in 1937 had decisively resolved a fundamental issue in the public mind: the revolutionary struggle would be pursued, first and foremost, by a mobilized citizenry that not only demanded independence but backed Congress's effort to gain control of central institutions to enable the People of India to break the grip of caste and class and achieve real-world justice for all.[10]

Upon the conclusion of the Second World War, Congress confronted a British Empire dramatically weakened by war against the Nazis. With the coming of peace, the arch-imperialist Winston Churchill was promptly voted out of office, and the new Labour government of Clement Attlee was unwilling to squander its scarce resources on a last-ditch struggle for imperial hegemony.

Attlee instead dispatched the last imperial viceroy, Lord Mountbatten, to establish a constitutional framework for an independent India before Britain's departure from the scene. Mountbatten initially aimed to establish a federal system for the entire subcontinent—permitting Muslims as well as Hindus to exercise substantial powers of self-government where they were a regional majority. This seemed a reasonable prospect, since the head of the Muslim League, Mohammed Jinnah, affirmed the same political principles advanced by Nehru. Both were democratic socialists with strong Enlightenment convictions, committed to creating a constitutional identity for the subcontinent that transcended religious and ethnic divisions.[11]

Nevertheless, Mountbatten's initial efforts at bridging the gap failed. Rather than spend more time and effort trying to gain broad support for a federal solution, the British simply gave up, and withdrew from the scene. This created a military vacuum, which allowed religious hatreds to explode into mass murders on a tragic scale—forcing millions of Muslims and Hindus to flee for their lives across the contested borders dividing India from Pakistan.

Asia has not recovered from this bloody disaster—which has generated a series of wars and continues to threaten the peace. But for our present purposes, only one point is important: the creation of Pakistan profoundly shaped India's path to revolutionary constitutionalism. It meant that the Constituent Assembly convened by Mountbatten was not the scene of complex bargaining between leaders of the Congress Party and the Muslim League over the terms of their subcontinent's political destiny. Partition reduced India's Muslim population to 11 percent, allowing Congress to dominate the proceedings.[12] The Assembly made a number of significant concessions to Muslims and other minority groups, but there was no longer any question that the Indian Congress Party was calling the shots. India, in short, serves as a paradigm case involving the construction of a new regime by a *hegemonic* movement party.[13]

Time Two: From Revolution to Constitution

When viewed through the standard legal lens, the Indian Constituent Assembly fails to qualify as a revolutionary assembly. Under prevailing forms of legal positivism, the status of the Assembly is resolved by the answer to a single question: Was it summoned in a fashion that marked a decisive break with the "rules of recognition" established by the previous regime?

The answer is no. All commentators recognize that the Constituent Assembly was constructed by Lord Mountbatten and operated in strict accordance with his legal grant of authority. Indeed, Mountbatten's procedures emphasized his organizing role in the affair. He refused to order new elections to allow the voters to choose their representatives to the Assembly—on the ground that a heated electoral contest would further inflame searing tensions between Hindus and Muslims. Instead, he asked the already existing provincial assemblies to elect representatives to his new creation.[14]

Even this gesture was compromised by a fundamental democratic deficit—the last election for these legislatures had been held in the winter of 1945–1946. While Congress had won a sweeping victory, constitutional questions were not then on the agenda—indeed, it was not even clear that the subcontinent would be subdivided into two. From a positivist point of view, the Constituent Assembly was *exclusively* Lord Mountbatten's creature, without any legal link to popular sovereignty.

Worse yet, once the Assembly's three years of hard work culminated in a draft Constitution in 1950, it did not submit its initiative to the wider public for self-conscious debate and decision at a referendum. Instead, it claimed that it had sufficient authority to promulgate the Constitution on its own. In many other places around the world, such top-down assertions of power have doomed the entire project—with the general public looking on with disbelief at the institutional hubris displayed in the nation's capitol.

Yet this didn't happen in the case of the Indian Constituent Assembly. Why not?

How could such a ghost of the British Empire *credibly* advance a Constitution in the name of "We the People of India?"

The positivist offers no resources for responding to this question.[15]

It is Jawaharlal Nehru, not Hans Kelsen, who provides the answer in his great speech of 1947, marking the moment at which India declared its independence from Britain on August 15:

> Long years ago we made a tryst with destiny, and now the time comes when we shall redeem our pledge, not wholly or in full measure, but very substantially. At the stroke of the midnight hour, when the world sleeps, India will awake to life and freedom. A moment comes, which comes but rarely in history, when we step out from the old to the new, when an age ends and when the soul of a nation, long suppressed, finds utterance. It is fitting that at this solemn moment we take the pledge of dedication to the service of India and her people and to the still larger cause of humanity.
>
> ... We end today a period of ill fortune and India discovers herself again. The achievement we celebrate today is but a step, an opening of opportunity, to the greater triumphs and achievements that await us. Are we brave enough and wise enough to grasp this opportunity and accept the challenge of the future?
>
> Freedom and power bring responsibility. The responsibility rests upon this Assembly, a sovereign body representing the sovereign people of India. Be-

fore the birth of freedom we have endured all the pains of labour and our hearts are heavy with the memory of this sorrow. . . . Nevertheless, the past is over and it is the future that beckons to us now. That future is not one of ease or resting but of incessant striving so that we may fulfil the pledges we have so often taken and the one we shall take today.[16]

Who is the "we" that is confronting this "tryst with destiny"? It is the Congress Party, whose millions of activists have made countless sacrifices over the "long years" of revolutionary struggle in the name of the people of India. It is this struggle, not the imperial legal forms, that brought India to "a moment [. . .] which comes but rarely in history, when we step out from the old to the new, when an age ends and when the soul of a nation, long suppressed, finds utterance."

Such an ecstatic assertion of charismatic authority has elsewhere served as the basis for the Supreme Leader and his party to express the "soul of the nation" in totalitarian fashion. But this is precisely the move that Nehru does not make. Instead, he is very self-consciously *transferring* the revolutionary authority earned by Congress to the Assembly—invoking his movement party's charisma to transform the viceroy's legal creation into the "sovereign body representing the sovereign people of India." This is the very first step in an ongoing dynamic that will yield the constitutionalization of charisma.

Nehru also sets out the Assembly's substantive agenda in a revealing fashion: the challenge, he explains, is to "fulfil the pledges we [the Congress] have so often taken and the one we shall take today." This serves as a concrete example of the *logic of reassurance* that played a key role in my abstract account of the revolutionary ideal type. In this model, the basic point of the Constitution is backward-looking as well as forward-looking—putting the People on notice that the new regime is determined to prevent the government from betraying the core ideals that justified the movement's earlier mobilization against the old regime: "Before the birth of freedom, we have endured all the pains of labour, and our hearts are heavy with the memory of sorrow. . . . Nevertheless the past is over, and it is the future that is beckoning to us now."

Nehru is here creating the link between Time One and Time Two that is central to the revolutionary constitution's logic of reassurance.

At the same time, the enduring meaning of the People's revolutionary ideals must be defined in a distinctive fashion: "Freedom and power bring responsibility." Nehru and Congress are not embarked on a great leap forward to Utopia: "we shall redeem our pledge, not wholly or in full measure, but very substantially." This is precisely the point of a revolution on a human scale: to construct a constitution that will establish a set of "pledges" that will serve as effective guides to the "incessant striving" for a better future.

The revolutionary character of these strivings was symbolized by B. R. Ambedkar's role in hammering out the constitutional text. Among all the members of the national leadership, he stood out as an Untouchable amid the generally upper-caste Hindus who dominated the commanding heights. By serving as the Constitution's principal architect, Ambedkar was breaking every legitimating principle of traditional Indian society, which condemned untouchables as pariahs.

But this was just the point—his shattering of tradition only enhanced the Assembly's authority to enact an Enlightenment Constitution in the name of the People.

Ambedkar's professional career carried the same message. Despite his despised caste status, he managed to obtain a Western education and proved to be a star student—gaining scholarships at Columbia University and the London School of Economics, at which point he also gained admission to the British bar. Returning to India, he could have readily enjoyed a distinguished career as an establishment lawyer. But he devoted his energies to spearheading a movement on behalf of the rights of untouchables. Such a high-risk engagement could have led to personal impoverishment and imprisonment. Yet this revolutionary troublemaker had now become the primary shaper of the constitutional will of the nation—a role he discharged with great distinction, bringing to the enterprise a brilliant mind and a cosmopolitan Enlightenment education.[17]

With Nehru's support, Ambedkar and his colleagues hammered out a revolutionary charter. Its transformative character is too easily ignored by conventional legalists, who emphasize that almost three-fourths of the text was derived from the Government of India Act of 1935.[18] But in revolutions on a human scale, a constitution's character can't be determined by a word count. The critical question is whether the new texts and institutional patterns fundamentally revise the meaning of the whole.

By this standard, the Indian Constitution clearly qualifies. For starters, the imperial order imposed dramatic restrictions on suffrage; in contrast, "We the People of India" opened the ballot box to every adult, regardless of caste, gender, or literacy. The Assembly followed up this vision of common citizenship with wide-ranging grants of power to the government to uproot the entrenched inequalities of traditional life—authorizing activist state in-

the First Amendment went much further than that. It granted all
parliamentary majorities the authority to insulate their legislative ini-
from judicial invalidation by listing the law on a special Schedule Nine
for this purpose. This key provision did not contain any explicit
—Parliament could exercise this extraordinary power to sideline the
by listing any statute on the Schedule.

vertheless, the Justices refused to challenge this blatant effort to con-
em to a subordinate role:

doubt our constitution-makers, following the American model, have in-
rporated certain fundamental rights . . . and made them immune from
erference by laws made by the State. We find it . . . difficult, in the absence
a clear indication to the contrary, to make those rights immune from con-
titutional amendment.[21]

ughout his fourteen years in office, Nehru made repeated use of the par-
ntary amendment power to overcome judicial resistance—and has
regularly criticized by legalists for doing so. But this critique takes too
-sighted a view.[22] The judges were right to recognize that they could not
n all-out struggle for judicial supremacy against Nehru. As we have seen,
Constitution's claim to speak for "We the People" had been established
through the exercise of charismatic authority by Nehru and Congress—
out even the need for a referendum in which the voters would ratify their
ative. During the founding period, it was the living memory of the great
ifices made by millions during the period of insurgency at Time One, not
constitutional text of Time Two, that was the primary engine of popular
timacy connecting the Parliament in New Delhi with the Indian people.
At the same time, both Parliament and the Supreme Court were acting in
s that would ultimately facilitate the deeper constitutionalization of cha-
ma when the vivid memories of these revolutionary times began to fade.
st fundamentally, Nehru chose to *amend the text rather than ignore it*
enever it threatened to undermine his parliamentary program. In this lim-
d but important way, he was entrenching the principle that the Constitu-
n, not personal or organizational charisma, would ultimately serve as the
ndation of legitimacy at later stages in the country's political development.
No less significantly, the Supreme Court was far from silent during the
urteen years of Nehru's ascendancy. Instead, it identified a host of issues on
hich it could speak authoritatively *without* provoking a parliamentary over-
de. These decisions not only helped establish the Court's authority as an

terventions on a previously unimaginable sc
of transformative authority remained limited.
safeguarded classic political liberties, and also
private property rights.

This self-conscious combination of transfc
mental limitation revolutionized another impe
tution's status as supreme law, it was no longer
Supreme Court to serve as a humble servant of a
Instead, the Court was expressly granted the auth
as unconstitutional.

Once again, this radical reform was constrai
Not only did the Constitution make it relatively
rule the judges by passing formal constitutional ar
the scope of judicial review to a (long) list of lib
Part Three of the text. In contrast, Part Four set
for egalitarian social and economic transformation
no similar authority to invalidate Parliament's effo
in the real world.

This neat and clean division, however, couldn't s
problems of jurisdiction—especially where private
Because Part Three afforded property rights substan
sive Court could readily sabotage the redistributive

How to resolve such tensions?[19]

This question quickly took on a very concrete form. /
tion came into effect, high courts in a couple of province
acts of expropriation of feudal landlords by their prov
the litigants raced to the Supreme Court, Nehru moved
imminent crisis. He was entirely unwilling to allow the
ment's commitment to property redistribution as part
campaign against pervasive poverty, illiteracy, and soc
Constitution allowed for amendment by two-thirds of Pa
Congress's majority exceeded this threshold, Nehru had
through the First Amendment to deal with the impending
ciary. The amendment retroactively denied the judiciary
pending lawsuits—putting an end to the immediate challe
of Congress's social democratic breakthroughs.

important—if not decisive—element in the emerging system of government. They also inaugurated a cultural revolution within the legal profession.

Previous generations of Indian lawyers had been thoroughly socialized into the Westminster tradition of parliamentary sovereignty—in which the very idea of judicial review was condemned as illegitimate. But the profession was increasingly obliged to cast this fundamental premise aside as the Court began to hand down important decisions declaring legislation unconstitutional. Once the Constitution began to be treated as law in the courtroom, skilled advocates had no choice but to adapt to this new juridical reality—otherwise they would be defeated by their more up-to-date opponents, who would invoke the accumulating constitutional precedents to win pending cases.[23]

During Nehru's long term as prime minister, these recurring court battles were setting the stage for new questions once the prime minister left the scene and handed over power to his successors. Would the new political leadership continue to insulate only some legislation from judicial review under Schedule Nine while allowing the courts to strike down other significant legislative acts as unconstitutional? Or would it insist instead that, just as in Britain, the judiciary should *never* claim authority to invalidate acts of Parliament?

At the same time, the judiciary would confront its own fateful decisions: Would it continue to allow Parliament to use Schedule Nine as an easy detour around its jurisdiction? Or would it put a stop to this device and make it far more difficult for the new parliamentary leadership to overrule judicial judgments?

Time Three: Succession Crisis

Within five days of Nehru's death, one of his intelligent but colorless aides, Lal Bahadur Shastri, was elected the nation's second prime minister. Acting with blinding speed, Congress's regional party bosses—known as the Syndicate—selected Shastri to preempt a challenge by an up-and-comer from Gujarat: the charismatic Morarji Desai was plainly bent on propelling himself forward as a strong Nehruvian leader of the nation.[24] When Shastri died of a heart attack in 1966, the Syndicate once again blocked Desai and chose Nehru's daughter as another safe replacement:

> Indira Gandhi was not inexperienced. She had long acted as hostess for her
> father, and had sometimes accompanied him on foreign trips. She had also

involved herself in politics. . . . More obviously, to an electorate primed on the heroics of the freedom struggle, she sounded perfect. A Nehru by birth, she had become a Gandhi by marriage . . . added to which she suffered from the considerable handicap of being a woman. While recognizing her appeal to the electorate, the kingmakers felt reassured by this. Once in office she should pose no challenge to their authority over the party or the government.[25]

We will see this move again: The family members of a dominant revolutionary spokesman have an obvious attraction for less charismatic party leaders. On the one hand, the candidate's familial association helps sustain the movement party's appeal to the masses; on the other, especially if the candidate is young and inexperienced, the established party elite may be quite confident of its capacity to manipulate the family member in ways that will ensure that it is they, rather than the youngster, who will be determining real-world policy.

In this case, the Syndicate's pseudo-charismatic gambit proved spectacularly unsuccessful. Despite the use of its revolutionary figurehead, the Congress Party suffered a big setback in the 1967 elections—with its share of parliamentary seats dropping from 73 to 55 percent. This represented the dawning of a new constitutional era, because Congress had lost the parliamentary supermajority required for formal amendments. In operational terms, this meant that the new prime minister could no longer overrule the Supreme Court by the simple expedient of ordering her backbenchers to follow party discipline at critical moments.[26]

At the same time, the Justices were building up their constitutional authority. In the year of Nehru's death, the Court reaffirmed Parliament's plenary power of constitutional amendment. But only three years later, a 6-to-5 majority in the *Golaknath* case declared that Parliament could not destroy fundamental rights (as interpreted by the Court) established by Part Three.[27]

The constitutionalization of charisma was proceeding apace: the revolutionary energy of the movement party was declining; the legitimacy of judicial intervention, rising. But the terms of the succession struggle shifted dramatically after Indira Gandhi's first election campaign of 1967. In a dramatic move, she turned on the Syndicate and announced her intention to reinvigorate her father's socialist vision. Though her electoral victory paled in comparison with Nehru's, she claimed a popular mandate to redeem her father's hope that future generations would deepen the founding generation's revolutionary commitment to social justice.

When the party bosses resisted, Gandhi led her supporters into a breakaway Congress (Reform) Party, leaving the old guard to preside over the established organization, which rapidly faded in influence. Together with other left-wing groups, she gained strong parliamentary support for a reinvigorated socialist program—nationalizing the banks, expropriating traditional property interests of the Indian princes, and advancing a host of welfare measures for the lower classes.

Entering the 1971 election campaign with a pledge "to end poverty," she crushed the opposition—with her party winning 352 of 518 seats, regaining the two-thirds majority required for formal amendments.[28] She proceeded to enact a series of constitutional provisions that insulated her statutory initiatives from judicial review—forcing a head-on collision with the Court.

Recall that, in 1967, a sharply divided Court had asserted its authority in *Golaknath* to invalidate amendments that violated fundamental rights. But the political situation had dramatically changed in the intervening period. When *Golaknath* was announced, Congress's revolutionary authority had reached a low point, with the Syndicate using Gandhi as a marketing device to sustain a bare parliamentary majority. But within six short years, the Justices confronted an entirely different situation. In her 1971 election campaign, Gandhi had attacked *Golaknath* as an illegitimate obstacle to her mandate from the People for a sweeping antipoverty campaign. Two years later the Justices were obliged to confront Gandhi's revolutionary reassertion of authority in the *Kesavananda Bharati* case,[29] which dealt with recent amendments authorizing key aspects of her nationalization and expropriation program.

The Court responded by overruling *Golaknath*. But the thirteen Justices on the panel wrote eleven opinions explaining what, if anything, should replace it. Six simply abandoned the field and recognized the plenary power of a parliamentary supermajority to amend the Constitution any way it liked. But seven asserted that the Court retained authority to strike down amendments that undermined "the basic constitutional structure."[30]

The meaning of this vague formula remained obscure—it was defined differently in different opinions, and the majority upheld all of Gandhi's nationalizations and expropriations. Nevertheless, the various dicta warned the prime minister that the Court had not yet given up its claim as ultimate guardian of the Nehruvian legacy inherited from Congress's struggle for independence.

Gandhi replied with a warning shot of her own. Until this point, the Chief Justiceship had been filled on the basis of seniority, without regard to the ascending jurist's constitutional views. But this time was different—Gandhi arranged for a dissenter in *Kesavananda* to take the top job instead of more senior judges backing the "basic structure" doctrine.[31]

This set the stage for another confrontation in the following year, arising out of case in which the prime minister herself was a party in the litigation. The dispute involved Gandhi's compliance with election laws in her own campaign for a parliamentary seat in 1971. After years of lawyerly contest, a lower court found Gandhi guilty of minor electoral violations. It then reached the explosive conclusion that these infractions disqualified her from further service as prime minister.

This bombshell prompted an expedited appeal to the Supreme Court. Gandhi had every reason to expect that the Justices would rapidly vindicate her position. The lower court's legal reasoning was very weak, and even a self-confident tribunal would pause before claiming the right to fire the sitting prime minister. Moreover, the Justices were anything but self-confident: Not only had they staged a disorderly retreat in *Kesavananda*, but Gandhi's newly appointed Chief Justice would predictably use his considerable powers to impress his colleagues with the need for self-restraint.[32]

Yet Gandhi refused to wait for her almost-certain vindication. She used the lower-court judgment as a pretext for declaring a sweeping State of Emergency—jailing her principal parliamentary opponents and other leading dissidents, including many leaders of the earlier independence struggle. Ignoring the opposition's boycott of Parliament, she pushed through another round of sweeping emergency legislation and enacted formal amendments insulating these measures from judicial review. At the same time, she launched a massive propaganda campaign, seeking to mobilize popular support for her Reformed Congress Party.

With mixed success. While aggressive censorship suppressed familiar opposition voices, one aspect of her program generated massive backlash. Emphasizing that India's future prosperity was threatened by overpopulation, she named her son Sanjay to lead an aggressive campaign for compulsory sterilization. No less remarkably, she did not even pass legislation granting her son an official position for the exercise of extraordinary powers—apparently, her word sufficed. There can be no better evidence of Gandhi's lawless assertion of charismatic authority.[33]

Despite her grave challenge to constitutionalism, the Court remained resolutely on the sidelines. With the new Chief Justice in control, it refused to intervene in cases involving the most egregious abuses of emergency power.[34]

But then Gandhi fell victim to her own propaganda. Convinced of her popularity, she ended the emergency after twenty-one months and called a parliamentary election in 1977 to ratify her brave leap into authoritarianism. To legitimate her expected triumph, she released her opponents from confinement and allowed them to contest the election. Once the prison doors opened, these old revolutionaries managed to transcend their big ideological differences to establish a new Janata Alliance, led by Gandhi's bitter rival, Morarji Desai. In his words, the newly united opposition pledged "to rectify the Constitution . . . to ensure that an Emergency like this can never be imposed [again]."[35]

Desai's desperate call to rally behind the Constitution seemed destined for failure. Janata had only two months to get its message across; and the four political parties in its broad coalition had suffered great organizational damage during the preceding period. Despite these overwhelming disadvantages, the anti-Emergency campaign resonated powerfully among ordinary Indian voters—who awarded Janata a decisive majority of 298 seats, as opposed to the 153 seats gained by Reformed Congress (a loss of 200 seats, compared to the previous Parliament!).[36]

Yet the new coalition failed to make the most of its popular mandate. Over the next three years, its ideologically divergent factions were unable to provide stable government; prime ministers rose and fell in an ongoing struggle for power.[37] Nevertheless, Janata's disciplined law minister carried through on its campaign pledge to eliminate the Emergency-era amendments that had "defiled" the Constitution.

The initiative put Mrs. Gandhi into a corner: As leader of the opposition, would she join the Janata majority in condemning her own conduct?

Whatever her personal feelings, she had no choice. From a practical political point of view, she would have to vote Yes. If she ever hoped to regain power, it was imperative to tell the electorate—in no uncertain terms—that she would never again engage in power grabs like those that provoked her popular repudiation. As the constitutional debate drew to a close in December 1978, the public witnessed a remarkable spectacle: both Morarji Desai of Janata *and* Indira Gandhi of Reformed Congress joined a large parliamentary majority to pass amendments guaranteeing that there would not be another round of Emergency abuses.

India's "succession crisis" was coming to an end—and in a way that bore a striking relationship to the Founding. In 1950 Nehru and Ambedkar created a Constitution that sought to prevent the Congress Party from betraying the revolutionary principles that had sustained the movement party during its decades-long insurgency. A generation later, the same logic of constitutional reassurance was being reenacted—with a historical twist: Just as Congress's revolutionary movement prepared the way for Nehru's Constitution at Time Two, Janata's insurgent outsiders, led by activists in the earlier independence struggle, prepared the way for a *popular reaffirmation* of the principles of 1950 at Time Three.

The paradoxical twist involved the identity of the entrenched insiders. The British imperialists were the target during Time One; but Nehru's own daughter (and her son) were the target during Time Three. Once entrenched in power, they had presented themselves as the legitimate heirs to the glory days of the revolution—this time insisting that their Reformed Congress Party had no need for constitutional restraints in its escalating struggle against the dark forces that were dooming the masses to ignorance, poverty, and subordination.

Yet by 1978 Gandhi's decision to join Desai in repealing the Emergency amendments was her public acknowledgment that she had failed. Her call for an *un*limited revolution had been repudiated by revolutionary means: it was Janata, and not the Reformed Congress, that had successfully mobilized the citizenry to recommit the Republic to a revolution on a human scale, based on the core principles hammered out by Ambedkar and the Congress Party in 1950.

Gandhi's turnaround in Parliament also served as a crucial preliminary for the Supreme Court's reentry onto the stage. Given the Justices' striking failure to stand up for the Constitution during the Emergency, there was an imperative need for them to rehabilitate their tarnished reputations. While Parliament had repealed many of Gandhi's amendments, it had not swept away all of them—leaving room for the Court to join in the clean-up operation.

Its 1980 decision in *Minerva Mills* represented an about-face from its chaotic 1973 judgment in *Kesavananda Bharati*. At that time, Gandhi was fresh from a sweeping victory at the polls and the Court repudiated its earlier claim, in *Golaknath,* to serve as the Constitution's ultimate guardian of fundamental rights. Not only had *Kesavananda* rubber-stamped Gandhi's recent amendments; only a narrow majority were brave enough to suggest, in dicta, that the Court reserved the right to defend the Constitution's "basic structure" on some future occasion. Since the judges could not even agree as to the meaning of "basic," the Court's determination to mount a serious defense of the Nehruvian Constitution was very much in doubt.

This time around, *Minerva Mills* transformed the "basic structure" formula into a powerful weapon. With only a single dissent, the Justices swept away key elements of the Emergency amendments that Parliament had left on the books.[38]

The Court's timing was important. When *Minerva Mills* was announced in 1980, the Janata coalition had collapsed, a caretaker government had taken its place, and Mrs. Gandhi had just won a landslide victory as India's only hope for stable government.

Minerva Mills, however, required her to confront the limited character of her renewed mandate from the voters. If she attacked the decision, it would have enabled her opponents to unite around the only issue that had permitted them to transcend their political differences. Once again, Desai and his Janata partners would have called upon their followers to take to the streets in defense of the Constitution. Perhaps this second counterrevolution would have proved less successful—but Mrs. Gandhi was in no mood to find out. She did absolutely nothing to oppose the Court's decision—pursuing an aggressive agenda that provoked many political crises but never raised issues that would have provoked a head-on confrontation with the Court.

Time Four: Codification

When Mrs. Gandhi was assassinated in 1984, leaders of her political party followed the same succession formula they used the last time around—selecting her only surviving son, Rajiv, as prime minister. But this time they got what they wanted: an attractive but inexperienced scion of the Nehru dynasty who wouldn't rock the boat.

Rajiv's rise reassured the party bosses, but it raised a serious problem on a second front. As Congress's revolutionary past faded in everyday life, its dominant political position was challenged by a new set of rivals. The country's federal structure enabled regional parties to gain powerful representation in provincial assemblies by appealing to locally dominant ethnolinguistic constituencies. Once these regional parties gained a footing in local politics, they could nominate their own slate of candidates for the national Parliament and compete with Congress's slate with increasing success.

This meant that Congress could no longer form a majority government on its own in New Delhi. Instead its leadership was obliged to engage in increasingly complex coalition building with the regionals to maintain control.[39] Over the decades, these Congress-led coalitions shifted away from socialist ideals and began to open up the economy for private enterprise—but this happened through elite politics and pressure from the World Bank, not through a new mass movement demanding a revolutionary embrace of neoliberalism.

As high-energy politics declined in Parliament, the Supreme Court became an increasingly confident guardian of the constitutional legacy. Particular decisions provoked heated political controversy, but none generated a legitimacy crisis resembling the intense struggles surrounding the Emergency.

Over time, judicial authority was reinforced by a feedback loop: the rising generation of lawyers was socialized into a professional culture that taught them to view the Constitution through a dense web of judge-made doctrines that resembled "lawyers' law" in traditional doctrinal fields; armed with these professional tools, they could strike down legislative initiatives with increasing professional confidence, while weak parliamentary coalitions struggled to respond decisively—sometimes succeeding, sometimes failing.

In short, the Indian experience provides a vivid example of the "consolidation" dynamic described more abstractly in Chapter 1. On the one hand, high-energy mass politics declined, replaced by elite wheeling and dealing in a remote capitol; on the other, the legal order's self-confidence increased, creating a supportive environment for the professionally disciplined development of constitutional doctrine.

Speaking broadly, much of the Court's case law emphasized the enduring relevance of the founding era's constitutional commitments. So long as socialist ideology was ascendant, the Justices did not greatly concern themselves with the vindication of social rights to health, housing, or minimum subsistence. But as revolutionary politics faded, the Justices have increasingly extended their concerns to the fate of the downtrodden—despite the fact that the political world has been evolving in the neoliberal direction.[40] Over the last decade, the Court has also broken new ground in imposing constitutional standards of transparency and accountability on the executive—enabling the Justices to present themselves as a bastion of integrity in a political system visibly scarred by crass opportunism.[41]

The past thirty years of case-law development has also enabled the Court to translate its special prerogatives to defend the "basic structure" into lapidary doctrinal elements:

> There is near unanimity that there are at least five features that can be regarded as essential and basic. The first is secularism; second, democracy; third, rule of law; fourth, federalism; and the fifth is an independent judiciary with the power of judicial review.[42]

The professional consensus on these five points allowed the Court to consolidate its position further in 2007. Its decision in *Coelho vs. State of Tamil Nadu* closed off the last "escape hatch" that allowed a parliamentary majority to evade the judicial effort to defend the basic structure against political attack.[43]

It pays to reflect on *Coelho*—both because it culminates a century-long path of constitutional development and because it frames the current effort by Prime Minister Narendra Modi to revolutionize the basic structure that the Court is seeking to defend.

Begin by recalling the moment when Nehru and Congress were triumphantly emerging from their long struggle for independence. Just as the revolutionary movement enacted its Constitution, Nehru immediately confronted a series of lawsuits attacking the constitutional validity of his land redistribution program. He responded by ramming the First Amendment through Parliament. This provision not only stripped the Supreme Court of jurisdiction in the impending cases. It authorized Parliament to insulate future controversial enactments from judicial review by placing them on a special Schedule Nine created for this precise purpose.

The Court's immediate response was total capitulation. Only when Nehru departed from the scene did it take a first step toward self-assertion in *Golaknath*. And even then, its declaration of independence turned out to be distinctly provisional—with the Justices utterly failing to safeguard the most fundamental constitutional rights during Indira Gandhi's Emergency. It was only after the popular repudiation of Gandhi's lurch toward authoritarianism that the Court took advantage of the succession crisis to gain broad political recognition as the Constitution's preeminent defender. There was nothing inevitable about *Minerva Mills*. If the Court had not seized the moment, its claim to serve as supreme guardian of the Constitution might never have been recognized.

Indeed, despite the Court's powerful reemergence after the succession crisis, Schedule Nine remained available for a series of coalition governments to avoid head-on confrontations with the judiciary. Moreover, these governments made energetic use of this escape hatch, placing 271 statutes (of varying importance) on the Schedule since the basic structure doctrine was first announced.[44]

But as the Court succeeded in consolidating its position on other fronts, it launched a direct attack on this final barrier to its constitutional supremacy in 2007.[45] *Coelho* reinterpreted Schedule Nine to bar its future use as an escape hatch. It then went further to declare that all the laws placed on the Schedule since 1973 would now be open to "basic structure" challenges.

To summarize: Schedule Nine first served as an expression of Congress's revolutionary charisma during Time Two; but by Time Three, the Court was going on the offensive and Parliament was making use of the Schedule to sideline the Court's ascendancy in special cases; yet it was only during Time Four, after the Court consolidated its constitutional authority on other fronts and the Congress Party further declined into patronage politics, that the Justices were finally in a position to terminate Schedule Nine and declare that the Court would henceforth defend the Nehruvian fundamentals against all forms of political assault.

But is such a declaration by an elite corps of judges truly compatible with the revolutionary paradigm that legitimates the larger Indian regime?

This was the question raised by the sweeping electoral victory of Narendra Modi, and his Bharatiya Janata Party, in 2014. This was the first time since 1984 that a single party had won an outright parliamentary majority. What is more, the BJP did not gain its majority through mere patronage politics (though, of course, this is never absent from the real world). It explicitly appealed to ordinary citizens to sweep out the political heirs of Congress's great past and use the BJP as a popular vehicle for revolutionizing the foundations of Indian political life.

The nature of this "new beginning" is, as always, controversial. For starters, Modi pledged to break away from the omnipresent state bureaucracy inherited from Congress's socialist past. But he was not merely promising to sweep away the legacy of bureaucratic overregulation. He was also aiming for a revolution in India's Nehruvian constitutional identity.

Modi's BJP is deeply rooted in the Hindu nationalist movement—which has, since the struggle for independence, raised a fundamental challenge to Congress's secularism—a core element of the "basic structure" that the Court has pledged to support.[46] To prepare for this high-stakes battle, Modi's first move recalled a similar tactic undertaken by Indira Gandhi as she prepared her own (very different) challenge to the Founding's legacy. Recall that Gandhi manipulated the process of judicial appointment to enable one of her followers to ascend to the Chief Justiceship and thereby engineer the Court's acquiescence in all of the Emergency's shocking assaults on constitutional fundamentals.

Soon after taking office, Modi made a similar effort—creating a super-majoritarian coalition for a constitutional amendment that would quickly enable his followers to gain control over the Court's leadership.[47] But unlike the judiciary's humiliating retreat before Gandhi, today's judges have refused to allow Modi's initiative to go forward. Their decision of October 2015 struck down the National Judicial Appointments Commission, created under Modi's amendment, as a violation of the constitution's "basic structure."[48]

The panel vote was 4 to 1, but the five Justices produced 1,000 pages of opinions, providing plenty of maneuvering room if interbranch confrontation escalates. If a serious contest does arise, Hindu nationalists in the government and Enlightenment secularists on the Court will tell very different stories about the struggle that gave birth to independent India. They will also advance rival interpretations of the Emergency and its aftermath. These debates about the meaning of the revolutionary past will frame a fundamental debate about the constitutional future.

Only time will tell whether the secularist or Hindu-nationalist version of India's Founding will decisively triumph, or whether a more complex combination of historical narratives and fundamental principles will emerge.[49]

One thing is clear: whatever the outcome, it will emerge only after another round of high-energy politics, in which one side finally gains the charismatic authority to reaffirm or modify Nehruvian principles in the name of We the People of the Twenty-First Century.

This is the key point for our purposes. As my argument proceeds, I will be comparing the revolutionary paradigm to the two other pathways marked out in the Introduction. When polities travel these alternative paths to constitutionalism, mass political mobilization can be a profound threat to legitimate order. From the establishmentarian and elitist perspectives, "populist" appeals are not a legitimate part of the process by which the People engage in acts of political redefinition. They are nothing more than rabble-rousing efforts by demagogues, seeking to destroy the constitutional achievements crafted through elite statesmanship.

Mobilized appeals to the People play a very different role in countries like India. In places with revolutionary traditions, they serve as a *legitimate* part of the process through which each generation confronts the ongoing project of constitutional self-definition. Sometimes, the result will be a mobilized reaffirmation of principles established by an earlier revolutionary generation; sometimes, the result will be their sweeping revision.

But at all times, these ongoing struggles will raise a more fundamental question: Will the victors use their popular mandate as a springboard for authoritarian repression? Or will they be obliged to recognize that the People have only authorized a revolution on a human scale, and that even the most triumphant movement parties are obliged to respect constitutional limits on their power?

CHAPTER 3

Struggling for Supremacy: South Africa

The decline and fall of empire will be a leitmotif in our investigations. Imperial disintegration opens a space for emerging nations to define their constitutional identities. But a mobilized mass movement will not invariably rise up to fill the vacuum left by the departing hegemon. In some cases, rising political elites manage to construct a new political order without large-scale popular participation—and I will be considering these scenarios in the next volume.

But as India demonstrates, the "declining empire scenario" also plays a key role in our current study—and following up with a comparison to South Africa permits us to begin an exploration of variations on this theme. Like India, modern South Africa emerges from the decline of the British Empire, but with one big difference—the nature of imperial collapse.

Effective British control over India disintegrated in the aftermath of World War II—with Lord Mountbatten desperately searching for terms that would enable the Attlee government to escape further responsibility for maintaining law and order on the subcontinent. Given the Indian National Congress's broad-based organization, it was the only plausible movement party to take up the burden of government. Once Congress assumed power (Time Two), it was in an ideal position to constitutionalize its charisma during the founding period. Given the absence of British resistance, and the lack of major political rivals, there were no external forces challenging the legitimacy of the Congress Party's constitutional project.

It would have been perfectly possible for Nehru and Ambedkar to refuse to take this task seriously. Indeed, this is precisely what was happening in China at the very same time: Mao and the Communist Party self-consciously refused to allow "bourgeois constitutionalism" to operate as a serious constraint on their revolutionary effort to lead the Chinese People to a breakthrough in their political identity.

My point is more limited: Not only did Congress reject Mao-style dictatorship, it was in an especially good position to channel its high-energy politics into the solemn commitments of a revolutionary Constitution. Undoubtedly, Nehru and Ambedkar could have botched the job. But given the decades of organizational work at the grass roots, and the absence of serious competitors, symbolic leaders in New Delhi were particularly well positioned to speak for the People in a way that tens of millions of engaged citizens found credible.

When we turn to South Africa, the postwar decline of the British Empire left the African National Congress (ANC) in a very different situation. It was white Afrikaners, not black Africans, who took charge of the nation's destiny as Britain gave up effective control. After winning a sweeping parliamentary victory in the (all-white) elections of 1948, the National Party (NP) hardened the lines of racial separation that had developed during the period of British dominion. One zone contained 90 percent of the land, and was reserved for whites; the other contained 10 percent of the territory, and was distributed among a number of native Bantustans ("homelands") organized on ethnic / linguistic / tribal lines. The Bantustan puppet regimes supplied the apartheid republic with a legal rationale for draconian restrictions on blacks living within the vast white area. After all, European states had traditionally limited the rights of "resident aliens" who chose to remain on foreign soil rather than return to their homelands. If this was good enough for Europe before the advent of the European Economic Community, why not for South Africa?

The UK responded ambiguously. Like the rest of the world, it refused to extend diplomatic recognition to the Bantustans; but it also refused to take the lead in penalizing the South Africans for the harsh treatment of millions of black "resident aliens" living in the white zone. The Americans were content to follow the lead of the British on the matter. It was only in the mid-1980s that Thatcher and Reagan reluctantly changed course and endorsed serious sanctions.

This meant that, for an entire generation, "decline of empire" generated very different scenarios in India and South Africa. Instead of smoothing the path for the Indian Congress to take power, the British retreat from South Africa served as a prelude to an all-out struggle between the apartheid Republic and the revolutionary ANC—which denounced the Bantustans as frauds and demanded equal rights for all South Africans, regardless of their race or place of residence.

To frame these two very different scenarios, I will begin with Time One. In India's case, Gandhi's tactics of civil disobedience prepared the way for the rise of the Indian National Congress (INC) as a well-organized movement party by the 1930s—allowing it to win sweeping victories in elections to con-sultative assemblies organized by the British. As a consequence, the INC's claim to speak for the People in its final campaign for independence in the 1940s had roots in time-tested relationships between national, regional, and grassroots levels of the organization.

In contrast, the ANC emerged from its liberation struggle against apart-heid in a shattered condition. While it too engaged in Gandhi-like campaigns of civil disobedience during the early decades of white rule, this only pro-voked an escalating show of force from the Republic of South Africa (RSA). Repression drove ANC activists underground, making it difficult for them to coordinate resistance efforts across different areas within South Africa. It also forced much of the ANC leadership out of the country. Oliver Tambo, the head of the ANC-in-exile, could maintain only intermittent contact with Nelson Mandela and other charismatic leaders during their twenty-five-year imprisonment on Robben Island and in Pollsmoor Prison.

The apartheid regime's crackdown also led the ANC to organize its own guerilla organization, the Spear of the Nation, which engaged in bitter mili-tary combat with the RSA's security forces. This meant that the ANC faced a Time One problem that simply did not arise in India: Could its fragmented civilian leadership sustain their control over the military commanders of the Spear's fighting force?

As the apartheid regime lost its grip on power during the 1980s, the ANC confronted a second problem. The RSA tried to co-opt the more mod-erate elements in the liberation movement by offering its leaders significant, but not decisive, power within reformed governing arrangements. The apart-heid regime had especially good reason to believe that this technique might be successful. Its sustained campaign of repression had shattered the ANC into at least four components: Mandela and his fellow prisoners, the official ANC-in-exile, the Spear of the Nation, and the domestic underground. This fractionation encouraged the apartheid government to try to create splits between the more "moderate" and the "extremist" factions—and to lure moderates into a subordinate role within a "reformed" white-dominated regime.

This is precisely the course taken by leading NP politicians during the late 1980s—though only with great difficulty, since they confronted a fractionation problem of their own. Many Afrikaners remained hard-liners, as were powerful leaders of the national security forces, and they were determined to continue the regime's all-out campaign against ANC "terrorists."

At the end of the day, President F. W. de Klerk managed to prevail over his white opponents—freeing Nelson Mandela and entering into negotiations on a new Constitution. The opening of these talks gripped the attention of the world—and earned Mandela and de Klerk the Nobel Prize for their remarkable acts of statesmanship. But all this praise has led to a major misunderstanding of their accomplishment.

Broadly speaking, observers have come to view South Africa as a paradigmatic example of a "third wave" revolution—in which moderate insiders successfully negotiate with moderate outsiders on the terms of a democratic transition.[1] This is a mistake. As we shall see, Mandela succeeded in forcing de Klerk to come to terms only by mobilizing the disparate elements of his movement—including the Spear of the Nation—and threatening to destroy the Republic and construct a revolutionary new order from the bottom up.

Even as the confrontation escalated to crisis proportions, Mandela aimed to keep the ANC forces committed to a revolution on a human scale—which is why the Constitution played such a central role in defining the terms of the movement party's ultimate victory.

Yet here again, conventional treatments of the ANC's constitutional revolution do not do it justice. Students of comparative law have rightly emphasized the worldwide influence of opinions written by leading justices of its Constitutional Court in expanding the scope of human rights. But I will be emphasizing a different dimension—pointing to the way in which Mandela used the Constitution as a central symbol for coordinating the disparate elements of the ANC and redeeming the movement party's claim to speak for We the People. Constitutional patriotism, in short, provided the vehicle for reconstituting the ANC as a well-organized grassroots organization that expressed the real-world aspirations for social justice expressed by the overwhelming majority of South Africans.

This *constitutive* feature of the Constitution permits a natural transition to the series of crises provoked by Mandela's departure from the presidency in 1999. I will be focusing on the ways his successors were constrained by the constitutional legacy of the Founding in their struggle for power—generating a series of shocks that most recently culminated in Cyril Ramaphosa's recent success in winning the presidency.

Once again I will be looking to the Indian experience for perspective. Nehru, no less than Mandela, was a charismatic leader who managed to constitutionalize the high-energy politics of his revolutionary movement. As in Mandela's case, Nehru's departure from the scene generated a series of power plays that threatened to sweep away the constitutional legacy of the Founding. How do these Indian struggles compare to those South Africa has experienced since Mandela left the presidency in 1999?

I propose, then, to consider the cases of India and South Africa as variations on common themes that my Introduction laid out in describing the legitimation crises confronting revolutionary regimes during succession crises at Time Three. But a serious effort along these lines requires us to begin the analysis at a much earlier point.

Time One: Totalizing Repression and Its Revolutionary Implications

Mahatma Gandhi provides a suggestive starting point—because he spent twenty years of revolutionary agitation in South Africa before making his way back to India in 1915. Gandhi arrived in South Africa in 1893 after completing his legal training in Britain, and soon spearheaded an ongoing campaign to win equal rights for Asians who were migrating from India to this resource-rich British colony. After two decades, his Natal Indian Congress gained only some very partial victories in the face of strong opposition from white settlers. Nevertheless, Gandhi's work helped inspire efforts by Westernizing black elites to establish the African National Congress in 1912.

Recall that the Indian National Congress had similar elitist origins in the 1890s—and it took twenty years for Gandhi and others to transform it into a mass movement. It also took a generation for the ANC to make a similar transition. The catalytic event was the creation of the ANC Youth League in 1943 by young university graduates like Nelson Mandela, Walter Sisulu, and Oliver Tambo. These activists then used the Youth League as a springboard for their takeover of the ANC's Executive Committee during the immediate postwar period.[2] As the Afrikaners swept into power to impose draconian apartheid measures on blacks, the ANC took the lead in the 1952 Defiance Campaign of mass protest. It then joined with Indian, colored, and white allies to organize a Congress of the People, which in 1955 endorsed a Freedom Charter defining the aims of the liberation movement. The Charter's vision was broadly similar to that set out by the INC in India—calling for a democratic South Africa that guaranteed fundamental rights to all citizens, regardless of class or color, and urging land redistribution and other interventions by the state to achieve social and economic equality.[3]

This would be the last time the RSA allowed a mobilized oppositional assembly to convene within South African territory for the next thirty years—and the Charter remained an ideological reference point throughout this bitter period. Nevertheless, its Enlightenment constitutionalism was increasingly challenged on two fronts. On the one hand, black nationalists in the breakaway Pan Africanist Congress (PAC) attacked the ANC's multiracial vision. On the other hand, Communist Party (CP) activists denounced the Charter's "bourgeois constitutionalism." This critique was particularly salient because Party members played a major role within the ANC itself—with Nelson Mandela serving as a secret member of the CP's Central Committee.[4]

The ANC reached a turning point in 1960 when police fired on nonviolent demonstrators protesting apartheid "pass laws" in Sharpeville. Confronting sweeping acts of repression, its leaders despaired at the prospects of peaceful change through Gandhi-like tactics of civil disobedience. Oliver Tambo had already been forced to flee the country, and had begun to set up an ANC-in-exile, establishing a permanent headquarters in Lusaka, Zambia, by 1963.[5] This became a magnet for militants who crossed the border for training as guerilla fighters in the ANC's military wing, the Spear of the Nation. Mandela himself fully backed this turn to violence before he was captured and sentenced to life imprisonment, along with other charismatic leaders who had remained in the country.[6]

During the following decades, and in stark contrast to the parallel Indian case, the ANC did not exist as a well-organized movement in the homeland. There were ongoing efforts to establish connections with unions and underground groups, but the Spear's guerilla attacks on vulnerable outposts provided the principal evidence of the ANC's presence within the country. Despite episodic outbreaks of civil unrest, government security forces were generally successful in maintaining order—and they further destabilized the exiled ANC through covert assassinations.

The ANC was more successful in gaining international recognition—though these efforts were severely compromised throughout the Cold War by the presence of Communists among the exiled leadership. With Moscow serving as the ANC's principal source of funds, Oliver Tambo was in no position to repudiate the South African Communist Party (SACP)—though as a social democrat, he tried to give the ANC a more inclusive political profile.[7]

Nevertheless, the apartheid government was very successful in portraying the ANC as a Communist front aiming to impose its revolutionary will through military force. As late as 1985, Margaret Thatcher was condemning it as a "terrorist group" similar to the Palestine Liberation Organization and the Irish Republican Army. She used her very considerable influence to block the Commonwealth from imposing economic sanctions on the racist South African regime, on the ground that it played an essential role in the world-wide struggle against Communism.[8] The Reagan administration displayed a similar reluctance.[9]

The catalyst for significant political change wasn't outside pressure, but massive student protest within the country during the late 1970s. The obvious alienation of the younger generation led the previously hard-line government of P. W. Botha to move in a more pragmatic direction. During the early 1980s Botha tried to co-opt moderate opposition forces into a common front against the ANC and SACP. His constitutional reforms created a "trilateral Parliament," in which the white-only chamber would be joined by assemblies elected by the Indian and Colored (mixed-race) communities. The white chamber would continue to play the dominant role in the reformed system; and blacks remained entirely unrepresented, but Botha's initiative marked a break with the rigid exclusionary past.

It also tapped into a worldwide trend toward "consociationalism" in multicultural societies. Consociationalists argue that the foundational principle of "one-person, one vote" is unsuitable for countries that include divergent cultural communities. They fear that equal suffrage allows a "winner-take-all" system that systematically suppresses discrete and insular minorities. They support constitutional structures, like multichamber parliaments, that require the numerically dominant group to engage in ongoing consensus-building before binding legislation is enacted.[10] In calling for consociational democracy, rather than the "one person, one vote" version, Botha's vision was well within mainline Western thinking of the era.

The "trilateral Parliament," however, fell far short of the consociational ideal, since Botha refused to create a fourth chamber granting the black majority a say in the new constitutional order. Instead, his government continued to insist that blacks were only citizens of tribal Bantustans and could be brutally subordinated as "resident aliens" in white areas. But Botha was not content to use police state methods in his campaign against the ANC. He provided political support to the Inkatha Freedom Party (IFP), a countermovement headed by Mangosuthu Buthelezi, who sought to invigorate government in his KwaZulu homeland and thereby provide a model for vibrant political self-rule in the other Bantustans.[11]

As moderates of other races considered Botha's overtures, hard-line white racists responded with alarm. Botha responded by calling a whites-only referendum to demonstrate broad support for his initiative by his core constituents in the dominant National Party (NP). But the hard-liners formed a new Conservative Party (CP) and urged whites to vote no, and were quite successful in appealing to their Afrikaner base. Nevertheless, Botha managed to gain the support of a broad coalition of progressives from the Afrikaner and Anglo communities—winning his referendum by a 2-to-1 margin.

This opened the way for elections to the Colored and Indian chambers in 1983 and 1984—generating another confrontation between radicals and moderates. This time the split occurred on the darker side of the color line. Moderates in the two minority communities viewed the new chambers as progressive moves, but radicals urged election boycotts to protest the continuing exclusion of blacks. The boycott rapidly escalated into the largest anti-apartheid movement on South African soil since the early 1960s. Because the ANC and SACP remained banned from politics, a new umbrella organization, the United Democratic Front (UDF), came to the fore. This "astonishingly diverse group in geographic and social terms" was a coalition of hundreds of distinct organizations, but "with a few exceptions, all were led by activists who considered themselves supporters or even members of the ANC."[12]

This allowed the ANC to sustain its symbolic centrality—even though its imprisoned and exiled leadership had only tenuous connections to the new round of protest.[13] While the Botha government managed to convene its new assemblies, the UDF sustained its momentum beyond the elections, gaining three million supporters by 1985, with leaders like Desmond Tutu and Helen Joseph gaining new prominence.

This groundswell culminated in a massive strike of 1.5 million workers by COSATU, a rising black labor union movement, in May 1986. With the Spear of the Nation escalating its armed attacks, the Botha government gave up its outreach efforts—declaring a State of Emergency in 1986, and unleashing a desperate effort by its military and security forces to crush the uprising and secure the frontiers.

Divide and Conquer?

Botha remained a steadfast defender of apartheid in public, but he began playing a different game in private. Just as he had previously tried to co-opt Indian and Colored moderates, he began a similar co-optation campaign with the black leadership.

Mandela was the key to this strategy. After two decades of daily humiliation at Robben Island, he had been transferred, along with his comrades,
to the maximum-security Pollsmoor Prison on the mainland. Nevertheless,
his contacts with the insurgents outside the prison were tenuous at best. If
Botha could persuade him to strike a pragmatic constitutional bargain that
preserved core elements of white power, this would predictably split the
rest of the movement—with the UDF, the ANC-in-exile, and COSATU dividing into pro- and anti-Mandela factions.[14] This would give his National
Party just the bargaining partner it wanted to reach a constitutional settlement that preserved the essentials of white supremacy—while black radicals
protested ineffectively from the sidelines.

Mandela was well aware of these dangers when first approached by government emissaries in 1985. Nevertheless, he decided to move ahead. Without
seeking the approval of his fellow political prisoners at Pollsmoor—much less
his exiled colleagues in the ANC Executive Committee—he began secret negotiations. Only then did he inform a few top leaders of his decision, and
gained their reluctant consent for him to serve as the ANC's one and only
representative at the top-secret negotiations with the NP government.[15]

Yet his fellow leaders' acquiescence did not blind Mandela to the realities
of his situation. In contrast to the ANC-in-exile, he lacked personal ties to
the new generation of activists from the UDF and COSATU coming onto the
scene. He could not count on their personal loyalty if he emerged with a secret deal with Botha that disappointed their hopes.

His relationship to the Spear of the Nation was even more problematic. If
the guerillas believed he was selling them out, they would respond to betrayal
by intensifying their armed campaign against black collaborators with the
enemy.

Recognizing these risks, Mandela refused to make the concessions required for serious progress with Botha emissaries. Negotiations went nowhere until Botha suffered a stroke in 1989, and F. W. de Klerk replaced him
as the head of the National Party government.

Agonizing Reappraisal

Even then, a great deal of violent confrontation would be required before
de Klerk could gain white support for a serious constitutional solution. In
the meantime, the ANC-in-exile would be a crucial site for rethinking the

movement's broader position on the role of constitutionalism in defining South Africa's future.

Two big international shifts triggered this agonizing reappraisal. On the one hand, Botha's State of Emergency of 1986 had a devastating impact on the apartheid Republic's standing abroad. Margaret Thatcher and Ronald Reagan were finally obliged to support economic embargoes and other initiatives aimed at forcing South Africa to engage in good-faith negotiations with the ANC. On the other hand, Mikhail Gorbachev's rise to power made it increasingly clear that the ANC could no longer rely on the Soviets to be its principal supplier of funds and arms in its ongoing struggle against the apartheid regime.[16]

Oliver Tambo, as head of the ANC-in-exile, moved quickly to explore the new possibilities opened up by these East-West shifts. For starters, he entered into top-secret talks in Britain with South African officials and the business community, aiming to lay a foundation for serious negotiations with the apartheid government. Tambo designated his protégé, Thabo Mbeki, to take the diplomatic lead for the ANC, and the two sides held twelve confidence-building sessions between 1987 and 1990 in the luxurious setting of Mells Park in Somerset. These talks were undoubtedly significant in building up mutual trust, but their importance has been exaggerated in later accounts. As everybody recognized, the key decisions were being taken by Mandela in the harsh conditions of Pollsmoor Prison, not by Mbeki in the posh surroundings of Mells Park. Only if Mandela stood firm, and rejected all the "compromises" offered by Botha, would businesses pressure the government to hand over real power to the black majority.[17]

A second initiative would prove more significant. With Thatcher and Reagan finally endorsing an effective economic boycott, Tambo encouraged the ANC to rethink its ultimate aims now that its revolutionary struggle had a real prospect of overwhelming white resistance. During the ANC's long decades of exile, there had been no need to move beyond the Freedom Charter of 1955—whose broad social democratic commitments sufficed to mobilize continued resistance at home and international support abroad. But as serious negotiations with the apartheid regime loomed on the horizon, it was now imperative for the ANC to transform the Charter into concrete constitutional proposals, so that it could go to the bargaining table with a clear set of priorities.

Yet in pushing forward, Tambo had a big political problem. Once the ANC got down to serious business, the drafting effort would precipitate deep ideological conflicts. Not only were Communists a strong force on the ANC Executive Committee, but they were even stronger among the armed cadres of the Spear of the Nation. The hard left looked with grave suspicion on Tambo's commitment to social democracy as a form of "bourgeois constitutionalism" that would betray their armed struggle against the entrenched racist power structure. It called instead for a "people's power" constitution, which would commit the ANC to the relentless destruction of white supremacy in all its economic and social forms.

Tambo not only opposed this vision of totalizing revolution. He recognized that its embrace would play into the hands of apartheid hard-liners and their overseas apologists, who had always insisted that the ANC was merely a Communist front. In January 1986 he deftly created a new constitutional committee, representing all factions, but carefully selected its members to push the internal debate in his direction. The chairman was Jack Simons—a distinguished scholar specializing in African traditional law, who had remained a member of the Party's Central Committee since his flight into exile in 1965. Despite his Communist commitments, Simon remained a strong believer in multiparty democracy. So too was Kader Asmal, who had fled South Africa to become a law professor in Ireland and a leading force in the international anti-apartheid movement.

Yet it was Albie Sachs who played a pivotal role—combining a commanding knowledge of constitutional law with a longtime personal commitment to the struggle. Working together, the committee hammered out a lapidary set of principles that focused on universal suffrage, multiparty democracy, and an entrenched bill of rights—while deferring questions of nationalization and other hot topics to a later point. Predictably, the committee draft was denounced as "too wedded to liberal-democratic notions" by a hard-left working group of the ANC Executive, who condemned it for failing to express the radical aims of the "revolutionary struggle."

As a Communist himself, Simons was the ideal chairman to deflect this critique. Here is an especially revealing paragraph in his committee's response to the ANC Executive:

> At a profound level, a constitution is the embodiment of the will of the nation; if it is to enjoy legitimacy, it must come from the people. In other words, the authors of a constitution must have a mandate from the people. This is why the Freedom Charter was so important. The Freedom Charter, drafted on the basis of the popular claims and aspirations brought to Kliptown from

across South Africa, embodied the genuine will of the people. But the Congress of the People back in the 1950s was also the last time the movement had been assembled and able to grant a mandate to its leaders. *To produce a constitution now would therefore be highly problematic; it would presuppose that a group of experts could draft the document and then present it to the people with attendant arguments as to why it served their best interests. Such an approach reversed the correct order because the constitution would come from leaders and technical experts, such as our committee, but not from the people. Therefore, to proceed with drafting a constitution at [this] time would undermine the nature of true constitutionalism in our country just at the moment that a free and democratic constitutional order was being seriously contemplated for the first time in South Africa's traumatic history.*[18]

It is hard to imagine a more self-conscious statement of the core principles of revolutionary constitutionalism. Within its historical context, this response was of more than intellectual interest. For starters, it helped propel Tambo's campaign forward, enabling him to win Executive Committee approval for the committee's basic approach in 1987. As it moved into the next stage, the ANC would settle for nothing less than universal suffrage—which would guarantee it a sweeping parliamentary majority at the first democratic election. At the same time, its recognition of the legitimacy of multiparty democracy, and a bill of rights, offered the white minority a continuing role in politics and a constitutional guarantee of their fundamental interests.

No less important, the ANC's constitutional principles provided a precious resource for Nelson Mandela as he finally emerged from prison in early 1990 to claim symbolic centrality of the still-disorganized movement. His heroic status was broadly recognized by the rising generation of UDF activists and COSATU unionists—as well as returning ANC exiles and the resurgent guerrillas of the Spear. But he had been isolated from the real-life struggles of the contending factions for decades—and would have had enormous difficulties if he had been left the task of gaining the consent of the different ideological factions to a common set of principles.

Yet Tambo and the constitutional committee had already done this job for him. Rather than generating a set of common principles, Mandela confronted a more manageable task. His success would be measured by the extent to which he could sustain broad popular support for the ANC's already-existing constitutional program.

This would not be easy. But for now, it is more important to emphasize a comparative point. While there are many similarities between the ANC and the Indian Congress Party, there was a crucial difference between their situations as the two revolutionary movements entered their founding periods (Time Two). Over the course of Congress's period of insurgency (Time One), it had created powerful institutional structures linking millions of local activists to regional and national leaderships. It was this buildup of *organizational charisma* that enabled Nehru and Ambedkar to claim, with broad credibility, that the Constitution of 1950 expressed the will of the People of India—despite the absence of referenda or any other specially compelling legalism to back up this claim. In contrast, given its systematic suppression by the apartheid regime, the African National Congress lacked any similar structure linking leaders to followers on a mass basis. The ANC served more as an evocative symbol than as an organizational reality that integrated the disjointed movement's aspirations for a "new beginning." As a consequence, Nelson Mandela faced a distinctive problem when he was finally released from prison in 1990. While Nehru and Ambedkar could credibly constitutionalize Congress's *organizational* charisma, he could not. He would instead be obliged to deploy his *personal* charisma in a campaign for the Constitution that would enable the ANC to build solid organizational links with its millions of followers.

South Africa, in short, was the site of *constructive* constitutionalism: the success or failure of Mandela's effort to mobilize mass support for the Constitution would play a key role in determining whether he could transform the ANC from an evocative symbol into a well-organized movement party that could *credibly* speak for We the People of South Africa.

Time Two: Constructive Constitutionalism?

Mandela's prison negotiations went nowhere until Botha suffered a stroke in 1989 and the National Party put F. W. de Klerk in his place as president. Yet it would be tough for de Klerk to offer Mandela a deal that dramatically weakened apartheid. A big turnaround would prompt a strong backlash from hardliners in his ruling National Party. If party rebels failed to topple their new leader, de Klerk could expect large numbers to defect to the far-right Conservative Party[19] and appeal to the all-white electorate to vote him out of office at the first opportunity.

The new president also faced a challenge from his military and security forces. After thirty years of war with "Communist ANC terrorists," would these forces obey his orders to make peace with the enemy?

This question became increasingly salient over the next five years as Mandela and de Klerk struggled to find a solution that could gain the assent of their fragile coalitions. When de Klerk took power in 1989, the battle between the Spear of the Nation and the RSA's security forces took the lives of 2,000 South Africans. But peace was not magically restored once de Klerk legalized the ANC and released Mandela from prison in 1990. To the contrary, the military struggle intensified—the death toll tripled from 2,000 to 6,000 per year as negotiations lurched onward through 1994. As the bloodbath continued, military leaders on both sides threatened to overthrow their civilian chiefs if they betrayed their bloody sacrifices by capitulating to the enemy.[20]

The next challenge is to describe how the political leadership of the RSA and the ANC confronted their internal challenges, and how the Constitution enabled both sides to resolve their conflict in a way that was broadly perceived as legitimate.

De Klerk's Turnaround

De Klerk was called "president," but he functioned like the prime minister of a Westminster system—rising to power in September 1989 only after gaining a narrow victory from National Party backbenchers. Given his tenuous support, de Klerk tried to bolster his position by calling a snap election among the white electorate—but in a fashion that intensified his legitimation problems in dealing with the revolutionary challenges posed by the United Democratic Front, the Spear, and the ANC-in-exile.

Since the 1940s the South African presidents had been strong defenders of apartheid—and when de Klerk's parliamentary colleagues voted him into office, they were by no means endorsing a big shift in the status quo. In seeking a mandate from white voters in the snap election, de Klerk maintained this hard-line stance.

Indeed, he ran an exceptionally reactionary campaign. In response to the escalating crisis, white liberals had organized a Democratic Party to gain parliamentary support for a more inclusive approach to race relations. De Klerk responded by denouncing his new rival as traitorous because some of its leaders had publicly met with the ANC.[21]

Race-baiting proved all too successful. Not only did the NP gain a parliamentary majority, the right-wing Conservatives won an additional 30 percent of the seats. This outcome seemed to give de Klerk little choice but to continue down Botha's path. After all, the voting returns had pushed the liberal

Democrats to the parliamentary sidelines with less than a fifth of the seats, giving the prime minister very little maneuvering room.[22]

Yet it was precisely at this point that de Klerk shocked his base by executing a 180-degree turnaround. He announced the liberation of Mandela and other political prisoners, the legalization of all banned groups, including the Communists and the Spear of the Nation, and the initiation of negotiations on a future Constitution.

Given the political and military context, it would be a mistake to misread the scope of this initiative. Although it required lots of courage, it did not imply a further decision to cede governing power to the black majority. To the contrary, de Klerk's preeminent aim was to negotiate a constitutional settlement that would guarantee the white minority a continuing veto. Just as Botha had reached out to the Indian and Colored communities with his tripartite Parliament, de Klerk offered an expanded vision of consociational democracy to the black community.

This was no small difference—it would permit blacks to play a leading political role for the first time since the beginning of white colonialism. But de Klerk continued to insist that any acceptable constitution must take a consociational form, enabling each racial community to veto any major change in the status quo. Despite his insistence on this key point, the hard-line Conservative Party denounced his "betrayal" of white supremacy—and proceeded to win a series of by-elections as voters rallied to their call.

This string of victories gave de Klerk little choice but to call a whites-only referendum to demonstrate that he did indeed have a majority of his constituents behind him. In returning to the voters in disarray, he made a key concession in a desperate effort to win a Yes vote: "We will not say yes to a suicide plan. . . . [T]here must be effective protection against domination of minorities . . . *whether it be a first phase or a fully encompassing constitution.*"[23]

This commitment allowed him to gain a convincing victory in the March 1992 referendum. But it placed him in sharp conflict with the key ANC demand "that the people shall have the right to vote under a system of universal suffrage based on the principle of one person, one vote." Rather than authorizing rapprochement, de Klerk's referendum "victory" seemed to create an unbridgeable gulf between his government and the ANC.

Mandela's Turnaround

At the same time, Mandela was struggling with problems of his own. His release from prison opened the way for a triumphant tour of Europe and southern Africa. Yet gaining support from his own fragmented movement proved far more difficult. As the exiled ANC leaders returned home, they joined Mandela in August 1990 to make their own conciliatory gesture to de Klerk—announcing the suspension of armed struggle while the two sides joined in serious constitutional negotiations.

But as in de Klerk's case, this proffer of an olive branch provoked a powerful backlash. Just as the president was challenged from the right, Mandela was rebuked from the left. He had joined with the returning ANC exiles to announce the suspension of hostilities without seriously consulting the new generation of UDF activists. When presented with a fait accompli, these upstarts reacted with outrage—organizing a series of protests that forced the old-guard leadership to reverse itself. With the Spear continuing its attacks, the ANC now proclaimed 1991 as "the year of mass action," endorsing mass strikes and protest marches in which Communists and other radicals played leading roles.

Secret negotiations between Mandela and de Klerk could not bridge the yawning gap separating their public positions. There was no official sign of progress until December 1991—almost two full years after Mandela's release from prison. This was the moment when the two sides finally managed to engage each other in public negotiations at the Convention for a Democratic South Africa (CODESA).

Existential Crisis?

The opening session was a great media event. The government and the ANC were at center stage, but CODESA included a very broad range of opposition parties across the political spectrum.

Matters immediately got off to a very bad start, with de Klerk impugning the very legitimacy of his principal bargaining partner:

> The heart of the problem is the following:
>
> The ANC has not yet terminated what it has itself defined as the "armed struggle." ...
>
> The stipulation in the Peace Accord that no political party shall have a private army places a question mark over the ANC's participation in a Convention which, essentially, is taking place among political parties.

An organization which remains committed to an armed struggle cannot be trusted completely when it also commits itself to peacefully negotiated solutions. . . .

The very stage of negotiation towards a new constitution we have reached at Codesa now makes it imperative that the ANC and others who wish to participate will have to terminate armed struggle before such participants can really enter into binding, legitimate, reliable and credible peaceful agreements.[24]

To which Mandela replied:

Mr. de Klerk today . . . has launched an attack on the African National Congress, and in doing so he has been less than frank. Even the head of an illegitimate, discredited, minority regime . . . has certain moral standards to uphold. He has no excuse. . . . [Given his failure] to uphold moral standards, . . . [it is] no wonder the Conservative Party has made such a serious inroad into his power base.[25]

To put it mildly, this opening does not support the now-standard view of South Africa as a paradigmatic case of "negotiated transition" in which elites managed the tricky business of change through enlightened collaboration. A shocked nation was witnessing something very different: a revolutionary confrontation between leading outsiders against leading insiders, each struggling to retain the support of their highly mobilized, militarized, and polarized partisans—by denouncing one another's right to sit at the same negotiating table.

CODESA did stagger on for a few months—at which a number of working groups generated reports on a series of fundamental issues. But it would be up to de Klerk and Mandela to determine whether they could patch things up behind the scenes.

The critical moment came when de Klerk emerged victorious from his white-only referendum in March: Would he engage in yet another turnaround, and drop his demand for a constitutional regime that contemplated a permanent National Unity Government (to wit, a white veto)?

The answer was no. As negotiations stalled, the apartheid regime once again began pumping up the Inkatha Freedom Party, led by the National Party's old KwaZulu ally Mangosuthu Buthelezi, as a rival to Mandela and the ANC—claiming that Buthelezi had broader support in the black community.[26]

At the same time, radicals in the ANC and the African labor federation abandoned CODESA to resume their mass-action campaign. This culminated in a sweeping work stoppage on June 12 that brought the country's industrial production to a complete halt.[27]

This demonstration of black solidarity was quickly followed up by an outbreak of black-on-black violence—with South African police looking on with indifference as thirty-nine peaceful ANC demonstrators were shot down by gunmen apparently allied with Inkatha.[28] These bloody scenes led to the formal breakdown of CODESA, and a further intensification of political violence—with 1,525 incidents, and 240 deaths, marking a new high the following month.[29]

De Klerk and Mandela responded with desperate efforts to pacify their militant wings. De Klerk condemned the ANC's "private army," and Mandela warned that "it would be a grave mistake if your government thinks that resorting to repression and the use the military and police power . . . can be a means of resolving the conflict."[30]

Yet the government remained resolute—its security forces fired upon 80,000 ANC protesters in September when they tried to overthrow the official government of one of the Bantustans established under apartheid.[31]

The sense of existential crisis was intensified by an approaching deadline. The existing Parliament's five-year term was scheduled to expire in 1994, and another election under the old apartheid Constitution would provoke a catastrophic escalation of the military and social conflict.

Constitutionalizing Revolution

With the time bombs ticking, legally and literally, there was only one way for Mandela to reassert his revolutionary leadership. He would have to demonstrate to his increasingly skeptical base that negotiations with de Klerk still provided a plausible path forward to a new South Africa.

This would require serious compromise: de Klerk was entirely unwilling to surrender his demand for consociational power sharing, while the ANC was firmly committed to a one-person, one-vote majoritarian democracy. At CODESA, the two sides had already tried to bridge this gap by deferring its final resolution to the next Parliament—which, for the first time, would be elected by South Africans of all races. In the meantime, CODESA participants concentrated on defining an interim Constitution that would, as a practical matter, guarantee the National Party an effective veto in a transitional government of national unity. Yet CODESA demonstrated that this sensible-seeming two-step could easily go nowhere—with the two sides breaking off talks and escalating the conflict further.

Mandela had little choice but to try again. If he gave up, he would jeopardize his standing as the symbolic leader of the entire movement. His public confession of failure would open up the path to militant radicals who had consistently denied the possibility of a peaceful transition. Indeed, his last-ditch effort at negotiations was already generating strong resistance from his increasingly militarized and radicalized base. He won an endorsement of his two-step approach at the ANC's annual meeting in December only with great difficulty—and only after pledging that power sharing would come to a decisive end when a permanent Constitution was written after the next round of elections.[32]

So the ANC and the government remained at loggerheads on the key issue—would power sharing be a temporary expedient or a permanent feature of the new South Africa? Nevertheless, the escalating violence and countermobilizations posed a deep threat to the continuing leadership of de Klerk as well as Mandela—forcing each of them to make a desperate effort to blaze a constitutional path forward.

On April 1, a full ten months after CODESA's collapse, a new "multiparty negotiating process" (MPNP) began at Kempton Park outside Johannesburg. The formal proceedings were even more elaborate this time, with a Negotiating Council drawn from a broad political spectrum ranging from right-wing Afrikaner parties to ANC rivals like the Pan Africanist Congress, the KwaZulu government, and delegations of traditional African leaders.

Much of this was window dressing. The government and the ANC focused their energies on bilateral negotiations, and only later confronted the other participants with the "choice" of rubber-stamping their hard-won accords. When confronting such *faits accomplis,* some important players—most notably, KwaZulu's Buthelezi—walked out and refused to return. Although most others signed on, nobody was fooled by this show of consensus. The fragility of the entire affair was dramatized at the outset when right-wing militants assassinated Chris Hani, a senior ANC leader and Communist Party chief—provoking a new wave of protest that threatened to undermine the talks when they were just beginning.

Although de Klerk was still president, it was Mandela who responded to Hani's murder with a televised speech to the nation, appealing for calm. He then got down to the lengthy business of reaching a deal with de Klerk. While the formal sessions of the MPNP proceeded apace, each leader dispatched a trusted emissary to sound out the other—with Cyril Ramaphosa playing this role for Mandela, and Rolf Meyer, for de Klerk. These secret top-down negotiations, not the elaborate bottom-up processes, were crucial to the success of the enterprise.

The Paradoxically Provisional Constitution

In a couple of months, the two sides made a momentous announcement: South Africans of all races would go to the polls for the first time in history on April 24, 1994.

Yet de Klerk and Mandela continued to remain far apart on a host of crucial issues. Initially, top ANC leaders wanted the first-stage "interim Constitution" to focus on the narrow set of questions necessary to get the new government off the ground: it should guarantee the political rights necessary for free elections, and establish the ground rules for a "government of national unity." But it should defer decisions on hot-button issues like social and economic rights until after the elections—when the first truly representative assembly would take on the task of drafting a permanent Constitution.

This demand made perfect sense from the perspective of the ANC. Everybody expected black South Africans to turn out at the polls in massive numbers and provide their movement party with a resounding parliamentary majority. This would give the ANC the upper hand when the time came to hammer out a permanent Constitution.

Unsurprisingly, de Klerk pushed in the opposite direction. He insisted that the "provisional constitution" should provide a comprehensive framework that would guarantee the white minority an effective veto on radical revisions of the social and economic status quo. As de Klerk's representatives pushed to expand the agenda beyond the narrow scope specified by Mandela, their initiative met with a paradoxical reception.

Recall that the ANC had already committed itself to a set of constitutional principles—and these principles emphasized the high importance of fundamental rights. As a consequence, the leading lawyers and political activists representing the ANC at Kempton Park were open to de Klerk's efforts to broaden the scope of the provisional bargain. To be sure, their drafting committee had not been given an open-ended mandate, and had been formally instructed to restrict itself to a narrow set of political rights.

But Mandela was not monitoring their work closely. Instead, his attention was focused on the crucial matter of defining the precise terms under which he would share power with de Klerk in the "national unity" government emerging after the coming parliamentary elections.

As a consequence, the ANC's legal team, supported by a variety of grass-roots activists, pressed for a far broader statement of fundamental rights than Mandela wanted. A leading participant was Albie Sachs, who had previously been a major force driving the ANC-in-exile to adopt its constitutional principles in 1987, and would later serve as justice on the country's new Constitutional Court. As he described it, "the drafting process was very much a hit and miss affair."[33] Driven by short deadlines, "we got a funny kind of Bill of Rights . . . neither complete, global, and polished . . . nor by any means a minimalist one."[34] At the same time, the de Klerk government was more than happy to sign on to Sachs's initiative—because his bill of rights included the protection of property rights, which was of crucial importance to the white minority.[35]

The two sides then created the Constitutional Court in the hope that their fine-sounding words would have enduring significance. By the 1990s, judicial review had come a long way since the 1940s, when the prevailing British and Continental consensus condemned it as an antidemocratic American novelty. Fifty years onward, successes in places as different as India and Germany had made supreme courts seem an obvious component in a liberal democracy. But this time around, the legal team gave their new Constitutional Court a precedent-breaking mission.

As we have seen, the entire Kempton Park Constitution was explicitly labeled as "provisional," which plainly indicated that the newly elected Parliament's permanent Constitution could change it in any way the new majority thought best. But it was precisely this basic point that the Kempton Park participants called into question. Their "provisional" text granted the newly created Constitutional Court the unprecedented power to invalidate provisions in the "final" charter that violated the fundamental principles of their "interim" text.

This remarkable proviso was both politically problematic and legally mind-bending. If, for example, black South Africans elected a parliamentary majority dominated by left-leaning members of the ANC, they might well decide to adopt a Constitution that would sweep away the property protections of the "interim" text and authorize sweeping redistributions to the victims of white oppression. If this happened, it was hardly likely that a few High Court judges could stop them.

Only one thing was clear: the very notion that a Constitutional Court *should* intervene to protect white property rights would have shattered foundational legal understandings. Under standard doctrines, it is *obvious* that a final Constitution trumps any "preliminary" accord leading up to it. If the provisional Constitutional Court had claimed that it had the "final say" over a popularly elected constituent assembly, it could not expect serious jurists—in South Africa or elsewhere—to rally behind such an implausible assertion of raw judicial power.

What, then, did the negotiators hope to achieve by their remarkable inversion of conventional legal wisdom?

The question once again challenges the current scholarly consensus on the judiciary's role in democratic transitions. As I have explained, the dominant view supposes that South Africa represents a classic case of a "third wave" transition in which the masses remain on the sidelines while political elites bargain their way to a peaceful transition of authority. Under this scenario, constitutional courts play an "insurance function," reassuring both sides that their agreement will be respected once elections shift the existing balance of power.

Mandela found himself in a very different situation. Although his decades on Robben Island had won him personal charisma, the ANC did not provide him with the organizational charisma required to secure control over the dynamic grassroots movements sweeping the country. What is more, the escalating confrontations between the government's security forces and the Spear challenged the very idea that a peaceful transition was a serious option. As Kader Asmal, a particularly perceptive participant, suggests, it is a mistake to view South Africa's "transition to democracy as a negotiated settlement. Maybe a more apt description would be a successful negotiation of a peace treaty between warring parties."[36]

From this vantage, Kempton Park's grant of veto power to the courts discharged a distinctive function. Although its grant of extraordinary judicial power disrupted standard jurisprudential categories, the emphatic legalisms of the "provisional" text managed to transform a "peace treaty" into something more—a means by which both Mandela and de Klerk could rally their fragile coalitions to embrace revolutionary constitutionalism.

On Mandela's side, the interim pact provided the ANC with the platform they needed to persuade voters to reject a future of violent upheaval and embrace the prospect of a revolution on a human scale. In presenting the "pro-visional" as *legally* binding, the Constitution was enabling Mandela *to constitute* the ANC as a movement party that could *credibly* speak for the People—provided, of course, the ANC succeeded in gaining an overwhelming victory at the polls.

Paradoxically, a leading opponent of the ANC helped consolidate Mandela's claims to authority. Mangosuthu Buthelezi, and his Inkatha Freedom Party, had long challenged Mandela's ideal of a unitary nation in which all South Africans were equal citizens—offering instead a consociational vision in which black communities would engage in grassroots democracy in their different homelands. After walking out of Kempton Park, Buthelezi initially was inclined to boycott the parliamentary elections, but he was persuaded to reconsider and sponsored a formidable slate of candidates to raise a funda-mental challenge to the ANC's call to South Africans of all colors and cultures to unite behind a common constitution. Yet Buthelezi's electoral intervention failed to deprive the ANC of an overwhelming parliamentary victory—thereby confirming the centrality of Mandela and his movement party in the collective effort to speak for the People.

The "provisional" Constitution performed a similar political function for de Klerk. Like Inkatha, the hard-line Conservative Party walked out of Kempton Park and announced a boycott of the elections. But unlike Inkatha, it remained on the sidelines, permitting a new Freedom Front to enter the field with a slate of candidates who urged white voters to repudiate the deal by sending the Front's candidates to Parliament.

The "interim" Constitution played a key role in enabling de Klerk to deflect this counterrevolutionary initiative. In his appeal to the white commu-nity, he emphasized that the courts could be counted on to sound the alarm if the ANC succumbed to sweeping expropriations and nationalizations—thereby providing his constituents with their best hope of peace and pros-perity within the new South Africa.

This appeal proved effective. But it would not suffice to protect de Klerk against a very different challenge. After waging decades of war against the "Communist-dominated ANC," leading generals looked upon de Klerk's deal as a cowardly surrender at a moment when victory was within their grasp. Recognizing the danger, de Klerk fired twenty-three military hard-liners. But this was not enough to prevent an attempted military coup just before the April 23 elections. Although the coup failed, violence on both sides was reaching new heights as the nation went to the polls.[37]

The choice between totalizing violence and revolutionary constitutionalism couldn't have been clearer.

The Mandate

The voters provided Mandela with the decisive mandate he needed to legitimate his claim to speak for the People: the ANC and its Communist allies won 62 percent of the vote, six times the 11 percent gained by Buthelezi's Inkatha party. At the same time, de Klerk's National Party gained the support of 20 percent of the expanded electorate, ten times that obtained by his Conservative rivals. Under the interim Constitution's ground rules, only parties winning more than 10 percent could participate in power sharing—with the top two parties selecting deputy presidents to serve under Mandela in his Government of National Unity.[38] At the same time, the interim arrangement committed the newly elected assembly to hammer out a permanent Constitution by the end of 1995.

Much would depend on how Mandela would deal with these commitments. If he treated his deputy presidents as mere underlings, subject to his command, he would quickly shatter the collaborative vision emerging from the elections. But Mandela resisted the authoritarian temptation—in part because he made a wise choice in choosing Thabo Mbeki as the ANC's deputy president to deal with Deputy President de Klerk. Mbeki had served with great intelligence and discipline as a principal diplomat for the ANC-in-exile. No less importantly, his public persona was distant and detached, posing no challenge to Mandela's great personal charisma. As a consequence, the president could allow Mbeki and de Klerk to dominate the public stage, especially where domestic policy was concerned, while reserving only the biggest decisions for himself. This emerging pattern gave political reality to the interim Constitution's commitment to a government of national unity.

It also set the stage for serious negotiations on its permanent replacement. The Kempton Park assembly tried to channel the upcoming debate by instructing the Constitutional Court to invalidate any "permanent" revisions that offended the statement of "fundamental principles" announced by the "provisional" text. But there was one issue that was too hot for courts to handle—the future of consociationalism. Would the permanent Constitution, like its predecessor, grant the National Party a veto on ANC initiatives? Or would it follow standard Westminster practice and empower the parliamentary majority to override the protests voiced by a minority coalition headed by the NP?

The ANC and the NP were at loggerheads on this critical issue—with de Klerk's party taking such a hard line in the negotiations that leading political scientists were predicting the likely success of a permanent consociational arrangement.[39]

Yet the ANC was not willing to bargain away the "one person, one vote" principle established by the Freedom Charter in the 1950s and confirmed by the party's statement of constitutional principles in the 1980s. Mandela had supported consociationalism in the short run, but the grant of a veto to the white community would effectively preserve a form of apartheid forever. This would have required him to betray a commitment that had sustained the revolutionaries through decades of insurgency.

On this core issue, the ANC followed down the Time One–Time Two pathway marked by the Indian National Congress: the country emerged as a majoritarian democracy redeeming the principle of voter equality that had served as the foundation for decades of collective sacrifice. On June 20, 1996, de Klerk's service as deputy president under the "interim" arrangement came to an end, and Mbeki remained Mandela's sole deputy under the new political order established by "We, the people of South Africa," who, in the words of its Preamble, "honour those who suffered for justice and freedom in our land."

At the same time, the permanent Bill of Rights enabled the National Party to protect its core interests—especially where private property was concerned. Because the interim document already afforded strong property protections, the extraordinary powers it had granted the Constitutional Court undoubtedly helped de Klerk give up his demands for a veto. It would be difficult for a few judges to face down a powerful ANC push for expropriation, but the brooding presence of the Court would serve as a caution against a dramatic assault on property rights.

The Bill of Rights also committed the country to wide-ranging social and economic guarantees, especially in dealing with racial discrimination in the private sector. Taken in its totality, the combination of majority rule and fundamental rights could serve as a platform on which both blacks and whites could join together in common citizenship. It is hardly surprising, then, that when the Constitution came before the Court for final review, the justices had little difficulty approving it, with relatively minor exceptions.

Of course, the practical meaning of the Bill of Rights would depend on the way the Court would interpret its meaning over time. The interim Constitution gave the ANC effective control over the selection of the eleven-member tribunal.[40] But it was crucially important for Mandela to reassure moderate whites that the Court would not be dominated by ANC party hacks. The president did a fine job in fulfilling these expectations. He not only appointed distinguished jurists, like Arthur Chaskalson and Albie Sachs, who had given their lives to the movement. He also selected judges who, while sympathetic to the ANC, had spent their professional lives within the legal framework of the old regime.

Mandela's balanced selections were not enough to establish the Court as a serious player in the system of checks and balances. The general public was unfamiliar with this new tribunal and was not inclined to give it the benefit of the doubt. Public polls in 1996 and 1997 indicated that "only 27.9% of the South Africans supported the Court in the strong sense indicative of institutional legitimacy."[41] At this founding moment of high-energy politics, it was the broad popular commitment to the ANC—as expressed by its sweeping victory at the polls and Mandela's entry into the presidency—that served as the paradigmatic expression of popular sovereignty.

In this respect the situation was broadly similar to the Indian case. As with Mandela and the ANC, Nehru and the INC did not rely on the judiciary to bestow legitimacy on their claim to speak for the People. Indeed, when the Indian Supreme Court challenged key aspects of Nehru's legislative program, the justices were obliged to retreat in disarray. It was only during the succession crisis at Time Three that the Indian justices managed to gain broad recognition as constitutional guardians of the revolutionary legacy left behind by Congress.

In South Africa, however, the Court did not wait for a generation to claim a similar guardianship role. It quickly asserted itself on a series of hot-button issues—in 1995, it invalidated the death penalty; in 1996, it struck down a Mandela decree that violated a parliamentary statute; and a decade later, it followed up with decisions legalizing same-sex marriage and challenging male primogeniture.[42]

These decisions were intensely controversial—with polls suggesting, for example, that 75 percent of the population was opposed to the abolition of capital punishment.[43] Why, then, did the judges press forward, despite the risk of political backlash that could have gravely damaged the Court's legitimacy for decades to come?

The answer lies in part in Mandela's remarkable statesmanship—best revealed in his response to the Court's early decision rejecting his authority to revise legislation through executive decree. While many triumphant movement leaders would respond aggressively to such a judicial rebuke, Mandela immediately signaled acquiescence, announcing that it was "not the first nor will it be the last, [time] the Constitutional Court assists both the Government and society to assure constitutionality and effective governance."[44]

Yet it is a mistake to overemphasize the role of personal character—Nehru was no less a statesman than Mandela. Their different responses also reveal the different roles the two Constitutions played in legitimating the claims of the different Congress Parties to speak for the People. During Time One, the Indian Congress had built a solid organization linking millions of grassroots members to regional and national leaderships. This lived experience of party unity was crucial in the legitimation of the Constitution at Time Two. In contrast, decades of RSA repression had badly fractured the South African liberation movement—making the ANC's appeal to constitutionalism a key method through which the different fragments could become a coherent political force at the moment of transition from Time One to Time Two.

It was precisely the ANC's success at Kempton Park in translating its fundamental commitments to human dignity and equality into the interim Constitution that permitted its disparate elements—ranging from returning political exiles to the guerilla leaders of the Spear to the grassroots activists and unionists of UDF—to view constitutionalism as an expression of their *joint* commitment to a new South Africa. These committed revolutionaries had no difficulty understanding that just as these egalitarian principles undermined apartheid, they also challenged other practices that were far more controversial among the general public—like capital punishment, gender discrimination, and social and economic inequality.

Once the ANC had won an overwhelming electoral victory, its political leaders were happy to enlist the Court's aid in filling out the ANC's revolutionary egalitarian principles in particularly controversial cases. Moreover, the Court's style of engagement greatly contributed to its remarkable early success. While its pathbreaking decisions have often gained worldwide attention, the Court did not impose its rulings on a "take-it-or-leave-it basis." Instead of telling Parliament or the general public that it had discovered the single "right answer" to questions posed by the constitutional text, it adopted a more flexible approach. On the one hand, it insisted that the Constitution did indeed raise a principled challenge to one or another aspect of the status quo.

But on the other hand, it gave Parliament a great deal of leeway in fashioning effective remedies that could realistically propel the country forward in meeting its obligations.

Recent scholarship has greatly illuminated this dynamic over the past two decades.[45] For present purposes, only one point needs emphasizing. The Court's ongoing success in collaborating with the ANC provided South Africa with a distinctive resource in confronting a series of succession crises it has confronted since Mandela resigned the presidency.

Time Three: Succession Crises

Although the permanent Constitution permitted Mandela two terms in office, he voluntarily retired after his first term expired in 1999—in sharp contrast to Nehru, who held on to power until death forced him out.

Mandela's self-restraint would set a constitutional precedent of great consequence a decade later. But in the short run, his departure generated a succession problem remarkably similar to India's.

Stage One: A Tripartite Power Struggle

Recall the scenario that followed Nehru's death. Three competitors emerged to claim the top spot. One was his trusted aide (Shastri), who lacked charisma but was skilled in organizational politics. Another was a politically dynamic up-and-comer (Desai), who promised to put new energy into the movement party. Finally, there was Nehru's daughter (Indira Gandhi), who tried to inherit the charisma her father had earned through decades of sacrifice.

The same choices presented themselves in South Africa. Mandela's Shastri was Thabo Mbeki, who had effectively handled the business of government as deputy president during the preceding five years but was aloof and distant in dealing with the public. His Desai was Cyril Ramaphosa, whose charismatic leadership style provided a sharp contrast to the technocratic Mbeki. Finally, the South African equivalent to Nehru's daughter was Mandela's wife, Winnie—who, like Indira, sought to revitalize the Congress Party's revolutionary commitments to social democracy and economic redistribution.

Because Nehru died in office, he left the ultimate choice of his successor to the party's regional and national leadership. In contrast, Mandela's voluntary resignation meant that he could play a large role in selecting his successor. If, for example, he had tried to obtain the presidency for his wife, this would have dramatically undermined South Africa's status as a constitutional republic, pushing the country down the path to a hereditary system of authoritarian domination. But for a variety of personal and ideological reasons, Mandela refused to keep the presidency in the family. He also rejected the more independent and dynamic Ramaphosa—choosing the faithful but colorless Mbeki over his more charismatic competitor. As in India, so in South Africa: the departure of the Great Leader opened the path for the Loyal Follower, despite the appeals of more charismatic figures.

At this point, our two case studies diverge. Shastri died within a year, reopening the succession struggle. This paved the way for Indira Gandhi's reassertion of socialist ideals—generating new rounds of popular mobilization, constitutional crisis, and the ultimate rise of the Supreme Court as the most credible institutional defender of India's constitutional inheritance.

In contrast, Mbeki remained a powerful force for the next decade. He successfully prevented Winnie from winning the ANC nomination for deputy president—promoting his longtime associate, Jacob Zuma, to the position after he won the presidency in 1999.[46] In the meantime, the charismatic but independent Ramaphosa abandoned the political sphere to his rival and turned to the private sector, where he became one of the richest black entrepreneurs of the new South Africa.

Once the new president deflected these more serious threats to his authority, he found Zuma's performance increasingly troubling. While Mbeki had magnificently discharged the role of "loyal follower" as deputy to Mandela, Zuma had neither the technocratic skills nor the sober temperament to serve a similar function. He had, however, served long years in prison alongside Mandela on Robben Island. By 2001, Mbeki was increasingly convinced that his deputy was conspiring with Ramaphosa and others to deny him a second term, and countered this threat before it could gather steam at the ANC party convention.

Acting with his usual prudence, the president did not try to deny Zuma renomination as his deputy, but he did try to discredit him and thereby maintain his grip on power even after his second term had expired.

His chance came in 2005. One of Zuma's close associates was sentenced to a fifteen-year jail term for scandalous acts of corruption. Though the deputy president declared his innocence, the president fired him from office—and added insult to injury by appointing his archrival to the post.[47]

Stage Two: Authoritarian Takeover / Constitutional Reinforcement

At the same time, Mbeki's backers began floating trial balloons in favor of a constitutional amendment allowing him to serve a third term. It was here that Mandela's precedent proved of large significance: if the Great Man refused to be tempted by a presidency for life, by what right did his Loyal Follower presume to attain such an exalted status?

The president was obliged by old-time ANC leaders to publicly disclaim his ambitions for a third term in 2006.[48] But his actions carried a very different message. In the words of a generally admiring biographer, he took an "increasingly authoritarian approach to power. . . . One consequence was to politicize the bureaucracy by rendering all appointments susceptible to patronage; another was . . . [to] impose all provincial and local appointments, such as premiers and mayors, from the center, rather than permitting them to be elected."[49]

As Mbeki was busy manufacturing an imposing group of apparatchiks, Zuma was launching his own presidential campaign in 2009. To put it mildly, he wasn't an ideal candidate. Apart from the corruption charges swirling around him, he was required to face trial for raping the daughter of a close associate. Although he gained an acquittal, the evidence presented was very damaging.

Nevertheless, his revolutionary credentials were impeccable. Before his imprisonment on Robben Island, Zuma had played a heroic role as the ANC's head of intelligence; and upon his release after a decade of imprisonment, he played an important role in the guerilla underground. Despite his personal flaws, his outgoing personality provided a vivid contrast with the cool and distant Mbeki. As the president's increasingly authoritarian actions threatened to push old-time activists to the periphery, in 2007 the movement base rallied behind Zuma's campaign to serve as head of the ANC—a position that had served as Mandela's and Mbeki's launching pad for their own presidential campaigns.

Appalled by the prospect of his rival's redemption, Mbeki broke with past precedent and announced that he too would run for another term as ANC president. This would have allowed him to continue ruling the country by controlling the ANC parliamentary delegation and ordering it to support one of his lackeys as figurehead president while Mbeki continued to exercise effective control.

The Mbeki-Zuma standoff transformed the 2007 ANC convention into a crucial constitutional arena. Both sides organized rival slates of convention delegates and made energetic efforts to gain grassroots support. Once the convention opened, it was the scene of desperate last-minute lobbying efforts. But at the end of the day, the old revolutionaries led by Zuma gained the upper hand over the new breed of apparatchiks appointed by the sitting president— obtaining 60 percent of the vote and repudiating Mbeki's grim determination to remain the power behind the throne.

This moment is broadly recognized as a "turning point almost as significant as Nelson Mandela's 1994 victory and the transition to democracy"—but of a rather different kind.[50] While 1994 marked the decisive breakthrough of revolutionary triumph, 2007 marked the point at which the once-triumphant revolutionaries managed to preserve their constitutional legacy against authoritarian assault.

India's response to emergency rule provides an illuminating comparison. On the one hand, Mbeki was going down a very different road from the one chosen by Indira Gandhi. She broke with the Nehruvian Constitution on the ground that the rising generation of establishment politicians had betrayed the socialist ideals of the revolutionary Congress Party, and that the State of Emergency provided the only means through which a new mass movement could revitalize these founding commitments. Mbeki made no similar appeal. Instead of dedicating himself to a renewal of the social democratic ideals expressed by the ANC during the Founding,[51] he was threatening to make a mockery of the Constitution by placing himself at the head of a bureaucratic party apparatus, and transforming the constitutional president into his puppet.

Yet Mbeki's maneuver was ultimately defeated by the same very same dynamic that stopped Gandhi. In both cases, the assault on the Founding Constitution at Time Three provoked a countermobilization by old-time revolutionaries. These old-timers had been pushed to the sidelines by Gandhi and Mbeki and they were further weakened by their own ideological disagreements. Nevertheless, the authoritarian threat posed by Gandhi and Mbeki led the fragmented opposition groups to suspend their bickering and make a desperate effort to save the revolutionary Constitution that had crowned their earlier successes. In each case, these last-ditch counterattacks seemed doomed to fail. Yet in each case, the revolutionary spirit was sufficiently alive to permit the old-time activists to rally popular support for their cause.

Their success took different institutional forms. When Gandhi tried to legitimate her Emergency by calling a snap election, the voters gave the Janata Party a stunning victory at the polls. Mbeki's power grab was stopped at an earlier stage. Old-time revolutionaries mobilized enough support at the ANC convention to head off his self-aggrandizing effort to maintain power indefinitely with the support of his party apparatus. This led, as in Gandhi's case, to a scenario in which the revolutionary Constitution's centrality as a symbol of political legitimacy was significantly reinforced.

Symbolic reinforcement occurred through different institutional means. In India, the voters' repudiation of Gandhi at the polls ultimately led her to acknowledge the Supreme Court's role as the ultimate guardian of the Constitution's basic structure. In South Africa, Mbeki's humiliation was accomplished without the need for a new election. Now that Zuma was head of the party, he immediately arranged for the ANC's parliamentary delegation to isolate Mbeki by appointing Zuma's followers to key cabinet posts. The president suffered another blow when a respected High Court judge condemned him for covertly encouraging the continuing criminal prosecution of Zuma on corruption charges. This precipitated a passionate emergency session of the ANC's Executive Committee, which ended with a decision to "recall" Mbeki from the presidency seven months before the official end of his term.

This move had no basis in the written Constitution—which only allows Parliament to remove a president through a no-confidence vote or an impeachment process. But because the ANC controlled Parliament, Mbeki left office without a fight. No less importantly, Zuma did not try to fill the vacuum by immediately occupying his rival's seat. Instead, he left the presidency in the hands of a caretaker and remitted his fortunes to the voters in the upcoming 2009 elections.

Zuma's act of self-restraint transformed the meaning of the election. If he had immediately taken power in 2008, he could have used all the resources of the presidency to transform the election into a rubber-stamp victory for his unconstitutional seizure of power. By deferring to a caretaker, Zuma entered the election campaign on an equal footing with his rivals—who made the dangers of continued ANC rule a major theme in their campaigns. It was only after leading his party to victory despite these challenges that Zuma gained the presidency.

This orderly transition vastly reinforced the constitutional precedent established by Mandela's refusal to serve beyond a single presidential term. Not only had Mbeki's top-down order collapsed, but Zuma had vindicated the Constitution by leaving it to the citizens of South Africa to determine Mbeki's successor.[52]

This crucial point is easily lost among the many headlines reporting on one or another of Zuma's peccadillos. None of his personal failings should obliterate the fact that, at this moment of constitutional self-definition, he took the high road.

Stage Three: Decline and Fall?

It has been downhill since then. During his time in office, Zuma was bent on transforming the constitutional system into an engine of personal enrichment for himself and his cronies.

This is the point at which the Constitutional Court's early rise to centrality began to make a difference. Given the pattern of institutional deference to its decisions over the past two decades, the Court has gained the real-world legitimacy required for a head-to-head confrontation with the president.

But not until other forms of checks and balances had been exhausted. When Zuma was serving as deputy president, his scandalous self-dealing had already exposed him to 783 criminal charges of corruption, fraud, and racketeering. These charges were suspended once he managed to oust Mbeki from power. Nevertheless, the Public Protector, Thuli Madonsela, used the independence granted her by the Constitution to launch her own investigation into Zuma's crimes.

The president's lawyers engaged in stalling tactics that prevented Madonsela from reaching a final judgment until 2014, when she published a searing condemnation of his wheeling and dealing. A particular point of controversy involved Zuma's appropriation of state funds to build a palatial estate on his own personal property. The Protector ordered him to pay back the money, and Zuma flat-out refused, directly defying the constitutional system of checks and balances.

Here is where the Constitutional Court intervened. In March 2016 it unanimously upheld the Protector's order and ruled that Zuma had "failed to uphold, comply and respect the constitution." It also condemned the ANC-controlled Parliament for "flouting" its obligations when it passed a resolution nullifying the Public Protector's findings and replacing them with a pro-Zuma statement of the "facts." The Court declared that "the rule of law is dead against" the ANC's erasure of the Protector's carefully considered decision.[53]

Within weeks, the parliamentary opposition followed up by filing the first impeachment motion in South African history. The ANC majority voted it down, but the debate put both the party and Zuma on the defensive—leading the president to return more than $12 million to the Treasury.

This gesture wasn't enough to insulate Zuma from backlash by the voters. Indeed, the ANC's parliamentary defense of its corrupt boss was a political gift to its opponents, led by the Democratic Alliance. This party was traditionally the home of liberal whites who had rejected apartheid. But the growing popular disenchantment with corruption within the ANC led the Alliance to broaden its appeal across racial lines—culminating in its election of a black parliamentary leader, Mmusi Maimane, in 2015. So far as Maimane was concerned, the time had come for South Africans to stop celebrating Mandela's great triumphs of the past and focus on the challenge of ensuring clean, constitutional, and effective government for the future. The impeachment proceedings in Parliament provided a compelling forum for Maimane to make his case. Though he lost the vote in Parliament, he was winning the battle for public opinion.

At the same time, the judiciary was dramatizing the president's loss of credibility in a second remarkable decision. Recall that, as Zuma was preparing his initial run for the presidency, he was already confronting 783 criminal charges—which were conveniently dropped by the prosecutor to clear a path for his presidential run of 2009. But suddenly in 2016, the country's second highest court held that this decision was "inexplicable" and "irrational," and that "Mr. Zuma should face the charges as outlined in the indictment."[54]

Against this background, Maimane's outstanding performance at the impeachment proceedings provided a national platform for the Alliance to score unprecedented victories in Cape Town and other municipalities in local elections in August 2016. If it sustained its momentum, it would have a fair chance of gaining an upset victory in the 2019 electoral cycle.

The country's succession crisis was reaching a climax—when voters might well repudiate the ANC's claim to be the enduring institutional vehicle of the heroic legacy of the liberation struggle. This clear and present danger loomed large as party loyalists met in December 2017 at an ANC Convention to pick their presidential candidate for the coming election.

The Constitution barred Zuma from serving a third consecutive term, but he was grimly determined to sustain his blatantly corrupt regime. In his hour of need, Zuma turned to his former wife, Nkosazana Dlamini-Zuma, who had kept up close personal ties despite their divorce in 1998. When push came to shove, he could count on her to intervene in the judicial proceedings that could otherwise result in criminal convictions. Her intervention on his behalf, however, would be a blatant assault on the rule of law—enabling Zuma and his pals to continue their multibillion-dollar fraud schemes while Nko-sazana Dlamini-Zuma presided over the wreckage.

To be sure, Dlamini-Zuma's past history could allow her to provide an appearance of respectability to the de facto destruction of the constitutional system. She was no mere crony. She had been a leading anti-apartheid activist, serving with distinction in a series of high cabinet posts since the days of Nelson Mandela. Her ascent to the presidency would serve to legitimate—to the extent it was possible—the reality of a kleptocratic regime.

Constitutional Redemption?

The question, quite simply, was whether the ANC convention would repudiate Zuma and Dlamini-Zuma and nominate a candidate who could *credibly* persuade an alienated electorate that, despite Zuma's corruption, Mandela's constitutional legacy could be revitalized under a new ANC president.

This was precisely the question raised by Cyril Ramaphosa, whose recent activities allowed him to present himself as an ANC presidential candidate who could restore the party's claim to integrity. Recall that Ramaphosa served as Mandela's trusted aide at the crucial Kempton Park negotiations, and Mbeki's principal competitor in the contest to succeed Mandela as president. Despite his political dynamism, however, he had failed to dislodge Mbeki from his inside track to power—leading him to abandon public life and transform himself into one of the country's leading black entrepreneurs.

After twenty years of success in the private sector, his great wealth made him a particularly attractive candidate. In contrast to Dlamini-Zuma's confirmation of the party's decline into corruption, Ramaphosa was not running to enrich himself. Instead, he could be presented to the voters as the ANC's last best hope of restoring its claim to speak for the People of South Africa.

In operational terms, the choice between Ramaphosa and Dlamini-Zuma would be determined by the 5,000 delegates sent to the convention by ANC local chapters and allied organizations. Given Zuma's control of the party apparatus, Dlamini-Zuma came into the competition with an overwhelming advantage. The question, quite simply, was whether the ANC's revolutionary tradition remained sufficiently robust among grassroots activists so that they could swing the balance to Ramaphosa's side.

The answer was yes, but only by the thinnest of margins. Ramaphosa won by 2,440 to 2,261—a mere 179 votes. No less significantly, the grassroots mobilization was so impressive that Zuma accepted the result, recognizing that legalistic nitpicking would only provoke massive demonstrations leading to his wife's humiliating withdrawal from contention.

The December convention, then, left Ramaphosa in control of the party, but Zuma was determined to hang on as president—even though, under identical circumstances, he had forced Mbeki out of the presidency in 2009 after he won the ANC nomination for the next election. At the very least, he was determined to remain in office unless Ramaphosa gave him a pardon that would allow him to escape future criminal prosecution. But Ramaphosa refused to make any such deal, since it would have profoundly compromised his credibility from the very moment he took charge of the government. He made it clear that if Zuma didn't agree to leave office, the ANC would join with the parliamentary opposition to impeach him.

When faced with the prospect of public humiliation, Zuma finally capitulated and "voluntarily" resigned, allowing Ramaphosa to take the oath of office as President of the Republic on February 15, 2018.

These dramatic events propelled themselves to the very center of national consciousness, with ordinary citizens bearing witness to the revitalization of the ANC with a complex mix of pride and anxiety—pride at Ramaphosa's vindication of Mandela's legacy; anxiety generated by the narrowness of Zuma's defeat.

The response from the rest of the world was less complicated. The news from South Africa generated great applause at a time when constitutional democracy was suffering shattering blows in so many other places. But the point of this book is to move beyond today's talk of the "crisis of democracy" and put current events in larger perspective.

This is precisely why I have paired South Africa with India throughout this exploration. Not only did the Congress Parties of the two countries share similar aspirations, but India's seventy-five-year history as a constitutional democracy provides a distinctive perspective on South Africa's twenty-five-year experience. If we look back to consider how India was faring at its quarter-century mark, we find that it too was confronting a wrenching succession crisis—but of a different kind. India's Constitution of 1950 was not in danger of serving as a symbolic fig leaf for a corrupt kleptocracy. It was under direct assault by Indira Gandhi, who threw old-time revolutionary leaders into detention during a twenty-one-month State of Emergency.

She then ended the Emergency to call a quick election, which she expected to win in a landslide that would give her a popular mandate for the utter destruction of the constitutional legacy left behind by Nehru and Ambedkar.

However, her snap election would not be credible if she and her New Congress Party ran unopposed. So she released her disorganized and demoralized opponents from jail so that they could offer some token opposition—and thereby legitimate her claim to speak for the People.

The obvious differences between South Africa's kleptocratic decline and India's revolutionary reassertion should not blind us to crucial similarities. In the Indian case, the crucial issue was whether Gandhi's opponents could overcome her tremendous organizational advantages and somehow organize a grassroots movement to defeat her New Congress at the coming election. In the South African case, the decisive question was whether Zuma's opponents could overcome his control of the party apparatus with a grassroots movement that could defeat Dlamini-Zuma at the ANC convention.

In both cases, the answer was yes—and the result was the reinvigoration of the constitutional legacies left behind by the Indian National Congress in 1950 and the African National Congress in 1995. Moreover, the South African dynamic at Time Three supports some cautious optimism—suggesting that the country's recent resolution of its succession crisis may well serve as a prelude to a system of political party competition that will break the monopoly of the ANC over the national government during Time Four.

My optimistic argument proceeds in three steps. First: In contrast to India, the kleptocratic threat posed by Zuma to South Africa's Constitution was far less serious than Gandhi's totalizing assault. I don't want to downplay the difficulties Ramaphosa faced in overcoming Zuma's control of the party apparatus in a 2,440-to-2,261 victory at the ANC convention. Nevertheless, they pale in comparison to those confronting Gandhi's jailed political opponents, who emerged from their confinement during the Emergency with only two months to challenge her New Congress in crucial elections. Their capacity to organize a new movement party—Janata—and achieve a sweeping nationwide victory over Gandhi's entrenched apparatus is a high-point in the history of revolutionary constitutionalism in the twentieth century.

Yet paradoxically, it is the relatively unspectacular character of Ramaphosa's triumph that sets the stage for the second step in my argument. As you will recall, once Janata won its decisive parliamentary majority, it immediately began to pay a price for its weak movement-party organization. The only thing that united its different ideological and regional factions was impassioned opposition to Gandhi's authoritarian ambitions. Once her New Congress Party had gone down to decisive defeat, Janata's ideological and regional factions had nothing to unite them—leading to a series of cabinet turnovers and generating divergent policy initiatives that undermined public confidence. This instability enabled Gandhi to defeat Janata at the next election, once she made it clear that she would never again mount a full-fledged assault on the constitutional legacy of the Founding.

In contrast, Ramaphosa has reinvigorated Mandela's legacy through the *internal reform* of the ANC rather than through its *external displacement* by a new movement party. He is therefore in command of the ANC's very considerable organizational resources as he tries to rally his party and his country behind concrete policy initiatives. In contrast to Janata, it is highly unlikely that his revitalized ANC will generate an acute governability crisis. Although Ramaphosa's policies may well provoke lots of opposition, leading critics will not come from the ANC but from rival political parties.

This leads to the third, and final, step in my argument. Given the ANC's revitalization, the way is clear for the leading opposition party, the Democratic Alliance, to emerge as a strong contender in a vigorous two-party system. To see the link between steps two and three, suppose that South Africa's succession crisis had come to a less happy conclusion. On this dark scenario, Zuma beats Ramaphosa by a narrow margin at the ANC convention and arranges for Dlamini-Zuma to run as the ANC's presidential candidate in 2019. This would have left the fate of Mandela's Constitution to the Democratic Alliance. Could it somehow mobilize a majority to defeat Dlamini-Zuma and repudiate the ANC's claim to be the privileged representative of the nation's revolutionary achievements?

If the Alliance were successful in this scenario, this could well have pushed the ANC onto the periphery of politics. Once installed in office, the Alliance might well have become the dominant political party for a very long time to come—leading to a variety of familiar authoritarian temptations. Yet because the ANC successfully renewed itself internally, the Alliance can gain power only by ousting Ramaphosa at the coming presidential elections in 2019.

This will be tough, given the enormous goodwill that the new president and the ANC have generated through their victory over Zuma. But there will come a time when ordinary South Africans get tired of the stale policies pursued by Ramaphosa or his successors, and decide to give the Alliance, or some other opposition group, a chance to try something new. So it isn't an idle pipe dream to suppose that by 2023, or 2027, South Africa will be governed by a non-ANC party—definitively heralding the transition from Time Three to Time Four in the life cycle of revolutionary constitutionalism.

The very different resolution of India's succession crisis at Time Three led to a very different transition to Time Four. Given Janata's failure to gain credibility as a governing party, the Congress Party remained dominant on the national scene through the early twenty-first century—trying to compensate for its obvious loss of revolutionary fervor by creating governing coalitions with provincial parties based in various regions of the country. It was only recently that Narendra Modi, with his BJP, has created a movement party that has successfully swept Congress to the political periphery—once again opening up the dangers that single-party domination poses to constitutional government.

Of course, things may turn out very differently over the next decade or three. Perhaps South Africa will be overwhelmed by crises that lead to the rise of a demagogic dictator. Perhaps Modi's threats to the Nehru / Ambedkar tradition will lead to modest modifications or the emphatic reinvigoration of the Enlightenment principles affirmed in 1950. The future is full of surprises.

Nevertheless, I hope that my initial pairing of India and South Africa will encourage you to read onward and consider additional exercises in revolutionary constitutionalism over the course of the twentieth century—and the ways in which they can enrich our understanding of the populist revolt against political establishments that is presently sweeping the world.

CHAPTER 4

From the French Resistance
to the Fourth Republic

For all their differences, the Indian and South African experiences are linked by four common features. In each country, revolutionary outsiders began as (1) a *social* movement that transformed itself into (2) a *political* party that ultimately gained (3) *organizational centrality* in the struggle against the old regime (4) in a fashion that endowed a small number of leaders with *symbolic centrality*. This conjunction enabled both the INC and the ANC to assert that their Constitutions were something more than legalistic scribbles on pieces of paper. The two Congress Parties could instead gain popular recognition of their revolutionary constitutions as *authentic* expressions of the principles that had inspired a generation to sacrifice greatly in support of the INC / ANC liberation struggles.

Many insurgencies do not display this fourfold conjunction. Revolutionary movements may lack a broad social base; or they may split into factions; or their symbolic leaders may attack one another in ways that undermine the Constitution's claims to authenticity. Each of these fragmentations, as I shall call them, can shape the dynamics of constitutional legitimation—for better and for worse. One of our aims is to understand how.

My discussions of postwar France and Italy take a step in this direction. But before we plunge in, some orienting reflections on the variety of possible fragmentations may prove useful.

Fragmentations

Talk about "social movements" is very popular right now. Because the term has many different meanings, it's best to begin by emphasizing that, for me, a movement's orientation to state power is all-important. Many movements don't direct their energies to the distant goings-on in capital cities, let alone attempt to revolutionize the basic principles of the existing regime. They focus on one or more spheres of social or economic life—the workplace, the family, the church, or other cultural institutions—and work at the grassroots level to change local practices of immediate concern to ordinary people. Over time these local efforts may cumulate into a broad bottom-up movement, which may lay the groundwork for a revolutionary transformation of peak institutions. But this is by no means inevitable.

Consider India. During the early twentieth century, Gandhi did not organize his civil disobedience campaigns in an effort to catapult the Congress Party into power over the central imperial institutions governing the Raj. His aim instead was to liberate local life from centralized British control. This would enable Congress to serve a different function. In Gandhi's anti-statist view, his movement should function as a vehicle for encouraging the subcontinent's diverse cultures to flourish on the grassroots level, without top-down interference by imperial bureaucrats. Gandhi's Congress certainly qualified as a powerful social movement, but it had not yet developed into a movement *party.*

This shift did not occur until the 1930s—when leaders like Nehru transformed the Congress Party into a vehicle for gaining electoral control of advisory assemblies created under the Government of India Act of 1935. Once the rising movement party won these elections, they used these assemblies as springboards for an escalating struggle for national liberation. In making this effort, Congress's organizational linkages between national, regional, and local activists were a precious resource. Even when activists were fully engaged in grassroots campaigns for social justice, it was easy for them to connect these engagements with initiatives generated at the regional and national level. Over time, these ongoing interactions led millions of grassroots party members to identify strongly with the efforts by leaders like Nehru and Ambedkar to break with the past and create a new constitutional beginning for the future.

This kind of mass engagement with national politics happens only rarely. Given the constant pressures of ordinary life—making a living, raising a family, and the like—most people have better things to do than follow the ceaseless wheelings and dealings of the power elite in distant capitals like New Delhi. Generally speaking, they ignore such matters and leave them to the small number of political junkies in their midst. These folks will pay attention for a variety of reasons—ranging from ideological commitment to self-interested efforts to gain office for themselves. But generally speaking, the mass of the population remains relatively detached—occasionally coming out to vote, or otherwise protest, but without demonstrating sustained commitment on a day-to-day (or even month-to-month) basis.

In contrast, the special conditions created by a movement party generate an *organic* connection between the revolutionary sacrifices of everyday life and the leadership struggles to vindicate the voice of We the People at the top. When Congress called for massive "Quit India" demonstrations during the Second World War, the millions who went into the streets were not content with Gandhi's vision of grassroots diversity. They were demanding a revolutionary breakthrough, led by the Congress Party, that would establish an Indian national identity based on fundamental principles of social democracy.

When compared to its Indian counterpart, the African National Congress had greater difficulty establishing compelling links between grassroots activists and national leadership during decades of military conflict with the apartheid regime. But as we have seen, the ANC ultimately succeeded in integrating its revolutionary fragments behind Mandela's struggle for the Constitution during the late 1980s and early 1990s.

In contrast, the constitutional experiences of France and Italy displayed a different structure in the aftermath of World War II. As in India and South Africa, revolutionary movement parties played the central role in legitimating new Constitutions—basing their authority to speak for the People on their engagement in the Resistance against Hitler and his French and Italian collaborators. But this time around, no single mass organization emerged from the wreckage of Pétain's France or Mussolini's Italy. In contrast to the ANC or INC, three distinct movement parties—the Communists, the Socialists, and the Christian Democrats—came to the fore with rival organizations and leaderships. This form of fractionation introduced a new problem into the dynamics of revolutionary constitutional creation at the end of the war.

Call it the problem of *disintegration:* During the period of insurgency, the struggle against the Pétain / Mussolini / Nazi regimes required the three movement parties to maintain a united front. But once they emerged victorious at Time Two, their ideological and organizational conflicts threatened to split them apart. Hence, the problem: Would the wartime coalition remain intact long enough to legitimate a new constitutional order in the name of We the People of France or Italy? Or would the competing movement parties disintegrate into rival fragments before they could jointly participate in the formulation of a revolutionary constitution for approval by the broader citizenry?

In both France and Italy, the three movement parties proved equal to the fragmentation challenge. They remained united long enough to hammer out a new Constitution and gain the consent of the voters to their "new beginnings."

The French situation was complicated by a different form of fragmentation. Even though the French Communists, Socialists, and Christian Democrats combined to win three-quarters of the popular vote to the postwar Constituent Assembly, Charles de Gaulle was unimpressed with the coalition's overwhelming electoral support. He based his own claim to revolutionary legitimacy on a different foundation. In de Gaulle's view, and that of his followers, his successful leadership of the Free French Forces' struggle against Vichy gave him an authority to speak for the People in a manner that transcended the petty ideological squabbles of the three Resistance parties.

Fragmentation between military and civilian branches of revolutionary movements isn't unique to France. We have already seen it, in a less acute form, in South Africa. But in de Gaulle's case, it generated open conflict during the revolutionary Founding of the Fourth Republic. As the three-party civilian coalition hammered out the constitutional terms of their "new beginning," General de Gaulle launched a vigorous campaign to defeat their initiatives when they were submitted for popular approval in national referenda. In the end the General's campaign failed, and the coalition of Resistance parties, like their Italian counterparts, gained the self-conscious support of the citizenry for the basic framework of the Fourth Republic.

Nevertheless, military-civilian fragmentation made a big difference over time. The Italian Republic of the twenty-first century remains anchored in the constitutional decisions shaped by the movement parties of the Resistance. But during the first decade of the Fourth Republic, General de Gaulle organized a movement party of his own to continue his campaign against the civilians' Constitution. By the early 1950s, however, the General's effort at countermobilization proved a dismal failure.

This was the final straw for the General. He abandoned the remnants of his movement party and retreated to self-imposed exile at his country estate at Colombey-les-Deux-Églises. As the glory days of his wartime leadership began to fade in public memory, he ostentatiously signaled the end to his active political career. Only an escalating crisis generated by the Algerian War created an opening for his return to center stage. With the civilian leadership of the Fourth Republic in disarray, the General made a last effort to lead the

French People to sweep away the postwar Constitution and endorse the Fifth Republic's radically different vision of democratic government.

This wasn't easy—and Part 2 will explore the complex dynamics that allowed de Gaulle to succeed in overcoming one obstacle after another during the course of his ten years as president of his new Republic. In this chapter I have a different purpose. My aim is to take the Fourth Republic seriously, rather than treat it as a prelude to the General's triumphant return. I will be trying to recapture a sense of the promise and perils of revolutionary constitutionalism as they were actually experienced at the dawn of the postwar era. When the leaders of the French and Italian Resistance struggled to hammer out their postwar frameworks of legitimate government, nobody could predict how their initiatives would work out over the decades; but the protagonists were very much aware that their enterprise would fail if they could not solve their fragmentation problems—and win the mobilized consent of ordinary French and Italian voters to the revolutionary Constitutions proposed in their name.

We have much to learn by comparing their efforts to do so.

Time One: The Duality of the Resistance

The French Resistance was famously divided between forces inside and outside the country. The internal Resistance expressed itself in complex social patterns—ranging from secret conversation circles to small-scale efforts at protecting particular victims of Nazi and Vichy oppression. These covert engagements merged into larger movement-party underground organizations, which gave their support to armed partisan bands engaged in guerilla attacks on the Nazi and Vichy regimes.

The domestic Resistance relied heavily on the Allies for financial and material aid. De Gaulle's claim to leadership was even more dependent upon foreign assistance. When the General fled to London in the wake of military defeat, it was only Winston Churchill's personal intervention at the BBC that enabled de Gaulle to make a dramatic radio appeal to his countrymen to take up arms against the Nazis. Six weeks later, only 7,000 Frenchmen had crossed the Channel in response to his call.

De Gaulle was not deterred by this meager response. In putting himself at the head of this small band as commander of the Free French, he insisted that he was the only legitimate spokesman for his captive People. Because the internal French Resistance did not yet exist, Churchill had little choice but to indulge de Gaulle's pretensions by providing the essential military resources to organize his "army." Yet as German forces increasingly dominated Europe during the early war years, de Gaulle's repeated shows of political independence led Churchill, together with Roosevelt, to try to replace him with a more tractable commander of the Free French Forces.[1]

To counter these efforts, de Gaulle mounted a skilled campaign to gain credibility with the underground movements against the Nazis that were gaining traction inside France. As his eloquent radio speeches began reaching larger audiences, his principal agent in occupied France, Jean Moulin, successfully established a National Council of the Resistance in May 1943. The Council then served as the General's vehicle for distributing arms and money to a wide range of opposition groups.

These groups came into the Resistance after years of intense political rivalry during the Third Republic—with Communists, Socialists, and Christian Democrats engaged in bitter ideological competition for popular support.[2] The National Council's provision of material aid helped secure their cooperation, but more fundamental factors were also at work. As François Goguel explains, "the resistants of all political beliefs" faced "common dangers . . . in the underground struggle," and it was "the personal contacts created by this solidarity" that led to the "reconciliation of parties which had formerly been opposed to one another."[3] To put Goguel's point in my terms: Despite the potential for fragmentation among traditional party leaders, grassroots activists of all parties were engaged in ongoing acts that put them in serious danger—and it was this experience of common sacrifice for the public good that bonded them together as a movement.

Given the support of party leaders, and the experience of underground activists, de Gaulle's eloquent radio broadcasts allowed him to emerge as the privileged spokesman for the Resistance to millions of more passive listeners living under the oppressive wartime conditions imposed by the Nazis. Over the same period, de Gaulle was making progress building up his military forces abroad—moving from London to Algiers and appealing to Frenchmen in North Africa to help build his army into a formidable fighting force, which ultimately reached 400,000 soldiers.[4]

Without these remarkable organizational achievements at home and abroad, it's impossible to make sense of the General's conduct upon his triumphant return to Paris in August 1944.

Time Two: From Triumph to Confrontation

The final battle for Paris involved a dramatic merger of the internal and external Resistance—outside the city, the Free French joined Allied forces in overcoming the German Army; inside, the partisan fighters of the Resistance launched an uprising that disrupted the Germans' desperate last-ditch defense.

De Gaulle's Moment

When the Germans collapsed under this two-pronged assault, de Gaulle set about establishing a provisional government in a remarkable fashion. He not only repudiated the legitimacy of the constitutional order established by Vichy. He also refused to treat the Constitution of the Third Republic as valid, creating a legitimacy vacuum that he then filled with . . . *himself.* Acting unilaterally in the name of the French People, the General established a provisional government to set the future course of the Republic.

In theory, spokespersons for the internal Resistance might have rebelled against de Gaulle's charismatic assertion of constituent authority. But given the General's success in building up the National Council of the Resistance during the war, it was far more sensible for Communists, Socialists, and Christian Democrats to continue their cooperation at de Gaulle's moment of triumph. The top leaders of all three movement parties accepted appointments in the General's interim government. But they emphatically believed that the sacrifices they all had made for the internal Resistance entitled them to speak for the People of France with an authority equal to de Gaulle's.

No less significantly, the General himself recognized that there were limits to his own legitimacy. While he had unilaterally repudiated the Third Republic, he had no interest in filling the "legitimacy vacuum" by staging a coup with the aid of his now-formidable Free French Forces. Rather than play the part of a latter-day Bonaparte, he quickly moved to constitutionalize his charisma. With the war in Europe coming to a close, his interim government called for free elections in October 1945, at which time the voters could authorize their newly elected representatives to hammer out a new Constitution for the Fourth Republic.[5]

In framing the Constituent Assembly's mandate, de Gaulle exercised significant self-restraint. He did not suppose that his previous pronouncements amounted to a decisive repudiation of the Third Republic. Instead, when they went to the polls, citizens were free to vote No to the question whether they wanted to authorize their newly elected representatives to draft a new Constitution for the Fourth Republic. If the No votes came out ahead, the new Assembly would simply reassume the powers it had previously possessed under the prewar regime, and continue with business as usual. But when the ballots were counted, 96 percent were marked Yes.

This meant that the legitimating source of the Constitution would not be de Gaulle's triumphant creation of a provisional government in April 1944, but the near-universal popular assent of October 1945. The remarkably strong voter turnout further enhanced the Assembly's legitimacy. Eighty percent of the citizenry cast ballots, with women participating for the first time in a national election. What is more, 75 percent of the voters favored one of the three movement parties, casting to the sidelines the political parties that had traditionally dominated the Third Republic. It is hard to imagine a more compelling demonstration that the French People were endorsing a "new beginning" in their political life.[6]

The election returns also emphasized the fragmentation problem that awaited the effort at constitutional construction. The Communists had come in first, with 26.1 percent of the vote, with the Socialists (at 23.8 percent) trailing close behind.[7] This was a stunning victory for the two Marxist parties. Even before the war, the two parties had already scored a major victory in 1936—winning 35 percent of the vote as part of a broader Popular Front that swept the moderate Socialist Leon Blum into power. But Blum required the support of non-Socialist groups in the Front to maintain parliamentary support. In contrast, the two Marxist parties now jointly controlled a majority of seats—expressing broad public recognition of their prominent role in leading the underground struggle against the Nazis.

At the same time, the Christian Democratic party, called the "Popular Republicans," also scored an impressive 24.9 percent, finishing ahead of the Socialists in second place behind the Communists. The leaders of this group also emphatically distanced themselves from the old parties of the Third Republic, demonstrating that more moderate voters were also determined to break free of the politics of the past. Nevertheless, these parties' wartime solidarities began to disintegrate as they began constitutional deliberations. The two Marxist parties split sharply on the question of democracy—with most Communists yearning for a Leninist "dictatorship of the proletariat" while most Socialists were Social Democrats. On this fundamental matter, they were closer to the Popular Republicans—who joined them in fearing a Leninist coup if the Communist Party continued its ascent at future elections.

At the same time, a second ideological conflict split the triumvirate along different lines—the two Marxist parties were strong secularists, but the Popular Republicans were committed Catholics. Communists versus Democrats, Secularists versus Catholics: these were serious conflicts, but as our next case study will suggest, the Italian Communists, Socialists, and Christian Democrats were able to hammer out a Constitution despite their strong disagreements on the same issues.

The big difference between the two cases had to do with General de Gaulle. The Italians had no military leader of the Resistance who was remotely comparable in stature. In France, the military / civilian fragmentation would have a decisive impact.

Presidentialism?

When the Assembly convened, the three movement parties reaffirmed de Gaulle's position as head of the provisional government. Accustomed to command, the General immediately began to push the civilian parties in a direction that none of them wanted to travel. The leaders of all three groups wanted to reform, but not abolish, the tradition of parliamentary government inherited from the French Revolution.

De Gaulle had something very different in mind. He demanded the creation of a powerful presidency that would allow him to move from charismatic leader of the Free French to constitutional leader of the Fourth Republic.

De Gaulle's presidentialism generated particularly intense suspicion from the Marxist majority. A devout Catholic, de Gaulle was closest to the Popular Republican (PR) orientation—affirming the need for a strong state to curb the excesses of capitalism, but opposed to Marxism in general and Communism in particular. If de Gaulle had publicly assumed leadership of the PR, he could have made it a powerful force in shaping the Constitution. The party had already scored 25 percent at the polls, and with the popular General at its helm, it could hope to outpoll the Communists in future elections. Given de Gaulle's conservative Catholicism, the PR delegation would also be attracted by his vision of a strong presidency. A president de Gaulle, together with a PR prime minister in Parliament, would serve as the most potent combination against the looming Marxist threat.

Despite this overwhelming political logic, the General refused to use the PR party as a vehicle for his constitutional ambitions. He understood himself to be *the* charismatic leader of the Nation, not a mere party chieftain. He refused to demean himself by taking on PR party leadership. Instead, he resorted to shock therapy to gain his objectives.

Without even notifying his potential allies in the PR, he abruptly announced his resignation as head of the interim government shortly after the Assembly began its deliberations. His aim was to demonstrate that, in his absence, the Communist/Socialist/Popular Republican coalition would quickly disintegrate into warring ideological factions that could not provide the strong direction the country needed to rise from its postwar misery. This would leave the triumvirate no choice but to call upon the General to save the Nation by presiding over a presidentialist Constitution that would grant him wide-ranging powers.[8]

De Gaulle's gambit failed. His resignation did generate short-term instability at the top of the provisional government, but it did not disrupt forward motion on the Constitution. Despite their opposition to Marxism, the Popular Republicans refused to support the General's errand into the wilderness. Instead, they joined with their wartime comrades in a common effort to define foundational principles.

The key issue was checks and balances. The two Marxist parties shared the Gaullist view that there was too much instability during the Third Republic. As a consequence, they advanced a variety of proposals that would help a government maintain itself in office once it had gained the support of a parliamentary majority.[9] But the PR rejected these initiatives, fearing that they could serve as a springboard for a Marxist dictatorship if the Communists continued their dramatic ascent at the polls.

This led the PR to try to convince the Socialists to abandon their Marxist allies and create an institutional mechanism that could effectively constrain the National Assembly. But after sustained efforts at compromise, the two sides failed to find common ground—and the Communist-Socialist alliance, along with some fellow travelers, passed their parliamentary Constitution through the assembly on a vote of 309 to 249.[10]

This vote only served to as a prelude to a final decision by the voters. Shortly after his triumphant entry into Paris, de Gaulle had proclaimed that it would be up to the People, in a special referendum, to decide the ultimate fate of the Assembly's proposal. Now that the General had gone into opposition, it was even more difficult to ignore this decree—since the referendum

provided the only way to establish that, despite de Gaulle's charismatic opposition, the Assembly's Constitution did indeed have the self-conscious
support of the French People.

A key element in the Assembly's initiative was centered on its effort to redefine fundamental rights for the twentieth century. Its proposed Constitution reasserted the enduring relevance of the liberal democratic rights set out
in the great Declaration of the Rights of Man and of the Citizen of 1789. But
it gave equal standing to the new Republic's commitment to social equality
and the dignity of labor, redefining the very meaning of "liberty, equality, fra-
ternity." This revolutionary transformation of the French revolutionary tradition served as the foundation for a coordinated effort by the Communists
and Socialists to root their initiative in popular sovereignty.

De Gaulle and the Popular Republicans failed to display a similar unity.
Different PR leaders presented disjointed critiques of the Marxist initiative. De
Gaulle himself utterly refused to enter the debate in any way whatsoever. His
ostentatious silence was eloquent in its own fashion—urging the voters to look
upon him, rather than the squabbling movement parties, as the true representative of the People.

The citizenry responded to this remarkable political display with another
80 percent turnout in May 1946. But the election returns revealed a sharp split
between the military and civilian representatives of the popular will—with
the electorate rejecting the Assembly's Constitution by the margin of 53 to 47.[11]
This outcome did not take the Communist / Socialist / Popular Republican triumvirate by surprise. They had had anticipated such a possibility, and explicitly provided that the defeat of their initiative should trigger the election of a
second Constituent Assembly to frame another constitutional proposal.

This follow-up vote took place the next month—and it revealed that de
Gaulle was beginning to pay a heavy price for his refusal to engage in party
politics. If he had organized a new Gaullist movement party, he could have
offered the electorate a list of candidates committed to his presidentialist vision. But because he remained aloof, the best he could hope for was a massive show of popular support for the slate of candidates presented by PR, since
it was this anti-Marxist party that had led the successful No campaign. Nevertheless, he even refused to issue a public endorsement of the PR slate, thereby
preventing the party from gaining maximum advantage from the momentum
it had gained by its stunning victory at the initial referendum.

As a consequence, the second Constituent Assembly looked very much
like the first when the votes were counted in June 1946. Despite its leadership

of the No campaign, the PR only added 3 percentage points to its tally, gaining 28 percent of the total vote. This was barely enough to beat out the 26 percent share earned by the Communists. Worse yet for the General, the Socialists won 21 percent. This meant that the two Marxist parties, together with their fellow travelers, would maintain majority control over the proceedings.

Yet the PR now held a trump card: If the Communists and Socialists pushed through another strong version of parliamentary democracy, the PR could lead another No campaign, urging the voters to teach the Left that it could not continue ignoring the People. At the same time, de Gaulle was changing course. After staying on the sidelines for so long, he finally broke his silence in a speech at Bayeux—sketching out a vision that anticipated the Constitution of the Fifth Republic.[12] On his view, the newly elected Constituent Assembly should design the presidency "to harmonize the general interest . . . with the general orientation of Parliament . . . to serve as arbiter of unexpected political difficulties . . . [and] if the country should be in danger, to be the guarantor of national independence." Given these great tasks, he insisted that a proper Constitution should create a special electoral college to choose the nation's "arbiter" and "guarantor"—since this would permit de Gaulle to ascend to his new and lofty position without ever acknowledging the legitimate role played by party politics in the life of his presidentialist Republic.

In finally intervening at a time when the new assembly was getting down to work, de Gaulle was intending to overwhelm their tactical coalition-building efforts with his grand vision. It had just the opposite effect. It forced the Popular Republicans to rethink their strategy: If they now played their trump card, and opposed the second Marxist-inspired Constitution, it would be the General who would lead the No campaign—perhaps organizing a Gaullist movement that would push the PR to the periphery. And if he emerged victorious, the third Constituent Assembly would have no choice but to bow to the General's will.

Once again the fragmentation between military and civilian authority was shaping the dynamic—especially for the PR, which was intent on preserving its position as a pivotal party in the life of the new Republic. As a consequence, its party leaders returned to the bargaining table and agreed to support the new initiative of the Left to create an upper house—the Council of the Republic—which could delay, but not defeat, the legislative initiatives of the National Assembly. Because the Council was gerrymandered in ways that favored conservatives, this promised a limited check on strong Marxist initiatives if the Communist/Socialist alliance continued to win majorities in the National Assembly. This check was further strengthened when it came to constitutional amendments, where the Council would play an even more significant role.[13]

The new Constitution also weakened the earlier draft's strong affirmation of the state's power to nationalize large-scale industry, enabling shareholders to claim compensation for sweeping seizures of property. But to make this guarantee effective, the second-round Constitution would have had to create a constitutional tribunal committed to its enforcement. While it made symbolic gestures in that direction, the text did not compel its creation, and nothing was ever done to make the tribunal into an institutional reality.[14] Socialist governments, if they had maintained their strong Left majorities in the National Assembly, would have been free to overcome opposition from the upper house and impose sweeping nationalization measures without confronting a decisive judicial demand for compensation to aggrieved capitalists.

In short, the second Assembly created a strong parliamentary framework similar to the one that the Popular Republicans had campaigned against the first time around. Nevertheless, the party reluctantly joined its wartime allies in defending the revision—at the same time minimizing its distance from de Gaulle by arguing that the Constitution could be "perfected" later, if necessary, with appropriate amendments.[15]

De Gaulle was not impressed. He condemned the PR for its "betrayal," and urged the country to vote No.[16] Yet once again, he paid a heavy price for his refusal to dirty his hands with the nuts and bolts of politics. His strong opposition led to lots of voter hesitation and a decline in turnout from 80 percent to 70 percent. But in the absence of a mobilized Gaullist party organization, the Resistance parties did a better job of convincing their followers to turn out at the polls. On October 13, 1946, the Constitution was ratified by a margin of 54 percent to 46 percent, with Yes votes outnumbering No votes by more than a million.[17]

This intense round of citizen engagement came to a close the following month with the election of a National Assembly to serve for the next five years. For the first time, a Gaullist Union entered the field—but the General failed to give it his explicit backing, and it received only 3 percent of the vote and none of the Assembly's 627 seats. The three Resistance movement parties won 72 percent of the votes and 457 seats—though their wartime solidarities soon disintegrated as strong ideological differences set them at loggerheads.[18]

As their conflicts escalated in Parliament, the General finally took the offensive. In April 1947 he announced the creation of the Rally of the French

People—calling upon all citizens to transcend rigid party commitments and devote themselves to the national interest (defined, of course, by you know who). In characteristic fashion, the General did not give advance notice of his plans to the existing party leaderships—not even the Popular Republicans, whom the public had come to view as his principal political supporter.

This virtually guaranteed a hostile response from the PR. To demonstrate its independence, the party required its members to make an existential choice: they could either remain loyal to the PR or join the Rally—but not both. The Marxist parties made an identical demand. Despite this emphatic show of civilian opposition, the General quickly attracted half a million followers to the Rally, whose candidates scored major victories in Paris and other large cities in the October 1947 municipal elections.[19]

The Rally also became a parliamentary force. It gained a foothold by offering the old parties of the Third Republic a means to rehabilitate themselves. Despite the fact that these old-regime legacies held 25 percent of the Assembly seats, the Resistance parties had refused to deal with them in organizing their coalition governments. But the more centrist representatives of the old-time Radical and Moderate Parties now joined an "intergroup" organized by the Rally, hoping to escape their pariah status by accepting de Gaulle as their titular head.

The Gaullist parliamentary threat escalated as the three-party alliance disintegrated. The precipitating cause was Communist opposition to the war in Vietnam, which led Socialist Paul Ramadier to dismiss the Reds from his government in May 1947. With both the Gaullist Right and the Communist Left on the attack, it was unclear whether the Center could hold. But much to de Gaulle's disappointment, the Socialists and Popular Republicans managed to reach out to enough moderate conservatives to sustain a series of Third Force governments for the Assembly's entire five-year term.

The election of November 1951 was a bitterly fought affair—with the voters dealing a body blow to the legitimacy of the Fourth Republic. The Communists and Gaullists came out on top—with 26 percent and 22 percent of the vote—leaving only 52 percent support for an ideologically disparate group of Third Force parties. Even though a last-minute change in the election law permitted them to translate their bare majority into 62 percent of the seats, it was going to be tough for this coalition to maintain stable coalition governments in the years ahead.

De Gaulle, however, helped the Third Force out by failing to provide his Rally with effective leadership. He had refused to lower himself by running for a seat in the National Assembly, and chose to deal with his delegation in a distant top-down fashion. This authoritarian style led members to defect on key parliamentary votes, and provoked the outright departure of 45 members from the party. With its national delegation in disarray, voters dealt the Rally a sharp setback at the municipal elections in 1953, accelerating its political decline.

The next big test would come with the 1956 elections to the National Assembly. Anticipating further humiliation, de Gaulle announced his withdrawal from politics, and the dissolution of the Rally, in November 1955—leaving a Gaullist rump in Parliament to struggle onward without his support. As he brooded silently in his country retreat at Colombey-les-Deux-Églises, the 65-year-old General seemed a man without a political future. Like Churchill, Roosevelt, and Stalin, he had secured a place in history as his country's heroic leader in the struggle against Hitler. But while his counterparts had—in one way or another—helped shape the emerging world order, he had utterly failed.

At this point the lesson of the revolutionary French experience seemed clear. To put the point in terms of the distinction developed in Chapter 1: The *personal* charisma of de Gaulle might suffice to damage the constitutional achievement of the *organizational charisma* generated by the Resistance movement parties; but it was not enough, by itself, to enable the military hero to win a second outsider-revolution in which he might lead the People to repudiate the civilian Fourth Republic in the name of a presidentialist Constitution.

How, then, did the defeated de Gaulle return to the political stage only three years later and succeed where earlier he had so dramatically and repeatedly failed?

I will defer my answer until we survey Italy's experience in revolutionary constitutionalism. Not only is this comparison revealing in itself, but it sharpens the questions raised by de Gaulle's ascent to power in 1958, and the remarkable ways in which his personal charisma has been constitutionalized over the next half century.

CHAPTER 5

Constitutional Revolution in Italy

Both India and South Africa emerged from the common-law tradition of the British Empire; and both managed to create constitutional courts as critical components in their revolutionary constitutions. France, in contrast, has served as Europe's paradigmatic civil-law system; but nothing resembling a constitutional court appeared during the Fourth Republic.

This simple point challenges a large claim advanced in the Introduction. I suggested that the classic divide between civil-law and common-law systems doesn't track the distinctive institutional dynamics driving the rise of world constitutionalism. Yet the absence of anything resembling a constitutional court in the Fourth Republic challenges this thesis. Worse yet, the counter-example is particularly troubling because I am purporting to describe the distinctive dynamics of revolutionary constitutionalism—and the rejection of judicial review has everything to do with the French Revolution. Ever since the glory days of 1789, the French tradition has consistently rejected "government by judges" as inconsistent with the rule of We the People.

The Italian experience suggests, however, that the Fourth Republic is an exception to the general rule. Since Italy's reunification in 1870, its judiciary has been organized along French lines—the Court of Cassation adjudicating disputes between private parties, and the Council of State dealing with lawsuits against public authorities. Like the French, Italian judges depended heavily on the legal academy for aid in dealing with difficult problems of statutory interpretation, yet the entire legal establishment drew the line when it came to invalidating statutes. No less than the French, Italian judges and scholars condemned such interventions as fundamentally illegitimate. Nevertheless, this deeply entrenched civilian tradition did not prevent the rise of judicial review under Italy's postwar revolutionary constitution.

The key difference between the two cases is the absence of an Italian military figure remotely comparable to General de Gaulle. As a consequence, the civilian politicians in Italy were not obliged to confront challenges to their authority raised by a charismatic general. They could instead give greater attention to the ways in which judicial review promised to consolidate their Constitution's revolutionary legitimacy over time.

The Italian case is a particularly congenial place to explore this hypothesis because its Constituent Assembly was dominated by the very same movement parties that controlled the agenda in France. Once again, we will see Communists, Socialists, and Christian Democrats struggling for power while simultaneously hammering out a constitutional framework to regulate their future competition. Yet this time around, we do indeed find the Assembly preparing the way for a Constitutional Court to emerge in response to a succession crisis at Time three.

My argument will also test a second major strand of contemporary scholarship. These observers view the rise of constitutional courts through the lens of a "rational actor" model of politics. In this now-familiar account, judicial review appears as a "rational" solution to a bargaining problem faced by the contending parties as they hammer out their new Constitution. As they try to reach an agreement, the wheeler-dealers around the table recognize that their relative power positions will change over time—leading newly empowered players to breach key terms of their hard-won compact. To reduce this danger, they turn to a relatively neutral court—giving it the power to invalidate legislation that undermines the terms of their initial constitutional bargain.[1]

Call this the *insurance function,* and I have been arguing that it does not do justice to the Indian and South African cases. This chapter shows that the Italian case also displays the four-stage dynamic characteristic of the revolutionary pathway. After elaborating the distinctive Italian variations on these increasingly familiar themes, Chapter 6 reflects on the larger lessons to be learned from the Indian, South African, French, and Italian experiences.

Time One: The Repudiation of Mussolini

During the nineteenth century, Italy followed the "establishmentarian" path to constitutionalism. In this ideal type, the existing regime successfully co-opts revolutionary mobilizations through strategic concessions.

The story begins in 1848. King Charles Albert of Sardinia-Piedmont had previously ruled as an absolute monarch. But he saved his throne from the populist threat by issuing a royal Statuto, which created a Parliament for the propertied classes—while reserving broad and ill-defined powers for the monarchy.[2] During the next generation, Albert's House of Savoy confronted a second revolutionary challenge when Garibaldi's military forces tried to overthrow it in their larger effort to unify Italy as a Republic. But Victor Emmanuel II and his prime minister, the Count of Cavour, managed to co-opt Garibaldi into their own successful campaign to make the monarchy the engine of Italian unity.[3] As a consequence, Albert's Statuto remained the constitutional reference point for the Kingdom of Italy from 1848 through the end of World War II—with the king and his royal counselors / bureaucrats engaged in a series of highly creative reinterpretations of the Statuto in response to dramatically changing political conditions.

The Statuto's famed "flexibility" was put to good use during the country's first half-century. When the House of Savoy seized the Papal States, it successfully concluded its campaign for Italian unification—but its seizure of Rome in 1870 came at a great political price. Declaring himself a "prisoner in the Vatican," Pius IX called upon Italy's Catholics to repudiate the triumphant monarchy. Given the papacy's intransigent opposition, the king had little choice but to rely on secular nationalists to govern the country.

The pope's call for true believers to boycott parliamentary elections was similarly counterproductive—leading a series of royal governments to enhance their legitimacy by expanding the franchise to maximize turnout. While admitting the working class to the franchise did help sustain the system, it also strengthened the parliamentary representation of leftist parties whose "godless" ideologies were most offensive to the papacy.

With the close of the World War I, the monarchy's continuing effort to adapt the Statuto to changing conditions led to disaster. When Benito Mussolini engineered his March on Rome in October 1922, Fascist forces were by no means in a position to overpower the existing parliamentary regime. King Victor Emmanuel III could well have used his constitutional authority to ask a liberal prime minister to form a government that was determined to keep the Fascists at bay. But the king used his "flexible" authority to appoint Mussolini instead, paving the way for Il Duce to crush parliamentary opposition and use the monarch as a symbolic figurehead for his Fascist system.

The king's fateful decision tainted his continuing claims to legitimacy once Mussolini's troops lost their grip on the country in 1943. Seeing the handwriting on the wall, Victor Emmanuel asserted his authority, under the flexible Statuto, once again to adapt his regime to changing times. Not only did he dismiss Mussolini from power on July 25, 1943. He immediately ordered Il Duce confined to a top-secret detention camp. At the same time, he named Field Marshal Badoglio as head of his new government.

These dramatic steps were not a clean break with the past. Badoglio had been field marshal of Italy's army in 1940, and lost his job only because his troops lost critical battles when the war broke out.[4] Once the king recalled him to power in 1943, Badoglio publicly reassured the Nazis that Italy would remain a loyal member of the Axis.

But at the same time, he began secret negotiations with the Allies to join their war against Hitler—managing to reach a provisional accord on September 3. He refused, however, to make the deal public, because he hoped to improve its terms through some last-minute negotiations. The Allies responded angrily to this bargaining ploy. On September 8 they unilaterally announced the terms of the secret deal they had reached with Badoglio.

The Germans responded decisively to this act of betrayal. Their massive army remained in control of the north of the country, and it immediately seized control over the Italian troops that had previously fought by their side—placing them in internment camps after disarming them. The Nazis also moved south with blinding speed—occupying Rome in two days, and forcing the king and his government to flee the city and seek safety with the Allies, who had been battling their way up the peninsula from Sicily.

The Germans then humiliated the monarchy further by quickly discovering the "secret" spot where Mussolini had been interned. After freeing Il Duce in a lightning raid, they dispatched him northward to serve as figurehead of a newly proclaimed Italian Social Republic. With the king's army thoroughly demobilized, there was only one force capable of challenging the Nazi's puppet regime: the guerilla fighters of the Resistance movement, who managed to create grassroots revolutionary governments in key areas and finally succeeded in seizing and killing Mussolini during the closing days of the war.

This symbolic triumph over Il Duce was long delayed. The Allies first landed in Sicily in July 1943, but they did not battle their way to Rome until June 1944 and only managed to win control of the great cities of the north during the spring of 1945—aided by a general uprising proclaimed by the Italian Partisans' Committee of Liberation. During this lengthy period, the Allies recognized the king as the head of the legitimate government of Italy; but given Victor Emmanuel's lengthy collaboration with the Fascist regime, would the Italian People agree?

This is precisely the question Palmiro Togliatti, head of the Communist Party, asked himself as he returned to Italy after seventeen years in exile. The Party played a leading role in the Northern Resistance—overshadowing the (significant) parts played by Socialists and Christian Democrats.[5] Many militants were looking for a sweeping repudiation of the king and an inspiring call for a Marxist revolution.

Togliatti disappointed them upon his return to Salerno, the provisional capital of the king's government. In his dramatic Turn of March 1944, he announced that the Communist Party would join the Socialists and Christian Democrats in a "government of national unity" under the monarchy.[6] Collaborating with Victor Emmanuel, he asserted, was the only way to resolve the legitimacy crisis generated by "a government invested with power but deprived of authority because it lacks the support of the mass parties." Otherwise, the existing situation would "create an atmosphere favorable to reactionary intrigues and thus for the rebirth of a fascist movement, while at the same time it weakens and discredits our country."[7]

In joining the government, Togliatti remained a steadfast Republican and refused to endorse the monarchy or its Statuto as appropriate foundations for the country's future. He simply postponed these ultimate constitutional questions until the Nazis could be decisively defeated. Socialist leaders took a similar position. Nevertheless, the entry of the Marxists into the king's government made a big difference at the next stage of the constitutional dynamic.

Time Two: Constitutionalizing the Revolution

When de Gaulle made his triumphant entry into Paris in 1944, he filled the legitimacy vacuum by unilaterally establishing an interim government. When the three French movement parties accepted positions in his interim regime, they immediately created a framework for ongoing competition between the civilian-led parties of the Resistance and the military commander of the Free French Forces for authority to speak for the People.

Victor Emmanuel's decision to fire Mussolini opened a different path. Rather than opening up a complete legitimacy vacuum, the king could fill the void by offering the ever-flexible Statuto as the basis for a transitional government to the postwar era.

This is what made Togliatti's Turn at Salerno so important. If the Communist leader had thrown his party's support to the Marxist militants who had seized control of northern cities and towns by the end of the war, their Committees of National Liberation would have proclaimed a Worker's State—propelling the country to the brink of civil war. Instead, Togliatti's entry into the king's "government of national unity" pushed politics in a different direction—postponing a head-on assault on the old regime and its Statuto until the final defeat of the Nazis.[8]

Once the Italian constitutional debate began, it immediately departed from the French path. Given the total collapse of Vichy, de Gaulle and the Resistance leaders of the three movement parties were essentially quarreling among themselves on the best constitutional design for their "new beginning." In contrast, when leaders of the Italian Resistance launched a strong critique of the Statuto, they confronted a strong response from constitutional conservatives. So far as they were concerned, there was no need for a revolutionary break with the monarchical past. The king should simply respond to postwar realities by endorsing yet another reinterpretation of the Statuto that had demonstrated its flexibility repeatedly over the course of the previous century.

As a consequence, ordinary Italians would soon be asking themselves a question that was different from the one their French counterparts faced. When the French went to the polls, they would be choosing between the revolutionary designs offered by de Gaulle and the civilian movement parties emerging from the Resistance. In contrast, Italians would be asking whether there was any need at all for a revolutionary break with the past or whether they should continue moving down the establishmentarian pathway marked out by the Statuto.

But I am getting ahead of the story.

I have already introduced the roles played by the king and Togliatti in framing this question, but it is time to turn the spotlight to another key actor: Alcide De Gasperi and his Christian Democrats.

De Gasperi as Revolutionary?

De Gasperi is typically portrayed as a master politician who successfully transformed the Christian Democrats into the dominant force in Italian government for the rest of the twentieth century. But at the time of Mussolini's fall, he was a revolutionary outsider, not a pragmatic insider, calling upon his fellow Catholics to repudiate the papacy's longtime contempt for democratic political engagement with secular liberals and Marxists.

Papal hostility to Italian nationalism went back to the unification of the country in the nineteenth century, but it began to soften when Benedict XV lifted the papacy's absolute ban on Catholic participation in parliamentary elections—giving rise to the formation of a left-center Popular Party (PP) in 1919, based on Church principles of collective responsibility for social welfare.[9] De Gasperi played a role in the PP from the beginning, but he only emerged as its effective leader in the final months of the PP's struggle against Mussolini's rise to dictatorship.

When Il Duce banned all public opposition in 1927, De Gasperi was immediately hunted down and thrown into detention.[10] With his health deteriorating rapidly, he could well have died for his democratic convictions. But in 1929 the archbishop of Trent managed to arrange his release—only for De Gasperi to find that he was now a pariah in Fascist society. He couldn't find a job, leaving him in desperate shape. Once again, however, the Church came to his rescue—offering him a lowly position as a cataloguer in the Vatican Library, which he gratefully accepted.[11]

At the very same moment, however, Pope Pius XI was repudiating the fundamental principles to which De Gasperi had dedicated his political career. In the Lateran Accords of 1929, Pius XI and Mussolini put an end to the bitter hostility between church and state that had prevailed during the preceding democratic era.[12] In its place, they formally established terms of mutual accommodation. Mussolini affirmed Catholicism as "the only religion of the State," and granted full sovereignty to Vatican City.[13] In return, the pope promised absolute neutrality in Mussolini's struggle against his foreign opponents—most notably, the Soviet Union, France, and Britain. Despite the dramatic differences between Soviet dictatorship and Western democracy, Pius XI considered all three countries as fundamentally alike in their repudiation of the Catholic Church's claim to privileged status as the state religion—and so he gave Mussolini freedom to ally himself with the side he believed would further the Fascist cause.

This was too much for De Gasperi.[14] Despite his deep religious convictions and personal indebtedness to the Church for his sheer physical survival, he refused to join leading Catholics in their chorus of praise for the Lateran Accords.[15] Nor did he play any part in the ongoing Vatican effort to encourage true believers to join Fascist organizations in support of Mussolini's regime.[16] Instead, he chose to remain in obscurity as a low-level librarian, and write a series of signed and unsigned essays that reaffirmed the need for a Christian *Democratic* approach to politics.[17]

Once Mussolini joined Hitler's war in 1940, De Gasperi went beyond personal pronunciamentos to take the lead in arranging a series of underground meetings with like-minded Catholics. By 1943 this collaboration yielded an elaborate Manifesto, issued under the pseudonym Demofilo, which was widely circulated throughout the underground. In contrast to the Marxists, this

program for Christian Democracy reaffirmed private property as a fundamental right. But it also emphasized the critical need for ongoing state intervention to eliminate the abuses of free-market capitalism. It insisted that
the state should

> eliminate those industrial and financial concentrations that are the artificial
> creation of economic imperialism, and modify laws that have favored con-
> centration in a few hands of means of production and wealth. That will
> lead, moreover, to the demolition of monopolies that are not . . . truly inevi-
> table. For those that remain, public control should be imposed, or, if it proves
> more efficient and a fair compensation is paid, these properties should be na-
> tionalized and put preferably into collaborative management with the workers.[18]

The Manifesto also supported strong forms of redistributive taxation and an
ambitious program of public works.[19]

De Gasperi then defied Fascist laws to issue a call for Catholics to emerge
from the underground and establish a new Christian Democratic Party at a
founding convention. By the time it met in 1944, Mussolini had fallen, and
the Christian Democrats had already joined the government of national unity.
But De Gasperi, upon his election as leader by the convention, continued to
make plain his party's revolutionary intentions:

> For the sake of the solidarity of the anti-Fascist parties, we are sacrificing many
> particular programs. Nevertheless, let no one delude himself; if tomorrow, the
> law were to be threatened and violated, and tyrannical and dictatorial desires
> were to be hinted at . . . , we would not allow ourselves to be surprised as the
> country was surprised in 1922 [when the king named Mussolini head of gov-
> ernment]. To the menace that comes from the Right or from the Left, we shall
> offer all the resistance, active or passive, of which the people will be capable.[20]

In appealing to the People to resist left- and right-wing totalitarianism,
De Gasperi found himself in the same place as Togliatti—though he had been
far more consistent than the Communist in insisting throughout his political
career on the importance of constitutionalism.[21] Nevertheless, their joint decision to join the Socialists in entering the king's government had a profound
impact on the course of higher lawmaking over the next few years.

When viewed through a comparative lens, De Gasperi's revolutionary trajec-
tory is hardly unique. Nelson Mandela's career provides a striking parallel.

Like De Gasperi, Mandela first gained political prominence as a leading opponent of an increasingly repressive regime, and he paid an even heavier price on Robben Island and Pollsmoor Prison. Both men reentered public life at a time when the established order lost its military grip. At that point, they were in their sixties, and decades of sacrifice had earned each man the charismatic authority that enabled them to serve as a central symbol for a movement party aiming for a new constitutional beginning.

Their fundamental principles were more similar than different. It is easy to ignore this ideological convergence because the two men began from different starting points. Mandela was a Communist who evolved into a social democrat; De Gasperi was a Catholic who broke with the pope to insist on a sweeping program of governmental intervention inspired by Catholic ideals of social justice. In both cases, their common social democratic commitments permitted pragmatic cooperation with other elements of the revolutionary movement whose long-term objectives ranged from a worker's state to laissez-faire liberalism.

The two men, however, faced different organizational challenges. When Mandela left prison, he had to consolidate his links with the returning ANC-in-exile, including the Spear of the Nation, as well as the domestic liberation movements emerging from the underground. De Gasperi confronted elaborate organizations created by the Fascists to mobilize millions of Catholic supporters for Mussolini's totalitarian regime. As a consequence, his first priority was to detach grassroots Catholic groups from their fealty to Il Duce and convince them to devote their energies to support the new Christian Democrat movement in its ongoing competition with their Marxist and liberal competitors.

Success was by no means certain. After more than a decade of Catholic praise for Mussolini and the Lateran Accords, the downfall of Il Duce could have simply led to widespread Catholic disillusionment with any form of political involvement whatsoever. But the Christian Democratic effort was remarkably successful over the next couple of years, generating a new movement-party network in support of its distinctive mission.[22]

I have already been emphasizing a final difference between the two cases. Although the African National Congress remained a site of conflict between Marxist militants and social democrats, the ANC's centrality to the entire movement made it easier for Mandela to gain broad recognition of his symbolic centrality to the entire revolutionary movement. In contrast, De Gasperi had to deal with the organizational gulf separating his new Christian Democratic movement from well-established Marxist competitors.

Here is where Togliatti's Turn at Salerno was crucial. If the Communist leader had endorsed an all-out proletarian revolution, De Gasperi would never have been in a position to build a credible united front with the Marxists. But Togliatti's Turn cleared the way for the Catholic and Communist movement parties to form a compelling coalition under the aegis of the king.

When faced with this show of national unity, the Americans and the British gave Victor Emmanuel's provisional government a surprisingly broad degree of political leeway. After all, the Allies could have treated Italy like Germany and Japan—and impose a lengthy military occupation on its war-ravaged enemy. But it treated the Italians more like the French—giving the coalition of Christian Democrats, Socialists, and Communists a great deal of leeway in defining their new constitutional identity on their own terms (more or less).[23]

The Birth of the Republic

Despite Victor Emmanuel's decision to fire and arrest Mussolini, it soon became apparent that the broader public would never forgive his intimate collaboration with the Fascists. In a desperate effort to save the House of Savoy, he named his son, Crown Prince Umberto, as head of state with authority to preside over the provisional government. Responding to the demands of the movement parties in the coalition, Umberto issued a call for a Constituent Assembly in June 1944. As in France, preparations moved into high gear in early 1946 after Hitler's defeat.[24]

This required the provisional government to confront a preliminary question. Should it propose a referendum to the voters in which they would explicitly decide whether Italy should repudiate the monarchy and establish a Constitution for the Italian Republic, or should it simply ask the voters to elect representatives to a national assembly who would make this decision on their behalf?

The Communists and Socialists saw no need for a referendum. They were emphatic republicans, and were confident that the Marxist slates would win a parliamentary majority—no need, then, for a plebiscite authorizing their revolutionary break from the Statuto. But De Gasperi took a different view. He had now become head of the provisional government, and although a clear majority of his party favored a republic, he recognized that southern Italy remained strongly monarchist. If this region were to accept the legitimacy of the new Republic, it would be best if the House of Savoy were not swept away by a decree handed down from Rome; its fate should be determined by a self-conscious act of popular sovereignty by the People.[25]

The popular response was tremendous, with turnout reaching almost 90 percent. A month before the vote, in June 1946, the king made a final effort to save the monarchy—formally abdicating in favor of his son Umberto II. This gesture proved insufficient: the Republic triumphed by a margin of 54 percent to 46 percent.[26] Voters also swept the Communist / Socialist / Christian Democrat coalition into a commanding position. Taken together, the referendum and the election conveyed a decisive message: the People had come out in overwhelming numbers to demand the construction of a democratic constitution that would mark a "new beginning" in their political life.

This was precisely the same mandate French voters had given their own Communist / Socialist / Popular Republican coalition eight months earlier. But the relationship between the three Resistance movement parties was different. In France, the Communists came out on top and the two Marxist parties won a majority of seats—permitting them to advance their first constitutional proposal over the dissent of the Popular Republicans (the French analogue to Italy's Christian Democrats).

In Italy, the Christian Democrats came in first with 35 percent of the vote (and seats), ahead of the Socialists (with 21 percent) and the Communists (with 19 percent). The two Marxist parties added up to a formidable 40 percent, but they could not impose their will in the manner of the French Left. They were obliged to reach an agreement with the Christian Democrats on a system of checks and balances that would impose significant restraints on the Chamber of Deputies.

The Italian debate differed in a second respect. In France, the great question centered on de Gaulle's critique of parliamentary government—which, according to him, accounted for the Third Republic's disastrous failure to defend the country against the Nazi threat. Italians were also confronting their prewar failure to preserve liberal democracy, but recent history taught them a different lesson. The source of their catastrophic collapse was the king's "flexibility" in interpreting the Statuto that precipitated the disaster. This enabled Victor Emmanuel to give Mussolini the chance to become prime minister in 1922 when other democratic leaders could have gained parliamentary support—and it was this tragic blunder that the new Constitution should avoid at all costs.

Never again should the political class be allowed to repeat Victor Emmanuel's catastrophic mistake—this was the central credo of all Italian revolutionaries, regardless of party. They insisted that the "flexible" Statuto must be replaced by a "rigid" Constitution imposing legally binding restraints on future strongmen. After twenty years of Il Duce, the Gaullist vision of strong presidential leadership was a nonstarter—especially for De Gasperi.

Since December 1945, De Gasperi had been serving as head of the king's government of national unity, exercising royal decree powers granted by the Statuto—and he continued using these powers, with the support of the newly elected representatives, during the eighteen months it took them to hammer out a constitutional proposal. The dynamic interaction of the assembly's roles as both constituent body and provisional legislature generated unanticipated complexities over time. But for clarity's sake, I'll begin by focusing on its constitutional challenges.

The "Rigid" Constitution

The referendum, together with the decisive victory of the revolutionary movement parties, made it clear that the Republic's "rigid" Constitution should aim to prevent the rise of future Mussolinis. The only serious question was how to accomplish this objective.

One target was the overcentralization of power. The creation of relatively autonomous regional governments would make a power grab in Rome more difficult to sustain. The Assembly also constructed a relatively powerful Senate to check a party leader commanding a strong majority in the Chamber of Deputies. But the creation of the Constitutional Court was a more controversial matter.

De Gasperi had insisted on the need for judicial review as early as the 1920s, and emphasized its importance in the underground Manifesto of 1943.[27] Marxists were more skeptical. It was one thing to construct popularly elected institutions in the regions and the Senate as checks and balances on the Chamber's assertions of power; it was quite another to assign this task to unelected judges. Taking to the floor, Togliatti saw a day in the not-distant future when a few judges might strike down socialist legislation advanced by a Marxist coalition that had gained majority support in both houses of Parliament—and condemned any constitution that would tolerate the frustration of the popular will by a tiny juridical elite.[28]

Yet the Marxists controlled only 40 percent of the assembly—so left-leaning Christian Democrats could respond to their concerns without abandoning their own campaign for a Constitutional Court. They did so by supporting a bill of rights that moved far beyond the classical liberal conception.[29] After proclaiming Italy to be a "Democratic Republic, founded on work," the initial provisions of the founding document insisted that "the fundamental duties of political, economic and social solidarity [shall] be fulfilled."[30] It followed up with a series of forty-two provisions that translated these grand abstractions into a complex set of affirmative rights and duties.[31] Rather than invite the Constitutional Court to impose its elitist notions of fundamental rights on parliamentary majorities, these detailed provisions were likely to trigger the legalistic instincts of the jurists, and invite them to engage in the disciplined readings of particular texts characteristic of the civilian tradition. While there could be no guarantees, this prospect managed to calm Marxist fears of a judicial coup and to accept the new Court as a legitimate part of the "rigid" Constitution's effort to preempt future Mussolinis.

To be sure, a small cadre of jurists played a large role in drafting the crucial constitutional provisions—since small changes in the text could invite large changes in doctrinal development. But their esoteric technical discussions should not divert attention from the big picture: It was the broad-based popular demand for a "rigid" Constitution enshrining social rights, not the legalistic opinions of a juridical elite, that drove the process forward. To borrow an insightful formulation from Piero Calamandrei, the assembly's leading jurist: "To compensate the forces of the left for a circumvented revolution, the forces of the Right showed no opposition to a promised revolution in the constitution."[32]

The Right's acceptance of a "revolution in the constitution" seems less surprising once it is recalled that De Gasperi had led his Christian Democratic Party to affirm the principle of private property only as part of a larger program of redistribution aiming for a strong welfare state.[33] Calamandrei's formulation emphasizes that *all three* Resistance movements were trying to channel the high-energy politics of the moment into a "rigid" Constitution establishing the Italian Republic as a social democracy distinct from both the Fascist and the classical liberal regimes of the first half of the twentieth century.

Given their common ambition to mark a "new beginning," the Assembly did not spend much time in floor debates on esoteric arguments invoking Hans Kelsen or John Marshall. They focused on a more practical problem.

During the preceding decades, many leading jurists were engaged in, or sympathetic to, the Fascist legal order. As a consequence, the Marxists insisted that all members of the Court should be appointed by Parliament—since this body would be controlled by anti-Fascist parties for the foreseeable future. But this approach was resisted by more traditional legalists, who feared that parliamentary leaders would favor the appointment of party hacks at the expense of serious jurists.

When faced with this genuine predicament, the Assembly struggled to reach a sensible compromise, which required Parliament to share power with less partisan institutions. Under this settlement, Parliament would select five members, but so would the judges from the ordinary court system. The drafters left the final five appointments to the president of the Republic, a senior statesman who typically exercised ceremonial functions, but whose institutional independence would invite him to move beyond petty political considerations in making appointments. To further enhance the new Court's credibility, the Constitution required distinguished legal credentials of all members, and limited their tenure to a single nonrenewable term of twelve years (later reduced to nine).[34]

At this point, the assembly confronted a different problem: How to fit its new Constitutional Court into the traditional judicial system that had deep roots in legal practice. Like the French, the Italians had constructed a professional culture that relied on two distinct institutions—the Court of Cassation and the Council of State—to develop legal doctrine in private and public law in close collaboration with leading scholars in the academy. These long-standing institutions and traditions would confront an existential challenge once the Constitutional Court came onto the scene. The Court could roam across the entire legal landscape, using the Constitution's revolutionary texts as a platform for proclaiming new doctrines previously unknown to Italian law. How to reconcile the coming revolution in constitutional law with the ongoing work of the courts and scholarly centers that had previously held unchallenged sway?

The Assembly didn't have the time to work out the answer. When it first convened in the fall of 1946, it selected a seventy-five-member commission to formulate a comprehensive proposal to serve as the basis for plenary discussions. When these debates began in early 1947, they proved very fruitful—with the full chamber substantially revising preparatory drafts in the effort to build broad support. During this ongoing process of give-and-take, it was sensible to defer sustained consideration of the precise mission of the Constitutional Court—given that this would depend on a host of other elements in the emerging structure. Only in November did the Assembly begin to focus on the issues raised by the design of the Court, and by this point it was running out of time. It had promised the Italian People that the Constitution would go into effect on New Year's Day of 1948—marking the passage of a century since King Alberto handed down his Statuto in 1848. It was determined to make good on this commitment.

More than symbols were involved. Once the Constitution placed the Republic on a firm foundation, the nation could turn to parliamentary elections that would set its political course for the next five years. If the Assembly had breached its January 1 deadline, the provisional government would have had an incentive to prolong the constitutional proceedings and continue using its powers under the discredited Statuto to enact more legislation without another electoral test. Since the competing parties all believed these elections could change the parliamentary balance in their favor, they were eager to bring the era of provisionality to an end.

As a consequence, the Assembly left the judiciary articles incomplete when the Constitution came into effect. The New Year's Day text simply empowered the president, the judiciary, and Parliament each to appoint five of the Court's fifteen justices, and granted the new tribunal the power to determine "the constitutional legitimacy of laws." The Assembly then returned on January 22 for a final session, at which it passed a "constitutional statute" filling in some of the blanks.[35] Yet even this supplementary text was incomplete, and would require the new Parliament to enact further legislation before the Court could actually come into existence.

Would Parliament, once elected, follow up on this commitment?

After all, the general public was entirely unfamiliar with the practice of judicial review. If Parliament killed the Constitutional Court through inaction, almost nobody would notice—other than a few specialists. So far as ordinary Italians were concerned, it would be business as usual—with the Court of Cassation and Council of State incorporating the new constitutional texts in ways that didn't require them to radically revise their traditional ways of doing justice.

Indeed, it took eight years before the Constitutional Court finally decided its first case. We will be exploring the politics that led to this lengthy pause, but we will also be asking a more fundamental question: Why didn't Parliament continue to let the Court remain in limbo forever, and refuse to allow it ever to come into existence?

The mystery deepens once a key feature of Italian jurisprudence is considered. Like their French counterparts, Italian courts were thoroughly convinced that American-style judicial review was profoundly illegitimate. So long as the traditional tribunals—the Court of Cassation and the Council of State—continued to operate at the top of the judicial hierarchy, they would never strike down important political initiatives passed by the reigning political majority. If, however, Parliament did pass the final bills required to bring the Court into life, its newly appointed judges could well take aggressive action to strike down legislation enacted by the current government. Why would any sensible politician go out of his way to construct such a constitutional Frankenstein when no great popular movement was demanding it?

From the Founding to the Succession Crisis

To answer this question, begin with the struggle for political power during the founding period. While Christian Democrats and Marxists collaborated in hammering out a credible Constitution, matters proceeded differently on a second front. Once elected to office in 1946, representatives were also serving as a provisional Parliament, with a coalition government exercising sweeping legislative powers under the Statuto. At the outset, De Gasperi included all three movement parties within his government, but he soon began preparations to expel the Communists and their close allies, and form a centrist coalition with the aid of democratic Socialists on the Left, and anti-Fascist conservatives on the Right.

As early as January 1947, De Gasperi had gone to Washington and gained Truman's support for his strategy. He returned to Rome with a financially modest, but symbolically significant, $100 million loan from the United States for Italian reconstruction.[36] His diplomatic success then provided him with some political capital when he confronted much more punitive demands for war-time compensation from London as the price for concluding a formal peace treaty with Britain the following month.

De Gasperi had no choice but to sign this treaty, and he was happy to share the blame with the Communists and left-wing Socialists in his cabinet. But once the deed was done, he dismissed them from the cabinet in May. This meant that, during its final months, the Assembly led a schizophrenic existence—with the centrist provisional government determining current policy while the coalition of all three Resistance parties continued to operate as the driving force on constitutional issues. The Assembly's split personality had a paradoxical effect. Instead of provoking partisan backbiting, it encouraged a certain sobriety—dare I say statesmanship?

With the Marxists controlling 40 percent of the Assembly, the Christian Democrats could not be confident that they would control the government after the next election. Calamandrei eloquently made this point when the Assembly finally focused its attention on the Constitutional Court. He rose to the floor on November 28 to protest a design that he believed was motivated by the governing coalition's pursuit of its narrow self-interest. He urged the De Gasperi government to take a different approach:

> [You should try] to solve problems the way you would see them if tomorrow you were to fill the opposition's seats. I have heard from a friend, a painter, that one of the ways of seeing if a drawing is well done is to flip it and look at it upside-down: that way mistakes come to sight more easily. The same applies when we have to study constitutional questions that should be solved *sub specie aeternitatis*. My honorable colleagues, put the frame upside-down, and put yourselves for a moment, forgetting your solid majority, in the conditions of the minority: Would you propose the amendments you are defending today, were you in the opposition?[37]

This is precisely the sort of thing that John Rawls would have said if he had been magically transported to Rome in 1947. But De Gasperi rejected this invitation, and refused to put himself behind a Rawlsian "veil of ignorance." He simply deferred the crucial design issues to some future time—leaving the constitutional text so indeterminate that the new court could not come into existence unless later politicians took a more decisive position.

As we shall see, key actors did indeed rise to the occasion in the 1950s. But they did not do so in a Rawlsian fashion. Rather than follow Calamandrei in a search for a "sub specie aeternitatis" solution that transcended their time and place, the political protagonists created the Court in response to a wrenching succession crisis that shook the new Republic to its foundations.

Succession Crisis

The crisis began in earnest in the aftermath of Italy's second parliamentary election in 1951. But to set the stage, we must begin with the first electoral contest, which quickly followed the promulgation of the Constitution on New Year's Day. In April 1948, Christian Democrats squared off against the Marxist coalition in a pitched battle over the future of the Republic.

Their struggle was heightened by the February coup in Czechoslovakia—in which Stalinists destroyed a government broadly similar to the Communist / Socialist / Christian Democratic coalition that had formerly ruled Italy. Now that De Gasperi had expelled the hard Left from his governing coalition, would the Communists and their Socialist allies persuade their countrymen to join the Soviet Union's side in the impending Cold War?

With the CIA pumping money into Italy's Christian Democratic Party, and the Comintern doing the same for the Communists, both sides put a massive effort into popular mobilization in the electoral campaign. The result was a ringing endorsement of De Gasperi's leadership—with the Christian Democrats winning 48.5 percent of the vote, which translated into an absolute majority of seats in both the Chamber of Deputies and the Senate. Moreover, a new Socialist party—the Social Democrats—gained 7 percent of the vote on an anti-Communist platform. This left the Democratic Front, dominated by the Communists, with only 31 percent of the votes and seats.[38]

De Gasperi could have used his victory to form an exclusively Christian Democratic government. But he refused this temptation, continuing to include other center-right parties in his governing coalition. At the same time, he made emphatic gestures to the Left—creating a system of social security, and other programs, that sustained the Constitution's social democratic commitments.

The Left dismissed these moves as mere fig leafs for a renascent capitalism. Nevertheless, it would be wrong to accept their claim that, as De Gasperi formed a series of coalition governments over the Parliament's five-year term, he was engaged in an all-out war against the constitutional principles laid down by the Constituent Assembly in the name of the People. To be sure, he was giving them a Christian Democratic, rather than a Marxist, spin. But whoever said that Marxists had a monopoly on social democracy?[39]

Nevertheless, the election returns did mark a shift in the contending parties' orientation to the revolutionary Constitution. At the Constituent Assembly, the Communists and Socialists were skeptical of a Constitutional Court—fearing that judicial elitists would veto sweeping Socialist initiatives when the Left came to power.[40] But now that they had been pushed to the political sidelines, they took a different view. They saw the Constitution as an enduring monument to their role as anti-Fascist leaders at the Constituent Assembly. Given this understanding, judicial review no longer seemed an elitist enterprise. Instead, the Constitutional Court seemed to be a promising mechanism for preserving the People's foundational commitment to social democracy against the threat of a politically ascendant capitalism.

The question was whether the Christian Democrats would agree. Now that the "veil of ignorance" had been lifted, they had little to gain—and a good deal to lose—by supporting the parliamentary enactment of a court bill. Once the Court came into existence, it might well strike down key elements of De Gasperi's legislative program. Why would he take this risk?[41]

De Gasperi was stuck between a rock and a hard place. His opposition to the "flexible" Statuto was central to his decades of struggle against Fascism, with his advocacy of a Constitutional Court playing a major role in his campaign for a "rigid" Constitution. But he was also unwilling to make it possible for a real-world Court to strike down his real-world initiatives.

He responded to this dilemma in Machiavellian fashion. He publicly supported the efforts of Calamandrei and other jurists to initiate the complex committee process required to prepare a court bill for parliamentary approval. At the same time, he worked behind the scenes to ensure that committee deliberation proceeded at a glacial pace.[42] As a consequence, Parliament did not take up the court bill until shortly before its term expired in 1953.[43]

This last-minute proposal would have guaranteed De Gasperi a dominant role in selecting appointees to the fifteen-member Court. Recall that the Constitution had given Parliament, as well as the president, the power to name five constitutional judges—with the professional judiciary choosing the remaining five. Under the bill that De Gasperi allowed onto the floor, a simple parliamentary majority would have sufficed to approve nominations—giving the prime minister effective control. De Gasperi would have also played a decisive role in the five presidential appointments, since the bill only permitted the president to appoint justices who had gained the prior approval of the prime minister and his cabinet.

The self-aggrandizing character of De Gasperi's initiative provoked a rebellion by Calamandrei and other constitutionalists, who denounced the measure in floor debate. Even more significantly, President Luigi Einaudi refused to support the prime minister's power play.

Einaudi had been elected by Parliament to his largely ceremonial office in May 1948 when De Gasperi was expelling the Communists and left-wing Socialists from his government. So far as the prime minister was concerned, Einaudi's ascent to the presidency was an ideal peace offering to the center-right parties he needed for his new coalition. Einaudi had been a lifelong monarchist, but he had broken with the king during the war and fled to Switzerland, where he proceeded to publicly denounce Mussolini. This dramatic step, as well as his recent success as head of the Bank of Italy, made him an ideal choice for the new parliamentary majority, which now included center-right parties that had campaigned for the monarchy at the 1946 referendum.

Because Einaudi had never been a Christian Democrat, there was nothing to stop him from denouncing the effort to make him De Gasperi's rubber stamp. He threatened to resign if Parliament passed the original proposal.

With general elections looming, the prime minister was unwilling to call the president's bluff. The prospect of Einaudi's condemning him for Mussolini-like behavior would have been a terrible blow to his campaign. Instead of playing with fire, De Gasperi accepted amendments that authorized the president to make five appointments without gaining the prior approval of the prime minister and his cabinet. Once obliged to retreat, the prime minister also accepted Calamandrei's demand for supermajority parliamentary support for its five nominees. As a practical matter, this left the prime minister with control of only two or three appointments—since he would be required to accept some nominations from the Left to gain the requisite supermajority for the entire slate. The bill then passed into law just as the old Parliament's term came to end.

This was a significant step: When all was said and done, De Gasperi had thrown his support behind a Court that could realistically operate as a constitutional defender of the revolutionary achievements to which the Christian Democrats—no less than the Marxists—had been committed in their struggle against Fascism.

Yet the Court was hardly De Gasperi's first priority as he looked forward to the coming elections. He was then 72, and recognized that the parliamentary elections of 1953 would serve as his final electoral test before his party's leadership passed on to his successors. (In fact, he died the following year.) It was now Communism, not Fascism, which was the principal threat to his vision of Christian Democracy. And he was determined to secure his political legacy by changing the electoral rules of the game.

De Gasperi's Defeat

Under the terms of his new electoral law, any political coalition that won 50 percent of the popular vote would be awarded *two-thirds* of the seats in the Chamber of Deputies. Because the Christian Democrats had received

48.5 percent in the previous election, this super-bonus promised to guarantee De Gasperi's party political supremacy for the indefinite future.

The legitimacy of this "scam law," as it was derisively called by opponents, became the central issue in the election—while the last-minute Court statute was ignored throughout the campaign. Predictably, the Left organized a united front to defeat this blatant effort to permanently consign it to the sidelines. But this time the Marxists were joined by smaller centrist groups—many with roots in the Resistance.

Nevertheless, the Christian Democratic coalition seemed sure to outmatch them. Not only did it begin with a strong electoral base; it could also point to real economic gains obtained under the Marshall Plan as proof to mainstream voters of the benefits of the American alliance and the dangers of alienating the West by voting Communist as the Cold War escalated.

These competing appeals generated a remarkable 94 percent turnout—and an even more remarkable result. The voters delivered a serious blow to Christian Democracy, reducing its support from 48.5 percent to 40.1 percent. Even more important, the party's center-right partners failed to make up for this shortfall—contributing only 9.8 percent of the votes to the coalition. This added up to 49.9 percent—just short of the majority required for the super-bonus.

Under normal circumstances, 49.9 percent would have amounted to an impressive victory, enabling De Gasperi to continue to serve as the country's only prime minister since the Founding of the Republic. Looking at the bare statistics, his position appeared even more impressive, since the Communists and their Left-Socialist allies only improved their vote from 31 percent to 35 percent—leaving him plenty of room to obtain a stable center-right majority.

So much the worse for number crunching. Everybody understood that 1953 wasn't an ordinary election. It represented the popular repudiation of De Gasperi's charismatic claims to leadership based on his historic role in the anti-Fascist Resistance. When the new Parliament came into session, De Gasperi immediately fell from power—leaving his successors to struggle inconclusively for political ascendancy. Nevertheless, they could agree on one thing: the hero of the Resistance should not only be denied the premiership, but should also be stripped of his formal position as head of the Christian Democratic party—a post that he had held continuously since he called for its creation during the dark days of Fascism.

De Gasperi died a few months later, provoking a popular outpouring of gratitude for his extraordinary contributions to the nation. But there was one item missing from his long list of achievements. While he had given greatly to the Nation, he had failed to cement his post-Resistance politics of anticommunism into the foundations of the Republic. The Center-Right sustained its political ascendancy throughout the Cold War period, but it never managed to win a decisive popular mandate for sweeping constitutional amendments that would have obliterated the revolutionary principles expressed at the Founding. To the contrary: despite the passage of three-quarters of a century, Italy's Constitution sets out the framework of social democracy constructed by the three movement parties of the Resistance.

The Rise of the Court

It is one thing for a Constitution to announce fundamental principles; quite another for the judiciary to transform them into the living law of the Republic. Although the legal foundations were now complete, the Court could not move into operation without a full complement of fifteen justices—and Parliament had great difficulty making its five appointments. The Christian Democrats and their close allies controlled about 45 percent of the seats; but the revised court bill required supermajority support; and without De Gasperi, the party's squabbling leaders lacked the authority to convince enough right-wing allies to vote for a plausible slate of center-right appointments. The impasse continued for two years, with the Left repeatedly demanding a share in the appointment power. As the months and years passed, the recurring failure became an increasing embarrassment to the governing coalition, now headed by Christian Democrat Antonio Segni.

The only way for Segni to appear decisive was to grant large concessions to the Left.[44] In November 1955, the Chamber of Deputies finally approved a five-judge slate that included only two Christian Democratic appointments—together with a Communist, a Socialist, and a Liberal. The ideological diversity of the panel was enhanced by Giovanni Gronchi, the new president of the Republic, who named "one pre-fascist Liberal, one independent Catholic, one Christian Democrat . . . , one technician with monarchist sympathies, and one republican jurist."[45] With the addition of five professional judges, the Court's personnel had a distinctive profile. Rather than looking like rubber stamps for the ruling coalition, the justices emerged from the political impasse with professional backgrounds that gave them the credibility they needed to establish an independent role for themselves.

This was by no means foreordained. Suppose, for example, that the 1953 election had turned out slightly differently—and that the Christian Democrats and their allies had won 50.1 percent, not 49.9 percent, of the vote. Under this scenario, a triumphant De Gasperi would have continued in office until his death. Governing with the benefit of the super-bonus, he would have been in firm command of a two-thirds majority in Parliament. With the Left pushed to the margins, he would have moved quickly to appoint five strong center-right judges to the Court. Given De Gasperi's lead, President Einaudi might well have added five more of the same.[46]

Under this scenario, the Court's claim to political independence would have lacked credibility. As the Center-Right and the Marxist Left squared off to debate the burning issues of the 1950s, the Court would have emerged as merely another political weapon deployed by the dominant Christian Democratic coalition.

In short, a strong and independent Court was a direct result of the succession crisis generated by De Gasperi's departure from the scene. Given its outcome, the group of politically diverse and professionally prominent justices could aspire to a very different role. Instead of taking sides in contemporary politics, they could emerge as defenders of the anti-Fascist Constitution that the Christian Democrats and Marxists had hammered out together at the Founding.

But they would have to act quickly. Otherwise, their infant institution would be sidelined by the traditional Italian judiciary. In a transitional provision, the Constituent Assembly had granted ordinary courts the power to interpret the constitutional text pending the creation of the new Court. Since the gestation period took eight years, these judges had responded to almost 200 concrete cases, in which they expressed an accumulating skepticism about the Constitution's claim to supremacy. Instead, they chose to understand their interim constitutional role within their legal tradition's deeply rooted opposition to "government by judges." In their emerging jurisprudence, the ordinary courts were only comfortable granting the Constitution the same status as ordinary legislation. Just as a statute of 1948 trumped earlier laws, so would the Constitution of 1948. But they were not inclined to claim that the Constitution empowered them to invalidate laws passed by contemporary political majorities after that date.

Even when dealing with earlier statutory eras, the courts followed longstanding tradition by granting Parliament and the bureaucracy wide-ranging discretion. These sweeping acts of deference insulated many Fascist laws from serious critique. They also trivialized the new Constitution's guarantees of social rights, treating them as mere programmatic ideals requiring further legislation. In short, as the new Court held its first session in 1956, the constitutional principles enacted in the name of the Italian People were headed toward legal oblivion.[47]

But the electoral repudiation of the "scam law," followed by the Christian Democratic repudiation of De Gasperi, created a "legitimacy vacuum" that cleared the way for the fifteen newly appointed Justices to take decisive action with remarkable speed.[48] The Court's very first decision involved a paradigmatic Fascist statute, requiring citizens to obtain formal police permission before they could publicize their views in posters or flyers. This set up a straightforward challenge under Article 21: "Everyone has the right to freely express their thoughts in speech, writing, or any other form of communication." Despite the sweep of this guarantee, the ordinary courts had upheld thirty criminal convictions against constitutional challenge. In defending these convictions before the new Court, the attorney general presented a broad argument that would have insulated all Fascist legislation from scrutiny. On his view, it was up to the ordinary courts to determine the continuing validity of statutes passed before 1948—since they could discharge this function under the traditional principle requiring judges to sweep away earlier statutes when inconsistent with later legislation. Instead of preempting the traditional judiciary, the new Court should confine itself to the assessment of modern statutes passed after that date—it was only here that the Constitution's status as *supreme* law came into play.

The justices rejected this gap-filling role. Not only did they strike down the Fascist law authorizing police censorship. They issued a sweeping rejection of the trivializing interpretation of social rights advanced by the ordinary courts during the previous eight years. The Court denied that these grants should be viewed as mere programmatic goals addressed to Parliament; they were instead vital sources of higher law requiring judicial elaboration. With the announcement of its Judgment #1, the Court put the political branches on notice that it was determined to serve as the ultimate guardian of the revolutionary Republic's Founding principles now that the struggle against Mussolini was receding into history.

The way the Court delivered Judgment #1 was almost as important as the message itself. Like their French counterparts, Italian judges typically render their decisions in lapidary form—citing relevant statutory provisions without advancing elaborate rationales for their legal conclusions. This latter task is performed by university jurists, whose commentaries provide the larger framework for case-by-case decision.

The justices broke with this deeply entrenched tradition. They refused to allow the scholarly community to explain the constitutional meaning of their judgments to the outside world. They would speak in their own voice, writing lengthy opinions that would anchor professional and public debate.

What is more, all pronouncements would be issued in the name of the Court, without any concurring or dissenting opinions. In taking this final step, the justices weren't doing anything extraordinary. Continental courts have for centuries abjured the individualistic opinion-writing familiar in the English-speaking world. But now that the Court was its own principal spokesmen, its insistence on unanimity escalated its claim to centrality. Scholars could not use dissenting opinions as platforms for critique. If they disagreed, they would have to launch direct attacks on the Court's reasoning—yet this confrontational posture was deeply uncongenial for a juristic community that had been engaged in ongoing collaboration with judges for centuries.

The Court's Judgment #1 is often likened to *Marbury v. Madison*. But the analogy greatly understates the revolutionary character of the Italian decision. Number 1 transformed the very idea of legal authority on the Continent. This wouldn't have happened if Italian politics had taken a different turn and managed to avoid the succession crisis generated by De Gasperi's defeat. It was only this crisis which created the legitimacy vacuum required for the appointment of judges with the independence required to advance the Court's radical assertion of constitutional supremacy.

Time Four: Consolidation

Yet even this assertion had limits. The justices decisively displaced traditional centers of legal authority, but they acted with great restraint on the political front. The next fifteen years saw the rise of the New Left and its challenge to the political establishment. While the Christian Democrats managed to sustain their electoral ascendancy, the 1960s generated a series of high-stakes confrontations that could have invited intervention by the Court. But the justices played no role in these struggles. Throughout this entire period, they only struck down laws passed during the Fascist, or earlier, eras.[49] These laws had few defenders, so judicial intervention carried little risk of political backlash. Moreover, the Court cleverly encouraged parliamentary recognition of its authority within this safety zone.

Once again, Judgment #1 can serve as a model. Although the justices invalidated the Fascist grant of absolute discretion to suppress political speech, they did not impose a flat ban on governmental efforts to restrict the distribution of political tracts and placards. They simply put the burden on Parliament to come up with appropriate rules that respected the fundamental importance of freedom of expression. This allowed the government of the day to enact legislation protecting its interests while simultaneously recognizing the Court's ultimate authority over the rules of the game. After fifteen years of repeated engagement, the Court's legitimacy was firmly entrenched in the political, no less than the legal, sphere.

Only at this point did the justices begin to intervene on hot-button issues of contemporary politics. Unsurprisingly, this ongoing encounter has propelled the Constitutional Court far beyond its first-generation jurisprudence.

But I will leave this story to others.[50] It is enough, for present purposes, to have traced Italy's developmental path through four stages—from (1) mobilized Resistance to (2) a revolutionary Founding to (3) the assertion of judicial supremacy after a succession crisis to (4) the political and legal consolidation of judicial authority during the next half century.

Italy versus France

This pattern is familiar by now, but it suggests a surprising conclusion. The rise of constitutionalism in Italy is broadly similar to the course of events in India and South Africa, despite all the obvious differences in their social, economic, and political conditions. But it is radically different from the path followed in France, despite Italy's many cultural and economic similarities to its northern neighbor. When the Court was announcing Judgment #1, no similar French institution had even come into existence. Instead, the Fourth Republic was still in power, and Charles de Gaulle remained in self-imposed political exile on his country estate. It was only General de Gaulle's later overthrow of the existing regime that ultimately generated a comparable assertion of authority by the Constitutional Council of the Fifth Republic—but only after a similar dynamic that propelled the Gaullist Republic from Time One through Time Four.

Before considering how the Fifth Republic complicates our understanding of revolutionary constitutionalism, let's step back to consider the larger themes suggested by our first four case studies.

CHAPTER 6

A Progress Report?

I have been focusing on two aspects of the transition from Time One to Time Two. The first involves the situation of revolutionary "outsiders" as they become "insiders"; the second deals with former "insiders" displaced by the triumphant "outsiders."

Begin with the outsiders as they become insiders. In contrast to the *hegemonic* Congress Parties in India and South Africa, the Resistance in France and Italy was fragmented into three parties—Communists, Socialists, and Christian Democrats. These groups emerged from distinct historical and ideological commitments, with different symbolic leaders, so they predictably experienced greater difficulty in sustaining the organizational unity required to win broad popular consent for a "new beginning" in constitutional life.

This *fragmentation problem* was rendered more acute in France by virtue of de Gaulle's success as a military leader of the Free French Forces. As Nazi collaborationists fell from power, the outsider General struggled with the outsider movement parties in competing efforts to mobilize the People in support of their rival constitutional visions.

In contrast, the fragmentation problem in Italy "merely" required the sustained collaboration of atheist Marxists and religious Catholics. This was no small task, but the Communist / Socialist / Christian Democratic coalition managed to hammer out a Constitution despite their escalating political disagreements. In contrast, it took their French counterparts two Constituent Assemblies to win a mandate from the voters—and even then, the General continued to appeal to the People to reverse their judgment.

Turn next to consider the flip side of the transition: How do former "insiders" respond to their displacement by revolutionary "outsiders"?

The "easy" cases—at least analytically!—are represented by India and France, where the revolutionary forces occupied a power vacuum left by the collapse of the old regime. In the French case, the political standing of Vichy collaborationists had been utterly destroyed by the end of World War II. While de Gaulle and the Resistance parties debated the nature of the constitution of the Fourth Republic, their debate wasn't complicated further by a credible movement seeking to preserve Vichy.

The Indian case also has its source in World War II, but this time it was the British victory, not the Nazi defeat, that generated the collapse of the old regime. The Attlee government could have chosen to maintain the military forces required to sustain law and order on the subcontinent, and give Lord Mountbatten adequate time to construct a constitution for the entire sub-continent that could gain the consent of both Congress and the Muslim League. But given the terrible losses sustained by Britain during the war, At-tlee refused to bear the military burden, allowing partition to proceed—and leaving both India and Pakistan to confront the challenges of constitution-alism on their own.

It would be worthwhile to consider why India succeeded and Pakistan failed to generate a credible constitution—especially since the Muslim League led by Muhammed Jinnah was inspired by a secular and social democratic program similar to Nehru's Congress Party. But I leave this tragic compar-ison to another time. For the present, it is more important to contrast the suc-cess stories in France and India with the very different success stories in Italy and South Africa.

In this second pair of cases, the defenders of the old regime did not simply collapse, but remained forces to be reckoned with during the transition from Time One to Time Two. But once again, the old-timers' sources of power were different. The apartheid government in Pretoria commanded formidable mil-itary forces, which required Mandela to engage in negotiations with de Klerk on an interim Constitution if he hoped to achieve a relatively peaceful tran-sition. Only then could the two sides clear a path for the decisive repudiation of apartheid in the permanent Constitution enacted by the first interracial Parliament.

The old regime also remained a force in Italy, but for different reasons. Unlike de Klerk in South Africa, the king's government was in no position to use military force to compel the revolutionary Resistance to the bargaining table—for the simple reason that the Italian army had utterly disintegrated once Mussolini fell from power. Instead, it was up to Togliatti and De Gas-peri, and their respective movements, to decide whether to accept the king's invitation to join his provisional government of national unity. Once they took this step, however, they were obliged to take the Statuto seriously, just as the ANC was obliged to take the interim Constitution seriously. As in South Africa, this did not stop the movement parties of the Italian Resistance from

TABLE 6.1. TRANSITION FROM TIME ONE TO TIME TWO

Insiders → Outsiders ↓	Hegemonic	Fragmented
Collapse	India	France
Constitutional Legacy	South Africa	Italy

transforming their provisional government into a platform for launching free elections that enabled them to replace the monarchy and its Statuto with a Republican Constitution that spoke in the name of the People.[1]

Nevertheless, other revolutionary movements have not had such success in liberating themselves from the *constitutional legacies* of the old regime—and we will be exploring the unhappy consequences of such entanglements in Part 2. But for now, Table 6.1 summarizes the basic insider / outsider points emerging from our work thus far.

We can now move to the next stages in the constitutional dynamic: succession crisis (Time Three) and consolidation of judicial supremacy (Time Four).

When Nehru, Mandela, and De Gasperi left the stage, they were replaced by leaders who lacked comparable personal charisma. The not-so-charismatic members of the political elite immediately began to compete for top positions. In each case, their infighting created openings for Justices to assert that it was they, and not the leaders of the old revolutionary parties, who should be relied upon to safeguard the constitutional principles for which the People had sacrificed so much during their struggle against the old regime.

It is one thing to advance such claims in landmark opinions at Time Three; it is quite another to gain their broad acceptance. This required a great deal of judicial statesmanship—both in timing the judiciary's pronouncements to exploit momentary political configurations that encouraged ruling elites to accept such claims, and in choosing cases that raise issues of principle that resonate with the general public. Even then, judicial claims to supremacy remained fragile, and required much more work before they became entrenched in the evolving framework of government.

This is the business of Time Four—in which an increasingly self-confident legal profession engages in an ongoing process that consolidates the judiciary's claims to supremacy.

India and Italy provide classic examples of these intergenerational dynamics; South Africa provides an important variation on the ideal-typical form of development. The French Fourth Republic, however, is the big exception—the judiciary made no similar claims to supremacy during the regime's brief existence. Nevertheless, the Fourth Republic's experience provides essential background for understanding the rise of judicial review during the Fifth Republic—which, I argue in Chapter 7, does indeed conform to the classic model typified by India and Italy.

So let's focus first on the Indian and Italian case studies. For all their differences, there is a fundamental similarity in their patterns of intergenerational evolution. During Time Two, courts in both countries fail to assert their constitutional supremacy over the charismatic leaders who have led their movement parties to adopt revolutionary Constitutions in the name of the People. This period of judicial subordination comes to an end only during the succession crises of Time Three.

To be sure, the modes of Time Two subordination were different in the two cases. As soon as the Indian Constitution came into effect, Nehru and the Congress Party pushed through a remarkable constitutional amendment authorizing the government to insulate their legislative initiatives from *all* judicial scrutiny by listing them on Schedule Nine. When this sweeping assertion of parliamentary supremacy came before the Court, the judges completely capitulated—refusing even to issue opinions that suggested, in dicta, that they might one day restrict Schedule Nine's scope. Instead, the Court contented itself with constitutional interventions on relatively uncontroversial issues that would not provoke parliamentary backlash. It was only the shattering succession crisis provoked by Indira Gandhi that gave the Court a political opening to declare that it would henceforth protect the Constitution's "basic structure" against parliamentary efforts to amend it.

The Italian story is structurally similar, if less dramatic. Where Nehru passed an aggressive constitutional amendment, De Gasperi preempted the threat of judicial review by stalling on implementing legislation required to create the Constitutional Court until the very end of his time in office.

Similarly, the Italian succession crisis was also far less intense than its Indian counterpart. Nevertheless, the voters' rejection of De Gasperi's "scam law" was a decisive rebuke to the Christian Democrats' continuing authority to speak in the higher-lawmaking voice of the Italian People. Even though it did not escalate to the epic heights reached by the popular repudiation of Gandhi's Emergency Rule in 1977, De Gasperi's resignation, like Indira Gandhi's, opened up an analogous legitimacy gap that permitted the Italian Court's decisive entry onto the constitutional stage.

To be sure, the initial interventions by the Italian Constitutional Court were more cautious than those of its Indian counterpart. Given the massive scale of Gandhi's defeat, that Court was in a position to sweep away key constitutional amendments passed during the Emergency—claiming the remarkable authority to safeguard the "basic structure" of the revolutionary Constitution of 1950 against repudiation by future politicians and parties. In contrast, the Italian Court moved more cautiously, contenting itself with invalidating Fascist laws for a couple of decades before it challenged more recent legislation. Moreover, it has never developed anything like a "basic structure" doctrine enabling it to assert absolute supremacy over transformative amendments approved by Parliament.

Nevertheless, as in India, the Italian Court's initial successes during Time Three laid the foundation for a much broader assertion of authority during the following generation, in which the Court has asserted its authority over an increasingly broad range of hot-button issues. To be sure, the high courts of these two countries expressed themselves in the distinctive juridical languages of Anglo-Indian common law and Continental-Italian civil law, and through different institutional arrangements. Yet these large differences between India and Italy should not blind us to the fact that the same four-stage dynamic emerged from their common revolutionary experience. Indeed, given the dramatic differences in almost all other aspects of Indian / Italian economic, social, and cultural life, this four-stage pattern is quite remarkable.

To a significant degree, the pattern expresses a predictable development in legal consciousness over time. During the founding period, Indian / Italian jurists had been rigorously trained to frame their arguments within a legal system based on the principle of parliamentary sovereignty. Great constitutionalists like India's Ambedkar or Italy's Calamandrei were truly exceptional in their self-conscious efforts to challenge this principle. While they succeeded in carving out a space for Constitutional Courts in the constitutional text, the members of these new tribunals were exquisitely aware that the bulk of the judicial profession would respond skeptically to their initial assertions of authority to strike down parliamentary legislation. What is more, they could be sure of an even more hostile response from the general public if their decisions provoked emphatic opposition from charismatic prime ministers like Nehru or De Gasperi.

It was only at Time Three, when these symbolic leaders were replaced by less charismatic successors, that the members of the new Court could seriously consider a grander role for themselves—in which they would claim that they, not Parliament, were the more legitimate guardians of the constitutional legacy of the Revolution.

Success was by no means guaranteed. In both India and Italy, it required judicial statesmanship of the highest order. Even if the legitimacy of its landmark opinions was sustained in the short run, the ascendancy of the Constitutional Court over Parliament was only consolidated over the next generation.

Once again, Indian / Italian histories suggest how the dynamics of legal culture aided this Time Four process. In both countries, early Court exercises of judicial review became the grist for a familiar kind of doctrinal debate among lawyers, judges, and scholars—serving as starting points for the elaboration of more general rules and principles required to resolve later controversies.

This developing jurisprudence also prepared the way for a fundamental change in the training of succeeding generations of legal professionals. They were no longer invited to view constitutional law as a new arrival on the scene containing revolutionary ideas categorically distinct from the "hard law" surrounding subjects like contract and property. Instead, lectures and course books provided an increasingly elaborate framework for the accumulating case law. This provided the rising generation of lawyers with the cultural tools they needed to treat constitutional *law* as fundamentally similar to other legal domains that they could discuss with professional self-confidence. Once again, this point is easy to ignore because standard Anglo-Indian doctrinal frameworks are so different from their Continental-Italian analogues.

In emphasizing this remarkable commonality, I do not suggest that the professionalization of constitutional law at Time Four guarantees that the past achievements of Indian or Italian jurists will endure as these countries confront the political, economic, and military challenges of the twenty-first century. We have already seen how India's current prime minister, Narendra Modi, is challenging the Supreme Court's defense of the Nehruvian revolutionary inheritance. I will defer a similar exercise in the Italian case, since this would require a more elaborate consideration of the country's efforts to integrate its revolutionary legacy with the rise of the European Union—a subject that I will be treating in the second volume.

For now, it is more important to integrate South Africa into the Indian / Italian analysis. When Ambedkar and Calamandrei were working in the late 1940s, judicial review seemed an American exception to the general rule of parliamentary sovereignty—and even the luster of the American example had been tarnished by Franklin Roosevelt's then-recent effort to pack the Supreme Court to overcome its decisions invalidating key New Deal legislation.

In contrast, when Mandela and de Klerk started their hard bargaining in the early 1990s, they were living in a different jurisprudential universe. The Constitutional Courts of India and the Continent had successfully consolidated their authority; and the Warren Court was inspiring emulation on a worldwide scale. The perceived success of judicial review opened up a new institutional possibility. Perhaps a Constitutional Court was not only a valuable tool for protecting the revolutionary legacy against its betrayal by political opportunists at later moments; perhaps it could also serve as a short-term vehicle for enforcing the constitutional bargain reached by Mandela and de Klerk as they tried to construct a peaceful transition from apartheid?

As we have seen, this "safeguard" function was assigned to the judiciary in the provisional Constitution established at the roundtable at Kempton Park in 1993, which required the Court to determine whether the permanent Constitution, negotiated by the first multiracial Parliament in 1997, was consistent with the fundamental principles reached in 1993. As we have also seen, the Court did not aggressively discharge its safeguard function in its real-world operation. Nevertheless, its novel role during the transition created institutional momentum that enabled it to emerge as a major constitutional actor during the Mandela years. In exercising strong forms of judicial review during the founding period, the court's activity contrasts sharply with the passivity of its Indian and Italian counterparts during the years when Nehru and De Gasperi were in power.

Mandela's conduct in office also helped. He did not respond in Nehruvian fashion when the Court imposed serious limits on his own powers in office. Instead, he made it clear that he would obey the Justices' opinions even when they circumscribed his sphere of independent action.

As a consequence, the Court was in a far stronger position when Mandela's departure opened the way for the competent but uncharismatic Thabo Mbeki to win the presidency in 1999. Although the Justices continued to generate landmark opinions, they did not play a key role in the country's first great succession crisis in 2007—when Mbeki tried to remain in power despite the Constitution's prohibition on serving a third term in office as president. Instead, it was the old-time revolutionaries of the ANC, not the Court, who played a decisive role in checking Mbeki's overweening ambitions.

Ten years later, the courts have played a more significant role in halting Jacob Zuma's similar effort to maintain himself in power despite the two-term limitation. Once again, however, the crucial decisions were made by old-time revolutionaries at the ANC convention, with the professional jurists only playing a supporting role.

It is far too soon to say whether South Africa's new president, Cyril Rama-phosa, will succeed in restoring popular confidence in the revolutionary Constitution left behind by Mandela and a very different ANC. Even if he and his successors manage to repair the damage done by Zuma and his corrupt cronies, the Indian / Italian stories still serve as cautionary tales. They suggest that constitutional courts still have lots of work to do before they can con-solidate their authority during Time Four. To be sure, South Africa's Court did have an early head start over its Indian / Italian counterparts in gaining respect for its landmark opinions. But as memories of the South African rev-olution continue to fade in lived experience, it remains an open question whether the Court will succeed in convincing the rising generation that it de-serves recognition as the authoritative guardian of South Africa's constitu-tional legacy.

Within this framework, the French experience appears exceptional. In con-trast to India / Italy / South Africa, the Fourth Republic failed to take judicial review seriously. When de Gaulle opposed the Constituent Assembly's ini-tiatives, his critique emphasized the importance of a strong presidency, not an independent Court.

The General's overthrow of the postwar regime, however, begins a very dif-ferent story—which I tell in the next two chapters. Chapter 7 deals with Times One and Two—exploring how the General and his allies managed to over-throw the parliamentary Fourth Republic and mobilize broad popular support for their vision of a presidentialist Fifth Republic. While the revolutionary Gaullist Constitution broke new ground in creating a Constitutional Council with the power to invalidate legislation, the Council refused to challenge De Gaulle's conduct even when it blatantly violated explicit textual commands. In subordinating itself to the charismatic Founder during Time Two, the Council conformed to the standard pattern played out in India and Italy.

Chapter 8, however, turns to consider key turning points in constitutional development in the decades after the General left the scene. As a series of po-litical leaders and parties struggled to gain control of the presidency, they created a series of opportunities for the Council to assert an increasingly aggressive role as the ultimate defender of the Founding constitutional legacy. By the 1990s, France had moved beyond Time Three to Time Four. Indeed, during the first decade of the twentieth century, it won a decisive confirmation of its guardianship role when France undertook a fundamental reassessment of its Gaullist inheritance in an extraordinary deliberative process. As we shall see, this resulted in the consolidation of the Council's constitutional authority across a broad range of issues over which it had not previously exercised its jurisdiction. All of this suggests that the country's short-lived experiment with the Fourth Republic should be treated as a truly exceptional exception to the general rule. Over the longer run, the Fifth Republic has followed its sister Republics of India and Italy down the same pathway from Time One to Time Four (with South Africa's shorter history only giving it the opportunity to continue its distinctive forms of Time Three struggle.)

The Fifth Republic's revolutionary dynamic is not only significant in itself. The French system has also served as a model for many other national efforts at constitutional reconstruction—indeed, the Fifth Republic's design has been far more influential than the American version of presidential government. Given its pervasive influence over the past few decades, it is important to consider how Gaullist institutional structures have shaped the political life of the nations that have adopted them.

We begin this inquiry with Poland's revolutionary break with Communist authoritarianism in 1989. Chapter 9 explores the historical accidents that led Lech Wałesa and Solidarity to borrow the Gaullist model, and use it as the basis for a provisional constitutional arrangement that enabled their movement party's rise to power in the name of the People.

But Wałesa was no de Gaulle. Despite his charismatic centrality, his election to the presidency did not enable him to win the support of other movement leaders who controlled Solidarity's delegation in Parliament. Instead, it led to a bitter power struggle which split the revolutionary movement party into fragments—generating a crisis of governability that increasingly alienated tens of millions of ordinary Poles who had enthusiastically backed Solidarity during its decade of revolutionary struggle against the Soviet Empire in the 1980s.

The Gaullist design also had a devastating impact on the formulation of a permanent Constitution. Despite their recognition of the importance of the task, the rival Solidarity factions failed to transcend their divisions to agree on the terms of a new Constitution. They were still quarreling over key provisions when the voters, disgusted by the ongoing factional strife, threw

Solidarity out of office and elected a new coalition, dominated by former Communists, who promised to establish the stable government that the country required to meet its future social and economic challenges.

Chapter 10 considers how this post-Solidarity coalition, led by well-known former Communists, finally managed to enact Poland's current Constitution in 1997. Given its political complexion, the coalition supporting the Constitution could not credibly claim that they were speaking for the revolutionary movement which had made such great sacrifices for a "new beginning" in the political life of the nation during the 1980s. Instead of serving as the culminating commitment of a revolutionary movement, the modern Polish Constitution is an elite construction.

This basic fact continues to haunt Polish politics. Since 1997, nationalist demagogues have repeatedly condemned the 1997 Constitution as the work of Warsaw elites who betrayed Solidarity's deepest aspirations. When their populist appeals propelled them to victory at the parliamentary elections of 2015, they deployed their authenticity critique to legitimate their authoritarian assault on the existing constitutional framework.

The Gaullist model bears a great deal of responsibility for this tragic turn of events. If Wałesa and Solidarity's other leaders had remained faithful to the parliamentary model, they would have had far greater success in constitutionalizing the charisma of their remarkable mass movement. But the Gaullist model seduced them into a form of fragmentation they would have otherwise rejected—and the Polish people may well pay a heavy price for the early fragmentation that prevented the triumphant legitimation of a Solidarity Constitution in the name of the People in the immediate aftermath of the revolution of 1989.

We will continue our inquiry into the worldwide influence of the Gaullist model in later case studies. Most notably Chapter 12 explores the surprising ways in which Iranian revolutionaries self-consciously used the Fifth Republic as a model in hammering out a Constitution for their Islamic Republic in 1979, and how this model has continued to shape Iran's constitutional development during the decades since Ayatollah Khomeini's death in 1989 passed on his legacy to his less-charismatic successors.

But for the moment, I hope I have said enough to encourage you to join me in exploring French developments that have had such a profound impact on the world since Charles de Gaulle spearheaded his revolutionary assault on the Fourth Republic in 1958.

❀ PART TWO

Elaborations

CHAPTER 7

De Gaulle's Republic:
The Outsider Returns

During its first decade, the French Fourth Republic displayed a familiar pattern—with movement parties losing their revolutionary unity and political energy as they confronted a series of divisive policy issues. But as the 1950s proceeded, the country endured an especially wrenching succession crisis— with Charles de Gaulle successfully overthrowing the parliamentary regime that he had failed to displace during the high-energy politics and constitutional referenda of 1946.

This dramatic turnaround was the result of an existential crisis provoked by the struggle of the National Liberation Front (Front de Libération Nationale; FLN) for Algerian independence. The Fourth Republic responded with brutal efforts to suppress the FLN and to preserve Algeria's status as an integral part of France. But when massive military escalations failed to crush the insurgency, the government in Paris reluctantly began to engage in an agonizing reappraisal—making it seem possible that the FLN might one day succeed in its campaign for independence. This prospect provoked an emphatic backlash from the million-plus Europeans who had settled in Algeria over the century of French hegemony. They were proud of their identity as French citizens. So far as they were concerned, the government would be engaging in a terrible act of betrayal if it caved and allowed the FLN to tear them away from their fellow citizens in metropolitan France.

In the autumn of 1958, the settlers rose up in outright rebellion against the central government, gaining the support of many military commanders who committed their forces to join in the struggle for the glory of France. Indeed, the commanding generals on the battlefield were not content to sponsor a local insurrection in Algeria. They initiated plans to invade the mainland to sweep from power the petty politicians in Paris. With the country on the brink of civil war, de Gaulle emerged from his self-imposed political exile at Colombey-les-Deux-Églises to offer himself as the savior of the nation.

Was it not obvious that only the Hero of the Free French Forces could bridge the gap between the outraged warriors and the squabbling politicians?

This was hardly the first time in French history that triumphant military leaders had cast themselves in this role. Napoleon I and Napoleon III had famously filled the legitimacy gap at earlier turning points in French history. Times had changed, and de Gaulle did not want to crown himself king, but president of France. To legitimate his rule, he would have to constitutionalize his charisma, and convincingly demonstrate that the French People had now finally endorsed his decade-long effort to create a powerful presidency that would enable him to transcend petty party politics and restore France to its former glory.

As we shall see, the General's success in mobilizing public support for his "new beginning" initiated a longer-term dynamic over the next sixty years that was similar to, but different from, the four-stage process of constitutional development marked out in Part 1.

One difference deserves emphasis from the outset. It involves the way de Gaulle went about establishing his claim to speak for the People in repudiating the Fourth Republic. Nehru, Mandela, and De Gasperi gained a comparable symbolic centrality by virtue of their leadership of a movement party with strong grassroots support. But de Gaulle was not propelled to power by a similar network of high-energy supporters. It was the collective memory of the General's heroic role in the Resistance that singled him out as the nation's last best hope for avoiding catastrophic civil war. Relying on de Gaulle's success in rallying France during the nation's darkest hour, the old leadership of the Fourth Republic granted the General emergency powers after reluctantly concluding that they could not counter the military rebellion without his assistance.

Once installed as the last prime minister of the Fourth Republic, de Gaulle acted with blinding speed to propose a new institutional framework that would grant him sweeping powers as president. But given the absence of a Gaullist movement party with deep roots in the country, how was he to convince the nation that his new Constitution for the Fifth Republic was something more than a piece of paper covering up the harsh reality of a military coup? How to establish instead that it represented an *authentic* effort by We the People to revolutionize the foundations of their government?

The General reached back to the glory days of World War II to find an answer. Recall that, upon his arrival in London, he went on the BBC to call upon the people of France to look beyond the scheming politicians of Vichy and continue the struggle for a Free France. This time around, he took advantage of television to make a similar charismatic appeal to the nation, following it up with a referendum at which they could demonstrate, by a decisive majority, that his proposed Constitution had a solid foundation in popular sovereignty.

Popular sovereignty = personal charisma + mass media + special referendum. As we shall see, the formula did indeed work to generate an overwhelming majority at the constitutional referendum—and broad acceptance of the new Constitution as a *legitimate* act of We the People. Given his initial success, de Gaulle repeatedly used the same formula to sustain the revolutionary legitimacy of the infant Fifth Republic when its implacable opponents repeatedly tried to destroy it.

But once he left the political stage, his less charismatic successors were reluctant to take a chance on melodramatic television appeals to the voters to legitimate their own efforts to reform the constitutional legacy that the General had left behind. Instead, presidents, prime ministers, and the jurists on the Constitutional Council engaged with one another in more incremental responses to a series of succession crises.

These ongoing reforms did not challenge the revolutionary premises of de Gaulle's original break with the Fourth Republic. But they did generate a dynamic of institutional adaptation that, a half century later, ultimately consolidated the Constitutional Council's role as legal guardian of the Republic in ways that invite comparison with the four-stage processes described in our earlier case studies.

Time One: De Gaulle as Revolutionary

During his long period in the wilderness, de Gaulle's critique of the Fourth Republic was clear and consistent. On his view, its parliamentary system generated a never-ending series of short-lived governments incapable of responding to the long-term problems confronting the nation. The root of the problem was selfish partisanship: rather than joining together in a stable government, party leaders repeatedly withdrew their support whenever they thought that they could bargain their way to a better cabinet position in the next coalition government. This endless game of musical chairs diverted the political class from the decisive actions that would enable France to regain its central position in European and world affairs. De Gaulle insisted that only a strong and independent president, serving for a long term, would be capable of restoring France to its former greatness. In his view, the Algerian "crisis" was merely a symptom of deeper problems with parliamentary government.[1]

What Was Wrong with the Fourth Republic?

This Gaullist diagnosis began to resonate broadly among the general public, as well as the demoralized officer corps, as they searched for an explanation for the series of humiliating French defeats in Vietnam, Suez, and North Africa during the 1950s.[2] Nevertheless, it is based on myth. To be sure, the average life of a coalition government in the Fourth Republic was less than a year. But as political scientist Duncan MacRae demonstrated long ago, the rapid turnover wasn't the product of shortsighted careerism.[3] Despite the claims of critics, rapid turnover was a positive force, enabling the National Assembly to resolve big issues that might have otherwise eluded decisive solution.

To see MacRae's point, begin with some numbers. In the 1950s, Communists, Gaullists, and other opponents of the regime controlled 200 seats in the National Assembly. This left a "Third Force," 400 representatives, who were available to form the parliamentary majority and a coalition government. But the political parties in this group had sharp ideological disagreements. For example, there was a long-standing conflict between secularists and Catholics on public aid for parochial schools. To win a parliamentary majority in favor of assistance, it was necessary to exclude strong secularists from the coalition government. But once this problem was resolved, secularists were essential for dealing with other hot-button issues—yet their entry into the government provoked the departure of strongly Catholic elements.

Over time, the series of shifting coalition cabinets—many containing only slightly different personnel—marked up a formidable list of achievements. For starters, Third Force governments created a distinctive institutional framework for economic development—relying heavily on a meritocratic civil service, and state ownership, to steer the market in positive directions.[4] This interventionist approach generated large gains for the working and middle classes by the mid-1950s—and provided the engine for further large gains during the early years of the Fifth Republic.[5]

Coalition governments also took aggressive action to realize the new Constitution's commitment to social justice. Breaking with the past, they created comprehensive systems to protect the elderly and the vulnerable—while vastly improving the educational achievements of the rising generation.

The Third Force also threw its support behind the Treaty of Rome of 1957. After de Gaulle gained power in 1959, he seriously considered repudiating this decision, but reluctantly accepted it. Similarly, it was the Fourth, not the Fifth, Republic that initiated the atomic bomb program that was so important to de Gaulle's efforts to assert France's independence from the United States in foreign affairs.[6]

There is, in short, remarkably little substance to the Gaullist image of Fourth Republic politicians swapping cabinet posts in blind disregard for the public good. To the contrary, the Third Force built an enduring institutional legacy promoting economic development, welfare guarantees, and the country's leading role in the construction of Europe.

The sudden collapse of the parliamentary regime took the general public by surprise.[7] In 1957, Maurice Duverger—the greatest French political scientist of the day—concluded that "no fundamental reform of French institutions appears imminent."[8] In January 1958, a public opinion poll reported that only 13 percent supported de Gaulle's return to power.[9]

Only one event provoked the General's remarkable reemergence later that year—the threat of a coup d'état by a politicized corps of military officers grimly determined to prevent the Fourth Republic from accepting Algerian independence.[10]

The General and the Parachutists

The military's estrangement cannot be attributed to halfhearted support by the Fourth Republic. The Third Force had consistently backed an escalating campaign to crush the FLN and sustain French hegemony in Algeria. Paradoxically, it was precisely this energetic support that led to the Fourth Republic's destruction.

The roots of the paradox run deep. In contrast to the British, French politicians refused to retreat from empire in Asia after the Second World War. Despite declining support from the general public,[11] coalition governments consistently poured vast military resources into a decade-long battle against Vietnamese independence—which generated large budget deficits and significant inflation.[12] It was only the shattering defeat at Dien Bien Phu in 1954 that provoked an about-face—which in turn suggested the Republic's constitutional resilience.

Pierre Mendès-France was at the center of the Vietnam drama. During the preceding decade, he was a moving force behind the political rehabilitation of the Radical Party. Radicals had played a leading role in the Third Republic but the party had been pushed to the sidelines by the Resistance movements during the founding of the Fourth Republic. Once the Communists were excluded from government, however, the Democratic Socialists and Popular Republicans had little choice but to reach out to the Radicals—whose liberal and secular traditions made them natural supporters of the regime.[13] While Mendès was broadly responsive to these overtures, he was a consistent opponent of the Vietnam War—making him the obvious Third Force choice to succeed Joseph Laniel as prime minister after the Dien Bien Phu disaster.[14]

Within a month of his investiture, Mendès had negotiated an armistice with Ho Chi Minh that recognized North Vietnam's independence. He then advanced similar initiatives for Morocco and Tunisia. But just at that moment, a new guerilla war broke out in Algeria—putting Mendès (and Socialist François Mitterrand, his minister of the Interior) on the defensive.

For his nationalist opponents, Mendès's "appeasement policies" were to blame for the FLN's campaign of organized violence. Mendès responded by sending more troops to suppress the revolt, but this did not calm right-wing anxieties—let alone those of the one million French settlers determined to maintain their political and economic domination over Algeria's nine million Muslims. When put to the test, Mendès lost a vote of confidence in February 1955—enabling his leading rival in the Radical party, Edgar Faure, to replace him as prime minister and continue a policy of military suppression.

Mendès was not to be denied. During the following year, his ongoing challenge led Faure to engineer the premature dissolution of Parliament—but this only further escalated their rivalry, enabling Mendès to expel Faure from the party. He then led his Radicals into a broader coalition, the Republican Front, which called for a peaceful resolution of the Algerian crisis. Although the Communists did not join the Front, they took the same line. The two peace campaigns won majority support at the polls: the Republican Front gaining 27 percent of the vote, and the Communists 25 percent.

When the new Parliament convened, Mendès had no chance of recapturing the premiership—his appointment would have so inflamed the Algerian settlers as to make a negotiated solution impossible. The top job went instead to Guy Mollet, whose Socialist Party had been a leading member of the Republican Front. With Mendès-France joining the government, Mollet dismissed the rabidly pro-settler Jacques Soustelle as Algeria's governor-general, replacing him with retired general Georges Catroux, who had publicly supported negotiations.[15] Mollet then followed up with a trip to Algiers—where he was greeted by a massive demonstration of 50,000 settlers surging through the streets shouting "Hang Catroux." Only the military intervention of parachutists, under the command of General Jacques Massu, managed to restore order after nightfall. Mollet returned to Paris profoundly shaken, and immediately executed a complete about-face—throwing 200,000 more troops into an all-out effort to crush the FLN's guerilla forces.

This escalation generated the dynamic that ultimately killed the Fourth Republic. Many officers were already attributing their humiliating defeat in Vietnam to Mendès-France and his ilk. They were determined to avoid another stab in the back—and, unlike Vietnam, their troops were within easy reach of metropolitan France. If push came to shove, would they launch a full-scale invasion to impose their will on the politicians?

Mollet and his successors did not want to find out. They continued a policy of all-out suppression for the next two years. But nationalist officers and civilians took nothing for granted, plotting together for a massive counterthrust if Paris engaged in a turnaround.[16] There can be no doubt that Jacques Soustelle, and other de Gaulle confidantes, were deeply immersed in this right-wing conspiracy—though it is uncertain how much they personally informed the General of their activities.[17]

One thing is clear: the General refused to repudiate the right-wing rebellion when it broke out in May 1958. The precipitating event was President René Coty's selection of Pierre Pflimlin to form the next coalition government. Unlike his predecessors, Pflimlin had made some gestures toward a negotiated settlement—though his statements contained plenty of weasel words and equivocations.[18]

Nevertheless, his selection was enough to arouse an immediate show of defiance from Raoul Salan, the commander in chief in Algeria. His telegram to General Ely, chief of staff in Paris, would have been explosive even if it had been kept confidential. But it was immediately leaked to the newspapers:

> The Army in Algeria is concerned with its sense of responsibility towards the men who are fighting and who are in danger of making a useless sacrifice if [Parliament] is not resolved to keep Algeria French. . . .
>
> The French Army would, to a man, consider the surrender of this part of the national heritage to be an outrage. Its desperate reaction is unpredictable. I request you to draw the attention of the President of the Republic to our anguish, which can only be assuaged by a government firmly resolved to keep the French flag flying in Algeria.[19]

Salan had previously distanced himself from more notorious right-wing plotters—so his warning, co-signed by other leading commanders, was even more ominous.

Pflimlin refused to be intimidated. He quickly convinced leading Third Force politicians to join his government, presenting his cabinet for approval by the National Assembly on May 12.

Algiers exploded the following day, with massive crowds seizing the governor-general's building and proclaiming a Committee of Public Safety under General Massu—whom the settlers idolized for his violent suppression of the FLN during the Battle of Algiers.[20]

But this outright act of rebellion failed to deflect the civilians in Paris. During the early hours of May 14, by a vote of 274 to 129 (with most, but not all, of the Right joining the majority), the National Assembly solemnly authorized the Pflimlin government to suppress the "insurrection."

This was the moment de Gaulle reentered the public stage. If he had backed Pflimlin unequivocally, his statement might have been decisive. While Massu was glorying in the adulation of the crowds, General Salan was leaving the building by the back door—refusing to commit himself, as commander in chief, to open insurrection. Given de Gaulle's heroic status, his condemnation of Massu's rebellion might well have led Salan to lead the officer corps to reaffirm its fidelity to the principle of civilian control.[21]

De Gaulle chose a different path: "In the past, the nation, from its heart of hearts, trusted me to lead it in unity to its salvation. Today, as it faces a grave new trial, may the country know that I hold myself ready to assume the powers of the Republic."[22] On the same day, Salan appeared on the balcony of the governor-general's building and endorsed the Committee of Public Safety: "Long live l'Algérie française! Long live de Gaulle!"

The commanding general then joined Massu to win the assent of regional commanders in France for an attack on Paris—with parachutists from Algeria, army battalions from Toulouse, and tank units from Rambouillet serving as key elements in the strategic adventure. The conspirators named it Operation Resurrection, but did not keep it a secret for long. By May 17 or 18 they had leaked their plans to de Gaulle, the Pflimlin government, and President René Coty—forcing a series of public and private confrontations over the following days.

The talks took on a new intensity on May 24, when the rebels seized Corsica, installing a Committee of Public Safety on an island that was officially considered a province of metropolitan France. Word reached Paris that Operation Resurrection was imminent—forcing negotiations to a climax on May 28, with de Gaulle threatening Coty and Pflimlin "to leave you to have things out with the parachutists [while I will] go back into retirement, with grief as my companion."[23] Declaring the country on "the verge of civil war," President Coty, with Pflimlin's backing, then offered to support de Gaulle's selection as prime minister by the National Assembly.[24] It was only at that point that Operation Resurrection was canceled.[25]

Others were not so easily intimidated. Rising political stars like Mendès-France and François Mitterrand were leading 250,000 Parisians in the streets, protesting de Gaulle's takeover as a threat to the Republic. Similar demonstrations throughout the country emphasized the dramatic contrast with the General's triumphant entry into Paris in 1944 amid the universal acclaim of the Resistance.[26]

De Gaulle could not respond in kind—only 500 loyalists rallied to his cause in a march down the Champs-Élysées.[27] He turned instead to the very politicians he had been denouncing for a decade—appointing a series of establishment types to his cabinet in exchange for their help in ramming two remarkable statutes through the National Assembly.[28]

The first granted the General and his cabinet the unilateral power to rule by decree for the next six months. The second authorized de Gaulle to guide the construction of an entirely new Constitution. There was no need, he explained, to follow the precedent he had helped establish in 1946 and ask the voters to elect a new Constituent Assembly for this purpose. So far as he was concerned, an "electoral campaign . . . would create agitation in people's minds," which "would be harmful" given the prevailing uncertainties.[29] Instead, his team of advisors would draft the Fifth Republic's Constitution on their own authority, and present the voters with a Yes / No choice on the finished product.

In seizing constituent power, de Gaulle was recalling some of the darkest moments of French history—when Napoléon III and Marshall Pétain browbeat earlier republican assemblies into committing suicide.[30] Once again, Mendès-France and Mitterrand eloquently opposed this move as a coup d'état—this time, on the floor of the National Assembly.[31] But they could not point to a technical violation of the constitutional rules of the Fourth Republic—and de Gaulle's newfound political allies rounded up the necessary votes for Parliament to sign its own death warrant on June 2, 1958.[32]

Constitutionalizing Charisma

Although de Gaulle had liberated himself from Parliament, he remained prime minister of the Fourth Republic, exercising his decree power with the support of a cabinet dominated by the old-regime parties. But he was careful to reserve the Ministry of Justice for his long-standing legal advisor, Michel Debré, who started moving forward on the project for a new Constitution at an extraordinary pace.

A Provisional Constitution?

Within a couple of weeks, the Ministry was churning out a working draft rooted in de Gaulle's 1946 Bayeux speech denouncing the Fourth Republic's Constitution. Debré's vision of a strong presidency was then submitted to a six-man review panel dominated by four leading politicians from the old parties. Predictably, they sought to shift the balance of power in favor of parliamentary control. The intense bargaining that followed took place in secret—and at a particularly contentious moment, the General was required to intervene personally. Within a month, a draft of working principles was submitted to an elite consultative commission; a majority of its thirty-nine members were drawn from Parliament.[33]

This establishment group deliberated from July 29 through August 16. Once again, it took aim at the still-powerful presidency—this time issuing a public critique. But alas, the rest of France was on vacation in mid-August, and the commission's voice could barely be heard among the waves crashing on the shore of seaside resorts.

Even more important, de Gaulle had met with the commission on August 8 and made it clear that he would not budge on key issues. The parliamentary statute establishing the commission specified that it was only advisory, so the prime minister was within his rights to declare that it was time to move on. He submitted the revised text to the Council of Ministers and President Coty on September 3, who approved it for presentation to the voters at a special referendum of September 28.

From beginning to end, the entire process took three months—and stood in stark contrast to the sustained and mobilized debate that attended the Founding of the Fourth Republic during the entire year of 1946. Nevertheless, de Gaulle's strategy of elite co-optation paid off handsomely at the polls. Because the old political establishment had actively cooperated in the process of constructing the Constitution, the four major parties came out in favor of a Yes vote, pushing opponents like Mendès-France and François Mitterrand into the political wilderness.

This made it easy for the Yes campaign to say that its isolated center-left opponents were merely pawns in a No campaign dominated by the Communists, the only major political party in opposition. The public had little understanding of the real constitutional issues, but the anti-Communist theme provided a compelling message during the four-week campaign, leading to a sweeping 80-to-20 victory on September 28.[34]

Co-optation had its costs. On the one hand, de Gaulle got much of what he wanted: a president who gained his office independently of Parliament, and who could transform himself into a dictator, with sweeping decree powers, if he unilaterally declared that a national emergency existed in Algeria or anywhere else.

Even during normal times, Parliament's lawmaking powers were restricted to enable the president to conduct foreign and military affairs largely without legislative interference. What is more, once a prime minister and his cabinet gained majority support in Parliament, the Constitution placed severe limits on Parliament's ability to vote them out of office, and made it very difficult for members to defeat the government's legislative program on the floor of the house.[35]

These were very substantial victories for de Gaulle's vision of presidential democracy, but they did not mark a final defeat for the principle of parliamentary supremacy. First and foremost, the National Assembly remained the only body that was directly elected by the voters. The much-empowered presidency would be selected by a specially created Electoral College, whose 80,000 members were drawn heavily from locally elected officials in rural areas. The College was certain to choose de Gaulle in the short run, but its composition posed a long-run problem once the hero of the Resistance departed from the political stage.

At that point, a profoundly conservative president selected by a gerrymandered Electoral College would confront a prime minister commanding a majority of the democratically elected National Assembly. Given the new president's problematic claim to authority, it would be tough for him to block the enactment of the prime minister's legislative program. Perhaps he could do so if the new Constitution clearly defined his powers in relationship to the prime minister and his cabinet. But the text was ambiguous on this score—the result of a compromise that Debré had made with the party establishment of the old regime to secure their support. This left the prime minister as the *only* leader chosen after a genuinely democratic election based on universal suffrage—giving him a priceless advantage in any confrontation with de Gaulle's gerrymandered successor. If the Constitution remained unchanged, the Fifth Republic would predictably revert to the pattern established during the Third and Fourth Republics—where the president played a largely symbolic role as head of state, and the prime minister was at the center of power so long as he could maintain his parliamentary majority.

De Gaulle was fully aware of this point—and he would later take dramatic steps to change the 1958 Constitution to secure his presidentialist legacy long after he passed from the scene. But for the moment he focused on securing his position in the short term. After he gained the cooperation of the Third Force in winning a decisive mandate for the Constitution in September 1958, he immediately went on the attack. Once he formally became president in October, de Gaulle faced his next political test in November, when voters returned to the polls for the first parliamentary elections of the Fifth Republic. This time around, the president called upon the People to reject the Third Force in favor of his newly established Union for the New Republic.

His appeal was remarkably successful. Despite its ad hoc character, the new Union won 198 seats for its candidates, and Gaullist allies picked up an additional 133—adding up to a strong governing majority for the Parliament's five-year term. In contrast, the Third Force parties together picked up a total of 124 seats, and the Communists did even worse—losing one-third of their votes and winning only 10 seats.

This meant that de Gaulle would not have to deal with a politically independent prime minister during the early years of the Fifth Republic. Instead, the Union's sweeping victory confirmed the decisive character of the preceding referendum—giving de Gaulle the parliamentary support he needed to establish that his vision of presidential democracy could actually work in practice. De Gaulle's centrality was further dramatized when the president turned to Michel Debré, the principal drafter of the Constitution, to serve as prime minister.

De Gaulle's Continuing Revolution

Despite their electoral triumphs, the president and prime minister soon found themselves confronting a very serious challenge, rooted in the Time One dynamics that had propelled the General into power in the first place. As we have seen, de Gaulle had artfully used the threat of a military coup to browbeat the established political parties into endorsing his new regime. But his ascendancy remained vulnerable if he could not gain the Algerian rebels' acquiescence.

Upon assuming office as the last prime minister of the Fourth Republic, de Gaulle had confronted an Algeria controlled by committees of public safety that had effectively displaced official governmental authority. He quickly responded by flying across the Mediterranean to personally reassure the settlers, and the military, of his intentions—famously proclaiming "Vive l'Algérie française!" in his speech of June 6.[36]

But over the coming months and years, de Gaulle's Algerian supporters became convinced that he was betraying their cause—and repeatedly tried to force him from power. De Gaulle replied with a series of charismatic appeals that were crucial in saving himself, and his Constitution, from destruction.

Even this success, however, did not conclude de Gaulle's exercise in the constitutionalization of charisma. Once he had tamed the specter of military overthrow, he turned to confront the party politicians of the Fourth Republic—who, like the Algerian rebels, had played a crucial role in propelling him to power. As we have seen, establishment types like Coty and Pflimlin had exacted a substantial price for cooperating with the General—insisting on a constitutional system in which the presidency would predictably lose much of its authority once the Hero of the Resistance had passed from the scene. If de Gaulle was to ensure his constitutional legacy for the future, there was only one way to do it—change the Constitution to allow the voters to choose the chief executive directly. Once the president was directly selected by popular vote, he would be in a position to claim that it was he, not the prime minister, who had the superior claim to speak for the People.

Changing the Constitution required supermajority support from both houses of Parliament, and members of the legislature predictably resisted his efforts to destroy their privileged status as the only representatives directly elected by the voters. Rather than risk defeat at the hands of the parliamentarians, de Gaulle reasserted his authority to revolutionize the very Constitution that he himself had established only a few years before. Once again, he used his standard formula—Media appeals + constitutional referendum = de Gaulle as popular sovereign. This move was especially remarkable because, as we shall see, it was expressly prohibited by the Constitution of the Fifth Republic!

Nevertheless, the General's second effort to constitutionalize his charisma proved successful—creating a firm foundation for the presidency, and setting the stage for his successors to struggle over the enduring meaning of his remarkable constitutional legacy during Time Three.

The Algerian Crisis

When organizing the ground rules for the constitutional referendum of September and parliamentary elections of November, de Gaulle followed up on his June commitment to "Algérie française." During the Fourth Republic, only a fraction of the Algerian population could vote for representatives to the National Assembly. Suffrage was limited to the one million French settlers in Algeria who had migrated from the mainland; the nine million Muslim inhabitants were excluded. But with the dawning of the Fifth Republic, everybody could vote—allowing all Algerians to demonstrate their status as full-fledged citizens of France.

Yet the manner in which these elections were conducted only confirmed the FLN's assertions that Algerians could never really become Frenchmen. By this point, de Gaulle had added Jacques Soustelle to his cabinet in recognition of his central role in the conspiracy that had propelled him to power. A right-wing ideologue, Soustelle was now minister of information, and was in a position to make a mockery of the Algerian referendum. Collaborating with his military allies, he launched the Ministry on an intensive propaganda effort for the Yes vote—systematically suppressing the No campaign. These authoritarian maneuvers turned out to be counterproductive: when officials reported that 96.5 percent of the votes coming out of Algeria were Yes, the news discredited the entire process. The November elections generated a similarly unbelievable outcome, with all 67 of Algeria's National Assembly seats going to candidates calling for the strong "integration" of their region into metropolitan France.[37]

At the same time as official election reports were proclaiming Algeria's determination to remain French, de Gaulle was reasserting his effective control over the rebellious committees of public safety. On October 13, General Salan, the Algerian commander in chief, was ordered to ensure "the immediate withdrawal" of the military from "all participation in organizations of a political nature." Confronting this unambiguous command, Salan forced General Massu to resign from the presidency of the Algiers Committee of Public Safety. De Gaulle then tricked Salan into accepting a "promotion" to an impressive-

sounding—but powerless—job in Paris. This created an opening that permitted him to replace Salan with General Maurice Challe, a de Gaulle loy-
alist who could be trusted to obey orders received from the metropole.

The president then embarked on an aggressive set of military, economic,
and social measures aiming to convince the Muslim majority to abandon the
FLN and reaffirm their French identity. Despite Challe's strong support, this
ambitious initiative proved a failure—leading de Gaulle to conclude that the
FLN was in Algeria to stay. In September 1959 he began to prepare the public
for this bitter truth, publicly stating that Algerians might one day gain their
independence if a majority voted to break their ties with France in a referendum. Nevertheless, he sought to postpone this day of reckoning by demanding that the FLN end its guerilla war and wait for four years to allow
passions to cool and negotiations to take place over the precise terms of the
referendum.

Despite these major caveats, de Gaulle's statement generated predictable
shouts of betrayal by French nationalists on both sides of the Mediterranean.
Worse yet, the president's success in bringing high-visibility generals into line
only drove military resistance underground—with many lower-ranking officers colluding with settler groups in Algeria and nationalists in France in
further acts of defiance.

This culminated in another uprising in the city of Algiers, in January 1960.
De Gaulle responded with decisive actions that quickly crushed the rebellion.
But he then sought to pacify die-hard nationalists by unleashing another
desperate effort to crush the guerilla movement.[38] Yet this renewed military
campaign failed to reestablish the semblance of law and order. After another
year of failure, de Gaulle took an additional step toward recognizing the inevitable. He advanced a more forthcoming, if vague, proposal that recognized
Algeria's right to self-determination.[39]

His announcement catalyzed more cries of outrage from the Right. As the
embittered cadre of military officers considered their next steps, de Gaulle
found himself at a crossroads. He could begin negotiating with the FLN on
the basis of his broad constitutional powers over military affairs—and then
try to impose his fait accompli on his political opponents—or he could try to
buttress his authority by calling on the French people to endorse his initiative at a special referendum.

French presidents after de Gaulle have generally refused to take such
gambles on the shifting tides of public opinion.[40] But the General was no
ordinary politician. Since his triumphant entry into Paris in 1944, he had

repeatedly appealed to the French people for a mandate to establish a "new beginning" in the political life of the nation. In calling for a referendum yet again, he was perfectly aware of the risk he was running. After all, it was precisely the use of referenda that had led to his resounding repudiation in 1946.

Yet he had now succeeded in constitutionalizing his charisma at the referendum of 1958. So it was entirely consistent with his public persona to deploy the tactic once again to establish that the People supported his call to transform the Republic's constitutional identity by allowing Algeria to cut its ties to France.

After a brief but intense campaign, de Gaulle won his referendum by an overwhelming majority. The results from Algeria, however, were more equivocal. Seventy percent of the recorded votes were Yes, but more than 40 percent of the Muslim community boycotted the election at the urging of the FLN.

Algeria's European settlers were also increasingly alienated—but they didn't need a boycott to send their message. Since most lived in the city of Algiers, they could convey their strong opposition by voting No at the city's polling stations—overwhelming the Yes vote by a margin of 70 to 30. This strong No sharply contrasted with the strong Yes from the nation as a whole, which approved de Gaulle's initiative by a margin of 75 to 25.[41]

Worse yet, the settlers and their military allies were utterly unwilling to accept the judgment reached by the voters in metropolitan France. General Salan had by now fled to Franco Spain and was busily organizing military and civilian conspirators into a Secret Army Organization to oppose de Gaulle's initiative by force. The Secret Army's first guerilla attacks were a prelude to another military uprising in the city of Algiers in April 1961.

Recall that, at an earlier stage, de Gaulle had replaced the rebellious Salan with General Maurice Challe, who had vigorously supported the president's efforts to turn the tide against the FLN. De Gaulle had then rewarded Challe by obtaining an appointment for him as commander in chief of all Allied Forces in Central Europe. But at this critical moment, Challe betrayed his benefactor.

He suddenly resigned his prestigious position to join Salan and others as the First Parachutist Regiment seized control of Algiers on the night of April 21. By the following day, the rebels had placed all loyal officials under arrest while the city's settler-population surged through the streets in support of the rebellion. Challe and Salan then waited expectantly for their fellow officers to initiate similar takeovers in the rest of Algeria, providing momentum for a replay of Operation Resurrection—but this time, with the aim of forcing de Gaulle out of office.

The officer corps was packed with rebels, but the ranks were full of civilian conscripts, and the fate of the uprising was in their hands. The "Challist" officers were in direct command of the rank and file, though, and believed that this gave them a great advantage in gaining their support against de Gaulle's "betrayal" of l'Algérie française. But the president responded with a decisive demonstration of his charismatic authority.

On the night of April 23, de Gaulle went on television to appeal directly to France's citizen-soldiers, calling upon them to reject the commands of their military superiors:

> An insurrectionary power has established itself in Algeria on the basis of a military pronunciamento. . . . This power has a façade—a quartet of retired generals—and it has a reality—a group of politicized, frenzied and ambitious officers. . . . In the name of France I order that all means, I repeat all means, be used to bar the route to these men until such time as they can be overcome. I forbid every Frenchmen, *and in the first place every soldier,* to carry out any of their orders.[42]

It was this assertion of authority, not the exercise of raw emergency power, that turned the tide. In response to the president's appeal, the conscripts overwhelmingly refused to follow their officers—forcing General Challe to recognize that his effort to reenact 1958 had failed. After two days of waiting in vain for further uprisings throughout Algeria, he handed himself over to the lawful authorities. Other bitter-enders like Salan refused to surrender but went underground with the Secret Army. Yet they could only express their opposition through guerilla warfare, not by ousting the lawful government from control over major regions.

De Gaulle's appeal to the conscripts had managed to carry the day. How did his television address overwhelm the face-to-face command authority exercised by the Challist officers?

In taking to the airwaves, the president was reenacting his glory days in 1941 when the BBC first projected his voice to his fellow citizens, urging them to stand up and be counted "in the name of France." But this revolutionary reenactment was only a necessary, not a sufficient, condition for success. His previous victory in the January referendum also played an essential part.

To see my point, suppose that de Gaulle had refused to call a referendum, and had begun negotiating with the FLN on the basis of the broad powers over military affairs granted him by the new Constitution. Under this scenario, his recognition of the FLN would have provoked fierce nationalist rejoinders from his opponents in Parliament and the press—generating great confusion among the conscripts as to the true state of public opinion. Within this context, it is far more likely that they would have obeyed their commanders' orders to continue their long struggle for Algérie française. It was only the massive Yes vote that made de Gaulle's appeal seem so compelling.

If you aren't convinced, consider a hypothetical scenario. This time around, assume (1) that de Gaulle did indeed call a referendum but (2) lost by a narrow margin yet (3) nevertheless pushed forward, claiming (correctly) that his broad grant of constitutional authority still allowed him to proceed with negotiations. Under this scenario, can there be any serious doubt that the conscripts would have heeded their "Challist" officers into open rebellion?

Revolutionary heroism + popular referendum = legitimation of a "new beginning." Paradoxically, this classic Gaullist formula served to justify the suppression of a military uprising of precisely the same kind that had propelled him into power three years earlier.

I should emphasize the limited character of de Gaulle's victory. After the failed coup, he found it difficult to reach an acceptable accord with the FLN. It took almost a year before the Evian Agreement of March 1962 set the stage for a final referendum on Algerian independence in July. As negotiations proceeded indecisively, the Secret Army continued its guerilla war against the FLN in Algeria, keeping settler hopes alive. Even the Evian Agreement wasn't enough to end resistance. Instead, the Secret Army launched a final desperate effort to sabotage the accord—launching a scorched-earth campaign that led to the desperate flight of 700,000 European settlers to mainland France, leaving almost everything behind. This tragedy made a mockery of de Gaulle's promises to the settlers of a bright future when he gained their support in 1958 for his revolutionary repudiation of the Fourth Republic.[43]

But it did not damage de Gaulle's political legitimacy in the slightest. To the contrary, the president presented the Evian Agreement as a triumph, and called upon voters on the mainland to endorse Algerian independence at another special referendum. When 90 percent responded on April 8 with an emphatic Yes, de Gaulle's authority to speak for the People was reinforced yet again.[44]

During the same period, the French military in Algeria managed to seize Salan and sentence him to life imprisonment. Overwhelmed by these setbacks, the Secret Army announced a cease-fire in early June.

This set the stage for the last phase of the Evian process. On July 1, all the voters of Algeria, including the shattered remnants of the settler community, went to the polls to cast a ballot on the ultimate question of national independence. When 99.72 percent voted Yes, the president gave formal recognition to the new sovereign state of Algeria in the name of the Fifth Republic.

In bringing the struggle to a close, de Gaulle had not only extricated metropolitan France from a traumatic defeat; he had not only reasserted his authority over the army; he had accomplished something even more fundamental. He had redeemed the revolutionary narrative that had given birth to the Fifth Republic: Just as in 1944, just as in 1958, so too in 1962, the revolutionary outsider had led the French people to redefine their constitutional identity after a profound military crisis.

Revolutionary Refounding

While he gloried in these triumphs, de Gaulle was all too aware of the fragility of his achievement. As he explains in his memoirs:

> In face of national crisis [in 1958], I chanced to have been pre-ordained as the country's savior, [allowing] me, with the direct concurrence of the people—that is to say on a pre-eminently democratic basis—to establish institutions designed to span the future.[45]

Nevertheless, he recognized that the presidency—the central institution in his new design—had emerged in a deeply compromised fashion, given the role of the gerrymandered Electoral College in presidential selection. The College would not pose a short-term problem, since "by reason of past history and present circumstances, the manner of my accession would be no more than a formality." But it would lead to a predictable crisis "when the dramatic circumstances and the exceptional person" who created the Fifth Republic "had disappeared."[46]

Speaking for myself, I find it hard to take de Gaulle's self-indulgent worship of himself as a hero. But his egocentric manner of self-presentation should not blind us to the validity of his basic insight. De Gaulle was right to insist that the constitutionalization of charisma is a long-term process—and that his departure from the stage at Time Three would predictably generate a distinctive succession crisis. He was also right to fear that indirect election by an Electoral College would put the next president at a grievous disadvantage in future power struggles with prime ministers who had the support of a

directly elected National Assembly. If de Gaulle was to preserve his presidentialist legacy, he had little choice but to lead the People in a campaign for
yet-another constitutional transformation:

> The only way was the election of the President of the Republic by the people.
> If he alone was chosen by Frenchmen as a whole, he would be "the nation's
> man," invested thereby in the eyes of all, and in his own eyes, with a para-
> mount responsibility precisely corresponding to the role assigned to him in
> the Constitution.[47]

"For the sake of the future," then, he continued, "I was determined to finish
off the [constitutional] edifice" by creating a truly democratic presidency "before the end of my seven-year term"—and he once again turned to the
popular referendum to gain legitimacy for this effort.[48]

But this time, he ran into a special problem. In dealing with the Algerian
crisis, the Constitution gave the president unilateral authority to call a referendum on a bill dealing with any "treaty which, although not contrary to the
Constitution, would affect the functioning of the institutions." Yet a call for a
popularly elected presidency required a formal amendment eliminating the
Electoral College—and Article 89 expressly declared that "the right to propose amendments to the Constitution belongs concurrently to the President
of the Republic . . . *and to members of Parliament.*"[49]

Additional provisions set out a significant obstacle course. The president's
newly appointed prime minister, Georges Pompidou, not only would be required to win the requisite majority in the National Assembly. He would have
to prevail upon the Senate to accept de Gaulle's initiative. The upper house of
Parliament played a secondary role on ordinary legislation, but it was granted
a veto on constitutional matters. Because it was composed of notables chosen
by an Electoral College similar to the one involved in presidential selection,
senators would predictably resist de Gaulle's assault on the principle of indirect election.[50]

These obstacles weren't insurmountable. Gaullists had won a large victory
in the 1959 elections for the National Assembly, allowing them to form a governing coalition that had loyally sustained the president's program during
very difficult times. To be sure, the president had recently replaced his first
prime minister, Michel Debré, with another loyal follower, Georges Pompidou. But this gave the newcomer an overwhelming incentive to establish
his political credibility by pushing de Gaulle's initiative through the Assembly.
Once Pompidou had executed this mission, it would be tough—to say the

least—for the Senate to turn down the joint initiative of a charismatic president and a prime minister who had the strong support of a directly elected
Assembly. Ultimate victory wasn't guaranteed, but the president and his new
prime minister could well have emerged triumphant after a sustained political
struggle.[51]

But de Gaulle chose an even riskier path. He simply refused to play by the
rules set down by his own Constitution. A dramatic incident undoubtedly
pushed him down the road to yet another revolution of the Republic. On August 22, bitter-enders in the Secret Army almost succeeded in assassinating
him and his family in retaliation for his "betrayal" in Algeria.[52] This shocking
event gave de Gaulle a dramatic opening to announce, while Parliament was
in recess, that he would unilaterally proceed with a referendum on the popular-
election amendment. This remarkable announcement provoked a hailstorm
of condemnation from all political parties—except, of course, the Gaullist
Union for the New Republic.[53]

The popular uproar was reinforced by the Republic's official guardians
of the Constitution. De Gaulle made his pronouncement on September 12.
By the end of the month, both the Council of State and the Constitutional
Council advised him that his initiative was flatly unconstitutional. Each acted
independently, but their condemnations were mutually reinforcing. The
Council of State had established itself as the great arbiter of public law over
the course of the preceding century, with its members representing the
most distinguished jurists in the nation. In standing up against the General,
it was crystallizing a professional consensus, condemning the action as a
profound assault on the rule of law.[54]

The Constitutional Council, in contrast, was an institutional newcomer,
with no analogue in earlier French experiments in republican government.
Quite simply, Michel Debré had designed the Council as an additional weapon
to support the strong presidency established by the Fifth Republic. He
recognized that the National Assembly would predictably try to reassert
its authority by aggressive use of its legislative powers. To guard against
this threat, Debré constructed the Council to operate as the president's
"watchdog"—granting it authority to strike down legislation that unconsti-
tutionally invaded presidential prerogatives, especially in the conduct of
foreign and military affairs.

To create the necessary appearance of impartiality, the Constitution required the president to share the power of appointment to the Council with
the heads of the National Assembly and the Senate. Each of them could select

three members for nine-year terms. To add to the Council's gravitas, former presidents of the Republic—René Coty and Vincent Auriol—also served as members. But during the founding period, this formula added up to a clear Gaullist majority of six—because, in addition to the president's appointments, the Assembly was under Gaullist control (the Senate, as we shall see, was less reliable).

The overwhelming majority of Councillors were politicians, with only a sprinkling of professors and judges providing legal perspective.[55] Since the Council was dominated by senior politicians broadly friendly to de Gaulle, it was a big surprise when this presidential "watchdog" turned around to bite its creator. Combined with the condemnation issued by the legal mandarins of the Council of State, the message was unmistakable: Charles de Gaulle, you are launching a revolutionary assault on your own Constitution!

The president responded with anger and contempt. As he later put it in his memoirs: "I myself was the principal inspirer of the new institutions . . . it really was the height of effrontery to challenge me on what they meant."[56]

At this stage, the advice provided by both Councils was advisory and strictly confidential. But in a shocking breach of protocol, the Council of State's opinion was leaked to *Le Monde,* and former president René Coty, now a member of the Constitutional Council, denounced de Gaulle's move as a "constitutional coup d'État."[57]

De Gaulle was unimpressed. When Parliament came back in session on October 2, he peremptorily informed it that the referendum would take place on October 28. The National Assembly responded with a "vote of no confidence." With only the Gaullist Union voting in support of Pompidou's government, the Assembly removed the government from power and censured the president for "violating the Constitution."[58] This was the first and only time that Parliament has overthrown a sitting prime minister in the sixty-year history of the Fifth Republic.

The president responded by escalating his own assault on Parliament. He retained Pompidou as interim prime minister, and ordered him to continue preparations for the October 28 referendum. He then dissolved the rebellious National Assembly and called for new elections in late November. He further increased the stakes in a televised address in the midst of the frenetic three-week referendum campaign:

> If you reject my proposal and follow the advice of the old parties who want to restore their disastrous regime and of all subversives who seek an outlet for

their sedition; or if the majority is feeble, mediocre, and indecisive, then it goes without saying that my task will be immediately—and irrevocably—ended.[59]

This is a truly remarkable passage. De Gaulle is equating his opponents in the democratically elected Parliament to the seditious conspirators who had tried to kill him. This is sheer demagogy worthy of a tin-pot dictator.

Yet there remains a significant difference: the president was not demanding unquestioning support for his cult of personality; he was threatening *to resign* if the voters did not support his illegal initiative. What is more, his proposal did not involve personal self-aggrandizement—say, by declaring him president for life. He was fully prepared to test his continuing popularity when his seven-year term came to an end in 1965, and he would be obliged to run for reelection. He was instead appealing to the People to preserve the constitutional principle of presidential democracy after he had departed from the scene.

His appeal succeeded—albeit not by the same margin that prevailed in 1959, when the original Constitution was approved. Voter turnout dropped from 85 percent to 78 percent, and the Nos increased from 20 percent to 38 percent. Nevertheless, the level of popular mobilization remained high, and the 62-to-38 vote amounted to a strong mandate. While de Gaulle had threatened to resign if he only won a "feeble" victory, he was on strong ground in declaring that he would remain in office since the voters had indeed given decisive support for his revolutionary refounding.

This left his opponents with only one card to play. The Constitution allowed them to appeal to the Constitutional Council for a declaration invalidating the referendum as unconstitutional. The Council had been designed for a very different purpose. It was created, not to impose its will on de Gaulle, but to aid him by striking down parliamentary laws that intruded upon his independent powers over foreign and military affairs. Yet, as we have seen, the "presidential watchdog" had already been growling ominously. In its earlier cautionary statement to the president, however, it had been acting in a purely advisory capacity. Now that the referendum had taken place, the Constitution granted it the power to invalidate its results—provided that one of the leading officials of the Republic invoked the Council's jurisdiction.

Only three officials had been granted this power—de Gaulle himself and the presidents of the National Assembly and the Senate. The Gaullist head of the National Assembly had no interest in challenging the president's fait accompli, but the president of the Senate was in a very different position. The

Gaullists did not have a majority in the upper house, which was largely selected by local officials, and more traditional conservatives held the balance
of power. As a consequence, the chamber had elected Gaston Monnerville, a
right-center member of the Radical Party, as its president. While Monnerville had been generally supportive of the Debré government, he was no
knee-jerk Gaullist, and he began denouncing the president's initiative as
"plainly illegal and unconstitutional" as soon as it was announced.[60] Just
as de Gaulle was dissolving the National Assembly in retaliation for its "vote
of no confidence" in Pompidou, Monnerville won reelection as Senate
president by a margin of 212 to 3—and became a leading voice in the No
campaign in the weeks before the October 28 vote. Once the results were
announced, Monnerville immediately played his trump card and called
upon the Constitutional Council to invalidate the results of de Gaulle's unilateral referendum.

This placed the infant Council in a no-win situation. Because its earlier
advice to de Gaulle had been leaked to the public, it would severely damage
its standing if it reversed itself and upheld the president's end-run around the
Constitution. Its sudden reversal would have particularly grave consequences
because the Council had not previously been a major player on the public
stage and a cowardly cave-in could discredit it forever.

If, however, the Councillors held firm and invalidated the referendum,
they faced an even greater danger. With de Gaulle having dissolved the
National Assembly, the voters would be returning to the polls at the end of
November to elect new representatives—and de Gaulle would make the
Council decision the centerpiece of the election campaign. He would predictably denounce the Council for defying the will of the People, and ask
voters for a mandate to enact a new constitutional amendment that not only
overruled the Council's decision, but might well cripple its capacity to defy
the president at later turning points.

Quite simply: whether it voted Yes or No, the infant Council confronted
a grave threat to its future standing. So it's not too surprising that it made
a desperate effort to evade its dilemma: It refused to make *any* decision
whatsoever on de Gaulle's unilateral end-run—declaring that it lacked all jurisdiction over initiatives that had been "adopted by the people following a
referendum, which constitutes the direct expression of national sovereignty."
To reach this conclusion, the Council was obliged to mangle the clear meaning
of the text.[61] Its legal credibility was further eroded when word leaked out
that the final vote was 6 to 4. But the Council's decision to make no decision

was plainly its least-worst option—permitting a strategic retreat that might allow it to rehabilitate itself at a more propitious political moment.[62]

Monnerville greeted the news with despair: "The Council has just committed suicide. If the Council does not have the competence to judge a violation so patent and so serious of the constitution, who does in our country?"[63]

This "suicide" announcement turned out to be distinctly premature. As we shall see, the Council would successfully reassert itself during a series of succession crises after de Gaulle had left the scene. Nevertheless, Monnerville's concluding question—"Who does" determine constitutional meaning?—was a very good one, and I have been trying to provide a foundation for a thoughtful response.

My own answer: It was Charles de Gaulle himself who was claiming the revolutionary authority to assert that the People authorized his "violation" of the Constitution. His effort to transform the presidency was only another in a series of episodes reenacting the same legitimating formula: Popular sovereignty = personal revolutionary charisma + media appeals + popular referenda.

This is different from the formula used by the movement parties of India, South Africa, and postwar France and Italy to legitimate their revolutionary constitutionalisms. While charismatic leaders played an important role, organized mass movements were even more critical. In contrast, *organizational charisma* supplied by grassroots supporters was notably absent in de Gaulle's top-down initiative. Nevertheless, his popular-sovereignty formula seemed to be operating with a similar legitimating effect.

Stabilization?

The Constitutional Council's humiliating retreat permitted it to evade a fatal blow, but it also gave de Gaulle new maneuvering room as he pondered his campaign strategy for the parliamentary elections coming up in November. In a televised address to the nation, he claimed that his referendum victory "highlighted a fundamental political fact of our time . . . the parties of the past, gathered together by a common professional passion of the moment, do not represent the nation."[64] He called upon his viewers to sweep the old parties to the sidelines and grant a decisive mandate to his Gaullist Union and thereby further vindicate his latest constitutional revolution.

The voters gave him what he wanted. His Union won an unprecedented 42 percent of the vote and 233 of the seats in the National Assembly—only nine short of an absolute majority. Close allies in the Popular Republican party (led by Valéry Giscard d'Estaing) gained 36 seats, so the president and his prime minister were in decisive command of the new constitutional order.

The new regime's next test would come in December 1965, when the Fifth Republic would hold its first presidential election. Although he was now 75, de Gaulle refused to stand aside and permit his loyal prime minister, Georges Pompidou, to take his place. Given his high opinion of himself, this wasn't very surprising.

His political opponents faced a more interesting question. Would they boycott the election and continue to challenge the legitimacy of de Gaulle's effort to transform the presidency into a plebiscitary institution? Or would the old parties of the Left and Center accept the new ground rules and try to defeat de Gaulle by uniting behind an attractive candidate who could persuade the voters to put an end to the General's charismatic upheavals and hand the presidency over to a rising spokesman for a new generation, who could better appreciate the distinctive problems confronting ordinary citizens in their daily lives?

A boycott was easier—at least organizationally. French elections are conducted in two rounds: each party runs its own candidate in the first round; if none wins a majority, the two leading contenders compete in a runoff. These rules required the anti-Gaullist parties to adopt a sophisticated strategy. If each opposition party nominated its own candidate in the first round, they would be playing into de Gaulle's hands. Since each candidate would predictably win only a small share of the vote, the General would tower above them all, and gain the majority vote he needed for a first-round victory.

To avoid this fate, the opposition would have to engage in a more coordinated effort. During the first round, a coalition of Left parties and a coalition of Centrists would have to join together to back their favorite candidate; they would then form a united front behind the Left or Center candidate who got the most votes in their second-round campaign against de Gaulle. This would require party leaders to cooperate with their traditional rivals from the very beginning of the electoral contest. Such public-spiritedness would be tough to sustain, especially since de Gaulle would be the odds-on favorite to win even if opposition leaders did unite behind a single champion in the runoff. Why not simply boycott the entire affair?

The parties of the Left resisted this temptation and rallied behind François Mitterrand; as did the parties of the Center, which nominated Jean Lecanuet. Left and Center then gained 32 percent and 16 percent in the first round—

together winning 48 percent against de Gaulle's 44 percent. This was a stunning setback for the General; everybody had been expecting him to repeat his recent electoral triumphs. Even though the General managed to beat Mitterrand in the runoff, 54.5 percent to 44.5 percent, the election was more a victory for the Gaullist Constitution than for de Gaulle himself.[65]

Mitterrand's success in competing on more or less equal terms had transformed the basis of de Gaulle's authority. During the General's first term in office, he had governed on the basis of his charismatic claim, confirmed by repeated plebiscites, to speak for the People during a time of extreme crisis. But as his second term began, he was governing as a duly elected president who had emerged after a clear, but hardly overwhelming, victory. The General's charisma had now been constitutionalized, but the engaged participation of the established parties of the Left and Center also served to legitimate the new presidentialist regime. For the first time since 1958, everybody seemed to be playing by the same rules of the game. But as events would prove, the new regime would have to survive a final test before its constitutional foundations were secure.

Revolutionary Reassertion?

The year was 1968, and the rise of the New Left was generating constitutional crises on a worldwide scale. But the French challenge was distinctive: New Left activists not only succeeded in mobilizing universities and other bastions of the middle class; they also won a strong response from the working class— generating the biggest general strike in modern French history. With students barricading the streets and workers circling the factories, the government was losing control.[66]

As the crisis escalated, François Mitterrand once again took center stage. On May 28 he proposed the formation of a provisional government, headed by Mendès-France, to conduct new elections for Parliament and the presidency. In case there was any doubt, Mitterrand announced that he would once again run for president in the name of the People.

De Gaulle's authority was visibly crumbling—and he made matters worse the following day, when he suddenly abandoned the Élysée Palace and left Paris without even telling Georges Pompidou where he was going, or why. Wild rumors swirled: Had de Gaulle resigned? Committed suicide?

The truth was no less ominous: The president had secretly crossed the Rhine to consult with the commander of French forces in Germany, General

Jacques Massu—the very same Massu who had, in 1958, led the Algerian Committee of Public Safety down the rebellious path that initially propelled de Gaulle into power. On the following day, the president returned to Paris for a television address, whose solemnity recalled his appeal to the nation when the military rebelled in 1962. This time he declared that the students and workers were merely pawns for a well-organized Communist conspiracy to seize power in the name of the proletarian revolution. Serious scholars have found no evidence to support this charge.[67] Nevertheless, de Gaulle announced that he was prepared, as in 1961, to invoke his sweeping emergency powers to use force to suppress the danger.[68]

But he deferred this ultimate weapon to propose a political solution. He ignored Mitterrand's call for new presidential elections and refused to concede interim authority to Mendès-France. Instead, he dissolved the National Assembly and transformed the new elections in June into yet another decisive test of his charismatic leadership. He ended his solemn address to the nation with a now-familiar formula—appealing to the voters to provide the Gaullist Union with a decisive mandate to defend the Republic.

Would the old formula work?

Mitterrand had proved a strong opponent in 1965. But he now faced a new challenge. He not only required the support of the established left-center parties. He also had to convince student and worker movements of the New Left to join the old left-center organizations in a mobilized effort to get out the vote. To put it mildly, it would be tough to build a credible movement party within the short space of a three-week parliamentary election campaign.

Mitterrand's coalition-building initiative turned out to be a miserable failure. Rather than uniting behind him, established party leaders attacked him for announcing his presidential candidacy without gaining their prior approval. While the Old Left bickered, emerging leaders of the New Left alienated the general public with their countercultural antics. At the same time, the broader grassroots movement fragmented into a series of disjointed strikes and disruptive demonstrations without a clear focus.

In contrast, the Gaullist campaign demonstrated its characteristic top-down discipline, while cleverly adapting to the temper of the times. Pompidou reached out to workers and students to satisfy some of their demands, while portraying the general chaos as further evidence of a "Communist plot." To establish their popular support, the Gaullists also organized disciplined mass marches in defense of the Republic.

Confronting the choice between order and chaos, the voters did not hesitate: they gave the Gaullists an absolute majority—the first time a single party had ever gained this distinction in the history of French politics. Indeed, the government could count on three-fourths of the National Assembly, once the votes of Giscard d'Estaing's Independent Republicans and other supporters were added into the tally.[69]

Only one month before, the Republic was visibly disintegrating; but its democratic legitimacy had now been revindicated, with the triumphant Georges Pompidou emerging with a sweeping mandate as prime minister after the Union's unprecedented victory.

This was not good enough for de Gaulle—because it propelled Pompidou, rather than himself, into the role of national savior. To the great astonishment of the general public, he responded to Pompidou's victory by unilaterally announcing that his prime minister had "resigned," and that he would nominate another longtime aide, Maurice Couve de Murville, to replace him.[70] The new Gaullist Parliament dutifully voted its support for the General's new prime minister when it convened in July, but this did not suffice to satisfy the president's need to reassert his symbolic centrality. He immediately proceeded to reassert his charismatic authority by calling for yet another referendum on a constitutional initiative.

His proposal represented a distinctive response to the New Left. In a gesture to the May uprising of students and workers, de Gaulle's proposed amendment would have enabled grassroots groups to participate in advising government on the regional level; and it would also have reduced the powers of the gerrymandered, and indirectly elected, Senate. But the General made it plain that there was something far more important at stake than the details of his proposal. He transformed the referendum into a vote of confidence in his own leadership—announcing that he would immediately resign if the No vote carried the day.

This was, of course, de Gaulle's standard technique for revitalizing his claim to speak for the People. But he was applying his formula to new conditions. From his first referendum in 1958 through the plebiscites on the Algerian crisis through the vote on the popular election of the presidency, de Gaulle's resignation would have shattered the Fifth Republic. But this time his resignation simply opened a path to the presidency for Georges Pompidou—whose triumph in the parliamentary elections made him the obvious choice of the Gaullist party if the General retired from the scene. In returning to the polls in April 1969, voters were not engaged in a life-and-death decision on the fate of the Fifth Republic. To the contrary, it was painfully clear that the 78-year-old General was reaching the end of his career, and that his Republic could not long endure if it continued to depend on his charismatic acts of self-assertion. Instead, the country would have to find a different way of sustaining the General's constitutional legacy.

Which leads us to a seeming paradox: By voting an overwhelming Yes for the Gaullists at the parliamentary elections in June of 1968, the citizenry had prepared the way to vote No on de Gaulle himself when they returned to the polls in April of the following year. To be sure, his margin of defeat in the April referendum was narrow: 52 percent to 48 percent. Yet the president was true to his word, and immediately resigned, requiring yet another national poll shortly afterward in June 1969—at which time Pompidou was swept into the presidency, 58 percent to 42 percent, over a fractured and demoralized opposition still reeling from its catastrophic 1968 defeat.

From June 1968 through June 1969, the French people had gone to the polls three times in a single year. Yet all this extraordinary activity was not a symptom of constitutional disintegration. Instead, the complex messages sent by the voters had allowed the Fifth Republic to survive its first succession crisis. With Pompidou and the Union in control of both the presidency and Parliament, the voters had given the Gaullists a fair chance to demonstrate that de Gaulle's Republic could endure without de Gaulle.

What would the Gaullists make of their extraordinary opportunity?

CHAPTER 8

Reconstructing the Fifth Republic

Once Pompidou was installed in the presidency, his situation was similar to that of other leaders who followed in the footsteps of charismatic founders— after Nehru, there was Shastri; after Mandela, Mbeki; after De Gasperi, Fanfani. All these successors had served for years within the top circle surrounding the symbolic leader. This enabled them to cultivate intimate connections with other party loyalists, and gave them a priceless advantage in gaining the top position once Nehru / Mandela / De Gasperi / de Gaulle left the scene.

Yet, like his counterparts, Pompidou confronted rivals occupying other important positions, who could plausibly assert that the Constitution empowered them to check and balance the new leader's assertions of power. When de Gaulle encountered similar shows of independence from his prime minister or the Constitutional Council, he successfully demanded that they abandon their pretensions to check and balance his charismatic authority and recognize that he, and he alone, could speak decisively in the name of the People.

But everybody—including Pompidou himself—recognized that he could not credibly make such grand claims. He did not owe his position to personal charisma but to his success in winning the presidential election under the constitutional rules of the game. Moreover, thanks to the politics of the 1960s, the legitimacy of these rules, and the Gaullist Constitution more generally, were broadly accepted by governing elites and the general public.

This put Pompidou in a bind when confronting other officials who aggressively asserted their own constitutional authority to act as checks and balances on his power. If the Gaullist Constitution was the basis for Pompidou's presidency, what gave him the authority to override claims that the very same Constitution gave his rivals the right to strike down his initiatives?

As in previous cases, the constitutional text was not clear enough to definitively determine the outcome of these power struggles. They were resolved instead through a series of confrontations that will reward comparison with analogous succession crises that arose in India / South Africa / Italy after the departure of Nehru / Mandela / de Gasperi.

Before engaging in comparative analysis, it is best to get a grip on the internal dynamics of the French experience—which developed in three distinct phases. The first was precipitated by a face-off between Pompidou and the Constitutional Council, which struck down a law as unconstitutional, and managed to gain the reluctant acquiescence of both the president and his Gaullist parliamentary party to its claim of authority.

This victory was extremely fragile, and could have readily been reversed by subsequent events. Only the outcome of a second succession crisis enabled the Council to gain recognition as a powerful actor in the struggle for legitimacy. When Pompidou died in office in 1974, the Gaullist Union split apart in its effort to replace him with his prime minister, Jacques Chaban-Delmas. The Gaullist implosion enabled Valéry Giscard d'Estaing to win the presidency on a centrist political platform. Once in office, Giscard had powerful reasons to distinguish himself both from traditional Gaullists like Chaban-Delmas and leftist rivals like Mitterrand. This led him to push through a constitutional revision that dramatically expanded the Council's jurisdiction—and thereby enable the new president to emphasize that, in contrast to his opponents on the left and right, he was profoundly committed to imposing fundamental limits on the legacy left behind by de Gaulle's repeated violations of the rule of law.

While Giscard's expansion of the Constitutional Council's authority was very important, it did not suffice to securely establish the Council as a compelling institutional presence. The last and greatest test came in the 1980s, when François Mitterrand and his Socialists gained a sweeping victory over their opponents and ascended to the presidency and Parliament to challenge the very foundations of the Gaullist Republic. The Council responded by aggressively defending the constitutional status quo—precipitating an escalating confrontation, which it only narrowly managed to survive. Its ultimate success in deflecting Mitterrand's assault finally generated the broad popular and elite support required for sustained legitimacy—paving the way for further consolidation of the Council's constitutional supremacy during the first decades of the twenty-first century.

From time to time this case study will pause for sustained comparative interludes. But it's best to begin by plunging into the particular dynamics propelling the Fifth Republic into Times Three and Four.

The Constitutional Council's Resurrection

Recall the paradoxical conditions under which de Gaulle left the political stage. Although the New Left had pushed him to the precipice of defeat in early 1968, he managed to regain the initiative and call new parliamentary elections in which Pompidou and the Gaullist Union scored a smashing victory over the disorganized leftist coalition. The General resigned only after he failed, in his follow-up referendum campaign, to reestablish his charismatic authority over the victorious Pompidou.

Once Pompidou ascended to the presidency, however, he confronted a legitimation problem of his own. He had won 44 percent of the vote in the first round of the election, but 35 percent of the ballots went to Leftist candidates—with the Communist gaining 21 percent, and four others splitting the remaining 12 percent among them. This split enabled the centrist candidate, Alain Poher, to squeeze into second place with 23 percent of the vote. While Pompidou soundly defeated Poher by a 58-to-42 margin in the runoff, the new president was perfectly aware that one-third of the country remained deeply alienated from the regime.

How should he deal with this fact? Should he and prime minister Chaban-Delmas seek some form of rapprochement with the Left or should they continue to base their leadership on the threat posed by the Red Menace?

The question forced itself onto center stage as the result of a low-level bureaucratic decision to ban a small left-wing political party, La gauche proletarienne, under a statute enacted during the Third Republic prohibiting private militias. This provoked an ad hoc citizen's group, led by Simone de Beauvoir (with Jean Paul Sartre in a supporting role), to organize themselves as the Association des amis de la cause du peuple—precisely the name employed by the banned party's newspaper.[1] When the Association applied to the Paris prefect for legal recognition, the authorities rejected its request, finding that the new organization was merely a continuation of the banned party. Upon appeal, an administrative tribunal reversed this decision, granting legal recognition to the New Left group—at which point Pompidou's government joined the fray.

In vindicating de Beauvoir, the administrative tribunal had based its decision on a long-standing interpretation by the Council of State of a famous statute passed in 1901—protecting the fundamental right of freedom of political association. The Chaban-Delmas government responded by proposing a statutory amendment that would have rejected organizations that were "trying to reconstitute an illegal association."[2] This initiative generated an uproar among the leftist members of the National Assembly, but the Gaullist majority stood firm and passed the bill on to the Senate. At that point, the chamber's leading constitutionalist, Pierre Marcilhacy, invoked a special procedure enabling a Senate majority to raise constitutional objections to Assembly bills and require the lower house to reconsider its earlier vote. When faced with the Senate's rebuff, the Chaban-Delmas government refused to give way. It pushed the bill through the National Assembly a second time, sending it down the path to enactment unless the Constitutional Council intervened to declare it unconstitutional.[3]

Once again, it was left to the president of the Senate to decide whether to invoke the Council's jurisdiction. By this point, Gaston Monnerville had given way to Alain Poher, who confronted a special credibility problem. He had been Pompidou's leading opponent in the 1969 presidential election—losing in a landslide in the second round. Many would view his appeal to the Council as a mere act of partisanship. Nevertheless, after "much hesitation," he responded to the civil-libertarian uproar by referring the bill to the Council "to throw some light on the matter."[4]

This thrust Gaston Palewski, the Council president, into the spotlight. He had served as de Gaulle's close associate since the 1930s, and his appointment came as a reward for decades of loyal service. But he had gained the General's special gratitude in spearheading the referendum campaign for the popular election of the presidency. As de Gaulle's public spokesman, Palewski repeatedly asserted that the president could bypass Parliament, despite the contrary command of the text. Looking back on his career, he explained his extreme deference to de Gaulle in revealing fashion:

> It seemed to me absurd to explain to the author of the Constitution how that text should be applied. When I tried to do so . . . the General would simply explain to me the precise reasons that had led him to adopt such and such an article—and I could not turn the Constitution against its own author![5]

If the General had remained at the helm in 1971, Palewski would have undoubtedly deferred again.[6] But Pompidou did not remotely possess the charisma of his predecessor. He, like Palewski, had reached his current position by faithfully serving the Savior of the Republic.

The case, in short, provoked a contest between two loyal followers over the legacy left behind by their charismatic leader. Pompidou asserted that he, no less than de Gaulle, deserved deference from the Council. But Palewski had it within his power to establish that Pompidou was no de Gaulle—and that the Council had a fundamental role in checking the pretensions of future presidents to de Gaulle's revolutionary authority as the unique embodiment of the People's will.

Would he do so?

This was a do-or-die moment. Given the Council's humiliating retreat in 1962, a second humiliation before Pompidou would utterly destroy its credibility as a serious guardian of the Constitution—and Palewski was well aware of this fact.[7]

A confrontation with Pompidou would inevitably be risky, but the chances of victory were enhanced by a political factor. If the Constitutional Council vindicated de Beauvoir's constitutional rights, it would not only bring cheers from the Left. It would also gain the support of many on the Right, who would appreciate its spirited defense of political liberty—leaving Pompidou in a vulnerable position.

Palewski, and other savvy Council politicians, seized the opportunity. The Council announced that the government's initiative violated the "fundamental principles recognized by the laws of the Republic," and that it was constitutionally invalid.

The View from Italy

I will analyze the legal basis of the Council's decision at a later point. For now it is more instructive to note some uncanny parallels between France and Italy at this initial moment of judicial ascent. Here too, the newly established Constitutional Court asserted its independence only after De Gasperi, the symbolic leader of Resistance to Mussolini, had passed from the scene, leaving a legitimacy gap open for aggressive jurists to fill.

What is more, the particular disputes confronting the two tribunals raised the very same constitutional values. Just as the French police had suppressed a dissenting newspaper, the Italians were suppressing the distribution of oppositional posters and flyers. In both cases, the legitimacy of the tribunals' intervention would be recognized, however grudgingly, by broad sectors of the government as well as the opposition.

There were important differences as well. Most obviously, the Italian Court was invalidating a law from the Fascist past, but the French Council was challenging a statutory amendment passed by the sitting government. No less important, the constitutional authority of the Italian Court was clear from the text—the only question was whether and when the tribunal would emerge from its textual limbo. In contrast, the authority of the French Council was deeply problematic. Indeed, the distinguished Gaullist professor who then sat on the Council, François Goguel, dissented from its decision along with two former Gaullist ministers.[8] If Palewski had joined them, he would have had little trouble leading the Council in the direction of restraint. In contrast to Italy, his activist leadership would generate a grave constitutional crisis over the coming decade.

But in the short term, the Council's decision catalyzed an important change in parliamentary attitudes that would assist it in future struggles for greater authority.

Political Reorientation

During de Gaulle's rule, most party politicians still yearned for the good old days of the Third and Fourth Republics, when the National Assembly was su-preme and "government by judges" was anathema. But the Constitutional Council's successful intervention on behalf of freedom of political associa-tion precipitated a change in prevailing sentiment on both the Left and the Right.

The most notable sign came in the run-up to the 1972 parliamentary elec-tions. This time around, Mitterrand succeeded in gaining broad support for a joint Socialist-Communist Common Program as the basis of the Left's cam-paign. In a dramatic shift, the Program endorsed the principle of judicial review—and even advocated the replacement of the Constitutional Council by a "Supreme Court" to defend fundamental rights. This was a stunning turn-around, especially by the Communists, who had long feared that bourgeois judges would exercise this power to defend property rights against socialist legislation passed by a working-class majority in Parliament.[9]

The Left's new position also raised a key issue: While the Council's judg-ments took the form of classical French judicial opinions, the panel was dom-inated by senior politicians with little or no inclination to distinguish law from politics. Moreover, the professional legal community had not yet orga-nized itself for serious doctrinal analysis of constitutional questions. A few professors offered up newspaper commentaries, but systematic juristic dis-cussion of the Council's work did not begin until 1975.[10]

The Left's Common Program of 1972 was pointing to a real problem: Unless it was radically reformed, the Council would have grave difficulties functioning as a credible legal tribunal. Why not simply replace it, as the Common Program suggested, with a serious institution modeled along the lines of the constitutional courts then operating successfully in Italy and Germany?

The need for reform would become increasingly apparent as the succession crisis moved on to its next phase.

Gaullist Disintegration and Council Ascent

In 1974 the sudden death of Georges Pompidou required the speedy organization of a special election to determine his successor. François Mitterrand was the Left's obvious choice, but the Gaullist Union was unprepared to fill the gap left by the loss of Pompidou. The party apparatus picked Pompidou's prime minister, Jacques Chaban-Delmas, as its candidate. This choice, however, provoked a political rebellion from many Gaullist politicians, who believed that the colorless Chaban-Delmas would be overwhelmed in public debate by the far more compelling Mitterrand.

The Gaullist dissenters, led by Jacques Chirac, threw their support to Valéry Giscard d'Estaing's independent candidacy. Giscard had backed de Gaulle once he became president of the Fifth Republic, but he had not been a confidante during the General's long political exile. His mentor was Antoine Pinay, a longtime conservative leader in the Fourth Republic who got him a job as a junior minister in the first Gaullist government. The young and dynamic Giscard then rose to lead the Ministry for Economy and Finance before he was forced out in 1966 by Pompidou, who was then prime minister. Giscard responded by organizing his own parliamentary party, the Independent Republicans, and embarked on a double strategy—supporting the government against the Left, but condemning de Gaulle for his "solitary exercise of power." After Pompidou's succession to the presidency, Giscard returned to his old post as economics minister—symbolizing the rise of a new generation of technocratic politicians who promised to lead the nation to ever-greater prosperity.

Yet he retained his political independence from Gaullism, continuing to lead the Independent Republicans. Upon Pompidou's death, he joined the presidential race—easily beating Chaban-Delmas in the first round, 33 percent to 15 percent. Mitterrand did even better, with 43 percent. This led to a hotly contested runoff, which Giscard narrowly won by 50.89 percent to 49.19 percent.

Upon taking office, he initiated a big shift in the system of checks and balances. Up to now, only the presidents of the two houses of Parliament, together with the president of the Republic, had the right to challenge a proposed law before the Constitutional Council. But Giscard pushed through a measure that authorized sixty members of either the National Assembly or the Senate to challenge pending legislation before the Council. This gave a small political minority the power to check and balance the claims of the governing majority on a continuing basis.

Giscard's move poses a fundamental challenge to the reigning school of "rational-choice" political science, which supposes that politicians are narrowly concerned with maximizing their chances for reelection. From this perspective, Giscard was starting off his tenure with a supremely irrational act. After all, it was going to be easy for his opponents on the Left (and maybe the Right) to put together the necessary sixty deputies to appeal to the Council. Since the Council had just claimed a broad interventionist mandate in de Beauvoir's case, it would be in a position to sabotage key elements of his program—making it tougher, not easier, for him to win reelection in 1981. Why would Giscard indulge in the political equivalent of Russian roulette?

His decision becomes intelligible only when viewed as a response to his distinctive position in the politics of succession left in de Gaulle's wake. Giscard's first task as president was to select a prime minister who could gain a solid majority in the National Assembly. This would be impossible if he chose somebody from his own Independent Republican party, which held only 55 parliamentary seats. To establish the basis for a solid center-right government, he asked Jacques Chirac to serve as prime minister, thereby gaining the support of the 183 Gaullists in the chamber. Chirac was happy to accept—after leading the rebellion against Chaban-Delmas, he was eager to demonstrate that he could also outperform Chaban-Delmas.

It was precisely Chirac's ambition that generated Giscard's problem. Giscard, no less than Chirac, wanted to demonstrate that his rise to power marked a break with the tired old government administered by de Gaulle's immediate successors—and here is where Giscard's constitutional reform offered a promising way to stand out.

During the 1960s Giscard had spent a great deal of energy castigating de Gaulle for his unilateral acts of presidential power. By enabling the parliamentary opposition to gain access to the Council, Giscard was signaling that de Gaulle's successors could not legitimately pretend to his founding charisma, and that the powers of the presidency could only be legitimately exercised within a larger framework of checks and balances.

Without Giscard's firm commitment on this matter, his initiative would never have passed through Parliament. Some true-blue Gaullists were reluctant to support any major change in the General's Constitution. Many on the Left opposed his reform as far too modest. On their view, the Council wasn't a credible site for the defense of fundamental principles because it was largely composed of Gaullist politicians who thought in terms of partisan political advantage. They continued to insist that, rather than expand the Council's jurisdiction, the Constitutional Council should be replaced by a serious Constitutional Court, with professional judges dedicated to the rule of law.

Giscard rejected such a radical change, believing that his more modest proposal was a more suitable evolutionary development. He made it clear to the conservative parliamentary majority that expanding the Council's jurisdiction was a central element in his program—and that he was prepared to retaliate against individual deputies who refused to give it their support. This was a potent threat at the beginning of a seven-year term, and the Center-Right finally delivered the votes required to pass the constitutional amendment.

The Great Succession Crisis

This set the stage for the last act in the succession drama. Long before he ran for reelection in 1981, Giscard's centrist policies had alienated the more conservative Chirac—who resigned in protest but returned to prominence when he won election as mayor of Paris in 1977. He then positioned himself as the Right's candidate to oppose Giscard's campaign for a second term. At the same time, Mitterrand renewed his challenge from the Left.

This constellation of political forces led to another intense three-way race in the first round of the presidential contest. Giscard (28 percent) narrowly beat Mitterrand (26 percent) for first place. Chirac finished third—and responded to his elimination with great bitterness. He refused to endorse Giscard in the second round, gravely weakening the president's effort to rally all conservative voters against the Left—and allowing Mitterrand to gain a 52 percent to 48 percent victory in the runoff.

This was a relatively narrow margin, but it provided the Left with political momentum as the nation turned to the parliamentary elections scheduled for the following month. When the votes came in, the Left had crushed the conservative parties in a landslide—gaining 58 percent of the vote and 333 out of 491 seats in the National Assembly.

It had taken twenty years, but the Left had finally recovered from Mitterrand's defeat by de Gaulle in the first presidential election of 1965. The arc of presidential succession had come to its conclusion: from the charismatic de Gaulle to his insider-successor Pompidou to his independent collaborator Giscard to his emphatic opponent Mitterrand.

The Gaullist domination of the Constitutional Council would endure during the early years of the Left's ascendancy. What is more, its institutional importance had been greatly reinforced by its two earlier transformations. As a result of earlier succession crises, it had not only established its authority to invalidate legislation proposed by the government; it could now invoke this power at the behest of sixty opposition deputies.

Yet it remained a transparently partisan body. Eight out of nine Councillors were conservative politicians, with Georges Vedel, a distinguished law professor, being the sole exception. Because only three members of the Council are replaced every three years, Mitterrand was guaranteed a hostile reception from the Gaullist holdovers throughout the entire five-year session of Parliament.

Nevertheless, the Socialists were determined to transform their electoral victories into a legislative program that would redeem the Left's historic mission. Mitterrand's new prime minister, Pierre Mauroy, proposed the sweeping nationalization of big business and high finance. Under his initiative, the state would own every major bank and thirteen of the largest corporations in the nation. But before it could become law, the Council would have to pass judgment on its constitutional validity—generating the final and fiercest stage of the succession crisis.

Juristic Paradoxes

Let's begin with the constitutional framework that organized the escalating confrontation. This requires us to examine some mind-bending puzzles that have their source in the legal logic deployed by the Council in its earlier intervention in Simone de Beauvoir's case.

In defending freedom of association in 1971, the Council based its case on the opening lines of the Fifth Republic's Constitution, which affirmed its "solemn . . . attach[ment] . . . to the Declaration of the Rights of Man . . . as confirmed and completed by the preamble of the Constitution of 1946."

This move endowed the *Fourth* Republic's Preamble with central significance for the *Fifth* Republic, leading to deep interpretive problems.

In drafting the Preamble in 1946, the Constituent Assembly gave it a two-part structure. Its first paragraph looked to the past:

> In the morrow of the victory achieved by the free peoples over the regimes that had sought to enslave and degrade humanity, the people of France proclaim anew that each human being, without distinction of race, religion or creed, possesses sacred and inalienable rights. They solemnly reaffirm the rights and freedoms of man and the citizen enshrined in the Declaration of Rights of 1789 and the fundamental principles acknowledged in the laws of the Republic.

But the rest of the Preamble looked to the future. It emphasized that "the necessities of our time" required the Republic to transcend the eighteenth century's liberal democratic vision of "the rights and freedoms of man and citizen." It then enumerated a long list of "political, economic and social principles" which added up to a very ambitious vision of social democracy. For present purposes, the ninth preambular commitment is key: "All enterprises that . . . acquire the character of a public service or de facto monopoly shall become the property of society."

This provision served as the foundation of the Socialist government's case for sweeping nationalization. For its conservative opponents, however, the Declaration of 1789 remained paramount. In their view, article 17 was the key text: "Since property is an inviolable and sacred right, no one shall be deprived thereof except where public necessity, legally determined, shall clearly demand it, and then only on condition that the owner shall have been previously and equitably indemnified." If this eighteenth-century provision remained decisive, it placed the burden of proof on the government and insisted on equitable compensation. In contrast, the twentieth-century provision gave a blanket authorization to nationalizations in cases involving "public" services and "de facto" monopolies; and it also undermined the right to claim compensation in such cases, since the text insists that private property holders should recognize that their assets have "become the property of society."

The Founders of the Fourth Republic were well aware of this tension. Recall that they succeeded in gaining public support for their postwar Constitution only the second time around, after their first draft had been rejected by the voters. This earlier version contained an elaborate bill of rights that, among other things, made a sharp distinction between the protections afforded personal property and the capital assets held by large enterprises—to the disadvantage of big business.[11]

The second Convention, however, tried to broaden popular support by addressing the hot-button issue of nationalization only in the Preamble. As a general rule, such prefatory statements are used as interpretive guides to the substantive provisions in the body of the text, not as independent sources of law.

This is the point, however, where the Council's 1971 decision in de Beauvoir's case revolutionized legal understanding. It gave the 1946 preamble an operative legal meaning in the Fifth Republic that it had entirely lacked in the Fourth Republic. No less important, it repudiated the Constituent Assembly's original understanding in a second way. In 1946, the overwhelming majority rejected the very idea that an eleven-member Council could legitimately strike down legislation supported by a democratically elected government. The Assembly was intent on preserving the French tradition of parliamentary supremacy. Yet in 1971, the Council's success in vindicating freedom of speech had established a form of "government by judges" that the National Assembly would have found to be intolerable. There can be no doubt, however, that the Leftist coalition in control of the 1946 Assembly did indeed intend to repudiate eighteenth-century notions of property rights. Andre Philip, the president of its constitutional committee, made it clear that "when private property . . . becomes monopolistic," the only "way for workers of these industries" to control their "management" is through "transfer to the collectivity." Addressing the Right's objections on the floor, he emphasized that "the difference between you and us is that you are still attached to a conception of economic liberalism, [but] the great majority of this Assembly has condemned [that idea]."[12]

Putting this history to one side, the language of the text itself compelled a similar conclusion: How else to interpret the assertion that the nationalization of "all enterprises that acquire the character of . . . a public service or de facto monopoly" are "especially necessary [in] our times"?

At the beginning of this section, I promised a legal "mind-bender." If I've done my job adequately, I can now deliver on this promise. If you were on the Constitutional Council in the early 1980s, how would you have interpreted the *clear* meaning of a 1946 provision that *none* of its authors had ever supposed would ever be legitimately invoked in a court of law?

Paradox Resolved?

From the very beginning, Mitterrand and Mauroy took extraordinary measures to arm themselves for the coming constitutional struggle. Traditionally, all French governments turn to the trained jurists of the Council of State for legal advice. But in this case, the cabinet called upon a team of sympathetic law professors to develop an impressive brief presenting its arguments even before the government submitted its proposed legislation to Parliament—fueling an intense debate on these foundational issues.[13]

When the Constitutional Council received the case, however, it took a strongly conservative position. Its opinion announced that the collectivist commitments of 1946 could only supplement, but not modify, the "inviolable and sacred right of property" proclaimed in 1789.[14]

To defend itself against the charge of blatant partisanship, the Council broke with past precedent when announcing its decision. Like all French tribunals, it had previously spoken with a unanimous voice in the name of the law, refusing even to reveal the name of an opinion's author. But in a departure from centuries of tradition, the Council identified Georges Vedel as principally responsible for its decision. Vedel, the only law professor on a Council otherwise populated by Gaullist politicians, was a jurist of distinction who had won genuine admiration for a lifetime of professional achievement. In singling him out, the opinion was suggesting that his undisputed legal competence could somehow compensate for the partisan political composition of the Council as a whole.[15]

Predictably, this gesture failed to calm the passionate opposition of the Leftist government and its millions of supporters throughout the country. A more consequential aspect of the Council's decision, however, did permit a pause for reflection. Vedel's categorical defense of private property could have invalidated the Socialists' entire program. Recall that the 1789 Declaration of the Rights of Man and of the Citizen required a showing of "public necessity" for expropriations. If the Council had denied that the sweeping nationalizations were "necessary," this would have triggered a life-and-death struggle with the government. But the Council refused to rule on this issue, only declaring that statutory levels of compensation offered to big business were insufficiently "equitable."

This finding sufficed to invalidate the government's legislation, but it also framed Mitterrand's options as he considered his next move. Most obviously, he could respond, in the manner of de Gaulle, by calling a national referendum

on a constitutional amendment overruling the Council's decision and reaffirming the centrality of the social democratic principles proclaimed by the
Preamble. This prospect was widely discussed in the press—with frequent
references to Franklin Roosevelt's confrontation with the Supreme Court in
the 1930s.[16]

But after mulling it over, Mitterrand chose a more accommodating
course.[17] His government passed a new wave of nationalizing legislation, but
added provisions that sought to comply with the Council's demand for more
equitable compensation. This forced the Council to confront the question it
had ducked previously and consider whether the entire nationalization program was "unnecessary."[18]

This time around, the government made it clear that another Council invalidation would indeed provoke a special referendum on a constitutional
amendment overruling its decision. As Prime Minister Mauroy explained
before the National Assembly, "We could have . . . , we can still, pose the institutional question [at a referendum]. We have chosen not to . . . for the stability of the country."[19] In case the Council missed this message, Mitterrand
was reported by the press as saying that further resistance would be intolerable: "One time, yes, two times, no, Mr. Mitterrand would never accept it."[20]

The Council responded by allowing the nationalization program to take
effect—bitterly disappointing the Right by its restraint. Yet this "switch in
time" hardly sufficed to guarantee its institutional survival. If Mitterrand had
followed up with more radical proposals, the conservative politicians on the
Council might have further escalated the struggle with additional declarations
of unconstitutionality.

But the path of constitutional politics took a different course. Because
Mitterrand's seven-year term extended to 1988, his next great test would
come when Parliament reached its five-year limit in 1986, requiring another
round of elections. When these results came in, the Left was narrowly defeated by a right-wing coalition led by Jacques Chirac. This led to a period of
"cohabitation"—with Chirac as prime minister confronting his archrival's
Socialist vision. Predictably, his governing parliamentary coalition quickly
moved to repeal its predecessor's nationalization program. Given Mitterrand's limited powers in domestic affairs, there was nothing he could do to
stop Chirac's initiative.

Nor was the Constitutional Council inclined to block the legislation. To
the contrary, it gave its wholehearted endorsement to parliament's repudiation of Mitterrand's transformation of the French economy.[21] Indeed, the

Center-Right's victory at the polls provided a very different perspective on the Council's resistance to the Socialist program. No longer did its initial objections seem to be a desperate effort by Gaullist politicians to reverse the Left's heroic struggle against capitalist oppression of the working class. Instead, it now appeared as part of a multistage give-and-take, involving the president, the Parliament, and the Council, which enabled the French nation to consider, and then reconsider, the shape of its politico-economic future. In short, the period of cohabitation between Mitterrand and Chirac enabled the construction of a distinctive *constitutional narrative* legitimating the Council's emerging role in the separation of powers.[22]

Even before the Socialists lost control of Parliament, they themselves began contributing to this broader reorientation. Between 1981 and 1986, four conservative members of the Council reached the end of their nine-year terms—permitting the appointment of left-leaning replacements. This sufficed to transform an emphatically right-wing institution into a bipartisan body.

The Council's legitimacy was further enhanced by François Mitterrand's selection of Robert Badinter as president. After a notable career as an activist lawyer, Badinter had entered the Socialist cabinet as minister of justice, and used his position to spearhead the enactment of a series of reforms, most notably the abolition of capital punishment. His appointment in 1986 marked the first time that the presidency was held by a distinguished jurist. By itself, Badinter's ascent would not have sufficed to pull the Council back from the brink of destruction. But it allowed him to build on the two-stage political dynamic of the preceding six years, in which the Council's personnel had been rebalanced and its initial act of invalidation had been legitimated.

In short, the paradoxical conjunction of three events—the appointment of a president (Badinter) with professional distinction, the change in the Council's political composition, *and* the defeat of the Socialists at the polls—operated to greatly enhance the institution's constitutional credibility. Over the next nine years, Badinter would lead the Council to take strong stands on a range of politically charged issues. But its very legitimacy was no longer in serious doubt. Two decades after de Gaulle's departure, it had successfully managed a series of "succession crises" in a fashion that had greatly enhanced its claim to serve as a legal guardian of the Gaullist Constitution.

A Comparative Interlude: France and India as Sister Republics

Is this French dynamic unique? Or does it bear a family resemblance to other cases in which jurists have risen to prominence during succession crises? If so, which case study casts the most light?

I vote for India. Nehru's departure, like de Gaulle's, initially led to the ascendancy of a loyal but colorless aide. Like Georges Pompidou, Lal Bahadur Shastri had initially accumulated power during the founding period by faithfully implementing the agendas set out by Nehru / de Gaulle—without ever challenging the charismatic authority of the head of state. Once these symbolic leaders left the stage, however, Shastri and Pompidou used their insider connections to win the top position in competition with rivals who had broader popular appeal.

But both men died suddenly after a couple of years in office, setting the stage for a more independent leader to emerge from the revolutionary elite. In the case of France, this role was played by Giscard d'Estaing—a supporter of de Gaulle, but never a member of his party, who reinvigorated the center-right politics that had brought de Gaulle to power in the first place. In the case of India, it was Indira Gandhi who used her "inherited charisma" to reinvigorate the Socialist commitments of the revolutionary Founding—to the shock of Congress Party bosses who had supposed that she would be a pliant tool for their wheeling and dealing. When Gandhi managed to mount a revolutionary challenge to these Congress Party insiders, the resulting succession crisis shook the constitutional regime to its very foundations.[23]

The French analogue had to wait until Mitterrand led the Left to victory over Giscard in 1981. But when it came, it once again led to a dramatic face-off against the legalistic guardians of the established regime. Mitterrand's struggle with the Constitutional Council was not on the same scale as Gandhi's confrontation with the Supreme Court. It only reached the stage at which he was threatening to override the Council with a constitutional amendment if it continued to resist his Socialist program. In contrast, Gandhi actually enacted amendments to guarantee her sweeping Socialist initiatives—and then went further to crush judicial efforts to protect civil liberties during her authoritarian Emergency period. Nothing like this happened in France.

Yet this big difference should not blind us to common patterns emerging in the life of the two revolutionary regimes. During both founding periods, Nehru / de Gaulle decisively humiliated the Supreme Court / Constitutional Council when these legalistic institutions attempted to block key elements of their transformative programs. But once these revolutionary leaders were succeeded by relatively colorless successors, the Court / Council quickly took steps to enhance their independence—asserting that they, not the political parties that had spearheaded the revolution, should be recognized as the ultimate guardians of the Constitution.

These initial claims, however, did not suffice to establish the Court / Council's authority. They were opening moves in an escalating confrontation with political institutions—culminating in a life-and-death struggle with the ascendant forces of the Left, whose sweeping initiatives challenged basic premises of the Nehruvian / Gaullist Constitutions.

In both cases, the Indian Court and the French Council played a waiting game—fearing that an all-out effort to block the Left's program would only result in a devastating demonstration of juridical powerlessness. To be sure, the French Council's strategic retreat in the first round of the nationalization crisis may seem modest when compared to the Indian Court's abject surrender during the Emergency. Nevertheless, both retreats were seen as dramatic victories for the Left—and both served to emphasize the provisional character of the Court / Council's previous claims to constitutional supremacy during the interim between de Gaulle / Nehru's departure and the rise of a fundamental challenge to the governing regime.

This *strategy of judicial avoidance* enabled the legalists to avoid direct attack by Mitterrand and Gandhi when they dramatically appealed for renewed popular support at parliamentary elections. At these decisive turning points, the crusading Left in both France and India met with defeat at the polls. Rather than enabling Mitterrand / Gandhi to revolutionize constitutional foundations in the manner of their Gaullist / Nehruvian predecessors, these defeats opened the way for their political opponents to repudiate their assaults on the established order.

It was at this point that Mitterrand / Gandhi engaged in dramatic turnarounds. They called a halt to their previous popular campaigns against the jurists on the Council / Court, and joined with their political opponents to affirm what they had previously denied: that the Council / Court was indeed a *legitimately independent* guardian of the constitutional legacy left behind by the founding generation.

This self-conscious affirmation took different forms in the two cases. In India, the moment of truth came immediately after Gandhi and her New Congress Party were defeated at the polls. While serving as a minority in the new Parliament, Gandhi and her party joined her opponents to back the repeal of constitutional amendments from the Emergency. This paved the way for the Court's reassertion of its claim, in *Minerva Mills,* as the ultimate guardian of India's constitutional legacy.

Mitterrand did not suffer a total defeat in the manner of Gandhi. Given the staggered French electoral calendar, he remained president even as his supporters lost the next parliamentary election to a center-right majority. Nevertheless, he could have readily continued his attack on the Council, especially because its opposition to his initial nationalization program played a key role in the Left's recent electoral defeat.

But like Gandhi, he pursued a different course—engaging in a dramatic turnaround to enhance, not disparage, the Council's legitimacy. Given the differing French and Indian institutional setups, these two reversals took different forms. In India, Gandhi's decision to vote for the repeal of her Emergency amendments to the constitution was a vital element in her political rehabilitation. It signaled that, in the future, voters could give New Congress renewed support on the understanding that Gandhi would *not* use her parliamentary majority to engineer another authoritarian putsch.

What is more, when Gandhi led her New Congress Party to victory at the next parliamentary election, she made good on this commitment. She did not reverse course yet again, and issue a fundamental challenge to the Court's claim as the ultimate defender of the constitution's "basic structure."

Her restraint reflected a renewed popular appreciation of the virtues of constitutionalism after the excesses of the Emergency period. But it was also the product of political calculation. Gandhi's enemies had made a mess of their effort to provide stable government, paving the way for her return to power. But an assault on the Court would have revitalized her demoralized and divided opposition. If there was one thing they could agree on, it was the need to prevent any return to Emergency Rule. If Gandhi once again attacked the Court, it would serve as a rallying cry for a new popular movement that would sweep her out of power at the next election. In short, a frontal attack on *Minerva Mills* not only would have generated a juridical crisis; it could well have precipitated a political crisis leading to Gandhi's decisive defeat by her reinvigorated political opponents.

A similar mix of principle and prudence is visible in Mitterrand's decision to end his struggle against the Council—though the French system provided a distinctive set of incentives. Three members of the Council retired every three years, and the president and the heads of the National Assembly and Senate each had the unilateral power to appoint a successor to one of these vacancies. As a consequence, the Socialists had a political incentive to continue eroding the Council's right-wing majority by naming left-leaning replacements. Even the Left's defeat in parliamentary elections still permitted Mitterrand to appoint Robert Badinter as president of the Council in 1986. While Badinter's professional achievements were very substantial, his appointment was also a reward for his loyal service as minister of justice during the crisis.

Once Badinter became president, he steered the Council away from its super-aggressive support of property rights, and toward a stronger civil libertarian interpretation of constitutional values. This permitted the Council to emerge in the 1990s with greatly broadened political support. The Left joined the Center-Right in endorsing its civil liberties initiatives, and the Right continued to applaud the Council's tempered, but continuing, protection of property rights.

The Council's success in broadening its political support also had a profound impact on the legal profession's evolving understanding of the preceding constitutional crisis. Mitterrand's turnaround permitted the next generation of lawyers to de-emphasize the near-death experience of the conservative Council in the wake of its initial opposition to the Socialists' nationalization initiative. As in the Indian case, the profession emerged from the succession crisis with an affirmative *professional narrative*—emphasizing how the decade-long constitutional crisis culminated in an emphatic recognition of the Council's legitimate role in elaborating a Gaullist framework embracing the enduring value of *both* civil liberties and property rights.

Further similarities between France and India emerge once we place Time Three against the background provided by the course of the countries' revolutionary developments during Times One and Two. As we have seen, both de Gaulle and Nehru successfully translated their revolutionary politics at Time One into an elaborate constitutional text at Time Two. Nevertheless, when the Council / Court threatened to interpret these texts in ways that blocked de Gaulle / Nehru's central political projects, they were immediately forced into a humiliating retreat. In the French case, this happened in connection with the Council's effort to block de Gaulle's referendum endorsing the popular election of presidents. In India, this happened when Nehru responded to the Court's protection of property rights by enacting Schedule Nine's sweeping restrictions on its power to engage in judicial review.

The balance of political / legal authority only began to shift with the departure of de Gaulle / Nehru from the scene, as the Council / Court made more aggressive claims to control their uncharismatic successors. In both cases, this first round of legalist assertion was distinctly provisional—as the dramatic retreats before the revolutionary politics of François Mitterrand and Indira Gandhi established. It was only when Mitterrand / Gandhi suffered political defeats at the polls at Time Three that the Council's / Court's central role in safeguarding constitutional foundations gained broader public recognition.

These decisive juridical breakthroughs did not come about through the inexorable workings of legalistic logic. They were the product of remarkable acts of judicial and political statesmanship—operating against the background of ongoing mobilizations and countermobilizations that gave deeper meaning to elite maneuverings in Paris and New Delhi. The combination of dramatic turnarounds by Mitterrand and Gandhi together with well-timed interventions by the Council and Court allowed these tribunals to gain bipartisan recognition of their role as legal guardians of their Republic's revolutionary legacy.

Now that the French Constitutional Council and the Indian Supreme Court had managed to win broad support in the aftermath of their succession crises, a new question emerged: Would they build on their success and manage to consolidate their position despite efforts by the next generation of politicians to evade or discredit their claim as supreme guardian of the country's revolutionary constitutional tradition?

Consolidation

We return to the French story with this question in mind. While the Left's parliamentary defeat forced Mitterrand to confront a right-center Parliament led by Chirac, this period of "cohabitation" was relatively brief. Mitterrand's seven-year presidential term was coming to an end in 1988—and his success or failure in gaining reelection would shape the future of political and constitutional development. The presidential campaign generated a remarkable level of public engagement, with 85 percent of the electorate going to the polls to cast their ballots in the final round—pitting Mitterrand against Chirac.

Mitterrand won by 10 percentage points, leading Chirac to resign as prime minister. The president named Socialist Michel Rocard to take Chirac's place, and then dissolved Parliament in the hope of sweeping his opponents out of power. In making this move, however, Mitterrand made it plain that he was not seeking a renewed mandate for another round of nationalization. Rocard was the leader of a modernizing faction of the Socialist party. He accepted the market economy and focused on initiatives requiring the rich to share their wealth with the working classes. His election campaign appealed to the Center, not the Left, urging voters to support a "United France."

He succeeded, if only barely. The Socialists and their allies won 276 seats while the "Union of the Right and Center" won 271. The swing votes were provided by the twenty-seven Communist members, who provided Rocard with a narrow parliamentary majority.[24]

This is the point at which Mitterrand's previous switch on the status of the Constitutional Council had a big impact. Even if he had continued his war of words against the tribunal, he was no longer in a position to force the Council to reconsider its position on nationalization. But now that he had appointed Badinter, the new president of the Council tried to gain support for a dramatic expansion of his tribunal's authority.

With the government's backing, Badinter led a campaign for a constitutional amendment that would have allowed ordinary citizens to invoke the Council's jurisdiction and call for the invalidation of statutes that violated their constitutional rights.[25] This proposal would have radically redefined the Council's mission. Thus far it had only participated in a Paris-based conversation between the president, prime minister, and members of Parliament. But the proposed amendment would have granted it jurisdiction to respond directly to individual litigants claiming that their constitutional rights had been violated in particular cases and controversies. This revision not only would have enabled the Council to transform itself into the country's preeminent defender of human rights. It also posed a threat to Rocard's own ambitious regulatory program. Even if sixty members of Parliament failed to challenge a new law proposed by the Socialist government before it went into effect, adversely effected individuals would now have the right to call upon the Council to invalidate the legislation later on. Nevertheless, Rocard took up Badinter's initiative as part of his modernizing program, and pushed it through the National Assembly and the Senate within a couple of years.

Only one problem remained: the versions approved by the two chambers differed in important details, and Badinter failed to resolve this dispute before Parliament's five-year term expired in 1993. When the Left lost this election, his initiative lost political momentum. Nevertheless, his near-miss provided a crucial precedent when the campaign to consolidate the Council's authority returned to the public agenda fifteen years later.[26]

During the interim, the Council remained active. Now that the Left was in the minority, sixty members of the Assembly or Senate regularly invoked their right to challenge major initiatives advanced by conservative governments—requiring the Council to engage in a series of concrete decisions that served as the grist for elaborate doctrinal discussions in the academy. At the same time, an increasing number of professional jurists became Councillors.[27] Although they remained in the minority, their presence enhanced the tribunal's professional standing.

Especially because the larger legal culture was evolving in supportive directions. For the entire century between 1870 and 1970, the French tradition had been deeply skeptical of the notion of "government by judges" implied by judicial review. A series of succession crises had enabled the Council to destabilize this consensus, but it would take the work of an entire generation before the legitimacy of its enterprise could be established within the larger legal community. As young jurists rose to maturity, they produced an endless stream of "serious" professional commentary provoked by this or that decision. Their ongoing engagement had a larger cultural consequence— adapting the broader French tradition to create a distinctively legal framework of analysis and critique that was entirely beyond the doctrinal horizons of the generation that had established the Fifth Republic.[28]

By the turn of the new century, young law students and rising judges would be creating a new orthodoxy. They would be immersed in commentaries that treated the Council's work-product as raising fundamental legal, not only political, questions. Paradoxically, the fact that only politicians in the legislative and executive branches could invoke the Council's jurisdiction facilitated this process. When it was politically expedient, the parliamentary opposition could readily appeal to the Council against a government initiative by obtaining the support of sixty dissenting representatives or senators. But these petitions, together with the relatively rare petitions from the government, only added up to fifteen a year. While the issues they raised were often extremely important, the slow pace of decisions permitted professional commentators to assimilate them into the larger French legal tradition in a deliberate fashion, without becoming overwhelmed by a flood of disparate controversies.

This evolutionary development set the stage for the most recent round of legalistic consolidation, catalyzed by Nicolas Sarkozy after his victory in the presidential election of 2007. As the candidate for the conservative Union for a Popular Movement (UMP), Sarkozy had emphatically sought to distinguish himself from Jacques Chirac, UMP's increasingly unpopular incumbent. As part of this larger effort, he cast himself as a constitutional reformer who would "modernize" the Gaullist legacy to meet the challenges of the twenty-first century. Upon gaining a victory over Socialist Ségolène Royal, he immediately redeemed his campaign pledge by appointing a special committee to come up with concrete proposals. The chairman, former conservative prime minister Édouard Balladur, reached out to leading politicians and jurists from the leftist opposition—who collaborated in the formulation of a sweeping reform program.

Their initiative fits perfectly into my broader theme: the constitutionalization of charisma. Consider the reform's treatment of emergency power. De Gaulle insisted on a constitutional text that gave him complete discretion to declare an emergency and rule by decree without regard to any fundamental rights secured by the Constitution. And as we have seen, he made full use of these powers in sustaining the Republic during its early years of crisis.

Yet the Balladur committee imposed strict limits on future presidents who claimed similar authority. Henceforward, they could exercise extraordinary powers only for a limited period, ultimately set at sixty days—at which point they would have to satisfy the Constitutional Council that the "grave and immediate" threat to the Republic's institutions continued to exist. Similarly, a two-term limit was explicitly imposed on presidents, who were also required to gain parliamentary approval for some of their top appointments.[29]

As part of this general program of executive limitation, the Balladur committee thrust the Constitutional Council into greater prominence. It not only gave the Council power to terminate presidential states of emergency. It adopted a version of Badinter's earlier initiative and authorized ordinary litigants to request Council review of lower-court decisions adversely affecting their constitutional rights.

In taking this step, Balladur also revolutionized the Council's relationship to the rest of the judiciary. Up to this point, it had passed judgment only on proposed legislation that was pending before the legislature—leaving it to the Court of Cassation (private law) and Council of State (public law) to interpret the Constitution in traditional lawsuits. But these institutions would now be required to recognize the Council's authority to revise their constitutional judgments.

With this reform, the Council finally gained a position similar to the one occupied by the Italian Constitutional Court, which had also struggled to gain ascendancy over the Italian analogues of the Court of Cassation and Council of State. To be sure, the Italian jurists achieved this objective much more quickly—taking advantage of the succession crisis left in the wake of De Gasperi's departure from power in 1953. In contrast, France experienced a half-century of succession crises before the Balladur committee could seize a similar opportunity. Nevertheless, we have come to a similar moment in Italian / French constitutional development. To state the Balladur committee's ambition in a single line: it aimed to entrench the Gaullist presidency within a much stronger rule-of-law framework.

In elaborating the complex terms of their comprehensive revision, the reformers added another element that gained a lot of attention. This particular provision involved more symbol than substance. But in contrast to its more fundamental rule-of-law initiatives, it enhanced the charismatic claims of the presidency. For the first time, it authorized the French president, like his American counterpart, to deliver an annual televised address to a joint session of Parliament and the nation at large.

When viewed from one angle, this proposal was hardly earth-shaking. As we have seen, de Gaulle repeatedly went on television to rally the People behind him at critical moments. Yet he appeared on the screen as a solitary figure, speaking to the French people on the basis of his heroic role during the Resistance. Sarkozy could not point to a similarly heroic narrative to back up his presidential authority—he was living in Time Four and he knew it. He embraced Balladur's proposal because it provided him with a new constitutional platform for upstaging his political rivals. His parliamentary opponents would have no choice but to remain in respectful silence while Sarkozy delivered his Address to a nationwide audience. The entire spectacle would annually reinforce the president's claim to serve as a worthy follower of de Gaulle.

Naturally enough, this prospect provoked passionate hostility from Sarkozy's opponents—who condemned the measure as a pseudo-royal ritual propelling the Republic toward "hyper-presidentialism."[30] They insisted that the government permit them a separate vote on this proposal, so that they could reject it without endangering the entire reform package. Predictably, Sarkozy and his prime minister, François Fillon, both rejected this demand. They gambled that, when push came to shove, they could gain the requisite parliamentary supermajorities required for the entire package.

This would not come easily. Constitutional amendments require the support of three-fifths of all senators and representatives at a special joint session called a Congress. The Balladur committee's moment of truth came at a dramatic meeting on July 21, 2008. After intensive lobbying by Sarkozy and Fillon, the sweeping revision passed by a single vote.[31]

The 2008 reforms had an immediate impact on the Constitutional Council, which had previously been considering about fifteen challenges annually from the political branches. Over the next five years, it was obliged to confront 465 constitutional questions raised by private litigants—expanding its docket by a factor of six.[32] Not only did this transform service on the Council into a full-time job, but it revolutionized the character of the Council's work. It would no longer be enough for members to confront high-visibility issues of current political concern; they would be obliged to master a host of complex legal issues raised by individual litigants seeking to vindicate their individual rights.

The Italian Constitutional Court confronted a similar problem at its inception, but it had greater institutional capacity to deal with it. From the very beginning, it was dominated by judges and law professors of great professional distinction. In contrast, most French Councillors are still senior politicians familiar with the challenges of statecraft, not the complexities of legal doctrine.

This means that the French Council will have a tough time making an Italian-style transition to its new role. Given the crush of legal business, there will be pressure to increase the numbers of accomplished jurists. If and when they gain a majority, the Council will become more aggressive in asserting control over the traditional supreme courts—which the Court of Cassation and the Council of State may well resist through a variety of legalistic expedients.[33]

This ongoing competition for juridical supremacy will generate great professional passion, and occasional political attention. Yet it should not obscure the main point: the recent success in "modernizing" the Constitution is another decisive step by the post-Gaullist generation to constitutionalize the charismatic Founding of the Fifth Republic within an entrenched system of checks and balances.

I don't suggest that the present institutional settlement marks the "end of history." New movement parties will arise, proclaiming the need for a new beginning in the political life of the nation—and they may one day succeed in mobilizing the French People to support the construction of a Sixth Republic.

My point is more modest. If and when a revolutionary movement party does gain control of the presidency and Parliament, it won't be in a position to sweep away the current Constitution in the rapid-fire way in which de Gaulle repudiated the Third Republic in 1945 and the Fourth Republic in 1958. Instead, it will confront a Constitutional Council whose authority to defend the fundamental principles of the Fifth Republic is broadly recognized and institutionally entrenched.

The majority of Councillors will be holdovers from the old regime, and they will vividly recall the Council's response at earlier turning points—most notably, its successful resistance to the Left's sweeping nationalizations of the 1980s. This will inspire the members to issue declarations of unconstitutionality that resonate in the professional and popular culture, and thereby help frame the key issues for the next series of electoral campaigns.

Only if the president and his or her movement party continues to win election after election will they ultimately gain the *legitimate* authority to repudiate the existing framework and inaugurate the Sixth Republic—and even then, their Constitution may well be profoundly shaped by the Council's earlier rounds of resistance to their transformative program.

I am no prophet. In this book I do not try to peer into the future, but to reflect on the past. I will conclude, then, by offering some reflections on the special difficulties haunting the postwar French experience and the distinctive ways in which they were overcome.

Recall the special "coordination problem" afflicting revolutionary efforts at constitutional construction. As Chapter 6 emphasized, symbolic leaders of revolutionary movements must—in one way or another—gain broad recognition from grassroots activists as legitimate spokespersons for the People during its period of insurgency (Time One).

This is always a tough job. But it is made easier if the leadership and followership manage to organize themselves into a single overarching movement party—in the manner of the Congress Parties of India and South Africa. In contrast, a hegemonic party did not emerge in postwar France or Italy. Instead, the defeat of Nazi-Fascist totalitarianism created an opening for three distinct movement parties—Communists, Socialists, Christian Democrats—to take on the task of hammering out constitutional terms for their nation's "new beginning."

In both European cases, these three distinct party organizations succeed in constitutionalizing the high-energy politics of Resistance—before they split apart as the Cold War gathered momentum. But the Italian and French cases differed in one fundamental respect. Civilian leaders like De Gasperi and Togliatti sacrificed greatly in the struggle against Fascism, but there was no military figure—like de Gaulle—who claimed to speak for the People in a fashion that transcended all three movement parties.

The presence of such a *trans-movement spokesperson* might well have made it easier for the three parties of the French Resistance to solve their "coordination problem" if de Gaulle had used his unique symbolic authority to support their effort at constitutional construction.

But the General moved in just the opposite direction—urging the People to repudiate the constitutional framework the movement parties had worked so hard to build. Even when he failed to gain a victory at the decisive referendum of 1946, de Gaulle did not give up. He refused to recognize the new regime's legitimacy, and seized the opportunity presented by the Algerian crisis to triumph over his old opponents in 1958.

These basic facts led to a big difference between the French and Italian experiences. France, but not Italy, has engaged in two exercises in revolutionary constitutionalism since the Second World War. This simple point has required me to spend many more pages on the French experience.

Nevertheless, our lengthy journey has led us to the same place: today's France finds itself in more or less the same place as today's Italy. Each country operates within a deeply entrenched constitutional order. At the same time, each is witnessing the rise of movement parties raising fundamental challenges to foundational principles. At present, these would-be revolutionaries are encountering formidable coordination problems of their own. Some offer strong critiques from the right, some from the left, and some from radically new directions. While these different "populist" insurgencies have sufficient appeal to gain substantial voter support, their visions of a "new beginning" are so disparate that they are not yet in a position to claim a broad and deep mandate for revolutionary change.

What is more, they confront constitutional tribunals that have won a long struggle to establish themselves as principled guardians of the existing Republic. As a consequence, if these disparate transformative movements do manage to win momentary political ascendancy, they cannot expect their initiatives to go unchecked. Their radical initiatives will be scrutinized by jurists who are deeply committed to the defense of the existing constitutional order.

It is impossible to predict the outcome of the ensuing confrontation. Perhaps it will lead the ideologically disparate insurgents to disintegrate into a host of bickering factions; perhaps it will provoke them to join together in a common front united by a coherent set of revolutionary principles; or perhaps it will lead the defenders of the existing constitutional order to mobilize a mass movement in its defense.

One thing is clear. Given the success of the Italian Constitutional Court and the French Constitutional Council in legitimating their authority over the past half-century, the partisans of a revolutionary breakthrough will not emerge victorious on the basis of a single electoral victory. The juristic defenders of the existing order will instead reject their initial efforts at radical revision, requiring them to return to the voters repeatedly, before they can *credibly* claim to revolutionize the Republic in the name of the People.

This is precisely the promise of revolutionary constitutionalism. It does not guarantee that the future will be better—or worse—than the past. But it does insist that political elites must gain the mobilized and self-conscious consent of their fellow citizens before breaking with the hard-won victories of the revolutionary past and gain the authority to chart a radically different path into the future.

CHAPTER 9

Solidarity's Triumph in Poland

The fall of the Berlin Wall provoked a triumphalist chorus. But a quarter-century's experience has served as a bitter reality check: the twenty-nine states of the former Soviet bloc have turned in a dismal performance, with sixteen currently failing minimal democratic tests.[1] Countries that looked promising a decade ago—like Hungary and Poland—are currently on the brink of breakdown.

The Polish case is of special interest, because most Eastern European transitions were led by political elites emerging from small dissident groups that were not backed by organized mass movements. In contrast, Solidarity was one of the largest revolutionary mobilizations of all time—and it was profoundly committed to constitutionalism and the protection of fundamental rights. Nevertheless, Lech Wałesa and his fellow revolutionaries failed to follow up with a new Constitution that their fellow citizens could recognize as an authentic expression of Solidarity's decade-long struggle against Communist oppression.

Why?

Particular contingencies and personalities play a large role—but so did the influence of the constitutional model provided by the French Fifth Republic. By 1989 the Gaullist regime had emerged from its decisive succession crisis in a fashion that greatly impressed Poles—and other Eastern Bloc nations—struggling to define the terms of their "new beginning." Despite the triumph of the United States in the Cold War, these emerging states did not base their constitutional designs on an American-style presidency. They constructed their new systems using the Fifth Republic as a model.

The French system is typically called "semi-presidential" in the scholarly literature. But this is a misnomer—in fact, the powers of the French president vastly exceed his American counterpart's. Not only is he explicitly protected from parliamentary interference with his conduct of military and foreign affairs. He can also threaten to dissolve the National Assembly and call new elections if it resists his initiatives. In contrast, the American president has no similar power to browbeat the U.S. Congress into submission. To emphasize these points, I will call the French system "super-presidentialist."

The Gaullist model poses a special problem when used in revolutionary transitions. It encourages the insurgent movement to split into rival camps—as some leaders focus on the presidency, and others focus on Parliament, to establish their claims to represent the movement as a whole. Moreover, the ongoing conflict between the rival branches may tempt the president to use his superpowers to dissolve Parliament in the hope that voters will send him a friendlier assembly for the next round of constitutional negotiations. Yet this strategy might only succeed in splitting the revolutionary movement into hostile political parties—which then proceed to accuse one another of betraying the revolutionary principles that united them all in their earlier struggle against the old regime. Once ordinary citizens begin to buy into their new party identifications, it will become ever more difficult for any Constitution proposed by the fragmented revolutionary elite to gain broad popular acceptance as a credible expression of We the People.

This cycle of fragmentation and alienation can, of course, be avoided by determined acts of statesmanship from revolutionary leaders in control of the presidency and Parliament. But bridge-building efforts were in short supply in Poland. The dynamics of disintegration are worthy of careful investigation, since Solidarity otherwise seemed in a particularly good position to redeem the revolutionary constitutional project. In contrast to India and South Africa, Poland was ethnically and culturally homogeneous—unlike the Congress Parties in these two countries, Solidarity did not confront the formidable challenge of uniting disparate linguistic and social groups into a single revolutionary movement in its struggle against the old regime.

Similarly, Communism was completely discredited in post-1989 Poland. As a consequence, Solidarity's leadership did not face the problem encountered in postwar France and Italy—where Democratic Socialists and Christian Democrats were obliged to hammer out a new political charter in negotiations with fellow revolutionaries who could barely conceal their disdain for "bourgeois constitutionalism." Instead, Polish leftists and rightists were united by their common opposition to the old regime's lawless abuse of fundamental rights.

Solidarity did confront sharp ideological divisions on other matters—most notably, on the question of church and state. But this hardly made Poland unique. The French and Italians faced the same split between Catholics and secularists after World War II. This did not prevent them from proposing and ratifying their revolutionary Constitutions.

The Poles failed where the French and Italians succeeded—even though Solidarity had won truly extraordinary levels of popular support. Because I believe that the Gaullist model should take a significant share of the blame, I will follow up the Polish story with some broader reflections upon the "perils of super-presidentialism."[2] But as always, it's best to begin by plunging into the particulars of our case study.

Time One: Revolutionary Beginnings

Solidarity was born in 1980 among a wave of work stoppages provoked by sweeping austerity measures imposed by the Communist government. But this show of resistance wasn't enough to shake the regime to its foundations. The Communists had overcome similar uprisings in the past, and it is best to begin with their first great crisis in 1956.

At that moment, the Soviets were crushing the Hungarian Revolution, and they also were threatening to crush Polish unrest with decisive military force. After a tense standoff, however, they took a different approach. The Kremlin allowed Władysław Gomulka to form a reformist Polish government, which relaxed the Communist Party's Stalinist grip on the country's economic and social life.

This break from totalitarian suppression earned Gomulka popular support, but it also made it easier for opposition groups to organize mass protests and strikes for more sweeping reforms in 1968, 1970, and 1976.[3] The Communists reasserted control on each occasion by a combination of strategic concessions and the use of force, but their opponents also learned a few lessons from the experience. In earlier waves of resistance, dissenting intellectuals and rebellious workers had failed to coordinate their activities. In the late 1970s, the Committee for Defense of Workers (KOR) tried to bridge this gap—with leading intellectuals like Jacek Kuroń and Adam Michnik calling for "reform from below."[4] The regime responded in a relatively tolerant fashion—allowing KOR, and similar groups, to operate openly in civil society.[5] This prepared the way for a new level of coordination.

The power of organized opposition was evident during the next round of unrest. Struggling with its poor economic performance, the Communist regime imposed a series of austerity measures. This provoked a strike at the Lenin Shipyards in Gdansk in August 1980, at which the workers displayed some organizational creativity of their own. They didn't merely stop work; they seized control of the entire facility. They didn't merely ask for wage hikes;

they challenged the core Communist claim to leadership of the proletariat, urging their fellow workers to join their movement. After expelling management from the Shipyards, they raised a banner over the entryway proclaiming "PROLETARIANS OF ALL FACTORIES—UNITE!"[6]

Lech Wałesa's emergence symbolized this message. He had been fired from the Shipyards during the earlier strikes of 1976, but he had managed to sneak through the gates as the takeover began. Like Mandela and Nehru and De Gasperi, he had already sacrificed for his convictions; but he came from a different place in the social order. These other revolutionary leaders were members of the educated elite who rejected cushy positions to join the insurgency. Wałesa was a social, as well as a political, outsider. But as a persecuted worker, he uniquely personified the revolutionary character of Solidarity's demands. Here was a worker leading a union of workers in their challenge to the Workers' State.

Wałesa's background enhanced his symbolic centrality, but it created a special problem. The Party would never allow Solidarity's revolutionary occupation of the Shipyards to last forever. Unless the union could somehow win a satisfactory agreement from the Communist establishment, military forces of the Warsaw Pact would crush its micro-revolution with brute force. Yet Solidarity's proletarian leadership lacked the skills required for serious negotiations with Party apparatchiks.

Here is where KOR and its allies entered the scene. After sixty-four leading intellectuals issued an appeal for a peaceful resolution, two of the signatories— Bronisław Geremek and Tadeusz Mazowiecki—traveled to the Shipyards to offer their assistance to the strikers at the very moment the government offered to begin negotiations.

The embryonic union greeted the two dissident intellectuals with enthusiasm: "We are only workers," Wałesa told them, "these government negotiators are educated men, we need someone to help us."[7] The two men were instantly constituted as a "committee of experts" to serve alongside Solidarity's strike committee. With Kuroń and Michnik joining in, the workers had acquired the intellectual firepower required to talk the language of the apparatchiks and get to Yes.

By the end of August the workers' high-energy politics, together with the intellectuals' mastery of the language of power, culminated in a breakthrough. On the surface, it took the form of a compromise. The Communists recognized Solidarity's right to operate as a trade union independently of Party control, and Solidarity recognized the Communists' "leading role . . . in the State."[8] This permitted both sides to claim symbolic victories.

But facts spoke louder than words: the supremely important point was that the Party was tolerating the union's claim to operate independently of its control. Did this remarkable concession provide an opening for the escalation of revolutionary struggle against the totalitarian regime?

Mass Mobilization

The Party's concession had an electrifying effect: within a couple of weeks, three million workers at 3,500 factories were forming their own Solidarity unions. By early spring, 9.5 million had signed up—representing 3 out of 4 of the nation's 12.5 million industrial and commercial employees![9] Over the same period, 1.5 million agricultural workers—half of Poland's smallholders—were joining Rural Solidarity.[10]

Such a populist explosion could have generated total chaos. But this didn't happen—and for one simple reason. By March, Solidarity was already paying 40,000 staff members for their work in organizing mass energies into a remarkable institutional structure. This was possible only because Solidarity members were voluntarily contributing 1 percent of their wages as union dues—enabling a corps of paid organizers to sustain union pressure on plant floors throughout the country. It also permitted Solidarity to create regional and national offices with full-time staffers who could coordinate grassroots protests into broader campaigns.[11]

At the same time, Solidarity was building on the precedent in participatory democracy established at the Lenin Shipyards. As work stoppages proceeded at other key sites, leadership decisions were subject to the approval of a workers' assembly. This was also true at the regional and national level, with "coordinating" committees of worker-representatives defining the terms of the ongoing struggle with the regime.

At the top of the emerging pyramid stood Wałesa. But he did not stand alone. He was surrounded by an impressive circle of dissidents emerging from KOR—and he was further reinforced when the Communist government allowed him to travel to the Vatican in January 1981 for a formal audience with the (Polish) pope.

All of this shocked the Communist Party to its very core. Immediately after the Lenin Shipyards Agreement, the Politburo fired First Secretary

Edward Gierek—making him a scapegoat for the country's poor economic performance over the past decade. Its new leader, Stanisław Kania, negotiated an uneasy path between reformist and hard-line factions as he framed a response to Solidarity's demands. But by the spring, the Party's three million members were plainly on the defensive—indeed, a quarter-million apparatchiks resigned, and a million more hedged their bets by signing up with Solidarity while retaining their Party membership![12]

Despite these defections, the Communist leadership had a trump card: it remained in firm control of Poland's formidable military and security forces. These could be readily reinforced by the 58,000 Soviet troops that were on Polish soil—as well as hundreds of thousands across the border. After all, the Soviets had invaded Hungary in 1956 and Czechoslovakia in 1968. Everybody recognized that it could happen again.[13] But Solidarity had its own ultimate weapon: a general strike that would shut down the entire country until the Party accepted its key demands.

These mutual threats generated lots of bobbing and weaving during the fall and winter, but they did not force decisive concessions from either side. The great challenge was posed by Solidarity's emphasis on constitutional issues—the protection of dissent and fundamental human rights; the control of bureaucratic arbitrariness through the rule of law. The revolutionary movement refused to be pacified by gestures on the economic front, and it backed up its constitutional demands with work stoppages.

Yet it did not yet escalate these stoppages into a nationwide strike. Wałesa and others threatened to deploy their ultimate weapon, but they did not pull the trigger.

Escalation or Negotiation?

As Solidarity's membership ascended to the ten-million mark in March, its national coordinating committee renewed its threat of a countrywide shutdown, but this time it meant business—issuing detailed instructions for a national "occupation strike" on the Lenin Shipyards model.

It also upped the ante by ordering an immediate general strike if the Party ordered its security forces to seize Solidarity's top leadership and impose martial law throughout the country. More ominously still, the Union issued instructions "in the event of invasion" by the Soviet army—calling upon its ten million followers to confuse the foreigners by obliterating street names, reversing signposts, and making it "impossible" for them to requisition food supplies.[14] With Party leaders rushing to Moscow to consult with Brezhnev, the question was: Who would blink first?

The answer: Wałesa. To be sure, he first sought advice from Mazowiecki and Geremek, who had served him well at the Shipyards; he also consulted Church representatives, who were providing Solidarity with increasingly public support. All of them advised that the risk of military intervention was too great. But it was Wałesa, and Wałesa alone, who made the final decision—telling the national coordinating committee it should retreat from its strike threat. He then reached a face-saving agreement with the government which failed to fulfill the movement's principal demands.

The wisdom of this decision will forever remain controversial.[15] Only one thing is clear. It demoralized the grass roots, undercutting Solidarity's revolutionary momentum.[16] Over the next half-year, moderates in the Communist government tried to co-opt the unionists into the system; but these efforts were finally overwhelmed by a hard-line faction, which gained the appointment of army general Wojciech Jaruzelski as the Party's First Secretary. On December 13 the general declared martial law[17]—seizing roughly ten thousand activists, including Wałesa and other leaders, for indefinite detention without trial.[18] At the same time, his forces overwhelmed workplace resistance.[19]

These massive acts of repression succeeded in imposing a surface calm on public life.[20] As Solidarity was pushed underground, activists could not help but reflect on the moment in March when Wałesa chose negotiations over a general strike. To be sure, his decision may (or may not) have avoided massive bloodshed; but it opened the way for demoralizing negotiations with the regime which ultimately enabled a hard-line response.

This would not be the last time that elite negotiations would undercut Solidarity's revolutionary thrust. But as we shall see, the dynamics of disintegration would look very different the next time around.

Time One: Revolutionary Resurgence

Jaruzelski had restored public order, but he could not crush the revolutionary underground—which demonstrated remarkable resilience over the next seven years.

Underground

Within three months, Solidarity announced its presence in Warsaw with a weekly newspaper, *Tygodnik Mazowsze*. Regular publication required immense organizational effort. To evade the secret police, staff was constantly relocating printing presses and distribution centers. The resistance also confronted the endless job of recruiting thousands of activists to deliver the paper to factories and offices. And yet the Warsaw region managed to circulate 80,000 copies a week on an ongoing basis. Similar if smaller efforts supported underground newspapers in other major cities.[21]

These remarkable achievements kept Solidarity alive as a real presence in Polish life. While the government had stripped the union of any role in labor negotiations, it could not prevent endless popular discussions provoked by the regular delivery of newspapers, pamphlets, and pronunciamentos at the workplace and at home.

Nevertheless, the shift to the underground generated a shift in authority—away from labor leaders like Wałesa and toward intellectuals like Kuroń and Michnik who were flooding the press with analyses of current events that challenged the Party line. These critiques prepared the way for a redefinition of Solidarity's objectives. When the Union seized factories in the early 1980s, it was still aiming for a democratic version of socialism—with Yugoslavia's experiment in worker-managed firms serving as an inspiration. But by 1988, the underground press had decisively turned to free-market economics as the force liberating Poland from economic stagnation. Under the new view, massive privatization of state enterprise was the best way to inject entrepreneurship and efficiency into the system.[22]

Wałesa did not challenge this ideological shift, but neither did he play a serious role in its articulation. His symbolic authority was enhanced by the Nobel Peace Prize awarded to him in 1983, shortly after his release from confinement. Yet it was Warsaw intellectuals like Kuroń and Michnik who gained increasing prominence, thanks to their incisive contributions to the underground press. Michnik's centrality was further enhanced when he, not Wałesa, was imprisoned in 1985 in an abortive strike at the Lenin Shipyards. As the years passed by, it was by no means clear that the hero of 1980 would ever regain the charismatic position he had won when leading the worker occupation of the Lenin Shipyards.

Revolutionary Reassertion

The test came in 1988, when Poland's poor economic performance provoked renewed strike activity. The regime's initial response was more of the same. In May, riot police brutally expelled workers occupying the Lenin Steelworks. In contrast to 1980, the government refused to concede Solidarity the right to organize independently of the Communist Party. Its hard line, however, was not successful in suppressing labor unrest. Within three months, a new strike campaign began disrupting the appearance of law and order.

The August strike wave did not compare to the upheavals of 1980. They "merely" involved thirty plants and 150,000 strikers—but they were largely driven by younger workers, who put new energy into Solidarity as it emerged from the underground. With Wałesa leading another illegal strike at the Lenin Shipyards, the stage was set for a revolutionary confrontation with General Jaruzelski, who remained first secretary of the Communist regime.

Jaruzelski found himself in a weakened bargaining position. It was no longer clear that Moscow would support him if he responded with brute force. There were still lots of Soviet hard-liners in the Kremlin, but Mikhail Gorbachev was not Leonid Brezhnev: Perhaps perestroika would lead the Politburo to greater restraint? If the Soviet troops remained in their barracks, would a resurgent Solidarity emerge triumphant over the demoralized Polish forces of law and order?

The regime's first instinct was, as always, to offer the strikers pay raises. But the workers refused to halt their strike unless the government granted Solidarity legal recognition. This response emphasized that Solidarity did not consider itself a mere trade union, but a revolutionary movement, raising a fundamental challenge to the Party's monopoly over political and social life.

Jaruzelski rejected Solidarity's demand outright. Given the uncertainty of Soviet support, he offered Wałesa half a loaf. In late August his minister of interior affairs, Army general Czesław Kiszczak, went on television to invite "social and worker" groups to Round-Table Talks "without preconditions"— opening a path for negotiations with Solidarity despite its formal illegality. At the same time, Kiszczak added a nonnegotiable demand: the strikers would have to go back to work, or the deal was off.[23]

Wałesa wanted to accept Kiszczak's offer. But would the strikers agree?

To reassert his symbolic centrality, Wałesa had already joined his old comrades at the Lenin Shipyards when they seized control of the operation.

While their strike committee supported Round Table negotiations, younger activists emphatically rejected Kiszczak's proposal. Wałesa recalled, "I was so struck by [their anger] that I couldn't utter a word. I didn't expect that degree of radicalism, the sort that can fuel a civil war."[24]

Five days later, Wałesa was locked in a three-hour meeting with Kiszczak—only to find him immovable on the key question of legal recognition. Nevertheless, Wałesa went along with the Round Table Talks—taking the "the biggest risk of his political career," in the words of a leading biographer.[25] During the next week, he returned to the shop floors and convinced the militants to go back to work and give negotiations a chance.

Time Two: Negotiated Transition?

Wałesa called on familiar allies like Geremek and Mazowiecki to join him at the Round Table. As they confronted their bargaining partners, they were creating an arrangement that defied standard legal categories. On the one hand, Wałesa and his team represented an *illegal* opposition; on the other, the *established* government was publicly prepared to deal with them over fundamental changes to *the regime's own Constitution.*

We have seen similarly unconventional frameworks emerge from other revolutionary situations. Mandela's confrontation with de Klerk at CODESA provides an obvious parallel. So do de Gaulle's negotiations with President René Coty during the last days of the Fourth Republic. But it is best to defer analysis of similarities and differences until we see how the Polish story turned out.

A Veil of Ignorance?

Secret negotiations began in mid-September—with Wałesa and a few aides bargaining with Kiszczak at the Magdalenka palace in a Warsaw suburb. Both sides believed that the government held most of the cards. Solidarity had not yet remotely reached the heights it had attained in 1981.[26] At the same time, the government still seemed willing and able to crush the movement with military force as a last resort.

This perceived asymmetry in bargaining power turned out to be mistaken—but it served as the basis for the negotiations. Given the apparent power imbalance, it wasn't even clear that the government was serious about reaching an agreement. Wałesa had already given away his main bargaining chip by stopping the strike wave. Now that he had restored law and order, Kiszczak refused to reciprocate.

Wałesa presented one key demand before he would consent to the formal opening of the Round Table Talks. He insisted that the government legalize Solidarity and recognize its negotiators as legitimate bargaining partners. This move had great symbolic significance—if Kiszczak agreed, he would be granting Solidarity the same status it had won after its 1980 strike in the Lenin Shipyards.

It also had great strategic importance. If the Round Table opened with Solidarity still bearing the stigma of illegality, this would sorely test the patience of grassroots activists who had only reluctantly called a halt to their strike campaign. If they relaunched a new round of worker unrest, this would make it clear that Wałesa, and other old-timers, no longer represented the new Solidarity's claim to speak for the People.

Nevertheless, Kiszczak adamantly rejected Wałesa's demand—dangling the prospect of legalization only if the talks succeeded. With the two sides hardening their positions, the Magdalenka negotiations were rapidly reaching an impasse.[27]

At the last moment, Jaruzelski tried to bridge the gap by appointing Mieczysław Rakowski as prime minister in late September. Rakowski presented a public persona that set him apart from the standard Communist apparatchik. When he appeared on state television, he didn't content himself with boring bureaucratic platitudes. He projected a strong image as a serious economic reformer determined to deliver real gains in the standard of living. By appointing him prime minister, Jaruzelski was signaling a new willingness to make a deal with Wałesa that would allow both sides to join in liberalizing the system without provoking the Soviet army.

Something analogous occurred in South Africa at a similar moment of impasse—with de Klerk reversing his hard-line bargaining position to gain Mandela's support for a power-sharing agreement that accepted many of the fundamental principles of the old regime. But Jaruzelski's effort at strategic co-optation was far less successful.[28]

Rakowski was no de Klerk. He had long detested Wałesa, and refused to follow through with good-faith gestures that would have suggested a serious desire to reach an accommodation. Instead he heightened the regime's confrontational stance by announcing his intention to close the Lenin Shipyards for "economic reasons." Though he never carried out this threat, it was an obvious assault on Wałesa's symbolic authority.[29] He then followed up with another maneuver. he permitted Wałesa to go on state television in November to debate the leader of the official Communist trade union movement—expecting that the uneducated electrician would make himself into a laughing stock.[30]

This was a big mistake. The regime had never allowed Solidarity's leader to appear on official television—and the debate was a media sensation. With tens of millions watching, Wałesa overwhelmed his apparatchik opponent in the cut-and-thrust of argument. Even the Communists' public opinion polls showed his support soaring into the stratosphere.[31]

With Wałesa's symbolic authority vindicated, Jaruzelski had little choice but to call a halt to Rakowski's provocations and accept the need for serious engagement with Solidarity at the Round Table. Before public talks could begin, however, the First Secretary had to beat back the opposition of Party hard-liners on the Central Committee—who feared that the Round Table Talks, once formally convened, might spiral out of control. Jaruzelski might well have failed to contain his critics if the Soviets had backed his opponents. But Gorbachev refused to commit himself—waiting to see whether the government would gain Solidarity's consent to a bargain that would satisfy Moscow's requirements (whatever they turned out to be).

This allowed Jaruzelski to gain the Central Committee's endorsement for his initiative. Only then did the Round Table formally commence, with much speechifying, at the Palace of the Council of Ministers on February 6, 1989. Once it got down to work, the negotiators divided into subcommittees—with the group focusing on political questions playing an especially critical role. The insurgents were represented by the "Citizens' Committee of the Chairman of Solidarity"—appointed entirely by Wałesa. The group included a hundred leading intellectuals and union representatives, led by the chairman's old confidantes, Geremek and Mazowiecki.[32] Wałesa himself did not play a direct role in day-to-day negotiations. Instead, he traveled around the country mobilizing support of his symbolic authority, and reserving himself for another round of secret top-level Magdalenka sessions if the public negotiations broke down. In the meantime, Geremek and Mazowiecki did an effective job in coordinating their negotiating team, enabling Solidarity to present a united front in dealing with the government.

Unity was especially important, given the Round Table format. Even though the subcommittee sessions were secret, Solidarity's negotiating team had been granted unprecedented access to official mass media—its spokespeople gained thirty hours of television time over the course of the proceedings.[33] They used it to great advantage. The Communist propaganda machine had regularly depicted Solidarity as a chaotic movement split among warring factions. But the negotiators' united front conveyed a sense of high seriousness. This not only increased popular support, but allowed the Solidarity team to focus public attention on its central demands.[34]

In contrast, the government was represented by four loosely coordinated groups from different ministries. This allowed for a certain degree of spontaneity at the bargaining table—with regime representatives making creative suggestions at subcommittee sessions before gaining formal approval from Jaruzelski and other top leaders. But it also led to disjointed media presentations, which sharply contrasted with the disciplined Solidarity performances.

Broadly speaking, the two sides' priorities were clear: Solidarity wanted legal recognition of its legitimacy; the Communists wanted a deal which in which the insurgents accepted a strictly subordinate role within the existing regime. But the Citizens' Committee rejected any "reform" that its mass following would condemn as a "sell-out."[35]

It was especially opposed to any scheme that resembled the "united front" technique the Party had deployed in the past to co-opt potential rivals. When Polish voters cast their ballots for Parliament every four years, they confronted a single slate that contained a majority of Communists but also included candidates from a few Catholic groups and the "United Peasant" and "Democratic" parties. Once elected, all members of this "united front" supported the Party's leadership on all important matters in the Sejm, which at that time was Poland's Parliament.[36] Predictably, the government repeatedly offered to include Solidarity members in its "united front" at the next election; and just as predictably, the Citizen's Committee found this utterly unacceptable. It insisted instead on an arrangement that would allow Solidarity to go before the voters as an independent political party.

Nevertheless, the Committee recognized that it could not press too hard— since the Party might still be in a position to respond with military force. As a consequence, it offered up a constitutional compromise that divided Sejm seats into two distinct groups. Its proposal allowed the government to reserve a majority of Sejm seats for the Party and its "united front" puppets; but in exchange, it would open up a significant minority of seats for free and fair competition. If Solidarity's candidates beat the Party's nominees in these "open" seats, this would allow its parliamentary delegation to assert that it was the *true* representative of the Polish People.[37]

After deflecting this initiative with a variety of halfhearted responses,[38] the Party finally came up with a serious counterproposal. It agreed to open up a minority of Sejm seats, but only if Solidarity accepted new institutional safeguards that would protect the Party's core interests. Here is where the Communists turned to the French Fifth Republic as the inspiration for their constitutional compromise. The Party's draft proposed the creation of a powerful presidency along Gaullist lines, under electoral ground rules that seemed to guarantee the selection of General Jaruzelski as president. This would allow him to use his super-presidentialist powers to maintain Communist Party control even if Solidarity's Sejm delegation rallied public support for hostile legislative initiatives.

Kiszczak's proposal required a fundamental change in the Polish Constitution of 1952, which had previously served as a fig leaf for totalitarian control. When viewed legalistically, this Constitution created a classic system of parliamentary supremacy modeled on the French Third and Fourth Republics—with a majority in the Sejm providing support for a Council of Ministers, which exercised executive authority and controlled the course of legislation and constitutional revision. In turning to the Fifth Republic to protect the Party's interests, Kiszczak not only adopted the Gaullist presidency, but also included a Senate to serve as an upper house that would share key powers with the Sejm.[39]

He suggested that, as in the early days of the Fifth Republic, the new Polish president would be selected by members of the Sejm and the new Senate sitting together as a National Assembly. This set up seemed to guarantee the selection of General Jaruzelski as president—since the Communists' "united front" was guaranteed 65 percent of Sejm seats and Kiszczak demanded Party control over the process which would fill all 100 seats in the newly created Senate.

Once Jaruzelski rose to the presidency, the Party's compromise would grant him superpowers of the Gaullist type. First off, he would possess large and independent authority in foreign and military affairs. This would allow him to reassure the Soviets that Poland would remain loyal to the Warsaw Pact—a key point, since Soviet military hegemony over Eastern Europe still seemed an unchallengeable fact of life in February 1989. As a consequence, the Citizens' Committee was not inclined to deny the general this presidential prerogative.

But it took a much darker view of a second aspect of the proposal. Once again taking a page from de Gaulle's playbook, the Party draft empowered the president to declare a state of emergency and exercise extraordinary powers to restore law and order.[40] This touched a raw nerve.[41] The Citizens' Committee bristled at the very idea that Jaruzelski would be empowered to crush Solidarity once again, and throw the country back into the dark days of

December 1981. Accepting such a provision would amount to a betrayal of Solidarity's revolutionary aspirations in the eyes of its millions of followers.

With both sides standing firm, the talks were on the verge of collapse. Outside the secret confines of the Round Table negotiations, violent confrontations were breaking out between students and police in Poznan, and a scattering of strikes warned of another wave of movement-party mobilization.[42] In a desperate effort to sustain the talks, Wałesa went to Poznan to make a direct appeal: "I beg you on my knees . . . let's give the round table a chance. . . . If they fail, then in April or May I will call for a resolute struggle for Poland and for reforms."[43]

After committing himself to a deadline, Wałesa returned to Magdalenka on March 2 for make-or-break talks with Kiszczak. (Jaruzelski was physically absent, but Kiszczak ostentatiously engaged him in lengthy telephone calls at crucial moments.)

Surrounded by their closest advisors, the two men resolved the Sejm problem with relative ease—agreeing that the Communists and their allies would get 65 percent of the seats, while Solidarity would be allowed to compete for the remaining 35 percent. The so-called "contract Sejm" would sit for four years and seemed to ensure Party control over the near term.[44] Given this concession, Wałesa was determined to reject the independent presidency that the Communists were also demanding—especially when they advanced yet another proposal. This is the point at which Kiszczak proposed the creation of a Senate, originally insisting that all of its one hundred members would be directly appointed by the president. While its powers would be modest, its existence would further emphasize the Communist refusal to cede real power to the minority of Solidarity representatives in the lower house.[45]

This was too much for Wałesa. With the support of the ever-present Geremek and Mazowiecki, he rejected the Communists' sudden embrace of checks and balances. So far as he was concerned, the contract Sejm had already provided the Party with the parliamentary majority it needed to govern over the next few years. There was no need to create a presidency and senate to further ensure Party supremacy. He could not go along with a Gaullist constitution that, to Solidarity supporters, would explicitly endorse Jaruzelski's authority to repeat the tragic repressions of 1981.

Kiszczak was equally intransigent. He made it clear that Party hard-liners would not accept the agreement unless Jaruzelski was granted the presidential power to shut Solidarity down if it threatened to overwhelm the system. The impasse continued for eight long hours. Then another member of the government team, Aleksander Kwaśniewski, broke the logjam by tweaking Kiszczak's pro-posal: Perhaps Wałesa would find the presidency acceptable if Jaruzelski were stripped of his power to appoint the Senate—leaving its hundred mem-bers to be freely elected by the voters?

Wałesa immediately expressed interest, but it was too late for the exhausted negotiators to discuss the idea seriously. The meeting adjourned with the gov-ernment delegation emphasizing that Kwaśniewski's last-minute suggestion had not yet gained Jaruzelski's approval. Nevertheless, Wałesa left with new hope. Geremek recalled:

> When we returned to Warsaw [from Magdalenka], I said that this would be a splendid proposal from our point of view, because, even if we didn't get any-thing else but this, it would dismantle the system for there would be one in-stitution which would be the bearer of Polish sovereignty. And the totalitarian system cannot be reconciled with the existence of even one structure which is really free, democratic, and independent.[46]

An elected Senate would, in short, provide Solidarity with a platform for con-stitutionalizing its claim to represent the People's revolutionary demand for a "new beginning" in Polish history.

The Communists were aware of the danger, but they underestimated the risk. They were party apparatchiks lacking all experience with competitive elections. It was easy for them to exaggerate their capacity to use their tradi-tional coercive tools to get voters to cast their Senate ballots in favor of "united front" candidates in Senate contests.[47]

They were also aware of a more immediate danger. If the Round Table Talks collapsed, Solidarity's activists would no longer remain quiescent. Vio-lent student demonstrations and strikes were already breaking out, as ordi-nary Poles began to despair at the negotiators' lack of progress. But unrest could easily escalate beyond control once Wałesa marched out of Magdalenka and appealed for public support.

This prospect explains the speed of the government's response. At the very next Magdalenka session, Kiszczak announced that Jaruzelski had endorsed Kwaśniewski's proposal. This shocked Wałesa and his team—and they imme-diately agreed to the outlines of a compromise: "Contract Sejm" + freely elected Senate + powerful president.[48]

A lot more work would be required to hammer out the details. Given its hopes for electoral victory, Solidarity's first priority was to ensure the Senate a significant role in the overall system. It did not challenge the Sejm's power to choose the prime minister, but it insisted on Senate participation in the legislative process. If a Senate majority rejected a bill, the Sejm could only override it with a two-thirds vote—slightly greater than the 65 percent guaranteed to the Party and its united front allies in the lower house.

When Solidarity made this proposal, it seemed largely symbolic—since it only required the Party to attract a couple of freely elected Sejm delegates to its side. But Kiszczak was adamant in rejecting it. For him, no less than Wałesa, the new constitutional settlement was much more than an exercise in realpolitik. It was a struggle over legitimating principles: the Party was utterly unwilling to accept Solidarity's revolutionary claim that its parliamentary representatives could reject the Communists' proud claim that they represented the Party of the People in the Workers' State.

For ten long days, the two sides growled at one another in a series of Magdalenka sessions. As a leading account reports, Solidarity appeared "to stake almost everything on this single issue." If the Senate override problem couldn't be solved, Geremek told the government team, they should "forget about the senate-president part of the package for the time being, and just go ahead with the contract Sejm elections."[49]

Note the paradox here: it was Solidarity, not the Party, that was insisting on retaining the classic parliamentary system that had formally governed the Communist regime since 1952. In contrast, Party hard-liners were now leading the charge for sweeping constitutional reform, since it enabled a Gaullist-style presidency to declare martial law if Solidarity got out of control. To save the Round Table from collapse, Kiszczak made a last-minute counteroffer: He suggested that the president, as well as two-thirds of the Senate, should be granted the power to veto legislation approved by the lower house.

At the time, Kiszczak's counter-offer was largely symbolic. The Sejm would be dominated by the Party, so it was unlikely to pass bills that would provoke Jaruzelski's veto. Nevertheless, Kiszczak's seemingly innocuous modification deflected the symbolic challenge to the Party's authority: While Solidarity had originally presented the Senate veto as an attack on Communist control of the Sejm, Kiszczak could sell his counter-offer to hard-line comrades as yet another enhancement of Jaruzelski's presidential power.

Solidarity went along reluctantly.[50] Kiszczak had given them what they really wanted—a freely elected Senate, where Union representatives might win a majority and confront the Party in the name of the People. The grant of a veto power to the presidency seemed a small price to pay for the prospect of such a victory in the struggle over legitimacy.

Yet this short-term concession had long-term consequences—operating as a constitutional time bomb once Solidarity swept the Communists from power. As I have suggested, the Gaullist model has the capacity to split revolutionary movements into factions as rival leaders compete for the presidency. But the additional grant of a presidential veto made the problem even worse. In contrast to France, it transformed the Polish president into a legitimate player in ordinary domestic politics—generating a grim prospect of escalating conflict if Parliament were dominated by Solidarity factions controlled by the president's political rivals. Under this scenario, the two sides could find themselves locked in combat as the Solidarity president vetoed the initiatives of the Solidarity prime minister. The escalating conflict might only succeed in alienating millions of Solidarity supporters—who would turn away in despair as their revolutionary heroes failed to establish a firm foundation for a "new beginning" at Time two.

We shall be describing the dynamics of Solidarity's disintegration shortly. For now, it's more important to assess the contribution of the Gaullist model to the Polish debacle. As we have seen, the Fifth Republic's great "succession crisis" of the 1980s could have had a very different outcome. Rather than redeeming the existing Constitution, the conflict between Mitterrand's Socialists and the Constitutional Council could have led to its revolutionary displacement by a Sixth Republic adopting a classic parliamentary constitution. Under this scenario, it is very doubtful—to say the least—that the protagonists at Magdalenka would have embraced the discredited Fifth Republic as a framework for their negotiations. Indeed, even given the recent French "success," only the Communists were aggressive advocates of the Gaullist model at the bargaining table. Solidarity was perfectly prepared to adopt a purely parliamentary system so long as it permitted the Union to gain an independent voice in governing arrangements.

At the same time, it's wrong to blame the French for Kiszczak's last-minute insistence on a presidential veto. While the Fifth Republic grants its president sweeping powers in foreign and military affairs, it draws the line when it comes to domestic legislation. Within this broad realm, it is the prime minister, and his governing parliamentary coalition, who plays the leading role. If the president doesn't like what the government is doing, he can dissolve Parliament and call for a new election—but at the risk of his own humiliation if the opposition gains a victory at the polls. So long as he allows Parliament to continue, he can't engage in ongoing warfare with his antagonists by vetoing particular initiatives. But in their effort to fulfill their short-term bargaining imperatives, the Magdalenka negotiators went beyond the French prototype to create a super-super-presidential system—without an adequate appreciation of the potential dangers looming on the horizon.

Although the outcome in the Polish case was particularly disastrous, it alerts us to a very common problem with elite bargains in revolutionary settings. Quite simply, both sides are under intense pressure to get to an agreement before popular mobilization explodes into violent confrontation. As a consequence, they can't afford the luxury of thinking through the middle-run implications of alternative constitutional designs. Instead, they take one or another familiar model off the shelf, adapt it to secure a quick agreement—and hope for the best.

This is why scholarly studies of each model's real-world operation are important—they may lead to a long-term reassessment of the different strengths and weaknesses of each model, and thereby point the next generation of revolutionary leaders toward more constructive constitutional options at future turning points.

This is, at least, my hope.

Solidarity's Moment of Truth

Whatever its long-term implications, the Round Table was a resounding short-term success for Solidarity's leadership. Its negotiating team had not only used the unprecedented grant of television time to refute the government's portrayal of them as irresponsible weirdos.[51] Wałesa's success in creating an independently elected Senate convinced his followers that he was indeed a serious statesmen. As the Round Table concluded in April, Wałesa's approval ratings soared to 82 percent.

Nevertheless, the leadership of the Communist Party had not given up their own effort to win the public to their side. To demonstrate their own reformist zeal, they turned to the current Sejm to pass the necessary constitutional amendments to formalize the Round Table system of checks and balances. It was easy for the leadership to gain the requisite support from the "united front," which remained in power until the coming elections. The Sejm enacted the amendments with blinding speed—demonstrating that the revolutionary Round Table had become the country's *legitimate* constitutional authority while the Communist Sejm had been reduced to a rubber stamp.

Legalistic approaches do not do justice to this revolutionary shift. A strict Kelsenian would view the Round Table as a mere "political" event that had no constitutional significance until the Communist-dominated Sejm approved it by the requisite supermajority. But our studies of India and South Africa have already challenged this strict dichotomy between law and politics. Even though constitutional revolutions sometimes involve a clean break with the past, they often involve a period of unconventional adaptation of existing institutions for transformative ends. Rather than seeming an anomaly, the transformative legitimation-relationship between (illegal) Round Table and (legal) Sejm is a common feature of revolutions on a human scale.

With new ground rules set in place, Wałesa pressed for early elections for the contract Sejm and Senate. Perhaps surprisingly, the government was happy to agree—first, because it was anticipating bad economic news over the summer and feared electoral retribution; second, because it supposed that an early date would give it an overwhelming political advantage. After all, the Party would come into the campaign in command of the official media and its propaganda machine. With the aid of its two million apparatchiks, it would be in a great position to organize a "get out the vote" effort in which millions of ordinary Poles would support the Party's candidates at the polls.[52] How could Solidarity, only emerging from the underground, win against such a formidable competitor?

The regime set the polling date for early June, giving the Union only two months to counter the Party juggernaut. It also enacted an election law that it hoped would facilitate a Communist victory even in the minority of Sejm seats open to competitive elections. Under the new rules, anyone could run in the election who obtained 3,000 signatures on their electoral petitions, which encouraged lots of revolutionary activists to enter the race. Solidarity only endorsed a single candidate in each race. But it was not allowed to indicate its support on the ballot provided to each voter. The Communists expected this setup to encourage an ill-informed electorate to split the opposition vote among a host of competing contenders. In contrast, they could use their bureaucratic machine to bring the Party faithful to the polls and cast all votes for a single favored apparatchik.

If no candidate won a majority, the law provided for a runoff between the top two vote-getters in the district. Under a plausible scenario, this would pit the Communists' "united front" candidate against a Solidarity opponent who had been damaged by his backbiting rivals during the first round of campaigning. All in all, this setup promised the Party the best of all possible worlds: Solidarity could not deny that it had a fair chance, but its poor showing would make a mockery of its claim to speak for the People.

It didn't work out that way. The Communists and their puppet allies, un-accustomed to competitive elections, ran diffuse and disorganized campaigns. Solidarity emerged from the underground with a remarkable display of organizational coherence and mobilized determination.

Movement-Party Triumph

When the Round Table Agreement was announced in April, Wałesa and his team had no tight links to the workers and demonstrators who had propelled the movement forward over the previous months.[53] Now that Wałesa had carved out a space for free elections, he made the obvious move. As head of the "Citizens' Commission of the Chairman of Solidarity," he called on activists to organize similar committees to gain ascendancy at the ballot box.

Talk is cheap, and such appeals typically go nowhere. But this time it triggered an extraordinary response, with hundreds of thousands of activists answering the call. By May, grassroots groups in larger cities were organizing at the neighborhood level, preparing for a compelling "get out the vote" campaign in early June. Significant efforts were gathering steam even in previously passive rural areas.

Citizens' committees were distinct from the Solidarity unions in membership and ideology. During the long period of repression, the unions had been banished from the workplace, and the new wave of strikes was largely led by younger workers who resisted control by older labor leaders. In contrast, the citizens' committees were organized by men and women in their thirties and forties who had records of activism from the heroic days of 1980.

There was also a difference in ideology. Solidarity remained a labor union, which used workplace issues as a springboard for a larger platform demanding human dignity, democracy, and the rule of law. The concerns of the citizens' committees were subtly different. Their leaders did not typically emerge from the shop floor—many were already starting businesses in the growing private sector. They answered Wałesa's call "to emphasize their Solidarity identity, to prove that it had not been lost,"[54] but they did it in a distinctive fashion. In spontaneously forming local committees, they emphatically denied that they were establishing a normal political party with an agenda keyed to the interests of workers or farmers or other interest groups. They adopted the characteristic stance of a movement party—insisting that they were speaking in the name of a unified national community determined to break with the Communist past.[55]

At this early moment, the differences between the unions and the committees were mediated by a common recognition of Wałesa and his team as preeminent spokesmen. This made it possible to build up a nationwide campaign infrastructure with remarkable speed. Within weeks, the National Commission was at the center of a regional network established by old-time Solidarity activists in each of Poland's forty-nine provinces. This allowed Wałesa and his circle to endorse particular candidates for each "open" race and to rely on the provincial committees to persuade their local activists to support the nationally endorsed candidate. With very few exceptions, the locals embraced Wałesa's designations—activists flooded public spaces with placards showing Wałesa embracing Solidarity's choice in each "open" race. Given this remarkable combination of personal and organizational charisma, the citizens' network transformed the voting ritual into a vehicle for ordinary citizens to demonstrate their determination to stand up and be counted in favor of Wałesa and his National Committee's revolutionary demands.

This collective engagement generated a massive landslide on election day. The citizens' committees' candidates won 160 of the 161 "open" Sejm seats, and 92 of the 100 Senate seats.[56] Because no candidate won 50 percent approval in the other 8 Senate seats, the French-inspired election law required a runoff—with Solidarity ending up with victories in 99 out of 100 constituencies!

The Communists were also humiliated in the race for their "safe" Sejm seats. To present an appearance of parity with the "open" seats, the Party's candidates were also required to pass the 50 percent threshold to win on the first round. To make this task as easy as possible, the election law stipulated that ballots for "united front" nominees would be counted as Yes unless voters took the trouble to cross out the candidates' names before depositing their ballot papers into the urn.

This electoral device was no match for the organizational energy of the citizens' committees. Grassroots activists convinced large majorities in *each and every one* of the 261 "safe" seats to cross out the names of the "united front" candidate sponsored by the Party.

But would the Communists cheat and declare themselves the winner in the official vote count? The East Germans had brazenly manipulated their election returns the month before—generating lots of anger but no large public demonstrations.[57] Then again, the East German opposition wasn't nearly as well organized as Solidarity. Given the Polish movement party's revolutionary momentum, the Communist leadership knew that it would confront massive strikes and street demonstrations if they reneged on the Round Table deal.

They quickly accepted the official results, and grimly proceeded to the second round to secure a victory in their protected Sejm seats.

This prospect was so uninspiring that second-round voter turnout collapsed to 25 percent. What is more, the citizens' committees intervened to endorse about seventy "united front" candidates who had distanced themselves, in one way or another, from their official sponsors. This tactic successfully allowed sixty of these quasi-independents to win second-round victories over regime stalwarts.[58]

As the demoralized candidates of the "united front" staggered across the finish line, the Party suffered yet another humiliation. The election law reserved 35 uncontested Sejm seats for a "national list" of leaders—provided, once again, a majority of voters refrained from crossing out their names before dropping their printed ballots into the urn. Amazingly, twenty-three of twenty-five Party bosses suffered this ignominious fate, including both Prime Minister Rakowski and Interior Minister Kiszczak.[59]

This shocking result threw into question the entire power balance in parliament. The drafters of the election law were so confident that the national leadership could leap over the 50 percent barrier that they failed to insert a fallback provision for a second-round election. If nothing were done, these 33 "national" seats would stay vacant, seriously weakening the Communists' majority control over the Sejm.

Time Two: The Turning Point

This forced Wałesa and his team to confront a fundamental question: Should they continue their Round Table collaboration with the Party leadership now that the Communists had been so decisively repudiated by the People?

It took only two days for Geremek to give an answer. Speaking at a June 6 news conference, he declared: "We signed the [Round Table Agreement] and we respect the principle: *pacta sunt servanda*."[60] Solidarity would not oppose the Communists if the existing puppet Sejm made a last-minute legislative change to permit a second-round election to fill the 33 vacancies—enabling the "united front" to enter the contract Sejm with its full 65 percent quota of reserved seats.

Geremek's announcement provoked bitter protest. After all, the Party had itself to blame for its legal predicament—its own puppet parliament had passed the election law that failed to provide for a runoff on the national list. Despite the leadership's cave-in, the National Committee's legal team publicly condemned the last-minute statutory change as a flat-out breach of the rule of law.[61]

They were right.[62] But legalisms did not get to the heart of the matter. Citizens' committee activists bitterly denounced a move by the national leadership that seemed to defy the will of the Polish People. They threatened to single out local representatives on regional and national committees for harsh retribution if they permitted the Party to maintain its grip on power.[63]

These grassroots demands also resonated among the 160 elected Sejm members who had joined the Citizens' Parliamentary Club. To be sure, the Club would follow the lead of Mazowiecki and Geremek, who would, in turn, follow the lead of Wałesa (who had not run for a parliamentary seat). But would its members join together to demand reconsideration of Geremek's hasty decision to abide by the Round Table Agreement?

The Moment of Truth

The question gained new force when the sweeping character of Solidarity's victory forced the Communist leadership to engage in its own agonizing reappraisal. On June 30, Jaruzelski shocked the nation by taking himself out of the race for the presidency. He urged the Party's Central Committee to ask Kiszczak to run in his place.[64]

This was hardly a serious proposal. The voters had explicitly rejected Kiszczak when he ran as a candidate on the national list (on which Jaruzelski's name did not appear, since he seemed destined for the presidency). Kiszczak was also a general who had participated in Jaruzelski's military campaign that crushed Solidarity in 1981. If Jaruzelski was no longer acceptable to the Polish people, Kiszczak wasn't either.

The Party's Central Committee reacted with alarm to Jaruzelski's announcement—unanimously asking him to reconsider. But the general hesitated, and refused to reenter the race unless and until Wałesa gave him the go-ahead.

The brute fact was that the Party could no longer guarantee his ascent to the presidency. Under the neo-Gaullist Constitution, the office would be filled by the Sejm and Senate sitting together as a National Assembly—with an absolute majority of 270 votes required for the successful candidate. But the Citizens' Parliamentary Club now controlled 249 seats (160 in the Sejm, 99 in the Senate), and the Communists' formerly subservient puppet parties were showing signs of independence. In a straw poll, 26 of the "united front" Sejm representatives in the Communist coalition indicated that they would vote against Jaruzelski. This was hardly surprising, since the political future of these "united front" parties depended on their ability to convince voters that they were no longer Communist puppets.[65]

Wałesa was confronting a moment of truth: Would he seize the moment and escalate Solidarity's revolutionary break with the old regime? Or would he continue to honor his Round Table Agreement with Kiszczak and his apparatchiks, despite their dramatic repudiation by the Polish People?

After some hesitation, Wałesa chose collaboration. He told his parliamentary supporters, in no uncertain terms, to arrange for Jaruzelski's ascent to the presidency in compliance with the Round Table Agreement.

This decision had fateful consequences. It not only threatened to alienate millions of voters who had stood up for Solidarity at the polls. It also tended to legitimate the Gaullist super-presidential model—even though it was the Communists, not Solidarity, who had originally insisted upon its embrace at the Round Table negotiations.

No need to exaggerate: As we shall see, Wałesa could have reversed course later on. Given its ultimate significance, it is worthwhile considering the implications of Wałesa's paradoxical refusal to accept Jaruzelski's recognition that he and his Party had been utterly discredited by the Polish People.

Gaullist Pathways to Power

If Wałesa had opted for a revolutionary challenge, he might have ousted the Party from power by traveling down two different institutional tracks. Most obviously, he could have claimed the presidency for himself—threatening the "united front" parties with electoral retribution if they did not shift their support from the discredited Jaruzelski to Solidarity's triumphant leader. Once installed in office, Wałesa could then appoint Geremek or Mazowiecki to serve as prime minister of a coalition government supported by the newly independent parties of the "united front"—consigning the Communists to the sidelines as a dissenting minority.

Or he could have pursued a second institutional route to the same destination: he could graciously allow Jaruzelski to assume the presidency, but only on condition that he publicly assure the public that he would not exercise his super-presidential powers, and would appoint Wałesa as prime minister and throw his support behind Solidarity's revolutionary program.

Once installed as president or prime minister, Wałesa would then be in a position to lead a decisive constitutional break with the past. In a speech to the nation, he could develop a Polish variation on themes elaborated by Mandela, de Gaulle, and De Gasperi at analogous points in their countries' development. The current Sejm, he would insist, had no legitimate authority to speak for the Polish people when only 35 percent of its members had been freely elected. At most, it should exercise strictly provisional authority until a genuinely popular assembly could convene in Warsaw—at which time it should hammer out a new Constitution that would definitively repudiate the principles of the old regime, and place it before the People for their final approval.

Wałesa's revolutionary logic would have been particularly compelling, given the existing state of the Constitution. Quite simply, the document was a mess. Many of the old provisions from the Communist-era Constitution continued to survive the wrenching revisions enacted after the Round Table—generating a host of ambiguities and inconsistencies on crucial questions that would predictably arise in the everyday business of government.[66]

At the same time, the call for new elections would have had great political attractions. The citizens' committees had performed with extraordinary vigor during the recent election; a quick follow-up would have enabled new movement party to gain another landslide victory, and play the dominant role in formulating Poland's new constitutional identity—in the manner of the Indian or African National Congress. Undoubtedly the citizens' committees contained competing ideological currents, and might well split into rival political parties over time. But for the immediate future, the movement would have remained sufficiently united to hammer out a Constitution that ordinary Poles could readily view as an expression of their revolutionary ideals in overthrowing the Communist regime.

Wałesa's Decisive Nondecision

Both of these scenarios were very much on Wałesa's mind as he made his fateful choice in early July.

He found the presidency tempting but dangerous. As Jarosław Kaczyński, Wałesa's closest political confidante at the time, recalled: "I thought then that there was no chance of Wałesa becoming president yet—although it seems to me that he was already thinking on these lines. The Russians were probably not the problem but our army and our police would not have agreed. Still, who knows—perhaps I was wrong?"[67]

The rest of Eastern Europe had not yet erupted in July 1989, so Kaczyński's question remained a real one—if Wałesa had demanded the presidency, it might well have provoked a bloody confrontation. What is more, when President George H. W. Bush visited Wałesa on July 9, he also urged caution, suggesting that Jaruzelski's rise to the presidency would provide useful reassurance to the Soviets; emissaries from the Vatican sent a similar message.[68] Nevertheless, the risk of Soviet military intervention was rapidly declining. At the same time, it wasn't clear how much Jaruzelski's ascent would alienate ordinary Poles from their revolutionary leadership.

Ironically, Wałesa announced his decision on Bastille Day, July 14. He declared that the "internal and external" situation required that "someone" from the Communist Party be selected president. Only then did Jaruzelski publicly resume his candidacy. Even so, it still proved difficult for him to gain the requisite majority. Although nobody ran against him, twenty-six Sejm members from the "united front" parties refused to support the general. So did the overwhelming majority in the Citizens' Parliamentary Club.

Jaruzelski squeaked into office by a single vote thanks to Geremek, the Club's newly elected leader. Displaying his skills as a wheeler-dealer, Geremek pressured just enough Club members to ensure the general's victory.[69] Reflecting on his handiwork, Geremek remarked that "there was no better way to accomplish [Jaruzelski's] election than just by one vote."[70]

The president got the message. During his tenure, he never invoked any of the sweeping powers granted by the neo-Gaullist text. With the presidency assuming a figurehead role, the designation of a prime minister became all-important. Jaruzelski first asked his minister of the interior, General Kiszczak, to form a government. But the Communists' former "united front" parties refused to support a man so deeply tainted by his prominent involvement with a discredited regime. By early August, Wałesa was publicly inviting these former puppet parties to join the Parliamentary Club in a coalition government; and by the end of the month, Jaruzelski reluctantly accepted the necessity of a non-Communist to serve as prime minister.[71]

The job was now Wałesa's for the asking. Not only would his ascent give him a decisive voice on crucial short-term issues, but it would also permit him to dissolve Parliament, call for a decisive round of fully free elections, and then preside, in the manner of Mandela, over the great task of promulgating a Constitution to serve as Solidarity's crowning achievement.

But Wałesa took a different course. If he became head of government, he would be required to engage in endless wheeling and dealing to sustain

Solidarity's uneasy majority coalition until the next round of elections. Instead of losing himself in the details of policy, he chose to remain in Gdansk as head of the Solidarity union, and appoint one of his trusted associates as prime minister.

Bronisław Geremek was the obvious candidate. Solidarity's parliamentary group had selected him as their leader, and he was already displaying formidable skills in assembling a shaky majority in the Sejm. Wałesa had repeatedly relied on his advice since the time when he, along with Tadeusz Mazowiecki, rushed to Gdansk to support him at the Lenin Shipyards in 1980.

Nonetheless, his appointment would have challenged Wałesa's symbolic centrality—since Geremek was skilled in public relations and the prime ministership would have given him the limelight on a daily basis. In contrast, Wałesa's other trusted "Warsaw intellectual," Tadeusz Mazowiecki, was notoriously weak at reaching out to the public—bringing a worn-and-weary demeanor to the television screen. As a consequence, his selection seemed to offer Wałesa the best of both worlds. He could leave it to Mazowiecki to handle day-to-day policy and political problems while he could make grand public pronouncements from Gdansk, without Geremek challenging his occasional "big picture" pronouncements on Poland's future. To make sure that the prime minister followed up on his vision, Wałesa could then dispatch his personal aides from Gdansk to monitor the government's performance and alert him to shortfalls.[72]

Wałesa's standoffishness also served as a form of political insurance. Ordinary Poles had long looked with admiration at the enormous economic gains achieved by the market economies of the West—and they were hoping to see a big boom as the revolutionary government liberated the country from heavy-handed command-and-control. If Wałesa became prime minister, he would take the blame if his government disappointed these great expectations. In contrast, if Mazowiecki failed, Wałesa would be in a position to save the nation once again by replacing him in Warsaw.[73]

All this strategizing might have seemed very sensible at the time. But as we shall see, the institutional dynamics let loose by the Gaullist constitution would lead to a constitutional tragedy within a very few years.

CHAPTER 10

Solidarity's Collapse:
The Perils of Presidentialism

During the first half of 1989, Solidarity had taken the lead in the larger Eastern European struggle against Soviet hegemony. Its sweeping victory in the June elections for the contract Sejm marked the first time that anti-Communists had gained the upper hand in dealing with the old regime. But during the second half of the year, Poland's triumph was superseded by even more dramatic events. As the Berlin Wall fell, the Round Table compromise began to seem increasingly obsolete. While dissidents were sweeping to power elsewhere, Jaruzelski still remained president, and Mazowiecki, as prime minister, still had to deal with a large bloc of Communist apparatchiks holding seats in the contract Sejm.

The anachronistic character of the Round Table's provisional Constitution was dramatized further by the Polish Communist Party's decision to dissolve itself in January 1990. In taking this remarkable step, the Communists decisively signaled their recognition that the People had repudiated the Soviet system—and that the only way they could rehabilitate themselves in future elections was to reorganize themselves, which they did as the Democratic Left Alliance. Their "united front" partners embarked on similar identity changes in their desperate efforts to detach themselves from the Communist past.

Nevertheless, Mazowiecki refused to ask the president to dissolve the contract Sejm and conduct fully free elections that would clear the path to a revolutionary Constitution. Instead of putting political legitimacy first, his main priority was the economy. His young finance minister, Leszek Balcerowicz, had initiated a sweeping plan for the rapid privatization of socialist enterprise. The long-term merits of the Balcerowicz Plan's massive dose of "shock therapy" will forever remain controversial. Only one thing was plain: the Plan was going to inflict lots of pain on workers in formerly state-owned industries, who would predictably take out their anger at the government in the next election. Mazowiecki responded to this clear and present danger by deferring a new election—hoping that the voters would begin to glimpse the longer-term benefits of the Plan's short-term dislocations by the time they returned to the polls.[1]

These delaying tactics were especially attractive because they promised to solve Mazowiecki's immediate problems of coalition management. Many members of Solidarity's parliamentary delegation were trade unionists and strongly opposed the sacrifices that "shock therapy" imposed on their members in state-owned enterprises. In contrast, many Communists in the Sejm were prepared to give the Plan their support. There was a political logic behind the sudden transformation of Marxists into free marketeers. Although the Party had dissolved, its old leadership remained in control and had a pressing need to persuade the voters that their freshly minted Democratic Left Alliance would never turn the clock back to the bad old days before 1989. The best way to establish their credibility was to back the legislation required for the Balcerowicz Plan, and thereby participate in the destruction of the Soviet system. This gave Mazowiecki a powerful incentive to continue the contract Sejm in power despite its patent lack of legitimacy.[2]

Things looked very different when viewed from Gdansk. As 1990 dawned, Wałesa began condemning the "Warsaw intellectuals" in Mazowiecki's government for their parliamentary rapprochement with the apparatchiks of the old regime. As leader of the Solidarity union, he increasingly presented himself as the defender of workers in publicly owned industries threatened by "shock therapy." After the heroic sacrifices of the working class during the 1980s, were the millions of Solidarity members willing to allow the Warsaw government to endanger their very livelihoods?[3]

Given the constitutional setup, there was only one way the hero of the revolution could halt this act of betrayal by the "Warsaw intellectuals." He could not simply demand that the government submit itself to a vote of no confidence, and trust the Sejm to do his bidding. To the contrary, now that Mazowiecki could count on the Communists to back the Plan, he could afford to lose many Solidarity representatives and still win in the Sejm.

Wałesa's only hope was the presidency. Although Jaruzelski had been guaranteed a six-year term, the Party's decision to transform itself into the Democratic Left Alliance had destroyed the residual legitimacy of the Round Table Agreement under which the general had gained office. Jaruzelski recognized this fact, and indicated that he was prepared to go gracefully even though his term formally ended in 1995.

Under the constitutional ground rules established at Magdalenka, this left the choice of his successor to a joint session of the Sejm and Senate. But given the Round Table's loss of credibility, the protagonists turned to consider whether they should follow the modern French example and transform the presidency into an elective office.

Wałesa dispatched his trusted aide, Jarosław Kaczyński, to explore the matter—and at first he reported that there was no need to change the system, since Wałesa could win a majority at the joint parliamentary session. But the Warsaw government refused to go along, insisting on a constitutional amendment providing for popular election. When offered this prospect, Wałesa was happy to agree—looking forward to the greatly enhanced legitimacy that would follow upon his direct election by the People.[4] With Solidarity united on this issue, the government worked out an electoral timetable: first, an election for the presidency in late 1990; then, a vote for a new Parliament in 1991.

The Perils of Super-Presidentialism

This hasty decision marked the death knell for revolutionary constitutionalism in Poland. Wałesa considered himself the obvious choice for the presidency, but Mazowiecki challenged his former boss in an effort to sustain the momentum behind his radical free-market program. The conflict between the two revolutionaries led to the chaotic dissolution of the high-energy network of citizens' committees that had been responsible for the massive electoral landslide in the preceding year.

Recall that, during the June 1989 electoral campaign, the Solidarity union had provided ample funds for forty-nine provincial citizens' committees to coordinate grassroots efforts. But after the election, the union became increasingly skeptical of the distinctively civic focus of its partner and cut off financial support. Nevertheless, the National Citizens Committee managed to maintain links among these grassroots movements, whose remarkable vitality was demonstrated at the next nationwide electoral contest.

While the Communist Party had been officially dissolved in January 1990, the apparatchiks were still in control of local governments throughout the country, and were using their power to frustrate reforms initiated by Warsaw. To break their stranglehold, the Sejm passed a law granting each of the nation's 2,300 communities authority to govern themselves on a broad array of issues—with a locally elected Council making the key decisions. This meant that Poles throughout the land would be casting their ballots for 50,000(!) councillors to mark their breakthrough into a new era of democratic life.

There was only one problem: If the citizens' committees remained on the sidelines, entrenched apparatchiks would make sure that their candidates won the elections—thereby providing a democratic fig leaf for their continuing control. This danger sufficed to motivate 100,000 activists to energize and deepen the citizens' network. By the spring, local groups throughout the nation were claiming to be the "only legitimate political force . . . whose mandate to rule derive[d] from the ten-year struggle with the communist regime."[5] And once again, these revolutionary efforts met with resounding success— just as the citizens' committees had crushed the Party in the parliamentary elections in the previous June, they swept the local apparatchiks out of power in a nationwide landslide in May.[6]

But as the committees looked forward to the upcoming contest between Wałesa and Mazowiecki in December, they faced a very different challenge. The activists were now confronting the painful task of choosing between two revolutionary heroes. As the rivals launched their presidential campaigns, the citizens' committees tried to organize a National Conference at which they could head off the split.[7] In late June, delegates came together at a preliminary nationwide Conference to hear appeals like this one:

> Poland is riven with discord, manifested by the inexplicable conflict between the Solidarity Chairman Lech Wałesa and Prime Minister Tadeusz Mazowiecki. Mr. Chairman! Mr. Prime Minister! You fought communism together. Together, you can and must build a democratic and independent Poland.[8]

It was not too late for the two protagonists to heed these pleas. As they began their campaigns, they framed the issues in ways that permitted reconciliation. On his side, Wałesa refrained from a frontal attack on his rival's sponsorship of the Balcerowicz Plan. Rather than targeting "shock therapy" directly, he accused the Warsaw government of destroying Solidarity's soul by continuing its parliamentary collaboration with the Communists.

Similarly, Mazowiecki did not mount a principled defense of his ongoing collaboration with the Communists. He described it as a pragmatic necessity: given the 35–65 partition of the contract Sejm, it was essential to sustain political stability during the transitional period.[9] Once a freely elected Parliament was seated the following year, it would be time enough to engage in a more aggressive campaign to sweep away the military and bureaucratic remnants of the old regime.

Because the two contenders' public positions were not deeply antagonistic, activists were perfectly realistic in agitating for a national Conference to pressure the two men into an "obvious" compromise. Under this scenario, Mazowiecki would endorse Wałesa for president and Wałesa would reciprocate by endorsing Mazowiecki's continuation as prime minister. The revolutionary leaders would then urge the citizens' committees to prepare themselves for another year of electoral engagement—first by mobilizing the People for a sweeping Wałesa victory, and then by ousting the former Communists and their fellow travelers in the coming parliamentary election.

Wałesa rejected these pleas. He relied instead on his close ally, Jarosław Kaczyński, to organize a new political party, the Center Accord (PC), to spearhead his election campaign.[10] On June 30, Wałesa came before the preliminary assembly of citizens' committees to denounce the entire effort to make them the foundation of a movement party propelling Solidarity's ideals into the future. He called upon the assembled activists to join PC and support his "war at the top" against Mazowiecki and his accommodationist policies. He then barnstormed around the country, denouncing the Communist politicians for covertly sabotaging a fair and effective response to economic stagnation—and insisting that their immediate removal was the key to Western-style prosperity.

Mazowiecki responded in his usual way—by presenting himself as a sober statesman, whose judgment Poles could rely upon in leading the nation forward to a modern market economy. What is more, the prime minister's strategy seemed to be paying off. Until the last month of the campaign, public opinion polls were putting him ahead of Wałesa, often by significant margins.[11] With the political winds behind him, the prime minister also formed his own political party, the Democratic Union (DU), to do battle with the Wałesa / Kaczyński PC.[12]

These top-down efforts at party building only served to alienate ordinary Poles from both protagonists. The two new parties, when added together, attracted only 20,000 members—in contrast to the 100,000 activists engaged with the citizens' committees during the preceding local elections.[13] These rival party efforts, however, did deliver a mortal blow to the citizens' network—which disintegrated rapidly as demoralized members either focused on local issues or simply gave up on politics to pursue their new lives in the rapidly changing social order.

Worse yet, the movement-party vacuum provided an opening for a political outsider to enter the race. The new rising star was Stanisław Tymiński, a multimillionaire who had emigrated from Poland in 1968 and accumulated a fortune under questionable circumstances. He had only returned to his homeland in 1989, and when he announced his presidential candidacy, nobody took it seriously.

For one thing, the ground rules for the election imposed a formidable obstacle on political independents—requiring them to gather the signatures of 100,000 Poles before they could enter the race.[14] But Tymiński could readily pay his minions to gather up the necessary signatures. Nevertheless, his campaign took on the appearance of a millionaire's ego trip: a month before the election on November 25, he stood at 2 percent in the polls.[15] But as the heroes of Solidarity denounced each other as a Communist collaborator or a ruthless demagogue, the general public turned away in disgust. Even though Poles knew almost nothing about Tymiński's character or achievements, at least this capitalist outsider was untainted by the struggle within Solidarity. This sufficed to persuade 23 percent of the voters to give him their support. When the results came in, this allowed the newcomer to beat out the boring and bland Mazowiecki, who only gained 18 percent support.

Wałesa finished first with 40 percent, but this was not enough to win the presidency under the constitutional ground rules. As usual, the Poles had followed the French model, creating a two-round system, requiring the front runner to win more than 50 percent of the vote to avoid a second round against the runner-up. Since Wałesa had fallen short, the country returned to the polls two weeks later to make their choice between Revolutionary Hero and Capitalist Savior.

During this interval, Mazowiecki resigned as prime minister and closed ranks behind Wałesa. But many other revolutionary leaders did not. Most notably, Adam Michnik issued a blistering denunciation in Solidarity's leading newspaper:

> A victorious charismatic leader becomes pathologically jealous of his power and popularity. He also becomes suspicious, sensing enemies and plots all around him. In order to get rid of rivals, that is, of ordinary democratic mechanisms, he will promise anything to one and all, and he will not discuss political programs: he himself becomes his own program. He always talks about himself, his merits and congenial achievements, describing his plans in the most scant and general terms. He promises accelerations: fast improvement for everyone. . . . Lech Wałesa will not be president of a democratic Poland.[16]

Wałesa could no longer respond to the "Warsaw intellectuals" by turning to the citizens' committees to rally behind his candidacy—he himself had destroyed their efforts to form a Solidarity movement party. With the committees demobilized, and the mass public demoralized, only 54 percent of eligible voters went to the polls to choose between Wałesa and Tymiński—compared to the 90 percent turnout generated by the citizens' committees in their sweeping victory over the Communists in June 1988.

When the electoral returns came in, Wałesa did win an impressive victory—beating Tymiński by a 3-to-1 margin. But in contrast to Nehru, Mandela, and De Gasperi, he was alone at the top, without the mobilized support of a grassroots movement party. In this respect, he resembled de Gaulle, who also won the presidency in top-down fashion.

With one big difference. Within eighteen months of gaining power, the General had moved decisively to enact the Constitution of the Fifth Republic and then sweep his political supporters into a commanding position in Parliament. In contrast, Wałesa failed to use the revolutionary moment to advantage. Now that he had gained the presidency, he continued to face a contract Sejm controlled by his embittered revolutionary rivals.

To put it mildly, this was not a congenial setting for Wałesa to work with Parliament to hammer out a common constitutional text they could present to their fellow citizens as an *authentic* expression of their decade-long struggle against Communist authoritarianism. Nevertheless, our earlier case studies have demonstrated that revolutionary leaders have sometimes managed to transcend personal rivalries to work together for the common good. Would Mazowiecki and Wałesa rise this challenge?

Breakdown

Mazowiecki had become prime minister in August 1989—sixteen months before Wałesa ascended to the presidency in December 1990. Although his first priority was the Balcerowicz Plan, he was very much alive to the pressing need for a new Constitution. Formally speaking, the current basis of the contract Sejm's authority was the Communist Constitution of 1952. But by 1989, this text had become a legal mess. During the decades of Communist ascendancy, it had been repeatedly amended to make a host of symbolic gestures to Moscow, the West, and the Polish people. Since it was the Party, not the Constitution, that ruled, there was no compelling need for textual coherence. Confusion was compounded by the neo-Gaullist innovations approved at the Round Table Talks and enacted into the Constitution by the Communist Parliament before it was dissolved for new elections. These last-minute revisions—describing the novel power relationships between president, Senate and Sejm—were full of ambiguities. This made the need for a new Constitution even more pressing.

The Mazowiecki government quickly gained Sejm consent for a special constitutional commission to confront this formidable task. But it had a hard time selecting its forty-six members. Solidarity only commanded 35 percent of the Sejm seats, so the commission would have to include representatives from the Communist "united front." Yet this would create a big problem when Parliament approved the proposal and placed it before the voters in a special referendum. At that point, opponents could readily call upon the People to vote No because Communist participation tainted the entire enterprise.[17] To counter this difficulty, Mazowiecki looked for a chairman whose large contributions to the revolution had given him an honored place in the popular narrative.

He turned to Bronisław Geremek, his disappointed rival for prime minister, and offered the chairmanship to his longtime revolutionary comrade as a consolation prize. Geremek's past career demonstrated the high intelligence and statesmanship needed to gain public support for the project. Nevertheless, his great contributions to Solidarity's struggle were not enough to deflect a powerful challenge from the Senate.

In contrast to the contract Sejm, 99 of the Senate's 100 freely elected members represented Solidarity. Untainted by Communist holdovers, the Senate appointed its own constitutional commission. Over the next year, this Senate group took an increasingly independent course—finally proposing a competing draft based on principles very different from those sponsored by Geremek's commission. By the time Wałesa gained the presidency, both the Sejm and the Senate were in the last stages of developing their competing visions of Poland's constitutional future—provoking a vibrant popular debate in the nation at large.[18]

Before turning to Wałesa's intervention into this conflict between the two chambers, it's important to consider a short-term initiative that would have an enduring impact on future developments.

A More than Symbolic Gesture

Mazowiecki and his allies were not prepared to await the Geremek commission's judgment on one key matter. The existing Constitution proclaimed that Poland was a People's Republic led by the Communist Party and allied with the Soviet Union. This was simply unacceptable for a revolutionary government swept into power by Solidarity. Within four months, Mazowiecki and his allies gained the supermajority required to enact constitutional amendments that erased such references from the text. Henceforth, the "Republic of Poland" would be a "democratic state ruled by law, implementing principles of social justice."[19]

For ordinary Poles, the key point was the amendment's decisive repudiation of the old regime. The precise meaning of the replacement terms—"democracy," "rule of law," "social justice"—did not generate significant debate in Parliament or the public. They were incorporated into the text by a few parliamentarians and jurists led by Janina Zakrzewska, whose revolutionary past gave her special authority in the drafting process. When she was a rising young jurist, she had joined an earlier wave of protest against the Communists in 1968, and she continued to speak out against the regime when she was fired from her post in the legal establishment. Over the next two decades, she refused to follow the example of so many of her peers who kept quiet and kept their jobs. Now that the old order was disintegrating, the Mazowiecki government rewarded Zakrzewska's two decades of revolutionary activity by appointing her to the Constitutional Tribunal. Once installed in office, she spearheaded a drive to transform 1989's "rule of law" formula into the foundation for an aggressive assertion of judicial review.

This too was a surprise, since the Tribunal was not originally intended to play an active role in overseeing the lawmaking process. It was created by the Communist Sejm three months after General Jaruzelski declared a State of Emergency to crush Solidarity in December 1981—in a desperate effort to suggest that the government was indeed committed to the ultimate restoration of the rule of law.[20]

This constitutional gesture was entirely incredible at a moment when Solidarity activists were still under arbitrary detention by Polish security forces. What is more, Jaruzelski's amendment explicitly authorized a two-thirds majority of the Sejm to overrule the new Tribunal if it found any law unconstitutional. Because the Party was then in complete control of Parliament, this guaranteed the Tribunal's purely "decorative" character.

Nevertheless, government hard-liners were opposed to the very idea that judges might legitimately intervene to control the Party. They successfully sabotaged the passage of implementing legislation for three years. Even when reform Communists managed to pass the necessary statute in 1985, its terms only served to emphasize the Tribunal's weakness. The "reformers" followed the Gaullist model and denied ordinary litigants any access to the Tribunal— permitting only Communist-controlled institutions to ask for a ruling. Their statute also explicitly barred the judges from considering a broad range of national security measures, including all those arising out of the Jaruzelski's Emergency.[21]

The justices got the message: Between 1986 and 1989, the new Tribunal refused to invalidate a single statutory provision—ostentatiously retreating from high-level confrontations with the Communist-controlled political branches. The Court demonstrated a good deal of independence on less contentious issues, but it was broadly perceived "as bowing to political expedience at the expense of constitutional coherence."[22]

Things began to change in 1989—at about the same time the Mazowiecki government was pushing its December amendments through Parliament.[23] For starters, six of the original twelve justices were scheduled to leave the Court—affording the new government the opportunity to make appointments that would change its direction. Given the Tribunal's evasions on high-profile issues, these openings did not tempt Solidarity's important politicians to give up their current jobs. Zakrzewska, in contrast, saw the chance to propel the Tribunal into a position of constitutional leadership. As early as 1964, she had already published a book on judicial review.[24] After she was expelled from the academy, she came forward in support of a resolution, endorsed by the Solidarity Congress in 1981, demanding judicial review of all legislation.[25] Now that Poland's first non-Communist government had substituted "rule of law" for the "leading role of the Party," she urged her colleagues to use this formula to redeem Solidarity's commitment to fundamental rights.

Her initiatives met with some success. The other five December appointees did not have Zakrzewska's strong revolutionary credentials. But neither were they hard-line apologists for the old regime. They were law professors and judges who had managed to carve out a degree of professional independence during the Communist era. This was also largely true of the six holdovers from 1985, who tended to express the views of the Party's reform wing.

To be sure, the Tribunal exercised great caution on hot-button issues. Remember that the existing Constitution placed them at the mercy of two-thirds of the Sejm—and there was also a very serious risk that either the government or the president would simply order their subordinates to ignore the Court's commands. Nevertheless, the Tribunal's early interventions on behalf of fundamental rights took some of the urgency out of the movement for a new Constitution. Because the justices were already transforming the open-ended 1989 formulas into hard law, it seemed less imperative to hammer out an elaborate Bill of Rights for immediate submission to the People.

To put the point in terms of my "three paths" model, the Tribunal was an elite construction, whose well-meaning efforts to secure fundamental rights were making it easier for Solidarity's political leadership to delay a big push down the revolutionary pathway to legitimate a full-blown Constitution, including a Bill of Rights, in the name of the Polish People.

Impasse

We return to December 1990 and Wałesa's rise to the presidency. By that point, both the Sejm and Senate were in the final stages in hammering out a draft Constitution. The plan was to submit the draft at a referendum at the same time voters returned to the polls to elect a new Parliament.

The two chambers were advancing rival visions. Under Geremek's leadership, the Sejm draft protected a wide range of social rights, but the Senate's Bill of Rights was largely restricted to the classic liberal freedoms. The two proposals also differed in institutional design. The Sejm's proposal constructed a parliamentary model, whereas the Senate refined the presidentialist model inherited from the Round Table.[26]

This last point was decisive for Wałesa. He had struggled mightily to establish that the People looked to him, not Mazowiecki, to carry on the work of Solidarity. He was not about to give the "Warsaw intellectuals" the chance to undercut his presidential victory by giving the voters a chance to approve a Constitution that would grant the leading role to the prime minister and his parliamentary coalition. Once Wałesa came out in favor of the Senate draft, there was no hope of reaching a compromise that would attract a Yes vote at the next election. Instead, the Sejm adjourned without advancing any proposal whatsoever, and Wałesa and his Solidarity rivals focused all their energies on gaining the upper hand in the upcoming parliamentary elections.

The shape of Poland's Constitution had become inextricably intertwined with the immediate power struggle between rival leadership factions.

Crisis

As the political campaign for Parliament began, voters confronted a radically new political situation. Now that Wałesa had destroyed the citizens' committees, competing political entrepreneurs formed a host of new parties to fill the legitimacy vacuum. Nine different organizations presented their own distinct slates of candidates in all 36 regions of the country—and 17 more ran slates in at least 30 regions. The cacophony of voices generated mass confusion and alienation—only 43 percent of eligible voters took the trouble to go to the polls in October 1991.

The former Communists were a major beneficiary. The Party had officially dissolved, and the leaders of its reformist wing had reorganized themselves as the Democratic Left Alliance. They could rely on old-time Party apparatchiks to use their still-substantial influence to get out the vote for the Alliance. A similar dynamic permitted the Polish Peasant Party to emerge from the remnants of the old regime's rural organization.[27] The old-regime politicians were now declaring their loyalty to the new democratic order, but it was nevertheless astonishing when the two old-new parties gained the same degree of support as the two leading parties emerging from the wreckage of Solidarity. More precisely, Mazowiecki's Democratic Union and Wałesa's Civic Center Alliance[28] won, respectively, 12.3 percent and 8.7 percent of Sejm seats—adding up to the same 20 percent scored by the Left Alliance–Peasant coalition.

To make matters even more confusing, Wałesa had relied on his trusted aide, Jarosław Kaczyński, to manage the Civic Center Alliance for him—only to see him betray his trust and wrest control of the Alliance from him. So far as Kaczyński was concerned, Wałesa had been unduly tolerant of Mazowiecki's marriage of convenience with Communists in the contract Sejm. His Alliance insisted that the new Sejm embark on a sweeping purge of Communist holdovers in the military and bureaucracy. This split the two Solidarity parties apart, setting Kaczyński at loggerheads with Mazowiecki's Democratic Union, which placed a high value on the bureaucratic competence of many holdovers from the old regime.

The resurgence of the former Communists, and the split between the Center Alliance and the Democratic Union, were only a prelude to the confusion created by Poland's first free parliamentary election. Six other parties, emerging from different Solidarity splinters, each gained 5 to 9 percent of Sejm seats. When added together, they held the balance of power.[29] But they too were quarreling among themselves—except on one important point. These splinter groups formed a "Right Solidarity" coalition emphatically opposed to the continuation of the "shock therapy" imposed by the Balcerowicz Plan. They called instead for aggressive welfare-state measures to ease the pain that had been inflicted on workers and their families. This part of their program seemed to place them on the left, not the right. Nevertheless, they gained their right-wing designation by linking Polish political identity to the Catholic Church, and opposing the secularist values advanced by both the Warsaw intellectuals of Solidarity and the former Communists of the Left Alliance.

Given their differences with the secularists, as well as their demand for the sweeping purge of old-time bureaucrats and military leaders, it would be tough for the Right to build a stable majority coalition on its own. At the same time, the Right's unremitting hostility to the Balcerowicz Plan would make it tough to collaborate with Mazowiecki and Kaczyński, who had committed their two parties to ongoing support of this increasingly unpopular initiative.

Only one thing was clear: Given Kaczynski's capture of the Center Alliance, Wałesa could—if he chose—use his super-presidential powers to undercut any prime minister who managed to gain the support of a majority coalition composed of the antagonistic factions that had filled the vacuum left by the collapse of Solidarity's citizens' committees.

Political party fragmentation also dealt a body blow to the new Parliament's effort to hammer out a permanent Constitution. This time around, the Sejm and Senate avoided their previous conflict by establishing a joint constitutional commission. Yet this wasn't enough to contain the ideological splintering of the rival parties—whose leaderships managed to generate six conflicting constitutional drafts. The continuing deadlock might have been used by Wałesa to demonstrate his leadership by working with the six factions to create a compromise draft which built on attractive features advanced by their different proposals.

But he took a very different course. Instead of spearheading a renewed effort, he exploited the inconsistencies of the existing Constitution for purposes of his own self-aggrandizement. Surveying the fragmented political scene, he claimed the right to appoint himself prime minister![30]

This was a shocker for legalists, who denied that the Round Table amendments authorized the concentration of presidential and prime ministerial power in the same man. It was politically unacceptable to the Solidarity Right, which had gained much public support by attacking "shock therapy," and feared correctly—that Wałesa would use his presidency / prime-ministership to sustain Balcerowicz in power.

These anxieties enabled Jan Olszewski to form a multiparty coalition that deprived Wałesa of the parliamentary majority he needed to serve as prime minister. Olszewski demanded that he be allowed to head the government himself. While the Round Table amendments left this decision to the president, Wałesa had little choice but to agree. The new cabinet then proclaimed itself the "first truly non-communist government." They immediately initiated an aggressive campaign to fire the old-time apparatchiks who remained prominent in the bureaucracy and military and denounced the previous Solidarity governments which had kept them in office.[31] The campaign escalated in intensity when Poland's first civilian defense minister, Jan Parys, challenged the president's role as commander in chief.

On Parys's view, the defense minister had the constitutional authority to force leading commanders into early retirement. He then cautioned his supporters that, rather than accept parliamentary control, Wałesa might attempt a military coup d'état to defend his presidentialist claims to ultimate authority.[32]

Wałesa responded by demanding Parys's resignation—even though his constitutional authority to do so was by no means clear.[33] Nevertheless, the defense minister complied; but other members of the cabinet escalated their attack. In particular, the minister of the interior threatened to disclose the secret police files of top officials, including Wałesa himself. Along with this threat came escalating rumors suggesting that Wałesa had been a phony all along—and that his file demonstrated his ongoing collaboration with the Communist intelligence services during the 1970s.[34]

In response to these dark rumors, the president threw his support behind an opposition effort to overthrow Prime Minister Olszewski's government with a motion of no confidence. This only led to a further escalation in the interbranch struggle—provoking Olszewski to assert, in a dramatic television speech, that his government's fall prefigured the return of the Communists to power.[35] Despite this melodramatic appeal, the Sejm ended Olszewski's twenty-four-week tenure in June—leaving chaos in his wake.

Wałesa had a tough time filling the gap. His search for a plausible ally to fill the post only succeeded in provoking the fractionated Sejm to organize a government independent of presidential control. To Wałesa's surprise, Hanna Suchocka emerged from Mazowiecki's Democratic Union in July to lead a disparate seven-party coalition—which, despite repeated policy disagreements, managed to sustain itself in power for fourteen months.

This moment of relative calm gave Parliament a chance to take stock of its escalating conflict with the president. Wałesa's recent efforts to name himself prime minister, and to dominate the peak military and civilian positions, dramatized the constitutional uncertainties left in the wake of the Round Table embrace of the Gaullist model. This led the Suchocka government to gain the requisite parliamentary supermajority required for constitutional amendments clarifying the terms of the presidential–parliamentary relationship. This "little Constitution" was a self-consciously provisional affair—aiming to stabilize institutional relationships without rethinking the basic premises of the French presidential system.[36]

At about the same time, Parliament relaunched its more ambitious effort to create a joint Sejm-Senate commission to begin work on a permanent Constitution. But this only led to the proliferation of six rival drafts over the next few months.[37] As the commission turned to the tough choices required to develop a coherent text to present to Parliament, its work came to a halt when the Suchocka government fell from power in October 1993.

As before, Wałesa confronted a Sejm that was broadly hostile to him and his policies—but this time around, he despaired of finding another prime minister who could sustain a semblance of collaboration. So he took an alternative path marked out by the "little Constitution," which once again followed the French model by allowing him to dissolve Parliament even though it had only served two years of its five-year term.

Despite the Sejm's brief period in office, it managed to come up with a new election law that aimed to eliminate the extreme party fragmentation that had generated such extreme political instability. Under the new ground rules, a political party could not send any representatives to the Sejm unless its slate won at least 5 percent of the national vote. In addition, parties passing a threshold of 7 percent would gain extra seats, thereby making it easier to create solid coalition governments.[38] In taking these steps, the Sejm was following in the footsteps of Germany and other countries that had used similar thresholds to create stable parliamentary systems.

But in Poland's case, these standard techniques had devastating consequences.

The Death of Revolutionary Constitutionalism

However heroic its struggle for freedom, Solidarity's performance in government had been a terrible disappointment. Without the organizing structure of a movement party, the scene had been dominated by Wałesa's bitter combat with his fellow revolutionaries—first in his "war at the top"; then in his combat with Parliament over his assertions of presidential authority. At the same time, the parliamentary coalition's continuing support of "shock therapy" had not yet produced decisive improvements in the living standards of the average worker or farmer.[39]

The political turmoil and economic disappointment led many Poles to look elsewhere for leadership—providing an opening for the former Communists of the Left Alliance and the Peasant Party to build on the surprising amount of support shown for them in the previous parliamentary election. Once again, these two parties emphasized that they had no intention of turning the clock back to the bad old days before 1989; but they offered the prospect of sensible and stable government, which was so conspicuously lacking during the past four years of postrevolutionary turmoil.[40] No less importantly, they could still call upon the apparatchiks of the old regime to use their considerable local influence to bring out the vote on election day. It was no surprise, then, that the "reformed" Communists improved on their previous electoral performance: the Democratic Left Alliance moved from a 12 percent share in 1991 to 20 percent in 1993; the Polish Peasant Party, from 9 percent to 15 percent—adding up to an impressive 35 percent of overall support.

In contrast, only three Solidarity parties managed to leap over the 5 percent barrier, gaining a bare 25 percent of the popular vote. Two of these represented the liberal and secular wings of the movement: Mazowiecki's Democratic Union (10.6 percent) and the Union of Labor (7.3 percent). The final splinter represented Wałesa's "Non-Party Reform Bloc" (5.4 percent). But the parties of the Solidarity Right fell just short of the 5 percent threshold, as did other religious and nationalist factions. Overall, one-third of the electorate "wasted" their votes on parties that did not gain Sejm seats. This extraordinary shortfall permitted the former Communists and their allies to transform their 35 percent vote share into a clear majority of seats in the new Sejm (and in the Senate as well).[41]

The problematic character of the turnaround was dramatized by the identity of the Left Alliance's parliamentary leader. He was none other than Aleksander Kwaśniewski, who had been the principal negotiator for the Jaruzelski government at the crucial Magdalenka sessions with Wałesa and his revolutionary comrades. Alive to the terrible symbolism in making this leading Communist into the country's prime minister, the Alliance refrained from pushing Kwaśniewski forward even though theirs was by far the largest party (37 percent) in the Sejm. It contented itself with supporting its ally, Waldemar Pawlak of the Peasant Party (17 percent), for the top spot. Nevertheless, everybody recognized that Kwaśniewski would be calling the shots for the governing coalition.[42]

Wałesa remained president, of course, and he retained the power to nominate the prime minister under the "little Constitution," but the composition of the Sejm gave him no choice but to accept Pawlak. Nevertheless, he still possessed large powers to veto legislation and make crucial appointments, which he could deploy to make it tough for the Left coalition to govern in a calm and coherent fashion.

He eagerly seized these opportunities—hoping that his revolutionary charisma would be redeemed by the voters when he ran for reelection at the end of his five-year term in 1995. On several occasions, his interventions went beyond the powers granted to him by the "little Constitution." But when his opponents cried foul, he relied on his legal team to provide strained constitutional interpretations to support his ongoing effort to disrupt the governing coalition.[43]

The battle continued when Parliament returned to its never-ending effort to provide Poland with a comprehensive replacement of the Communist-era Constitution. To emphasize the importance of this task, Kwaśniewski got himself appointed chairman of the new constitutional commission. Wałesa responded with a campaign against Kwaśniewski's initiative. On his view, it was utterly wrong for an old-time Communist to take advantage of quirks in the election law, excluding representatives of one-third of the voting public, to pretend that he could hammer out a Solidarity Constitution in the name of the People.

Wałesa's challenge was self-interested—since it was likely that the new Sejm majority would propose a parliamentary system that would only grant the presidency a figurehead role. Nevertheless, his challenge hit a nerve—and Parliament responded with a law that allowed non-parliamentary groups to participate in deliberations and to submit constitutional drafts signed by 500,000 supporters.

This was a formidable barrier—but within six months, the Solidarity labor union gained almost a million signatures for a draft that endorsed parliamentary government with a strong commitment to social rights.[44] This had the paradoxical consequence of slowing down the process further, since the union's impressive showing required the commission to take its draft seriously. Moreover, it was also obliged to consider the six drafts inherited from the previous Parliament, each of which offered different understandings of fundamental rights and presidential powers.[45]

As deliberations slowed to a crawl, Kwaśniewski's attention turned to the forthcoming presidential election, scheduled for 1995. He was emerging as Wałesa's principal challenger, and he came to the campaign with very substantial assets. Old-time Communist apparatchiks were still very good at bringing out millions of disaffected Poles to the polls on election day. In contrast, Wałesa had utterly failed to fill the void left by his destruction of Solidarity as a broad movement party. He would go into the election "without a political machine . . . [or] a stable following among the electorate."[46] The best he could do was urge his fellow citizens to remember his revolutionary leadership during the glorious struggles of the 1980s. In contrast, Kwaśniewski could point to the generally sober conduct of his parliamentary coalition in providing the stability that was sorely lacking under previous Solidarity governments.

The struggle for the presidency between Revolutionary Hero and Reformed Communist provoked a spike in public engagement—in the second round of balloting, 68 percent of eligible voters turned out at the polls to have their say on the shape of Poland's future.

Kwaśniewski emerged victorious by a 52-to-48 margin.[47] Now that Solidarity had been banished from the presidency and sidelined in Parliament, the constitutional project could finally proceed to a "successful" conclusion—although the process would not involve anything resembling revolutionary legitimation.

The Left Alliance made a gesture of reconciliation by reaching out to Bronisław Geremek to occupy the chair of the constitutional commission that was vacated when Kwaśniewski became president. But this symbolic gesture to Solidarity's heroic past could not change the reality that it was the Left Alliance, not the old revolutionaries, which controlled all the levers of power.

The key decisions were made by a small group of parliamentary leaders and law professors on the constitutional commission, who proceeded with their work without the broad popular debate which accompanied earlier efforts at constitutional construction.[48] The commission then lobbied its draft through Parliament, making ad hoc concessions to gain overwhelming legislative majorities.[49]

The top-down character of decision-making was constrained, however, by a final factor: the Constitution could not come into effect without voter approval at a referendum. Solidarity and the religious parties had been frozen out of the drafting process, and the constitutional commission tried to preempt popular opposition by searching for a middle ground on the divisive issues of the day. Its proposal cut back on the independent powers of the chief executive, but rejected the strong form of parliamentary democracy where—as in Germany—the president plays a largely ceremonial role. The commission's bill of rights moved beyond the classical liberal conception, but endorsed a rather limited notion of social rights. Finally, the draft made desperate efforts to accommodate secular and Catholic understandings of the foundations of the Republic.[50] After lobbying the Constitution through Parliament, the Left Alliance called a special referendum for May 1997 to gain popular consent for its elite construction.[51]

Only to find that its efforts to pacify the opposition had been a failure. With Wałesa a force behind the scenes, the Solidarity union led the No campaign. Its president, Marian Krzaklewski, headed a coalition of thirty-seven (!) parties that denounced the Constitution as the work of former Communists. Although the Church officially remained neutral, many parishes served as organizing points for the No campaign—finding the proposal too secular in general and too weak in its guarantees of the "right to life."[52]

The government tried to deflect these assaults by reframing the debate. The key question, President Kwaśniewski argued, was Poland's future relationship to the West. By making a clean break with their much-amended Communist Constitution of 1952, the Polish people would demonstrate that they were committed to liberal democracy and were ready to assume membership in the European Union and NATO. In response, opponents denounced the Left Alliance for replacing Poland's hard-won independence from Moscow with new forms of subordination to Brussels and Washington.[53]

On the surface, at least, this confrontation between Solidarity's Christian nationalism and the Left's secular internationalism raised large questions about the enduring legacy of the past revolutionary struggle. Nevertheless, the Polish people responded with a collective yawn. They had been thoroughly alienated by the battles of the Wałesa years. In 1989 more than 90 percent of eligible voters had come out to repudiate the Communists at the opportunity provided by the quasi-free elections in June; even the 1995 presidential race between Wałesa and Kwaśniewski drew 68 percent to the polls, but this time around, only 43 percent bothered to cast a ballot. When the votes were counted, the Yeses beat the Nos by 53 percent to 47 percent. This meant that only a quarter of the voting-age population gave its affirmative consent to the effort by former Communists to replace the Communist Constitution with a new charter for the Polish Republic.[54]

The low turnout generated a big legal problem: Did the new Constitution require approval by an absolute majority of voters in order to be valid?

The answer required an interpretation of two provisions in the "little Constitution" enacted in 1992 to clarify the powers of the president and Parliament. One provision addressed the general problem posed by referenda, and it authorized the Sejm and the president to use the device whenever they jointly deemed it appropriate. But to prevent the abuse of this populist technique, it explicitly insisted that an absolute majority of eligible voters must go to the polls before a referendum could be deemed valid.

A second provision, however, specifically addressed the procedures for the validation of the new Constitution. On this matter, the president and Parliament were affirmatively required to use a referendum to establish that the People had indeed endorsed the terms of their revolutionary break with the old regime. But in contrast to the general provision, this special one did not explicitly require a 50 percent turnout.[55]

This led to an obvious legal question: How to construe this silence?

A host of litigants rushed to the Supreme Court to find out: After all, if a 50 percent turnout was required as a general rule, wasn't it even more vital in a referendum aiming to establish that the People of Poland did indeed support their new Constitution?

On July 15 the Court said no.[56] Over a couple of dissents, the judges found that the drafters of the "little Constitution" intended to exempt the referendum from the general requirement of an absolute majority. This was a plausible, but by no means an inevitable, interpretation of Polish law. If the judges had taken the principle of popular sovereignty more seriously, they would have forced the former Communists to make more concessions to Solidarity and the Church to gain broader popular support in a follow-up referendum. If this second appeal to the People had gained broader support, it might well have enhanced the legitimacy of the Constitution's redefinition of the country's political identity.

But, of course, this desperate attempt at national reconciliation might well have failed—with another low turnout only reemphasizing the citizenry's pervasive political alienation—leaving the "reformed" Communist elite to govern under a text whose lineage went back to the Communist Constitution of 1952. Even if the second referendum had generated a strong Yes vote, it could not have disguised the large role that former Communists had played in setting the constitutional terms of Poland's alleged "new beginning."

Countries traveling down the revolutionary path may reasonably hope for something more—as the histories of India, South Africa, France, and Italy demonstrate. But by 1997, Solidarity's fragmentation had made such a broad and decisive endorsement of an authentically revolutionary Constitution a political impossibility.

It would be a mistake, then, to judge the judges too harshly when they allowed the 1997 Constitution to go into effect without another round of popular debate and decision. Their decision expressed a deeper truth: the moment for revolutionary constitutionalism had passed. No court could have changed this fundamental reality.

The roots of this tragedy go back to short-term decisions made by Wałesa and Geremek as they struggled to gain initial concessions from the Communist government at the Round Table Talks of 1988. Recall that it was the Communist Party, not Solidarity, that insisted on the creation of a powerful presidency. The adoption of the French super-presidential model was the product of a deal in which Solidarity won a freely elected Senate at the cost of accepting General Jaruzelski as a super-Gaullist president with extraordinary emergency powers that would enable him to reassure the Kremlin that Poland would remain faithful to the Warsaw Pact.

This short-term decision could have been revised during the early period of the Solidarity's political ascendancy if its revolutionary leadership had made the construction of a new Constitution their highest priority. But for very different reasons, both Wałesa and the Mazowiecki government deferred this task for what they considered more pressing priorities. Moreover, the French success in managing the tensions of super-presidentialism during the 1980s lulled the Polish protagonists into a false sense of security in relying on Fifth Republic models.

Later acts of statesmanship might have sustained Solidarity's political coherence long enough to redeem the promise of revolutionary constitutionalism. But once Wałesa and Mazowiecki decided to compete for the presidency, their "war at the top" made it impossible for Solidarity to survive as a movement party that could serve as the basis for broad-based consent to a Constitution worthy of the collective sacrifices of the Polish People. Wałesa's ascent to the presidency in 1991, in short, had already made it virtually impossible for Poland to repeat the successes achieved in India, Italy, France, and South Africa.

It did not, however, guarantee the terrible irony involved in the former Communists' successful rise to power. Even though Solidarity had been fractured into a series of small parties, Wałesa might have maintained good relations with Parliament through sustained acts of statesmanship. But his continuing war with the Sejm opened a path for the Democratic Left Alliance to present itself as the country's best hope for stable government. Once Solidarity had disintegrated, the former Communists were in a position to transform their shattered Party organizations into an effective force for mobilizing the voters at the constitutional referendum. This allowed the former Communists to present themselves as the principal sponsors of Poland's constitutional breakthrough to democracy.

It also set the stage for a final paradox, which concerns the Constitutional Tribunal. Recall that, when it was originally created in the aftermath of Jaruzelski's suppression of Solidarity in 1981, the Tribunal was hemmed about by stringent limitations on its authority. Most notably, it did not have the last word on the constitutionality of legislation—its adverse decisions could be overruled by two-thirds of the Sejm, which was then under the total control of the Party.

This override provision did not deter the Tribunal from initiating a rights-jurisprudence after 1989, but it did encourage caution—since repeated legislative overrides would have delegitimated the entire project. The 1997 Constitution, however, eliminated the Sejm's veto, and reinforced the Tribunal's legitimacy by incorporating some of its decisions into the constitutional text itself. This greatly encouraged the dynamic development of a rich jurisprudence protecting fundamental rights over the next two decades—as did the need for Poland to secure its successful admission to the European Union by demonstrating its respect for human dignity. To put the paradox in a single sentence: A Tribunal initially created by the Communist dictatorship was invited to develop a powerful jurisprudence of human dignity by a Constitution enacted through the efforts of former Communists.

Founding Failure and the Current Crisis

Poland is currently in a grave crisis—with the Warsaw government attempting an all-out assault on the 1997 Constitution, climaxing in an attack on the independence of the Constitutional Tribunal. This has rightly set off alarm bells throughout the world—with defenders of fundamental rights calling for urgent action to prevent a grievous setback to liberal constitutionalism.

I have joined this call, but whatever happens next, my aim here is to put the present crisis in deeper comparative perspective.[57] From this vantage, the larger lesson is the peril involved in importing French super-presidentialism into revolutionary situations.

To flesh out my argument, begin by considering the biography of Jarosław Kaczyński, the leader of the Polish political party that is spearheading the current government's assault on constitutional democracy in general, and judicial independence in particular.

Kaczyński played an important role in organizing Solidarity's last-ditch effort to defeat the Constitution at the 1997 referendum. At that time, he denounced the proposed draft as the handiwork of leftist internationalists bent on erasing the revolutionary contributions of Solidarity's Catholic and nationalist wings. When his No campaign failed, Kaczyński did not give up. His defeat only convinced him of the imperative need to build a new movement party out of the fragments left in the wake of Solidarity's disintegration. By 2001 he had joined his brother Lech in establishing the Law and Justice Party, and organized a successful grassroots campaign leading to his brother's election as president in 2005. Jarosław functioned as the party's parliamentary leader with less success—and when his brother was killed in an air crash, he failed in his effort to replace him as president in 2010.

But five years later, Law and Justice reemerged as an even more powerful movement party, gaining 38 percent of the popular vote. As in 1993, this strong showing was translated into an absolute majority in both houses of Parliament because the Left split into two factions and each narrowly failed to fulfill high threshold requirements—leaving 15 percent of the electorate unrepresented in Parliament.[58] Even with this artificial boost, Law and Justice doesn't currently command the parliamentary supermajority required for formal constitutional amendments. Nevertheless, it is already taking strong steps to shift the course of constitutional doctrine and practice in conservative nationalist directions, passing statutes that would disable the Constitutional Tribunal from invalidating laws that threaten fundamental rights.

A grim future is emerging. The current crisis has many causes—not least, Kaczyński's lust for absolute power. But the current constitutional tragedy should not divert attention from more structural factors—most notably, the acceptance of the French Fifth Republic as an appropriate baseline for the Polish exercise in revolutionary constitutionalism.

The baleful influence of the Gaullist model is best appreciated through a thought experiment: Suppose that history had taken a different turn in 1989, and that Wałesa and Mazowiecki had rejected the strong French-style presidency that they had accepted only with great reluctance at the Round Table Talks. Under this alternative scenario, they would have refused to allow Jaruzelski to become president, but would have permitted the Communists to retain their power position in the "contract Sejm"—propitiating Party hardliners by accepting a reduction of the open seats from 35 to 25 percent of the total. How would this single decision have transformed the future of Poland's constitutional development?

Under this scenario, once the victorious Solidarity delegation arrived in Warsaw, there would have been only one way in which Wałesa could push the transition forward from Time One to Time Two. He could not bide his time and wait for Jaruzelski to resign from the super-Gaullist presidency, since the office didn't exist. If he wished to play a central role in shaping the new era of Polish democracy, he would have had no choice but to become prime minister by leading Solidarity's embryonic movement party to a sweeping victory at Poland's first free parliamentary elections. With his charismatic authority confirmed by the electorate, he would then call upon his Warsaw colleagues to serve in his Cabinet, and work with him, as they had in the past, to build the country's future.

Once their popular mandate had been reaffirmed, the Wałesa-Mazowiecki-Geremek government could have confidently presented a Solidarity Constitution to the People at a referendum in 1991 or 1992. In hammering out a common text, the ideological splits between Christian nationalists and secular liberals would have predictably emerged—just as similar divisions arose at Time Two in the postwar French and Italian Republics. But as at these comparable moments, Wałesa and his Cabinet could have called on their Solidarity movement party to mobilize the citizens' committees for a landslide Yes vote.

Over time, the ideological divisions between Christian nationalists like Kaczyński and "Warsaw intellectuals" like Michnik might well have split the citizens' movement into contending parties. But during the early founding period, there would have been time enough for Wałesa, Mazowiecki, and Geremek to hammer out a common constitutional text to bring before the voters in 1991 or 1992—and gain broad-based consent for a Solidarity Constitution.

Comparatively speaking, my hypothetical Polish scenario would have resembled the real-world developments that actually took place in South Africa at about the same time. Like its counterpart, Poland would have operated under a parliamentary government—though one modeled more on the German model than on the British system.[59] Like the ANC, the Solidarity movement party would have integrated a broad range of activists and organizations—ranging from strong socialists to emphatic free-market liberals. Such splits did not defeat the effort by Mandela and other ANC leaders to contain these ideological disagreements long enough to unify behind a Constitution expressing the core principles that unified them during their decades of common struggle at Time One.

The very opposite dynamic prevailed in Poland. The 1997 Constitution was enacted during a moment of popular alienation from politics. Worse yet, Kaczyński played an important part in the effort to organize fragments of Solidarity to defeat the top-down Constitution at the low-turnout referendum—and he has continued, throughout his career, to view its enactment as a profound betrayal of Time One principles.

In contrast, he would have played a very different role if Wałesa had demanded new parliamentary elections in 1990 to prepare the way for a Solidarity Constitution of 1991. During these early days, he was still one of Wałesa's most trusted aides, and would have been a key player in Wałesa's effort to reach out to Geremek and Mazowiecki to sustain the broad-based movement party required to win a resounding victory at the polls in the constitutional referendum.

Under this alternative scenario, the Kaczyński-of-today would not be looking upon the Constitution of 1997 as an act of betrayal. He would be looking back to the Constitution of 1992 as an occasion when he had played a central role in organizing citizens' committees for an overwhelming Yes vote. Even more important, ordinary Poles would have viewed the Solidarity Constitution as a culminating achievement in their revolutionary struggle for a new beginning in their collective life as fellow citizens of a liberal democracy.

I do not claim that this dramatic shift in the character of collective memory would have totally transformed the current situation. There are many other important economic and social forces that Kaczyński is exploiting in his drive toward dictatorship. But constitutional legitimacy is *an* important factor, isn't it?

My thought experiment also invites further reflection on the Gaullist model's contribution to the Polish tragedy. As we have seen, the Solidarity leadership was initially opposed to the use of the Fifth Republic model as the basis for a transitional arrangement with the Communist regime. At the crucial bargaining sessions at Magdalenka, it was Kwaśniewski, not Wałesa, who insisted on the Gaullist-style presidency to ensure that General Jaruzelski could keep a more democratically elected Parliament under control. Wałesa only accepted super-presidentialism when the Communists sweetened the deal by providing for a freely elected Senate that enabled Solidarity to gain control of at least one branch of the Communist-dominated state. This deal made short-term sense. But it was a disaster in the middle run, once Solidarity had swept the Communists from their dominant position in the other branches.

I have mentioned a variety of context-specific reasons to account for the failure of Wałesa and Mazowiecki to constitutionalize Solidarity's charisma. But there is one trans-contextual point that needs emphasizing—and that involves the high international reputation the Gaullist model had gained by the late 1980s when Solidarity was making its deal with the Communists. By this point, the Fifth Republic had just survived the great succession crisis provoked by Mitterrand's first term in office, and its presidentialist model seemed to offer a promising alternative to the classic forms of parliamentary government on the Continent. In keeping the Round Table system intact, Solidarity was simply accepting the conventional wisdom of the moment. Like many other countries liberating themselves from the Soviet empire, it treated the Fifth Republic as if it were a "one-size-fits-all-solution" to the problem of democratic transition.

Poland's disastrous experience, however, should serve as a wake-up call for the twenty-first century. While I have foresworn prophecy, the coming decades will almost certainly witness future revolutions on a human scale, and the Polish story suggests caution in adopting the Gaullist framework as a transitional pathway for the construction of an enduring Constitution.

Poland is hardly the only place in which the Gaullist super-presidentialist model has had a baleful effect on the success of revolutionary constitutionalism over the last quarter-century. The Russian case also serves as a textbook illustration. When Boris Yeltsin gained a momentary ascendancy in Russian politics in the 1990s, the Gaullist-inspired system prevailing at the time of transition enabled him to win the presidency without trying to build a grass-roots movement party devoted to constitutionalizing the liberal democratic revolution. This failure created an organizational vacuum that Vladimir Putin and his coalition of Party apparatchiks and billionaire oligarchs have managed to fill over the past two decades.

I have focused on Poland, however, because it provided a far more promising site for the construction of a constitution that the overwhelming majority would consider an authentic expression of the ideals expressed during Solidarity's sustained period of revolutionary sacrifice. In contrast to Russia, Wałesa and Solidarity did not have to deal with the bitter resentments of a host of nationalities and religious groups that had been brutally suppressed during the Soviet era; nor did they have to deal with the international humiliations imposed on Russia after 1989 as it struggled to find a new place in the world. Instead, the Poles gloried in the fact that the triumph of Solidarity had gained widespread admiration in the West, and that they had finally won long-sought independence from their Russian overlords. Given these far more propitious conditions, it's far more difficult to dismiss the French model's disruptive capacity on revolutionary constitutionalism.

More generally, the Polish story carries a larger lesson. Future revolutionaries—and there will be many—should recognize that they are running a race against time at the Founding. If they fail to constitutionalize the high-energy politics of commitment during the first few years of their ascendancy, the resulting alienation can cast a dark shadow on their country's political development for a long time to come.

CHAPTER 11

The Race against Time: Burma and Israel

Burma and Israel are important in their own rights, but treating them together adds complexity to our reflections on the race against time. As in Poland, revolutionary leaderships in both countries deferred the task of constitutional construction at the Founding—only to see their movement parties splinter in ways that made it impossible to generate an authentic constitution later on. But the consequences of these two lost "races against time" have been very different.

In Burma, it has led to tragedy on a scale beyond anything that Poland has experienced. In Israel, it has led to a more complicated and hopeful story. Despite David Ben-Gurion's refusal to constitutionalize the commitments of the Zionist revolution, a powerful Supreme Court ultimately emerged as the guardian of fundamental rights. The Israeli counterexample complexifies the grim diagnosis suggested by our other case studies. What accounts for the difference?

Burma at the Crossroads

After a sweeping electoral victory in 2015, Aung San Suu Kyi and her National League of Democracy confronted the same problem facing Lech Wałesa and Solidarity in 1989. Despite the strong support of a mobilized public, the League's elected representatives were operating under a Constitution, designed by an oppressive military regime, that dramatically limited parliamentary powers of Suu Kyi and her movement to govern the country.

Suu Kyi could accept these limits on her rule, and reach an accommodation with the generals—at the cost of alienating her mass following. Or she could demand a constitutional revision stripping the generals of their powers—and risk that the military would close down Parliament, and try to crush her movement with brute force.

Like General Jaruzelski and the Communists, Burma's military government would be confronting an equal and opposite dilemma: If they refused to cooperate with Suu Kyi, they might not be able to suppress the massive League demonstrations called to back up her demands. Indeed, the murder of civilians might provoke an escalation in resistance, finally inducing the military to allow the League to establish civilian rule.

The first move belonged to Suu Kyi and the League. Would they play by the rules laid down by the generals, or insist on a sweeping constitutional transformation?

Setting the Stage

Begin with Burma's original struggle for independence in the 1930s and 1940s, led by Suu Kyi's father, Aung San—and not only because Suu Kyi's symbolic centrality is based on her paternal descent. Aung San also helped establish an enduring revolutionary tradition that still shapes current understandings.

Our story starts in the 1930s. Until that time, present-day Burma was just another distant province of the Indian Subcontinent which the British ruled from New Delhi. The Government of India Act of 1935 marked a fundamental change—enabling inhabitants to elect consultative assemblies and participate in more constructive forms of engagement with regional and central authorities. But because Burma was so distant from New Delhi, it was given special treatment in a Government of Burma Act, which separated it from India in 1937 and created a 36-seat Senate and a 132-seat House of Representatives to increase popular support for continued imperial rule.

This initiative was a defining moment for university students like Aung San. He emphatically rejected the British call for Burmese elites to play a supportive role in the government of the empire, and presented himself as a revolutionary outsider, organizing a broad alliance—ranging from Buddhist monks to Communist militants—which sought to compel the British to recognize Burmese independence.

The Government of Burma Act vastly complicated this revolutionary project. Without giving it serious thought, the Act defined "Burma" in an expansive fashion. It not only included the Burmese-speaking zone of Buddhists who had long been ruled by their own monarch. It extended the new "Burma" to a large area inhabited by groups who didn't think of themselves as Burmese at all, but spoke their own languages, affirmed Hindu or Moslem beliefs, and often considered themselves distinct national communities. Aung San took special care to define his revolutionary movement in ways that respected these profound differences. But these early efforts were interrupted by the British authorities—who responded to Aung San's revolutionary agitation by prosecuting him for subversion, and forcing him into the underground during the late 1930s.

World War II added further complexity. Until then the Burmese revolutionaries largely deployed Gandhian techniques of civil disobedience. The Japanese invasion of Burma led them to take a military turn, organizing a Burma Independence Army (BIA) to collaborate with Japan in a joint effort to destroy British imperial rule. With Hirohito's forces on the offensive, the emperor reciprocated by naming Aung San a major-general in the Japanese army.

As Japanese forces began to crumble, Aung San switched sides and the BIA joined an alliance of convenience with imperial Britain to expel the Japanese from Burma. As a reward, the British offered to make Aung San a general in their newly organized Burmese Army. But Aung San rejected the offer, reasserting himself as a revolutionary outsider at the head of a broad Anti-Fascist People's Freedom League demanding a decisive break from the empire.

When the Attlee government abandoned Britain's imperial pretensions over the entire subcontinent, Aung San traveled to London in January 1947 to win an agreement for Burmese independence within the coming year. He then triumphantly returned to lead the League to a landslide victory in elections to a Constituent Assembly. At a preliminary convention of the League's grassroots leaders, he emphasized that "it is not an inherent law of Revolution to resort to violence." It was better to "compare Revolution to childbirth. . . . [Some] child-births are easy and some are difficult. A great deal depends on the health of the parents and the skill of the mid-wife." The coming Convention should hammer out constitutional principles to give "the masses themselves" a sense of "direct participation . . . [in shaping] their own destiny."[1]

It is hard to find a more self-conscious statement of constitutionalism's role in legitimating revolutions on a human scale. Given his time and place, it was hardly surprising that the substantive principles Aung San advanced on behalf of his Democratic League were broadly similar to those elaborated by Nehru and Congress in India: secularism, social democracy, and Westminster-style government. The biggest difference involved the status of ethnic and religious minorities—with Aung San and the League guaranteeing minorities far greater rights to parliamentary representation and regional self-government than did their Indian counterparts.[2]

Then disaster struck: Before the Constituent Assembly could complete its work, the governor-general had called Aung San and other revolutionary leaders to a session of his executive council, where suddenly they were mowed down by gunmen on the orders of a political rival. These assassinations did not prevent the League's delegates from adopting a Constitution that expressed the core principles laid out by Aung San's speeches. But it left a legitimacy vacuum at the top.

The contrast with India is telling: Over the next decade, Nehru and Congress sustained their revolutionary momentum to demonstrate that, despite a series of very serious challenges, the Indian Constitution provided a practical form of government. In contrast, given its premature succession crisis, the League confronted a more uncertain future, fracturing into rival components.

The leader who emerged as prime minister, U Nu, was a very considerable statesman, but had only been a secondary figure in the revolutionary movement. To sustain his position, he gradually committed his government to a stronger version of Burmese nationalism than Aung San had endorsed—alienating the ethnic and religious groups that comprised one-third of the entire population.[3] Because these minorities were concentrated in border areas, the frontier regions became hotbeds of civilian resistance and guerilla warfare over the next decade.

The battle for control escalated further when armed Communist insurgents joined the struggle. Faced with formidable resistance, the civilian government increasingly relied on its military arm—opening up a space for a decisive coup by General Ne Win in 1962, which inaugurated a half-century of military dictatorship.

Ne Win was ethnic Chinese—a big disadvantage, given the nationalist turn in Burmese politics. But he was also a leading commander of Burmese forces during and after the struggle for national independence—and this gave credibility to his claim that the Army provided the best hope for the nation to continue down Aung San's path toward a "Burmese Way to Socialism." Despite leftist sloganeering, Ne Win did not in fact create a strong civilian bureaucracy to propel economic development or deliver a broad range of social services to the poor. His aggressive Burmese nationalism, moreover, condemned the country to decades of brutal warfare against minorities in border regions.

Yet the military regime was more successful in maintaining law and order in the Burmese heartland—ruthlessly suppressing dissenters as traitors who were aiding the ongoing rebellions in the borderlands. This mix of war and suppression sustained itself for an entire generation—until it was over whelmed by the democracy movement that swept Southeast Asia in the late 1980s.

Here is where Aung San Suu Kyi comes in. She was only 2 years old when her father was murdered, and she had spent her adult life abroad—studying at Oxford, marrying a British scholar, and raising two kids in a quiet neighborhood in north Oxford. She occasionally visited her family in Burma but had not developed significant connections to pro-democracy activists. It was sheer happenstance that she was in the country tending to her aging mother when open defiance broke out in 1988. She remained on the sidelines for months as mass protests escalated, playing no role in the demonstrations that forced the 77-year-old Ne Win to leave office in July.

Only in late August did she finally appear before a crowd of a half-million people to provide symbolic support for the uprising. Her eloquent speech, calling on the movement to commit itself to her father's statement of principles, enhanced the legitimacy of the revolutionary effort. But her strategic advice was more equivocal. She refrained from demanding an immediate end to military rule. She also kept her distance from the cultural and religious minorities that had been engaged in decades of guerrilla war against the army. Instead, she urged the renascent Burmese movement to chart an independent campaign of civil disobedience that might gradually push the generals down the path to democracy.

The high command was unimpressed by Suu Kyi's gradualism. In the following month, a younger cadre of generals responded with a decisive show of force—with General Than Shwe ultimately emerging as the supreme commander of the State Law and Order Restoration Council (SLORC). The coup provoked another round of protest, which SLORC suppressed with brutal efficiency—though guerilla resistance continued in the countryside, and universities were closed for long periods in response to recurrent protests.[4] As part of its "law and order" campaign, SLORC also seized Suu Kyi and placed her under severe confinement. It was this seizure that decisively transformed her into a figure like Mandela or Wałesa, whose dignity in adversity represented a symbolic challenge to the legitimacy of the established regime.

SLORC's brutality, and Suu Kyi's dignity, guaranteed widespread international condemnation at a moment when the Soviet Empire was collapsing and the struggle for democracy in China was hanging in the balance. In a desperate effort to regain legitimacy, SLORC announced plans for "free" elections to a constituent assembly in 1990—expecting that its puppet political party would have no trouble gaining a victory over the shattered movement led by a confined Suu Kyi.[5]

They were wrong: Suu Kyi and her National League of Democracy won 392 of 492 seats.[6] The generals responded by annulling the results, imprisoning many delegates, forcing others into exile, and keeping Suu Kyi under confinement—where she would remain for fifteen of the next twenty-one years.[7] SLORC then proceeded to rule the country as a brazen dictatorship, without even the fig leaf of a Soviet-style Constitution. In response to international sanctions, it convened its own constitutional convention in the mid-1990s—but the assembly went nowhere, failing to generate a serious proposal. (SLORC later changed its name to the State Peace and Development Council—SPDC—the new name did not change power realities.) During all this time, the junta continued its campaign of repression—killing or imprisoning the leaders of the democracy movement in the Burmese heartland while making war against guerilla fighters in the border areas.[8]

Militarized Constitutionalism

With the turn of the century, the generals began a new effort to legitimate their rule. In 2002 the SPDC released Suu Kyi from prison—only to see her mobilizing major demonstrations during the following year. This led to more bloody suppression, and more imprisonment for Suu Kyi. When the United States threatened sanctions in 2003, the SPDC announced a long-term plan for democratic transition. But as in the 1990s, real movement proceeded at a snail's pace. Only another massive wave of unrest in 2007, in which Buddhist monks took the lead, forced the military's hand. Without engaging in serious public consultation, the SPDC responded to the "Saffron Revolution" by presenting a draft Constitution to the voters in a May 2008 referendum—and then announced that 94 percent had marked Yes on their ballots.[9]

This incredible result, together with widespread reports of intimidation and ballot manipulation, discredited the referendum at home and abroad. Nevertheless, the regime pushed forward with its effort at auto-legitimation, giving institutional substance to its paper proposals.

At first glance, the new Constitution appeared to be relatively benign. It established a bicameral legislature, which elected the president by majority vote in a joint session. It also created an independent judiciary, a formidable set of rights, and a federal system expressing the country's cultural and religious diversity. Nevertheless, a host of provisions made it clear that Senior General Than Shwe, who still controlled the SPDC, would continue to exercise decisive authority. For starters, the Constitution granted the commander in chief the unilateral power to name one-fourth of the members of each house of the legislature.[10] This gave the SPDC a big advantage in the coming elections, enabling it to gain a parliamentary majority if regime-friendly political parties won a third of the open seats.

Than Shwe then demanded additional reassurances. Specific provisions guaranteed the generals control over key ministries and required the president to collaborate with a National Defense and Security Council, in which the military exercised effective veto power.[11] Even more ominously, the text allowed the junta to reimpose martial law,[12] and immunized the military against criminal prosecution for any past or future abuse.[13]

The SPDC then made it practically impossible for constitutional amendments to loosen its stranglehold on power. Revisions would require the consent of a majority exceeding three-fourths of Parliament. Because the commander in chief filled one-quarter of the seats, no changes could be made without the military's consent.[14] Than Shwe then took decisive action to insulate himself from the charismatic threat posed by Suu Kyi. Without naming her specifically, his Constitution prohibited Parliament from selecting "any person" to the presidency whose children were dual nationals—precisely her situation. Since her British-born children "owe[d] allegiance to a foreign power," their mother could not be trusted to guide the nation.[15] The best she could hope for was a seat in Parliament.

The 2008 Constitution, in short, made no effort to hide the military's continuing claim to hegemony—offering the democratic movement a subordinate role in politics, but only at the cost of legitimating the larger system through their ongoing participation. The SPDC then proceeded to announce that, for the first time since the fiasco of 1990, the people of Burma would have a chance to go to the polls in 2010 to fill the open seats in Parliament.

This raised an obvious question: Should Suu Kyi and the League play by the generals' rules, or should they maintain a revolutionary stance and boycott the elections? Nelson Mandela found himself in precisely the same position as he emerged from prison in 1990—with de Klerk offering the ANC the chance to gain parliamentary representation within a constitutional arrangement that conceded an absolute veto to his National Party on crucial matters.

Mandela refused to play the game by de Klerk's rules. The ANC instead declared 1991 to be a "year of mass action" for a truly democratic constitution—and the revolutionaries remained defiant until the apartheid government, and its powerful military, accepted a negotiating framework that firmly adopted the principle of one person, one vote. As part of this deal, Mandela and de Klerk reached a power-sharing arrangement that gave white South Africans veto power on key issues for five years. But this proved to be a transitional step toward a new Constitution codifying the country's revolutionary break with its authoritarian past.

Suu Kyi adopted the same strategy. She condemned the junta's constitutional gesture as a sham and called upon the League to boycott the elections. The regime responded by banning the League and other revolutionary parties, keeping Suu Kyi under detention during the campaign.[16] The election itself was characterized by massive abstention, blatant manipulation, and voter fraud. When the junta announced that its political puppet, the Union Solidarity and Development Party (USDP) had won 77 percent of the contested seats, this pseudo-victory only confirmed everybody's worst suspicions: the junta's attempt to legitimize itself had once again proved an abysmal failure.[17]

The SPDC responded to blistering international condemnation by taking small steps at rehabilitation. Shortly after announcing the election results, Suu Kyi was released from detention—inspiring a new round of activism from the democracy movement. Although the new speaker of the House had previously served as a commanding general, he conducted its sessions in a surprisingly tolerant manner—allowing the small minority of independent representatives to denounce government initiatives on the floor of the chamber.[18]

None of this was enough to disguise the military's iron grip. Nevertheless, the new institutions were generating halting moves toward more open politics.

Constitutional Transformation?

This led Suu Kyi to a moment of reappraisal. Under the new Constitution, members of Parliament were required to resign upon taking important positions in the executive branch—leading to the exodus of forty-five MPs when they entered the USDP government. By-elections were scheduled to fill these vacancies in 2012. At this point, Suu Kyi abandoned her boycott and the League plunged into the race—even though, unlike Mandela, she had not obtained any concessions on a longer-term transition to genuine democracy.

One factor helps account for this difference: while both the Burmese League and the African Congress could mobilize mass demonstrations to support their demands, Mandela's bargaining position was reinforced by the presence of the ANC's military arm, the Spear of the Nation. The ANC's military threat fundamentally changed de Klerk's political calculus: if the Spear launched an all-out battle for revolutionary transformation, he knew that his own political supporters would abandon him and select a more extreme defender of apartheid as prime minister. As a consequence, it was in de Klerk's interest, as well as Mandela's, to recognize the need for an explicitly transitional arrangement.

The Burmese junta had no similar incentive. It had repeatedly shown its ability to crush open opposition in the Burmese core of the nation. Given Suu Kyi's refusal to establish a united front with guerilla forces in the border regions, the military was reasonably confident that it could drive the League into the underground yet again. In this key respect, Suu Kyi was confronting a dilemma that was more like Wałesa's in 1989 than Mandela's in 1991.

General Jaruzelski—like Than Shwe—had brutally crushed Solidarity in 1981 when it began to push for real democracy. Like Suu Kyi, Wałesa was also uncertain whether Jaruzelski would crack down once again in response to a new wave of mass demonstrations and plant seizures in 1988. As a consequence, he accepted the Communists' Round Table proposals of April 1989, which seemed to entrench the old regime for the foreseeable future—both by guaranteeing the Communists and their allies a majority in the lower house of Parliament, and by guaranteeing General Jaruzelski the presidency. Despite Jaruzelski's effort to stack the deck in his favor, Wałesa bet that voters would support Solidarity candidates in the "open" parliamentary seats created by the Round Table Agreement—and deliver a crushing blow to the regime's legitimacy.

Suu Kyi made the same bet—and won it. Though the 45 seats open at the 2012 by-elections were only a small share of the total, the League swept 44 of them, with Suu Kyi entering Parliament as leader of the opposition. At the very least, this mini-landslide demonstrated that sustained military repression had failed to destroy the League's capacity to harness the energies of a mass movement for real democracy in the Burmese core of the country.

Nevertheless, the differences with Poland remained significant. Most importantly, the Polish Communists did not try to secure their permanent rule at the 1989 Round Table Talks. At most, their pact guaranteed the Party and its allies a supermajority in the Sejm for five years and General Jaruzelski control of the presidency for six. But there was no explicit bar against the fully democratic election of future Parliaments and presidents after the interim period.

Suu Kyi had won no similar commitments. Indeed, she had not engaged in any explicit bargaining with the generals at all. She simply switched tactics and left it to the junta to react to her fait accompli. From this vantage, the seemingly modest character of the 2012 elections might have given the military a false sense of security. The League's victory of 44 seats posed no immediate threat to the SPDC's overwhelming parliamentary position. By allowing Suu Kyi to enter the lower house, the junta could, at the very least, win a public relations victory that would allow it to gain economic advantages in dealing with Western democracies.

By co-opting Suu Kyi in the short term, however, the generals were playing a risky constitutional game. The 2010 Parliament had a five-year term, giving the League an opportunity to mount a more serious electoral challenge in 2015. During the interim, Suu Kyi could use Parliament as a platform to enhance her position as a national spokesperson for genuine democracy—inspiring another round of grassroots activity, especially in traditional rural areas where the League previously had a weak presence.

The Moment of Truth

The construction of a deeper and broader revolutionary movement was the indispensable precondition for the League's stunning electoral victory in November 2015. In elections for the more powerful lower House, the League beat the military's puppet party by a margin of 2 to 1, winning 255 of the available 323 seats. Even after the junta designated 116 additional representatives, the League remained in the majority—though the generals still retained their veto over constitutional amendments.[19]

Here was the point at which our key question arose: Would Suu Kyi and the League seize the moment to force the military to recognize that their old Constitution had lost all claim to legitimacy—and that the military should give way to a new Constituent Assembly that would codify the popular demand for genuine democracy?

Suu Kyi was in a perfect position to dramatize this demand by focusing on a particularly absurd provision. This section barred her from the presidency merely because she had given birth to her babies in Britain, making her the mother of dual citizens. Now that she had won such a sweeping mandate, this was plainly an unacceptable reason for preventing her from leading the People of Myanmar down the path to democracy.

Recall, however, that the junta's Constitution also gave the commander in chief the power to appoint one-quarter of the delegates to each house—providing him with the votes he needed to deprive the amendment of its requisite supermajority. Yet if General Than Shwe insisted on his constitutional ban on Suu Kyi, this could provoke a massive uprising on a scale even greater than the one that forced Ne Win from power in 1988.

If, however, Than Shwe allowed the clause to be repealed, he would demonstrate that his paper veto over amendments was no longer credible under prevailing revolutionary conditions. This would have allowed Suu Kyi, once she ascended to the presidency, to escalate her assault on the system by issuing a proclamation that called for an election to a new constituent assembly.

Suu Kyi would be taking a risk if she demanded repeal of the absurd provision barring her from the presidency. The junta might reject her demand, crush the popular protests, and displace parliamentary government with martial law. Nevertheless, given the League's sweeping electoral victory, together with its grassroots mobilization, the military would be taking grave risks in adopting this confrontational course.

In the run-up to the election, the junta laid down the gauntlet. After three days of debate in the old Parliament, the military's representatives rejected a proposal to reduce the share of votes required for constitutional amendment to 70 percent, thereby stripping them of their veto. They also rejected a proposal to eliminate the bar on Suu Kyi.[20]

How would Suu Kyi respond? Would she call the generals' bluff? And if so, would the generals retreat or attack?

When faced with this dilemma, Suu Kyi chose to retreat. She did not demand that the generals allow the newly elected Parliament to reverse their decisions and recognize her right to the presidency. Instead of taking the first step toward a revolutionary Constitution, she reached an understanding with the junta that evaded a frontal challenge to their established framework.

Under this ad hoc arrangement, she arranged for her parliamentary majority to elect her longtime confidante, Htin Kyaw, to the presidency; he then granted Suu Kyi the title First and Incumbent State Counsellor. Since this position was entirely unknown to the 2008 Constitution, he also appointed her to multiple cabinet positions in both foreign and domestic affairs.[21] The message was clear: it would be the First State Counsellor, not the president, who would be making the big decisions for the government—but her authority would be limited by the massive constraints imposed by the generals' constitution.

This was precisely when the Burmese revolution lost its race against time. As it came out of the underground, the League of Democracy served as a vehicle for a host of disparate organizations and local leaders who joined together in a common struggle against the old regime. These grassroots groups not only emerged from the Burmese-speaking heartland, but from the many ethnic and religious minorities in the borderlands. The broad, if unsettled, character of this revolutionary mobilization gave Suu Kyi a price-less opportunity for constitutional leadership.

Recall that Suu Kyi's father had pointed the country in the direction of an inclusive democratic order radically different from the repressive national-istic regime created by the military junta. Before his assassination in 1947, he had urged Burma's first Constituent Assembly to grant substantial autonomy to the non-Burmese regions while committing the nation as a whole to the protection of the fundamental rights of all citizens, regardless of race or reli-gion. Since her own claim to symbolic centrality was intimately connected to her father's martyrdom, Suu Kyi would have had every incentive to urge the new Constituent Assembly to return to Aung San's vision and repudiate the Burmese nationalism that had justified the endless bloody war against one-third of the country's inhabitants.

Once again, an analogy to South African developments clarifies the di-mensions of Suu Kyi's lost opportunity. During the 1980s, the escalating rev-olutionary mobilizations in South Africa had put the apartheid government's security forces increasingly on the defensive. But like the League of Democ-racy, the ANC was composed of disparate cultural groups holding different political ideologies.

In response to this predicament, Mandela elaborated a narrative that urged all ANC factions to remember the last time the country's liberation movements had met on South African soil to hammer out a statement of fundamental principles. This took place in 1955, before the apartheid regime's escalating repression drove activists into exile or underground. Despite the passage of a generation, Mandela urged the disparate elements of the rising movement to recognize the Freedom Charter of 1955 as a common bond uniting them in revolutionary struggle. Support for the Charter, in turn, served as a key ele-ment in creating the foundation for the broad-based legitimation of a breakthrough Constitution for the new South African Republic.

A strategy like Mandela's would have been even more compelling in Suu Kyi's case—given her father's leadership at the Founding Convention. But once she took charge as First State Counsellor, and accepted the legitimacy of the junta's constitutional restrictions, she quickly gave up her halfhearted efforts to redeem these commitments.

Her retreat, in turn, alienated minority activists who had rallied to the League's call for a radical breakthrough, opening a space for hard-line guerillas to disrupt the fragile peace that had prevailed during the height of revolutionary agitation and military uncertainty. This allowed the junta to reinvigorate the Burmese nationalist ideology which had served as its principal raison d'être in the past—leading to an escalating campaign of repression, which culminated in the tragic genocide of the minority Rohingya in 2017. Within the space of a few months, the military obliterated 4,000 settlements long inhabited by this Muslim group—killing tens of thousands and forcing 700,000 across the border to Bangladesh, where they are living in miserable detention camps. Matters may well take a turn for the worse if the overwhelmed Bangladeshi government decides to force the Rohingya to return to Burma, where they will be corralled into death camps recalling those in Hitler's Germany.

Suu Kyi can do nothing to halt these horrific events, now that she has trapped herself in the junta's Constitution. Not only has her earlier failure to demand a new Constituent Assembly alienated her supporters in minority areas; the League's popular appeal has also been undermined in the Burmese heartland by the junta's propaganda machine. Movement activists are still visibly engaged in leading protests in urban centers and universities, but the League's inclusive vision of democracy may well have suffered a setback in other parts of the Burmese-speaking heartland.

I hope I am wrong. Only one thing is clear: It will take more than solemn condemnations by the United Nations or the Nobel Prize Committee to change these dynamics. At best, international repudiation may lead Suu Kyi and her puppet president to resign, leading to a new round of parliamentary elections in which her demoralized League would suffer significant electoral losses—which would doubtless be exaggerated in the official vote counts.

At this point, the junta's victorious puppet parties might authorize the military to force the 72-year-old Suu Kyi to live out the rest of her life under detention. Even if she remains free, the fate of the League will be up to the next generation of activists—who are unlikely to reverse the current authoritarian tide soon enough to prevent the death of countless Rohingya and other minorities in the borderland regions.

Despite this tragedy, I do not wish to judge Suu Kyi too harshly. As we have seen, if she had refused to take the position of First and Incumbent State Counsellor, the military might have responded to her demand for a constitutional revolution with a counter–coup d'état. At her moment of truth, it was not clear that her decision to reach a compromise with the junta would generate such a terrible outcome in such a short time.

It is not for me, sitting in the comfort of my office at Yale, to undertake a pseudoscientific "cost-benefit analysis" that points conclusively to the "correct" decision.

My aim instead is to reinforce my Polish case study's challenge to the "third wave" paradigm that currently prevails in comparative constitutional law. Neo-Huntingtonian approaches emphasize the imperative need for revolutionary outsiders to reach a peaceful compromise with authoritarian insiders that would permit the system to gradually evolve into a stable democratic order. These scholars entirely ignore the possibility that such a bargain, under revolutionary conditions, can generate mass demoralization and authoritarian resurgence—and destroy the very forms of constitutional government that neo-Huntingtonians seek to promote.

The case studies of Poland and Burma demonstrate the grim realities of the race against time, but they do so in different ways. In Poland, the principal villain in the story was the Gaullist model of presidential democracy—which enabled the premature fragmentation of the revolutionary movement, making it impossible to enact a credible Solidarity Constitution.

The Gaullist model cannot be held responsible for the Burmese tragedy. The great stumbling block here was the brazen refusal by the junta to allow the League to amend the Constitution to permit Suu Kyi to serve as president. If we are to enrich our understanding of the operation of the Gaullist model under revolutionary conditions, we will have to engage in further case studies. I take up this challenge in my study of Iran in Chapter 12.

Before doing so, however, I want to complexify my pessimistic diagnosis of the "race against time" by considering a counterexample. Like Poland and Burma, the modern state of Israel was born in revolutionary struggle; and like Lech Wałesa and Aung San Suu Kyi, David Ben-Gurion very self-consciously refused to focus the energies of his movement party on the task of constitutionalizing the principles that had inspired the Zionists' long struggle for a homeland. Yet Ben-Gurion's rejection of a Founding Constitution at Time

Two did not prevent the emergence of a strong constitutional court, committed to the protection of fundamental rights, at Time Three.

Why?

Revolutionary Legalism in Israel?

Israel emerges from its founding moment without a revolutionary Constitution. Yet seventy years later, the country is a functioning democracy with a strong Supreme Court. The system imposes oppressive burdens on Palestinians in the occupied territories, but for present purposes it is more important to ask how Israelis have managed to create a system of checks and balances to govern their own intense competition for political power.

As always, our story begins with the early Zionist struggle, for more than half a century, to establish Israel as a homeland dedicated to a "new beginning" in the life of the Jewish people—and only then proceeds to later critical moments in the country's history.

Time One: Political and Cultural Zionism

The French Revolution offered the Jews of Europe the prospect of a new political identity. Perhaps they need no longer be condemned to live on the Continent as "Christ-killing" pariahs; perhaps they might join their fellow citizens as free and equal members of an Enlightenment political order?

Over the course of the nineteenth century, urban elites took this prospect seriously and developed a reformed version of Judaism which broke free of Orthodox traditions. Reform Jews rejected cultural patterns that forced them to live a life that set them apart from prevailing social mores. But these assimilationist efforts generated nativist backlashes throughout Europe—with the Dreyfus Affair demonstrating that, even in Enlightenment France, vicious anti-Semitism was rampant.

This led to a moment of agonizing reappraisal. In his book *The Jewish State,* Theodor Herzl called upon secular and Reform Jews to give up on the promise of assimilation. Published in 1896, his book immediately propelled Herzl to the forefront of the effort to create a worldwide Zionist organization for securing a homeland for the Jewish people.

Its overriding aim was to convince one or another colonial power to reserve a portion of its empire for the Zionists. The physical location of the Jewish homeland was not of fundamental importance—indeed, Herzl's book dealt with the competing claims of Palestine and Argentina, and early Zionists continued to debate the merits of modern-day Uganda.[22] The key point was to create a place of refuge for Jews threatened by anti-Semitic violence, and to demonstrate that they were fully capable of organizing a modern Western society—thereby refuting anti-Semitic assertions to the contrary. While Herzl welcomed Orthodox Jews to the homeland, he did not expect them to play a leading role. His aim was to create a place where Jews could redeem the Enlightenment ideals that Europeans had betrayed by succumbing to anti-Semitism.

Herzl's creation of the World Zionist Organization (WZO) marked a decisive breakthrough, but his particular vision launched a larger debate. The rising generation of Eastern European Jewish leaders looked to the agricultural and working classes, inspired by Socialist ideals, to be the movement's revolutionary vanguard. So far as they were concerned, Herzl (who had died in 1904) spoke for an Austrian and German bourgeoisie, whose liberal ideals had little appeal to the Jewish masses fleeing massive pogroms in the Russian Empire. These Jews were now shipping out to the New World in a desperate effort to build new lives for themselves; but for rising young Zionists like David Ben-Gurion, the challenge was to convince them to go to Palestine (which he had always favored as the Jewish homeland). The New World was far more prosperous than the Middle East, so the Zionist project would fail unless it promised Jews something more than bourgeois riches. It must offer them the opportunity to build a country that would, once and for all, refute anti-Semitic caricatures depicting them as money-grubbing opportunists. Inspired by Socialist ideals, they would build a Jewish state based on the dignity of labor.[23]

Ben-Gurion had already moved to Jerusalem before World War I to help develop the first worker cooperatives. But Palestine decisively emerged as the site for Zionist settlement only when Chaim Weizmann convinced the British government to recognize it as the "Jewish homeland" in its Balfour Declaration of 1917. This remarkable diplomatic coup permitted the reconciliation of Herzl's original emphasis on state building with Ben-Gurion's Socialist emphasis on the dignity of labor.[24]

The Zionist synthesis was made more compelling by an act of cultural redefinition involving the status of Hebrew. For centuries Hebrew had served only as the language of religious practice and Talmudic study. In the conduct of ordinary life, European Jews spoke Yiddish or Ladino among themselves and tried to master the dominant language of their locale when dealing with outsiders. (Reform Jews reversed this priority, and increasingly spoke German or French or English at home and in their synagogues.) The reinvigoration of Hebrew required an enormous scholarly enterprise aimed at transforming a Bible-based discourse into a language capable of expressing modern social realities. As this was accomplished, Zionist schools in Palestine began, in the 1920s, to churn out youngsters speaking modern Hebrew as their "native" language—inspiring their parents to join them in constructing a distinctive Israeli culture that marked a sharp break from the European past.[25]

Hebrew, Socialism, and a Jewish State. Different leaders emphasized different aspects of this revolutionary trinity. Weizmann's astonishing diplomatic triumph in obtaining the Balfour Declaration propelled him to an ascendant position in the World Zionist Organization—allowing him later, at critical moments, to gain decisive support from the Roosevelt administration and the United Nations for Israeli statehood. But Weizmann's political campaign, and his incessant efforts to raise money from wealthy elites in Europe and America, led him to downplay the collectivist aspirations of the settler movement.

In contrast, Ben-Gurion left no doubt that he was a strong supporter of the Socialist ideals inspiring his fellow settlers in Palestine. He took on the leadership of Histadrut, the General Federation of Hebrew Workers, which was established at a joint conference of socialist parties in 1920. Its constitution created a "Society of Workers," who refused to "exploit the labor of others." To give substance to this commitment, the Federation threw its support behind the burgeoning kibbutz movement, as well as an ambitious program of vocational training and cooperative industrial production.

At the same time, the settler community went about organizing its own National Assembly along broadly Westminster lines—and soon gained official recognition for their efforts from the authorities governing the British Mandate.[26] As leader of the Workers' Federation, Ben-Gurion proceeded to organize a political wing which quickly emerged as the largest parliamentary group, though it never controlled a majority and was obliged to engage in coalition building with other socialist parties to speak in the name of the Assembly.

By 1930 Ben-Gurion used these early successes to obtain the WZO's endorsement, and its formidable financial resources, for Workers' Federation projects. As World War II approached, the Federation's ongoing political activities crystallized in the formation of a social democratic movement party, the Mapai, which would be the leading political force throughout the founding period.[27]

The National Assembly's practices during the Mandate laid a promising foundation for the future. Regularly scheduled elections were conducted with scrupulous fairness—there were no efforts by Ben-Gurion or the Federation to convert their pluralities into majorities by manipulating the vote count. Instead, the ongoing need to generate majority coalitions encouraged the competing socialist parties to avoid ideological extremism and engage in mutual accommodation—although the small Orthodox parties were left on the sidelines.[28] Similarly, the Workers' Federation was remarkably successful in channeling the World Zionist Organization's massive economic assistance into the sustained development of rural and urban cooperatives.[29]

Both in his politics and as head of the Federation, Ben-Gurion was demonstrating to the settlers, and to the outside world, that the revolutionary promise of Zionism was no dream: Jewish immigrants to Palestine were building a vibrant social democracy that compared favorably to those constructed in Europe and the New World during the interwar period.

This success had an extraordinary impact on migration patterns. Between 1882 and 1903, only 25,000 Jews had sought a haven in Palestine; and only 35,000 joined them in the decade before World War I. But once the United States dramatically restricted immigration in the early 1920s, large numbers of Jews began to choose the inspiring example of Palestine over the economic attractions of Latin America.

By the time of Israel's independence in 1948, the settler community had grown to 750,000 from 100,000 at the end of World War I. It then doubled to 1.4 million over the next three years.[30] Half of these newcomers were refugees from Nazi death camps; most of the others were fleeing Arab countries in the wake of Israel's military struggle for independence.

This leads to a final factor in the Time One equation: the military. During World War I, Vladimir (Ze'ev) Jabotinsky had already organized the Jewish Legion, which fought with the British to liberate Palestine from the Turks.[31] His militancy propelled him onto the Zionist stage as a rival to the diplomat Weizmann and the social democrat Ben-Gurion. Taking up Herzl's grand theme, he remained a stalwart defender of modernity, science, and freedom, and condemned Orthodoxy with fervor. At the same time, he was a foe of socialist / communist collectivism, which he saw as a threat to human dignity. Throughout the 1920s and 1930s, he eloquently urged European audiences to support armed struggle to win independence in Palestine before the next wave of anti-Semitism overwhelmed the Jews of Europe.[32]

This was anathema to Weizmann and Ben-Gurion, who saw continuing British cooperation as central to the settlement project. Ben-Gurion did support the creation of a settler militia, the Haganah, to take necessary actions in self-defense. But he was convinced that only British troops had sufficient firepower to maintain the fragile peace prevailing between Jewish settlers and the Arab majority. With the brutal persecutions of Hitler and Stalin, however, Jabotinsky's eloquent praise of the "new specimen of Jew . . . the FIGHTING JEW"[33] drew increasing support in Europe and America. Nevertheless, he was in no position to challenge Ben-Gurion's leadership in the settler community, since he chose to spend his last years abroad.

This gap was filled by Menachem Begin, one of Jabotinsky's younger followers. Begin was in Poland when the Nazis were preparing their invasion in 1939, and he narrowly escaped to the Soviet Union—where he was seized by the Communists and sent off to the Gulag. Upon his release in 1941, he somehow managed to make the long journey to Palestine, and arrived at a critical moment.[34]

Militant Israeli nationalists, under the leadership of Avraham Stern, had launched a series of terrorist attacks against the British to prepare the way for independence. When Stern was gunned down in April 1942, an uneasy peace prevailed—until Begin called upon Irgun militants to renew their terrorist campaign in 1944 and force the British to give up their Mandate to the Jewish state.

Ben-Gurion was appalled by this Quixotic enterprise. At this point in the war, the British were following up their decisive victory over Rommel in North Africa with mop-up operations that ultimately sent 100,000 troops to Palestine. In Ben-Gurion's view, it was folly to alienate these forces when they could play an essential role in a successful handover of power to the state of Israel after the Nazis were defeated. As a consequence, he turned decisively against Begin—arranging for his own Haganah guerillas to cooperate with British forces in rounding up Irgun militants and their underground supporters.

He continued collaborating even when the British took strong measures to limit further Jewish immigration and barred the entry of ships from Europe carrying refugees from the death camps. In the British view, this was necessary to contain a violent Arab backlash that would precipitate all-out war. Ben-Gurion reluctantly went along—refusing to order Haganah to intervene to prevent the departure of the ships, even though there was no guarantee that they would find a safe harbor elsewhere.

Ben-Gurion quickly terminated this humiliating alliance as soon as the war came to an end. In October 1945 his Haganah joined Begin's Irgun in a Hebrew Resistance Movement to prepare their forces for the day when Israel declared its independence.[35] But this show of cooperation was merely symbolic. The two leaders split on the critical issue of real-world military tactics. In Begin's view, the best way to hasten the day of Israeli independence was to engage in a bloody terror campaign that imposed unbearable costs on British troops and civilians. This would give the government in London no choice but to hand over power as quickly as possible. Irgun's ongoing campaign reached its climax in July 1946, when it bombed the headquarters of the British Mandate at the King David Hotel in Jerusalem, causing major casualties.

Ben-Gurion was moving in a different direction. He was well aware that the Attlee government was abandoning its imperial pretensions on a broad front from Asia to South Africa, and Chaim Weizmann was saying that Attlee would be withdrawing from Palestine as well. If this turned out to be true, the only sensible thing was to allow the 100,000-strong British army of occupation to maintain public order. This would buy time to enable the settlers to prepare their military forces for the terrible moment when British forces left the scene, and Arab armies would try to crush the infant Jewish State in its cradle.

Ben-Gurion's strategy proved successful. He called upon the Workers' Federation to use its formidable organizational apparatus to provide intensive military training to Jews working in rural and urban cooperatives. These soldiers made up the core of the new Israeli Defense Forces (IDF), which also incorporated new migrants into its ranks. Given Ben-Gurion's success in transforming the IDF into an effective fighting force, Begin had little choice but to permit his militants to enter the new Israeli army and lose their distinct command structure which had allowed Irgun to operate as an independent fighting force.[36]

But Begin turned to politics to continue his challenge to Ben-Gurion's leadership—organizing a revisionist movement party, Herut, to oppose Mapai's socialist ideals with an alternative vision emphasizing the central significance of individual freedom.

Begin's individualist challenge is an indicator of the complexity of Israeli politics on the eve of Israeli independence. At the same time that Herut was attacking Mapai's brand of socialism, Communists and Socialists were attacking Mapai from the left—organizing a rival movement party, Mapam, which won strong support in labor circles.

To complexify matters further, Orthodox Jews were rethinking their position on critical issues. For a long time, the dominant opinion considered it sacrilegious for Zionists to insist on a new Constitution when the Old Testament established that it was God, not man, who had granted the Jewish people the right to rule the territory. But as the moment of truth approached, significant elements of the Orthodox community refused to stand on the sidelines. They formed the United Religious Front to enter into the political fray.

Could all these rivals find common ground?

Time Two: The Lost Constitutional Moment

Israel's situation was by no means unique. Movement parties in France and Italy were displaying similar divisions, at about the same time, as they emerged from their wartime Resistance against the Nazis and Fascists. Devout Christian Democrats, like Orthodox Jews, opposed the aggressive secularism advanced by Social Democrats and Communists. But at the same time, they joined with Social Democrats to oppose hard-line Communists who derided constitutionalism as a "bourgeois myth." Despite their divisions, the three parties managed to hammer out a Constitution when unelected provisional governments in France and Italy called elections for constituent assemblies that would establish the relative degree of Communist / Socialist / Christian Democratic support among the general citizenry.

Israelis took the same basic approach. During the Mandate, the democratic legitimacy of the National Assembly had been regularly reinvigorated by periodic elections. But with the outbreak of war between the Jewish community and the Arabs in 1947, elections became impossible, and so holdovers (together with the British) continued to govern the Jewish community until the Mandate came to an end with the Declaration of Independence in 1948. Until then, Ben-Gurion served as head of the preexisting National Executive, with the solid support of the National Assembly as well as local representatives of the World Zionist Organization. Once Ben-Gurion announced the Declaration on May 14, the structure of government changed. He now operated as head of a thirty-seven-member Provisional Council of State, which included representatives of all significant groups within the settler community as well as members from the WZO.[37]

Ben-Gurion was unwilling to wait until the Declaration to prepare the country for its fateful moment of constitutional self-determination. His minister of justice asked Leo Kohn, a distinguished jurist, to take the lead in drafting a serious constitutional framework. Kohn responded with a series of drafts, which were repeatedly revised in ongoing confidential consultations with a broad range of groups in the larger community. The second of these drafts became the basis for the deliberations of a formal Committee on the Constitution created by the Provisional Council of State in 1948. The Committee's seven members represented the very different ideologies held by dominant secular and religious groups on the Council. For the next year and a half, the Committee met twenty three times before it submitted its final version to the thirty-seven-member Provisional Council after it came into existence once independence was declared in May.[38]

I will consider its decision shortly. But it's better to begin with the ways in which the competing political parties framed the constitutional issues as they tried to gain the support of the voters who were going to the polls to cast their ballots for the first time as citizens of the State of Israel.

Betrayal

It fell to David Ben-Gurion, as president of the Council, to speak out the words of Israel's Declaration of Independence in a radio address from his Tel Aviv headquarters on May 15. After recounting the turning points in Jewish history that legitimated Israel's claim to independence, the Declaration set out an explicit deadline of "1 October 1948" for an "Elected Constituent Assembly" to "adopt" a "Constitution." During this four-and-a-half-month period, the Declaration assigned interim authority to the Provisional Council, enabling the Assembly to concentrate all its energies on an intense effort at constitutional construction.[39]

In setting out this two-stage process, the Declaration sent Israel down a path that was different from the one traveled in France and Italy. In both these places, the same assembly operated as the basis for provisional government and constitutional construction. The Israeli Declaration kept these functions distinct—explicitly instructing the Provisional Council to keep on operating while the Constituent Assembly did its work. This division of labor, together with the eighteen-week deadline, emphasized the centrality of constitutionalism to the Declaration's understanding of Israel's state-building project.

Nevertheless, the Council was twice obliged to postpone the Declaration's deadline when Arab armies and Palestinian militias launched all-out efforts to destroy Israel before it could organize itself in a proper fashion. But once the Israeli Defense Forces managed to beat back these initial assaults, the

Council moved rapidly to redeem its commitment despite the continuing military threats. On January 25, 1949, *90 percent* of the men and women of the settler community cast ballots to decide which movement parties should take the lead in constructing Israel's framework of government.

In the run-up to the election, Ben-Gurion's Mapai committed itself to the constitutional enterprise: "While the task will take years, the Constituent Assembly will lay down principles, mark a path, and establish a government which will steer the ship of state within the stormy waves of these tropical seas."[40] This commitment was affirmed by Begin's Herut, which elaborated a formidable set of constitutional principles to guide its delegates at the Assembly.[41] Although the leftist Mapam did not explicitly mention the Constitution in its official electoral program, its political leaders consistently supported the project once the Constituent Assembly came into existence.[42] Only the United Religious Front asserted the need to build the state on biblical foundations—and even here, there was significant support in the Orthodox community for a Constitution that expressed a Zionist understanding of the national project.[43]

As the election campaign was reaching its climax, however, the Provisional Council posted a formal notice of an initiative that suggested a radical departure from the course laid out in the Declaration. Under its proposed Transition Ordinance, the Council would not permit the Constituent Assembly to concentrate its energies, and those of the general public, on the task of constitutional construction. Instead, it would immediately hand over its interim powers of provisional government to the Assembly as well.

The Council published a formal announcement of its Transition Ordinance only twelve days before the election, but it was barely noticed during the campaign's final days.[44] Certainly Ben-Gurion did nothing to alert the public to its existence—let alone justify it. If he had, it would have provoked a heated debate. Given his silence, Israeli citizens had every reason to believe, as they went to the polls, that Ben-Gurion would remain faithful to the division of authority between the Constituent Assembly and the Provisional Council that he himself had proclaimed when giving voice to the Declaration in May 1948.

But once the Assembly convened three weeks after the election, Ben-Gurion immediately turned his back on the Declaration and made the Assembly's first order of business the enactment of a Transition Law that granted it the powers of a Westminster-style parliament. To signify this transformation, the Assembly would henceforward call itself the "Knesset." On February 15, 1949, the minister of justice in Ben Gurion's provisional government rose to the floor and moved its immediate adoption. This provoked Menachem Begin to rise in protest and propose the following amendment:

> The primary duty of the Constitutional Assembly is to establish a Constitution for the state and to legislate laws for Israel. The Constituent Assembly's role will conclude with the passage of a Constitution for the state. Within three months, elections will be held for the legislative authority, in accordance with the Constitution.[45]

Given the divergence between the Declaration of Independence and the Transition Law, such a motion would ordinarily give rise to a wide-ranging debate—requiring Ben-Gurion to explain to the Assembly, and to the people at large, why such a change in course was in the national interest.

Nothing like this happened. Instead, the newly elected speaker of the assembly refused to allow any debate at all on Begin's motion, but proceeded at once to an up-or-down vote. No less remarkably, ordinary Israelis were not even able to learn how their representatives cast their ballots on this fateful measure. Assembly records simply report that a vote was held and that "the proposal of Mr. Begin was not accepted."[46] On the very same day, the Transition Law was pushed through the Assembly by a margin of 77 to 0, with 11 abstentions—although 42 members chose to absent themselves from the chamber.

This boycott dramatized the power play involved. The Assembly was refusing to make the slightest collective effort *to justify* its betrayal of the Declaration. Instead, the majority was intent on seizing the enormous powers of a Westminster-style parliament without Ben-Gurion saying a single word defending his extraordinary ascent to power as prime minister. During the year that followed, the Assembly spent all of its time acting as a parliament (Knesset) and devoted zero minutes of floor debate to the Constitution. When it finally turned its attention to constitutional issues a full year later, the nation's political leaders squared off against one another in a highly revealing fashion.

But before analyzing these debates, we should get a better grip on the dynamics that propelled Ben-Gurion and his provisional government to betray the Declaration of Independence at such a critical moment.

The Fate of the Kohn Draft

Recall that, long before the Constituent Assembly met, Ben-Gurion's minister of justice had asked Leo Kohn to engage in an ongoing drafting effort in consultation with a broad range of interested groups. As the moment of Independence approached, the provisional government created a formal Committee on the Constitution, which adopted the latest Kohn draft as the basis for its own deliberations. The Committee's seven members expressed the radically different ideologies held by major secular and religious groups in Palestine. They proceeded under conditions of strict confidentiality, lest premature disclosures would make it impossible to achieve broad-based support for the final product. Yet its public silence belied an intensive effort to reach common ground as it formulated its final draft in October 1948.[47]

From a juristic point of view, the draft was an extraordinary achievement—containing a tightly organized system of seventy-eight articles (with many subsections), backed by extensive and insightful commentaries highlighting critical issues for decision.[48]

The Kohn text was framed to gain the broadest possible political support. It made a series of symbolic gestures to the religious community, beginning with a Preamble that declared it was "establish[ing] our State on foundations of peace and justice as in the vision of the prophets of Israel . . ." But it also contained hard-edged provisions forbidding "discrimination of any kind . . . on the grounds of race, religion, language, or sex," and insisting that "all citizens shall enjoy equal political and civil rights . . . and shall not be put at a disadvantage as a candidate for public office or employment . . . on account of his race, religion, language or sex." These unconditional guarantees made it clear that Jews claimed no privileged status over Muslims or Christians or atheists in the new constitutional order. At the same time, the draft responded directly to the horrors of the Holocaust by declaring that Israel would be constituted by its commitment to "uphold the dignity of Man."[49]

Kohn's Committee took emphatic steps to ensure that these large principles would be redeemed in the real world. Their draft created a High Court with the power to "decide all questions relating to the validity of any law having regard to the terms of the Constitution."[50] If the Court rendered a negative judgment, it could be overruled by parliament only under stringent conditions. Not only would the government (presumably led by Ben-Gurion) be required to gain a two-thirds majority to enact a formal amendment reenacting the challenged law, it would be required to do so on two different occasions, with the second supermajority vote occurring at least six months after the first.[51]

These override provisions were sure to provoke resistance from the future prime minister. But Ben-Gurion was not paying attention to the Committee's proceedings as it was hammering out the terms of its final proposal. His attention was concentrated on immediate life-and-death issues—most notably, the reception of hundreds of thousands of Jewish refugees flooding into the homeland at a time when the IDF was battling against Arab military invasions. When Ben-Gurion finally got a chance to review Kohn's draft, Committee members saw, to their dismay, that he was "almost fainting."

His principal complaint did not involve the judicial review provisions. Eyewitness accounts report that, as he was recovering from his initial shock, he barely managed to exclaim that "he didn't want Kohn's vision of Israel but a *secular* Jewish state."[52] Ben-Gurion then led the Council to approve a Transition Ordinance that granted the Constituent Assembly power to serve as a Westminster-style parliament throughout the period when they were engaged in their effort to frame a Constitution worthy of the Jewish People.[53]

The Will to Power?

Ran Hirschl reports, "Historians and legal scholars, even those inclined to resist cynicism," have adopted a consensus view of this dramatic turn-around. So far as they are concerned, Ben-Gurion's "opposition to a constitution was fundamentally attributable to his fear of losing all or some of [his] power."[54]

Start with some basic mathematics. If Ben-Gurion had been seriously disturbed by Kohn's symbolic gestures toward the religious community, it would have been easy to put together a broad coalition in the Assembly to eliminate these provisions from the final Constitution.

Just count up the votes. Ben-Gurion's strongly secular Mapai had emerged as the leading political party from the elections—winning 36 percent of the popular vote and 46 of the Assembly's 120 seats. With this strong base, he only needed 16 more delegates to win a majority in support of a suitably revised Kohn text.

He could have readily leaped over this hurdle. On the one hand, the hard-left Mapam had won 15 percent of the vote and 15 seats,[55] and despite the skepticism of some members, its leader, Meir Ya'ari, was a strong proponent of a "progressive, socialist, secular" Constitution.[56] Even if a few of Mapam's hardcore Marxists deserted Ya'ari, Ben-Gurion could have picked up the votes of a dozen or so members from smaller secular parties.[57]

So it wouldn't be difficult to find at least 70 or 75 votes for a draft that resembled the Franco-Italian Constitutions enacted at about the same time—which synthesized socialist demands for real-world equality with more traditional demands for democratic freedom.

This was even before Menachem Begin's Herut entered into the headcount. His political party came to the table with 14 seats based on 12 percent of the votes. As his opening protest against the Transition Law demonstrates, Begin was particularly emphatic about the importance of giving undivided attention to the Assembly's constitutional mission. The French and Italian cases suggest, moreover, that it would have been perfectly possible to incorporate Begin's strong commitment to individual liberty in the artful drafting of the bill of rights.[58] All in all, it would have been perfectly possible for Ben-Gurion to assemble ninety or more supporters for a Constitution expressing Israel's revolutionary commitment to secular Zionist principles.

Yet this broad support would come only at a price. Once Ben-Gurion had joined forces with Mapam and Herut, it would be difficult to deny cabinet positions to their leaders in the coalition government.

In contrast, another mathematical option allowed Ben-Gurion to monopolize power without effective checks and balances. Recall that the traditional Orthodox community had formed a United Religious Front, which gained 16 seats in Knesset. This delegation, when joined together with Mapai's 46, added up to a majority of 62.[59] The Orthodox would, of course, object to any principled affirmation of the secular character of the Jewish state. So long as Ben-Gurion did not challenge the rabbis' religious prerogatives, however, he could act decisively on all the urgent issues on the immediate agenda. As Bernard Avishai put it, Ben-Gurion gave up "the chance to promulgate a constitution, but it gave Mapai the undreamed-of chance to form a cabinet without any real partners."[60]

I have no inclination to deny that this pure power-maximizing account has a lot going for it. Nonetheless, I will be arguing that the revolutionary context adds an essential dimension to Ben-Gurion's fateful refusal to constitutionalize the high-energy politics of the Founding.

Parliamentary Push-Back

Once Ben-Gurion made his choice, and rammed the Transition Law through the Assembly / Knesset, it was up to his secular opponents to make the next move: Would they admit defeat or keep pushing for a serious attempt at constitutional construction?

After a year of agitation, the prime minister finally accepted the need for serious debate. During February 1950, Zionist critics repeatedly denounced Ben-Gurion's turnaround as a cynical power grab that betrayed the profound meaning of the Jewish community's long struggle for independence.[61] The prime minister's arch-nemesis, Menachem Begin, not only insisted on a strong bill of rights, but on the need to severely restrict Ben-Gurion's exercise of sweeping emergency powers under statutes inherited from the Mandate.[62] Left-wing leaders of Mapam made similar demands—even Communists joined in the defense of constitutionalism.[63] All in all, about forty members of the Assembly advanced eloquent statements of constitutional principle— which provoked angry confrontations on the floor that sometimes led to outright chaos. Most notably, when Menachem Begin asserted that only a written Constitution could restrain abuses of martial law by the government, he was shouted down and denounced for presenting a "speech of incitement, not a speech on the constitution."[64]

As the nation watched, the debates took a turn that eludes the power-maximizing account. This standard interpretation supposes that Ben-Gurion could rely on the 46 members of his Mapai party for their unconditional support, and thereby ensure a majority together with the 16 members of the United Religious Front (and a few other Ben-Gurion allies). Generally speaking, the presumption of party loyalty makes sense in a Westminster-type system, since prime ministers can destroy the careers of members who refuse to support the government on key votes. Nevertheless, this presumption of loyalty may no longer make sense within revolutionary contexts, when prime ministers repudiate movement-party principles.

This is precisely what happened in Ben-Gurion's case. Despite his symbolic centrality and political savvy, leading members of his own party began to attack his failure to follow through on the Declaration's constitutional commitments. Listen to Mapai's Ben-Zion Dinaburg addressing the chamber at an early stage of the debate:

What, in essence, is a constitution? A constitution is first of all the expression of persons' common will to live together under a common authority. The constitution establishes the framework and the principles, according to which people wish and commit to build their lives together. . . .

Do all the immigrants who come here now understand what national life is? I am not even sure that all of those who have been here a long time understand what a national life is, and what each citizen owes to the state . . . Is not a constitution the greatest instrument for placing the state in the heart of the soldier?[65]

Dinaburg also confronted the frequent objection that a written Constitution gave too much power to unelected judges to make crucial decisions at a perilous time:

Why must it be a court? In our circumstances we can decide that the Knesset will select a specific body, the constitution committee of the Knesset, that will review each law that is under consideration and submit its view to the Knesset. This could be an ad hoc committee specific for this purpose and could have representatives from all parties and qualified persons.[66]

Ben-Gurion only came to the floor late in the debate—and when he entered the argument, he didn't repeat his earlier anxieties about the religious symbolism deployed by Kohn's final draft. Instead he launched a fundamental critique of the very idea of a written Constitution.

He emphasized that the French, and many other nations, had repeatedly failed to sustain their democracies despite their paper constitutions. In contrast, the British did not waste their time proclaiming grand constitutional principles. They focused instead on the particularly pressing problems of their era—and developed commonsense solutions that had broad appeal. This "inductive" method permitted them to build a vibrant democracy in step-by-step fashion—and the prime minister urged his countrymen to take the same approach. Rather than wasting time debating a Constitution, the Knesset should be focusing all its energies on defending the country against external threats, assimilating new immigrants, settling the Negev, and building the massive infrastructure required for a modern economy.

In making his case, Ben-Gurion ignored Dinaburg's innovative institutional proposals and repeated familiar warnings about judicial supremacy.[67] But his antagonism to jurists was secondary to his insistence that the Knesset and ordinary citizens should follow Britain's problem-solving path to democracy and freedom.

Everything we know about Ben-Gurion suggests that his admiration for Westminster-style government was entirely sincere, and not merely a spur-of-the-moment effort to prettify his power grab. It was a significant factor in his very self-conscious decision to lose the "race against time."

The Harari Resolution: A Revisionist View

Despite Ben-Gurion's counterattack, his critics continued to press their objections during the following months—forcing the issue back onto the floor in June 1950. At that point Ben-Gurion swerved again. Instead of continuing his root-and-branch resistance, he offered his opponents an olive branch. He threw his support behind a resolution offered by Yizhar Harari, a member of a small liberal party, who offered a way forward that might enable both sides to move beyond their escalating confrontation. The Harari Resolution renounced Menachem Begin's demand that the Knesset immediately take up its assigned task of adopting a comprehensive Constitution in the name of the People. Yet it also rejected Ben-Gurion's insistence on concrete problem-solving. Instead, it set out a pragmatic approach that authorized the Knesset to enact Basic Laws in a step-by-step fashion.

So far as Harari was concerned, the challenge was to learn from experience. As government responded to the concrete problems arising in one or another sphere of public life, it should be trying to generate principles that deserved elaboration and codification after serious parliamentary debate. But until that happened, it was best to avoid the grand pronunciamentos associated with French or American paradigms. Over time, the Knesset's efforts to write Basic Laws in a piecemeal fashion might ultimately culminate in a comprehensive Constitution for the People of Israel.[68] But the Resolution offered up this prospect for the remote future; in the here and now, principled pragmatism should be the order of the day.

Given Ben-Gurion's earlier twists and turns, it is easy to see his endorsement of Harari in purely opportunistic terms. He was already 64 in 1950, and it was the next ten years that were important to him as a practical matter. If his overwhelming position as a Westminster-style prime minister was secure for the next decade, that would be good enough for him. From a self-interested point of view, the operational question was whether the Resolution would provide Mapai leaders like Dinaburg with a face-saving way to remain loyal to their party and continue to support him as prime minister. From this angle, the Resolution had the great advantage of allowing them to preserve their commitment to a written constitution while giving Ben-Gurion everything he needed in the short-run.

But once again, this power-maximizing account doesn't do justice to the revolutionary logic of Ben-Gurion's situation. He was not merely concerned with the next decade. He was also concerned with the founding legacy he would be leaving to future generations of Israelis. From this perspective, the coming vote on the Harari Resolution would have a special significance.

If Dinaburg and others defected, and forced the Knesset to embrace a written Constitution, Ben-Gurion would be in a precarious position. To sustain his leadership of Mapai, he would have to demonstrate that he was prepared to follow through on Dinaburg's demands, and enact a Kohn-type draft as Israel's supreme law. But he would have to share the glory with a rising star who had played a central role in forcing the issue onto center stage: none other than his nemesis, the 37-year-old Menachem Begin.

Worse yet, once Ben-Gurion left the scene, Begin would emerge as the surviving Founding Father of the Republic, and would use his enhanced symbolic stature as a powerful weapon to defeat the next generation of Mapai's leaders in their struggle for political ascendancy.

In contrast, if Ben-Gurion could prevent Mapai defections and gain majority support for Harari, he would be in a position to secure his founding legacy in the proper British manner—by providing examples of statesman-like problem solving that would serve as concrete precedents for future generations to emulate. Indeed, if these precedents finally did culminate in a comprehensive Constitution, this would only serve to consolidate Ben-Gurion's role as the revolution's decisive leader.

Ben-Gurion's olive branch, in short, was not merely the product of short-term power maximization—though this certainly was a vital factor. It also arose from a concern that collaborating with Menachem Begin would allow Begin to emerge as the country's last Great Founding Father and enhance his effort to destroy Mapai and its ongoing efforts to preserve the social democratic legacy of the Zionist revolution.

But now that Dinaburg and others had rebelled, Ben-Gurion could no longer determine the fate of the Harari Resolution. Unless the rebels returned to the fold, Harari would go down to defeat and Ben-Gurion would have had no choice but to put together a Mapai–Mapam–Herut coalition that would enact a written constitution broadly similar to those constructed in postwar France or Italy.

The moment of truth came on June 13, 1950, when Harari was put up for a final vote. How would the Assembly decide?

The answer is stunningly equivocal. On the one hand, none of the fence-sitters joined the 38 Zionists who voted No on the Resolution. On the other hand, the government managed to convince only 50 members to vote Yes. The remaining 19 in attendance refused to jump off the fence—3 abstained and 11 left the chamber.[69]

50 to 38 to 19: the tally did in fact prove decisive, leading the secularists to abandon their campaign for a founding Constitution. Nevertheless, it raises all sorts of jurisprudential puzzles. Recall that the Declaration of Independence *explicitly* required the Assembly to concentrate all its energies on its constitutional function. By what right did a *minority* of fifty members turn its back on the Declaration and refuse to accept *any* responsibility to come up with a comprehensive proposal, leaving this task to the remote future? Didn't this power grab by fifty members transform the Constituent Assembly into an utterly lawless Knesset, especially given the voters' prevailing understanding of its mission at the time they went to the polls to elect delegates to the Assembly?

I leave such puzzlers to positivist theorists of the "pure science of law," who suppose that there is a sharp line dividing constitutional from unconstitutional assertions of political authority. The point of this book is to show how revolutionary dynamics characteristically lead actors to straddle the positivist line in unconventional ways—combining legal and illegal appeals in complex mixtures as they attempt to establish their authority. From this perspective, the challenge is to demonstrate how, for all its seeming lawlessness, Ben-Gurion did manage *to legitimate* a collective decision to depart from the Declaration and pursue Harari's path of principled pragmatism.

Before moving forward to Times Three and Four, I want to pause to reflect on one immediate consequence of the prime minister's refusal to constitutionalize his charisma at Time Two.

Human Dignity and the Holocaust: The Lost Israeli Contribution

At the same time as Israel was turning its back on a written Constitution, the United Nations was propelling a big new idea onto the world stage. The Universal Declaration of Human Rights of 1948 committed all its signatories to the "recognition of the inherent dignity . . . of all members of the human family."[70] In the very same year, West Germany's new Basic Law began with the proposition "Human dignity shall be inviolable." Until that time, constitutional appeals to "human dignity" had been virtually unknown—the only exception was its appearance in the Constitution of the Irish Republic in 1937.[71] Yet ever since the UN's Universal Declaration and West Germany's Basic Law endorsed the concept, "human dignity" has been one of the overarching themes propelling constitutionalism forward, profoundly shaping worldwide understandings of the legitimate uses of power.

But I am focusing right now on the 1940s, not the 2010s. At this early moment, it is unquestionable that Israel's Constituent Assembly, if it had been allowed to fulfill the mission marked out by the Declaration, would have made an early and decisive contribution to dignitarian jurisprudence.

Recall that Kohn's final draft explicitly declared that "the state shall . . . preserve the dignity of man." The choice of this formula was by no means accidental—Kohn had been a consultant to the Irish when they first introduced the principle into their 1937 Constitution.[72] But in Israeli hands, the same principle would have gained worldwide significance in the light of the Holocaust. The Kohn draft developed this link further, but I leave it to the reader to imagine the profundity of the constitutional statement that would have emerged after full Assembly debate.[73]

Only one thing is clear: an Israeli constitution would have emerged as one of the three pillars of human rights law, along with the Universal Declaration and the German Basic Law, during the 1950s. Whatever else it may or may not have accomplished, Ben-Gurion's rejection of a founding Constitution made it impossible for Israel to make a unique contribution to the most important development in human rights law in the modern era.

Time Three: Succession Crisis

Since the 1990s the Israeli Supreme Court has in fact elaborated a powerful jurisprudence of "human dignity"—engaging in the very same worldwide legal conversation from which it was conspicuously absent during the first postwar generation. Under the leadership of its president, Aharon Barak, the Court's opinions have transformed the abstract dignitarian principle into a set of hard-edged doctrines that could serve as a rigorous analytic framework for the protection of fundamental rights.[74] This ongoing effort has profoundly influenced courts in many other places. Given the Barak

Court's leading role, its particular decisions have been the object of intense critical scrutiny—some judges and commentators denounce them for their "judicial activism," while others applaud their interventions on behalf of the powerless.[75]

I won't be engaging in this ongoing debate. Instead I will consider whether the very existence of the Barak Court refutes a principal thesis advanced in my other case studies. In particular, the Polish and Burmese cases emphasize the high significance of the "race against time" at the Founding, and the tragic consequences of losing this race. How, then, has the Barak Court managed to vindicate the principle of human dignity at Time Three despite David Ben-Gurion's refusal to constitutionalize it at Time Two?

Our studies of India, Italy, and France offer some insight. Revolutionary movement parties in all three places were more successful than Israel in constitutionalizing their charisma immediately after the Second World War. Nevertheless, their constitutional courts did not immediately begin to make aggressive use of their powers of judicial review. They asserted this authority only later on, once the symbolic leaders of the revolution had died or resigned, leaving a "legitimacy vacuum" that judges tried to fill during the succession crises that followed.

Time Three was a messy business in each case: it took a lot of political and judicial statesmanship, as well as sheer luck, for the Courts to win recognition as the ultimate guardians of their revolutionary constitutional legacy. These earlier case studies provide the entry point for my analysis.

Commentators on the Barak Court generally begin their discussion in the 1990s, when it began to assert its dignitarian jurisprudence in remarkably broad terms.[76] But I will start at a much earlier point, when the departure of Ben-Gurion, and the decline of Mapai, created a succession crisis that exhibits structural similarities to those experienced in France, Italy, and India. As in these cases, the rise of the Israeli Supreme Court is best understood as the product of judicial statesmanship at a time when the country was struggling to resolve its own succession crisis.

I start my story in 1963, when a 76-year-old Ben-Gurion decided that the time had come to pass on his leadership of Mapai to a handpicked successor. As in the analogous French / Indian / Italian cases, he picked an utterly uncharismatic aide who had skillfully handled a host of complex policy issues while Ben-Gurion confronted the large questions of national identity left in the wake of the country's successful revolution. In this particular case, Ben-Gurion turned to Levi Eshkol, who as finance minister had done an outstanding job attracting massive inflows of capital from America and Europe that propelled Israel's economy forward with remarkable success.

He then quickly regretted his decision. When Eshkol proved resistant to his commands, Ben-Gurion melodramatically quit Mapai and organized a new movement party, Rafi, seeking to throw Eshkol and his uncharismatic cronies from power, and restore the great spirit of the revolution. But Mapai wasn't as tired as Ben-Gurion supposed. Eshkol formed the Workers' Alliance with a smaller leftist group, Ahdut HaAvoda, and won a smashing victory over Rafi.[77] Then came the astonishing military triumph of the Six-Day War, which gave Mapai a big boost and led Eshkol to organize a full-scale merger of Rafi into the Labor Party.[78]

Ben-Gurion loudly dissented and tried to form yet another rival movement party just before his death, but Labor seemed to be managing his departure quite well. Yet its wartime boost in popularity came at a significant cost. During Ben-Gurion's twenty-five-year ascendancy, he had steadfastly treated his old rival, Menachem Begin, as a political pariah—never allowing Herut to join Labor's governing coalition. But in the run-up to the Six-Day War, Eshkol appointed Begin as minister without portfolio in a "government of national unity," and Ben-Gurion's old nemesis continued in the cabinet when Golda Meir became prime minister upon Eshkol's death in 1969.

Begin's entry into government significantly improved his standing before the wider public, but he soon reasserted his outsider status in 1970 by resigning in protest against Golda Meir's cautious pragmatism. Yet he did not stay on the outside for long. The Yom Kippur War marked a decisive turning point. The army's poor performance on the battlefield forced Meir to resign, and left Yitzhak Rabin in charge of a Labor government reeling from a series of corruption scandals.

This gave Begin his opening. He was the last remaining revolutionary hero who was not tainted by Labor's corruption and incompetence. He also had much greater sympathy for the plight of a new wave of religious immigrants from the Middle East and Africa, who bitterly resented being treated with disdain by Jews who had immigrated from Europe. Begin himself held secular convictions, but he was genuinely sympathetic to the plight of this new generation of immigrants whose religious beliefs required them to flee their homelands and seek refuge in Israel. He moved decisively to present himself as the spokesman for these outsiders.

Moreover, his increasingly emphatic free-market positions could appeal to the rising generation of European Jews. After thirty-five years of massive capital inflows, these young Israelis were far more interested in the challenges of entrepreneurship than in reinvigorating the socialist ideals of their parents—many of whom had also shifted their focus to free-market opportunities.[79]

All of this enabled Begin and his party—now called Likud—to transform the 1977 elections into a "political revolution" or HaMahapakh—as it has come to be called. The revolutionary characterization might seem exaggerated if one only looked at the electoral results. Likud beat Labor by 33 percent to 25 percent, gaining 43 seats to its rival's 32 seats. Begin only managed to gain control of the Knesset by cobbling together a slim 61-seat majority with the aid of the religious parties.[80] Indeed, Likud and Labor competed on relatively equal electoral terms for the next two decades.

Nevertheless, if one looks beyond the numbers, HaMahapakh did represent a moment of revolutionary transition. It marked the end of an era in which Labor could credibly present itself as a privileged representative for the ideals of We the People established at the Founding. While the party would continue to invoke Ben-Gurion and other revolutionary heroes, the general public would no longer grant Mapai the symbolic centrality it had successfully asserted previously. Henceforward, it would be competing with Likud and other rivals on the basis of its forward-looking proposals, not its heroic past. HaMahapakh, in short, marked Israel's relatively successful resolution of its "succession crisis."

So it is revealing to find Aharon Barak moving onto the public stage at precisely this Time Three moment. The scandal-ridden Labor government of Yitzhak Rabin turned to him in 1975 as part of its desperate effort to regain public support. The 39-year-old Barak was then an academic superstar who had recently become dean of Hebrew University's Law School. When Rabin named him attorney general, Barak gained broad applause for his integrity in dealing with highly charged prosecutions. This led Begin to retain him as attorney general once Likud defeated Labor at the 1977 elections. Begin then asked Barak to serve as his principal legal advisor during the Camp David negotiations—where once again the young superstar earned praise for his professionalism.

The joint recognition by both Labor and Likud made Barak an obvious choice when a vacancy on the Supreme Court opened up in 1978. Once appointed, his bipartisan support gave Barak special credibility in urging his colleagues to fill the legitimacy vacuum left by the departure of the founding generation. With Labor and Likud locked in partisan conflict, it was left to the Court to elaborate the nation's fundamental commitments in ways that could bring all Israelis together. If the Court didn't do it, who would?

Barak's emphasis on human dignity provided the Court with a particularly compelling way to discharge this mission. As we have seen, if Ben-Gurion had led the country to embrace a founding Constitution, he would have left behind a text responding to the horror of the Holocaust by proclaiming Israel's determination to defend human dignity. In taking up this theme, the Court was rooting the country's contentious present in a common commitment to its revolutionary past.

To put the point within the framework of my larger argument: Time and again, we have seen courts taking constitutional leadership to preserve core revolutionary principles once the founding generation has left the scene. These founding commitments were framed in different terms in different countries, so judges discharge this preservationist function by developing legal languages that are contextually appropriate in their time and place.

Nevertheless, the same legitimation dynamic drives these preservationist enterprises despite their different doctrinal appearance. From this vantage, the Israeli Court's dignitarian turn shouldn't come as a surprise. When viewed in comparative perspective, it is simply another example of courts exercising their preservationist function during a succession crisis.

This conclusion emerges, however, only when the Barak Court is placed within the intergenerational framework that has served to organize this book. Only by linking together Times One, Two, and Three in systematic fashion can we glimpse a deeper logic legitimating the rise of judicial review over the course of Barak's thirty-year tenure on the Court. But most discussions take a shorter-term perspective—divorcing Time Three from its revolutionary roots at Times One and Two—and, unsurprisingly, come to very different conclusions.

Ran Hirschl's influential discussion provides a case in point.[81] On his view, the Barak Court provides a particularly vivid example of a worldwide pathology: While contemporary judges indulge in grand talk of "human dignity," they deploy this rhetoric as a smokescreen for judicial intervention on the side of the rich and powerful. These economic elites are deeply committed to liberal individualism, free markets, and global cosmopolitanism. But the lower classes are more attracted by appeals to collective solidarity and social welfare. When democratic politicians respond to these popular demands in ways that threaten elite commitments, talk of "human dignity" provides an attractive legal language which the judicial super-elite deploys to veto democratic demands for social justice.

For Hirschl, Israel provides a spectacular example of this worldwide tendency toward "hegemonic preservation" of elite power. The Barak Court speaks for Jews whose parents or grandparents escaped European oppression during the first half of the twentieth century. This old-time "Ashkenazi bourgeoisie" is increasingly outnumbered by newer arrivals with very different backgrounds and beliefs. But they refuse to accept their diminished role in democratic politics and applaud the Barak Court's ongoing struggle to maintain their constitutional hegemony in the name of "human dignity."

Hirschl's analysis begs a big question, which is aptly illustrated by that paradigmatic member of his so-called Ashkenazi bourgeoisie: Aharon Barak. Israel's future chief justice was born in Kovno, Lithuania, in 1936. His father was a lawyer and his mother was a teacher. When the Nazis invaded, they were confined in the oppressive conditions of Kovno's Jewish ghetto. At the end of the war, the family fled Russian occupation and wandered for years through Europe as displaced persons before they managed to reach Israel in 1947—enabling the 11-year-old Aharon to emerge into adulthood amid the great political and military struggles of the Founding.

On Hirschl's account, these biographical details only serve to explain Barak's enthusiastic enlistment in the "hegemonic preservation" of elite bourgeois values as the Ashkenazi settlers struck it rich during the late twentieth century. In my account, Barak's leading role in developing the Court's dignitarian jurisprudence is the product of lifelong reflection on the meaning of the Holocaust's significance in the revolutionary struggle for Israeli independence.

This is not to say that Hirschl is wrong in describing the country's political challenges in the early decades of the twenty-first century. As I write these lines, the government of Benjamin Netanyahu is making a dramatic effort to reorient Israel's constitutional identity—emphasizing its biblical origins rather than the Enlightenment ideals of the Zionists who fought and won Israel's struggle for independence. From this vantage, there are parallels to current developments in India, where Narendra Modi and the BJP are trying to reinterpret the struggle for Indian independence in ways that emphasize its Hindu roots at the expense of the Enlightenment commitments of Nehru and his Congress Party.

Yet there is an obvious difference as well. In contrast to the Indian Supreme Court, the Israeli Court cannot appeal to incisive texts inherited from the founding Constitution—since there isn't one. The best it can do is point to the more recent Basic Law on Human Dignity passed by the Knesset as part of a larger effort in the 1990s to reinvigorate the Harari Resolution's authorization of a piecemeal approach to constitutional construction. As we shall see, the new Netanyahu initiative was itself provoked by the Barak Court's use of the Human Dignity law as a launchpad for its dignitarian initiative—and so it is attempting to pass new Basic Laws repudiating the Court's initiatives.[82]

As always, it is best to proceed step by step—tracing the way the Basic Law tradition has evolved from the Harari Resolution through the 1990s, when it became the basis for the Barak Court's dignitarian initiatives—and only then assess the current Netanyahu effort to repudiate the Court's jurisprudence by passing a new set of Basic Laws that propel Israel's constitutional identity in a radically different direction.

So let's begin the story with Time Two. As long as Ben-Gurion and his party remained in power, the Harari Resolution played an insignificant role. The few Basic Laws passed dealt primarily with uncontroversial matters. But once Likud took over, leading law professors and jurists began to take Harari seriously—recall that Begin and his political party were vocal opponents of Ben-Gurion's founding act of constitutional sabotage. Given Likud's historical commitment to a written Constitution, legal elites advanced an ambitious Basic Law agenda during the 1980s. Yet matters proceeded at a snail's pace. The government focused on more urgent matters of foreign and domestic policy, and failed to devote sufficient energy to the project of constitutional construction. Nevertheless, there was some movement over time—with the Basic Law on Human Dignity finally making it onto the action agenda in 1992.[83]

This initiative finally passed the Knesset, but it never gained the sustained consideration it deserved. Instead, the attention of parliamentarians and the public was diverted by a second constitutional initiative presented at the very same session. The Basic Law on Government proposed a big change in the country's Westminster system. No longer would Israel be led by a prime minister who depended on the support of a fragile majority coalition in the Knesset. Reformers instead proposed to create a popularly elected presidency, which they hoped would facilitate a more decisive form of quasi-Gaullist government.

Unsurprisingly, this presidentialist proposal provoked a storm of debate in parliament. By shifting the choice of the country's leader to the electorate, Knesset members would be stripping themselves of their principal source of power. The government finally gained the public support needed to overcome the Knesset's passionate resistance. But this great debate pushed serious and sustained public consideration of the Human Dignity law to the sidelines. Indeed, when its dedicated proponents finally managed to push it on to the floor, most parliamentarians did not bother to show up in the Knesset to cast a vote on their proposal. Rather than gain the support of a resounding majority, this Basic Law was approved by a vote of 32 to 21—with only a quarter of the 120-member assembly saying Yes to Human Dignity![84]

This brute fact casts a long shadow over present-day politics. The Netanyahu government's recently enacted Basic Law radically redefines the country's constitutional identity. It not only declares that Israel is the "national home of the Jewish people, in which it fulfills its natural, cultural, religious and historical right to self-determination." It goes on to proclaim "Jerusalem, complete and united" as Israel's capital, threatening to kill off Palestinian hopes for a state of their own. It even strips Arabic of its standing as an official language alongside Hebrew—merely assuring Palestinian citizens that this depreciation of their culture does not impair "the status given to the Arabic language before this law came into effect."[85]

It is far too soon to say how the courts and the larger public will respond to this remarkable assertion of Jewish primacy. For present purposes, it is more important to emphasize the no less remarkable way in which it was accomplished. Despite the bitter protests of dissenters, Netanyahu rammed it through parliament by a vote of 62 to 55.

I have no doubt that the government's apologists will compare this tally with the 32-to-21 vote for the Basic Law on Human Dignity two decades ago. They will emphasize that an absolute majority of the nation's 120 elected representatives have affirmed their fellow citizens' demand for a truly Jewish state—and contrast this majoritarian affirmation to the feeble expression of popular sovereignty accompanying the Law on Dignity.

This predictable rhetorical maneuver, however, only serves to reinforce my basic thesis—which is to emphasize the enduring significance of Ben-Gurion's self-conscious refusal, at Time Two, to constitutionalize the charisma of the revolutionary struggle for independence. Recall the Kohn draft's insistence that the Constitution could be amended only through an extended process, lasting many months, requiring Knesset supermajorities to approve revisions on two separate occasions. Remember also that, when Ben-Gurion was finally obliged to allow the Knesset to debate its constitutional responsibilities, speaker after speaker emphasized the high importance of entrenching fundamental Zionist principles in a fashion that would make their amendment extremely difficult. Indeed, the broad parliamentary coalition voicing these concerns almost forced Ben-Gurion down the pathway to written constitutionalism. If a Constitution had emerged in 1951 under this alternative scenario, only one thing is clear: it would never have allowed a single 62-to-55 vote to repudiate core commitments of the Zionist revolution.

From this vantage point, Netanyahu's recent revolutionary redefinition has been achieved through decidedly unrevolutionary means. Rather than attempting to mobilize a broad-based citizen movement to generate an authentic act of popular sovereignty, he is taking advantage of the Harari Resolution to impose a top-down redefinition of constitutional identity on a bitterly divided nation.

Israel is, in short, a very special case. While Harari enabled Barak to reassert the centrality of Zionist principles at Time Three despite the absence of a revolutionary Constitution at Time Two, it is also enabling Netanyahu to repudiate these principles at Time Four. Netanyahu's new Basic Law, I should emphasize, does not explicitly reject the Barak Court's dignitarian jurisprudence; but it is perfectly possible that future governments will gain razor-thin support for additional Basic Laws that achieve this result.[86] If this happens, the Israeli repudiation will have a significant impact on the worldwide constitutional conversation to which the Barak Court has so greatly contributed over the past twenty years.[87]

Even if Israel does abandon its commitment to human dignity, I can offer some small consolation to foreign jurists and politicians witnessing this tragic turn. It won't be nearly as easy for countries with strong revolutionary Constitutions to engage in similar acts of repudiation. In places like India or South Africa, defenders of existing commitments will be in a far better position to force their opponents to engage in massive grassroots efforts of the kind that legitimated the Indian and South African Constitutions in the first place.

This does not imply that defenders of revolutionary constitutions in places like India or South Africa will emerge victorious over the course of the coming generation. This will depend on their success in mobilizing popular support behind a revitalized vision of Enlightenment ideals that can meet the challenges of social and economic life in the twenty-first century—and convincing their fellow citizens that their new programmatic initiatives respond far more constructively than authoritarian efforts to exploit discontent by demonizing enemies at home and abroad. But it does suggest that the ground rules for determining the fate of the ongoing struggle against authoritarianism will be very different in Israel than elsewhere.

In countries which have constitutionalized their revolutions at Time Two, it will take a good deal of time and effort for authoritarian movements to win their struggle. A single victory at the polls may be enough to put their critique on the table for serious debate. But it won't be enough to legitimate a plunge into despotism. Instead, aspiring authoritarians will predictably encounter the resistance by courts (and other entrenched institutions) to their initiatives. This in turn will provide time and space for defenders of the constitutional regime to mobilize a renewed citizen effort to halt the slide to despotism before it is too late. As a consequence, it will require the authoritarian movement to win *a series* of elections in a *decisive fashion* before it can gain the broad legitimacy required to revolutionize their legacy.

In contrast, we are only now beginning to appreciate the fateful consequences of Ben-Gurion's refusal to allow his fellow Zionists to inscribe the lessons of the Holocaust into a Constitution of the State of Israel. While it did not make it impossible for the Barak Court to reassert the protection of human dignity as an enduring principle rooted at the very heart of its revolutionary identity, this achievement can be erased by a series of parliamentary maneuvers that manage to gain narrow Knesset majorities for Basic Laws without the necessity of sustained popular debate, and repeated popular endorsement, by We the People.

CHAPTER 12

Constitutionalizing Charisma in Iran

It may seem odd to consider Iran in a book dealing with revolutions on a human scale. Hasn't the country repudiated "Western constitutionalism" in supporting Ayatollah Khomeini's great leap forward to an Islamic utopia?

This is, at least, the conventional wisdom. But a glance at recent events is enough to raise doubts. During his first presidential campaign in 2013, Hassan Rouhani ran as a strong advocate for détente with the West, placing special emphasis on a sweeping nuclear arms agreement. The current Supreme Leader, Ali Khamenei, squarely opposed this initiative. He threw his support behind Saeed Jalili, who had served as Iran's principal arms negotiator and continued to advocate a hard-line stance. As voters went to the polls, they were offered a clear choice.[1]

They voted for Rouhani in a landslide. The Supreme Leader responded with a strategic retreat. Given Rouhani's powerful democratic mandate, Khamenei recognized that he lacked *legitimate* authority to block Rouhani's diplomatic breakthrough. Rather than invoke his constitutional powers to veto the nuclear weapons deal, he allowed it to go into effect without any public show of opposition.

But he did not give up. Instead, he saw the presidential election of 2017 as an opportunity to carve out a space enabling him to reassert control over foreign policy. To nobody's surprise, Rouhani made his nuclear agreement the centerpiece of his election campaign, calling on voters to provide a ringing endorsement of his dramatic initiative. But this time around, he would confront the archconservative Ebrahim Raisi, whose long-standing commitments to the Ayatollah would lead him to defer to Khamenei's views on foreign affairs.

When faced with this prospect, the voters went to the polls to vindicate Rouhani's position, granting him a 57-to-38 landslide victory over Raisi. Given the reinforcement of the president's democratic mandate, the Supreme Leader now lacks the legitimate authority to demand that Iran withdraw from Rouhani's nuclear agreement—even in the face of its repudiation by Donald

Trump. Despite this blow, Khamenei has not tried to sabotage Rouhani's efforts to sustain his arms-limitation deal in cooperation with Europe.

The Supreme Leader is the single most powerful official in Iran's government. But calling him Supreme does not make him all-powerful—even when the country is dealing with existential questions of nuclear annihilation. To the contrary, Iran's Constitution is based on the separation of powers—in which different branches engage in an ongoing competition for effective authority. As in many other countries, the balance of legitimate power shifts over time, sometimes dramatically. But so long as Iran does not collapse into a top-down system of autocratic rule, it falls within my definition of constitutional government.[2]

The Iranian government is hardly unique in authorizing unelected officials to play a leading role. American Supreme Court justices, like the Supreme Leader, have life tenure—and also claim the right to safeguard the regime's fundamental values when they are endangered by popularly elected institutions. Obviously, the value commitments of the two regimes are different; and the Iranian Constitution gives the Supreme Leader greater institutional resources to resist backlash from elected institutions. These differences are important. But they should not disguise the feature that the United States and Iran share in common: both are separation-of-powers systems that emerge from revolutionary constitutional traditions.

This chapter will be taking France, not America, as its source for comparative insight. As we shall see, Ayatollah Khomeini—not to be confused with his successor, Ali Khamenei—spent long years in exile as a consequence of his repeated acts of defiance against the Shah's regime. For fourteen years he served as a distant symbol of revolutionary resistance—first in Turkey, then in Iraq, and finally in Paris. As Khomeini watched a new wave of Iranian insurgency escalate in 1978, he prepared for a return to his homeland in a distinctive fashion.

He did not content himself with inspirational appeals to his fellow countrymen. He asked his closest collaborators to work out an elaborate constitutional draft providing the Iranian people with a framework for self-government after the revolution. The "Paris draft" initiated a dynamic process of deliberation and decision upon the Ayatollah's return to his country in early 1979. Within months the public was debating a variety of proposals provoked by the Paris initiative. This broad and multidimensional debate led up to elections, on August 3, 1979, in which Iran's voters chose a constituent assembly to hammer out a final draft. In mid-November, the Assembly presented its proposal to the voters—who approved it at a referendum on December 3. This set the stage for a second series of elections in early 1980, at which Iranians returned to the polls to fill the powerful positions that their Constitution had created to govern in their name.

Iran, in short, provides a sharp contrast to our case studies of Poland, Burma, and Israel. While the revolutionaries in these countries lost the race against time, the Iranians did not allow other pressing issues—and there were many!—to deflect them from prioritizing the Constitution as a central object of concern. This founding success, I shall argue, was the starting point of a fascinating historical dynamic that, forty years later, imposes very substantial checks and balances on the current Supreme Leader.

The Iranian counterexample takes on even greater interest once we explore the distinctive features of its constitutional construction. Khomeini's initial draft was not only written in Paris; it borrows very heavily from the Constitution of the Fifth Republic—in both its text and its institutional design.

This was not merely because the Ayatollah had been forced to find refuge in the City of Light. The educated Iranian elite had been profoundly influenced by French culture throughout the entire twentieth century. Khomeini and other Shiite leaders were more interested in adapting, rather than repudiating, French ideas in their effort to construct a system that was both Islamic *and* Republican. As a consequence, the Fifth Republic provided the "obvious" model for their own efforts to design a plausible framework for Iran's future Islamic Republic.

Under its Constitution of 1979, the Supreme Leader was checked and balanced by a president, prime minister, parliament, and constitutional council, all speaking for the People in ways inspired by the Fifth Republic. This means that our analysis of Iranian developments will require revision of the dark conclusions emerging from our Polish case study. I argued there that the Gaullist "super-presidentialist" system was a major factor leading to a "war at the top" that made it impossible for Walesa and other revolutionary leaders to hammer out a credible Solidarity Constitution to mark Poland's "new beginning." But in Iran's case, the Gaullist legacy had the opposite effect.

In explaining how and why, I will be hauling out my familiar four-stage model. As in India, South Africa, Italy, and France, the Iranian system of checks and balances did not entrench itself until Time Three, when Ayatollah Khomeini's death opened up a profound "succession crisis." It is precisely at this moment that the French-inspired constitutional order played a central role in defining the terms under which the remaining members of the revolutionary elite could legitimately compete for power.

None of these rivals remotely commanded the charismatic authority of the Ayatollah—which is why the 1979 Constitution provided a crucial baseline in their struggle for ascendancy. As competition intensified, Khamenei emerged as the next Supreme Leader, but as part of a deal that required him to accept the legitimacy of checks on his power imposed by a Gaullist-inspired presidency.

The Iranian pattern at Time Three involves big variations on themes developed in earlier "success stories" involving India, South Africa, Italy, France, and Israel. In all these cases, it was nonelected jurists who gained greatly as a result of Time Three's succession crisis. In Iran, by contrast, it was the popularly elected president who emerged as a powerful constraint on the Supreme Leader, also known as the Guardian Jurist.

This is a key difference, but it should not blind us to deeper similarities: Like Nehru and Mandela, De Gasperi and de Gaulle, Khomeini made founding decisions at Time Two that profoundly shaped the constitutional order emerging at Time Three—imposing constraints on the next Leader's authority that would not have arisen if Khomeini had not constitutionalized his charisma at the high point of revolutionary ferment in 1979 and 1980.

Iran will soon be reaching another turning point. The current Guardian Jurist is 79, and the time is coming to choose his replacement. Depending on the circumstances, the next Supreme Leader may try to break free of all the checks and balances that have been entrenched over the past thirty years— or he may entrench them further by explicitly endorsing them. Even if he mounts a frontal assault, this may only serve to provoke a successful democratic counterattack led by the presidency.

My aim isn't to predict the future. Nor is it to judge the Islamic Republic's performance by my own liberal values. It is to reveal the ways in which Iranian developments have proceeded along the four-stage path traveled by the other countries we have investigated. The fact that Iran's principles are so different only serves to reinforce my central thesis: that the intergenerational dynamic of revolutionary constitutionalism is worthy of study in its own right.

On then, to Time One—since Iran's revolutionary "new beginning" only makes sense in terms of the distinctive character of the regime it was repudiating.

Time One: The Struggle for Iranian Identity

Since the founding of the Achaemenid Empire by Cyrus the Great in 550 BCE, Persian dynasties built a series of great civilizations in the land that is now Iran. But I will begin our story in the nineteenth century, with the Qajar dynasty's struggle to defend its borders against the military threats posed by imperial Britain (from the south) and imperial Russia (from the north). While the Qajar monarchs retained formal sovereignty, British and Russian interventions intensified with the discovery of vast oil reserves in the early twentieth century, further weakening the dynasty.[3]

This provided an opening for Westernizing Iranian elites to mobilize a campaign that forced the Qajars to accept a constitutional monarchy along European lines—with the Shah's powers checked by a parliament (Majlis) under the Constitution of 1906.[4] But the destabilization of the traditional regime helped to provoke outright military intervention by Russian and British troops aiming to secure their grip on the country's oil. When the last Qajar Shah proved incapable of expelling British and Soviet troops after World War I, he was displaced by Reza Shah, a brigadier-general of the Persian Cossack Brigade, who established the Pahlavi dynasty.

The new Shah retained the Majlis as a matter of royal prerogative, but thoroughly dominated its affairs. Nevertheless, he gestured toward popular sovereignty by authorizing the upper classes to choose representatives to the National Assembly.

This gesture took on new meaning when the monarch's son, Mohammad Reza Shah, assumed the throne in 1944 and allowed serious party competition to emerge in Assembly elections. This soon forced the Shah to confront a series of prime ministers who claimed popular mandates for one or another of their initiatives. The struggle between the Shah and Majlis reached its climax in 1951 when the Assembly, by a vote of 79–12, nominated the 70-year-old Mohammad Mossadegh as prime minister.

Mossadegh's strong opposition to the Pahlavi dynasty was rooted in the experience of a lifetime. Like many other children of the established elite, he was given a French-inspired education by parents who were trying to adapt to Western ways. He then launched an electoral campaign in the first-ever Majlis convened in 1906—where his strong and self-confident democratic views won him a seat at the age of 24. Two years later, in 1908, he went off to Paris to study law—and became, in 1913, the first Iranian to receive a doctorate from a European university. He was preparing himself for a brilliant political career as a Westernizing constitutionalist in his homeland. But the downfall of the last Qajar, and the first Pahlavi's clampdown on free expression in the Majlis, led Mossadegh to abandon these ambitions.

In 1944, when the Shah's son reopened the Majlis to democratic politics, Mossadegh seized the opportunity to reenter the arena. He organized a broad-based mass movement for national self-determination. So far as his National Front was concerned, the Shah was merely an imperialist puppet—who gave unstinting support to a concession agreement with the British-dominated Anglo-Iranian Oil Company that gave away to foreigners almost all the economic benefits of the country's oil.[5]

The only way to break the imperialist grip was to break the power of the Shah. Iran's constitutional legacy provided the most obvious path forward. Although the early promise of the Majlis was shattered by later events, Mossadegh's National Front considered itself as the spearhead of a new and more successful effort to reduce the Shah to a figurehead of a European-style constitutional democracy. If the Shah refused to cede power to a democratically elected parliament, it might prove necessary to sweep the monarchy away and create a new republic. In either event, constitutionalism was a key to the realization of the National Front's economic program, which demanded the nationalization of the oil industry so that ordinary Iranians—not Western plutocrats—could profit from their country's natural resources.

When viewed comparatively, there was nothing especially distinctive about the Front's initiatives—its commitment to nationalization and social democracy have ready analogues in revolutionary projects in France, Italy, India, and Israel during the immediate postwar period. What is more, Mossadegh and his fellow activists were increasingly successful in mobilizing mass demonstrations—which included both secular and Islamic groups—to back up their demands.

Fearing a revolutionary upheaval, the Shah rubber-stamped the Assembly's nomination of Mossadegh as prime minister, but this only further escalated the conflict. When the Majlis voted to nationalize Iran's oil in 1951, British interests responded with a worldwide boycott. But Clement Attlee recognized that his government was no longer capable of backing up the boycott the old-fashioned way—with direct British military intervention against Iran. Instead, Britain turned to America as the only force that remained capable of taking decisive action.

This was precisely the moment when Churchill returned to power at Westminster, and his operatives convinced Secretary of State John Foster Dulles to view the crisis through Cold War lenses. On this view, there was more at stake than a classic conflict between an autocratic monarch and a democratic movement demanding social justice. Mossadegh was instead threatening to make Iran into a pawn of the Soviet Union—allying the country with the Reds in their global struggle for world domination. To eliminate this clear and present danger, Churchill persuaded Dulles and his brother Alan, the head of the CIA, to engineer a coup that overthrew Mossadegh, reversed the nationalizations, and provided the Shah with massive military assistance to impose public order on the unruly masses.[6]

The Shah reciprocated by making Iran into a showcase for the Eisenhower administration's market-friendly approach to Third World development. During the rest of the 1950s, the Shah's neoliberal policies enabled an increasingly secular middle class to begin transforming Iran's growing cities into powerful engines of economic growth. When Kennedy succeeded Eisenhower in 1960, the Shah realigned his policies accordingly. Once again with American support, he initiated a "White Revolution," which, like Kennedy's "New Frontier," proclaimed a renewed battle for social justice. The Shah shocked traditionalists by granting voting rights to women, and advanced a sweeping social program, including land redistribution to peasants, profit sharing for workers, and a massive effort to educate the rural and urban poor.[7]

This leftward turn created the first opening for public engagement since the American-inspired coup of 1953. Mossadegh-era nationalists denounced the White Revolution as a sellout to the West, because the Shah refused to nationalize the country's oil wealth in the name of the People. The Communist-dominated Tudeh Party went further, emerging from the underground to insist that only a working-class revolution could bring about real-world justice. At the same time, the Shah's celebration of Western secular ideals generated opposition from traditional Muslims, who went into the streets to protest two of the Shah's initiatives: the grant of suffrage to women and the elimination of the legal requirement that all officeholders be Muslim.

Ayatollah Khomeini became their leading spokesperson. He had recently gained a central position in the city of Qom, the center of Shia theological study. The clerics of the holy city traditionally eschewed political involvement, but Khomeini broke this taboo to denounce the Shah's initiatives in favor of women and religious minorities.[8]

So far as the Shah was concerned, Khomeini was falling into his trap. Pahlavi had already been condemning the Shia clergy as "black reactionaries" whose "little, empty and antique" views would be overwhelmed by the rising tide of modernity. He now took the unprecedented step of issuing a letter singling out the Ayatollah's public protest and insisting that Khomeini's reactionary appeals should not be allowed to block his government's revolutionary calls for social equality and religious toleration.[9]

The Shah's special attention proved a boon to the Ayatollah, granting him a symbolic centrality among the many other leaders of the proliferating protest movements. The contest between Khomeini and the Shah escalated further when the Shah called a referendum in 1963 to demonstrate public support for his revolution—with women going to the polls for the first time in Iranian history. Khomeini responded by urging his followers to boycott the election, which he saw as the entering wedge for further American intervention in Iranian affairs.[10] He also strongly encouraged the creation of an Islamic underground, which quickly made its presence known by organizing the nationwide distribution of 250,000 copies of Khomeini's escalating denunciations of the Shah's modernizing initiatives. At the same time, Khomeini was encouraging the organization of an armed Islamic militia.[11]

The Shah found all this intolerable and arrested Khomeini on June 3—provoking bloody street confrontations throughout the country. Responding to widespread fears that he would be executed, leading clerics rallied to Khomeini's defense, proclaiming him "a source of emulation"—the very highest honor in Shiite Islam. Fearing chaos, the Shah backed down and released the Ayatollah.[12] But when Khomeini continued his blistering public campaign, Pahlavi took decisive action, forcing the Ayatollah into fourteen years of exile. Public protest was suppressed by his dreaded secret police, the SAVAK, inaugurating a sustained period of economic growth. By 1978, the 76-year-old Khomeini seemed fated to die in Paris, bitterly disappointed by the seeming success of the Shah's modernizing project.

Yet time was also running out for the Shah, who was then dying of cancer. As the monarch disappeared from public view, a broad coalition surprised everybody by successfully organizing a new wave of protests against the regime. Tens of thousands were soon demonstrating in the streets. The military responded with bloody repression, but this only provoked massive counterdemonstrations. Although the regime still prevented Khomeini from returning to Iran, the Ayatollah moved beyond symbolic assertions of leadership to create, in November 1978, a secret five-man Revolutionary Council to represent him in the homeland.[13]

The mass mobilization reached new heights on December 11, when two million people surged through Tehran denouncing the Shah as an American puppet. With the military overwhelmed by the continuing upheaval, the Revolutionary Council (now expanded to include more secular representatives of the National Front) emerged in public as the Shah left the country forever on January 16, 1979.

Despite his abdication, Pahlavi did not give up the effort to sustain the old regime. He appointed a "regency council" headed by his last prime minister, Shapour Bakhtiar, who called upon insurgents to join him in a government of national unity under the existing imperial Constitution. To demonstrate good faith, he dissolved the savagely repressive SAVAK and dramatically invited Khomeini back from Paris—leading to the Ayatollah's return, on February 1, with millions of Iranians pouring into the streets of Tehran to celebrate this great turning point in their history.

The Ayatollah disdainfully rejected Bakhtiar's offer of a negotiated transition, and his Revolutionary Council threw its support behind a provisional government headed by Khomeini's longtime associate Mehdi Bazargan. By mid-February the Shah's army abandoned Bakhtiar and switched sides to support the Council. This quickly led to the collapse of Bakhtiar's desperate attempt to save the old regime. Though the Shah's army was demoralized and disorganized by recent events, it nonetheless reinforced the efforts by fragmentary bands of revolutionary militia, known as the "republican guard," to impose a semblance of order.[14]

Yet military shows of force would not be enough to stabilize the situation. The Ayatollah and the Council quickly filled the legitimacy vacuum with a constitutional initiative for an Islamic Republic. What should such a regime look like?

Time Two: Constitutionalizing Charisma

The Ayatollah had been asking this question for a very long time. When gaining prominence in Qom in the early 1960s, Khomeini had suggested that a future Iran might be governed by a Guardian Jurist selected for his religious commitment and insight. But during his long years in exile, he had not developed this theme, which challenged long-standing religious principles. In contrast to Sunni practice in the Islamic world, the dominant Shiite tradition in Iran rejected ongoing clerical participation in affairs of state, leaving secular affairs to a series of reigning dynasties. The clerical elite instead committed themselves to lives of scholarship and spirituality in Qom and elsewhere, untainted by worldly involvements.[15]

During most of his extended exile, Khomeini's refusal to challenge this tradition was politically prudent—since advocacy for a Guardian Jurist would predictably provoke widespread denunciations from leading clerics in Qom. But as the Ayatollah observed the final months of the revolutionary uprising from Paris, he confronted a critical decision: In setting out his vision of an Islamic Republic, should he renew his advocacy of a Constitution that would give pride of place to a Guardian Jurist?

His answer was no. Khomeini asked a top aide, Hassan Habibi, to take the lead in drafting a constitution. The "Paris draft" produced by Habibi's team contained absolutely no mention of a Guardian Jurist. Its institutional framework was entirely based on the Gaullist model then prevailing in France. The Islamic character of the new Republic was principally signified by modifications of a French-style bill of rights to protect traditional religious practices.[16]

With the Ayatollah's approval, the Paris draft served as the basis for further development by a specially selected constitutional committee in Tehran during the early months of 1979. When the committee's draft was published in the spring, the Fifth Republic continued to serve as the model and the office of the Guardian Jurist remained conspicuously absent.[17]

The Course of Constitutional Decision

The Provisional Council kicked off the process of constitutional decision with a special referendum at the end of March, at which voters went to the polls to confront the implications of the Shah's downfall: Were they for or against an Islamic Republic?

The voters' response raised more questions than it answered. In many places, there was no effort to keep ballots secret. Dissenters had reason to fear retribution if they cast a No vote.[18] At best, the referendum put the general public on notice that the imperial Constitution was dead, and that something was needed to fill the void. Would the gap be filled by the Ayatollah's fiat?

This was the moment when the Tehran drafting committee initiated a serious constitutional debate. By mid-April it published its first draft in the newspapers, providing a concrete reference point for sustained public discussion. By mid-June, the Council formally approved this draft, but made it clear that it should only serve as a preliminary stage in a more elaborate two-step process. The first step would culminate in August 3 elections for a constituent assembly, called the Assembly of Constitutional Experts. After the Experts hammered out a final draft, it would then be submitted to the public at a second referendum, which, unlike the March vote, would involve a serious exercise in democratic decision. The Constitution would go into effect only if it gained majority support from the People of Iran.

Given the central role of the first draft in shaping this larger debate, let's begin with a sketch of its principal features. The draft's institutional framework followed the French model in providing for (1) a powerful and popularly elected president, (2) a prime minister supported by a majority of the Majlis selected on the basis of universal suffrage, and (3) a Council of Guardians exercising powers of judicial review like those deployed by the French Constitutional Council.

Both president and Majlis based their legitimacy on an emphatic commitment to popular sovereignty. The election rolls would be open to all Iranians—women no less than men, secularists no less than the religious.[19] This inclusive act of democratic empowerment was coupled with a Gaullist system of checks and balances—the Majlis would be sharing lawmaking power with a popularly elected president, whose direct mandate from the People could often catapult him into a commanding role—especially because, as in the Fifth Republic, the president would have a large say in the process by which parliament would select the prime minister and departmental heads. Overall, the first draft provided a structure enabling the new republic to generate strong democratic leadership during the tumultuous period looming ahead.

At the same time, the draft imposed significant constitutional limits on top-down power. It elaborated a formidable set of fundamental rights that protected ordinary Iranians from political abuse. Many provisions were verbatim copies of the French text, but others emphasized distinctively Islamic values that recast the nature of fundamental rights.[20]

A final French-inspired institution would ensure that the politicians would take these rights seriously. The Iranian Council of Guardians was an adaptation of the French Conseil Constitutionnel. Like the Conseil, the Guardians would hear challenges to the constitutionality of laws passed by parliament before they came into effect. But its membership was altered to reflect the distinctive aspirations of the *Islamic* Republic. The Council would be composed of eleven members—six secular jurists and five clerics. While leading members of the clergy would nominate the five religious jurists, parliament had the final say on their election—once again emphasizing the Republic's foundation in popular sovereignty, not the will of God. The selection of the six secularists would be guided by similar principles—with judicial and scholarly elites each nominating three jurists, and parliament retaining the final say.

When proposed legislation was brought before the Council, only a two-thirds majority could raise a constitutional challenge. This meant that five clerical members required the support of three secular jurists to exercise their constitutional prerogative.

The drafters also defined the Council's relationship to the Majlis in a way that would prove significant. If two-thirds of the Council concluded that a legislative initiative offended the Constitution, this required the legislators to "reconsider or revise" the law. Its new version would then be resubmitted for Guardian approval in a back-and-forth process until the Council lifted its objections. In contrast, the French Council rendered a single decision on the statute, and left it to the president or prime minister to decide, on their own, how to respond.[21]

To sum up: The first draft rejected the need for a Guardian Jurist to safeguard the Islamic character of the Republic. This role was assigned to a Council of Guardians on which clerics were in the minority, and which would engage the Majlis in ongoing negotiations until it satisfied the Council's objections. So long as it operated within the limits established by the Council, it would be up to a democratically accountable president, prime minister, and Majlis to sustain the revolutionary Republic's commitment to Islam.

The newspaper publication of the first draft in April kicked off an intense debate that set the stage for the August elections. A host of prominent intellectuals flooded the media with constitutional critiques and counterproposals—many strongly secular in character. These were countered by religious leaders urging revision of the draft in more Islamic directions.

During the next couple of months, the contending sides held elaborate scholarly conferences proposing concrete alternatives to the first draft. At one end of the spectrum, the Iranian Lawyers Association conducted an eight-day session at which forty-eight largely secular groups targeted the more emphatic Islamic commitments of the draft; at the other end, the Congress of Muslim Critics of the Constitution opposed its overly secular character. No fewer than sixty (!) constitutional proposals emerged from sessions like these—as well as a steady stream of media commentary.[22]

This cacophony, however, should not conceal mainstream support for the first draft's tempered Islamicization of the original Paris design. The most significant voice was the Ayatollah's. He directly addressed the issue when the first draft was formally endorsed by the Revolutionary Council in mid-June:

> We must support and confirm the constitution so that the constitution will be as Islam requires. It must be approved quickly. It is a blueprint made by the government and this blueprint is correct.[23]

The secular National Front, rooted in Mossadegh's earlier struggle for national liberation, moved in the same direction. Its leader, Karim Sanjabi, was "moderately satisfied" with the draft, describing it as "progressive, based on Islam, on national sovereignty and on individual and social freedoms."[24]

Given later events, Khomeini's refusal to demand a dominant constitutional position for himself was remarkable; but it was not unique. Most notably, Nelson Mandela faced a similar problem, which he resolved in a similar fashion.

Call it the problem of *political isolation*. Like Khomeini, Mandela had spent long years far removed from the leadership cadres and grassroots movements that were engaged in the hard work of insurgency. As a consequence, he confronted a special difficulty in convincing these independent activists to accept his leadership once he returned to real-world political life—especially because these independent groups advanced a broad range of ideologies. Within this setting, Mandela used the Constitution to legitimate his symbolic centrality by encouraging contending factions to emphasize what they had in common— their long struggle against the illegitimate impositions of the old regime.

Khomeini was following the same strategy. After his long years in exile, advocacy of Supreme Leadership would have utterly alienated the secular nationalists and Marxists who were playing key roles in organizing strikes and protests in urban areas. It would have also generated strong protests from leading clerics in Qom, who viewed Khomeini's vision as an intolerable breach with fundamental Shia principles—and who could convey their opposition in mosques throughout the land.

The Ayatollah's embrace of the French model had the opposite effect. By endorsing the principles laid down in the first draft, he was calling upon all revolutionaries to unite behind their common aspiration to bring a definitive end to imperial rule and enable the Iranian People to construct a new Islamic Republic.

Despite their very different revolutionary ideologies, Khomeini and Mandela were traveling down the same path in leading their countries toward a revolution on a human scale.

Revolutionary Boycott and Popular Sovereignty

The Revolutionary Council then made a decision that disrupted this fragile consensus. When it endorsed the first draft in mid-June, the Council also issued its formal call for the Assembly of Constitutional Experts to serve as a constituent assembly to hammer out a final draft for approval at a referendum. But it did so in a highly controversial fashion.

First, it set the election date for August 3, allowing only six weeks for the campaign. Next, it divided up the country into districts that permitted the election of one Assembly representative for each 500,000 voters. But it gerrymandered district lines to increase conservative religious representation. Because secularists were concentrated in urban areas, the Council could reduce their influence by strategically drawing district boundaries to maximize the influence of rural areas where clerical influence was at a maximum.

The secularists responded with outrage. They demanded a revision of the scheme of representation—or, at the very least, a delay in the August 3 election date to permit them to organize more effectively in the countryside.[25]

The Council ignored these demands and pressed forward with its plans. The secularists answered with another round of strikes and street protests, denouncing the effort to stack the deck against them. But this time around, the religious revolutionaries struck back. They had already organized the Islamic Republican Party (IRP), which was becoming a potent political force, and urged its members to disrupt the secularist protests. These activists were joined by armed religious militants—already known as the Revolutionary Guard—who, though relatively disorganized, were already battle-hardened by their struggles against the Shah and his army. Pitched battles broke out in Tabriz and other places, but the Guard proved quite successful in suppressing this new wave of defiance.[26]

At this point the secularists confronted a big decision: Should they boycott the elections and try to discredit the Assembly's claims to speak for the revolutionary People? Or should they accept the Assembly's legitimacy and urge their followers to go to the polls and win at least some of the seats in the urbanized centers?

The National Front chose the boycott—as did other important movements. Paradoxically, the only major exception was the Tudeh (Communist) Party—which, despite its contempt for "bourgeois constitutionalism," fielded candidates in the hope that secularly inclined voters would have no choice but to rally behind them.[27]

This didn't happen—even in the cities, only small minorities were willing to endorse the Communist views that mainstream secular leaders had harshly condemned. Instead, the alienated secularists simply refused to show up at the polls. Despite the Revolutionary Council's efforts to demonstrate public support for its constitutional project, it only managed to induce half of eligible voters to come out to the polls and cast their ballots.[28]

This poor showing emphasizes the significance of the boycott. If the secular movement parties had urged their followers to vote, they could have won a significant number of seats. But given their refusal to participate, the number of powerful secular voices defending the first draft in the constituent assembly was precisely zero.

In contrast, the Assembly contained some strong Khomeini supporters who wanted a constitution that installed him as Guardian Jurist.[29] If the secularists had been present, their strong defense of the first draft would have created an opening for more moderate religious figures to occupy the middle ground. Traditional Shia opposition to clerical involvement in politics remained strong in Qom, and the secularists' defense of the first draft's rejection of the Jurist's role would have resonated among religious traditionalists. Given the passionate debate between the secular Left and the Khomeini-ite Right, it would have been natural for these centrists to operate as swing votes—joining the secularists to reject a Guardian Jurist while joining the Khomeini-ites to strengthen the first draft's Islamic commitments and the Guardians' powers to enforce them.

But the boycott propelled the Assembly in a different direction. Since the secularists were absent, they could not join a campaign to elect a religious traditionalist to preside in a neutral fashion over the ideologically charged disputes between themselves and the Khomeini-ites. Instead, when the Assembly convened in late August, it chose Khomeini's intimate associate, Hussein-Ali Montazeri, to serve as president. On Montazeri's view, the Assembly's mandate was clear: "Since the People voted for an Islamic state, then the Guardian Jurist must be at the pinnacle to ensure that the regime is indeed Islamic." This was true "by definition [of an] Islamic Republic," because "only an expert in Islamic laws and not a Western-educated person can discern the Islamicity of laws."[30] Given the Ayatollah's symbolic centrality, and the absence of dissenting voices, the traditionalists were in no position to disagree. After all, hadn't the most esteemed clerics at Qom declared Khomeini to be a "source of emulation" for all the faithful?

The Assembly's final draft broke new ground in creating a position for the Ayatollah as Supreme Leader. Nevertheless, it did not permit a clerical elite to monopolize his selection, in the manner, say, in which the pope is chosen by the College of Cardinals. Instead, it required leading Islamic clerics to compete for the approval of ordinary voters for election to a special Council of Experts. This meant that the legitimacy of future Guardian Jurists would ultimately rest on decisions by voters, who could determine whether hard-liners or more tolerant clerics should select the next Guardian Jurist of their Islamic *Republic.*

This point was emphatically reinforced by the Assembly's retention of the first draft's Gaullist framework—with a directly elected president sharing power with a prime minister dependent on the support of a democratically elected parliament. These political leaders would predictably invoke the will of the People in defense of the legislative and executive powers granted to them by the Constitution. So long as Khomeini served as Guardian, there was little risk that presidents or prime ministers would challenge him on important issues. But his less charismatic successors would confront far more serious challenges to their authority.

Anticipating this problem, the Assembly provided the Leader with a more powerful Council of Guardians to assist him in defending his claims to supremacy. The first draft gave secular jurists a six-to-five majority over their religious counterparts. The final draft added a sixth religious Councillor, and granted the six religious members a special veto over proposed legislation they believed to violate Islamic law. In contrast, all twelve members would consider whether legislation violated the republican principles inscribed in the Constitution, and if a majority raised an objection, it would engage in ongoing negotiations with the Majlis until the Guardians were satisfied with the revised legislation.

These changes definitely enhanced the Supreme Leader's position, but they were virtually invisible to the broader public. The Council was a French import, with no roots in previous Iranian practice, and so long as the charismatic Ayatollah remained Leader, he would not require its assistance to vindicate his supremacy. Only time would tell how much his successors could rely on the Guardians to oppose initiatives by the popularly elected branches.

During the Founding, there were far more pressing matters to worry about. Just as the Assembly was putting the final touches on its final draft, a group calling themselves the Muslim Students of the Imam Khomeini Line seized the American Embassy to denounce the Great Satan for admitting the

Shah into the United States (for cancer therapy). This seizure provoked an outpouring of patriotic fervor that ensured broad popular support for the new Constitution. However bitterly the secularists opposed particular Assembly initiatives, it would have been political suicide for them to launch an aggressive campaign for a No vote. This would have allowed their religious opponents to portray them as traitorous allies of the American imperialists.[31]

The Assembly took full advantage of its political opportunity and moved forward with great speed. On November 15, ten days after the embassy seizure, it published its final draft and called for a referendum in three weeks to enable the People to constitute themselves as citizens of the Islamic Republic.

The Ayatollah now had a big decision to make. Up to now, he had stood apart from the Assembly's proceedings, and he remained aloof as Montazeri led the campaign for his Supreme Leadership. But once the Assembly had presented its draft to the nation, the Ayatollah had two options. On the one hand, he could declare himself the Guardian Jurist before the referendum took place. This would have transformed the Yes vote of December 3 into a public acclamation of *his divinely inspired assertion* of authority as Guardian Jurist. On the other hand, he could remain silent until the results of the referendum were announced—implying that it was the will of the People, not the will of God, that served as the ultimate ground for his claim to Supreme Leadership.

It was this decision, more than anything inscribed in the draft, that would convey the character of the Ayatollah's authority to ordinary Iranians. How would Khomeini respond?

By remaining silent.

The Ayatollah made his constitutional position more explicit at the next stage—when the voters returned to the polls in February 1980 to elect the Republic's first president. Khomeini's closest confidante, Ayatollah Mohammad Beheshti, emerged as the obvious front-runner. Over the years he had established himself as a commanding presence in his own right—combining philosophical depth and leadership skills in a compelling fashion. Nevertheless, Khomeini barred his way—declaring that it was wrong for a cleric to compete for this secular office.[32]

When three non-clerics entered the race, the Ayatollah professed complete neutrality between them. Abolhassan Bani-Sadr, however, had the most impressive claim to the position. As a young man, he had actively engaged in the great uprising against the Shah in 1963—and had been rewarded for his efforts by long periods of exile. Over time he had become one of Khomeini's confidantes, and he would predictably support the Guardian's vision of an Islamic Republic. In granting him a landslide victory, the voters expressed their solidarity with the revolutionary regime. But Bani-Sadr's ascent to the presidency also symbolized the division of powers established by the Constitution—a secular president, elected by the voters, was a constitutional force to be reckoned with in the new regime.[33]

The May 1980 elections to the Majlis reinforced this point. Mohammad-Ali Rajai, who emerged as prime minister, had the same profile as Bani-Sadr. He was a committed Muslim, but not a cleric. His Islamic Republican Party (IRP) gained 85 of 270 seats in the Majlis. Since this fell far short of a majority, Bani-Sadr was obliged to temper the ardor of his own movement party by forming a coalition with other religiously oriented groups that had different opinions on many matters. At the same time, secular political parties also won substantial representation.[34]

In short: Even though the Ayatollah was an immensely popular figure, he had consistently constitutionalized his charisma into a complex structure firmly grounded in popular sovereignty. Given his charismatic authority, he had little to fear from this formal system of checks and balances so long as he remained in command. But as in the cases of de Gaulle and Mandela, the priority he placed on creating a Constitution at the Founding would profoundly shape the struggle for power when his less charismatic successors tried to replace him at the top.

Succession Crisis

The Ayatollah remained at the helm until his death in 1989. During almost all this time, Iran was at war with Iraq. This eight-year struggle has been the subject of a vast literature. But I will focus on how it transformed the concrete operation of the Iranian Constitution. This will permit a clearer appreciation of the paradoxical ways in which the institutions created in 1979 shaped the succession crisis of 1989.

Wartime Transformations

Saddam Hussein launched a surprise attack on September 22, 1980, shortly after Iran's new government was up and running. Saddam was expecting an easy victory—the surviving fragments of the Shah's army were demoralized, and the militants of the Revolutionary Guard remained disorganized. In fact, his "whirlwind campaign" scored sweeping triumphs in the short run, enabling Iraq to occupy vast areas of Iran along the frontier.

Yet Tehran did not capitulate. The new government successfully rallied Iranians for a heroic defense of their revolutionary Republic. This led to a long and bloody struggle, costing the lives of more than half a million Iranian soldiers and civilians. (Total population was about 50 million at the time.)[35] By war's end, a battle-hardened Revolutionary Guard had succeeded in recapturing the lost territories.

Iranians had paid a terrible price for this victory. With families throughout the country grieving the loss of loved ones, and many suffering war injuries, the Ayatollah's Guardianship provided a deeper meaning to their years of self-sacrifice. They were not enduring this ordeal merely to support an endless battle against a tin-pot dictator. They were engaged in a holy war to save the Islamic Revolution against Saddam's militant secularism.

This patriotic appeal had profound political consequences.[36] While the secularist boycott of the constituent assembly had propelled the Constitution in a religious direction, their political parties had still won significant representation in the first Majlis. Moreover, the Ayatollah himself had blocked a leading cleric from the presidency, paving the way for one of his civilian confidantes, Abolhassan Bani-Sadr, to gain office.

But with the country reeling from its early defeats, Khomeini made Bani-Sadr into a scapegoat for the disorganized military's failure to defend the country's borders against Saddam's massive assault. In June 1981 he called upon parliament to impeach the president, despite his landslide electoral victory eighteen months earlier. The Majlis complied and, even more ominously, enacted legislation banning the secularists' principal party, the National Front, from future engagement in electoral politics.[37]

The transformation of the Ayatollah into a symbol of national unity also challenged Islamicists who were committed to the separation of mosque and state. From the early days of the Revolution, this traditional Shiite view had been the creed of the Mujahideen, a powerful guerilla force that embarked on a terrorist campaign in retaliation for Bani-Sadr's ouster. The most spectacular attack occurred in late June, when a bomb exploded amid a conclave of leading members of the Islamic Republican Party (IRP), killing seventy of them in a single blow. This included the Ayatollah's closest advisor, Mohammad Beheshti.[38] Khomeini's personal loss reinforced his grim determination to ensure that committed clerics would henceforth occupy all key government positions in his holy war against Hussein—which now also included a brutal campaign of repression against the traitors inside the country who had taken up arms against the Islamic Republic.[39]

The shift to a clerical monopoly was on display at the next presidential election—which was held in the wake of further assassinations, dramatizing the imminent danger of catastrophic collapse. Upon Bani-Sadr's impeachment, prime minister Mohammad-Ali Rajai ascended to the presidency—only to be killed by a terrorist bomb in August, along with Mohammad-Javad Bahonar, the prime minister who would have succeeded him. The embattled IRP's response was to call a special presidential election under the appropriate Gaullist-inspired constitutional provision—and give Iranians a collective opportunity to demonstrate that, despite their external and internal enemies, they would fight to the end for the Islamic Republic.

To symbolize this commitment, the IRP chose as its presidential candidate one of the mullahs closest to the Ayatollah, Ali Khamenei. With the National Front banned from the ballot, Khamenei essentially ran unopposed in the October 1981 election. Yet despite his certain victory, and chaotic wartime conditions, ordinary voters managed to make their way to the polls in large numbers, casting 95 percent of their ballots for Khamenei, thereby committing themselves to more years of bloody sacrifice for the Revolution.[40]

Khamenei was typical of the new breed of cleric coming to the fore. He had spent long years in exile with the Ayatollah, but it was his political acumen, not religious distinction, that gained Khomeini's trust. Indeed, he had not even obtained the status of *marja* accorded to the most respected clerics in the Shia hierarchy.[41]

The same was true of the mullah who would emerge as Khamenei's principal rival over the next few years: Akbar Rafsanjani. Like Khamenei, he had made great personal sacrifices for the Revolution. In his case, he remained at home and served as a leading spokesman for the Islamic cause—spending years in prison as a punishment for his persistent dissent to the Shah's secularizing policies. After the Revolution, he was speaker of the Majlis but increasingly served as de facto military commander of the Republican Guard's campaigns against Hussein.[42] Despite his prominence, he too did not receive the status of *marja* from the leading Shia clerics in Qom, who continued to emphasize spiritual depth, not military prowess, in their assessments of religious distinction.

Nevertheless, these two second-rate mullahs were remarkably successful in confronting the great practical challenges raised by Saddam's early victories. Along with other power-minded clerics, they set to work transforming the Revolutionary Guard into an effective fighting force, while also organizing an enormous relief effort for cities and villages devastated by the ongoing conflict. As their military counteroffensives beat back Saddam's troops, they were rewarded by ringing electoral triumphs at the polls.

Despite wartime chaos, the constitutional calendar was punctiliously observed. Since the secular National Front had been banned, only the Islamic Republican Party offered the voters a slate of movement-party candidates. Nevertheless, the IRP's slate did not run unopposed. A host of independent candidates entered the race. But they first had to convince the Ministry of the Interior that they believed in Islam.[43] The Ministry aggressively excluded suspected secularists, so these "independents" would generally be sympathetic to the IRP. The remaining nonviolent secularists of the "Freedom Movement" once again urged a boycott, but unlike 1979, voters ignored them and went to the polls in overwhelming numbers. They gave the IRP 48 percent of the vote and 130 seats; the independents won 140, but most were reliable supporters of the IRP.

Nevertheless, this resounding reaffirmation of the war effort did not ensure Khamenei's control over parliament.[44] To the contrary, the Iranian constitution adapted the French model in a fashion that favored the country's prime minister, Mir-Hossein Mousavi, in his contest for power against the president. Like Khamenei, Mousavi had gained office in 1981 in the bloody aftermath of Bani-Sadr's impeachment. But he represented a very different faction of the IRP. Khamenei advanced the "rightist" views of the merchant class—the bazaaris—who wanted to commit the government to the protection of its traditional free-market prerogatives. Mousavi was a strong leftist, who used his control over cabinet ministries to advance an elaborate statist program that aimed at providing immediate relief and reconstruction assistance to the devastated population.[45]

Khamenei was determined to push policy rightward once he scored a sweeping 87 percent majority in his 1985 reelection campaign—with the Ministry once again barring his major contenders from the ballot. On four different occasions during the Majlis' four-year term, Khamenei tried to replace Mousavi with a rightist prime minister of his own choosing; and he failed all four times. This demonstration of presidential weakness permitted his rival to gain the upper hand in the 1988 elections. His left-leaning forces organized their own slate of candidates and appealed for support from voters if they hoped to preserve the statist programs that were providing immediate relief for their suffering. The result was an overwhelming electoral mandate. When the new Majlis met, it granted Mousavi their highest-ever vote of confidence, supporting his reelection as prime minister with 204 of the 217 votes cast. But Mousavi then overplayed his hand when he encountered resistance in parliament to some of his ministerial nominations. In order to establish his primacy, he surprised everybody by announcing that he was resigning as prime minister—expecting that this would lead his shadowy opponents to beg him to continue in power with the full complement of his ministerial choices. To Mousavi's surprise, his opponents stood their ground—and despite the leftist's mandate from the People, Khamenei finally succeeded in ousting him from office.[46]

The increasingly bitter struggle between Khamenei and Mousavi did not, however, prevent them from joining together in support of an escalating reign of terror against secularism in all its forms. The Revolutionary Guard had crushed the Islamicist guerillas of the Mujahideen by early 1982. But operating under martial law, the Guard engaged in massive roundups of suspected secularists—with vague suspicions increasingly justifying torture and mass murder on a horrific scale.[47]

Wartime hysteria seemed to be making the founding debates and decisions of 1979 and 1980 utterly irrelevant to real-world politics. Rather than operating as a collaborative enterprise between the religiously inspired Guardian and the secular leaders of a democratic republic, Iran was propelling itself down the path toward a brutally repressive theocracy led by Khamenei as president and Rafsanjani as commander-in-chief.

While all this was happening, the Ayatollah was retreating from day-to-day decision-making. Now in his 80s, he spent much of his time in seclusion in the Tehran suburbs addressing theological issues—relying on a very few confidantes to convey his views to the powerful clerics controlling the army and the government. Chief among them was Hussein-Ali Montazeri, who was the Ayatollah's principal spokesman at the Assembly of Constitutional Experts—and, as its president, had demonstrated his loyalty and statecraft in winning broad support for the incorporation of the Supreme Leadership into the governing framework. After the Ayatollah's previous advisor, Beheshti, was assassinated in 1981, Montazeri increasingly became the Ayatollah's principal representative in dealing with the powerful clerics in the government and army.[48]

The Emerging Succession Crisis

Unlike Khamenei and Rafsanjani, Montazeri was a marja whose spiritual depth had gained broad recognition in Qom. Given this fact, his intimate association with the Ayatollah marked him out as his obvious successor as Guardian Jurist. Recall, however, that the Constitution of 1979 did not authorize Khomeini to make this appointment. Instead, it explicitly assigned this task to a special Council of Experts—and the first Majlis had quickly created a two-step system for their selection. During the first step, leaders of the clerical establishment would nominate a wide range of spiritual leaders for Council membership; but in the second step, the general electorate would make the final choice. The Ayatollah fully supported this resolution, because it was in harmony with then-prevailing commitments to the democratic foundations of the Islamic *Republic.*

Despite the disruptions created by Saddam's War and Bani-Sadr's impeachment, elections for the Council took place in 1982 and its eighty members remained in office for the next eight years. But by 1985, the Ayatollah had reached the age of 83, and the Council chose to smooth the transition by naming his successor ahead of time—unanimously appointing Montazeri as the next Guardian Jurist.

Perhaps its decision might have been more difficult if the supporters of President Khamenei had advanced his candidacy. He had just gained a sweeping reelection victory, in recognition of his initial success in turning the tide against Saddam's armies. Given that the Constitution barred him from a third consecutive term as president, why not designate him as the next Guardian?

There was an easy answer: Khamenei was not a marja, and the Constitution explicitly barred lesser clerics from the Guardianship. Since Montazeri's religious insight and dedication had been recognized by his fellow marjas, and Khamenei failed to qualify, nobody on the Council took his candidacy seriously. Once it unanimously selected Montazeri, its choice gained support among the governing elite and the general public.

With his future Guardianship ensured, Montazeri began to take a more independent stance in dealing with the Ayatollah. In a series of letters, he began questioning the Islamic character of some regime policies, especially the ruthless repression of political prisoners. These critical comments suggested that, once installed as Supreme Leader, he could well repudiate the Islamic character of some key decisions made under the Ayatollah's Guardianship.[49]

This implication increasingly troubled Khomeini, and in March 1989 he did something about it. He ordered Montazeri to resign his position as his appointed successor. Khomeini's demand had no constitutional foundation. Only the Experts, not the Ayatollah, could dismiss Montazeri, and only if they found his conduct "deficient" when judged by the high standards of spiritual excellence set out in the text. Montazeri was perfectly aware of this point. After all, he had served as president of the constituent assembly that wrote it into the Constitution in the first place. Nevertheless, he refused to appeal to the Experts to defend his claims to succession, and humbly recognized the Ayatollah's charismatic authority—submitting a letter of resignation that declared his loyalty to the regime.[50]

Montazeri's announcement shocked the nation, because it was already obvious that the Ayatollah's health was rapidly declining—in fact, he would die three months later. It was no surprise, then, that another distinguished marja, Mohammad-Reza Golpayegani, quickly emerged in public discussions as the leading candidate for the Supreme Leadership.

But in their private deliberations, the Experts did not consider Golpayegani to be a serious contender. He was indeed a distinguished marja, who had devoted his life to spiritual devotions of such intensity that his colleagues had granted him special distinction. But he had no political experience and was utterly unknown to the general public. The appointment of such a novice would have destroyed general confidence in the very idea that Iranians should rely on a Guardian Jurist to guide the Republic. Indeed, Montazeri was the *only* marja "who possessed adequate theological learning, as well as sufficient revolutionary credentials," to sustain the legitimacy of the system—in the words of Ray Takeyh's particularly convincing account.[51] By firing Montazeri from his deathbed, Khomeini was putting into question whether *anybody* with established religious authority could reliably serve to guide the Islamic Republic.

Quite remarkably, the Constitution had anticipated such a possibility. It provided that, if no single holy man emerged as a suitable successor, Supreme Leadership could be exercised by a Council of Three—only one of whose members needed to be a marja. This would have allowed Khamenei and Rafsanjani to join Golpayegani on the Council, thereby providing the practical statecraft and public recognition that the marja so painfully lacked.

The Council of Three had the further advantage of allowing the country's president to avoid a public power struggle with its military leader at a moment when the nation would be mourning the death of its greatest revolutionary hero. Rather than discredit one another by publicly competing for Supreme Leadership, the two men could greatly enhance their stature by endorsing the Council of Three, and then use Golpayegani as their mouthpiece to announce final decisions after they had reached a mutually satisfactory compromise in behind-the-scenes negotiations.

But this obvious solution had one big weakness. Khamenei and Rafsanjani held starkly different views on many of the pressing problems facing the country after its long years of wartime devastation. If they joined Golpayegani on a Council of Three, they would be constantly pushing in different directions, and it would be up to Golpayegani to cast the deciding vote—transforming the bewildered novice into the Supreme Leader in fact if not in name.

The Ayatollah had set a precedent as Guardian Jurist that would be tough for anybody to follow. But the prospect of three squabbling Guardians serving as his successor would have utterly demoralized the nation—once again putting the very legitimacy of supreme clerical leadership into question. As a consequence, it isn't surprising that it was considered and rejected a few weeks before the Ayatollah's death. This meant that Khomeini and Rafsanjani now found themselves in a desperate race against time—made more urgent by the Ayatollah's deteriorating condition.[52]

They confronted two obvious problems. First, the ascent of either man was patently illegal, since the Constitution expressly limited the position to marjas. Second, they had to decide which one of them should ascend to the Leadership. If they couldn't agree before the Ayatollah died, their public competition could readily degenerate into violent street confrontations between their committed partisans.

Begin with the second issue—call it the problem of *mutual consent*. Here is where the Gaullist legacy became a precious resource. As in France and Poland, the division of power between president and prime minister had already generated intense conflict in Iran, where Khamenei had been locked in an ongoing struggle for power with Mir-Hossein Mousavi as prime minister. But as a consequence of Mousavi's failed effort to establish his supremacy, there was no powerful figure currently serving as prime minister who was in a position to defend the institutional prerogatives of this office. As a consequence, Khomeini and Rafsanjani could use the prime ministership as a bargaining chip in their effort to solve their mutual consent problem. If the Constitution were amended to abolish the office of prime minister, the president would now emerge as the *only* figure with a popular mandate from the People.

A super-Gaullist presidency was particularly attractive to Rafsanjani. He had developed great skill in presenting himself on public occasions in a highly persuasive fashion. This would vastly increase his legitimacy in any standoff against the Guardian Jurist. Even if the Guardian opposed presidential initiatives on their merits, he would be hard-pressed to call on the Guardian Council to veto them so long as the super-Gaullist president had a strong democratic mandate.

In contrast, Khamenei projected an austere public persona that made it impossible for him to compete against his rival in a popularity contest. He was perfectly aware of his limitations as a populist politician. Nevertheless, his severe public persona was more in keeping with the Guardian Jurist's claim to spiritual supremacy. Although Khamenei recognized that he could not inherit the Ayatollah's charismatic authority, the Ayatollah's precedents would help legitimate Khamenei's own efforts to shape the country's future.

It took intense and secret negotiations, under enormous time pressure, for both men to see that a super-Gaullist presidency was in their mutual self-interest. To the present day, we don't know what went on behind closed doors. But my simplified analysis suffices to introduce my first key thesis: the deal could never have occurred if the original Constitution had not been based on the model of the Fifth Republic.

To see why, suppose that the constituent assembly of 1979 had rejected the Gaullist model, and had unequivocally placed the Supreme Leader at the very top of the governmental hierarchy. Under this scenario, the Constitution would have granted the Supreme Leader authority to govern in a top-down fashion—in collaboration, let us suppose, with leading clerics in the manner of the Catholic Church. Within this purely theocratic framework, Rafsanjani would have been faced with a stark choice in 1989: If he failed to compete with Khamenei for Supreme Leadership, he would have had to accept a clearly subordinate position in the power structure.

The only thing that allowed Rafsanjani to escape this dilemma was the 1979 decision to integrate the Supreme Leadership into a Gaullist system in which president, prime minister, and Majlis gained their authority on the basis of popular sovereignty without any pretense to divine inspiration. In other words, it was the *democratic* framework established at Time Two that made it possible to resolve the *religious* succession crisis at Time Three. This is the first big—albeit paradoxical—thesis that I shall be advancing here.

No less paradoxically: the creation of a democratic super-presidency came at a moment when the holy war against Hussein was reaching its triumphant conclusion, and the theocratic character of the regime was otherwise propelling itself to new heights. If we don't take into account the relationship between Time Two and Time Three, it would be hard to explain why the regime's reinforcement of its *democratic* foundations occurred at such an emphatically *theocratic* moment.

A final problem remained. If Khamenei and Rafsanjani adopted the super-Gaullist solution, this would only compound the illegality of their arrangement. It was already unconstitutional for either man to ascend to the Leadership, given their status as second-class clerics. But the creation of a super-Gaullist presidency required another sweeping series of constitutional amendments. Not only would it be necessary to abolish the prime minister's office, but this necessitated a systematic revision of a host of provisions that would recalibrate the super-Gaullist president's relationship to the Supreme Leader, the Majlis, and the other branches of government.

The Experts had no power to make these changes. They had the exclusive right to appoint the next Supreme Leader, but they had no authority to propose or enact amendments. Indeed, the Constitution ratified by the voters in 1980 did not contain any provisions for its subsequent revision. Somehow or other, the revolutionary leadership had to convince the country that, when Khamenei and Rafsanjani began exercising their powers as Supreme Leader and super-president, they were not engaging in utterly lawless acts of authority.

Or was such an exercise in public legitimation really necessary?

There are plenty of places in the world where power grabs occur without any serious effort to constitutionalize them. It is of great significance, then, that Iran's revolutionary elite made a determined effort to blaze a constitutional path that could, as quickly as possible, rectify the anomalous situation in which Khamenei and Rafsanjani would find themselves when the Ayatollah died.

On April 24, 1989—two months after Montazeri's resignation and six weeks before the Ayatollah's death—Khomeini sent a letter to the office of the presidency creating an "Assembly for the Revision of the Constitution." He named twenty top officials to serve, and the Majlis followed up by naming five others. It is impossible to determine whether Khomeini was sufficiently alert to make these appointments during the final weeks of his life. During the summer of 1988 the Ayatollah's serious illness had already become a matter of public knowledge, and it is quite possible that Khamenei and Rafsanjani played a key role in the selection of the ad hoc group.[53]

Whatever the truth may be, once the members convened, they immediately went into overdrive to complete their assignment before the Ayatollah passed away.[54] Given the sweeping textual changes required to constitutionalize the new arrangement between the two leaders, the revisionary assembly was very far from completing a final draft by June 3, when the Ayatollah died. Nevertheless, Khamenei and Rafsanjani were sufficiently confident that a satisfactory solution would be forthcoming that they implemented their deal in the only way that was remotely credible. Both men emerged from Khomeini's death chamber to declare that the Ayatollah himself had named Khamenei as his successor.

As a constitutional matter, their joint appeal to the Khomeini's charismatic authority was entirely inadequate. As we have seen, the Constitution refused to allow the Ayatollah to pick his successor and granted this authority exclusively to the Council of Experts. As a consequence, the two men followed up their joint announcement by immediately entering the chamber where the Experts awaited them. After a period of deliberation behind closed doors, Rafsanjani reemerged to declare that the Experts had indeed named Khamenei as the next Guardian of the Republic.

Very recently, however, the full video of the Experts' actual deliberations has finally leaked out to the public. It dramatizes the legitimacy problems I have been exploring. Once Rafsanjani formally informed the Council of the Ayatollah's wishes, Khamenei rose to the floor to tell the Experts that he simply would not accept the appointment:

> I had also mentioned this to Mr. Hashemi (Rafsanjani) a few weeks ago when this issue came up. . . . I told [Rafsanjani], in all seriousness, that I will not accept this. Let's put aside the fact that I am truly not worthy of this position—which is a fact that I know, and you all perhaps also know. There is a technical problem here. This would be an illusionary Leadership, not a real one. Neither am I qualified pursuant to the Constitution, nor am I qualified as a religious Leader as many of you. My command will not carry the weight of a Leader. What kind of a Leadership would this be? . . . The Constitution requires a Leader to be a Marja.[55]

Khamenei's unequivocal rejection of Leadership provoked general pandemonium, with one of the Experts shouting that the constitutional bar was "only temporary," given the revisionary assembly's plan for a constitutional amendment to legalize it retroactively. But Khamenei refused to retreat, and continued to oppose his appointment to an "illusionary Leadership."

With the Council's decision hanging in the balance, Rafsanjani rose to the floor to insist that the Experts yield to his demand for an immediate vote. But this time he did not content himself with a problematic invocation of the Ayatollah's will. He not only repeated that the illegality problem would be "temporary." He also addressed the deeper question posed by Khamenei's candid assertion that a change in the Constitution would not suffice to resolve the widespread belief that he simply lacked the spiritual excellence demanded for Supreme Leadership. So far as Rafsanjani was concerned, these pervasive doubts could also be resolved over time "with some help from others."[56] But for now, he insisted that nothing productive would come from further debate—and that the time had come for the assembly to stop talking and start voting.

The Council complied. But behind closed doors, eighteen members continued to be appalled by the illegality of it all and cast dissenting votes for Marja Golpayegani. Nevertheless, the other sixty members recognized that they had no real choice but to elect Khamenei to provide the country with effective government at a critical moment in its history.

Interestingly, the protagonists were overly optimistic about the ease with which the ad hoc constitutional assembly would reach its objective. It took until late July, after an additional twenty-three formal sessions, before members finally converged on a common approach. Once the interim government came into formal existence, it then appointed its own six-man commission to build on this work and advanced an elaborate set of provisions for popular approval at a referendum in early December.[57] At the same time, voters cast their ballots to fill the super-presidential office created by the sweeping constitutional revisions. When the results came in, it revealed that ordinary Iranians gave their overwhelming approval both to the constitutionalization of Khamenei's rise to Supreme Leadership and to the election of Rafsanjani to the super-presidency—with 98 percent voting Yes on the Constitution and 96 percent voting Yes on Rafsanjani.

All in all, a remarkable performance. Recall that the succession crisis had begun only seventeen months before—when the Ayatollah forced Montazeri to renounce the Supreme Leadership in March 1988. This sheer assertion of charismatic authority by Ayatollah Khomeini threatened to inaugurate a bloody era of theocratic dictatorship. Yet the December 1989 referendum ushered the country into a new era of checks and balances, based on a democratic show of consent by We the People of Iran.

Checks and Balances

To gain a better sense of the new balance of power, we must return to another fateful decision made during the final days of the Ayatollah's rule. This concerned the future of the Islamic Republican Party, the organized religious movement that had dominated political life since the secular National Front was banned in 1981.

As I have suggested, the IRP was divided against itself on fundamental issues. The left flank, led by prime minister Mousavi with the support of the Revolutionary Guard, emphasized the need to continue wartime reconstruction and relief projects. The right flank, led by Khamenei with the support of the traditional merchant class, pushed for more market-friendly approaches.

Foreign policy generated similar divisions. Khamenei and the religious right emphasized the continuing danger posed by American imperialism. Opponents, led by Rafsanjani, urged that a policy of rapprochement with the West would allow Iran to reap vast oil revenues on world markets and then use this enormous fund to inaugurate a decisive economic advance.

While these ongoing debates were shaped by Iran's particular history and situation, many other countries were confronting similar issues in 1989—with free-market cosmopolitanism challenging the relatively socialist and nation-centered policies of the previous generation. For example, the Congress Parties of India and South Africa were debating the same questions at about the same time.

There was one big difference. The Congress Parties in both these countries managed to sustain their unity in the midst of these bitter disputes, but the IRP did not. By mid-decade, the Left and Right were engaged in outright conflict, organizing rival slates for parliamentary elections and competing for control of the legislative agenda.[58] This split had unanticipated consequences once the Ayatollah had left the scene. When Khamenei was president during the 1980s, he also served as president of the IRP. If the party had remained in existence after his ascent to Supreme Leadership, he could have used his influence among old-time IRP leaders as a counterweight to Rafsanjani's appeal to the masses. But once Rafsanjani was freed from IRP restraints, there was nothing to stop him from using his democratic mandate to enact a sweeping free-market program that Khamenei had repeatedly opposed in his earlier public life.

This led to an early test of the new powers granted to the Supreme Leader by the sweeping constitutional amendments resolving the succession crisis.

These revisions did not simply eliminate the provision that required the Islamic Guardian to be a marja; they declared that the Khamenei, and his successors, should be recognized as the *Absolutely* Supreme Leader of the Republic. Moreover, it gave him new institutional tools to insist on his supremacy.

These innovations had their roots in earlier institutional developments. Even before the IRP finally broke apart, the party's ongoing factional strife generated serious constitutional problems. As shifting left- and right-wing coalitions enacted legislation in the Majlis, these statutes frequently encountered opposition from the twelve jurists on the Council of Guardians.

Council objections met with a mixed reception. Some pronouncements induced significant legislative changes, but others were greeted by bitter denunciations from disappointed parliamentarians.[59] They not only disputed the Guardians' interpretations of the relevant texts, but engaged in their own intramural disputes over the best legislative response to the Guardians' objections. In the meantime, matters of large importance were left in limbo, without any decisive resolution—requiring the Ayatollah, typically working through Montazeri and other confidantes, to engage in ad hoc efforts to resolve particular deadlocks. But as these impasses multiplied, and the Ayatollah's energies declined in 1988, Khomeini once again created an ad hoc institutional response to a systemic problem that had not been anticipated by the 1979 Constitution. His decree of February 1988 created an "Expediency Council" authorized to break interbranch deadlocks and endow its own solutions with the force of law.

The amendments adopted by the People in 1989 affirmed this deathbed decision. They also gave Khamenei unilateral power to appoint a group of permanent members who could play a dominant role in defining the agenda for the more transient officials from other governmental organs who would serve as Expediency Council members.[60]

But paradoxically, this grant of power only demonstrated that the text's assertion of Khamenei's *absolute* supremacy was hardly enough to earn him the genuine respect of the religious and political elite. Because he could not rely on the loyalty of devoted followers, he used his appointment authority to co-opt the support of potential opponents. Rather than use Expediency as a weapon against the president's initiatives, he made Rafsanjani the head of the Expediency Council itself!

This made good sense, given Khamenei's diagnosis of his own predicament at the crucial session of the Council of Experts that authorized his ascent. At that time, he openly expressed the fear that, as a second-class cleric, his "command[s] will not carry the weight of a Leader." Instead of blinding himself to political reality, he accepted the advice tendered at the very same session by Rafsanjani, who assured him that his deep problem of legitimacy could be resolved, over time, "with some help from others."

Similarly, Khamenei could not confidently expect the Guardians to back him up if he condemned the president's initiatives. The six religious jurists on the Council were, as a group, far more distinguished clerics than the Supreme Leader himself. Khamenei could not count on them to support his claims to power if they believed that Rafsanjani's initiatives were better supported by the holy texts. Similarly, Khamenei could not count on the Council's six civilian jurists, especially if his views were inconsistent with those rooted in the French tradition that had had such a profound impact on the country's legal culture. All members of the Council consistently deferred to Ayatollah Khomeini's charismatic authority, but the new Supreme Leader would have to *earn* the respect of these skeptical elites through his conduct in office. Recognizing these realities, Khamenei refused to provoke a premature test of his legitimacy by calling on the Guardians to block Rafsanjani's initiatives. Despite his history of opposition to similar measures, he remained silent as Rafsanjani pushed through his ambitious program of deregulation and privatization.

During the early years of his presidency, moreover, the Guardians had not yet invoked another French-inspired provision that would become important in later power struggles. Like the French Conseil Constitutionnel, the Guardians had been assigned two distinct functions by its governing constitutional text. They were not only charged with the task of evaluating the constitutionality of new legislation. They were also required to "supervise" all national elections.

As Rafsanjani prepared to run for a second term in 1992, the Guardians interpreted this provision in an exceptionally aggressive fashion—asserting that they could exclude candidates from the ballot if they found them "morally or religiously unfit" for the office. During the 1980s the Ministry of the Interior had repeatedly abused a similar authority to exclude opponents of the governing clerical establishment from electoral competition—but at least it could invoke the wartime emergency to justify its exclusionary actions. But the Guardians' claim of authority normalized this practice within the constitutional framework of the postwar Republic.[61]

The Council has exercised its exclusionary power in different ways—provoking a series of populist countermovements that attempted to vindicate democratic principles over time. But even when its exclusions had a big short-term impact, they did not necessarily give Khamenei the advantage over his presidential competitors. As we shall see, it was Rafsanjani, not the Supreme Leader, who gained the advantage from the Guardians' decisions in his reelection campaign in 1993.

Time Four: The Shifting Pendulum of Power

I cannot hope to provide a blow-by-blow account of the struggle between Supreme Leader and super-president since the Ayatollah's death. The best I can do is provide an overview suggesting how the pendulum of power has swung from democratic to religious authority, and back again, without either side emerging with a final victory.[62]

Begin, then, with Rafsanjani's success in pushing his ambitious program through the Majlis without Khamenei or the Guardians raising any objections. The president's sweeping pro-market reforms stirred great hopes of a postwar boom, but they did not produce the quick results he had promised the public. His privatization program was also tarnished by corruption scandals. As a consequence, Rafsanjani's campaign for reelection in 1993 generated a weak response. Only half of all voters bothered to go to the polls—and the president won an extremely narrow victory over three relatively undistinguished competitors. Khamenei's severe persona, and undoubted personal integrity, were now transformed into a large advantage in his ongoing confrontation with a president who could no longer claim a decisive democratic mandate—and the balance of power shifted strongly in the Leader's direction during Rafsanjani's second term.

The next electoral cycle, however, threw the Supreme Leader back onto the defensive. Mohammad Khatami's victory in the 1997 presidential election presented him with a profound challenge. Khatami had campaigned on a program of cultural liberalization at home and détente abroad—positions starkly inconsistent with Khamenei's deeply conservative views. Yet his candidacy inspired an enormous wave of popular support. Only half the electorate had turned out to vote in 1993, but 80 percent went to the polls in 1997—and they awarded Khatami a landslide victory, giving him 75 percent of the vote while his two more-conservative rivals together gained only 25 percent.

The next test was provided by the parliamentary elections of 2000—in which the "Khordad Front," representing the forces of reform, faced off against the Followers of the Imam and the Leader ("Imam" referred to Khomeini, and

"Leader" referred to Khamenei). When the returns came in, the Front crushed the Followers, winning an absolute majority of 222 seats to their opponents' 74 seats.

The time had come for a showdown, with Khatami driving a radical reform agenda through the Majlis, and Khamenei invoking all the powers of the Guardians and the Expediency Council to block these initiatives. The ongoing confrontation dramatized the stakes as Khatami appealed to the People to back him in his campaign for reelection in 2001. The voters responded by granting him an even more emphatic mandate—giving him 77 percent of the vote while his closest rival scored 16 percent.

Nevertheless, Khamenei refused to budge, and took desperate measures to break the reformists' momentum. As the 2004 parliamentary elections approached, the Guardian Council invoked its powers of disqualification in draconian fashion. Not only did it deny ballot access to 2,500 would-be candidates (half of all who applied). It prohibited 80 sitting members of the Majlis from running for reelection—finding that their support for Khatami's efforts at cultural liberalization had made them "morally" or "religiously" unfit." As a consequence, the reformists could only field 191 (weak) candidates in the race for 285 Majlis seats—and only 47 of them managed to gain election. Khatami left office two years later without anything significant to show for his efforts to liberalize the Islamic Republic, other than some scattered protests and street demonstrations.[63]

At this point the Supreme Leader went on the offensive. The presidential election of 2005 witnessed a mass movement, based on a nationwide network of mosques, in support of Mahmoud Ahmadinejad, who denounced Khatami and other cosmopolitan elitists for betraying the fundamental principles of Islam. He faced off against Rafsanjani, the paradigmatic modernist president. (While the Constitution requires presidents to leave office after two terms, it follows the French paradigm in allowing them to run again after somebody else has filled the position). Ahmadinejad won 62 percent of the vote, signaling the dawn of a new era, symbolized by his precedent-breaking decision to kiss the Supreme Leader's ring at his inauguration ceremony.

Ahmadinejad confronted a very different political reality when he embarked on his reelection campaign in 2009. Four years earlier, the reform movement had been grievously demoralized by Khatami's utter failure to realize his program during his eight years in office—leading to large drops in turnout in the urban regions that were most favorable to Khatami during his earlier campaigns. But Ahmadinejad's radical turn to the right triggered a strong reaction from reformist opponents determined to repudiate an increasingly oppressive orthodoxy.

Sensing that his time had come at last, the leftist prime minister of the 1980s—Mir-Hussein Mousavi—suddenly reemerged from decades of political retirement to declare his candidacy. His announcement catalyzed an effort by old-time revolutionaries and youthful activists to join together in a collective effort to propel his candidacy forward. As election day approached, Mousavi was leading in the polls and reformers confidently looked forward to a sweeping victory.

But for the first time in the Republic's history, the clerical establishment resorted to massive cheating to suppress the democratic threat to their authority. The Interior Ministry rapidly announced, to the general astonishment, that Ahmadinejad had won in a landslide, scoring a 63 percent majority over his opponents. This incredible result immediately provoked massive demonstrations denouncing the vote count. Flying the banner of the Green Revolution, in emulation of the "Color Revolutions" in Eastern Europe and the Philippines, the protestors demanded a new election—or at least an honest recount. Security forces responded with brutal violence, throwing thousands into prisons notorious for rape and torture.

The regime's constitutional response only further undermined its legitimacy. As part of its supervisory authority over elections, the Guardians took up the task of reviewing the charges of voter fraud and coercion pouring in from the country. When it upheld Ahmadinejad's victory, it lost its integrity in the eyes of the public. Given the blatant vote-rigging involved, the president was utterly dependent on Khamenei's religious authority to support his claim to power—but by providing him with crucial support, Khamenei implicated himself in the fraudulent scheme.

Recall that Shia teachings had traditionally warned that the lust for power would profoundly corrupt the character of religious experience. Was the second-class cleric, posing as the Ayatollah, providing a dramatic example of this profound truth?

The next presidential election would be a crucial test. If the Council of Guardians eliminated all serious challengers to Khamenei's preferred candidate, or cheated on the vote count, this would predictably provoke a rerun of the popular uprising that erupted four years earlier. Only this time, the Supreme Leader could not be confident that another harshly repressive response would prove successful. Khamenei vividly remembered that similar efforts by the Shah to restore law and order had failed to crush popular protests in 1978.

They led instead to a revolutionary escalation that overwhelmed the old regime. Even though these dramatic events in the history of the Revolution were not something the younger generation had lived through, they nevertheless loomed large in collective memory. Would Khamenei run the risk of a rerun, in which he might be condemned to play the Shah's tragic role?

The answer was no. This time around, the Guardians enacted a new parliamentary law that delegated the supervision of elections to a special eleven-member commission, from which Guardians were entirely excluded. Under the new statute, seven seats were reserved for "trustworthy characters" and only four represented the ministries in charge of organizing the election-day balloting in a professional fashion. In 2013, for example, the "trustworthy characters" included a university president, an esteemed cleric, two members of parliament, and similar notables.[64]

Chastened by the elimination of their general supervisory jurisdiction, the Guardians also took a more measured approach to screening presidential candidates. They refused to allow Rafsanjani or Khatami to enter the race and renew their old challenges to Khamenei's Leadership. But they permitted a more pragmatic reformer, Hassan Rouhani, to run on a program that renewed the campaign for a more tolerant Islam at home and a pro-Western breakthrough abroad.

To minimize the risks to Khamenei involved in their decision to allow Rouhani a place in the spotlight, the Guardians also allowed seven other candidates to enter the race. They expected that these rivals would attract enough votes from their different constituencies to deprive Rouhani of a powerful democratic mandate even if he came out in first place.

This clever strategy proved to be an utter failure. Rouhani's campaign inspired a massive increase in citizen engagement. Although in 2007 only a minority of Iranians bothered to cast a ballot, 70 percent vote came out to the polls in response to Rouhani's call for a breakthrough in Iran's relationship to the West. What is more, the proliferation of rival candidacies did not prevent Rouhani from emerging with a 51 percent majority—while the Supreme Leader's favored candidate, Saeed Jalili, who took an especially hard line against Rouhani's sweeping nuclear initiative with the West, ended up in the single digits. As we saw in this chapter's introduction, their defeat at the polls required Khamenei and the Guardians to allow Khatami to commit the country to a dramatic nuclear agreement with the West, which symbolized the voters' determination to mandate a radical change in foreign policy.

Four years later, however, the Guardians hit upon a very different strategy to bring this "new beginning" to a rapid end by defeating Rouhani's effort to win reelection. Instead of permitting a host of candidates to run, they only allowed a single strong candidate, the religiously conservative Ebrahim Raisi, to enter the field against him. But this strategy failed as well: Rouhani crushed Raisi in a landslide, 57 percent to 38 percent.

The president's renewed popular mandate has once again thrown Khamenei on the defensive. However much he may want to repudiate Rouhani's nuclear agreement, he lacks the support of the Iranian people to do so—even though Donald Trump has done his best to discredit Rouhani's opening to the West. The truth is plain for all to see: it is the super-Gaullist president, not the Absolutely Supreme Leader, who is currently decisive on this life-and-death question for the Islamic Republic.

I do not wish to exaggerate. Perhaps Khamenei may find that Trump's continuing opposition may enable him to sabotage the deal. Perhaps the next election will give a democratic mandate to a conservative president, who will seize the opportunity to lead the country back in Khamenei's direction. But similar swings in the balance of authority between elected and unelected branches have regularly occurred in all our other case studies. They do not mark Iran out as radically different from the others we have explored in this book.

To be sure, the Iranian Constitution gives the Guardian Jurist far greater power to repel the advances of his democratic adversaries than the vetoes possessed by his juristic counterparts in other countries—at least on paper. But history has shown that the authority of the Leader to make effective use of these powers depends on something more fundamental—the extent to which he, as opposed to his rivals in the presidency and parliament, has *earned* the authority to define the enduring meaning of the values affirmed by Iran's revolutionary Constitution.

This basic point defines the bright line I have drawn between constitutionalism and despotism in the modern world. Dictators also encounter resistance to their commands, but they refuse to recognize that such shows of opposition are legitimate. Constitutional regimes, in contrast, require the most powerful officials to engage in ongoing competition with institutional rivals for the final say over the future course of political development.

Iran passes this test; many other Middle Eastern countries don't. They are poorly disguised despotisms.

This is not a point that should be forgotten amid the tweets and tragedies of the current day.

CHAPTER 13

American Exceptionalism?

Rooted Cosmopolitanism

Is America unique?

Over the past quarter-century, the U.S. Supreme Court has famously split into two warring camps on this question. American exceptionalists, led by Scalia and Thomas, have contended that the country's fundamental law will be distorted and degraded if judges heed the voices of their foreign counterparts. Constitutional cosmopolitans, led by Breyer and Kennedy, have replied that such acts of willful ignorance only succeed in depriving Americans of the deep insights other nations have gained in confronting fundamental questions.

I want to move beyond this simplistic dichotomy. For starters, I will take one step in the Scalia / Thomas direction and insist that there was indeed something very special about the American Founding. Americans of the eighteenth century were profoundly influenced by memories of Oliver Cromwell's earlier struggle to sweep away monarchy and establish a new Republic during the 1650s. This bloody British effort ended in chaotic failure, and the return of royal rule. American colonists were well aware that their struggle against King George III might lead to a similar disaster. It was not enough to expel the king; they were fighting to prevent the return of autocracy by establishing a constitutional order that could gain broad popular recognition as an *authentic* expression of the revolutionary principles motivating their struggle.

Easier said than done. Scalia / Thomas are absolutely right about the enduring significance of the Founding's success in constitutionalizing charisma. Nevertheless, this book shows that Breyer / Kennedy are also right to insist that the early American achievement is no longer unique. The challenge is to reflect on the lessons learned from more recent experiments in revolutionary constitutionalism, and consider how they can inform an understanding of America's past, present, and future.

In searching for insight, Americans should be wary of an indiscriminate form of cosmopolitanism. While some countries have traveled down the revolutionary pathway to constitutionalism, many have not. The list of rejectionists is long and impressive. It includes Germany and Japan and Spain, Great Britain and Australia and Canada, as well as the European Union. It also includes some especially revealing examples emerging from Latin America. These countries' constitutions have been built and sustained by elites without the revolutionary engagement of mass movements.

I will be considering these elitist constitutions in the next volume. But for now, the success of some elitist regimes should caution Americans against an overly enthusiastic form of cosmopolitanism, which fails to appreciate that the same legal formula can take on very different meanings in radically different cultures. To take one example, the principle of "human dignity" is used in very different ways within the revolutionary culture of Israel, the anti-revolutionary culture of Germany, and the Anglo-establishmentarian culture of Canada. It's possible, of course, that German or Canadian doctrines of "dignity" have more to offer the United States than Israeli approaches.

But Americans should consider the matter carefully before coming to this conclusion. They should not assume that dignity talk supports a one-size-fits-all framework for analysis. Sometimes it does make sense to embrace doctrinal structures emerging across the divide that separates revolutionary from elite constitutions; but sometimes it doesn't. The key thing is to appreciate the need for self-conscious reflection on the boundary-crossing question before resolving the issue.

Americans should treat the constitutional experience of nations like India or France, South Africa or Poland, with special respect. These countries are traveling down the very same Enlightenment pathway that the United States has been following since the Founding. As a consequence, they do indeed offer us valuable lessons in our own continuing journey down the revolutionary road to constitutional legitimacy.

To put my point in a single phrase, I am calling for a *rooted cosmopolitanism*—an approach that recognizes that America's constitutional culture is indeed exceptional when compared to many other relatively successful systems; but that it is by no means unique, and that we have something special to learn from sister nations whose constitutions have emerged from revolutions on a human scale.

It is easy to issue grand pronunciamentos calling for new approaches to old debates. The tough part is to show that rooted cosmopolitanism does in-

deed generate new insights. I don't pretend that this chapter suffices to resolve all reasonable doubts. At best, my explorations will prove sufficiently
revealing that they encourage others to join in the hunt.

I begin by inviting you to view the American Founding from the perspectives afforded by the revolutionary experiences of Charles de Gaulle's France
and Nelson Mandela's South Africa. I then jump forward a couple of centuries to the age of Donald Trump. I suggest that the roots of the Trump crisis
go back to the New Deal—and that we have something valuable to learn about
Roosevelt's effort to constitutionalize social democracy in America by comparing it to similar efforts by Nehru in India and Ben-Gurion in Israel. In contrast to Nehru, Roosevelt refused to codify the New Deal's sweeping assault
on laissez-faire capitalism in a series of formal constitutional provisions elaborating foundational principles of social and economic equality. Like Ben-
Gurion, he feared that judges would use their powers of "interpretation" to
transform these new textual commitments into new juridical weapons against
the New Deal vision of the welfare state. Rather than write things down on
paper, he believed it was wiser to force courts to recognize that they suffer
from a profound "counter-majoritarian" difficulty, which required them to
defer to the political branches.

FDR's refusal to lead a popular campaign for the proposal and ratification of New Deal amendments has had a profound impact on the next sixty
years of constitutional development. As my discussion moves from the period of New Deal ascendancy to the Reagan Revolution and beyond, I will be
invoking a larger range of comparisons to explore the ways in which Roosevelt's refusal to constitutionalize charisma in the 1930s continues to haunt
twenty-first-century America as it confronts President Trump's demagogic
parody of government by the People.

The Founding Revisited

Begin at the beginning—and consider what we might learn about America's
eighteenth-century Founding from the revolutionary experiences of modern
France and South Africa.[1]

Start with some striking parallels between George Washington and Charles
de Gaulle. It was overwhelming defeat, not triumphant victory, that propelled
these men to the center of the revolutionary stage. In contrast to his fellow
generals, de Gaulle did not respond to France's military defeat in 1940 by
giving up the fight. Instead, he retreated to London to call upon his fellow

citizens to organize themselves for sustained revolutionary resistance to the Nazi regime.

The same was true of Washington. Once appointed commanding general in the spring of 1775, he managed to lose Boston, New York, and Philadelphia in quick succession—retreating to Valley Forge in the winter of 1777 on the verge of total defeat. Nevertheless, he refused to collaborate with the enemy in the manner of Benedict Arnold and other opportunists. Instead, his guerilla attack on the British at Trenton inspired demoralized American revolutionaries to continue their struggle for national liberation against all odds.

A second parallel arises at a later point in Time One—when the two military leaders finally gained decisive victories over their enemies after a long period of uncertain struggle. With their victories at Yorktown in 1781 and in Paris in 1944, Washington and de Gaulle emerged as unchallenged charismatic leaders of their national liberation movements. Yet despite their symbolic centrality, they failed to play a central role in constructing the first constitutions that governed the political lives of their newly liberated Peoples.

De Gaulle did attempt to take the lead, but his efforts were defeated by his fellow revolutionaries of the Resistance. With the voters repeatedly repudiating his presidentialist vision of constitutional democracy, the Hero of the Free French was forced to retreat in despair to Colombey-les-Deux-Églises. In contrast, Washington maintained cordial relations with his fellow revolutionaries. Nevertheless he too retreated, to his estate at Mount Vernon, and left it to his comrades to do the hard work required to win the unanimous assent of all thirteen states to America's first Constitution: the Articles of Confederation *and Perpetual Union*. (Please note that the official text includes the last three italicized words, not only the first three.)

The de Gaulle / Washington parallel continues to the next stage, when the Fourth Republic and the American Confederation confront existential crises. At this point, the two generals dramatically reemerge on the political stage—for the same two reasons.

First, their wartime struggles marked them out as paradigmatic patriots who sacrificed greatly for the Revolution at its moment of peril. Second, their failure to engage directly in the politics of the Fourth Republic / Confederation meant that they were untainted by the alleged failings of these regimes. With their revolutionary charisma intact, their call for a second "new beginning" would predictably gain a respectful hearing from the public, which vividly remembered the People's triumphant response to earlier calls by de Gaulle / Washington during the darkest hours of the revolutionary struggle against the Nazis / King George III. To put this charismatic dynamic in a formula: Past triumph + later disengagement = charismatic reassertion of revolutionary authority.

Call this *the logic of charismatic reengagement,* and we have seen it on vivid display in France. But two centuries earlier, James Madison was already well aware of its importance. As we shall see, the Constitutional Convention met under circumstances that gravely damaged its *legal* authority to sweep away the Articles of Confederation and replace them with a new revolutionary framework in the name of We the People. So far as Madison was concerned, Washington's presence at the Convention was absolutely necessary to fill this legitimacy gap. In revealing correspondence, he pleaded with the general to end his posture of detachment and return to the fray by presiding over the Convention—dramatizing to his countryman the imperative need to save the Revolution by endorsing a radical transformation in the Republic's constitutional arrangements.

Washington was hard to convince. But in the end, he responded positively to his friend's plea, and endowed the Convention with his charismatic authority.[2] To be sure, the general's dramatic support was not sufficient to guarantee the Convention's ultimate success in gaining legitimacy for its rerun of Time Two. Nevertheless, it was absolutely necessary—for precisely the same reason General de Gaulle's past success in speaking for the People during the Second World War was essential in gaining broad popular legitimacy for his effort to sweep away the Fourth Republic and replace it with the Fifth.

Despite this similarity, there were two large differences in the way de Gaulle and Washington deployed the logic of charismatic reengagement. In France, the revolutionary takeover of the Fourth Republic begins on a strongly militaristic note—with de Gaulle backing up his claim to speak for the People by threatening a military coup d'état. In contrast, before coming to Philadelphia, Washington had previously resisted the militarist temptation—refusing to heed calls from his army to seize power from the Continental Congress, and insisting that his comrades-in-arms must bid farewell to military life once they had defeated the British. This meant that the Philadelphia Convention's success in ousting the Confederation would be determined on civilian terrain.

The two generals also differed in their personal relationship to the radical constitutional proposals that gained their endorsement. De Gaulle had been repeatedly denouncing the Fourth Republic since its founding in 1946. As a consequence, there was no secret about his constitutional ambitions in overthrowing the established regime in 1958—everybody recognized that, if he succeeded, the new Republic would be reorganized on presidentialist lines.

Washington's concrete constitutional views were a mystery to the general public—and perhaps to himself as well. As a consequence, the prospects for his success in leading a campaign against the Confederation's authority seemed relatively bleak. Not only had he refused to supplement his charismatic capacity "to speak for the People" by engaging in Gaullist threats of military force. He had not even made it clear what, if anything, he thought "the People" were demanding as he took his place at the head of Madison's illegal Convention.

Madison was more like Washington than is generally recognized. He famously joined Hamilton and Jay in writing the Federalist Papers *after* the Convention advanced its initiative. But neither he nor his collaborators took to the newspapers *before* the Convention to explain to their fellow citizens why the Articles of Confederation needed fixing in the first place. Worse yet, Madison & Company did not clearly state that they were bent on repudiating, rather than amending, the Articles.

Once they met in Philadelphia, the Convention delegates found themselves bitterly divided on this very question. Only during the closing days did a majority vote decisively in favor of a revolutionary break with the existing system. Nevertheless, they kept this decision—and all others—secret during the entire four months it took to reach a full agreement on their revolutionary Constitution. They only told the general public what "We the People" were trying to accomplish as they were leaving Philadelphia. The conspiratorial character of their meeting further undermined the legitimacy of their enterprise.

The Articles themselves had been constructed in a far more open and deliberative fashion. Once representatives of the revolutionary state governments had declared their independence at the first Continental Congress, they immediately set to work on a constitution for the new Republic. By 1777 the Second Continental Congress had hammered out the terms of the Articles after extended debate, sending them out to the states for approval.

The ratification campaign was remarkably successful. Despite their divergent interests and ideologies, twelve revolutionary governments agreed to the Articles within two years. When Maryland went along in early 1781, its assent represented a remarkable triumph in the art of self-government. In joining the Confederation, the states explicitly gave up their claims to sovereignty, solemn affirming that "the Union shall be perpetual," and that its government will be called "the United States of America." In exchange, each state insisted on retaining the right to veto any effort to alter the Articles defining their perpetual Union. The final provision declared that no proposed amendment would be valid "unless such alteration be agreed to in a congress of the United States and be afterward confirmed by the legislatures of every state."

These words emphasize the truly revolutionary character of the Philadelphia Convention's assault on the "United States of America." It not only usurped the exclusive authority of the Confederation Congress to propose sweeping amendments in the name of the American People; it asserted that only nine, not thirteen states, needed to agree before the new government could come into existence.

Moreover, once the Articles of Confederation gained unanimous approval in March 1781 and "the United States of America" came into constitutional existence, the newly established Continental Congress was not, as legend has it, transparently unequal to the great challenges facing the nation. To the contrary, it passed its first great test with flying colors.

When George Washington beat the British at Yorktown in October 1781, the critical question was whether Congress could negotiate a peace treaty that would convince the liberated colonists that their wartime sacrifices were worthwhile. Predictably, different interest groups made different demands, but one issue was absolutely fundamental.

This involved the territorial definition of the United States. As the Declaration of Independence made clear, the revolutionaries insisted on claiming vast areas of the wilderness for their new nation. Yet this demand was resisted not only by the British, but by America's essential ally, Louis XVI of France. The French king's government had grown tired of spending vast sums to support the American rebellion, and it pressed Congress to accept a treaty that would have granted the United States sovereignty only over a narrow strip of land extending from the Eastern seaboard to the Appalachian Mountains.[3] If American negotiators had succumbed to French pressure, Congress would have indeed confronted a legitimation crisis of the first order. But the American negotiating team, led by John Jay and John Adams, managed to save the day. In a brilliant diplomatic coup, they induced the British to recognize the sovereignty of the United States over the "Northwest Territories," including all Crown lands south of Canada.[4]

No less remarkably, the Continental Congress followed up this diplomatic victory with a series of ordinances that not only provided settlers in the Northwest with a system of self-government, but the conditions under which they could gain admission to the Union. Most famously, the last of these ordinances provided that "neither slavery nor involuntary servitude" shall ever prevail within lands obtained from the British. The Continental Congress enacted this famous Northwest Ordinance on July 13, 1787—at the very same moment that the Philadelphia Convention finally reached its Great Compromise, which barred its proposed government from abolishing the slave trade for twenty years, and provided the South with a formula for congressional representation that would ensure its ability to protect domestic slaveholding for many decades to come.

The Continental Congress was also on the verge of a breakthrough on a second critical issue. As originally formulated, the Articles denied Congress the power to force the states to pay their allocated share of national expenses—leading to grave fiscal weakness. Until Maryland signed on to the Articles in 1781, Congress had little choice but to appeal to the patriotic sentiments of each state's legislature to supply the needed funds to sustain the war effort—with limited success. But now that the Confederation had come into constitutional existence, Congress appointed Robert Morris as superintendent of finance to strengthen its fiscal capacities. Morris took a host of controversial steps to deal with short-term problems, and also led Congress to propose a constitutional amendment that would authorize the federal Treasury to force the states to pay up. Within two years, the amendment gained the approval of twelve states, but Rhode Island refused to go along. Rather than taking no for an answer, Morris and Congress immediately proposed a new amendment granting it taxing power in 1783. Even Rhode Island gave its consent this time around, and by 1786 the initiative "came close to adoption," with all thirteen states passing resolutions approving the amendment.[5]

But New York's resolution posed a problem. Although it explicitly approved the amendment, it attached so many caveats that Congress refused to accept it unless the state endorsed Congress's new taxing power in a more affirmative fashion. In the meantime, Congress created a committee to implement the amendment "as soon as the State of New York shall have passed an Act acceding to the said system."[6]

Not for the last time, the fate of a stronger Union depended on New York. But despite his powerful position in the city, and his strong nationalistic convictions, Alexander Hamilton refused to throw his support behind the pragmatic reform of the existing system. He would settle for nothing less than a revolution against the "perpetual Union" established five years earlier—and by 1786 he was already joining Madison and others in issuing a call to the states for a Convention that would ultimately assemble in Philadelphia during the summer of 1787.

While the desertion of strong nationalists like Hamilton sufficed to undermine New York's wholehearted delegation of taxing power to the Confederation, the Philadelphia Convention predictably confronted a familiar obstacle in gaining unanimous support from state legislatures for their own revolutionary assembly. Predictably, Rhode Island denounced the entire enterprise, boycotting the Philadelphia meeting on the ground that the Articles authorized only the Continental Congress, and nobody else, to propose amendments to the *perpetual* union.

New York also posed a big problem. Its legislature had sent three delegates to the Convention, but only allowed a majority to approve any proposals on behalf of the state. Yet two of the New Yorkers—John Lansing and Robert Yates—walked out to protest the centralizing character of the emerging initiative, leaving only Alexander Hamilton at the secret sessions. As a consequence, the Convention did not even pretend that Hamilton's signature sufficed to bind his state. On the final roll call, only eleven state delegations are enumerated as approving the Constitution—New York and Rhode Island are omitted from the list.

Worse yet, other delegates followed the New Yorkers' example and walked out in response to the centralizing demands of the majority. These boycotts didn't stop the remaining delegates from signing the final text in the name of their states. Nonetheless, they cast a dark shadow on the legitimacy of the proceedings. At the end of the day, only 39 of the 55 delegates who arrived in Philadelphia actually stuck it out to the end and signed the final document.

The lawless conduct of yet another delegation also called the Convention's initiative into doubt. Delaware's legislature had expressly instructed its representatives to reject any proposal that deprived it of equal voting power in Congress. But Delaware's delegates chose to ignore this express command, and agreed to an arrangement in which more populous states would greatly outnumber their own state in the newly created House of Representatives. The Convention chose to include Delaware among the eleven states that had approved the final document, despite its delegates' blatant violation of their legislature's commands.

To further compound their legitimation problem, all the signatories defied the Articles' amendment provision in two more ways. First, the Convention entirely cut the state legislatures out of the ratification process, asserting that only specially elected ratifying conventions could determine the fate of their initiative. This assertion of power, in Article Seven of the Constitution, was especially remarkable, given that all delegates had been sent to Philadelphia by the very state legislatures they were now cutting out of the ratification process. Delegates came to Philadelphia as agents of the constitutionally established governments of their states, and they left as self-proclaimed revolutionaries purporting to speak in the authentic voice of "We the People of the United States."

This set the stage for a final act of self-aggrandizement. The Articles explicitly required all thirteen state legislatures to agree to any amendments of its original plan of revolutionary self-government. Nevertheless, the Philadelphia Convention proclaimed that if only nine state ratifying conventions approved, the new government would come into constitutional existence. Indeed, when President Washington and the first U.S. Congress took power in New York City in 1789, two states—Rhode Island and North Carolina—had not yet entered the Union. Constitutionally speaking, they remained faithful members of the "perpetual Union" that all thirteen states had previously established as the "United States of America."

So the new Republic began life as an oxymoron: It was a *secessionist* association of *nationalists* revolting against the perpetually *United* States. The Constitution's oxymoronic status came to an end only in May 1790 when the final holdout, Rhode Island, signified its consent. Even then, this state's ratifying convention met in blatant violation of Rhode Island law, and only consented to the new Union in response to a congressional threat of a devastating economic boycott if it continued to remain faithful to the Articles of Confederation.

Rhode Island's coerced consent was the last in a long series of deeply problematic episodes, illegal under the Articles, through which Madison & Company conducted their assault on the Perpetual Union and emerged triumphant by the narrowest of margins. I have provided a blow-by-blow account of this history in *We the People*. But my previous work framed this story in purely American terms—without asking how its revolutionary dynamics compare to those that have emerged more recently in other parts of the world.

When we view the Philadelphians' assault on legality from a comparative perspective, two points help account for their improbable success. The first is cultural. Many other constitutional cultures teach their inhabitants to equate illegality with illegitimacy, but the eighteenth-century English recognized a third possibility. In their constitutional tradition, a "convention" was the name of a *legally defective* parliament. Rather than looking upon such "conventions" with suspicion, the British celebrated their constructive possibilities—since the great achievements of the Glorious Revolution of 1688 would have been impossible without this boundary-crossing vehicle.

To see why, consider that a parliament, under English law, is a tripartite body consisting of Monarch + House of Lords + House of Commons. This meant that once King James II fled the country, his triumphant opponents confronted a constitutional conundrum: Since the king was absent, a proper parliament could not be convened to call William and Mary to the throne. Even more important, the victorious Whigs were determined to prevent the new line of Hanoverians from ever repeating the abuses of the Stuarts. As a consequence, the two Houses at Westminster passed a Declaration of Right during the time that the throne remained vacant, and then insisted that the new king and queen swear to obey the Declaration before they would be allowed to ascend to power.

To achieve these ends, the Whigs confronted a final obstacle. The membership of both the Commons and the Lords had been greatly depleted in the struggle to oust the Stuarts, and the ragtag remnants sitting in Westminster could not even pretend to operate as fully legitimate chambers of parliament. Rather than impose their will by fiat, the victors issued a call for the election of a new House of Commons to join the Lords in a "Convention" to govern the kingdom in the absence of a king.

It was this self-conscious embrace of a legally problematic "convention" as a *legitimate* higher lawmaking body that served as the American colonists' great precedent in their own liberation struggle against George III's arbitrary rule. From the very beginning of their revolt, they called innumerable "conventions" to make their demands on London for reform of the Crown's established modes of colonial rule which the Americans found increasingly unacceptable.

Nevertheless, rule by convention generates an obvious problem: it is all too easy for one or another group of local troublemakers to call themselves a "convention" and make demands in the name of the People. How, then, to prevent a multiplicity of revolutionary "conventions" from splintering the movement, thereby enabling King George's troops to crush the divided revolutionaries in their struggle for national liberation?

Here is where a second fundamental factor helps account for the American success. From the very beginning, British settlers had been granted substantial powers of self-government in their colonial assemblies—and it is these assemblies that spearheaded the revolution. They signaled their rejection of imperial demands *by calling themselves* "conventions" and refusing to meet with the king's representatives in the standard fashion. Because these "conventions" had been elected in a fashion rooted in a century of practice, nobody considered them garden-variety "troublemakers." If anybody could appropriately decide that the time had come for a revolutionary "convention," these duly elected members of their community were the ones to do it!

It was this logic that enabled state conventions to invoke the precedent of the Glorious Revolution in a broadly credible fashion. This, in turn, provided the context within which Washington and other revolutionary heroes could credibly assert that the time had come for *responsible* revolutionaries to use "conventional" methods to launch a *second* revolution against the government established by the Articles.

To sum up: Washington's symbolic leadership was important—but it should not be understood in a cultural vacuum. When the Federalists persuaded most state legislatures to send delegates to another "Convention" in Philadelphia, they were building on both a distinctive boundary-breaking idea inherited from England and a deeply entrenched practice of self-government developed over the course of the preceding century.

Theory + practice = a *legitimately* illegal assembly. Our previous case studies reveal a series of variations on this theme—though I have called them "*un*conventional adaptations," given the subsequent evolution of the meaning of "convention" in ordinary language. Several of these cases, moreover, provide particularly insightful perspectives on the Founders' situation, but for now, let's focus on only one. This involves another struggle for independence against the British Empire—this time, in India.

Once again, the British provided local residents with institutions for self-government, culminating in the Government of India Act of 1935. As we have seen, Nehru and other leaders of the Congress Party used these assemblies to demonstrate that their movement aimed for something more than episodic acts of civil disobedience—but was entirely capable of engaging in responsible acts of self-government. To be sure, the Indian assemblies were not nearly as historically entrenched, or as powerful, as their counterparts in British North America. Nevertheless, the combination of engaged self-government *and* organized civil disobedience from 1935 was crucial in preparing the way for a broad recognition of Congress's *legitimate* claim to speak for the People at India's moment of independence in 1948.

Of course, Washington and the Convention had a much tougher job than Nehru and his assembly. While the Congress Party was occupying a vacuum left by the British, the Philadelphians were rebelling against a perpetual Union already established by their fellow revolutionaries. Little wonder, then, that their desperate efforts to legitimate their takeover generated powerful protests against their power grab.

The most significant came from the New York ratifying convention, which gave its consent by the narrowest of margins. As part of the final compromise that enabled passage of its ratification resolution, the New York convention called upon other states to join with it in organizing yet another nationwide Convention to rethink the radical changes that the Philadelphians were imposing on their country. In its circular letter to sister states, the New Yorkers explained that "several of the articles appear so exceptional to a majority of us, that nothing but the fullest confidence of a revision of them by a general convention . . . could have prevailed a sufficient number [of us] to ratify it."[7]

New York's effort to repudiate the Philadelphia Convention explains why Madison pushed the Bill of Rights through Congress with blinding speed at its opening session. By September 28, 1789, he and his allies had won the two-thirds majorities required to send the amendments to the state legislatures for their consent. This was a moment when neither North Carolina nor Rhode Island had yet signed on to the Constitution. Madison's aim was to persuade them, and the skeptics in New York and elsewhere, to give up their demands for another revolutionary Convention, and to channel their energies into the ratification of amendments that were responsive to their fears of centralizing tyranny.

His rapid response was a strategic success, and greatly enhanced the legitimacy of the entire Federalist project. By joining the campaign for Madison's amendments, leading anti-Federalists were now building on the framework constructed at Philadelphia, rather than devoting their energies to the mobilization of a nationwide movement to sweep it away.

Madison's outreach effort was broadly comparable to the French and Italian dynamic that gained broad credibility for their revolutionary constitutions after the Second World War. As in the American case, the ideological differences separating the wartime Resistance movements of Communists, Socialists, and Christian Democrats quickly reemerged when the Nazis were defeated. Nevertheless, these bitter rivals managed to suspend their *future*-oriented disagreements long enough to construct a Constitution that expressed the common principles unifying their *past* resistance to totalitarian oppression.

The Federalists were the first, but by no means the last, to succeed in transforming the act of constitutional creation into a unifying enterprise—and the great significance of their achievement is only emphasized by the failure of other revolutionaries, in places like Poland and Israel, to gain a similar success. Nevertheless, this founding triumph did not ensure the Constitution's short-term survival, let alone its long-term endurance.

Time Three: Succession Crisis

Washington had gained his charismatic centrality in the manner of Charles de Gaulle, but he was determined to conduct his presidency in the manner of Nelson Mandela. In forming his government, he reached out to other revolutionary leaders who pursued very different ideologies and regional interests. At the same time, he tried to stand above the fray as president of all the People.[8]

He was far less successful than his South African counterpart, however, in preparing the way for a smooth transfer of power to his successors. Mandela left the presidency after the collapse of the Soviet Union had put an end to the worldwide struggle between communism and capitalism that had dominated the postwar era. This greatly advantaged Thabo Mbeki, who had made his peace with the emerging neoliberal consensus, in his competition with unrepentant class warriors for the top job.

George Washington, in contrast, left the presidency at a time when the French Revolution was challenging Americans to redefine the very foundations of their constitutional identity. When the president took his oath of office in 1789, Parisians had not yet stormed the Bastille; when he took his second oath in 1793, Louis XVI had been sent to the guillotine by a revolutionary Republic that, like its New World counterpart, asserted its authority to speak in the name of the People. These dramatic events gripped the American public imagination—as rival newspapers provided competing accounts that fueled countless local debates that divided citizens into pro-French and anti-French camps, splitting the broad coalition that had previously thrown its support behind the Constitution and Bill of Rights.

The leading candidates to succeed Washington—John Adams and Thomas Jefferson—outstripped their competitors precisely because, as ambassadors to Britain and France during the 1780s, they expressed these competing positions with unrivaled clarity. The French-speaking Jefferson was engaged in an extraordinary balancing act during his five-year stay between 1785 and

1790—involving himself both in complex diplomatic initiatives with the royal government at Versailles and in remarkably fruitful conversations with leading Enlightenment intellectuals in Paris. Called back by Washington to serve as secretary of state, Jefferson insisted that America's treaty of 1778 with Louis XVI had taken on even greater significance now that the French had overthrown their king in the name of the very same Enlightenment ideals that had inspired the Philadelphia Convention. It was only right, then, for the United States to reaffirm its treaty obligations and assist its sister republic in its struggle for survival against King George III and his Continental allies.

For John Adams, such talk was nothing more than idealistic nonsense, obscuring crucial military realities. His basic point: If America sided with France, this would invite a British invasion from Canada and an ongoing assault on the high seas from the Royal Navy. America was militarily unprepared to withstand this two-pronged attack. The only way to save the American Republic was to abandon France and keep the peace with Britain.

Adams was in a unique position to make this case. As ambassador to Britain in 1783, he had already declared his independence from France when negotiating a peace treaty with Britain recognizing American independence. Recall that the French king, tiring of the Americans' endless drain on his resources, had demanded that the Confederation Congress accept a treaty that recognized American sovereignty only over a thin strip of the Eastern seaboard bounded by the Appalachian Mountains. It was only by convincing the British that a more generous offer was in their economic self-interest that Adams secured a diplomatic coup by gaining their recognition of American sovereignty over the Northwest Territories. If rapprochement with King George III had been so successful in 1783, why wouldn't it work again if Adams won the presidency in 1797?

Jefferson and Adams were standard-bearers in the struggle over America's political identity, but their long stays abroad had detached them from real-world politics at home. Neither had a chance of winning the presidency without the aid of leaders who had deeper domestic roots—and it is here that Madison and Hamilton provided essential assistance. They had previously joined forces in support of the Philadelphia Convention's assault on the Confederation. But they now split apart, with Hamilton taking a pro-British line as Washington's Secretary of the Treasury and operating as de facto leader of a radically reorganized Federalist Party. Madison began organizing the anti-Federalist opposition when serving in the House of Representatives while giving broad support to Jefferson as secretary of state.

Despite his Mandela-like aspirations, Washington had far more difficulty rising above these bitter debates. He increasingly threw his support behind a pro-British foreign policy—as well as Hamilton's campaign to create a Bank of the United States that was modeled on the Bank of England. This led Jefferson to resign as secretary of state in 1793 and retreat to a self-imposed political exile at Monticello. In the meantime, Madison had spearheaded a series of statewide Republican electoral challenges to Federalist ascendancy. When Washington shocked the nation by refusing to run for a third term in 1796, both movement parties mobilized their supporters to win the presidency for their rival ideological champions.

When the results came in, Adams emerged victorious by a narrow margin while his fellow Federalists gained strong majorities in both the House and the Senate. As a consequence, the new president was in a position to vindicate his pro-British views. With the consent of Congress, he imposed an embargo on trade with France—backing it up with orders to his small navy to capture any vessels daring to defy the ban. At the same time, he took aggressive steps to prevent his opponents from challenging his anti-French position, encouraging Congress to pass the Sedition Act of 1798, which made it a crime to make false statements critical of the federal government.

This provoked Jefferson and Madison to denounce the statute in resolutions that were endorsed by Republican-dominated legislatures in Kentucky and Virginia. Both resolutions not only declared that the sedition law violated the Bill of Rights; they claimed that because Congress had broken the constitutional compact, the states had the sovereign right to block any effort to enforce the sedition law within their boundaries. This dramatic reassertion of state sovereignty was a radical about-face, especially for Madison, who had led the campaign for national supremacy at the Philadelphia Convention.

But such logic-chopping objections were beside the point: the Republicans were battling for their political survival. As they organized themselves for a desperate effort to win the presidency for Jefferson in 1800, the federal judiciary responded by throwing a string of Republican newspaper editors in jail for their seditious opposition to Adams's military campaign against the French Revolution.

So far as the Republicans were concerned, this framed the 1800 presidential election in especially stark terms: the Federalists were not only betraying France; they were allying themselves with the very same British king whose oppressive behavior had provoked the Declaration of Independence. So the election of 1800 boiled down to a simple question: Would the American people choose Jefferson, the author of the Declaration, or Adams, the ally of King George III?

When viewed from a comparative angle, the election posed a classic case of a succession crisis, in which Washington's departure opened up a fierce competition between rival views of the meaning of the Founding. Once again, the emerging scenario most closely resembled the Time Three dynamic that played out in India. Here, too, Indira Gandhi and her New Congress Party spearheaded a radical break with core commitments codified by the Constitution of 1950—throwing old-time revolutionary defenders of the Nehruvian legacy into jail during her notorious State of Emergency. When Gandhi called new elections to ratify this move, and released her opponents from prison, they managed to rally the country against her efforts to repudiate the constitutional framework established at Time Two.

The same logic played out in America, though in less dramatic fashion. The Jeffersonian newspaper editors were thrown in jail for opposing Adams's alliance with King George III, but there was no Indira-like roundup of opposition leaders. Instead, Republican party networks in each state remained intact. At the same time, Adams did not suffer a crushing electoral defeat of the kind that swept Indira Gandhi from power in the immediate aftermath of the Emergency. Instead, he was narrowly defeated by Jefferson, who claimed the presidency on the basis of a 73-to-65 Electoral College vote. Both candidates relied heavily on support from their home regions, with Adams carrying New England and Jefferson much of the South. But in Jefferson's case, his vice-presidential running mate, Aaron Burr, made a critical contribution—carrying the 12 electoral votes from his home state of New York for the Republican ticket.

Without Burr's victory, Adams would have won a second term. If he had done so, there is good reason to believe that Jefferson would have continued his public protests against Adams's pro-British policies, advancing claims that Federalist partisans would have denounced as "false" under the Sedition Act. Since federal judges had willingly presided over sedition trials during the run-up to the 1800 elections, there is every reason to expect that they would have continued throwing prominent Republicans into jail throughout Adams's second term. Indeed, sedition prosecutions continued in Federalist New England until 1803 before the Jefferson administration managed to force their termination.

Worse yet, the succession crisis had not been resolved by Jefferson's seeming victory in the Electoral College—the result remained in doubt because of the way the Philadelphia Convention designed the system of presidential selection in 1787. Although much of the Constitution is framed in terms of relatively abstract principles, this isn't true when the text turns to presidential selection. Instead, the constitutional text puts forth an elaborate set of hard-edged rules governing the process—devoting almost 500 words of its 4,500-word text to this single subject. Nevertheless, all this textual detail was not the product of sustained deliberation. It was a rush job that emerged only late in the day, as a result of the delegates' grim determination to leave Philadelphia and get back home by mid-September. In their eagerness to get out of town, the delegates made a string of serious blunders that called Jefferson's Electoral College victory into question and generated a succession crisis that threatened to spiral out of control and sweep away the entire institutional system that the Founders had created.

Before turning to a blow-by-blow account of the Electoral College crisis of 1800, let's first consider the mistakes made in 1787, and how they propelled the Republic to the precipice of destruction at the turn of the century.

Founding Blunders

During earlier debates at the Convention, the Philadelphians repeatedly found themselves at loggerheads when confronting basic issues defining the powers and selection of the president. As their energy began to fade in the heat of summer, the delegates passed the buck to a special three-member committee and charged it with proposing sensible compromises on key issues. To ensure its impartiality, David Brearley, not James Madison, was put in charge.

This effort at reconciliation turned out to be a fiasco. Given the Convention's eagerness to bring their business to a close, Brearley had hoped to issue a report by September 1. But on August 21 he was writing his fellow delegate, William Paterson, that he had "no prospect of getting through" before the end of September. In his letter, he implored Paterson, who was in New Jersey at the time, to return to Philadelphia to help him out:

> Every article is again argued over, with as much earnestness and obstinacy as before it was committed. We have lately made a rule to meet at ten and 'til four, which punctually complied with [so as to permit the members to attend plenary sessions]. Cannot you come down and assist us,—we have many reasons for desiring this; our duty, in the manner we now sit, is quite too hard for three, but a much stronger reason is, that we actually stand in need of your abilities.[9]

The Convention wasn't willing to wait for Paterson's return. Instead it provided Brearley with reinforcements the same day he wrote his despairing letter—transforming his small group into an eleven-member Committee on Postponed Parts, with a representative from each of the states then in attendance. This broadened the committee's potential base of support, but it was then given the impossible deadline of September 1 to begin reporting its recommendations to the Convention as a whole.

On Tuesday, September 4, Gouverneur Morris presented the case for the committee's proposals on the presidency. Although its concrete plan went nowhere, two of its proposals shaped the following two days of rapid-fire debate—with the Convention casting nine up-and-down votes on Wednesday and twenty on Thursday in a desperate effort to get to Yes before they began their exodus from Philadelphia.

In making his presentation, Gouverneur Morris made it clear that "many" members were in favor of "an immediate choice by the people" of the nation's president. Yet the committee refrained from advancing a "direct election" proposal to the floor. If they had done so, America might not have repeatedly witnessed candidates gaining the White House despite their loss of the popular vote.

This brings us to the committee's second key decision. Instead of moving ahead with direct election, it proposed the creation of an Electoral College to choose the country's head of state. While its particular design of the College was rejected, its formula for state representation endured. This famously guaranteed three delegates to the smallest states—two based on their equal representation in the Senate, one on their single representative in the House.[10]

At the same time, it assured the most populous states many more electors, based on their more numerous House delegations. In 1800 this meant that Virginia obtained 24 electoral votes while Delaware only got 3. But the mathematical implications were already obvious in 1787, and the small states insisted on some device that would prevent three or four big states from getting together and throwing all their votes behind a single candidate—giving that candidate an Electoral College majority even if the remaining states were overwhelmingly opposed. After a rapid series of (inconsistent) votes on Thursday, September 6, the Convention hit upon a particularly clever way of calming these small-state anxieties.

This involved the vice presidency.[11] Instead of instructing electors to designate one candidate as president and another as vice president, the Convention instructed each elector to cast *two* votes for the top spot—with the proviso that only one candidate could come from their home state. This required electors to look beyond their boundaries for at least one candidate with a truly national reputation for public service—"continental characters," as they were called at the time.

This double-vote system seemed perfectly plausible in 1787. Given Washington's past acts of statesmanship, it was clear that the College would elect him president by an overwhelming majority. Once he set a precedent for public-spirited statesmanship, it was reasonable to expect that members of future Electoral Colleges would be on the lookout for candidates who, like Washington, would make a serious effort to transcend provincial concerns in pursuit of the national interest. Even if such a continental character came from tiny Delaware, electors from Virginia or New York might well vote for him—given the fact that they couldn't cast their second ballot for another home-stater. By imposing this restriction on each elector's second vote, the Convention did the best it could to ameliorate small-state anxieties while preserving the big-state advantage in choosing the country's head of state—and so it was no surprise that the "double-vote" proposal gained the support of a strong majority.

Nevertheless, this super-clever solution generated a new set of technical problems. Even if the "double vote" rule did motivate the search for Washington-equivalents, several continental characters might emerge as front-runners without any of them winning an electoral vote majority. Or, on rare occasions, two front-runners might each win a majority, but end up in a tie—requiring some institution to operate as a tiebreaker. To its great credit, the Convention immediately saw this problem and did not end its Thursday session without resolving it. The delegates ultimately decided to deny the Senate any role as a tiebreaker—because, unlike the House, its members were not directly elected by the voters, but chosen by state legislatures, and therefore lacked the democratic legitimacy to decide close cases.

This sensible solution, however, once again threatened to give a few big states the decisive voice, so the Convention tried to respond to small-state objections by creating a special voting rule to govern decisions by the House when the Electoral College failed to pick out a clear majority winner. In this special case, each House delegation—whatever its size—would cast a single vote in deciding who would ascend to the presidency. If a majority of state delegations didn't initially converge on a single candidate, they would be required to keep on voting until enough delegations switched from their top choice to a "compromise" candidate who was acceptable to at least a majority of the states.[12]

All in all, the Convention had put in a tremendous day's work in resolving so many technical problems in their effort to achieve a sensible solution to the ongoing struggle for power between large and small states in the new federation. But when the delegates returned the next day to polish up their draft, they made a last-minute change that jeopardized their entire achievement. As Roger Sherman pointed out to his colleagues, their draft had thus far left the vice president "without employment" unless the sitting president was incapable of performing his duties.[13] In response, the Convention voted to give him a steady job, and named him presiding officer of the Senate.

This created an obvious problem. The sitting vice president, after all, had finished second in the previous electoral contest—and so was a likely candidate for the top job the next time around. If the vice president was a candidate in that next election and a tiebreak was needed, the sitting vice president could use his position as presiding officer over the tie-breaking procedure to manipulate the rules in his own favor. The Convention, in short, was in danger of violating a fundamental principle of justice—"nobody should be a judge in his own case"—in a situation where it could allow a candidate to weasel his way into the White House. Nevertheless, in their rush to move on to other issues, the delegates failed to appreciate the link between their decision to make the vice president the presiding officer of the Senate and their earlier decision to give the Senate's presiding officer the task of chairing the process of presidential selection by the House.[14]

Americans would be paying a high price in 1800 for this blunder of 1787. Because Adams narrowly defeated Jefferson in 1796, his rival would become vice-president and preside over the electoral vote count in February 1801. When Georgia's ballot was opened, it contained very serious irregularities—which, if acknowledged, would have gravely endangered Jefferson's ascent to the presidency. As we shall see, Jefferson's self-interested ruling on the Georgia ballot precipitated a grave crisis.

But first, it's important to see how another last-minute blunder at Philadelphia escalated the crisis to truly existential proportions. As the Convention delegates rushed to the exits in early September, they failed to revise the constitutional text to guarantee that the newly elected House would be casting the tiebreaking vote if the Electoral College didn't select a clear majority winner. Instead, their final draft permitted the lame-duck House, elected in 1798, to stay in existence until the new president took office on March 4, 1801.[15]

In practical terms, this made all the difference. There were sixteen states in the Union in 1800, and Jefferson needed the support of nine House delegations to gain the presidency. But the old House, elected in 1798, was controlled by a Federalist majority—which was distributed among the states in a fashion that deprived Jefferson of the nine states he needed to win.

Of course, if the Republicans had gained a decisive victory in the Electoral College, they could avoid the threat of a fierce confrontation between the Federalist majority supporting Adams in the House and the self-interested efforts by Jefferson, as presiding officer, to propel himself into the White House.

This is the point at which a final factor entered into the mix. This problem cannot be fairly attributed to the Philadelphians' desire to get out of town by mid-September. Even if they had taken more time, they could not have anticipated the storming of the Bastille in 1789, or the way the French Revolution would split apart the broad coalition that had managed to gain broad public support for the Constitution of 1787.

Impasse in the House, Crisis in the Country

By the time Washington left office, the tie-breaking provisions of the text presented unanticipated challenges to Federalists and Republicans as they struggled to gain control over the presidency. In 1796, for example, both parties found it easy to settle on Adams and Jefferson as their presidential standard-bearers. Yet they had not yet achieved the same degree of organizational discipline when it came to their vice presidential choices. While Adams won the top spot with 71 votes, only 59 Federalist electors voted for Thomas Pinckney, their party's pick for the second spot. This is why Jefferson's 68 votes were good enough to gain the vice presidency.

By 1800 each party's electors had learned from this mistake. Federalists solidly backed Pinckney and Republicans backed Burr on their second ballots for president. But the Federalists were mindful of the fact that, under the 1787 rules, they would throw the election into the House if both Adams and Pinckney won precisely the same number of votes. As a consequence, one of their electors cast a ballot for John Jay as vice president—leaving Pinckney with only 64 votes compared to Adams's 65. So if Adams had won, he would have emerged with a clear Electoral College majority and taken a detour around the House to ascend immediately to the presidency.

The Republicans weren't as well organized. They allowed all 73 of their electors to vote for Burr as well as Jefferson—generating a tie that threw the election into the House. This shouldn't have been a problem, since Republicans had also swept into power in the House, giving them control of more than 60 percent of the seats—making it easy for them to deliver a majority of state delegations for Jefferson. But this is precisely where a terrible result was generated by the Philadelphians' failure to guarantee that the newly elected House would be making this decision. With Burr and Jefferson in a dead heat, it would be up to the lame-duck Federalist House to choose between them as it convened on February 11, 1801, to select the incoming president.

Worse yet, under the timetable authorized by the Constitution, the four-year terms of both the Federalist House and President Adams would expire on March 4—leaving the country utterly at sea if the Federalist House refused to elect Jefferson as his successor. With anxiety sweeping the country at the prospect of an empty presidential chair, Federalist newspapers published an essay by John Marshall that added further fuel to the flames.

It was published in early January, a month before the House would begin casting ballots in early February—giving lots of ordinary citizens, as well as all the protagonists, time to appreciate its threatening message. Adopting the custom of the time, Marshall published his essay under a pseudonym—Horatius, for a Roman warrior who had heroically sacrificed his life to save the ancient Republic from destruction. He argued that John Adams could constitutionally appoint his secretary of state to serve as interim chief executive while the states organized a second round of elections for the presidency.

Horatius made his case with characteristic Marshallian vigor—providing powerful textual support for his position. Nonetheless, the argument took on a dramatically self-interested character because Marshall himself was Adams's secretary of state! By the time the House began voting for the next president in early February, moreover, the Federalist Senate had also confirmed Marshall's appointment as Chief Justice of the United States!!

Horatius was setting the stage for a struggle that would shake the very foundations of the new republic. As the clock ticked toward midnight of March 3, Marshall not only threatened to emerge as interim president, but he would also be serving as acting secretary of state and permanent Chief Justice. Jefferson, in contrast, would enjoy no official position whatsoever, now that his vice-presidential term had expired. Yet the fact remained that he had won the election, and nobody could expect his mobilized followers to allow the Federalist power play to go unchallenged.

Jefferson was well aware of the escalating danger as he took the podium to preside over the opening of Electoral College ballots on February 11. Nevertheless, he refused to reach out to the Federalists to encourage its bipartisan resolution. As the clerk opened Georgia's documents, it was perfectly plain that they had not been prepared in the fashion required by the constitutional text. Yet they reported that Georgia's electors had chosen Jefferson and Burr for the two top spots. If Georgia's four votes were excluded, both Republican candidates would be left with only 70 votes—one less than the 71 each needed for to win an Electoral College majority. The fact that this still put them ahead of Adams (65) and Pinckney (64) was not enough, under the rules, to eliminate their rivals from contention. Instead, the Federalist House would be free to vote for the Federalist candidates to serve as president and vice president instead of their Republican rivals.

Seeing their opening, the Federalists rose to the floor to demand that Georgia's votes be set aside—and that, at the very least, proceedings be suspended while a special commission of inquiry was dispatched to Georgia to find out the truth. At this point, Jefferson confronted a moment of truth of his own. If he were to discharge his duties as an impartial presiding officer, his next move was clear: allow a full and free debate on the issue to give the House an opportunity to reach a sober judgment on the proper way to respond to Georgia's voting irregularities. Yet he took a very different course. He peremptorily ruled Federalist objections out of order—and, with pandemonium breaking out on the floor, ordered the clerk to count Georgia's four votes in his own column.

Jefferson's blatantly self-interested conduct ended all hope for a bipartisan settlement of the crisis. During the next seven days, the country witnessed the House engaging in thirty-five rounds of voting, each time with the same result. Since Adams was now out of the race, Federalist delegations in six states did the next best thing and voted against Jefferson by marking their ballots for Burr; two states found themselves split down the middle and abstained. The eight remaining states voted for Jefferson, leaving him one short of the nine required by the constitutional text.

As the clock ticked onward to March 4, another figure added his considerable ego into the dispute. Aaron Burr had it within his power to break the impasse by making it clear that he would never accept the presidency despite the six Federalist votes on his behalf. But he refused to do so. Instead, his partisans began to campaign for a "compromise" in which the House would turn to Burr instead of Jefferson in an effort to unify the country. After all,

New York's twelve electoral votes had provided the Republicans with their margin of victory. If the state had gone Federalist, Jefferson would have lost to Adams 77 to 61. So was it really wrong to make Burr president?

Loyal Republicans immediately denounced the Burrites for raising this question. Everybody knew that it was Jefferson who had been the standard-bearer in the Republicans' campaign for their "Revolution of 1800" against Adams's Anglophile politics. A "compromise" under which Jefferson would serve as vice president under Burr would transform the recent election into a farce.

With Republican ranks in turmoil, and Marshall's emergence as acting president / secretary of state / chief justice increasingly likely on March 4, news arrived of an even grimmer prospect. Rival militias in the North and South had begun organizing themselves for a march on Washington, D.C., to resolve the impasse by force. Once again, the parallel with France was striking—chaos at the National Convention was the ultimate source of Napoleon's rise to power from the ashes of the revolutionary republic.

This is the moment when Alexander Hamilton emerged to play a decisive role in preventing a disastrous conclusion to the House impasse. As secretary of the Treasury during Washington's administration, he had long-standing connections with Federalists in the House, but he had broken with Adams in recent years and opposed his reelection. As a consequence, he had been content to sit on the sidelines as the protagonists lurched toward the precipice. But the rise of Burr as a potential "compromise candidate" spurred him into action. Over the past twenty years, the two men had engaged in a fierce struggle for power in New York politics, which would soon culminate in a duel leading to Hamilton's death. At this point, however, Hamilton seized the opportunity to prevent Burr from becoming president since this would have permitted him to use his executive powers to destroy Hamilton's political position in New York.

This clear and present danger made Hamilton's philosophical disagreements with Jefferson seem trivial by comparison. He suddenly intervened in the contest, and played a key role in breaking the impasse on the thirty-sixth ballot—persuading Federalists in Maryland and Vermont to stop voting for Burr and throw their states into Jefferson's column, giving him his nine-state majority. In taking this step, Hamilton was also motivated by the seriousness of the crisis; but his past passivity suggests that the prospect of a Burr presidency played a key role in breaking the House impasse before the militias moved into action.

There is, of course, a lot more to say about this story, which I have elaborated elsewhere at greater length.[16] Yet modern-day jurists like Scalia and Gorsuch, as well as their scholarly supporters, have erased it from their so-called originalist understanding of the Constitution—because it challenges the basic premise of their entire approach. It is just plain wrong for so-called originalists to view the Constitutional Convention as a "miracle at Philadelphia" that firmly set the nation on a path to greatness over the next two centuries. The truth is very different: Given the delegates' blunders as they rushed to the exits, the miracle is that the Constitution managed to survive beyond 1800.

To put the point comparatively: If we contrast the Philadelphians with the other case studies considered in this book, only Solidarity did a worse job in hammering out a constitution at Time Two that sustained the government's legitimacy during its succession crisis at Time Three. To be sure, other revolutionary republics also had a difficult time filling the "legitimacy vacuum" left by the departure of Nehru or Mandela or de Gaulle or De Gasperi. In each case, the constitutional order established at the Founding managed to survive only through a combination of statecraft, compromise, and sheer luck. But it is sheer parochialism for originalists to suppose that the Convention was unique and had magically put the country on a solid path to progress.

Instead, 1787 inaugurated a revolutionary cycle. As each new generation of Americans rose to power, new movements came to the fore demanding radical revisions of established constitutional understandings. Sometimes these revolutionary movements succeeded and sometimes they failed, but their challenges to the status quo have always had an impact on the pre-existing constitutional framework.

This is especially important to recognize at the present moment. While Donald Trump's blatant self-promotion and fact-free tweets are quintessentially twenty-first century, his message resonates within a long tradition. Like it or not, his angry call to "drain the swamp" marks him out as yet another revolutionary outsider determined to sweep away the old insider-elite in the name of the American People. In this fundamental respect, he does not differ from George Washington or Abraham Lincoln or Franklin Roosevelt, or less-successful revolutionaries in other generations who used their presidencies as vehicles for radical "new beginnings."

Trump's message, and his uses of power, differ dramatically from these earlier exercises in presidential leadership. Nevertheless, if we consider him unique, we blind ourselves to the possibility that twenty-first-century Americans have something valuable to learn from the precedents set by previous revolutionary presidents as they try to gain perspective on their present predicaments.

There are many past presidencies that can provide much-needed context, but I will be focusing on the effort by Franklin Roosevelt to win constitutional legitimacy for the New Deal in the 1930s. I will argue that the legacy left behind by the court-packing crisis of 1937 contributes significantly to the authoritarian dangers posed by Trump—and that, if Americans are to successfully defeat this very real threat, they should reverse some basic decisions made by Roosevelt in his epic struggle with the Supreme Court.

The New Deal Revolution

The United States has been the scene of three great constitutional revolutions. The first was led by Federalists in the eighteenth century; the second, by Radical Republicans in the nineteenth; the third, by New Deal Democrats in the twentieth.

All three shared a common aim—a radical transfer of power from the states to the central government. Without such a transfer, the country could not confront, let alone resolve, the looming crises that threatened to overwhelm it—or so the revolutionaries asserted in all three eras. In each century, the insurgents focused their critique on a different aspect of the power-sharing arrangement between center and periphery. In 1787 the Convention targeted the state-centered system established by the Articles and transferred some important powers to the central government. But as the founding generation passed from the scene, it handed on a federation in which the states still played a dominant role.

After the Civil War, Radical Republicans in Congress reversed this balance. Their Reconstruction Amendments put an end to slavery and authorized federal intervention in local political and social life in ways that were previously unthinkable. Nevertheless, the nation-centered federation that emerged during the following decades still reserved a great deal of autonomy to the states.

It was only the New Deal revolution of the 1930s that repudiated "state sovereignty" as a fundamental restriction on the exercise of national power. By Roosevelt's third term in office, the New Deal Court was making it clear that federalism imposed no limits on the national government's newly won authority to pursue social justice and economic welfare for the nation as a whole. This didn't imply that federalism was unimportant. But from now on, it would be up to the president and Congress to determine when states' rights got in the way of the wide-ranging national mandate that had been recently granted by "We the People of the *United* States."[17]

The New Dealers' victory did not come easily. Like their predecessors, they had revolutionary aims that provoked bitter opposition from traditionalists who struggled mightily to defend the status quo. But by the 1940s, mainstream politicians in both parties had accepted the basic premises of the New Deal regime, consigning bitter-enders to the political periphery. It was only with the Reagan revolution of the 1980s that opponents of unlimited national government began a serious comeback. I suggest, however, that these more recent efforts to repudiate the New Deal are best understood by first considering some defining aspects of the Roosevelt revolution that set the stage for more recent efforts to restrain the regulatory ambitions of politicians and bureaucrats in Washington, D.C.

My key point: The New Dealers did not achieve their victory by following the script provided by the Founding Federalists and Reconstruction Republicans. They did not try to legitimate their nationalist revolution by hammering out a set of constitutional texts in the name of We the People. They accomplished the same end by different means. In the aftermath of Roosevelt's unprecedented electoral landslide in 1936, the president famously threatened to pack the Supreme Court if it continued to veto his initiatives. When the conservatives on the Court made their "switch in time" and called off their offensive, Roosevelt sealed his victory by replacing them with committed New Dealers as the old-timers left the bench.

By the 1940s, Americans were witnessing a dramatic turnaround. On the juristic level, the Supreme Court's opinions were sweeping away the remnants of Old Court jurisprudence and constructing the foundations of the New Deal order that would replace it. On the political level, mainstream Republicans were turning to candidates, like Thomas E. Dewey, who had made their peace with the New Deal. These dual developments conveyed a clear message—the Roosevelt Revolution had indeed gained the broad and sustained support of the American people.

Nevertheless, Roosevelt's failure to codify the high-energy politics of the New Deal into decisive constitutional texts was a matter of great importance. This is the lesson suggested by comparing leaders like Nehru or de Gaulle, who constitutionalized their charisma, with leaders like Wałesa or Ben-Gurion, who didn't. Yet American analysts typically fail to reflect on the implications of Roosevelt's decision to choose Ben-Gurion's path over Nehru's.

It's perfectly understandable that commentators typically dismiss the New Deal amendment scenario—given Article Five's requirement of approval by two-thirds of both chambers and three-fourths of the states, presidents usually don't take the amendment option seriously if they really want to get things done. But the 1936 electoral landslide was so massive that Article Five was no longer a significant obstacle—and written constitutionalism was very much a live option.

Presidents generally consider it a big win if their party controls Congress by a 60–40 margin. But this time around, Democrats won three-fourths of the seats in both the House and the Senate. This gave Roosevelt lots of room to assemble two-thirds majorities to constitutionalize the fundamental principles of the New Deal revolution, especially because he could also count on significant support from progressive Republicans.

Prospects for state ratification were also bright. The president had just swept 46 out of 48 states in his campaign against Alf Landon—10 more than required by Article Five. Moreover, Congress had recently adopted a technique that would vastly increase prospects for success. In 1933 the New Deal Congress seized the opportunity to propose the repeal of the Eighteenth Amendment, enacted in 1920, which prohibited the sale of alcohol anywhere in the country. But they feared that if ratification were left to state legislatures, thirteen of them would refuse to endorse their initiative. So they invoked the provision of Article Five that authorized Congress to require the states to call specially elected ratifying conventions to determine the amendment's fate.

This opened the path to rapid ratification. On February 20, 1933, two-thirds of Congress proposed the repeal amendment; by December 5 of the same year, three-quarters of the states had approved it. In organizing elections for their ratifying conventions, each state provided ballots that enabled rival slates of delegates to precommit to a Yes or a No vote on repeal. This converted the ratification process into a rolling popular referendum. The early Yeses registered by voters in states like Michigan, Wyoming, and New Jersey catalyzed a nationwide debate over the next few months, as citizens in different regions went to the polls. Only South Carolina voted No, indicating stronger southern resistance to repeal. But the other regions unanimously voted Yes, providing a compelling demonstration of broad popular support.[18]

It was only natural, then, for Roosevelt to begin confidential talks with top advisors on the amendment option as they discussed potential responses to the first round of Old Court vetoes of key New Deal initiatives in 1935. During his first term, however, Roosevelt limited himself to public denunciations of the Old Court and waited for a renewed popular mandate before taking decisive action.[19]

As the 1936 election approached, however, the Democratic platform, written at the president's express direction, explicitly pledged to seek clarifying amendments if "pressing national problems" could not be solved "through legislation within the Constitution." In the meantime, New Dealers in Congress submitted a broad range of proposed amendments—thirty-nine in all—to be given serious consideration after the voters went to the polls.[20]

With the pathway to written constitutionalism prepared in advance, congressional leaders immediately prepared the country to take it seriously in the aftermath of the New Deal landslide. Here is Speaker of the House William Bankhead making it a top priority as the new Congress was opening for business in early January 1937:

> I hope a way can be found to reach [our objectives] without resort to a constitutional amendment, but, unless the personnel of the Supreme Court changes, we will run head on into the same situation we faced before. I do not see how we can escape a constitutional amendment.

This was front-page news in the *New York Times*, as was a similar statement by Senate majority leader Joseph Robinson.[21]

There can be no question, then, that Roosevelt was making a highly self-conscious decision when he rejected his congressional leaders' initiative and chose court-packing as the way to sustain his overwhelming mandate from the People.

His plan, announced in early February, had one large short-term attraction. It did not require the two-stage process of debate and decision—first by Congress, then by ordinary Americans—laid out in Article Five. Instead, he could obtain a quick victory by using his massive congressional supermajorities to pass an ordinary statute expanding the size of the Supreme Court, and use the rest of the legislative session to enact another round of social welfare programs that would pave the way for more sweeping electoral victories in 1938 and beyond. Moreover, there was ample precedent for Congress to expand the Court through the passage of a regular statute. During the nineteenth century, this had happened frequently. So Roosevelt was not breaking new ground, by any means.[22]

Although the president's initiative made short-term sense, it came at a long-term cost to the higher lawmaking system. Court-packing merely required the House and Senate to agree that the Old Court was an obstacle to "progress," but it left it to the president's judicial appointments to define the nature of the progressive commitments of the Roosevelt revolution. It didn't require the political branches to lead a broad popular debate as they worked to hammer out affirmative principles of New Deal constitutionalism. No less important, court-packing did not require progressives to move beyond Washington, D.C., to mobilize broad popular support to win the endorsement of their proposed amendments in state referenda. Rather than make popular sovereignty a living reality, court-packing would leave it to the judges to create a new constitutional order through legal opinions that spoke in a legalistic language that required professional training to comprehend.

When Roosevelt first announced court-packing on February 5, he ignored these points. He presented his plan as a mere efficiency measure, allowing youthful new appointments to permit the elderly Justices on the Court—five were over 75—to do their work effectively. By evading the big issues, he had a strong chance of ramming the bill through Congress in a matter of weeks, not months. There were only 89 Republicans in the House and 16 in the Senate, so they were powerless to block the initiative. Indeed, their loud opposition would only play into the president's hands. He had defeated these "economic royalists" in 1936, and he could count on his congressional supporters to defeat them again if they made court-packing into a partisan issue.

Recognizing this, Republicans did something quite extraordinary. They kept quiet, and tried to recruit progressive Democrats to lead the opposition. But this desperation tactic seemed likely to fail. Roosevelt would long remember the Democratic turncoats who betrayed him when he launched his first post-landslide initiative. They could expect him to retaliate in all sorts of ways, especially if they succeeded in defeating court-packing. So the political costs for a leading Democrat to defect to the opposition were enormous. Moreover, the chances of success were very low, since so many Democrats owed their seats to Roosevelt's endorsement and could easily lose at the next election if he backed a rival who seemed more faithful to the president's program. So why would any serious New Dealer stick his neck out to lead such a "mission impossible"?

Burton Wheeler fully understood the danger. Yet he rose to the occasion. He was a leading New Dealer, with serious presidential ambitions, and he would be taking an especially big risk in joining Republican bitter-enders in a campaign against the triumphant Roosevelt. Nevertheless, within a couple of weeks he announced his public opposition to the president's plan.

Wheeler's critique went to the very heart of the New Deal's higher law-making responsibilities. He completely agreed with Roosevelt that the Supreme Court should be required to abandon its desperate defense of the old constitutional order. But court-packing was an illegitimate shortcut—it repudiated the past without giving Congress and the states a chance to define and debate the affirmative constitutional principles to guide the activist regulatory state in the future. Once New Deal amendments were on the books, Wheeler was confident that the Court would fall in line, even if none of the Justices retired in the meantime.

Wheeler's remarkable act of political courage provoked an immediate outpouring of debate in the press and Capitol Hill—focusing public attention on crucial issues that could have readily been obscured by controversies over details of the president's plan. It also provided political cover for many other congressional Democrats to remain noncommittal until they saw how the broader public would respond. This made it impossible for the president's initial steamroller tactics to succeed, giving him no choice but to respond to Wheeler's critique before it could gain further momentum.

Roosevelt's counteroffensive reached its climax in his "fireside chat" of March 9, when tens of millions of radio listeners heard Roosevelt deliver a point-by-point attack on Wheeler's position:

> There are many types of amendment proposed. Each one is radically different from the other. . . . It would take months or years to get any substantial agreement upon the type and language of an amendment. It would take months or years thereafter to get a two-thirds majority in favor of that amendment in both Houses of the Congress.
>
> Then would come the long course of ratification by three-fourths of the states. No amendment which any powerful economic interests or the leaders of any powerful political party have had reason to oppose has ever been ratified within anything like a reasonable time. And thirteen States which contain only 5 percent of the voting population can block ratification even though the thirty-five States with 95 percent of the population are in favor of it. . . .
>
> And remember one thing. Even if an amendment were passed, and even if in the years to come it were to be ratified, its meaning would depend upon the kind of Justices who would be sitting on the Supreme Court bench. An

amendment, like the rest of the Constitution, is what the Justices say it is rather than what its framers or you might hope it is.[23]

The president's defense rested on a question-begging premise. It supposed that, if he had taken the course set out by Wheeler, Roosevelt would have remained on the sidelines and allowed senators and representatives to bicker endlessly on the terms of appropriate New Deal amendments.

Nothing like this would have happened. Roosevelt had already been paving the way to New Deal amendments before the election. Together with top advisors, he was in a perfect position to put together an amendment package on short notice. Given his super-super-majorities, Roosevelt could have readily gained two-thirds support from both chambers after a few months of engaged debate. He could also urge Congress to follow the precedent of prohibition repeal and call for ratification by specially elected state conventions. If it took only nine months for voters in 36 states to approve this amendment in 1933, there was every reason to anticipate another rapid victory now that Roosevelt had carried 46 states of 48 states—with the Republicans scoring more than 40 percent of the vote in no more than 10 of them. It follows that the president was entirely unpersuasive in claiming that Congress's initiatives would suffer from intolerable delay over the "long course of ratification by three-fourths of the states."[24]

Roosevelt's final counterargument was also unconvincing. Even if amendments were enacted, he claimed that their "meaning would depend upon the kind of Justices who would be sitting on the Supreme Court bench"—so getting New Dealers onto the Court would be decisive in any event. At the time of his "fireside chat," two recently enacted landmark statutes—the Wagner Act and the Social Security Act—were pending for decision by the Court. So the president seems to be suggesting that the "Nine Old Men" would strike these statutes down even while Congress was about to advance Article Five amendments endorsing their constitutionality. But the Court's politically astute Chief Justice, Charles Evans Hughes, would never have allowed such a counterproductive confrontation to occur. A judicial veto of either statute would have provoked Congress to pass the president's amendment package immediately. Instead of committing institutional suicide, Hughes would have led the majority to postpone decision on the cases until the 1938 term, scheduling them for re-argument while the amendments were up for decision by the states. As New Deal Democrats piled up Yes votes for their amendments in state after state, the Hughes Court might have simply waited for 36 Yeses to moot these challenges to landmark legislation. But it would never have done lasting damage to the Court's legitimacy by launching a counterattack on be-half of a dying constitutional order.

When taken literally, however, Roosevelt's remarks could be read to envi-sion a different, if equally implausible, scenario. On this interpretation, hard-line conservatives on the Court would wait until the amendments were ratified. Only then would they embark on a campaign to "reinterpret" their terms in ways that nullified the intentions of the New Dealers who had worked so hard to enact them.

Yet it was perfectly obvious that Hughes and other centrists would also re-fuse to back such an effort. Judicial conservatives like Justices Butler and Van Devanter were very old indeed, and would soon be leaving the Court even if the president didn't try to pack it. Chief Justice Hughes would soon have to deal with an increasing number of Roosevelt appointees in a constructive fashion. As a consequence, he would never redeem Roosevelt's pseudorealistic predic-tion and alienate the newcomers by endorsing a final round of 5-to-4 opinions striking out against the New Deal. Regardless of court-packing, Roosevelt was flat-out wrong in his pseudorealist predictions. But if amendments had been enacted, the ultimate authority upholding these breakthroughs would have been We the People, not We the Justices.

Regardless of its merits, Roosevelt's "fireside chat" was a dramatic effort to mobilize public support for his administration's defense of court-packing to the Senate Judiciary Committee, which began the following day on March 10. While the president did not expect these more formal presenta-tions to persuade Wheeler and other critics, he only needed the support of 49 of 79 Democrats to push his bill through the Senate. The faster the Senate hearing moved, the easier it would be for the Democrat's majority leader, Joseph Robinson, to pass the bill onto the House, where Speaker William Bankhead would assure its rapid approval by its 334 Democratic members.

To speed this process along, the administration limited its presentations to the Senate Judiciary Committee to two weeks, so that its bill could get to the floor by mid-April once Wheeler and his critics were afforded an equal opportunity for rebuttal. All this seemed like a sensible strategy in early March, when the big New Deal cases were still pending before the Court. But the poli-tics of court-packing changed dramatically once the Justices began their "switch in time"—which culminated in decisions upholding the Wagner Act on April 12 and the Social Security Act on May 24.

These opinions, together with Willis Van Devanter's retirement, dramati-cally changed the political equation. New Dealers on Capitol Hill no longer believed that Roosevelt's initiative was necessary to save the New Deal. Even though court-packing had become a luxury, however, they found it very difficult to reject their president's demands. Roosevelt only narrowly failed to gain majority support after floor debate in the Senate reached its climax in July.[25]

The enduring meaning of the Court's switch, and the president's defeat, has been an endless source of controversy for generations of American lawyers. But from the comparative point of view, the president's earlier confrontation with Wheeler is more consequential. It required Roosevelt to address the very same question raised at similar turning points in each of our previous case studies: the constitutionalization of charisma. Given the fateful character of this choice, it pays to consider the road not taken. The adoption of revolutionary Constitutions made a big difference at later stages in India, South Africa, Italy, France, and Iran. So it is only reasonable to suppose that the ratification of New Deal amendments had comparable long-range consequences in shaping American developments.

Rewriting the Constitution?

If Roosevelt had taken the country down the Article Five path, it would no longer be possible for modern Americans to look upon Madison & Company as the principal authors of their Constitution. Like French citizens of the Fifth Republic, they would still take pride in their eighteenth-century Bill of Rights and other enduring principles laid down at the Founding. But the New Deal amendments would also require them to recognize that the Constitution had moved decisively beyond eighteenth-century notions of liberty, and that the People of the twentieth century were insisting that all Americans be granted the social and economic rights required for the meaningful exercise of freedom. In taking this step, the United States would have taken its place among revolutionary republics in India and South Africa, France and Italy, and many other places, whose twentieth-century constitutions have explicitly committed their People to the systematic pursuit of social justice.

With the New Deal amendments securely anchored in the exercise of popular sovereignty, the written Constitution would serve as a standing rebuke to originalist judges who currently pride themselves in their textualist approaches to legal interpretation. This approach has led jurists like Antonin Scalia and Neil Gorsuch to view the Founding as the basis for a sweeping constitutional condemnation of a powerful national government committed to the general welfare. But under the New Deal amendment scenario, a different vision of the Founding would emerge—one that would emphasize its basic similarities to the New Deal project.

I have set the stage for this reorientation in my revisionist reading of the founding era. My argument emphasized that the Philadelphia Convention's main challenge was to convince the country that the Confederation gave too much power to each individual state—and that the only way to solve America's problems was to transfer crucial aspects of state sovereignty to the central government.

This was precisely the same diagnosis that Roosevelt was presenting to Congress in 1937. Under the "written amendment" scenario, he would have engaged in a Madisonian-style exercise—calling on Congress to redefine the powers of the central government so as to enable it to confront the economic and social problems of twentieth-century life. As in the summer of 1787, so in the spring of 1937, Roosevelt's call would have provoked a two-stage process of debate and decision. The first round would have occurred on Capitol Hill—where New Dealers would have hammered out their proposed amendments in a more publicly accountable fashion than occurred during the secret sessions in Philadelphia. Once they had gained the requisite two-thirds Congressional majorities, they would have followed precisely the same path blazed by the Convention—calling on the states to convene specially elected ratifying conventions to determine the fate of these measures.

This would have made 1938 into a rerun of 1788. In state after state, Americans would have been called upon to debate the big issues as they decided between rival slates of convention delegates. As New Dealers mobilized their grassroots supporters to go to the polls and vote for Yes, the accumulating series of Yeses would have culminated in a demonstration of popular sovereignty similar to the one achieved by the Federalists 150 years earlier—enabling the American People to show their self-conscious support for a decisive breakthrough to "a more perfect Union."

Indeed, the New Deal version of the Federalist two-step would have been far more convincing than the original Madisonian exercise. Recall the escalating series of legitimacy deficits that impaired the Philadelphia Convention's claim to speak for the People. These problems were compounded by the Federalists' difficulties in winning the consent of state conventions to their centralizing initiatives—to the point where the first Congress began its political life as a secessionist assembly representing, at best, only eleven of the thirteen states.

In contrast, the New Dealers' movement for a constitutional "new beginning" had the mobilized support of an overwhelming majority of Americans. This is why Article Five's super-majoritarian barriers would not have prevented Roosevelt from gaining the endorsement of We the People for activist national government with the powers necessary to achieve economic justice and social welfare under the real-world conditions of modern life.

I do not deny that the 17 million Americans who voted for Alf Landon and other Republican candidates in 1936 would have been bitterly disappointed if the New Dealers had followed up their 1936 landslide by mobilizing tens of millions of grassroots supporters to win 36 state ratifications of transformative amendments over the next year or two. But in contrast to the Founding, there was one thing these bitter-end opponents could not have denied—that an overwhelming majority of Americans, at a rare moment of high mobilization and political self-consciousness, had come to this fateful decision with their eyes wide open.

We the Judges?

Roosevelt's choice of court-packing set the country down a different path. Its larger implications, however, did not become apparent until much later. Despite his Senate defeat in 1937, Roosevelt in fact succeeded in packing the Supreme Court. As old-line conservatives left the bench, the president systematically replaced them with dedicated New Dealers—who, by the early 1940s, were unanimously handing down sweeping precedents that served as the foundations for activist government during the rest of the twentieth century.

This judge-made revolution only began to unravel with the ascent of Ronald Reagan to the presidency in 1980. Reagan's election marked the first great success in an ongoing effort by conservative activists and intellectuals to transform the Republicans into a classic movement party. Their overriding aim was to mobilize the People against the New Deal legacy of "big government" and inaugurate a new era of freedom based on the free market. Once in power, Reagan followed Roosevelt's precedent in claiming a mandate from the People to revolutionize constitutional law.

He also followed Roosevelt in the way he tried to achieve this objective. He did not rely on Article Five amendments to define the Republican party's new constitutional vision for America. Instead, he went about appointing legal intellectuals like Antonin Scalia to the Supreme Court to supply it with the brainpower required to repudiate the New Deal principles left behind by the likes of Felix Frankfurter and Robert Jackson.

Call this *the strategy of transformative appointment*. It began to unravel when Reagan nominated Robert Bork to reinforce the judicial revolution set in motion by Scalia. If the Senate had approved the Bork nomination, Reagan would have been well on his way to reenacting Roosevelt's precedent—but this time he would have used Roosevelt's technique of transformative appointment to repudiate the New Deal doctrines that Frankfurter and Jackson had formulated, and their successors had elaborated, over the following decades.

Bork made no secret of his ambitions. He used his testimony before the Senate Judiciary Committee to declare an originalist war on the status quo—elaborating the different ways in which New Deal doctrines had darkened the splendor of the founding vision of limited central government. With these pronouncements, Bork put the country on notice that Reagan was determined to repudiate Roosevelt's revolutionary legacy by the very technique of transformative appointment through which his predecessor had created it in the first place.

If this gambit had succeeded, Bork's rise to the Court would have ensured Reagan's place in history as the greatest president of the twentieth century. But in his ambition to surpass Roosevelt, Reagan failed to appreciate some basic arithmetic. When Scalia was nominated, the Republicans were in control of the Senate; but they had suffered a big defeat in 1986, and the Democrats were now in command by a margin of 55 to 45. As a consequence, they were in a good position to use the public uproar generated by Bork's provocations to defeat his nomination—leading ultimately to the appointment of Anthony Kennedy in his place.

Kennedy was no Bork—that was the key message he conveyed at his Senate hearings when he affirmed the continuing vitality of leading precedents of the post-Roosevelt era. Instead, he was a firm believer in step-by-step interstitial changes in existing doctrine—whose character was utterly obscure (perhaps even to himself).[26]

The shift from Bork to Kennedy taught future presidents an important lesson. They simply had too much to lose if their nominees issued radical pronunciamentos at their confirmation hearings. They could gain their constitutional objectives more effectively through "stealth nominations." Under this strategy, the president claims a "mandate from the People" for his stealth nominations, but nominees refuse to follow the precedents set by Frankfurter and Bork and explain to the Senate judiciary committee the character of the doctrinal revolution they will endorse once they ascend to the bench. This makes it far harder for ordinary citizens to understand the stakes involved in the nomination—since opponents' predictions can be readily dismissed by the nominee's defenders as partisan exaggerations. Given widespread confusion among the public, the president's chances of success are high, especially if his party happens to be in control of the Senate.

Stealth appointments make Supreme Court nominations into occasions for partisan power plays without any serious effort to engage the American people in self-conscious debate on the nation's constitutional future. They would be perceived as radically illegitimate if Roosevelt had not established the precedent of revolutionizing the Constitution through judicial nominations.

Roosevelt backed his claim of a popular mandate with super-supermajorities that remain unprecedented to the present day. In contrast, revolutionary presidents of the present era want to achieve the same end by stealth on the basis of razor-thin majorities. The pathological character of this dynamic was dramatized by the recent controversy over Merrick Garland, Obama's nominee to replace Antonin Scalia in 2016. The Republican Senate's refusal to accord Garland a hearing was unprecedented in the modern period. But recent "stealth" practices made it more acceptable because everybody expected Judge Garland to make the hearing as boring and uninformative as possible—depriving the general public of a Bork-like opportunity to understand what Garland was really planning to do when he ascended to the Court. So why not wait for the newly elected president to make this fateful choice? After all, if Scalia's seat remained vacant, won't the issue play a role in the next presidential election—permitting the voters to have their say?

It is at this point that the long-term consequences of Roosevelt's turn away from written constitutionalism can be fully appreciated. After seventy years, nobody expects a president to revolutionize the status quo through a two-stage process in which Congress's proposal of formal amendments is only a prelude to a countrywide debate provoked by elections for ratifying conventions. Given stealth appointments, the nature of the critical issues are not even conveyed in vivid fashion at the Senate hearings—the only moment at which ordinary citizens are tuning in. Instead, they are only taken into account during presidential election campaigns—where they must compete with many other issues advanced by the Republican and Democratic nominees. Voters who oppose a candidate's judicial philosophy might well favor the candidate's economic and social policies—and cast their votes on that basis. Worse yet, successful politicians in the internet age will typically avoid elaborate constitutional disquisitions on the campaign trail. While Donald Trump certainly gave Americans fair notice that he aimed to use the presidency to "drain the swamp" in Washington, D.C., he had no interest in elaborating the constitutional implications of his position. Instead, he merely signaled to a very disparate set of conservative interest groups that they could count on him to back their favorite judges when a Supreme Court vacancy opened up.

While Trump's refusal to take the Constitution seriously was especially spectacular, most other candidates will follow their pollsters down a similar path—searching for evocative sound-bites while burying their constitutional commentaries deep in their campaign sites. Barack Obama was an exception, of course, but he managed to discredit the process in a different way. Although he took the Constitution seriously in some of his stump speeches, once he made it to the White House he betrayed his most emphatic commitments against unilateral presidential war making—thereby teaching the public to discount constitutional rhetoric on the campaign trail, even when it sounds sober and sincere.[27]

It is only by rethinking Roosevelt's turn away from written constitutionalism that today's Americans can once again engage in the kind of public debate that will make popular sovereignty a living reality in the twenty-first century. In earlier work I have sketched out a path toward this alternative constitutional future.[28]

My proposed Popular Sovereignty Initiative would authorize a president, upon his or her successful reelection, to ask Congress to put proposed amendments before the voters in a *national* referendum at the next presidential election. If Congress agrees, this means that the voters will be making their decision while its presidential proponent is about to leave office. Even if the president manages to convince a majority to approve the initiatives, this should not be enough to make them part of the living Constitution of the twenty-first century. Instead, it would set the stage for a second referendum at the next presidential election four years later. During the interim, the amendment package would be exposed to countless conversations at work, at home, and in civil society—at a time when its initiating president is now in retirement, and must rely heavily on rising political leaders to make the case. Only if this second referendum generates a strong Yes vote should the amendment package be recognized as a part of the twenty-first-century Constitution.

The Initiative represents a decisive departure from the parody of popular sovereignty currently on display as Donald Trump, with a razor-thin majority of the Senate, claims the authority to revolutionize the Constitution through stealth appointments.

The true cost of Trump's power play will become clear only over the next decade. The country is currently divided between two competing movement parties, with conservative Republicans and progressive Democrats pushing for radically different futures, while centrists shake their heads in disbelief. Even if, for example, Democrats win the presidency and Congress in 2020, it is perfectly possible that their ascendancy will be brief, and that a revitalized Republican party will successfully renew its campaign against "big government" and return to power in 2024.

The shifting pendulum in Washington, D.C., can readily generate a constitutional crisis that will make the court-packing struggle of 1937 seem tame by comparison. Suppose, for example, that President Trump and the Republican Senate succeed in following up their appointments of Neil Gorsuch and Brett Kavanaugh with another so-called originalist, and that the victorious Democrats of 2020 enact a strong legislative program reinvigorating New Deal and Great Society commitments to economic and social justice.

This will leave the Trump Court in a tough position. If it strikes down the new wave of progressive legislation, it will put court-packing back on the action agenda. After all, if the newly elected president and Congress meekly accept the Court's vetoes, they will be betraying tens of millions of grassroots activists whose energies fueled their recent triumph over Trump. But if the originalists on the Court engage in their own version of the 1937 "switch in time," and uphold the Democrats' New New Deal, the Justices will be betraying the millions of conservative supporters who were relying on them to defend the Scalia/Gorsuch vision of the Founding against progressive distortions. Whatever choice the Court makes, the result will profoundly alienate vast numbers of ordinary citizens.

To fully appreciate the dimensions of the problem, suppose that the Trump Court refuses to switch and strikes down key elements of the Democratic program for greater economic and social justice. This will force the president and Congress to make some tough choices of their own. If they allow the Trump Court's veto to stand, they alienate their most committed supporters. But the only way to redeem their campaign commitments is by packing the

Court to overcome the resistance of hard-line conservative justices who may well be in a position to invalidate progressive legislation for the next decade or even longer. Under this scenario, the Democrats ram through legislation which expands the Court from 9 to 13, and appoint four progressive justices to the newly created vacancies—ignoring the bitter protests of the Republican minorities on Capitol Hill.

This will put America's constitutional future at the center of the presidential campaign in 2024—though even here, the court-packing drama will compete with other hot-button issues raised by rival candidates in their struggle for the White House. Suppose that, when all the votes are counted, the Republicans emerge victorious—only to confront a new dilemma. Should they follow up its victory by shrinking the Court back to nine, ordering the four new justices to take up their judicial duties on courts of appeals? After all, court-shrinking is not unprecedented in American history—the Republicans could appeal to major examples from Reconstruction to back up their case.[29] Of course, they would concede that court-shrinking is a very serious step. But isn't it even more important to reverse the Democrats' outrageous court-pack and enable the so-called originalists to preserve the Founders' vision of the Constitution?

Whatever happens next, matters may take an even darker turn if the pendulum keeps on swinging from right to left, and back again, in 2028 and beyond. I will leave it to readers to play out these dark scenarios on their own.

In short: Now that Trump's stealth campaign has succeeded, it will be very difficult to avoid a crisis of shattering proportion. Great acts of statesmanship will be required to preserve something of value from our constitutional tradition. If future leaders of the Right and the Left do seize such an opportunity, I urge them to reflect on the tragic consequences that have followed upon Roosevelt's embrace of constitutional revolutions through transformative appointments—and make written constitutionalism a serious option for the next generation of Americans.

The Popular Sovereignty Initiative marks out a formidable obstacle course for political movements aiming to redefine the country's constitutional commitments. But that is precisely its aim. Given the current degree of polarization, it *should* be required for activists on the right and the left to reach out to the center in order to hammer out enduring contributions to America's constitutional identity. If the Initiative were enacted into law, it would also temper the ardor of judicial revolutionaries on the Court—who would be obliged to recognize that their brand of "originalism" may well provoke We the People of the United States to repudiate the Trump Court by enacting a very different amendment package to guide the country in the future.

I have no stake in the details of my proposal. Nor do I suppose that the Initiative will immediately gain a prominent position on the short-term agendas of the Democratic or Republican parties. But if, as I fear, America is on the verge of a very grave crisis, something like the Initiative might well offer itself to serious political leaders as a constructive response to the wave of constitutional alienation that is likely to poison national politics over the next decade.

I recognize, of course, the enduring Madisonian truth that "enlightened statesman may not always be at the helm." It is perfectly possible that the post-Trump leadership of both parties will allow the "Constitution" to degenerate into an ideological smokescreen for the judicial majority that is temporarily ascendant in Washington, D.C.

Yet statesmen in other places have managed to bridge bitter divisions and work together to enable their fellow citizens to take charge of their constitutional destiny—think of Italy and France after the Second World War. American history also offers more hopeful examples of constructive responses to constitutional crisis. Perhaps the current generation of Americans will also rise to the occasion, and do their share to ensure that the promise of government by the People shall not perish from the earth.[30]

Notes

INTRODUCTION: PATHWAYS

1   Readers interested in my political philosophy should turn to *Social Justice in the Liberal State* (1980); "What Is Neutral about Neutrality?," 93 *Ethics* 372 (1983); "Why Dialogue?," 86 *J. Phil.* 5 (1989); "Temporal Horizons of Justice," 94 *J. Phil.* 299 (1997).

2   Jo Murkens, "Unintended Democracy," in Kelly Grotke & Marcus Prutsch eds., *Constitutionalism, Legitimacy, and Power* 351–370 (2014).

3   Juan Linz & Alfred Stepan, *Problems of Democratic Transition and Consolidation* (1996); Alfonso Fernandez-Miranda & Pilar Fernandez-Miranda, *Lo que el Rey me ha pedido* (1995). Jose Maravall, in *The Transition to Democracy in Spain* (1982), emphasizes the role of mass strikes in pushing the process forward, but does not challenge my basic claim.

4   Stephen Gardbaum, *The New Commonwealth Model of Constitutionalism* (2013); Scott Stephenson, *From Dialogue to Disagreement in Comparative Rights Constitutionalism* (2016).

5   David Butler & Uwe Kitzinger, *The 1975 Referendum* (1996).

6   The Brexit referendum, along with its aftermath, has provoked a storm of commentary, which I will not try to summarize. For the UK Supreme Court's remarkable assertion of its authority to prevent the prime minister from assaulting the principle of parliamentary sovereignty through her appeal to the royal prerogative, see R (Miller) v. Secretary of State for Exiting the European Union [2017] UKSC 5.

7   For further reflections on darker scenarios, see Ackerman, "Why Britain Needs a Written Constitution—and Can't Wait for Parliament to Write One," 89 *Political Quarterly* (June 2018), at: https://doi.org/10.1111/1467-923X.12524.

8   Ackerman & Tokujin Matsudaira, "Dishonest Abe," *Foreign Policy* (June 24, 2014).

9   For a more complex account of the Parliamentary Council's defiance, see Bruce Ackerman, "Populismus heist Angst vor dem Volk," in Bernd Scherer & Sven Arnold eds., *Die Alte und die Neue Welt* (2008).

10 Donald Kommers, *Germany's Constitutional Odyssey* chap. 3 (forthcoming).

11 Ernst Mahrenholz, *Die Verfassung und das Volk* (1992).

12 For a book-length treatment of the revolutionary features of German reunification that are typically ignored in German constitutional accounts, see Stephan Jaggi, *The 1989 Revolution in East Germany and Its Impact on Unified Germany's Constitutional Law* (2016).

13 For recent discussions, see Justin Collings, *Democracy's Guardians* (2016); Hailbronner, "Rethinking the Rise of the German Constitutional Court," 12 *Int. J. Con. Law* 626 (2014).

14 I analyze the development of America's revolutionary tradition over the centuries in *We the People,* vols. 1–3 (1991, 1998, 2014).

1. CONSTITUTIONALIZING REVOLUTION?

1 Harold Berman, *Law and Revolution* (1983); Hauke Brunkhorst, *A Critical Theory of Legal Revolutions* (2014).

2 My thinking has been influenced by Hannah Arendt, *On Revolution* (1963); Hans Blumenberg, *The Legitimacy of the Modern Age* (1966); and Eric Voegelin, *The New Science of Politics* (1951). But as this chapter suggests, I also disagree with each of these writers in fundamental respects.

3 For a thoughtful review of the current literature, see Jacobsohn, "Theorizing the Constitutional Revolution," 2 *J. Law & Courts* 1 (2012).

4 When viewed in interdisciplinary terms, this book is part of a broader methodological turn emphasizing the role of mobilized social organizations in social change. Doug McAdam, Sidney Tarrow, & Charles Tilly, *Dynamics of Contention* (2001) (sociology); Knott, "Narrating the Age of Revolution," 73 *Wm & Mary Q.* 3–7 (Jan. 2016) (history); Andreas Kalyvas, *Democracy and the Politics of the Extraordinary* 65–78 (2008) (political science).

5 I differ from Professor Jacobsohn, supra n. 3, who assesses the "revolutionary" status of constitutions by passing judgment on their long-term impact. Participants in a revolution are not equipped with crystal balls—long-range impact can only be assessed retrospectively. This book, in contrast, aims to describe the basic dilemmas, as the protagonists themselves understand them, raised by efforts to constitutionalize revolutions as they arise at different phases of revolutionary development.

6 For a more positive view of recent scholarly developments, see Ran Hirschl, *Comparative Matters: The Renaissance of Comparative Constitutional Law* (2014).

7 Juan Linz & Alfred Stepan, *Problems of Democratic Transition and Consolidation: Southern Europe, South America, and Post-Communist Europe* (1996).

8 Tom Ginsburg, *Judicial Review in New Democracies* 22–35 (2012).

9 The work of the Comparative Constitutions Project is available at: http://comparativeconstitutionsproject.org/.

10 This process of trivialization is on display in Ginsburg, Lansberg-Rodriguez, & Versteeg, "When to Overthrow Your Government: The Right to Resist in the World's Constitutions," 60 *UCLA L. Rev.* 1184 (2013), linking constitutions that enshrine the "right to resist" to scenarios involving the sudden disruption of the previous order. After measuring "disruption" in quantitative terms, the authors—to their credit—recognize that these numerical measures are inadequate. As a consequence, they provide a series of "anecdotes," drawn from particular cases, to help account for the selective incorporation of the "right to resist" in cases of disruptive transitions. But these bits of qualitative analysis, focusing on a particular clause and particular episodes, do not serve as adequate substitutes for the holistic and multigenerational accounts of revolutionary legitimation of the kind advanced here.

11 Elster has elaborated on this theme, with increasing depth, throughout his career. See *Ulysses and the Sirens* (1984); *Ulysses Unbound* (2000); *Securities against Misrule* (2013). Stephen Holmes has also made important contributions, starting with *Passions and Constraint* (1995).

12 Arendt, supra n. 2.

13 Recent efforts to invigorate a Schmittian approach include Paul Kahn, *Political Theology: Four New Chapters on the Concept of Sovereignty* (2011); Chantal Mouffe, *Agonistics: Thinking the World Politically* (2013).

14 Joseph Schumpeter, *Capitalism, Socialism and Democracy* (3rd ed. 1950).

15 Adam Przeworski is the leading contemporary scholar who brings neo-Schumpeterian themes to comparative constitutional analysis. *Democracy and the Limits of Self-Government* (2010).

16 Tarrow, "The People Maybe? Opening the Civil Rights Revolution to Social Movements," 50 *Tulsa L. Rev.* 415 (2014). For promising interdisciplinary trends in other fields, see the sources cited at n. 4, supra.

2. MOVEMENT-PARTY CONSTITUTIONALISM

1 Sarbani Sen, *The Constitution of India: Popular Sovereignty and Democratic Transformations* 45–52 (2007).

2 Mantena, "On Gandhi's Critique of the State," 9 *Modern Intellectual History* 535 (2012).

3 For different views of the competing visions, see Perry Anderson, *The Indian Ideology* (2012); Martha Nussbaum, *The Clash Within* (2007); B. R. Nanda, *Gandhi and Nehru* (1979). The Socialist and Communist Parties also played a role in the independence struggle, but they never successfully challenged Congress's dominant position. Ramachandra Guha, *India after Gandhi* 24–25 (2007).

4 The Council Act of 1861 created the basic consultative framework, which slowly evolved in inclusionary directions. Mithi Mukherjee, *India in the Shadows of Empire* 97–98 (2010); Sumit Sarkar, *Modern India* 12, 14–19 (2005).

5 S. P. Sathe, "From Positivism to Structuralism," in Jeffrey Goldsmith ed., *Interpreting Constitutions* 215 (2006).

6 Anderson, supra n. 3, at 49–55; Martha Nussbaum, supra n. 3, at 120; Nanda, supra n. 3.

7 B. R. Tomlinson, *The Indian National Congress and the Raj* 32–48, 71–72 (1972). Imperial appointments still bulked large in the Central Legislative Assembly, but Congress won 44 of the 88 of the elected seats. Id. at 42–43.

8 Perry Anderson notes the importance of Gandhi's emphasis on organizational links between national and subnational levels, supra n. 3, at 17.

9 Id. at 43–44 ("The Quit India movement was imposed by Gandhi on a reluctant Congress Leadership, which was not convinced by it. It was his final throw").

10 As the postwar conflict between Hindus and Muslims escalated, Gandhi recognized that he had been sidelined: "There was a time when mine was a big voice. Then everybody obeyed what I said; now neither the Congress nor the Hindus

nor the Muslims listen to me." Javeed Alam, "The Nation and the State in India," in Zoyz Hassan et al. eds., *India's Living Constitution* 83, 96 (2005).

11 In contrast to Congress, the Muslim League lacked well-developed linkages between top leaders and followers characteristic of a full-fledged "movement party." As late as 1943, for example, the League lacked a strong grassroots organization in Punjab, a linchpin of the new state of Pakistan. Maya Tudor, *The Promise of Power* 123–124 (2013).

12 After partition, Congress's share of seats in the Indian Constituent Assembly increased from 69 to 82 percent. Sathe, supra n. 5, at 215.

13 Hanna Lerner, *Making Constitutions in Deeply Divided Societies* 109–151 (2011)— who sees the point, but fails to reflect sufficiently upon its significance.

14 For a brief summary, see Uday Mehta, "Indian Constitutionalism: The Social and the Political Vision," in Niraja Jayal & Pratap Mehta eds., *The Oxford Companion to Politics in India* 15, 19 (2010). For the numerical breakdown, see B. Shiva Rao, *The Framing of the Indian Constitution* 292–294 (1967).

15 In its Indian Independence Act of 1947, the British Parliament formally confirmed the Constituent Assembly's authority to promulgate a constitution. It also authorized the Assembly to serve as the basis for an interim government, headed by Nehru, who enacted broad legislative initiatives required by a host of pressing problems. As part of this interim arrangement, Britain retained nominal sovereignty. Mountbatten no longer served as viceroy, but became governor-general. While he continued to play an important political role until he left the country in June 1948, his formal position consigned him to the same limited functions exercised by representatives of the Crown in other self-governing dominions. Upon his departure, a leading politician from the Congress, Chakravarti Rajagopalachari, became the first and last Indian to serve as head of the British Raj— with his office disappearing upon the promulgation of the Constitution in 1950. At this transitional moment, the Constituent Assembly emphasized that it was speaking in the name of "We the People of India" by refusing to submit its Constitution for formal approval by the governor-general, since the newly created Republic would henceforth be totally independent of Britain. For a thoughtful engagement with the jurisprudential paradoxes raised by this final end-run around the governor-general's assent, see Swaminathan, "India's Benign Constitutional Revolution," *The Hindu* (Nov. 3, 2016), at: http://www.thehindu.com/opinion/lead /India%E2%80%99s-benign-constitutional-revolution/article12318419.ece.

16 J. Nehru, "Speech on the Granting of Independence, 14 August 1947," in Brian Arthur, *The Penguin Book of Twentieth Century Speeches* 234–237 (1992).

17 Christophe Jaffrelot, *Dr. Ambedkar and Untouchability* 106–114 (2005), which suggests how Ambedkar's liberal democratic ideals softened the more socialistic commitments of Nehru's Congress without eliminating them. These points are recognized, however grudgingly, in Perry Anderson's fiercely critical account of the birth of the Indian Republic. Anderson, supra n. 3, at 137–139.

18 In a standard text, Subhash Kashyap emphasizes that "the founding fathers made it very clear that they were not writing on a clean slate. They took a conscious

decision not to make a complete departure from the past, but to build on the existing structure and experience of institutions already established." *Our Constitution: An Introduction* 4–5 (2004). The key word here is "*complete* departure," which supposes that anything less than a totalizing break marks the Constitution as un-revolutionary.

19 I cannot do justice to all the revolutionary commitments of the Founding text—many of which have generated vast literatures. For a perceptive holistic account, see Mehta, supra n. 14, at 15–27.

20 H. C. L. Merillat, *Land and the Constitution in India* 126–136 (1970); Granville Austin, *Working a Democratic Constitution: The Indian Experience* 69–98 (1999).

21 Shankari Prasad v. Union of India, 1951 AIR 458.

22 Chandrachud, "Nehru, Non-Judicial Review and Constitutional Supremacy," 2 *Indian J. Con. & Ad. Law* 45 (2018) (discussing parliamentary overrides during Nehru's ascendancy). The ongoing exercise of this revisionary power was only one expression of Nehru's continuing assertion of charismatic authority. For another, see Harshan Kumarasingham, *A Political Legacy of the British Empire* 55 (2013) (describing Nehru's personal involvement in selecting 4,000 Congress Party candidates for regional and national parliaments and his unchallenged hegemony over the cabinet).

23 For a pathbreaking account of constitutional litigation during Nehru's ascendancy, see Rohit De, *A People's Constitution: The Everyday Life of Law in the Indian Republic* (2018).

24 During his brief tenure, Shastri in fact exhibited more independence than the Syndicate desired. Guha, supra n. 3, at 389–441.

25 Jon Keay, *Midnight's Descendants* 149 (2014); Guha, supra n. 3, at 405–406.

26 Sanjay Ruparelia, *Divided We Govern: Coalition Politics in Modern India* 57–59 (2015); Guha, supra n. 3, at 420 (table 6).

27 *Compare* Sajjan Singh v. State of Rajasthan, 1965 AIR 845, 1965 SCR (1) 933, reaffirming Shankari Prasad, *with* Golaknath v. State of Punjab, 1967 AIR 1643, 1967 SCR (2) 762.

28 Guha, supra n. 3, at 447. Gandhi's political ascendancy was reinforced by India's lightning-fast military victory over Pakistan in December 1971. For a more elaborate discussion of the entire period, see Austin, supra n. 20, at 293–534.

29 AIR 1973 SC 146.

30 At the very last moment, the Chief Justice circulated a "summary" of the Court's decision, which affirmed the "basic structure" doctrine. While seven Justices elaborated their views of this doctrine in their opinions, nine signed the "summary" without further comment. For a blow-by-blow account, see T. R. Andhyarujina, *The Kesavananda Bharati Case* 50–62 (2011).

31 Austin, supra n. 20, at 278–282; Guha, supra n. 3, at 472–473.

32 When dealing with constitutional questions, the Court sits in panels of five or more, with larger benches having the power to overrule judgments made previously by smaller ones. By convention, the Chief Justice "plays a strong role not only in deciding which cases are heard by larger benches, but also which cases are heard

by which judges." Robinson, "Structure Matters: The Impact of Court Structure on the Indian and U.S. Supreme Courts," 61 *Am. J. Comp. Law* 173, 186–187 (2013).

33 Guha, supra n. 3, at 509 (Sanjay Gandhi operating as an "extra-constitutional center of power"); Bipan Chandra, Mridula Mukherjee, & Aditya Mukherjee, *India since Independence* 327 (2008).

34 A. D. M. Jabalpur v. Shivakant Shukla, 1976 SC 1207. Gandhi's newly appointed Chief Justice selected the five-judge panel, which ruled, with a single dissent, that habeas corpus was entirely unavailable during the Emergency. Austin, supra n. 20, at 340–344 (the "darkest chapter" in the Court's history); Ramnath, "ADM Jabalpur's Antecedents: Political Emergencies, Civil Liberties, and Arguments from Colonial Continuities in India," 31(2) *Am. U. Intl. L. Rev.* 209 (2016).

35 Guha, supra n. 3, at 523–530.

36 Id. at 522.

37 Id. at 332–334.

38 Austin, supra n. 20, at 505–507.

39 Ruparelia, supra n. 26, at 95.

40 At the same time, the Justices framed their new doctrines to permit continuing adaptation to changing political realities. For an insightful analysis, Khosla, "Making Social Rights Conditional," 8 *ICON* 739 (2010).

41 Pratap Mehta, "The Indian Supreme Court and the Art of Democratic Positioning," in Mark Tushnet & Madhav Khosla eds., *Unstable Constitutionalism* 233 (2016), although I part company when it comes to Mehta's treatment of judicial dynamics, which embraces an extremely strong version of legal realism that ignores the independent role of legitimacy in accounting for judicial behavior.

42 Sudhir Krishnaswamy, *Democracy and Constitutionalism in India* 159 (2009). See also S. R. Bommai v. Union of India (1994) 3 SCC 1.

43 I. R. Coelho (Dead) by LRS v. State of Tamil Nadu and Others, AIR (SC) 861 (2007).

44 Venkatesan, "Judicial Challenge," 24 *Frontline* 5, 8 (2007).

45 Interestingly, a Supreme Court panel made an earlier effort to dethrone Schedule Nine in the immediate aftermath of Mrs. Gandhi's assassination, e.g., Ajoy Kumar Banerjee v. Union of India, AIR 1984 SC 113, but the Court failed to follow up with a full-scale assault.

46 Krishnaswamy, supra n. 42, at 159.

47 Parliamentary Research Service, "The National Judicial Appointments Commission Bill 2014," at: http://www.prsindia.org/billtrack/the-national-judicial-appointments-commission-bill-2014-3359.

48 Supreme Court Advocates-on-Record Association v. Union of India, 2015 SCC OnLine SC 1322.

49 Anuradha Needham & Rajeswari Rajan, *The Crisis of Secularism in India* (2007).

3. STRUGGLING FOR SUPREMACY

1 I am indebted to Willie Esterhuyse, *Endgame: Secret Talks and the End of Apartheid* (2012), and similar sources, for many insights. Nevertheless, Esterhuyse's "in-

sider account" greatly underestimates the decisive role of mass mobilization in overwhelming the established order.

2   Sheridan Johns & R. Hunt Davis Jr., *Mandela, Tambo, and the African National Congress: The Struggle against Apartheid, 1948–1990: A Documentary Survey* 17–21 (1991).

3   *The Freedom Charter* at: http://www.historicalpapers.wits.ac.za/inventories/inv _pdfo/AD1137/AD1137-Ea6-1-001-jpeg.pdf.

4   Stephen Ellis, *External Mission: The ANC in Exile, 1960–1990* 21–24 (2013); Jeremy Seekings, *The UDF: A History of the United Democratic Front in South Africa* chap. 1 (2000).

5   Hugh Macmillan, *The Lusaka Years: The ANC in Exile in Zambia* (2013).

6   Ellis, supra n. 4, at 21.

7   6 Gail Gerhart & Clive Glaser, *From Protest to Challenge: A Documentary History of African Politics in South Africa, 1882–1990: Challenge and Victory, 1980–1990* 149–152 (2010); Macmillan, supra n. 5, at 16–17, 190, 202, 212.

8   Esterhuyse, supra n. 1, at 49.

9   Macmillan, supra n. 5, at 209 ("It was only in 1986 that the British high commissioner in Zambia, Kelvin White, and the American ambassador, Paul Hare, were permitted by their governments to meet Tambo").

10   Arend Lijphart, *Patterns of Democracy: Government Forms and Performance in Thirty-Six Countries* (2nd ed. 2012). Lijphart continued to argue for a South African Constitution based on consociational principles as late as 1998, even after the country had adopted "one person, one vote." "South African Democracy: Majoritarian or Consociational?," 5 *Democratization* 144–150 (1998).

11   Buthelezi founded the Inkatha Freedom Party in 1975 with the consent of the ANC, but he had transformed the IFP into an independent force by 1979.

12   Seekings, supra n. 4, at 59 (2000).

13   Allister Sparks, *Tomorrow Is Another Country* 57 (1994).

14   Id. at 71:

> Despite the denials one hears today from those who were involved, it is difficult to escape the conclusion that the purpose of the government's talks with Mandela was to explore the possibility of co-opting him as leader of ... [the] moderates—along with members of the exiled ANC whom the government's analysts regarded as nationalists and moderates, as compared with the communists and other militants.

15   Nelson Mandela, *Long Walk to Freedom* 464–467 (1994). For an insightful analysis, see Read & Shapiro, "Transforming Power Relationships: Leadership, Risk, and Hope," 108 *Amer. Pol. Sci. Rev.* 40 (2014).

16   Heinz Klug, *Constituting Democracy: Law, Globalism, and South Africa's Political Reconstruction* 78 (2000).

17   Macmillan, supra n. 5, at 254.

18   Kader Asmal, *Politics in My Blood: A Memoir* 109 (2011) (quoting passages in text and placing them in context). Italics added.

19 Courtney Jung, Ellen Lust-Oskar, & Ian Shapiro, "Problems and Prospects for Democratic Settlements: South Africa as a Model for the Middle East and Northern Ireland," in Ian Shapiro ed., *The Real World of Democratic Theory* 80, 103 (2011).

20 Peter Stiff, *Warfare by Other Means: South Africa in the 1980s and 1990s* (2001); Anthony Turton, *Shaking Hands with Billy* 300 (2010) (fig. 2, presenting annual death counts compiled by South African Institute of Race Relations).

21 Sparks, supra n. 13, at 94.

22 "South Africa House of Assembly Election Results: 1989," at http://www.ipu.org /parline-e/reports/arc/2291_89.htm.

23 SABC Network (Johannesburg), Feb. 24, 1992 (de Klerk's statement, kicking off his referendum campaign) (italics added). See generally, Courtney Jung & Ian Shapiro, "South Africa's Negotiated Transition: Democracy, Opposition, and the New Constitutional Order," in Ian Shapiro ed., *Democracy* 194–294 (1996).

24 *CODESA: Opening Statement by State President F. W. de Klerk* (Dec. 20, 1991), at: http://www.anc.org.za/content/codesa-opening-statement-state-president-fw -de-klerk.

25 *CODESA: Response by Nelson Mandela, to the Opening Statement by State President F. W. de Klerk* (Dec. 20, 1991) at: http://www.anc.org.za/content/codesa -response-nelson-mandela-opening-statement-state-president-fw-de-klerk.

26 Jung & Shapiro, supra n. 23, at 201.

27 Richard Spitz with Matthew Chaskalson, *The Politics of Transition* 28 (2000).

28 Sparks, supra n. 13, at 133–152, provides a compelling reportorial account.

29 Jung & Shapiro, supra n. 23, at 199 (1996).

30 Hassen Ebrahim, *The Soul of the Nation* 577, 587 (1998) (Mandela's reply to de Klerk, July 9, 1992). For the entire series of public exchanges, see id. at 532–576.

31 Jung & Shapiro, supra n. 23.

32 Id.

33 Spitz, supra n. 27, at 255.

34 Id. at 408.

35 Id. at 313–329.

36 Asmal, supra n. 18, at 132–133.

37 Peter Stiff, *Warfare by Other Means* 557–586 (1996).

38 Because Inkatha (barely) passed the 10 percent threshold, it was also granted a seat in the cabinet, though it had no significant influence on major developments.

39 Lijphart, supra n. 10.

40 Theunis Roux, *The Politics of Principle* 166–168 (2013).

41 Id. at 34.

42 S. v. Makwanyane, 119 (3) SA (CC), 1995 (6) 665 (CC); Executive Council of the Western Cape Legislature v. President of the Republic of South Africa, 1995 (4) SA 8787 (CC), 1995 (10) BCLR 1289 (CC); Minister of Home Affairs v. Fourie, 2006 (1) *SA* 524 ((CC) 2006 BCLR 335 (CC)); Bhe v. Khayelitsha Magistrate, 2005 *SA* 580 (CC), 2005 (1) BCLR 1 (CC).

43 Du Plessis, "Between Apology and Utopia—The Constitutional Court and Public Opinion," 18 *S. Afr. J. on Human Rights* 1, 5–6 (2002).

44 Klug, supra n. 16, at 150.

45 James Fowkes, *Building the Constitution: The Practice of Constitutional Interpretation in Post-Apartheid South Africa* (2016); Roux, supra n. 40.

46 Mark Gevisser, *A Legacy of Liberation* 322 (2009), for the political wheeling and dealing involved.

47 Id. at 323.

48 Ian Shapiro & Kathleen Tebeau, "Introduction," in Shapiro & Tebeau, *After Apartheid* 2 (2011).

49 Gevisser, supra n. 46, at 325.

50 Id. at 327. See also Shapiro & Tebeau, supra n. 48, at 2–3.

51 The Indira Gandhi scenario might well have become a South African reality if Winnie Mandela had emerged victorious during one of the succession crises generated by her husband's departure from the presidency.

52 Zuma was well aware of the constitutional significance of self-restraint. Indeed, he opposed the ANC's initial "recall" of Mbeki, arguing privately that the president "should be allowed to depart with dignity and that his remaining in place was necessary for a smooth transition." Gevisser, supra n. 46, at 335.

53 *Daily Telegraph*, "Jacob Zuma Faces Impeachment as Court Rules He Failed to Uphold South Africa's Constitution" (Mar. 31, 2016), at: http://www.telegraph.co .uk/news/2016/03/31/zuma-faces-impeachment-bid-as-top-court-rules-he -broke-constitut/.

54 *Daily Telegraph*, "Jacob Zuma 'Should' Face 783 Criminal Charges, Declares South African Court" (Apr. 29, 2016), at: http://www.telegraph.co.uk/news/2016/04/29 /south-african-court-clears-way-for-jacob-zuma-to-face-783-crimin/.

4. FROM THE FRENCH RESISTANCE TO THE FOURTH REPUBLIC

1 International recognition of de Gaulle's authority to represent France came slowly—first from the Soviet Union, then from Great Britain, and finally from the United States. But by 1943, de Gaulle had finally secured his position. Jean-Louis Crémieux-Brilhac, *La France libre* (1996); Andrew Shennan, *De Gaulle* 16–36 (1993).

2 "Christian Democracy" was a familiar term in Italy, referring to Catholics who rejected the Pope's call to boycott secular politics. But it was not used in France to describe similarly inclined Catholics, whose activists expressed this commitment in the Popular Republican Party, as well as other groups. Given the terminological variety, I sometimes use the term "Christian Democrats" to make later comparisons with Italy more readily comprehensible.

3 François Goguel, *France under the Fourth Republic* 6 (1952) (Pierce transl.).

4 Eric Jennings, *La France libre fut africaine* (2014).

5 Looking back at this early decision near the end of his life, here is how de Gaulle described his motivations:

From the moment the guns stopped firing, I had decided on my line of action. Short of ostracizing the elected representatives, assuming the characteristics of a new oppressor succeeding others, and destroying myself by adopting a position which the general trend of opinion in France and the whole of the West would soon have made untenable, I must, for whatever length of time was necessary, let the party system display its noxiousness once more, determined as I was not to act as a cover or a figurehead for it. So I would depart, but intact. In this way, when the time came, I could once more be the country's refuge, either in person or through the example which I should have left behind. *Meanwhile, with an eye to the future, and before the Assembly had been elected, I introduced the referendum system, made the people decide that henceforward its direct approval would be necessary for a Constitution to be valid, and thus created the democratic means of one day founding a good one myself, to replace the bad one which was about to be concocted by and for the parties.*

Charles de Gaulle, *Memoirs of Hope: Renewal and Endeavor* 7–8 (1971) (Kilmartin transl.) (emphasis added).

6 For a penetrating account, Pierre Rosanvallon, *Le sacre du citoyen: Histoire du suffrage universel en France* 393–412 (1992).

7 Philip Williams, *Crisis and Compromise: Politics in Post-War France* 20–22 (3rd ed. 1964); Frank Giles, *The Locust Years: The Story of the Fourth French Republic* 19–20 (1991).

8 As Goguel reports:

In his letter of resignation, the General explained that . . . he had long held that his task "should end when the representatives of the nation were reassembled and when the political parties would be in a position to assume their responsibilities." He said that he had agreed to remain in power after the election of the Constituent Assembly only "in order to facilitate a necessary transition" and stated that "this transition is now accomplished." The last statement had no basis in fact. . . .

The real reason for the General's resignation was the desire to force the parties to pay greater heed to his wishes than they had been disposed to until that time. He undoubtedly thought that if he resigned, the Constituent Assembly, divided into several parties which were clearly antagonistic to one another, would be incapable of electing a new Provisional President, and he hoped that after an indefinite period of impotence it would be forced to make a new appeal to him. Then he would be in a position to impose his views on the parties.

Goguel, supra n. 3, at 7–8.

9 Jeannette Bougrab, *Aux origines de la Constitution de la IVᵉ République* 284–313 (2002).

10 Goguel, supra n. 3, at 10.

11 Marcel Morabito, *Histoire constitutionnelle de la France de 1789 à nos jours* 395 (12th ed. 2012).

12   On the long-run influence of this speech, Janot, "Du discours de Bayeux à la Constitution de la Vᵉ République," 108 *Espoir* 12 (1996) (by a drafter of the 1958 Constitution). On Michel Debré's influence, Wahl, "Aux origines de la nouvelle Constitution," 9 *Revue française de science politique* 30, 51 (1959).

13   The second draft also marginally enhanced the authority of the largely ceremonial presidency.

14   Article 91 provided for a "constitutional committee," chaired by the president of the Republic, consisting of ten members selected by the National Assembly and the Senate, along with the presidents of both chambers. Its job was to "examine whether the statutes enacted by the National Assembly imply a revision of the Constitution," but it failed to play any role during the life of the Fourth Republic. Similarly, the Conseil d'État, in its adjudicatory capacity, consistently followed its rule, first promulgated in 1936, barring litigants from appealing to the Constitution in their particular challenges to the exercise of public authority.

15   Goguel, supra n. 3, at 16.

16   De Gaulle's speech at Épinal was paradigmatic. See "Speech Delivered at Épinal on September 29th, 1946," *Discours et messages II Dans l'attente* 26 (1970).

17   Goguel, supra n. 3, at 16–17.

18   For a rich discussion of party politics, see Williams, supra n. 7, at 59–182.

19   Id. at 28–47.

5. CONSTITUTIONAL REVOLUTION IN ITALY

1   Tom Ginsburg, *Judicial Review in New Democracies* 22–35 (2012), who elaborates the "insurance function" in the context of rational-actor models within elitist constitutions. This chapter explores the different—more populist and ideological— dynamic that can generate an analogous "insurance" role for a constitutional court in revolutionary scenarios.

2   Anna Manca, "State Building by Means of Constitution in the Italian Constitutional Monarchy," in Kelly Grotke & Markus Prutsch eds., *Constitutionalism, Legitimacy and Power: Nineteenth Century Experiences* 49, 56 (2014).

3   Denis Mack Smith, *The Making of Italy: 1796–1866* (1988); Lucy Riall, *Risorgimento: The History of Italy from Napoleon to Nation-State* (2009).

4   David Ellwood, *Italy 1943–1945* (1985).

5   See generally, Frank Coppa & Margarita Repetto-Alaia eds., *The Formation of the Italian Republic* (1993).

6   Generally, Ellwood, supra n. 4.

7   Pietro Secchia & Filippo Frassatti, 2 *Storia della Resistenza: La guerra di liberazione in Italia* 527–530 (1965); Aldo Agosti, *Palmiro Togliatti* 149 (2008).

8   In addition to the Communists, Socialists, and Christian Democrats, three other parties played a secondary role in the Committee of National Liberation: the Labor Democrats (DDL), the Action Party (PDA), and the Liberals (PLI). Robert Ventresca, *From Fascism to Democracy* 29 (2004).

9   Piero Craveri, *De Gasperi* 79–85 (2006).

10   Id. at 101–102.

11 Elisa Carrillo, *Alcide De Gasperi: The Long Apprenticeship* 45–100 (1965).

12 David Kertzer, *The Pope and Mussolini* 3–111 (2014).

13 *Lateran Treaty*, art. 1 (1929).

14 De Gasperi's revolutionary convictions were perhaps most eloquently expressed in a letter written to his wife during the last months of his imprisonment by the Fascists:

> Could I, perhaps, have sustained my ideas with less ferocity? I would have certainly done so if those who call themselves Catholics like me ... had not applauded the [Fascist] success so much and, with that attitude, make others believe that the Church was abandoning [us] ... This is the tragedy of my, our, sacrifice.

Alcide de Gasperi, *Lettere dalla Prigione*, prefazione di M. Romana C. de Gasperi, 102–104 (1974) (my translation).

15 Even Togliatti grudgingly recognized De Gasperi's anti-Fascist credentials. Palmiro Togliatti, *De Gasperi il Restauratore* 74–75 (2004).

16 Francesco Traniello, "Political Catholicism, Catholic Organization, and Catholic Laity in the Reconstruction Years," in Coppa & Repetto-Alaia, supra n. 5, at 29–35; see also, David Kertzer, supra n. 12.

17 For an insightful essay, emphasizing this aspect of De Gasperi's thought, see Cau, "Alcide De Gasperi: A Political Thinker or a Thinking Politician?," 14 *Modern Italy* 431–444 (2009).

18 Alcide de Gasperi (a cura di Nicola Guiso), *Idee Sulla Democrazia Cristiana* 17–27 (1974) (my translation).

19 Id.

20 Giorgio Tupini, *I Democratici Cristiani* 83–5 (1954).

21 Even when De Gasperi was struggling against Mussolini in the 1920s, he had emphasized that the crucial division was "not between liberalism and fascism, but between the rule of law developed in modern constitutions and the old police state that is threatening to reappear in disguise [under Fascism]." Paolo Piccoli & Armando Vadagnini, *De Gasperi: Un Trentino Nella Storia D'Europa* 161 (2004) (my translation).

22 Gianfranco Pasquino, "Italy's Transition to Democracy: 1943–1948," in Guillermo O'Donnell et al. eds., *Transitions from Authoritarian Rule: Southern Europe* 60, 66 (1986).

23 While he remained in office, Churchill threw Allied support behind the King, not the Resistance. Once Churchill left office, the Americans took charge: "But, contrary to Churchill's determination, the Americans did not have a specific policy for Italy, or any clear-cut design for the shaping of the Italian political system." Gianfranco Pasquino, supra n. 22, at 60.

24 See generally, Andrea Buratti & Marco Fioravanti eds., *Costituenti Ombra—Altri Luoghi e Altre Figure Della Cultura Politica Italiana (1943–48)* (2010).

25 While his advocacy of the referendum permitted De Gasperi to paper over a division within his party, Antonio Gambino, *Storia del Dopoguerra* 130–131 (1975), it was entirely consistent with his ongoing commitment to popular sovereignty.

26 The poll also revealed a sharp regional split: two-thirds of the South voted for Monarchy, but the more populous North endorsed the Republic by an equally lopsided margin. See Ministry of Interior, at: http://elezionistorico.interno.gov .it/index.php?tpel=F&dtel=02/06/1946&tpa=I&tpe=A&levo=0&levsuto =0&eso=S&ms=S.

Tensions increased when monarchists on Italy's highest court stalled on certifying the final vote. Despite this judicial slowdown, the national unity government immediately issued a proclamation declaring Italy a Republic and designating De Gasperi provisional head of state. 9 Indro Montanelli & Mario Cervi, *Storia d'Italia* 306–317 (2006).

It was up to Umberto II to make the next move. Would he obey the government's command that he leave Italy immediately, or would he escalate the confrontation by remaining in the country until the court made a final decision?

Umberto responded by calling it quits. Montanelli & Cervi, supra, at 317–322. Umberto's final act redeemed De Gasperi's insistence on a popular referendum: Would the same smooth transition have occurred if the 600-member Constituent Assembly, rather than the People themselves, had repudiated the king and proclaimed a Republic?

27 Demofilo (pseudonym of Alcide De Gasperi), "Le Idee Ricostruttive della Democrazia Cristiana," in Edizione Cinque Lune, *Atti e documenti della Democrazia Cristiana* 12–15 (1959) (arguing for a court that "would protect the spirit and the letter of the Constitution . . . against every abuse by public powers").

28 Togliatti, for example, denounced the "oddity *(bizzarria)* of the Constitutional Court," asserting that it was proposed simply because his opponents "fear[ed] that tomorrow there could be a majority which is a direct and free expression of working classes, which deeply desire to renew the social, economic and political structure of the country." Seduta Pomeridiana 1998 (Mar. 11, 1947).

29 Agosti, supra n. 7, at 187; Craveri, supra n. 9, at 339.

30 Italian Constitution (1948), art. 2.

31 Id., arts. 13–54.

32 Leopoldo Elia, "Opening Address: The Republican Constitution and the Development of Democracy in Italy," in Coppa & Repetto-Alaia, supra n. 5, at 13 (quoting Calamandrei).

33 Maurizio Cau notes De Gasperi's emphasis on "corporativism" in the postwar years, supra n. 17, at 442.

34 Vittoria Barsotti et al., *Italian Constitutional Justice in Global Context* 12–16 (2015).

35 Id. at 17–19.

36 Paul Ginsborg, *A History of Contemporary Italy* 103 (1990).

37 Piero Calamandrei, *House of Representatives, Session n.* 597. 24052/3 (Nov. 28, 1950).

38 Ginsborg, supra n. 36, at 115–118.

39 See generally, Samuel Moyne, *Christian Human Rights* (2015).

40 While he was minister of justice, Togliatti had carefully vetted the Fascist judiciary to ensure their loyalty to the new regime. This move significantly ameliorated anxieties over the judiciary's future role. Agosti, supra n. 7, at 164, 186.

41 There was, of course, a countervailing consideration: perhaps the political tide would turn in the long run, and the Christian Democratic court would strike down some future Socialist initiatives. But given De Gasperi's sweeping victory at the polls, this seemed a distant prospect—whereas the short-term risk of Court invalidation of Christian Democratic initiatives was very real.

42 Calamandrei denounced Christian Democratic obstructionism both in Parliament and in a series of three essays. 1 Piero Calamandrei (a cura di Norberto Bobbio), *Scritti e discorsi politici* 546–595 (1966). For a recent appraisal, see Simoncini, "L'istituzione della Corte Costituzionale e la sua Affermazione," 11 *Giornale di Storia Costituzionale* 295 (2006).

43 Barsotti, supra n. 34, at 19–24, for further elaboration of the discussion presented here.

44 L. Paladin, *Per una Storia Costituzionale dell'Italia Repubblicana* 130 (2004) (political science account).

45 F. Bonini, *Storia della Corte costituzionale* 95 (1996).

46 Einaudi was not only a strong supporter of American-style judicial review, but a defender of the Old Court resistance to the New Deal. Einaudi, "*Major et Sanior Partes,* or on Toleration and Political Adhesion," in 3 Domenico da Empoli et al. eds., *Luigi Einaudi: Selected Political Essays* 122, 126–127 (2014).

47 Barsotti, supra n. 34, at 24–27.

48 For a trenchant analysis of the Court's opinion, see id. at 30–35.

49 Id. at 35–36.

50 For insightful accounts, see Sergio Bartole, *Interpretazioni e Trasformazioni della Constituzione Repubblicana* (2004); Barsotti, supra n. 34.

6. A PROGRESS REPORT?

1 For recent reflections on the distinctive problems posed by constitutional legacies, see Diego Arguelhes, *Old Courts, New Beginnings: Judicial Continuity and Constitutional Transformation in Argentina and Brazil* (Yale J.S.D. dissertation, 2014).

7. DE GAULLE'S REPUBLIC

1 If revolving-door government was the problem, de Gaulle never seriously considered the West German solution. Under its Basic Law of 1949, a parliamentary majority could not oust a coalition government through a simple "vote of no confidence." Before this happened, its opponents would be required to assemble a new majority that would affirmatively vote for a new government to replace it. This requirement of a "constructive vote of no confidence" has in fact operated to ensure a remarkable level of government stability. Yet in framing the Gaullist constitution, Michel Debre never seriously considered this device as a serious alternative to the presidentialist model, since it would have required de Gaulle to engage in direct negotiations with parliamentary leaders to form governing coalitions at the beginning of each newly elected National Assembly.

2 Michel Winock, *L'agonie de la IVᵉ République,* 116–123 (2006); Georgette Elgey, 5 *Histoire de la IVᵉ République* 193–254 (2008) (*La République des Tourmentes (1954–1959)*). For an impressionistic account of public opinion, coming to a similar conclusion, Chastenet, "Après la Tourmente," *La Vie Française* 1 (1958).

3 Duncan MacRae Jr., *Parliament, Parties and Society in France, 1946–1958* (1967). This paragraph, along with the next, summarizes key findings in MacRae's important book.

4 Philip Nord, *France's New Deal: From the Thirties to the Postwar Era* 147 (2012); Serge Berstein, *The Republic of de Gaulle, 1958–1969* 102 (Morris trans.) (1993).

5 Frank Giles, *The Locust Years: The Story of the Fourth Republic, 1946–1958* 230–231 (1991).

6 Vaïsse, "France's Nuclear Choice, 1945–1958," 36 *Vingtième Siècle Revue D'Histoire* 21 (1992).

7 Jean-Jacques Chevallier et al., *L'histoire de la Vème République* 13 (2015) suggests that, after Dien Bien Phu, some members of the political elite came to recognize that "broad institutional reform by the insiders" was necessary "in order to avoid a reform by outsiders." But all functioning systems contain their share of insider skeptics. Such calls for reform do not, by themselves, suggest that the Republic was on the verge of imminent collapse.

8 Maurice Duverger, *The French Political System* 190 (1958).

9 Giles, supra n. 5, at 290.

10 Leading historians, as well as engaged intellectuals like Raymond Aron and Pierre Avril, share this judgment. Giles, supra n. 5, at 329–365; Philip Williams, *Crisis and Compromise: Politics in the Fourth Republic* 55–57 (1964); Winock, supra n. 2 (providing a detailed account).

11 Giles, supra n. 5, at 205.

12 Hugues Tertrais, *Le piastre et le fusil: Le coût de la guerre d'indochine 1945–1954* (2002).

13 Williams, supra n. 10, at 115–131.

14 Between 1952 and 1955, military expenditure amounted to one-third of the entire budget. Giles, supra n. 5, at 195.

15 Id. at 262–263.

16 Id. at 297–328; Elgey, supra n. 2, at 496–497.

17 Giles, supra n. 5, at 310–311.

18 Id. at 318–319; Jean-Marie Denquin, *1958: Le genèse de la Vème République* 143–144 (1988).

19 Giles, supra n. 5, at 321 (Giles transl.). The telegram was also signed by other leading officers.

20 Id. at 324–328.

21 Id. at 329–331.

22 Id. at 330.

23 Id. at 351.

24 Id. at 352.

25 Jean Lacouture, *De Gaulle: The Ruler* 175 (1991) (Sheridan transl.). French constitutionalists have typically trivialized the role of Operation Resurrection in overwhelming the governing elite's resistance to de Gaulle's takeover. See, for example, the single cryptic paragraph that Professor Jean-Marie Denquin devotes to the subject in his important book, supra n. 18, 170.

26 *Le Monde*, "En Province" (May 30, 1958).

27 *Le Monde*, "Plusieurs blessés" (June 2, 1958).

28 De Gaulle, *Address to the National Assembly (June 1, 1958)*, at: http://www.charles -de-gaulle.org/wp-content/uploads/2017/03/Discours-prononcé-place-de-la -République-à-Paris.pdf.

29 Lacouture, supra n. 25, at 179.

30 President Coty engaged in a brow-beating exercise of his own. He threatened to resign if the National Assembly did not support his nomination of de Gaulle. This would have deprived the Fourth Republic of a head of state at a moment of existential crisis. Coty's unprecedented threat provoked such protest that André Le Troquer, the president of the Assembly, had trouble finishing Coty's speech over the loud denunciations from the floor. Nevertheless, when confronting the abyss, the National Assembly appointed de Gaulle by a vote of 329 to 224. Winock, supra n. 2, at 266–274.

31 Lacouture, supra n. 25, at 178.

32 Francis Hamon & Michel Troper, *Droit Constitutionnel* 420–424 (36th ed. 2015).

33 Berstein, supra n. 4, at 6–8.

34 Id. at 13–16.

35 Chevallier, supra n. 7, at 29–35; Michel Troper, "Constitutional Law," in George Bermann & Etienne Picard eds., *Introduction to French Law* 22–29 (2008).

36 The official text of de Gaulle's speech does not include "the celebrated phrase 'Vive l'Algérie française!' even though numerous witnesses confirm that he made this declaration "rather than the 'Vive l'Algérie' which appears in the text." Berstein, supra n. 4, at 31. De Gaulle's *Memoirs*, written after his retirement, reveal a similar tendency to rewrite history; see Lacouture, supra n. 25, at 188–189.

37 This remarkable result was also due to an FLN boycott of the parliamentary elections. Berstein, supra n. 4, at 31. In previously providing statistics on the Gaullist landslides in these elections, I was only reporting the results from metropolitan France, without adding these phony Algerian numbers into the total.

38 Id. at 41–42.

39 Lacouture, supra n. 25, at 287–300 (de Gaulle's "zigzag to peace").

40 Hamon & Troper, supra n. 32, at 535–536. The only—very important—exception to this rule deals with referenda on France's relationship to the European Union. I will be discussing these referenda in the next volume.

41 Mark Walker, *The Strategic Use of Referendums: Power, Legitimacy, and Democracy* 26–28 (2003).

42 Berstein, supra n. 4, at 50 (Berstein trans.; my emphasis); Nassif, "Generals and Autocrats," 130 *Pol. Sci. Q.* 245 (2015) (ultimate dependence of high command on obedience of rank and file).

43 Berstein, supra n. 4, at 70.

44 Lacouture, supra n. 25, at 312–314.

45 Id. at 306.

46 Id. at 306–307.

47 Id.

48 Id.

49 My emphasis.

50 Section 89 also allowed for an amendment without the need for a referendum if it obtained a three-fifths majority of both houses meeting in joint session.

51 I disagree, however, that de Gaulle's proposed referendum would have "certain[ly]" been rejected by the Senate—though there is no way, of course, to verify such counterfactuals. But see Lucien Jaume, "Constituent Power in France: The Revolution and Its Consequences," in Martin Loughlin & Neil Walker eds., *The Paradox of Constitutionalism* 82 (2008).

52 Berstein, supra n. 4, at 71.

53 Lacouture, supra n. 25, at 488–495.

54 Chevallier, supra n. 7, at 84.

55 The Council's first president was de Gaulle's longtime strategic advisor, Leon Noel, who continued to serve as an advisor during Noel's six-year term of office.

56 De Gaulle, *Memoirs of Hope: Renewal and Endeavor* 315 (1971) (Kilmartin trans.)

57 Viansson-Ponté, "Le Conseil d'État juge inconstitutionnel le recours à l'article 11," *Le Monde* 1 (Oct. 3, 1962) (reporting leak from "reliable" informant).

58 Berstein, supra n. 4, at 73.

59 Id. at 75–76.

60 Barrillon, "A l'appel de M. Monnerville, les radicaux s'élèvent contre 'un référendum manifestement illégal et inconstitutionnel,'" *Le Monde* (Oct. 2, 1962).

61 The Council's rationale is so far-fetched that the leading textbook can barely contain its incredulity in dealing with its decision. Hamon & Troper, supra n. 32, at 753.

62 Alec Stone Sweet, *The Birth of Judicial Politics in France: The Constitutional Council in Comparative Perspective* 65–66 (1992).

63 Id. at 66 (quoting Monnerville).

64 Charles de Gaulle, "Television Address of November 7, 1962," at: http://www.ina.fr/video/CAF89051357.

65 Berstein, supra n. 4, at 96–100, 200–201 (table 21).

66 Ingrid Gilcher-Holtey, *Die Phantasie an die Macht* 171–278 (1995); Martin Klimke & Joachim Scharloth eds., *1968 in Europe* (2006).

67 Lacouture, supra n. 25, at 557.

68 De Gaulle did not deign to mention Mitterrand by name, but he clearly had his arch-rival in mind when warning that hard-line Communists would "mak[e] use of the ambition and hatred of second-rate politicians" to gain political ascendancy. "Speech of May 30th 1968," *Discours et messages 5 Vers le terme* 344–345 (1970).

69 Gilcher-Holtey, supra n. 66, at 339–420, 471–475.

70 Berstein, supra n. 4, at 228.

8. RECONSTRUCTING THE FIFTH REPUBLIC

1 Wolin, "Le moment maoïste parfait de Sartre," 187 *Revue l'Homme et la Société* 273 (2013).

2 Boudou, "Autopsie de la décision du Conseil constitutionnel du 16 Juillet 1971 sur la liberté d'association," 97 *Rev. Fran. de Droit Con.* 5–120 (2014); Beardsley, "The Constitutional Council and Constitutional Liberties in France," 20 *Amer. J. Comp. Law* 431–452 (1972).

3 Alain Poher, *Trois fois president: Mémoires* 213–216 (1993).

4 Alec Stone Sweet, *The Birth of Judicial Politics in France* 67 (1992).

5 Palewski, "Propos," *Rev. des Deux Mondes* 138–139 (Jan. 1981).

6 Poher, supra n. 3, at 213–216 (quoting Palewski as confiding that he "need[ed] to make Pompidou understand that he is not de Gaulle, one must give him a lesson and call him to order").

7 Id. at 138 (quoting Palewski as emphasizing that the switch to popular election in 1962 made it essential to "introduc[e] actual counterweights in our Constitution").

8 Laurens, "Le Conseil constitutionnel donne un coup d'arrêt au pouvoir et affirme son indépendance," *Le Monde* (July 19, 1971).

9 *Programme commun de gouvernement du Parti Communiste et du Parti Socialiste* 145–146 (1972).

10 *Les grandes décisions du Conseil constitutionnel* 267–287 (1975).

11 *Constitution de la République française adoptée par l'Assemblée nationale constituante le 19 avril 1946,* art. 36, at: http://mjp.univ-perp.fr/france/co1946p.htm.

12 *Official Gazette, Constituent Assembly* 3375 (Aug. 28, 1946), at: http://4e.republique .jo-an.fr/numero/1946_i84.pdf.

13 Louis Favoreu ed., *Nationalisations et Constitution* 105–193 (1982).

14 Martin Rogoff, *French Constitutional Law: Cases and Materials* 210–212 (2011) (text of decision).

15 Stone Sweet, supra n. 4, at 159.

16 Maurice Duverger invoked the New Deal precedent in "Volonté générale et texte des lois," *Le Monde* (Dec. 3, 1981). His opponents appealed instead to the Supreme Court's decision in the Nixon Tapes Case, which "led to the rapid exclusion of a president with one of the strongest popular mandates." Gantier, "Devra-t-on, pourra-t-on dénationaliser?," *Le Monde* (Feb. 17, 1982).

17 Because Mitterrand wanted the statute to pass quickly this time, he was willing to accept higher levels of compensation than did other Socialist leaders. Jacques Attali, 1 *Verbatim* 156 (1993).

18 Stone Sweet, supra n. 4, at 162.

19 *Débats parlementaires, Assemblée Nationale* 550 (Jan. 26, 1982).

20 John Keeler & Alec Stone, "Judicial Confrontation in Mitterrand's France," in Stanley Hoffman et al. eds., *The Mitterrand Experiment* 170 (1987); Rollat, "Exprimant les réserves du gouvernement le PS met en cause, à son tour, le role du Conseil," *Le Monde* (Jan. 20, 1982).

21 Rogoff, supra n. 14, at 103–105 (text of decision); Jean Lacouture, 2 *Mitterrand: Une histoire de Français* 242–248 (1998) (political context).

22 Louis Favoreu, *Le politique saisie par le droit* (1988) (paradigmatic statement of emerging narrative).

23 De Gaulle also had a son, Philippe, who attempted to deploy his inherited charisma to establish a new party, the Centre des Républicains Libres—which never got anywhere. Philippe de Gaulle, *Mémoires accessoires: 1946–1982* (1997).

24 Jean-Jacques Chevallier et al., *Histoire de la Vᵉ République, 1958–2015* 29–35 (15th ed. 2015).

25 On the amendment, see *Projet de loi constitutionnelle n°1203* (Mar. 30, 1990), at: https://www.senat.fr/evenement/revision/pjlc90.html.

26 Carcassonne, "Le Parlement et la QPC," 137 *Pouvoirs* 73–81 (2011) (describing 1993 precedents).

27 Between 1959 and 1984, 31 percent of Council members were jurists and 69 percent were politicians. Between 1986 and 2016, 44 percent were jurists and 56 percent were politicians. Carcassonne, "Les membres du Conseil Constitutionnel: 1958–2008," *Cahiers du Con. Con.* 10–13 (2009) (supplemented with more recent data).

28 The decisive shift occurred in the 1990s, with the creation of the *Revue Française de Droit Constitutionnel*.

29 Comité de réflexion et de proposition sur la modernisation et le rééquilibrage des institutions de la Vᵉ République présidé par Edouard Balladur, *Une Vᵉ République plus démocratique* 20–21 (2008).

30 Bastien Francois, *La Constitution Sarkozy* 80–81 (2009).

31 Journal Officiel de la Republique Francaise, *Loi constitutionnelle n°2008-724 du 23 juillet 2008 de modernisation des institutions de la Vᵉ République;* Avril & Gicquel, "Chronique constitutionnelle française (1ᵉʳ juillet–30 septembre 2008)," 128 *Pouvoirs* 156, 179 (2008).

32 54 *Nouveaux Cahiers du Conseil constitutionnel* 309 (2017) (statistical data through Sept. 2016).

33 Francis Hamon & Michel Troper, *Droit Constitutionnel* 757–771 (2015); Tusseau, "La fin d'une exception française?," 137 *Pouvoirs* 5–11 (2011).

9. SOLIDARITY'S TRIUMPH IN POLAND

1 Freedom House, *Nations in Transit (2015)* at: https://freedomhouse.org/sites /default/files/FH_NIT2015_06.06.15_FINAL.pdf.

2 My formula recalls similar concerns expressed by Linz, "The Perils of Presidentialism," 1 *J. Democracy* 51 (1990).

3 Gale Stokes, *From Stalinism to Pluralism* (1991).

4 Arato, "Civil Society against the State: Poland 1980–81," *Telos* 23 (1981); Zuzowski, "The Polish Intelligentsia: KOR and Solidarity," 26 *Austral. J. of Pol. Sci.* 307 (1991).

5 Maryjane Osa, *Solidarity and Contention: Networks of Polish Opposition* 135 (2003); Zuzowski, "The Origins of Open Organized Dissent in Today's Poland: KOR and Other Dissident Groups," 25 *East Eur. Q.* (1991).

6   Timothy Garton Ash, *The Polish Revolution: Solidarity* 67 (1983).

7   Id. at 55.

8   The agreement also committed the government to a wide-ranging series of fundamental rights, id. at 73–76, but the Party extracted its own guarantees against "disturbing the established system of international alliances," id. at 67.

9   Id. at 80, 163.

10 R. J. Crampton, *Eastern Europe in the Twentieth Century—and After* 157 (2nd ed. 2002).

11 Ash, supra n. 6, at 55.

12 Id. at 178.

13 Mark Kramer, "The Soviet Union, the Warsaw Pact, and the Polish Crisis of 1980–81," in Lee Trepanier et al. eds., *The Solidarity Movement and Perspectives on the Last Decade of the Cold War* 27, 64 (2010).

14 Ash, supra n. 6, at 263–264.

15 Id. at 172–173 (analysis of alternative scenarios).

16 "Revolution" was the word consistently used to describe the struggle—both by Solidarity and by its opponents—throughout the entire period. Id. at 287.

17 The decision to suppress Solidarity was most likely taken at the meeting between Jaruzelski and Brezhnev in the Crimea. Kramer, supra n. 13, at 48; Arthur Rachwald, *In Search of Poland* 20 (1990).

18 Grzegorz Ekiert, *The State against Society* 23 (1996). One year after the crackdown, only a small number of Solidarity's leaders remained in custody—with Wałesa gaining his release in November 1982. Gale Stokes, *The Walls Came Tumbling Down* 109 (1993).

19 Christopher Andrew, *The Sword and the Shield* (2000); Roman Laba, *The Roots of Solidarity: A Political Sociology of Poland's Working-Class* 148 (1991).

20 David Ost, *Solidarity and the Politics of Anti-Politics* 49 (1990).

21 For an especially vivid description, see Shana Penn, *Solidarity's Secret: The Women Who Defeated Communism in Poland* 148–178 (2005).

22 Dorothee Bohle & Gisela Neunhöffer, "Why Is There No Third Way?," in Dieter Plehwe et al. eds., *Neoliberal Hegemony: A Global Critique* 89, 94 (2006); David Ost, *Labor and Union Identity in Poland: 1989–2000* 6 n.8 (2000).

23 Wiktor Osiatynski, "The Roundtable Talks in Poland," in Jon Elster ed., *The Roundtable Talks and the Breakdown of Communism* 21, 28 (1996).

24 Roger Boyes, *The Naked President* 168 (1994); Marjorie Castle, *Triggering Communism's Collapse* 44 (2003).

25 Boyes, supra n. 24, at 169.

26 Jan Kubik & Amy Linch, "The Original Sin of Poland's Third Republic," in Dariusz Aleksandrowicz et al. eds., *The Polish Solidarity Movement in Retrospect: A Story of Failure or Success?* 23, 32 n.11 (2009).

27 Gregory F. Domber, *Empowering Revolution: America, Poland and the End of the Cold War* 215 (2014).

28 Boyes, supra n. 24, at 170.

29 Wałesa denounced the planned closure as a "personal provocation . . . against the birthplace of Solidarity." See Associated Press, "Walesa Says He'll Fight Government's Plans to Close Gdansk Shipyard" (Oct. 31, 1988).

30 The head of the Communist unions, Alfred Miodowocz, apparently issued his debate challenge on his own initiative. But Rakowski allowed it to go forward. See Wojciech Koszkowski, "Points of Departure," in Jan Chodakiewicz et al. eds., *Poland's Transformation: A Work in Progress* 38 (2003).

31 Castle, supra n. 24, at 47.

32 Jan Kubik, *Power of Symbols against the Symbols of Power* 284 (2010); Castle, supra n. 24, at 67–68.

33 Castle, supra n. 24, at 134.

34 Osiatynski, supra n. 23, at 33–34.

35 Id. at 25.

36 Piotr Sula, "Post-Communist Parties in Poland after 1989," in Uwe Backes & Patrick Moreau eds., *Communist and Post-Communist Parties in Europe* 311, 312–314 (2008).

37 Castle, supra n. 24, at 72, 104.

38 Id. at 104–114.

39 Jacqueline Hayden, *The Collapse of Communist Power in Poland* 76–81 (2006).

40 Id.

41 Castle, supra n. 24, at 116.

42 Id. at 118.

43 Reuters, "Walesa Begs Workers to Give Talks a Chance" (Mar. 1, 1989).

44 Joseph Rothschild, *Return to Diversity* 184 (2007).

45 Hayden, supra n. 39, at 81–85.

46 Castle, supra n. 24, at 123. See also Jacek Kuroń's revealing report in Solidarity's leading underground newspaper:

> In that moment a certain dogma of the communist system crumbled: there will be free elections in Poland. Their result will be to show, and from then on we can say: you do indeed rule here, but not by right. . . . *After all, if we win by an overwhelming majority there will come into being in Poland an authentic representation of society, speaking with its own voice.*

Castle, supra n. 24, at 123 (quoting *Tygodnik Mazowsze*, Mar. 8, 1989) (emphasis added).

47 Castle, supra n. 24, at 121–122.

48 Hayden, supra n. 39, at 81–85.

49 Castle, supra n. 24, at 133.

50 Id. at 123–124, 133.

51 Id. at 134.

52 A. Kemp-Welch, *Poland under Communism: A Cold War History* 369 (2008) (2.2 million party members on eve of Round Table Talks).

53 Grabowski, "The Party That Never Was: The Rise and Fall of the Solidarity Citizens' Committees in Poland," 10 *East European Politics and Societies* 214 (1996) (detailed description of developments); Castle, supra n. 24, at 41–44 (briefer summary).

54 Grabowski, supra n. 53, at 222 (translation from the Polish original).

55 Id. at 220–222.

56 Solidarity won 64 percent of the vote in the "open" Sejm seats and 73 percent in the Senate races. Castle, supra n. 24, at 196.

57 Gareth Dale, *Popular Protest in East Germany* 264 (1999).

58 Castle, supra n. 24, at 205.

59 Id. at 195–196 (election results).

60 Id. at 202 (quoting *Rzeczpospolita*, June 7, 1989); Kemp-Welch, supra n. 52, at 405 (describing confrontation between Geremek and leading Communists).

61 *Gazeta Wyborcza* (June 14 and 15, 1989); Castle, supra n. 24, at 202.

62 The legal problem was created by the refusal of the Communist notables to risk further humiliation by running again on a nationwide basis. As a consequence, the Sejm abolished the national list and created thirty-three new election districts. In doing so, it violated the constitutional rules that had constructed the new Sejm in the first place. Castle, supra n. 24, at 203.

63 Id.

64 Id. at 206.

65 Tagliabue, "Jaruzelski, Changing Mind, Will Seek Presidency," *N.Y. Times* (July 19, 1989); Castle, supra n. 24, at 206–207.

66 Mark Brzezinski, *The Struggle for Constitutionalism in Poland* 87, n. 16 (2000) (citing commentary by a leading jurist).

67 Boyes, supra n. 24, at 191.

68 Castle, supra n. 24, at 206, 206 n.52.

69 Tagliabue, "Jaruzelski Wins Polish Presidency by Minimum Votes" *N.Y. Times* (July 20, 1989); Castle, supra n. 24, at 206 n.55.

70 Castle, supra n. 24, at 207. Reflecting on his handiwork, Geremek remarked that "there was no better way to accomplish [the] election than just by one vote." Id. at 207 n.58.

71 Id. at 208–210.

72 Krzysztof Jasiewicz, "Poland: Wałesa's Legacy to the Presidency," in Ray Taras ed., *Postcommunist Presidents* 130, 155 (1997).

73 Ivo Banac, *Eastern Europe in Revolution* 65 (1992); Frances Millard, *Democratic Elections in Poland, 1991–2007* 24 (2010).

10. SOLIDARITY'S COLLAPSE

1 Lucja Cannon, "Polish Transition Strategy," in Jane Zacek & Ilpyong Kim eds., *The Legacy of the Soviet Bloc* 148–149 (1997).

2 Mazowiecki's construction of a coalition with the Communists is a common theme in leading accounts. Roger Boyes, *The Naked President* 203 (1994); Timothy Garton Ash, *The Polish Revolution: Solidarity* 372 (1983); Frances Millard, *Democratic Elections in Poland, 1991–2007* 11 (2009).

3   Wałesa became increasingly disenchanted with his treatment by the Warsaw government soon after he had installed it in office. To his dismay, Mazowiecki had appointed his Council of Ministers without even consulting him. As the government moved into high gear, Wałesa regularly phoned in his advice, and Mazowiecki dutifully listened—but then ignored it to pursue his own neo-liberal policies. Jacqueline *Hayden, Poles Apart: Solidarity and the New Poland* 104–105 (1994); Simpson, "The Troubled Reign of Lech Wałesa in Poland," 26 *Pres. Stud. Q.* 317, 320 (1996).

4   Millard, supra n. 2, at 23; Krzysztof Jasiewicz, "Poland: Walesa's Legacy to the Presidency," in Ray Taras ed., *Postcommunist Presidents* 130, 132 (1997).

5   Grabowski, "The Party That Never Was: The Rise and Fall of the Solidarity Citizens' Committees in Poland," 10 *East Eur. Pol. & Soc.* 214, 229 (1996).

6   Id.

7   Id. at 243–245.

8   Id. at 245.

9   Szulkin, "The 1990 Presidential Election in Poland," 16 *Scan. Pol. Stud.* 359, 362 (1993); Millard, supra n. 2, at 23.

10 Grabowski, supra n. 5, at 242–246.

11 Boyes, supra n. 2, at 251; Borrell, "Poland: Electrician vs. Intellectual," *Time* (Nov. 19, 1990) (Mazowiecki still had a 5-point polling advantage as late as October); Mitchell Orenstein, *Out of the Red* 38 (fig. 3) (2001).

12 Grabowski, supra n. 5, at 248.

13 Id. (reporting data one month before the election).

14 Millard, supra n. 2, at 23.

15 Id. at 25–26; Boyes, supra n. 2, at 256–257; Simpson, supra n. 3, at 321.

16 Adam Michnik, "My Vote against Walesa," in Irena Grudzinska-Gross ed., *Letters from Freedom: Post-Cold War Realities and Perspectives* 156, 160 (1998).

17 In fact, Geremek allowed old-time Communists to dominate a crucial subcommission dealing with basic questions of institutional design. Andrzej Rapaczynski, "Constitutional Politics in Poland," in A. E. Dick Howard ed., *Constitution Making in Eastern Europe* 93–131, 100 (1993).

18 In contrast to later periods, constitutional questions provoked broad popular discussion at this time. Wyrzykowski, "Constitutional Changes in Poland 1989–1991," 17 *Bull. Austl. Soc'y. of Leg. Phil.* 25, 45 (1992).

19 Mark Brzezinski & Leszek Garlicki, "Polish Constitutional Law," in Stanisław Frankowski & Paul Stephan eds., *Legal Reform in Post-Communist Europe: The View from Within* 21, 33 (1995).

20 Brzezinski, "The Emergence of Judicial Review in Eastern Europe: The Case of Poland," 41 *Am. J. Comp. L.* 153, 169–173 (1993).

21 Lech Garlicki, "Constitutional Court of Poland: 1982–2009," in Pasquale Pasquino & Francesca Billi eds., *The Political Origins of Constitutional Courts: Italy, Germany, France, Poland, Canada, United Kingdom* 13, 16–19 (2009).

22 Bond, "Concerning Constitutional Courts in Central and Eastern Europe," 2 *Int'l Public Pol'y R.* 5, 10 (2006). The Tribunal demonstrated greater activism when

dealing with administrative regulations, as opposed to legislation. See Garlicki, supra n. 21, at 19–20.

23 Brzezinski, supra n. 20.

24 Janina Zakrzewska, *Kontrola Konstytucyjności Ustaw: We Współczesnym Państwie Burżuazyjnym* (Control over the Constitutionality of Laws in the Modern Bourgeois State) (1964).

25 Brzezinski, supra n. 20, at 169.

26 Osiatynski, "Special Report: Poland's Constitutional Ordeal," 3 *East. Eur. Con. Rev.* 29–38 (2009). See also, Rapaczynski, supra n. 17.

27 For important insights, see two books by Anna Grzymala-Busse: *Redeeming the Communist Past: The Regeneration of the Communist Successor Parties in East Central Europe* (2002) and *Rebuilding Leviathan: Party Competition and State Exploitation in Post-Communist Democracies* (2008).

28 During this election, the Center Accord had formed a coalition with some small parties to run as the Civic Center Alliance. To prevent reader confusion, I am sticking with the Center's previously established name.

29 Millard, supra n. 2, at 48–49. Twenty other parties won very small numbers of Sejm seats. The Senate pattern was similar.

30 Wiatr, "The President in the Polish Parliamentary Democracy," 37 *Politička misao* 89–98, 92 (2000).

31 Jasiewicz, supra n. 4, at 138–141.

32 Frances Millard, *Politics and Society in Poland* 21 (2002).

33 Wałesa claimed that his authority to "coordinate" national security implicitly empowered him to name the ministers of internal affairs, national defense, and foreign affairs to the Council of Ministers. He ultimately won this fight. Brzezinski & Garlicki, supra n. 19, at 40.

34 Millard, supra n. 32, at 58–59.

35 Jasiewicz, supra n. 4, at 141.

36 Brzezinski, supra n. 20, at 111 (on the provisional character of the "little Constitution").

37 Id. at 114–115 (detailing salient differences between the drafts).

38 Id. at 115–116 (for further details).

39 The economic situation began to improve in 1991, but GNP did not reach 1989 levels until 1994. De Broeck & Koen, "The 'Soaring Eagle': Anatomy of the Polish Take-Off in the 1990s," IMF Working Paper (Jan. 2000), at: http://www.imf.org/external/pubs/ft/wp/2000/wp0006.pdf.

40 Generally, Grzymala-Busse, *Redeeming*, supra n. 27, at 208–214.

41 The two major Solidarity parties in the Sejm were the Democratic Union (10.6 percent) and the Labor Union (7.3 percent)—both secular and relatively liberal. Wałesa's "Non-Party Reform Bloc" (5.4 percent) also managed to leap over the threshold, taking just enough votes away from the Solidarity union to deprive it of representation. See Millard, supra n. 2, at 56–78 (tables 4.2–4.4 provide relevant statistics).

42 Id. at 77–78.

43 Jasiewicz, supra n. 4, at 151–154.

44 Brzezinski, supra n. 20, at 118.

45 Id. at 123.

46 Jasiewicz, supra n. 4, at 154.

47 Id. at 158–162. Turnout in the final round of the presidential election was 68 percent. Turnout in previous parliamentary elections had been 43.2 percent in 1991 and 52.08 percent in 1993. Millard, supra n. 2, at 209.

48 Lech Garlicki & Zofia Garlicka, "Constitution Making, Peace Building, and National Reconciliation: The Experience of Poland," in Laurel E. Miller ed., *Framing the State in Times of Transition: Case Studies in Constitution Making* 391, 399 (2010).

49 Ewa Karpowicz & Wlodzimierz Wesolowski, "Committees of the Polish Sejm in Two Political Systems," in David Olson & William Crowther eds., *Committees in Post-Communist Democratic Parliaments: Comparative Institutionalization* 44, 47–49 (2002).

50 Osyatinski, "A Brief History of the Constitution," 6 *E. Eur. Con. Rev.* 66 (1997) (overview of constitutional provisions); Tóth, "From Uneasy Compromises to Democratic Partnership: The Prospects of Central European Constitutionalism," 13 *Eur. J.L. Reform* 80, 88–89 (2011) (describing concessions to the Church).

51 Anna Grzymala-Busse, "Redeeming the Past," in Grzegorz Ekiert & Stephen E. Hanson eds., *Assessing the Legacy of Communist Rule* 157 (2003) ("Because the drafting process took place in the lion's den of daily politics, the very legitimacy of the framers was repeatedly called into question. . . . More often than not, compromises were struck by adding into the draft constitution everything that everyone wanted.").

52 Eberts, "The Roman Catholic Church and Democracy in Poland," 50 *Europe-Asia Studies* 817, 835 (1998).

53 Grzymala-Busse, supra n. 51.

54 To be exact, only 22.6 percent of the eligible population voted in the referendum. Levent Gönenç, *Prospects for Constitutionalism in Post-Communist Countries* 133 (2002). In his perceptive discussion, Andrew Arato concludes that the Constitution "seemed an imposed and illegitimate product" from the perspective of "major forces in Polish society, including the Church, Solidarity, and its offspring." See *Civil Society, Constitution, and Legitimacy* 228 (2000).

55 Under article 19, the president can trigger a referendum only with the consent of the Senate; the Sejm can do it on its own.

56 "Uchwała Sądu Najwyższego z dnia 15 lipca 1997 r. w sprawie ważności referendum konstytucyjnego przeprowadzonego w dniu 25 maja 1997 r". (Resolution of the Supreme Court of July 15, 1997, on the validity of the constitutional referendum held on May 25, 1997), *Dz.U. 1997 nr 79 poz. 490* (July 15, 1997).

57 Ackerman & Kisilowski, "Obama Is Poland's Only Hope," *Foreign Policy* (Jan. 21, 2016).

58 See id. If the two leftist factions had joined forces, their entry into the Sejm would have made it impossible for Law and Justice to convert its 37.5 percent share of

the vote into a majority of the seats—requiring it to enter a coalition with more moderate center-right forces.

59 Recall that, during the early 1990s, Geremek's constitutional commission in the Sejm did in fact favor a parliamentary model.

11. THE RACE AGAINST TIME

1 Bokyoke Aung San's Address at the Convention, on May 23, 1947, in Josef Silverstein ed., *The Political Legacy of Aung San* 151, 159 (rev. ed. 1993).

2 Silverstein's introduction to his edited volume, supra n. 1, provides an outstanding overview.

3 Richard Butwell, *U Nu of Burma* chap. 10 (1963).

4 Generally David I. Steinberg, *Burma: The State of Myanmar* chap. 1 (2001).

5 Id. at xxviii.

6 For a more elaborate breakdown of the election results, see Europa Publications, *Regional Surveys of the World: The Far East and Australasia 2003* 863 (34th ed. 2002).

7 Aung San Suu Kyi was placed under house arrest from July 20, 1989, to July 10, 1995; from September 23, 2000, to May 6, 2002; and again from May 30, 2003, to November 13, 2010. See generally Peter Popham, *The Lady and the Peacock: The Life of Aung San Suu Kyi* (2012).

8 Karen Human Rights Group, *Suffering in Silence* (2001).

9 BBC, "Burma 'Approves New Constitution'" (May 15, 2008) (expressing skepticism about the 94 percent Yes vote) at: http://news.bbc.co.uk/2/hi/asia-pacific /7402105.stm.

10 Constitution (2008), art. 109 (reserving one-fourth of the seats in the House of Representatives); art. 141 (same for House of Nationalities); at: http://www.wipo .int/wipolex/en/text.jsp?file_id=181169.

11 Article 201 granted the commander-in-chief authority to appoint—directly or indirectly—five of the eleven members of the Council, enabling him to overrule the president by gaining the support of one more member.

12 Constitution (2008), art. 410 (defining emergency); art. 420 (suspending "fundamental rights"); art. 296 (suspending habeas corpus and due process).

13 Constitution (2008), art. 445 (amnesty).

14 Constitution (2008), art. 436.

15 Constitution (2008), art. 59(f).

16 Reneaud Egretaud, "Emerging Patterns of Parliamentary Politics," in Donald Steinberg ed., *Myanmar: The Dynamics of an Evolving Polity* 59, 62 (2015).

17 Id. at 62–63 (table 4.1).

18 Lloyd-George, "The Dicey Democrat," *Foreign Policy* (Nov. 28, 2012).

19 The junta's party won 9.1 percent of the seats in the lower house and 6.5 percent in the upper house. See Union Election Commission: http://uecmyanmar.org /index.php/2014-02-11-08-31-43/863-20-11-2015-amyothar93 (official Burmese source); http://psephos.adam-carr.net/countries/b/burma/burma2015.txt (En-

glish language report). But this jumped to 31.8 percent and 29.9 percent once the commander in chief made his appointments.

20 Parameswaran, "Constitutional Reform Fails in Myanmar Ahead of Polls," *The Diplomat* (June 26, 2015).

21 Moe & Ramzy, "Aung San Suu Kyi Nominated as Minister in Myanmar's Government," *New York Times* (Mar. 22, 2016).

22 Herzl himself considered the pros and cons of Palestine and Argentina as homelands in *The Jewish State* chap. 2 (1896), and the choice between Palestine and Uganda was a serious matter for debate at the Sixth and Seventh Congresses of the World Zionist Organization in 1903 and 1905. See Adam Rovner, *In the Shadow of Zion: Promised Lands before Israel* 54–81 (2014). After those congresses, British Zionist Israel Zangwill broke off from the WZO, and established a Jewish Territorial Association, which "very nearly succeeded in establishing a 'Portuguese Palestine' in Angola in the years leading up to World War I." Id. at 92.

23 Mitchell Cohen, *Zion and State: Nation, Class and the Shaping of Modern Israel* 97 (1992); Anita Shapira, *Berl: The Biography of a Socialist Zionist: Berl Katznelson, 1887–1944* (1984).

24 Jonathan Schneer, *The Balfour Declaration: The Origins of the Arab-Israeli Conflict* (2012).

25 Jack Fellman, *The Revival of a Classical Tongue: Eliezer Ben Yehuda and the Modern Hebrew Language* 96 (2014); Liora Halperin, *Babel in Zion: Jews, Nationalism, and Language Diversity in Palestine, 1920–1948* (2015).

26 Samuel Sager, *The Parliamentary System of Israel* 11–21 (1985) (evolution of Jewish self-government under the Mandate).

27 Anita Shapira, *Ben-Gurion: Father of Modern Israel* 98–100 (2014) (Ben-Gurion's coalition-building activities under the Mandate); Itzhak Galnoor, *The Partition of Palestine: Decision Crossroads in the Zionist Movement* 224 (1995) (Ben-Gurion's coalition-building inclinations during the early years of independence).

28 For different perspectives on self-government by the Orthodox community during the Mandate, see Ben Halpern & Jehuda Reinharz, *Zionism and the Creation of a New Society* 188–194 (1998); Martin Sicker, *Pangs of the Messiah: The Troubled Birth of the Jewish State* 57–64 (2000); Aaron Klieman, *The Rise of Israel: Zionist Political Activity in the 1920s and 1930s*, 98–108 (1987); Sheneur Abramov, *Perpetual Dilemma: Jewish Religion in the Jewish State* 90 (1976).

29 Michael Brown, *The Israeli-American Connection: Its Roots in the Yishuv, 1914–1945* (1996); Raymond Russel, *Utopia in Zion: The Israeli Experience with Worker Cooperatives* 30–35 (1995).

30 Israel Central Bureau of Statistics (Sept. 1, 2016), "Population, by Religion," at: http://www.cbs.gov.il/shnaton67/st02_02.pdf; Israeli Ministry of Aliyah and Integration, "The First Aliyah (1882–1903)," at: http://www.moia.gov.il/English/FeelingIsrael/AboutIsrael/Pages/aliya1.aspx); Jonathan Kaplan, The Jewish Agency for Israel, "The Mass Migration of the 1950s," at: http://www.jewishagency.org/society-and-politics/content/36566.

31 Joseph Schechtman, *The Life and Times of Vladimir Jabotinsky: Rebel and Statesman* 206 (1986).

32 Bernard Avishai, *The Tragedy of Zionism* 129–131 (2002).

33 Id. at 167–168.

34 Id. at 166.

35 Shapira, supra n. 27, at 138.

36 Daniel Gordis, *Menachem Begin: The Battle for Israel's Soul* 80–90 (2014).

37 Sager, supra n. 26, at 23.

38 Radzyner, "A Constitution for Israel: The Design of the Leo Kohn Proposal, 1948," 15 *Israel Studies* 1 (2010).

39 The Declaration makes it clear that "the People's Council shall act as a Provisional Council of State, and its executive organ, the People's Administration, shall be the Provisional Government of the Jewish State," and that these provisional institutions shall continue "until the establishment of the elected, regular authorities of the State in accordance with the Constitution which shall be adopted by the Elected Constituent Assembly not later than the 1st October 1948." *Declaration of Independence* at ¶12.

40 Platform of the Workers of Israel Party (Mapai) for Elections to the Constituent Assembly, "The Task of the State of Israel" (1949) (on file with the author).

41 Herut's constitutional program called for the wide use of public referenda, direct elections for many public offices, strong local governments, and the protection of civil rights against governmental assertions of emergency powers. "The Election Platform for the Constituent Assembly of the Herut Movement, Founder of the National Military Organization," at: http://www.infocenters.co.il/jabo/jabo _multimedia/%D7%94%201/%D7%941%20_%2019_1.pdf.

42 Emanuel Rackman, *Israel's Emerging Constitution* 18 (1954).

43 Id. at 31.

44 There was a bit of media coverage when the State Council formally announced its decision on January 13. See, e.g., JTA, "Israeli State Council to Transfer Activities to Constituent Assembly; Will Then Dissolve" (Jan. 14, 1949), at: https://www.jta.org/1949/01/14/archive/israeli-state-council-to-transfer -activities-to-constituent-assembly-will-then-dissolve. But this formal decree was buried during the final days of the campaign—with the media focusing on issues that the political parties had explicitly placed at the center of their election platforms. Because I don't speak Hebrew, I asked one of my outstanding law students, Yishai Schwartz, to undertake a systematic review of the materials available in the Yale library. He failed to uncover sustained and serious commentary on the Transition Ordinance. The Yale library is one of the world's great archives, but even its formidable specialists may not have obtained all election pronunciamentos for their collection—though others are now available on the internet. So it is possible there was a greater awareness of the Ordinance's significance. But if the matter had gained genuine prominence, the systematic searches that I organized should have led to its detection.

45 *Proceedings of the Fourth Meeting of the Constitutional Assembly* 31 (Feb. 16, 1949).

46 Id. at 37.

47 The Kohn draft was published on December 10, 1948. *Proposed Constitution for the State of Israel to Be Voted on after January 1949 Elections,* at: https://israeled .org/proposed-constitution-state-israel-2/. But it seems to have been completed in October. See Kohn, "A Constitution for Israel: Draft and Explanatory Statement," at: http://storage.archives.gov.il/Archives/0b0717068003715a/Files/0b07 170680757b89/00071706.81.D0.6C.F7.pdf at 191 (English version).

48 Id.

49 Id. at arts. 4(1), 4(2), 12.

50 Id. at art. 70.

51 Id. at art. 75.

52 Philippa Strum, "The Road Not Taken: Constitutional Non-Decision Making in 1948–1950 and Its Impact on Civil Liberties in the Israeli Political Culture," in S. Ilan Troen and Noah Lucas eds., *Israel: The First Decade of Independence* 88 (1995).

53 Constituent Assembly (Transition) Ordinance (1949) 2 L.S.I. 81.

54 Ran Hirschl, *Towards Juristocracy: The Origins and Consequences of the New Constitutionalism* 54 (2007), citing Gary Jacobsohn. See also Avishai, supra n. 32, at 187. For a more sympathetic view, see Hanna Lerner, *Making Constitutions in Deeply Divided Societies* 60–62 (2011).

55 Knesset Election Results, "Elections to the Constituent Assembly" (Jan. 25, 1949), at: https://www.knesset.gov.il/description/eng/eng_mimshal_res1.htm.

56 Statement of Meir Ya'ari, *The 115 Meeting of the Knesset* 769 (Feb. 13, 1950).

57 Some smaller parties could have been readily recruited into a political coalition seeking to redeem the Declaration's commitment to written constitutionalism. These include the General Zionists (7 seats), the Progressives (5 seats), the Sephardim (4 seats), the Democratic Party of Nazareth (2 seats), and the Women's International Zionist Organization (1 seat). For further discussion, see Rackman, supra n. 42.

58 Herut Platform, supra n. 41, chap. 8. See also the position later advanced by Menachem Begin on the floor of the assembly, *The 113 Meeting of the Knesset* 736–740 (Feb. 1950) (demanding a constitution that would restrict the Ben-Gurion government's use of emergency orders, invasive searches, and military censorship).

59 Ben-Gurion's first cabinet, which governed from October 1949 to January 1950, had the support of Mapai (46 seats), the United Religious Bloc (16), the Progressive Party (5), the Sefardim (4), and NDP (2), adding up to 73 seats. "First Knesset: Government 1," at: https://www.knesset.gov.il/govt/eng/GovtByNumber_eng.asp ?govt=1.

60 Avishai, supra n. 32, at 187.

61 Statements of Meir Ya'ari (Mapam), Meir Wilner (Maki), Yaakov Meridor (Herut), and Yaakov Klivnonv (General Zionists), presented at *Meetings 115–117 of the Knesset* 766–767, 800, 823, 835 (Feb. 13–20, 1950).

62 Statement of Menachem Begin, *Proceedings of the 113th Meeting of the First Knesset* 737–740 (Feb. 7, 1950) (demanding a constitution that would restrict the government's use of emergency orders, invasive searches, and military censorship).

63   Statement of Meir Ya'ari, *Proceedings of the 115th Meeting of the Knesset* 766–767 (Feb. 13, 1950); Meir Wilner (Communist), *Proceedings of the 116th Meeting of the Knesset* 80 (Feb. 14, 1950).

64   *Proceedings of the 113th Meeting of the First Knesset* 736, 738 (Feb. 7, 1950).

65   Statement of Ben Zion Dinaburg, *Proceedings of the 113th Meeting of the Knesset* 741–742 (Feb. 7, 1950). Other leading figures, including Zerach Warhaftig of the United Religious Bloc, also emphasized a constitution's pedagogical role. See id. at 731.

66   Id. at 743.

67   Statement of David Ben-Gurion, *Proceedings of the 117th Meeting of the Knesset* 812–820 (Feb. 20, 1950), which placed special emphasis on the *Lochner* era:

> The Supreme Court took upon itself the right—despite there being no mention of this in the Constitution—to decide that statutes passed by the representative of the people in Congress violate the Constitution, and that it is in its power to nullify the law even if a great majority of the people and its representatives support it . . . and thus the Supreme Court became a blocking, conservative, obstructive power that privileges property rights over human rights. (Id. at 816)

68   Addenda to the Protocols for the 150th through 152nd meetings for the First Knesset 1743 (1950) ("The First Knesset charges the Constitution, Law and Justice Committee to draft a proposal for a constitution for the state. The constitution shall be compiled one section at a time in such a manner that each section shall constitute a Basic Law. The sections shall be brought before the Knesset when the committee completes its work, and all the sections together shall combine to form the Constitution of the State of Israel").

69   *Proceedings of the 151st Meeting of the First Knesset* 1721–1723 (June 13, 1950). Previously a ballot had been taken on considering, alongside Harari, an alternative motion "by 37 members" instructing the Constitution Committee to return a full constitution to the floor before the Knesset dissolved. The vote on this demand was 50 for Harari, 39 for the alternative motion, 13 abstentions, and 11 members departing the chamber. Id. at 1720.

70   *Universal Declaration of Human Rights* (1948), Preamble, at: http://www.ohchr.org/EN/UDHR/Documents/UDHR_Translations/eng.pdf.

71   McCrudden, "Human Dignity and Judicial Interpretation of Human Rights," 19 *Eur. J. Int. L.* 655–724 (2008).

72   Radzyner, supra n. 38, at 3.

73   Kohn, supra n. 47, art. 12:

> The State shall ensure the sanctity of human life and uphold the dignity of man. There shall be no penalty of death, nor shall anyone be subjected to torture, flogging or humiliating punishment. The application of moral pressure or physical violence in the course of police interrogations is prohibited; evidence obtained by such methods shall not be admissible in Court.

74 Wagner, "Transnational Legal Communication: A Partial Legacy of Supreme Court President Aharon Barak," 47 *Tulsa L. Rev.* 437 (2013); Christopher Mc-Crudden, supra n. 71.

75 Fiss, "Law Is Everywhere," 117 *Yale L.J.* 256 (2007); Bork, "Barak's Rule," *Azure* 125 (Winter 2007).

76 For an enlightening exception, see Rivka Weill, "The Strategic Court of Aharon Barak and Its Aftermath" (forthcoming 2019).

77 With voter turnout at 86 percent, Eshkol's Alliance won 37 percent of the vote and 45 seats, while Ben-Gurion's Rafi won 9 percent of the vote and 10 seats. The Alliance then formed a coalition with the National Religious Party (11 seats) and Mapam (8), as well as a bevy of smaller parties: Independent Liberals (5 seats), Poalei Agudat Yisrael (2), Progress and Development (2), and Cooperation and Brotherhood (2). Yehuda Avner, *The Prime Ministers* 109 (2010); Zaky Shalom, *Ben-Gurion's Political Struggles, 1963–1967: A Lion in Winter* 64 (2006).

78 Jonathan Mendilow, *Ideology, Party Change, and Electoral Campaigns in Israel, 1965–2001* 53 (2003).

79 Peretz, "The Earthquake: Israel's Ninth Knesset Elections," 31 *Middle East Journal* 251–256 (1977).

80 "Ninth Knesset, Government 18," at: https://www.knesset.gov.il/govt/eng /GovtByNumber_eng.asp?govt=18. Begin later expanded his majority by including a new centrist party, Dash, which imploded after two years. Etzioni-Halevy & Livne, "The Response of the Israeli Establishment to the Yom Kippur War Protest," 31 *Middle East Journal* 281–296 (1977).

81 Hirschl, supra n. 54.

82 "Israel's Justice Minister Imposes Four New Supreme Court Justices," *The Economist* (Feb. 24, 2017); Heller, "Bill to Declare Israel a Jewish State Back on National Agenda," Reuters (May 7, 2017).

83 Professor Amnon Rubinstein was a member of the Knesset who played a leading role in sponsoring an ambitious Basic Law project during the 1980s. To emphasize Herut's deep-rooted commitment, the first version of the Basic Law: Human Dignity that Rubinstein submitted to the Knesset was a verbatim copy of a proposal that Herut had submitted during the early 1960s. See Amnon Rubinstein, "The Struggle over a Bill of Rights for Israel," in Daniel Elazar ed., *Constitutionalism: The Israeli and American Experiences* 139 (1990). Rubinstein analyzes the difficulty of gaining serious political attention for his dignitarian initiative in "Israel's Partial Constitution: The Basic Laws 4 (April 2009)," at: https://ssrn.com /abstract=1406945; see also, Sapir, "Constitutional Revolutions: Israel as a Case-Study," 5 *Int'l. J. Law in Context* 355 (2009).

84 For Israeli commentary emphasizing the problematic democratic genesis of the Law on Human Dignity, see Weill, "Hybrid Constitutionalism: The Israeli Case for Judicial Review and Why We Should Care," 30 *Berkeley J. Int'l L.* 349 (2012); Gavison, "Legislatures and the Quest for a Constitution: The Case of Israel," 11 *Rev. Const. Stud.* 370 (2003).

85 Jerusalem Post, "Final Text of Jewish Nation-State Law, Approved by the Knesset Early on July 19," at: https://www.timesofisrael.com/final-text-of-jewish-nation -state-bill-set-to-become-law/.

86 The Netanyahu government has also proposed legislation authorizing the Knesset to overrule Supreme Court decisions opposed by 61 of its members. But it is unlikely that parliament will pass this measure anytime soon. Heller, "Israeli Legislation Reigning in Supreme Court Wins Preliminary Approval," Reuters (May 6, 2018).

87 For Barak's complex views, which deny the authority of the Knesset to repudiate core dignitarian values, see his *Human Dignity: The Constitutional Value and the Constitutional Right* 283–286 (2015).

12. CONSTITUTIONALIZING CHARISMA IN IRAN

1 Hosseinian & George, "Presidential Hopefuls Clash on Iranian Nuclear Policy," Reuters (June 7, 2013) at: https://www.reuters.com/article/us-iran-election-debate -idUSBRE9560UR20130607. I return to the presidential elections of 2013 and 2017, and provide further documentation of my claims about them, after I establish a firmer foundation for constitutional analysis in the following discussions of Times One, Two, and Three.

2 For a pathbreaking study that has influenced my own effort to extend the principle of constitutionalism to theocratic states, see Ran Hirschl, *Constitutional Theocracy* (2010).

3 Martin Ewans, *The Great Game: Britain and Russia in Central Asia* (2004).

4 Tilmann Röder, "The Separation of Powers: Historical and Comparative Perspectives," in Rainer Grote and Tilmann Röder eds., *Constitutionalism in Islamic Countries* 321–372 (2012).

5 Farhad Diba, *Dr. Mohammad Mossadegh: A Political Biography* (1986).

6 Mark Gasiorowski & Malcolm Byrne, *Mohammad Mosaddeq and the 1953 Coup in Iran* (2004).

7 Nikki R. Keddie & Yann Richard, *Modern Iran: Roots and Results of the Revolution* 145 (2006).

8 Heather Wagner, *The Iranian Revolution* 39–45 (2010) (the Shah's expansion of suffrage and officeholding to women and non-Muslims); Ayatollah Khomeini, 1 *Sahifeh: The Corpus of Khomeini's Writings, Letters, Speeches* 267–272 (2009) (speech denouncing the Shah's actions).

9 Abbas Milani, *The Shah* 291–295 (2011).

10 Khomeini's call for a boycott was a flop. Turnout was over 90 percent, and the referendum gained near-unanimous approval. Ralph Kauz et al., "Iran," in Dieter Nohlen et al. eds., *Elections in Asia and the Pacific: A Data Handbook* 72 (2001).

11 Milani, supra n. 9, at 296; Ruhollah Khomeini, *Sahifeh-ye Imam* 414 (1999) (text of speech).

12 Mohsen Milani, *The Making of Iran's Islamic Revolution* 91 (1988).

13 Shaul Bakhash, *The Reign of the Ayatollahs: Iran and the Islamic Revolution* 51 (1984); Ervand Abrahamian, *Iran between Two Revolutions* 505 (1982).

14 Kurzman, "The Qum Protests and the Coming of the Iranian Revolution, 1975 and 1978," 27 *Social Science History* 287–325 (Fall 2003).

15 Mohammad-Ali Khosravi & Asghar Mir-Shekari, *Daily Life and Socio-Political History of Imam Khomeini* 348–349 (2013); Tabrizi, *Memoirs of Ayatollah Syed Hossein Mousavi Tabrizi* 180 (2008); Khomeini, supra n. 8, at 11 (Ayatollah recognizing traditional Shia rejection of a governmental role).

16 *Draft of the Constitution of the Islamic Republic* (1979), at: http://www.iran-amirentezam.com/node/31.

17 Katoozian, "A Review of the Development of the Draft of the Constitution," 1 *J. of Con.* 124 (2005).

18 Koven, "Khomeini Decrees Islamic Republic after Vote in Iran," *Wash. Post* (Apr. 2, 1979); Kauz et al., supra n. 10, at 72.

19 Though the Ayatollah had risen to prominence by opposing the Shah's grant of women's suffrage in 1963, he raised no objection to the draft's reaffirmation of their voting rights in 1979. Wagner, supra n. 8, at 39–45.

20 *Draft*, supra n. 16, art. 2, provision 13 (Islam as state religion), art. 5, provision 27 (right to pursue a profession conditioned on Islamic values).

21 Id. at arts. 10, 142–147.

22 Asghar Schirazi, *The Constitution of Iran: Politics and the State in the Islamic Republic* (1997).

23 Id. at 23.

24 Bakhash, supra n. 13, at 76.

25 Khomeini himself acknowledged the presence of widespread dissent; see Office of Imam Khomeini, Qom (Moharram 11,1400 [Dec. 1, 1979]) at: http://tarikhirani .ir/fa/events/3/EventsList//%D9%88%D9%82%D8%A7%DB%8C%D8%B9 .%D9%88.%D8%B1%D9%88%DB%8C%D8%AF%D8%A7%D8%AF%D9%87%D 8%A7.html?Page=&Lang=fa&EventsId=460&Action=EventsDetail.

26 Ahvazi, "Imam Khomeini as Seen by Ayatollah Hashemi Rafsanjani," *Institute for Organizing and Publishing Imam Khomeini's Oeuvres* 115–117 (2015). For a report on armed conflict in Tabriz, go to: http://www.imam-khomeini.ir/fa/c78 _60869/10243_==_F_NewsKindIDInvalid/%D8%AD%D8%B2%D8%A8_%D8% AC%D9%85%D9%87%D9%88%D8%B1%DB%8C_%D8%AE%D9%84%D9%82_ %D9%85%D8%B3%D9%84%D9%85%D8%A7%D9%86.

27 David Menashri, *Iran: A Decade of War and Revolution* 86 (1990).

28 "The 1979 Assembly of Experts for the Drafting of the Constitution Election," Iran Data Portal, at: http://irandataportal.syr.edu/the-1979-assembly-of-experts-for -the-drafting-of-the-constitution-election.

29 Mehdi Moslem, *Factional Politics in Post-Khomeini Iran* 27–28 (2002).

30 Id. at 29.

31 Different groups took different positions, with the Communists even urging their followers to support the Islamic Republic with a Yes vote. See Tudeh Party, *Documents and Statements of the Tudeh Party of Iran* (1980).

32 Daniel Brumberg, *Reinventing Khomeini: The Struggle for Reform in Iran* 111–112 (2001).

33 For the election results, go to: http://irandataportal.syr.edu/1980-presidential
    -election (Bani-Sadr wins 75 percent of vote).

34 For the election results, go to: https://www.parliran.ir/majles/fa/Content/articles
    /%D8%AF%D9%88%D8%B1%D9%87%20%D8%A7%D9%88%D9%84.

35 Pierre Razoux, *The Iran-Iraq War* 471 (2015).

36 Menashri, supra n. 27, at 168–393 (1990).

37 Kenneth Katzman, "Iran: The People's Mojahedin Organization of Iran," in Al-
    bert Benliot ed., *Iran: Outlaw, Outcast, or Normal Country?* 101 (2001).

38 Moojan Momen, *An Introduction to Shi'i Islam: The History and Doctrines of
    Twelver Shi'ism* 297 (1987).

39 Dilip Hiro, *Iran under the Ayatollahs* 186–223 (1985) (describing terrorist cam-
    paign and its suppression).

40 Saskia Gieling, *Religion and War in Revolutionary Iran* (1999).

41 John Murphy, *Ali Khamenei* (2008).

42 Jafar Shiralinia, *Narrative of the Life of Ayatollah Akbar Hashemi Rafsanjani*
    (2nd ed. 2016). Toward the end of the war, Rafsanjani was ultimately appointed
    acting commander in chief—but he had in fact assumed a central position long
    before. Shireen Hunter, *Iran after Khomeini* 48 (1992).

43 Menashri, supra n. 27, at 124.

44 Mohammad Ali Zandi, "The Second Majlis Elections," Bagher-ol-Olumn Re-
    search Institute (2014).

45 Siavush Randjbar-Daemi, *The Quest for Authority in Iran* 38–52 (2018).

46 Id.

47 Michael Axworthy, *Revolutionary Iran: A History of the Islamic Republic* 285–289
    (2013); Hiro, supra n. 39, at 186–223.

48 Hossein-Ali Montazeri, *Memoirs of Ayatollah Montazeri* 322 (2000).

49 Although there is no authoritative edition of Montazeri's letters, the most impor-
    tant ones can be found at: https://shabtabnews.com/2016/09/27/%D8%A7%D9%8
    6%D8%AA%D8%B4%D8%A7%D8%B1-%D9%86%D8%A7%D9%85%D9%87
    -%D9%81%D9%88%D9%82-%D9%85%D8%AD%D8%B1%D9%85%D8%A7%D9
    %86%D9%87-%D8%A2%DB%8C%D8%AA-%D8%A7%D9%84%D9%84%D9%87
    -%D9%85%D9%86%D8%AA%D8%B8%D8%B1/.

50 Asghar Schirazi, *The Constitution of Iran: Politics and the State in the Islamic Re-
    public* 72–73 (1997); Milani, supra n. 12, at 220. Article 107 of the 1980 Constitu-
    tion explicitly granted the Experts the power to dismiss a Guardian if he "be-
    comes deficient in one of the spiritual qualifications" specified in other articles,
    or if it "becomes evident that from the outset he has been lacking in some of the
    qualifications."

51 Ray Takeyh, *Guardians of the Revolution: Iran and the World in the Age of the
    Ayatollahs* 117 (2009).

52 At the Council of Experts' session that formally appointed him to the Supreme
    Leadership, Khamenei remarked that the Council of Three option had come up
    "a few weeks ago," and it is reasonable to suppose that the Experts rejected it at
    a confidential session held at that time—though the records from that period re-

main confidential. The recently leaked video reporting on the Experts' secret deliberations leading to their choice of Khamenei indicates, moreover, that they explicitly rejected the Council of Three option before making their final decision. BBC Persian, "A Recently Surfaced Video of the Assembly of Experts Election of Ayatollah Khameini as the Supreme Leader," at YouTube (Jan. 8, 2018), https://www .youtube.com/watch?v=u_UvvEwAqZo; see also, Randjbar-Daemi, supra n. 45, at 62. It is indisputable, then, that the Council of Three was perceived as a constitutionally available option at the moment when the Experts acted illegally in selecting a non-marja as Leader.

53 Axworthy, supra n. 47, at 297. I am relying on Professor Axworthy's report that the Ayatollah's serious illness had already come to the public's attention in the summer of 1988, but I should emphasize that Axworthy makes no judgment as to Khomeini's mental capacities. If revealing documents on this issue continue to exist, the Iranian government has successfully prevented them from leaking out to the general public.

54 Randjbar-Daemi, supra n. 45, at 59–61.

55 BBC Persian, supra n. 52.

56 Id.

57 Randjbar-Daemi, supra n. 45, at 65.

58 Nikki Keddie & Yann Richard, *Modern Iran: Roots and Results of Revolution* 260 (2003).

59 Randjbar-Daemi, supra n. 45.

60 *Constitution of Iran,* art. 112 (1990).

61 Id. at art 99. The Guardians' self-aggrandizing interpretation is at: http://www .shora-gc.ir/portal/Home/ShowPage.aspx?Object=News&ID=9c349336-a860 -4b81-b498-b9e0d414dc93&LayoutID=41ac3004-064d-4591-9605-3bb7 5173947b&CategoryID=e2beada8-28bd-4ff4-a9f8-84d4ee0a2973.

62 My overview is broadly consistent with the far more detailed analysis presented in a recently published book by Randjbar-Daemi, supra n. 45, at 68–273. Because this work provides exhaustive citations to the scholarly literature and original sources, I particularly recommend it to readers who wish to explore the issues more intensively.

63 For a thorough discussion of Khatami's presidency, see Ghoncheh Tazmini, *Khatami's Iran: The Islamic Republic and the Turbulent Path to Reform* (2009).

64 Under the new statute, the majority of the committee is composed of seven members especially noteworthy for their "trustworthy character." The other four represent the bureaucracies charged with running the election in a professional fashion—three representing the Interior Ministry, one the intelligence services. Go to: http://www.shora-gc.ir/Portal/File/ShowFile.aspx?ID=bb3d98d1-8f15-4586 -99f1-233c61080f9e.

13. AMERICAN EXCEPTIONALISM?

1 This section builds on the blow-by-blow analysis of the Founders' revolt against the Articles presented in Ackerman, *Transformations* 32–95 (1998). Like other

work in this genre, e.g., Michael Klarman, *The Framers' Coup* (2016), my earlier book engaged in sustained exploration of the original sources. Rather than cite again the documentation provided in *Transformations,* I use these notes only to refer to texts that gain new importance within the comparative perspective presented in this chapter.

2 Gary Wills, *Cincinnatus: George Washington and the Enlightenment* 92–148 (1984).

3 Richard Morris, *The Peacemakers* 179–181(1965); Bemis, "The Rayneval Memorandum of 1782 on Western Boundaries and Some Comments on the French Historian Doniol," 15 *Proc. Amer. Antiquarian Soc'y* 15–92 (1937).

4 David McCullough, *John Adams* chap. 5 (2001).

5 I am quoting from the leading scholarly book on the period, Jack Rakove, *The Beginnings of National Politics* 338 (1979).

6 Fizpatrick ed., 30 *Journals of Continental Congress* 443 (July 27, 1786). More modest conditions were also imposed on Delaware and Pennsylvania, but if New York had complied, there was every reason to expect these two states to comply as well.

7 2 Elliott ed., *The Debates in the Several State Conventions on the Adoption of the Federal Constitution* 322 (2nd ed. 1854); Ackerman, supra n. 1, at 63 (providing further analysis).

8 Ackerman, *The Failure of the Founding Fathers* 3–108, 269–275, 298–327 (2005), provides a more detailed account of the events discussed in this section. The notes provided here should be viewed as a supplement to the much more elaborate documentation provided in my earlier work.

9 Letter from David Brearley to William Paterson, Aug. 21, 1787, in Max Farrand, 3 *The Records of the Federal Convention of 1787: Appendix A, Supplementary Records of Proceedings* 73 (1911).

10 2 Max Farrand, *The Records of the Federal Convention of 1787* 508, 520 (1911, 1937) (Journal Entries, summarizing vote counts); id. at 500 (Madison's Notes, reporting Morris's speech); 3 Farrand, supra n. 9, at 76 (letter from Edmund Randolph to his wife, Sept. 2: "I expect to leave this place Saturday Seventh"); (Letter from Madison to his father, Sept. 4: "The Convention has not yet broken up, but it's session will probably continue but a short time longer").

11 2 Farrand, supra n. 10, at 527–528 (Madison's Notes, reporting Williamson's proposal of selection by the House operating under a special rule in which each state delegation cast a single vote).

12 Id.

13 Id. at 537 (Madison's Notes, attributing remark to Roger Sherman).

14 Id. at 537–538 (Madison's Notes, Sept. 7, 1787, reporting a variety of objections that failed to notice the central problem posed by the vice president's presiding role).

15 Only in 1933 did the Twentieth Amendment call an end to the practice of lame-duck sessions authorized by the Founders. Bruce Ackerman, *The Case against Lame-Duck Impeachment* 17–41 (1999).

16 Ackerman, supra n. 8, at 111–266, argues that the election of 1800 is only the first of a series of succession crises, continuing through the Jefferson and Madison Administrations, that shook the very foundations of the new constitutional order. But for present purposes, it suffices to show how the crisis of 1800 explodes the myths surrounding the "miracle at Philadelphia" offered up by the so-called originalists of the present day.

17 The preceding paragraphs summarize the basic argument advanced in my three-volume trilogy, *We the People*. The endnotes in this section supplement the more extended citations in Ackerman, supra n. 1, at 255–382, 476–490.

18 Donald Bacon et al. eds., 4 *Encyclopedia of the U.S. Congress* 1996 (1995).

19 William Leuchtenberg, *The Supreme Court Reborn* 86 (1995).

20 Ackerman, supra n. 1, at 306–311 (describing Democratic platform and closing campaign speeches by Landon and Roosevelt dealing with election's revolutionary constitutional implications).

21 *New York Times*, "Amendment Rises as a Session Issue," at 1 (Jan. 3, 1937) (quoting Joseph Robinson, Senate Majority Leader); *N.Y. Times,* "Basic Law Change Gains in Congress," at 1 (Jan. 8, 1937) (reporting the views of House Speaker Bankhead).

22 Ackerman, supra n. 1, at 239–241.

23 Radio Address, Feb. 17, 1937, NBC 737–12, disk 3691–2 (NBC archives); Ackerman, supra n. 1, at 326–327 (providing the text of the speech quoted here); id. at 324–44 (putting the speech in its larger context).

24 Id.

25 Leuchtenberg, "FDR's Court-Packing Plan: A Second Life, a Second Death," 1985 *Duke L. J.* 673 (1985).

26 Ackerman, "Transformative Appointments," 101 *Harv. L. Rev.* 1164 (1998); Ackerman, supra n. 1, at 394–395.

27 Ackerman, "Lost inside the Beltway: A Response to Professor Morrison," 124 *Harvard Law Review Forum* 13 (2011); Ackerman, "Is America's War on Isis Unconstitutional?," *N.Y. Times* A23 (May 4, 2016).

28 Ackerman, supra n. 1, at 403–420; Bruce Ackerman, "What Is to Be Done?," in Stephen Skowronek et al. eds., *The Progressives' Century: Democratic Reform and Constitutional Government in the United States* 478–494 (2016).

29 Ackerman, supra n. 1, at 239–41 (summarizing "court-packing" and "court-shrinking" precedents of Reconstruction).

30 I do not suggest that a Popular Sovereignty Initiative will serve as a constitutional cure-all. I offer additional proposals for serious reform in the *Decline and Fall of the American Republic* (2010). But this is not the place for a comprehensive presentation of my reform agenda.

Acknowledgments

I embarked on this exploration during the 1980s. The Cold War was drawing to a close, and I threw myself into very rewarding interdisciplinary discussions at Yale and Columbia on the promise and predicaments of the dawning new era—leading me to arrange summertime stays with scholarly communities at the University of Rome and the Institute of Applied Systems Analysis in Vienna to enrich my understanding.

These European encounters led me to apply for a year-long fellowship at the Institute of Advanced Study in Berlin. When I arrived in Autumn 1991, the Wall had fallen only two years before—transforming the Institute into a site of intense debate by leading scholars and political actors from Germany and the former Communist bloc. Without the extraordinary insights generated by these discussions, I would never have written *The Future of Liberal Revolution* (1992) to try to make sense of the brave new world that was then emerging. This initial effort propelled me in a direction that has shaped my life to the present day. I will be forever grateful to the Berlin Institute for giving me this opportunity.

Yale was especially generous in supporting my continuing comparative research over the next quarter century. In addition to the assistance provided by my Sterling Professorship, the University allowed me to obtain research leaves that enabled me to engage in face-to-face discussions with serious constitutionalists throughout the world. I am indebted to the Woodrow Wilson Institute in Washington, the Kyoto Seminar in American Studies in Japan, the Collegium Budapest, the Center for Advanced Study in Palo Alto, the University of Paris II, the American Academy in Berlin, the Rockefeller Institute in Bellagio, the Stellenbosch Institute for Advanced Study in South Africa, and Queen Mary University of London for providing me with the time and conversation partners required for the ongoing research, writing, and revision which has finally allowed me to offer you this volume.

During all the time it took to compose this work, the great hopes generated by the fall of the Berlin Wall have been betrayed by an escalating cycle of popular alienation and lawless authoritarianism. This legitimacy crisis will require inspired acts of statesmanship and citizenship if we are to reverse the worldwide slide to dictatorship. But it also invites us all to place our present predicaments in historical perspective.

The challenges we confront today are by no means unique. They are rooted in the successes and failures of the great exercises in constitutional construction over the course of the twentieth century. While understanding the past is never enough to resolve the crises of the present, it does provide precious insights into the roots of current dilemmas and the risks and rewards of potential solutions.

I have been encouraged in this belief by the reception accorded to earlier drafts of this book.

Thanks to a generous grant from the Oscar M. Ruebhausen Fund, twenty judges and scholars flew to New Haven from around the world to debate the questions raised by *Revolutionary Constitutions* in August 2018. Professor Richard Albert of the University of Texas played a key role in organizing this three-day event. He then devoted much energy and insight to editing the participants' essays into a form which will permit their publication. Two months later, I flew to Milan and Trieste to participate in another series of outstanding discussions that were a central part of the ceremonies awarding me an honorary doctorate of laws. These too will ultimately appear in publishable form. The entire point of this book is to encourage such spirited debates—which help increase the chances of emerging from the present darkness with constitutional structures responsive to the challenges of the twenty-first century.

Portions of the Introduction were first published in "Three Paths to Constitutionalism—and the Crisis of the European Union," *British Journal of Political Science* 45, no. 4 (2015): 705–714, doi:10.1017/S0007123415000150, © 2015 Cambridge University Press, and are reprinted with permission.

On a more personal level, my comparative pursuits have provided the occasion for building a web of professional relationships which have blossomed into some very real friendships. With apologies to those inadvertently omitted, I will single out Aharon Barak, Denis Baranger, Luis Roberto Barroso, Sergio Bartole, Olivier Beaud, Stephen Breyer, Steven Calabresi, Guy Canivet, Marta Cartabia, Sabino Cassese, Victor Ferreres Comella, Olivier Dutheillet de la Mothe, Alessandro Ferrara, Lech Garlicki, Stephen Gardbaum, Ruth Gavison, Dieter Grimm, Menaka Guruswamy, Brenda Hale, Noelle Lenoir, Miguel Maduro, Ernst Gottfried Mahrenholz, Federico Mancini, Adam Michnik, Andrzej Rapaczynski, Franco Romani, Carlos Rosenkrantz, Amnon Rubenstein, Albie Sachs, Wojciech Sadurski, Laszlo Solyom, Michel Tropez, Pedro Cruz Villalon, and Patrick Weil.

I am also indebted to a remarkable series of young scholars who have served as research assistants and have now embarked on outstanding careers of their own: Diego Arguzlhes, Jack Boegelin, Joshua Braver, Ana Beatriz Robalinho Cavalcante, Chintan Chandrachud, Justin Collings, Tomas Dumbrovsky, Francois Expert, Juliana Ponde Fonseca, James Fowkes, Pardis Gheibi, Farshad Ghodoosi, Sebastian Andres Guidi, Alon Gur, Michaela Hailbronner, Daniel Hessel, Stefan Jaggi, Andrea Katz, Alyssa King, Brendan Lim, Marianna Mao, Avi Nuri, Daniel Rauch, Yishai Schwartz, Bart Sczweczyk, Scott Stephenson, David Stoleru, Raeesa Vakil, Rivka Weill, and Youlin Yuan.

For all my foreign explorations, Yale has been my academic home for half a century. It has not only provided a remarkably stimulating intellectual environment, it has also been the site of my deepest relationships. Anne Alstott, Ian Ayres, Jack Balkin, Oona Hathaway, Paul Kahn, Robert Post, Jed Rubenfeld, Scott Shapiro, and Reva Siegel have become parts of my life. Other friendships go back even further. Some of these sources of inspiration have now passed away—Juan Linz, Al Stepan, Harry Wellington. But others continue to guide my future—Guido Calabresi, Mirjan Damaska, Owen Fiss, George Fletcher, Tony Kronman, and Jerry Mashaw.

I owe my deepest debt to my wife, Susan. Ever since we fell in love as graduate students, she has been the foundation of my very existence—making me a far better person than I would have been without her daily displays of compassion, intelligence, and moral integrity. I also tried my best to help out in raising our two children, Sybil and John. But in retrospect, I did not do enough. Nevertheless, my failings did not prevent Susan from blazing her own brilliant interdisciplinary career at the intersection of law and political economy. As we celebrate our fiftieth wedding anniversary, we also rejoice in the ongoing efforts by both our children to make the world a better place.

Thank you.

Index

Adams, John, 367, 374, 375, 376, 377

Afghanistan, constitutional collapse in, 18

African National Congress (ANC): appeal to constitutionalism by, 103; Communist Party and, 82, 87; constitutional legacy of, 113; Constitution and, 96, 98–99, 106–107, 116; de Klerk and, 91; emergence of, 79, 81; government response to, 55; imperial disintegration and, 78; internal reform of, 114; international views of, 82–83; Mbeki and, 108; as movement party, 80, 118; Ramaphosa and, 111–112; reappraisal of role of, 85–89; Zuma and, 106, 109–110. *See also* Mandela, Nelson; Spear of the Nation

Ahmadinejad, Mahmoud, 357–358

Algeria, 169–170, 173, 174–175, 176, 181, 182–187

Ambedkar, B. R., 52

ANC. *See* African National Congress

Anti-Fascist People's Freedom League (Burma), 284–285

Arendt, Hannah, 41–42

Articles of Confederation (U.S.), 364, 365, 366–370

Asmal, Kader, 87, 98

Attlee, Clement, 58, 301, 329

Aung San, 283–285, 293

Auriol, Vincent, 190

Australia / New Zealand, democratic constitutionalism in, 54

Authenticity problem in elite construction, 18–21

Authoritarianism: in Algeria, 182; constitutionalization of revolutions and, 322–323; of de Gaulle, 129–130; of I. Gandhi, 68–71, 73; in Israel, 322; of Mbeki, 106–108; in Poland, 166, 261, 295; of Trump, 387

Avishai, Bernard, 308

Badinter, Robert, 213, 217, 219

Badoglio (field marshal), 133–134

Bakhtiar, Shapour, 332

Balcerowicz, Leszek, 255

Balfour Declaration, 297, 298

Balladur, Édouard, 221

Bani-Sadr, Abolhassan, 340–341, 342, 343

Bankhead, William, 390, 394

Barak, Aharon, 314–315, 317–319

Bazargan, Mehdi, 332

Begin, Menachem, 300, 301, 305, 308, 309, 316–317

Beheshti, Mohammad, 340, 342

Benedict XV, 136

Ben-Gurion, David: betrayal of Declaration of Independence by, 303–305; critique of idea of constitution by, 310–311; Harari Resolution and, 311–313; as head of Provisional Council of State, 302–303; as prime minister, 305, 309; retirement of and successor to, 315–316; settler militia and, 300–301; short-term power maximization by, 307–308, 312; Socialist ideals of, 298, 299; as Zionist, 297

Bharatiya Janata Party (BJP, India), 74, 115, 319

Bill of Rights: for French Fourth Republic, 209–210; for Iran, 333; for Israel, 308, 309; for Italy, 143; for Poland, 265, 273; for South Africa, 87, 88, 97, 101–102; for United States, 373

Blum, Leon, 123

Bork, Robert, 398

Botha, P. W., 83–85, 89, 91

Brearley, David, 378–379

Brexit referendum, 14–18

Breyer, Stephen, 361

Burma: case study overview, 52, 282–283; Constitution of 2008 in, 287–289; independence struggle of, 283–284;

Burma (*continued*)
  India compared to, 285; military regimes
  in, 285–287, 292, 294–295; moment of
  truth in, 291–295; Poland compared to,
  290–291; South Africa compared to, 290;
  Time One in, 283–287; Time Two in,
  287–295. *See also* Suu Kyi, Aung San
Burr, Aaron, 377, 382, 384–385
Bush, George H. W., 253
Buthelezi, Mangosuthu, 83, 93, 95, 99

Calamandrei, Piero, 143, 147, 149, 150
Cameron, David, 14–15
Case studies, overview of, 43–53
Catroux, Georges, 174–175
Center Accord (PC, Poland), 259, 266
Chaban-Delmas, Jacques, 200, 201–202, 205
Challe, Maurice, 183, 184–185
Charisma: forms of, 35–36; Schmitt and, 42.
  See also Constitutionalization of
  revolutionary charisma; Organizational
  charisma; Personal charisma
Charismatic reengagement, logic of, 365
Charles Albert (king), Statuto of, 132–133,
  142, 145, 146, 149, 158–159
Chaskalson, Arthur, 102
Checks and balances system. *See* Judicial
  review
Chirac, Jacques, 205, 206, 207, 212, 213,
  218, 220
Christian Democrats (Italy), 136–138, 148,
  150–151
Churchill, Winston, 58, 120, 121, 329–330,
  416n23
Citizens' Parliamentary Club (Poland),
  250, 253
Civil-law tradition, 131. *See also* France;
  Germany; Iran; Italy; Poland
Civil Rights Revolution (United States),
  22, 163
CODESA (Convention for a Democratic
  South Africa), 92–95
Coelho vs. State of Tamil Nadu, 73, 74
Coercion of insurgencies, 55
Collective agency and revolutionary
  project, 40–41
Committee for Defense of Workers (KOR,
  Poland), 229, 230, 231

Committee on the Constitution (Israel),
  302–303, 306
Common-law tradition, 131. *See also* India;
  South Africa; United States
Communist Party (CP): in France, 179, 204;
  in Iran, 337–338; in Italy, 134–136, 148; in
  Poland, 229–232, 233, 239–242, 246–247,
  248–251, 255; in South Africa, 82–83, 87
Comparative law, 37–38, 295
Congress Party (India): dominance of, 115;
  government response to, 55; I. Gandhi
  and, 66–67, 216; Nehru on, 60–62;
  regional parties and, 71–72; Syndicate of,
  65–66; transformation of, 56–59, 117, 118.
  See also Indian National Congress (INC)
Conservative Party in South Africa, 84, 89,
  91, 99; in United Kingdom, 13–15
Consociationalism, 83, 91, 100–101
Consolidation phase. *See* Time Four
  (Consolidation)
Constituent Assembly: in France, 122–123,
  124, 125–128; in India, 59–60, 61; in Iran,
  325–326, 333–334, 337–340; in Israel, 303,
  304–305, 309, 313, 320–321; in Italy,
  140–147, 153
Constituent power, 40–41
Constitutional Convention (U.S.), 365, 366,
  368–373, 378–382, 386
Constitutional Council (Conseil Constitutionnel, France): Balladur committee and
  reform of, 221–223; de Beauvoir case and,
  208–209, 210; de Gaulle and, 189–190,
  191–193, 214–215, 217–218; Gaullist
  domination of, 207, 208, 211; Giscard and,
  200, 206; members of, 219–220, 223–224;
  Mitterand and, 215–217, 219; nationalization legislation and, 209–213; Pompidou
  and, 201–205; views of, 204–205
Constitutional Court: in Italy, 142–146,
  148–150, 152–156, 203–204, 223; in South
  Africa, 97–98, 101–104, 109, 110
Constitutionalism: constructive, 89;
  despotism compared to, 360; ideal types
  of, 3–7; insider pathway to, 4–6, 157–159;
  legitimation problems of, 7–10; outsider
  pathway to, 3–4, 157; pathways to, 1–2;
  rise of, 1; "third wave" of, 38–40, 80, 98,
  295. *See also* Constitutionalization of

revolutionary charisma; Elite construction; Establishmentarian path to constitutionalism

Constitutionalization of revolutionary charisma: de Gaulle and, 178, 181, 187–188, 195; in French Fifth Republic, 221, 223; fundamentality and, 34–35; as ideal type, 3–4; of Khomeini, 341; legitimation problems of, 7–10; overview of, 4; phases of, 4, 8, 10, 37, 43; promise of, 225–226; Roosevelt and, 388–395; self-consciousness and, 30–31; transition dilemmas for, 32–34, 38–40, 227–228. *See also* Fragmentations of revolutionary movements; Movement parties

Constitutional Tribunal (Poland), 263–265, 276, 277

Constructive constitutionalism, 89

Continental Congress (U.S.), 367–369

Convention for a Democratic South Africa (CODESA), 92–95

Co-optation: de Gaulle and, 178–179; into established regimes, 4–5; of insurgencies, 55; in Iran, 354; in Italy, 132–133; in Poland, 233, 237, 239; in South Africa, 79, 83, 84; of Suu Kyi, 290–291

Coordination problem, 46, 55, 224–225

COSATU, 84, 85

Cosmopolitanism, rooted, 361–363

Coty, René, 175, 176, 177, 178, 181, 190

Council of Guardians (Iran), 334–335, 339, 354, 355–356, 357, 358, 359–360

Council of State (France), 189, 190, 201, 211, 221, 223

Court of Cassation (France), 221, 223

Court-packing (United States), 163, 363, 390–395

Courts: insurance function of, 132; legitimation and, 38. *See also* Constitutional Court; Judicial review; Judiciary; Supreme Court

Couve de Murville, Maurice, 197

Cromwell, Oliver, 361

Czechoslovakia, coup in, 148

De Beauvoir, Simone, 201

De Beauvoir, Simone, legal case, 208–209, 210

Debré, Michel, 178, 179–180, 188, 189

De Gasperi, Alcide: Christian Democrats and, 136–138; Constitutional Court and, 149, 150; constitution and, 142–146; defeat of, 150–152; elections and, 148; Mandela compared to, 138–139; provisional government and, 140–141, 142, 146–147

De Gaulle, Charles (General): Algeria and, 182–187; appeals to nation by, 170–171, 185, 190–191, 196, 222; challenges faced by, 180–182; constitutionalization of charisma and, 178, 181, 187–188, 195; Fifth Republic and, 117, 119–120; Fourth Republic and, 170; Free French Forces and, 120–121; Giscard and, 206–207; movement parties and, 119; Palewski and, 202; party politics and, 126, 128; as president, 179–180, 187–193; presidentialism and, 124–125, 127; provisional government of, 122–124, 125; Rally of the French People and, 128–130; reelection campaign of, 194–195; reemergence of, 169–170, 173, 176; referendum defeat of, 197–198; as revolutionary, 171–172; Washington compared to, 363–366; withdrawal from politics of, 130. *See also* French Fifth Republic

De Klerk, F. W.: as head of government, 85–86, 89–91, 94; Mandela and, 80, 92–93, 94, 95–96, 100; provisional Constitution and, 99

Democratic Alliance (South Africa), 110, 114

Democratic Left Alliance (Poland), 255, 256, 266, 270–271, 272, 276

Democratic Party (U.S.), 387, 389, 390

Democratic reorganization, problem of, 33

Democratic Union (DU, Poland), 259, 266, 270

Desai, Morarji, 65, 69, 70–71, 104

Despotism compared to constitutionalism, 360

Dewey, Thomas E., 388

Dinaburg, Ben-Zion, 309–310, 312

Disestablishment problem in establishmentarianism, 10–18

Dlamini-Zuma, Nkosazana, 110–112, 113–114

Dulles, Alan, 330

Dulles, John Foster, 329–330

Duverger, Maurice, 173

Einaudi, Luigi, 149–150, 153
Elite construction: authenticity problem of, 18–21; as ideal type, 6–7; Japan and, 54; legitimation challenges of, 38; negotiated solutions emerging from, 33; in Poland, 265; populist appeals and, 75; problems of, 245
Elite power, preservation of, 318–319
Elster, Jan, 40
Eshkol, Levi, 315–316
Establishmentarian path to constitutionalism: Australia, New Zealand and, 54; Canada and, 362; Great Britain and, 21; in Italy, 132–133; legitimation challenges of, 38; overview of, 10–18; populist appeals and, 75
European Union, 12–18, 21–23
Evian Agreement of 1962, 186–187
Evolutionism, as mode of self-presentation, 31

Faure, Edgar, 174
Federalist Party (U.S.), 372, 373, 374, 375, 376–377, 382–384, 387
Fillon, François, 222
Founding phase. See Time Two (Founding)
Fragmentations of revolutionary movements: in France, 123–124, 127–129, 157–159; Gaullist model and, 228, 244; in Italy, 157–159; overview of, 116–120, 157; in Poland, 259, 260, 275–276
France: as ally to American colonies, 367; case study overview, 48, 157–160, 164–165, 224–226; Declaration of the Rights of Man and of the Citizen, 209, 211; India compared to, 214–218; Italy compared to, 46–48, 131–132, 141, 156, 203–204, 225; judicial review in, 131, 164, 189–190, 201–203, 220; movement parties in, 118–119, 121, 122, 123–129, 169; presidential role in, 221–222; United States compared to, 373. See also Constitutional Council; De Gaulle, Charles; French Fifth Republic; French Fourth Republic; Gaullist model; Mitterrand, François
French Fifth Republic: constitutionalization of charisma in, 221, 223; de Gaulle and, 119–120, 177; elections in, 193–194; Electoral College in, 179, 187–189; as

model for Iran, 326; nationalization program in, 209–213; New Left in, 195–196, 197, 201–202; power struggles in, 199–200; provisional constitution for, 178–180; role of president in, 227–228; Time One in, 171–177; Time Three in, 207–213; Time Four in, 218–226
French Fourth Republic: Algeria and, 169; coalition governments of, 172–173; constitution of, 208–210; de Gaulle repudiation of, 170; military and, 173–177; movement parties in, 169; Operation Resurrection in, 176–177; Time One in, 120–121; Time Two in, 122–130
French Revolution, 5, 374–375, 382
Fundamentality and revolutionary constitutionalism, 34–35

Gandhi, Indira, 65–71, 107, 112–114, 214, 215–216, 218
Gandhi, Mahatma, 56–58, 81, 117
Gandhi, Rajiv, 71
Gandhi, Sanjay, 68
Garland, Merrick, 399
Gaullist model: Iran and, 326, 333, 334, 339, 348–350; overview of, 227–229; Poland and, 240–241, 244–245, 275, 278; Russia and, 280–281. See also Super-presidentialism
George III, 361, 371, 375, 377
Geremek, Bronisław: Citizens' Parliamentary Club and, 253; constitutional commission and, 262; Round Table Agreement and, 249–250; Round Table Talks and, 236, 238, 242, 243; Shipyards strike and, 230; Wałesa and, 233, 254
Germany, 19–21, 314, 418n1 (chap. 7)
Gierek, Edward, 232
Ginsburg, Tom, 39–40
Giscard d'Estaing, Valéry, 194, 197, 200, 205–207
Goguel, François, 121, 204
Golaknath case, 66, 67, 70, 73
Golpayegani, Mohammad-Reza, 347–348, 352
Gomulka, Władysław, 229
Gorbachev, Mikhail, 86, 235, 238
Gorsuch, Neil, 386, 395, 401

Government of Burma Act of 1937 (Great Britain), 283–284
Government of India Act of 1935 (Great Britain), 57, 62, 283, 372
Great Britain: Ben-Gurion and, 300–301; Burma and, 283–284; conventions in, 370–372; European Union and, 12–18; India and, 56–59, 372; Iran and, 329–330; Israel and, 296–302; Persian Empire and, 328; as precedents of responsible government ideal type, 4–5; Royal Prerogative in, 15; South Africa and, 78
Gronchi, Giovanni, 152

Habibi, Hassan, 333
Hamilton, Alexander, 366, 368–369, 375–376, 385
Hani, Chris, 95
Harari, Yizhar, resolution offered by, 311–313, 320
Heath, Edward, 12–13
Hebrew, reinvigoration of, 297–298
Hegemonic movement parties, 59
Herut (Israel), 304
Herzl, Theodor, 296, 297
Hirschl, Ran, 307, 318–319
Histadrut (General Federation of Hebrew Workers), 298–299, 301
Htin Kyaw, 292
Hughes, Charles Evans, 393, 394
Human dignity: appeals to, 313–314; Israeli Basic Law on, 319–320, 321; jurisprudence of, 314–315, 318; as principle, 362
Human scale, revolutions on: Arendt and, 41–42; fundamentality and, 34–35; legitimation of, 284; movement parties and, 31–32; overview of, 28–30; self-consciousness and, 30–31; transition dilemmas and, 32–34
Huntington, Samuel, Third Wave, 38
Hussein, Saddam, 341, 349–350

Imperial disintegration, 77–78
India: Burma compared to, 285; case study overview, 43–44, 157–164; Constitution of, 62–64; democratic constitutionalism in, 54–56; France compared to, 214–218; imperial disintegration and, 77–78; Israel

compared to, 319–320; Italy compared to, 160–162; judicial review in, 63–65; revolution on human scale in, 30; South Africa compared to, 45–46, 54–56, 112–115, 116; struggle for independence in, 372–373; Time One in, 56–59, 78–79; Time Two in, 59–65, 88–89; Time Three in, 65–71, 80–81, 104, 105; Time Four in, 71–76, 115; United States compared to, 377. See also Government of India Act of 1935
Indian National Congress (INC), 77, 78–79, 81, 88–89, 103, 113, 116. See also Congress Party
Inkatha Freedom Party, 83, 93, 94, 99, 100. See also Buthelezi, Mangosuthu
Insider pathway to constitutionalism, 4–6, 157–159. See also Precedents of responsible government
Insurance function of courts, 132
Insurgencies, government responses to, 55
Iran: balance of power in, 353–356; case study overview, 49–51, 324–327; clerical monopoly in, 342–344; Constitution of 1979 of, 327; Council of Experts in, 339, 346, 347, 351–352; Council of Three in, 347–348; Gaullist model and, 326, 333, 334, 339, 348–350; Great Britain and, 329–330; judicial review in, 334–335; "Paris draft" and, 325–326, 333; Provisional Council and constitution of, 333–336; Revolutionary Council in, 331–332, 337, 338; Supreme Leader / Guardian Jurist in, 325, 327, 332–333, 338–339; Time One in, 328–332; Time Two in, 332–341; Time Four in, 356–360. See also Khamenei, Ali; Khomeini; Time Three (Succession Crisis) in Iran
Iraq, 18, 341–345, 349–350
Islamic Republican Party (IRP, Iran), 337, 341, 342, 343, 344, 353–354
Israel: Ashkenazi bourgeoisie in, 319; Basic Laws of, 319–321, 322, 323; case study overview, 49–50, 295–296; debate over constitution in, 309–310, 311–313; Great Britain and, 296–302; India compared to, 319–320; judicial review in, 314–315, 317–318; Kohn draft of constitution for,

Israel (*continued*)
306–307, 314, 321; settler community in, 299; Six-Day War of, 316; Time One in, 296–302; Time Two in, 302–314; Time Three in, 314–323; Transition Law of, 304–305, 309; Zionist principles of, 321–322. *See also* Ben-Gurion, David
Israeli Defense Forces (IDF), 301
Italy: case study overview, 131–132, 157–164, 224–226; France compared to, 46–48, 131–132, 141, 156, 203–204, 225; India compared to, 160–162; judicial review in, 131, 142–146, 148–150, 152–156, 203–204, 221; movement parties in, 118–119; "rigid" constitution for, 142–146; Time One in, 132–135; Time Two in, 135–146; Time Three in, 147–155; Time Four in, 155–156; United States compared to, 373

Jabotinsky, Vladimir, 299–300
Jalili, Saeed, 324, 359
Janata Alliance (India), 69–70, 113–114
Japan, 19, 54, 284
Jaruzelski, Wojciech: Communist Party and, 233, 238; as president, 240, 253, 256; Rokowski and, 237; Solidarity and, 235; withdrawal from campaign by, 250–251
Jay, John, 366, 367
Jefferson, Thomas, 374–375, 376, 377–378, 381, 382, 384
Jinnah, Mohammad, 58–59
Joseph, Helen, 84
Judicial avoidance strategy, 215
Judicial review: case study overview, 315; in France, 131, 164, 189–190, 201–203, 204, 220; hard and soft forms of, 11–12; in India, 63–65; in Iran, 334–335; in Israel, 314–315, 317–318; in Italy, 131, 142–146, 148–150, 152–156, 203–204, 221; in Poland, 264–265, 276; in rational actor model of politics, 132; in South Africa, 97, 102–104; in United States, 162–163. *See also* Constitutional Council; Constitutional Court; Supreme Court
Judiciary: in constitutionalization process, 9–10; in elite constructionism, 21; in responsible government ideal type, 10–12, 16. *See also* Judicial review

Kaczyński, Jarosław, 252, 257, 259, 266, 277–278, 279–280
Kania, Stanisław, 232
Kavanaugh, Brett, 401
Kennedy, Anthony, 361, 398
Kesavananda Bharati case, 67, 68
Khamenei, Ali: IRP and, 353; Khatami and, 357; merchant class and, 344; Mousavi and, 348; as president, 345, 346; presidential elections and, 343, 358–359; public persona of, 349; Rouhani and, 360; as successor to Khomeini, 351–352; Supreme Leadership and, 324, 347–348, 353–355
Khatami, Mohammad, 356–357, 359
Khomeini (ayatollah): Assembly for the Revision of the Constitution and, 350–351; Bani-Sadr and, 342; on constitution, 336; constitutionalization of charisma of, 341; constitution and, 340; Expediency Council and, 354; Montazeri and, 345, 346–347; as Supreme Leader / Guardian Jurist, 339; as symbol of national unity, 342–343; Time One and, 325, 330–332; Time Two and, 332–333; Time Three and, 346–347, 350–352
Kiszczak, Czesław, 235, 236, 237, 240, 241–242, 243, 249
Knesset (Israel), 303, 304–305, 309, 313, 320–321
Kohl, Helmut, 20
Kohn, Leo, 302–303, 306
Kommers, Donald, 19
KOR (Committee for Defense of Workers, Poland), 229, 230, 231
Krzaklewski, Marian, 273
Kuroń, Jacek, 229, 230, 234
Kwaśniewski, Aleksander, 270–271, 272, 273

Labor Party (Israel), 316, 317
Lansing, John, 369
Law and Justice Party (Poland), 277
Lawyers in constitutionalization process, 9–10
Leadership charisma, 35–36
Lecanuet, Jean, 194
Legal positivism, 36–37
Legitimacy vacuum, 8–10. *See also* Time Three (Succession Crisis)

Legitimation problems: comparative law and, 37–38; of constitutionalism, 7–10; of mass political mobilization, 75–76; of movement parties, 36; of referenda, 12–18

Likud Party (Israel), 317, 320

Linz, Juan, 38

Logic: of charismatic reengagement, 365; of reassurance, 61

Louis XVI, 367, 374, 375

MacRae, Duncan, 172

Madison, James, 365, 366, 373, 375–376

Madonsela, Thuli, 109

Mahrenholz, Ernst Gottfried, 20

Maimane, Mmusi, 110

Majlis (Iran), 328, 334, 335, 354

Mandela, Nelson: ANC and, 88–89; ANC Youth League and, 81; backlash against, 92; Botha and, 85; Communist Party and, 82; consociationalism and, 101; Constitutional Court and, 102–103; De Gasperi compared to, 138–139; de Klerk and, 80, 92–93, 94, 95–96, 100; freeing of, 80, 88, 91; imprisonment of, 55, 79; mandate for, 100–104; political isolation problem of, 336; power-sharing and, 95, 97; provisional Constitution and, 98–99; succession crisis and, 56, 104–105; Suu Kyi compared to, 288–289, 293–294; Washington compared to, 374. See also Spear of the Nation

Mandela, Winnie, 104–105

Mapai (Israel), 304, 309, 311–312, 315–316

Mapam (Israel), 304

Marcihacy, Pierre, 202

Marshall, John, 383, 385

Mass political mobilization: in Burma, 292–293; elite bargains and, 245; engagement with national politics and, 117–118; in France, 119, 191; in India, 56, 61; in Iran, 329, 331–332; in Italy, 148; outcomes of, 30; in Poland, 227, 231–232; in revolutionary paradigm, 3–4, 7–8, 75–76; in South Africa, 81–82, 95, 111–112; as threat, 75; in United States, 398. See also Movement parties

Massu, Jacques, 175, 176, 182, 195–196

Mauroy, Pierre, 208, 212

May, Theresa, 15–16

Mazowiecki, Tadeusz: constitution and, 261, 262, 263; as presidential candidate, 257, 258–259; as prime minister, 254, 255–256; Round Table Talks and, 236, 238; Shipyards strike and, 230; Wałesa and, 233

Mbeki, Thabo, 86, 100, 104, 105–106, 107–108

Meir, Golda, 316

Mendès-France, Pierre, 173–174, 177, 179, 195

Meyer, Rolf, 96

Michnik, Adam, 229, 230, 234, 260

Military: in Algeria, 184, 185, 186, 189; in Burma, 285–287, 292, 294–295; defeat of, and elite construction, 18–20; in French Fourth Republic, 173–177; in Iran, 337, 342, 344, 345; in Israel, 300–301; in Poland, 233; in South Africa, 55, 79, 82, 84, 90, 91

Minerva Mills case, 70–71, 73, 216

Mitterrand, François: campaigns of, 194–195, 196, 205, 207, 218; Constitutional Council and, 200; constitution and, 179; de Gaulle and, 177; judicial review and, 204; nationalization program and, 211–213; as president, 208, 218–219

Modi, Narendra, 73, 74–75, 115, 319

Mollet, Guy, 174–175

Monnerville, Gaston, 192, 193

Montazeri, Hussein-Ali, 338, 340, 345–347

Morris, Gouverneur, 379

Morris, Robert, 368

Mossadegh, Mohammad, 328–329, 330

Moulin, Jean, 121

Mountbatten, Louis Francis, 58–60

Mousavi, Mir-Hossein, 344–345, 348, 353, 358

Movement parties: coordination problems of, 224–225; disintegration problems of, 118; family members of dominant spokespersons in, 66; in France, 118–119, 121, 122, 123–129, 169; hegemonic, 59; in India, 58, 59, 117, 118; in Israel, 301–302, 304, 309; in Italy, 141, 146, 415n8; legitimation problems of, 36; overview of, 31–32; in Poland, 277. See also African National Congress (ANC); Fragmentations of revolutionary movements; Indian National Congress; Solidarity

Muslim League (India), 58–59
Mussolini, Benito (Il Duce), 133, 134, 137, 138
Mutual consent problem, 348
Myanmar. *See* Burma

Narrative: constitutional, 213; professional, 217; revolutionary, and symbolic leaders, 35
National Assembly: British Mandate (Palestine), 298, 299, 302; France, 128, 129, 130, 179, 190–191, 196
National Council of the Resistance (France), 121
National Front (Iran), 329, 332, 336, 337, 342
National League of Democracy (Burma), 282, 287, 289, 290, 291, 294–295. *See also* Suu Kyi, Aung San
National Liberation Front (FLN, Algeria), 169, 173, 174–175, 182, 183, 186
National Party (NP, South Africa), 78, 79, 84, 89, 90–91, 100, 101. *See also* De Klerk, F. W.
Nehru, Jawaharlal, 56–58, 60–62, 63–66, 73, 104, 105, 117
Neo-Huntingtonian approaches, 295
Neo-Schumpeterianism, 42–43
Netanyahu, Benjamin, 319, 321, 322
New Deal Resolution (United States), 387–397, 400
Ne Win, 285, 286
Normalization of revolutionary politics, 9
Northwest Ordinance of 1787, 368

Obama, Barack, 399, 400
Olszewski, Jan, 268
Organizational charisma: in France, 130; Mandela and, 89; overview of, 35–36; in Poland, 248
Outsider pathway to constitutionalism, 3–4, 157. *See also* Constitutionalization of revolutionary charisma

Pahlavi dynasty, 328–329, 332
Pakistan, creation of, 59
Palewski, Gaston, 202–203
Pan Africanist Congress, 82
Parliament Act of 1911 (Great Britain), 5, 13
Parys, Jan, 268
Paterson, William, 378

Pawlak, Waldemar, 271
Persian Empire, 328
Personal charisma: of de Gaulle, 130, 193; of Mandela, 89, 98, 100; in Time One, 33; of Wałesa, 248
Pflimlin, Pierre, 175, 176, 177, 181
Philip, Andre, 210
Pinay, Antoine, 205
Pinckney, Thomas, 382
Pius IX, 133
Pius XI, 137
Poher, Alain, 201, 202
Poland: Balcerowicz Plan in, 255–256, 267; Burma compared to, 290–291; case study overview, 48–49, 165–166, 227–229; citizens' committees in, 247–248, 250, 257–258, 259; constitutional commissions in, 262, 265, 267, 269, 271, 272–273; current crisis in, 277–281; Gaullist model and, 240–241, 244–245, 275, 278; judicial review in, 264–265, 276; labor unrest in, 229–231, 235, 241; martial law in, 233; need for new constitution in, 261–262; parliamentary elections in, 247–249, 266–269, 270–271, 277–278; revolutionary constitutionalism in, 270–276; Time One in, 229–236; transition from Time One to Time Two in, 278–279; vote on Constitution in, 273–274. *See also* Time Two (Founding) in Poland
Polish Peasant Party, 266, 270
Political change: historical views on, 27; legal positivism and, 36–37
Political isolation problem, 336
"Political" revolutions, 29–30
Pompidou, Georges: Constitutional Council and, 201–205; death of, 205; de Gaulle and, 194; election campaign of, 196; legitimation problem of, 201; as president, 198, 199; as prime minister, 188–189, 190, 197
Popular reaffirmation of Founding in India, 69–70
Popular referenda in establishmentarianism, 12–18
Popular Republican party (PR, France), 124–125, 126–127, 128, 129
Popular sovereignty: in France, 171, 181, 193; in Iran, 334, 349

Popular Sovereignty Initiative, 400–401, 402–403

Populism, 2, 5, 10, 15–16, 75, 115, 132, 166, 226, 231, 274, 349, 356, 386–387, 400–401

Precedents of responsible government: disestablishment problems of, 10–18; as ideal type, 4–6

Presidential role in France, 221–222. See also Super-presidentialism

Property redistribution in India, 63

Property rights in South Africa, 97–98, 101

Putin, Vladimir, 281

Qajar dynasty, 328

Rabin, Yitzhak, 316, 317

Race against time: Ben-Gurion and, 311; in Burma, 293–295; at Founding, 281; in Iran, 325–326, 348; in Poland, 295

Radical Republican Party (U.S.), 387

Rafi (Israel), 316

Rafsanjani, Akbar: background of, 343; Council of Guardians and, 359; Council of Three and, 347–348; Khamenei and, 345; as president, 349, 352, 353, 355; reelection campaign of, 356, 357

Raisi, Ebrahim, 324, 360

Rajai, Mohammad-Ali, 341, 343

Rakowski, Mieczysław, 237–238, 249

Rally of the French People, 128–130

Ramadier, Paul, 129

Ramaphosa, Cyril, 96, 104, 105, 111–112, 114

Rational actor model of politics, 132, 206

Reagan, Ronald, 86, 388, 397–398

Reassurance, logic of, 61

Reform Act of 1832 (Great Britain), 5, 13, 15

Reformed Congress Party (India), 68, 69–70

Republican Party (U.S.), 376–377, 382–383, 385

Republic of South Africa (RSA). See South Africa

Revolutionary Council (Iran), 331–332, 337, 338

Revolutionary Guard (Iran), 337, 342, 344, 345

Revolutionary path to constitutionalism. See Constitutionalization of revolutionary charisma

Revolutions: "political," 29–30; secular relegitimation of, 27; totalizing variant of,

27–28. See also Constitutionalization of revolutionary charisma; Human scale, revolutions on; Time One (Revolution)

Reza Shah Pahlavi, Mohammad, 328, 330–331, 332

"Right to resist" and disruptive transitions, 406n10

Robinson, Joseph, 390, 394

Rocard, Michel, 218–219

Rohingya, genocide of, 294–295

Roosevelt, Franklin, 162–163, 212, 363, 387–397

Rooted cosmopolitanism, 361–363

Rouhani, Hassan, 324–325, 359–360

Rule-of-law principles, 2–3

"Rule of recognition," 36–37

Russia: Gaullist model and, 280–281; Persian Empire and, 328

Sachs, Albie, 87, 97, 102

Salan, Raoul, 175–176, 182–183, 184–185, 186

Sanjabi, Karim, 336

Sarkozy, Nicolas, 220–221, 222

Scalia, Antonin, 361, 386, 395, 398

Schmitt, Carl, 42

Schumpeter, Joseph, 42–43

Secret Army Organization (Algeria), 184, 185, 186, 189

Segni, Antonio, 152

Self-consciousness and revolutionary constitutionalism, 30–31

Shastri, Lal Bahadur, 65, 214

Sherman, Roger, 381

Simons, Jack, 87–88

Sisulu, Walter, 81

Socialist Party (France), 200, 204, 208, 209, 211, 212–213

Solidarity: constitutional commissions and, 273; Constitution and, 275–276; elections and, 246–249; emergence of, 229–231; failure of, 227, 228; mass mobilization and, 231–232; No campaign and, 273; parliamentary government plan of, 272; performance of, in government, 270; Round Table Agreement and, 255, 256–257; Round Table Talks and, 236–238, 245–246; strike threat of, 232–233; success of, 245–247; as underground, 234. See also Wałęsa, Lech

Soustelle, Jacques, 174, 175, 182
South Africa: Burma compared to, 290; case study overview, 157–160, 162–164; Great Britain and, 78; imperial disintegration and, 78; India compared to, 44–46, 54–56, 112–115, 116; Italy compared to, 162–163; judicial review in, 97, 102–104; M. Gandhi in, 81; Poland compared to, 279; revolution on human scale in, 30; Time One in, 78–79, 81–89; Time Three in, 80–81, 104–115. See also Mandela, Nelson; Time Two (Founding) in South Africa
Spain, 6–7, 18–19
Spear of the Nation (South Africa), 55, 79, 82, 84, 90, 91
State Law and Order Restoration Council (SLORC, Burma), 286–287
State Peace and Development Council (SPDC, Burma), 287–288
Stealth judicial appointments (United States), 396–400
Stepan, Alfred, 38
Stern, Avraham, 300
Strategy of transformative appointment, 397–398
Succession crises. See Time Three entries
Suchocka, Hanna, 268–269
Suffrage in Algeria, 182
Super-presidentialism, 227–228, 229, 257–261, 275, 277, 349–350, 352. See also Gaullist model
Supreme Court: of India, 63–65, 66, 67–68, 70, 72–75, 214–218; of Israel, 314–315, 317–319; of Poland, 274; of United Kingdom, 405n6
Supreme Court of United States: American exceptionalism and, 361; originalists on, 386, 395, 401, 402; Reagan and, 397–398; Roosevelt and, 388, 389–390, 390–395, 397; stealth nominations to, 398–400, 401–402; Supreme Leader of Iran compared to, 325
Suu Kyi, Aung San: as barred from presidency, 292; electoral victory of, 282, 290, 291; life and education of, 286; Mandela compared to, 288–289, 293–294; moment of truth of, 291–295; release from detention of, 289; seizure and confinement of, 286–287

Tambo, Oliver, 55, 79, 81, 82, 86–87
Than Shwe, 286, 288, 292
Thatcher, Margaret, 82–83, 86
Third Force (France), 172–173, 180
"Third wave" paradigm in comparative constitutional law, 38–40, 80, 98, 295
Thomas, Clarence, 361
Time One (Revolution): in Burma, 283–287; definition of, 4; in French Fifth Republic, 171–177; in French Fourth Republic, 120–121; in India, 56–59, 78–79; in Iran, 328–332; in Israel, 296–302; in Italy, 132–135; in Poland, 229–236; in South Africa, 78–79, 81–89; transition to Time 2 from, 157–159; in United States, 361, 363–365
Time Two (Founding): in Burma, 287–295; definition of, 4; in French Fourth Republic, 122–130; in India, 55–56, 59–65, 88–89; in Iran, 332–341; in Israel, 302–314; in Italy, 135–146; transition to, 157–159; in United States, 365–374
Time Two (Founding) in Poland: citizens' committees in, 247–248, 250; movement party in, 247–249; Round Table Agreement and, 245–247; Round Table negotiations in, 236–245; turning point, 249–254
Time Two (Founding) in South Africa: Constitutional Court and, 97–98, 101–104; constitution and, 94–102; de Klerk and, 90–91; existential crisis and, 92–94; India compared to, 55–56; Mandela and, 92; overview of, 89–90
Time Three (Succession Crisis): case study overview, 159; definition of, 8; in France, 207–213; in India, 65–71, 80–81, 104, 105; in Israel, 314–323; in Italy, 147–155; in South Africa, 80–81, 104–115; succession crises of, 9–10
Time Three (Succession Crisis) in Iran: checks and balances and, 353–356; emergence of, 346–352; wartime transformations, 341–345
Time Three (Succession Crisis) in United States: overview of, 374–378; presidential election and, 378–382; presidential election impasse in, 382–387

Time Four (Consolidation): case study overview, 159–160; in French Fifth Republic, 218–226; in India, 71–76, 115; in Iran, 356–360; in Italy, 155–156; overview of, 10, 43

Togliatti, Palmiro, 134, 135–136, 140, 142

Totalitarian dictatorship, 7–8, 32

Totalizing variant of modern revolutions: in India, 113; overview of, 27–28; in South Africa, 87, 99–100

Transformative judicial appointments (United States), 397–398

Transition dilemmas for revolutionary constitutionalism, 32–34, 38–40, 227–228

Trans-movement spokespersons, 224–225

Trump, Donald, 324–325, 386–387, 400, 401, 402

Tutu, Desmond, 84

Tymiński, Stanisław, 259–260

Umberto II, 140, 141

Unconventional adaptation, 34, 246, 313, 326, 372

Union for a Popular Movement (UMP, France), 220–221

Union for the New Republic (France), 180, 189, 193–194, 197, 198, 200, 205

Union Solidarity and Development Party (USDP, Burma), 289

United Democratic Front (UDF, South Africa), 84, 85, 92

United Nations Universal Declaration of Human Rights, 313–314

United Religious Front (Israel), 304, 308

United States: case study overview, 52–53; colonial assemblies in, 371–372; India compared to, 377; Iran and, 329–330; judicial review in, 162–163; revolutionary paradigm and, 22; rooted cosmopolitanism and, 361–363; Time One in, 361,

363–365; Time Two in, 365–374. See also Supreme Court of United States; Time Three (Succession Crisis) in United States

U Nu, 285

Van Devanter, Willis, 394

Vedel, Georges, 208, 211

Victor Emmanuel II, 133–134, 135, 140, 141

Vietnam and France, 173–174, 175

Wałesa, Lech: approval ratings for, 245; collaboration decision of, 251–253; constitutional commissions and, 265; debate appearance of, 238; defeat of, 272; direct populist appeal of, 241; election of, 261; emergence of, 230; ideological shift and, 234; labor unrest and, 235–236; as president, 267–269, 271; as presidential candidate, 257, 258–259; prime minister role and, 253–254; Round Table Talks and, 236–238, 241; as spokesperson, 247, 248; strike threat and, 233; support for, 231; on "Warsaw intellectuals," 256. See also Solidarity

Washington, George, 363–366, 370, 372, 374, 376

Weber, Max, 1, 4, 8, 23

Weizmann, Chaim, 297, 298, 299, 301

Wheeler, Burton, 391–392, 395

Wilson, Harold, 12, 13–14

Women's movement, 29–30

World War II, Italy in, 134

World Zionist Organization, 297, 298, 299

Yates, Robert, 369

Yeltsin, Boris, 280–281

Zakrzewska, Janina, 263, 264

Zionism, political and cultural, 296–302

Zuma, Jacob, 105, 106–107, 108–112, 113